# MORE THEATRES

APOTHECARY (*Max*) TO ROMEO (*Harris*):
'My poverty, but not my will, consents.'

# MORE THEATRES
# 1898–1903

MAX BEERBOHM

WITH AN INTRODUCTION BY
RUPERT HART-DAVIS

RUPERT HART-DAVIS
London
1969

© Eva Reichmann 1969

First published 1969
Rupert Hart-Davis Ltd
3 Upper James Street
Golden Square London W1

Printed in Great Britain by
Western Printing Services Ltd
Bristol

SBN: 246 63894 X

# CONTENTS

| | Page |
|---|---|
| Introduction | 11 |
| G.B.S. Oblige | 17 |
| Mr Shaw's Profession | 21 |
| Mr Shaw's Profession II | 25 |
| *The Beauty Stone* | 27 |
| *The Ambassador* | 30 |
| Two Plays | 35 |
| *Pelleas and Melisande*, and Sarah | 38 |
| *Ragged Robin* | 42 |
| A Poor Farce | 43 |
| A Startled Faun | 46 |
| *The Termagant* | 48 |
| Mr George Bancroft as Casabianca | 52 |
| *The Great Ruby*, &c | 56 |
| Max, Mr Archer, and others | 60 |
| An Awful Warning | 64 |
| Mr Davidson and his Play | 69 |
| Mr Jones | 72 |
| *The Jest* | 77 |
| Dumas Debased | 81 |
| One Thing and Another | 85 |
| A Play and a Book | 89 |
| Two Pantomimes | 92 |
| R.I.P. | 97 |
| An Exquisite Matinée | 101 |
| Pat and Sandy | 104 |
| Olla Podrida | 109 |
| Oxford Revisited | 113 |
| Pinerobertsoniana | 116 |
| More from Maeterlinck | 120 |
| A Triptych | 123 |
| *Silet, Sapit* | 128 |
| Two Comedies | 128 |

## CONTENTS

| | |
|---|---|
| Background in Foreground | 133 |
| Mr Rose Rampages | 137 |
| In Dublin | 140 |
| *Such Stuff as Dreams are Made of* | 144 |
| Mr Carton's New Play | 147 |
| Playwrights and their Betters | 151 |
| Two Very Different Things | 154 |
| No Common Denominator | 158 |
| The Art Workers' Masque: as Drama | 162 |
| The Old Pack | 166 |
| Discursion | 169 |
| Ibsen, After All | 173 |
| The Flavour of the Lees | 177 |
| *The Degenerates* | 179 |
| *The Ghetto*, and other Plays | 184 |
| At Drury Lane | 187 |
| *King John*, and other Plays | 191 |
| A Melodrama and its Makers | 195 |
| Greeba in London | 199 |
| Two Plays | 202 |
| A Plea for the Mimes | 206 |
| Miss Fletcher's Play | 210 |
| Bellona in Oxford Street | 214 |
| *Children of the Ghetto* | 218 |
| Ancient and Modern | 222 |
| Two Farces | 227 |
| At Her Majesty's | 230 |
| Mr Anthony Hope's Talent | 233 |
| *Dandy Dick* | 237 |
| At the Adelphi | 241 |
| At the Lyceum | 245 |
| *The Man of Forty* | 248 |
| Acting Good and Evil | 252 |
| *Samson Agonistes* and *Zaza* | 256 |
| Mr Carton's Play | 259 |
| Lord Hopetoun's Unstrengthened Hands | 263 |

## CONTENTS

| | |
|---|---|
| A Migniard Play | 266 |
| *Rip Van Winkle* | 269 |
| Demos's Mirror | 273 |
| Drama of This Year | 277 |
| The St James's Theatre | 281 |
| Caesar and Cromwell | 285 |
| Farce for Merrie England | 289 |
| A Hint to the Druriocracy | 292 |
| This Inimpedible Mr Jones | 297 |
| Advice to Old Playgoers | 302 |
| *Style* and the Stage | 305 |
| Enter Mr Frank Harris | 310 |
| *Herod* | 315 |
| *Herod* as Dramaturgy | 318 |
| Aeschylus made Ridiculous | 323 |
| Two Plays | 327 |
| A Satire on Romantic Drama | 331 |
| *Captain Brassbound's Conversion* | 335 |
| Shakespeare in Two Directions | 338 |
| *The Merchant of Venice* | 342 |
| *Twelfth Night* | 346 |
| Metropolitan, Transmarine, and Transpontine | 350 |
| Melodrama and the Seventh Standard | 355 |
| *Hamlet* in Panton Street | 359 |
| Mr Lyall Swete in Two Plays | 363 |
| *Coriolanus* and Other Plays | 366 |
| Anstey versus the Middle-Class | 370 |
| Three Plays | 374 |
| Phillips and Philistinism | 377 |
| Several Theatres | 381 |
| Mainly about Mimes | 384 |
| A Bibliomantic View of the Stage | 388 |
| Phèdre and Mascarille | 391 |
| In a Music Hall | 395 |
| *Everyman* | 398 |
| Two Padded Plays | 402 |

## CONTENTS

| | |
|---|---:|
| Parlour Melodrama | 406 |
| Luck among Theatres | 410 |
| Two Plays, Professional and Amateur | 414 |
| Ought Theatres to be Rased? | 418 |
| Two of the Christmas Plays | 421 |
| An Anomaly in Theatrical Ethics | 425 |
| Mr Grundy in Two Samples | 429 |
| *Ulysses* | 433 |
| The Lyric, the Garrick, and the O.U.D.S. | 437 |
| A Triple Bill | 441 |
| A Tragedy and a Curtain-Raiser | 444 |
| An Indiscreet Play | 448 |
| Drury Lane, and Wyndham's | 452 |
| Two Antique Novelties in Drama | 456 |
| The Threshold of a Theatre | 459 |
| Miss Syrett's Play | 463 |
| Mr Hawtrey, Recurring | 467 |
| A New Play and an Old | 470 |
| Crawford versus Dante | 474 |
| The Case of *Monna Vanna* | 477 |
| A Non-Theatrical Criticism | 481 |
| *Hamlet* and *The Hedonists* | 485 |
| *Chance the Idol* | 488 |
| *What Would a Gentleman Do?* | 492 |
| The Triumph of the 'Variety Show' | 496 |
| *My Lady Virtue* | 499 |
| Mrs Humphry Ward's Play | 503 |
| *Lyre and Lancet* | 507 |
| A Play in a Suburb | 511 |
| A Feuilleton-Play | 514 |
| *Othello* Re-interpreted | 518 |
| Drama for Epicures | 522 |
| Mr Arthur Collins as Symbolist | 525 |
| *Fiamma* | 529 |
| Ibsen's 'Epilogue' | 532 |
| A Chaotic Play | 535 |

## CONTENTS

| | |
|---|---|
| At the Garrick Theatre | 539 |
| *The Prophecy* | 543 |
| Three Plays | 546 |
| *Old Heidelberg* | 550 |
| *The Altar of Friendship* | 554 |
| *Everyman* Revisited | 558 |
| At the Imperial Theatre | 562 |
| Sardou's Antidantedote | 565 |
| Drama at Oxford | 569 |
| *Much Ado* and Mr Craig's Setting | 573 |
| A New Farce | 577 |
| A Triple Bill | 580 |
| Advice to those about to Translate Plays | 584 |
| A Play without Words | 588 |
| A Contrast in Hospitality | 591 |
| *Little Mary* | 595 |
| A Play with an Idea | 599 |
| *The Professor's Love Story* | 603 |
| Index | 607 |

# INTRODUCTION

Max Beerbohm was the dramatic critic of the *Saturday Review* from 28 May 1898 to 16 April 1910. For the ten-volume collected edition of his works he selected roughly a third of his dramatic criticisms, which were published in two volumes as *Around Theatres* in 1924 (a one-volume reprint appeared in 1953). In his Epistle Dedicatory to Gordon Graig he admitted that in what he had suppressed there was quite as much of his best as in what he had selected, and it is in this belief that *More Theatres* and its successor are presented to the public. Between them they contain all Max's uncollected dramatic criticism arranged chronologically.

When *Around Theatres* was first published in America, in 1930, Max contributed this new Note:

> My entry into dramatic criticism was informal—nay, was grossly irregular. For about two years I had been writing occasional articles for the *Saturday Review*, tilting at this and that personage as the fancy seized me. In the Spring of '98 George Bernard Shaw's *Plays Pleasant and Unpleasant* were published. There was much in them that I didn't admire, and in two successive numbers of the periodical whose dramatic critic was G.B.S. I tilted fervidly at G.B.S. A week or so later I received from him a post-card, in which he announced to me that he was about to quit his post on the *Saturday*, and that I was 'the only man to carry on the business.'

Max answered (BM. Add. Mss. 50529):

> My dear G.B.S., I was very much pleased, as you may imagine, to receive your letter and the great compliment it implied. But your decision to retire from dramatic criticism rather depresses me —and I hope that you will still reconsider it. You may be tired of the job, but 'stale' you certainly are not—you are a weekly marvel of freshness and agility—and you certainly don't repeat yourself, though I am sure you would bear repetition.
> Whether *I* could succeed you, I am by no means certain. There would be several difficulties. My mind is not very fertile, and any

success I may have had is due to my own shrewdness in not doing much. I am afraid I might come an early and nasty cropper off the hebdomadal tightrope. Also, I have no enthusiasm for the theatre—in fact I don't care a damn about the theatre. This would handicap me for decent criticism. Also, I have a big brother at Her Majesty's, and he would be rather compromised by my position, and I by his. Also I am an amiable person, and might be unable to speak ill of any bad actors, except those whom I have never met. And I have met so many, so many!

However, the position of dramatic critic to the *Saturday* is a dignified position—and regular emolument must be very nice. And I will wait and see what Frank Harris says—and whether you remain adamant.

The most obvious difficulty for me would be in following you. You have done so much in dramatic criticism, and I should be always tripping up in your large and deep footprints. Meanwhile I am sincerely yours. MAX BEERBOHM.

The 1930 Note continues:

After some hesitation I drove to the office. Frank Harris was away at Cannes or somewhere. His secretary, however, seemed to think Shaw's idea quite a good one. So did Runciman, the musical critic, who was by way of editing the paper in Harris's absence. I suppose one of them wrote to Harris about it. But I was unaware of any sanction from the holiday-taker when, after G.B.S. had written his valedictory article, I entered on my new career. A few weeks later Lord Hardwicke became proprietor of the paper, and Harold Hodge its editor. I thought I might now lose the appointment that had never been conferred on me; nor should I have grieved over my dismissal, for I had not yet acquired keenness on my job. But I was retained. And it was only in 1910 that I was dismissed—by myself.

Keen enough though I did become, my friends mostly seemed to think that in doing weekly journalism I was wasting my time. This was a gratifying idea; but I think it was a mistaken one. I believe that the obligation to write every week a fugitive article for a largish public is no bad thing for a writer inclined, as I was, to 'preciosity'. I believe that my way of writing became more chaste, through journalism, and stronger. You think this boast unjusti-

## INTRODUCTION

fied? Then let me claim for my years of bondage merely this: that without them I could not have had the delicious sense of freedom that filled me when they were over—that fills me even now whenever I think of them. My interest in theatres didn't survive my freedom by a single moment. I never go to a theatre of my own accord. But when I am invited to one, or taken to one, I never fail to revel there. Whether the play and the acting be good or bad I don't care a straw. All that matters is that I shan't have to sit down subsequently and write well-reasoned opinions of the affair. Bliss! Rapture!

For the sake of completeness, those early 'tiltings' at Shaw, written before Max became a dramatic critic, are printed at the beginning of this volume. I have also included 'A Non-Theatrical Criticism' (p. 481), since, although it is accurately titled, it seems to fit better here than in the final volume of Max's essays which I am preparing for the centenary of his birth in August 1972. Everything here apeared in the *Saturday Review*, on the date given at the end of each article.

Knowing how much Max would have disliked editorial footnotes, I have avoided using any except those that appeared in the *Saturday Review*, hoping that a full index will take their place.

My chief gratitude is to Mrs Eva Reichmann, Max's sister-in-law and the owner of his copyrights, for her patience and trust. My beloved friend the late Allan Wade spent the spare time of years in copying out all these articles from files of the *Saturday Review*, and his impeccable typescripts have proved invaluable. Mr Basil Lee, the owner of the frontispiece, very kindly photographed it and gave permission for its reproduction. Professor B. R. McElderry Junior generously told me of Max's letter to Shaw in the British Museum.

*Last Theatres*, the final volume of Max's dramatic criticism, should appear in a year's time.

*May 1969*                                         RUPERT HART-DAVIS

# MORE THEATRES

## G.B.S. OBLIGE

Last Saturday I studied Mr Bernard Shaw's excursus on Mr Heinemann's play, and my interest in the excursus was all the keener for that I had just read the play itself, to which I had first been lured by another excursus, signed 'W.A.', in the *Daily Chronicle*. Mr Archer had written partly in disparagement, partly in praise of *Summer Moths*, but I confess that, for me, the value of his criticism had been somewhat discounted by the fact that Mr Heinemann was his publisher. I know Mr Archer to be so meticulously fair, so awfully, so painfully upright, that in undertaking to criticise the work of a personal enemy, though he would honestly endeavour to judge it without reference to his own feelings, he would yet despite himself, and as it were almost unconsciously, praise it beyond its merits, whilst, in criticising the work of one to whom he were bound by ties of friendship and business, he would be almost sure to err on the side of undue severity. For aught I knew, then, Mr Heinemann's play might be a masterpiece, and I hurried to its perusal. Briefly, I thought it bosh. I must admit, however, that I am no expert in dramaturgy. Mr Archer, who knows far more than I know of such matters, and in comparison with whom Balmoral and the Judicial Bench can only be regarded as foul hot-beds of corruption, had seemed to think that Mr Heinemann's work displayed a wonderful insight into human character. Well! Saturday came round, and with it Mr Bernard Shaw, honestly wondering 'whether Mr William Heinemann is the coming dramatist.' Mr Shaw seemed to have arrived at his conjecture by a process of elimination. According to him, Mr Heinemann has no wit, no humour; power of construction has been denied him; of literary instinct he shows no symptom; he cannot write. 'But for my part,' says Mr Shaw, 'when I find the characteristic devotion of the born artist accompanied by a hopeless deficiency in all the fashionable specific talents—and this appears to be Mr Heinemann's case—I immediately give him my most respectful attention, and am particularly careful to indulge in none of those prophecies of extinction which were so confidently launched at Wagner, Ibsen and Meredith.' Thus, in his ruthless candour, does Mr Shaw define and give away a whole position. In their efforts to rid our stage of its old conventions, he and his co-propagandists have long been drawing their arguments from this unspoken premiss: that a bad play is necessarily a good play. Any unbiased person who frequented the Independent Theatre will admit that a large proportion of the plays enacted there made no more appeal to the intellect than is made by the plays at quite trivial theatres. The authors chose more or less unpleasant themes, and they did not know their business. That was all. And that was why their plays were produced at the Independent Theatre. But I, as a timid Boeotian, believe that, unless a man have some talent for dramatic writing, the fewer plays he writes the better. He may be (unlike the average Independent author) a thinker, or a poet, or a wit, but he will be wise not to write plays, unless he have that natural instinct which is as necessary to the good dramatist as to the good painter or musician, cricketer or shot. Ibsen is a thinker and (according to latest advices) a poet. But what is it, if not his genius for dramatic invention and construction, that has enabled him to use these advantages in the theatre and to create of them great plays? I admit that an innate gift for any art involves what Mr Shaw calls the 'confounded aptitude for doing what other people have done before.' Every great man in art has begun by imitating one or another of his forerunners. Ibsen himself had that confounded aptitude which enabled him to begin by doing good work of a conventional kind. Yet it did not prevent him from developing, in course of time, a new dramatic method of his own, did it? Without the innate gift and the confounded aptitude which it involves, he would have been quite helpless. So would Wagner and Meredith have been. But even if you accept Mr Shaw's thesis that natural aptitude is baneful, does it follow that natural ineptitude, *plus* perseverance, is likely to bear great fruit? When a sturdy little boy tumbles off a rocking-horse, is he the more likely to be a superb equestrian when he grows up? Mr Shaw admits that *Summer Moths* is *pas grand' chose*, but he accepts the author's ineptitude as a presage of possible genius, and gravely compares Mr Heinemann, in that he is 'original' and drives 'as hard as he can at real life,' with Maupassant —Maupassant, who was, if ever was any man, an artist; who, under the direct influence of Flaubert, slowly developed his natural talent, until he was able to depict life through it worthily and in his own way; Maupassant, whose first printed story was 'Boule de Suif,' a masterpiece in literary art. To drive as hard as one can at real life may be excellent advice for many writers, but Mr Shaw must surely be aware that the goal can only be reached through literary art. Even supposing for one moment—I really cannot give a longer time —that Mr Heinemann, as a man, has Maupassant's broad grasp of life, I cannot see why one should wonder whether he be 'the coming dramatist,' when it is quite obvious that he has no dramatic talent. A kind man should be very careful in the bestowal of encouragement. The same slap on the back which does but invigorate a strong man will send a weak one off his balance. Art aside, what is Mr Heinemann's strength? In what way is he original? What strange evangel is he brewing? I advise my readers to read *Summer Moths* and then to ask Mr Shaw, in a quiet chorus, whether that play be anything if not an imitation of Ibsen's 'specific talent,' whether it be a sign of original genius to imitate a realist and a sign of slavishness to imitate a romanticist, and, finally, whether that which is sauce for the goose could ever, under any possible combination of circumstances, be sauce for the gander.

I know that every master of a new method in art is vilified at first. Am I another instance of obtuseness and brutality in criticism? I think not. Mr Heinemann is only the slave of a quite familiar method in art. But I said that every great man in art began with imitations? I did. But Ibsen, Wagner and Meredith imitated well. Mr Heinemann's imitation is far from good. Besides, I am not vilifying Mr Heinemann; I have merely ventured to take him as a stalking-horse, from whose shelter I may shoot the cat which Mr Shaw has let out of the bag. Mr Shaw is too explicit by far. He has let his contempt for artistic ability run away with him. A fumbling imitation of Ibsen moves him to exultation, whereas, I remember, those adroit essays in mimicry, *Mrs Tanqueray* and *Mrs Ebbsmith*, positively infuriated him. Mr Pinero may be as 'reactionary' as Mr Shaw declares him to be, but, if so, the reason is to be found, not in Mr Pinero's great talent for dramaturgy, but in the fact that Mr Pinero himself is not a man of elemental force. Mr Pinero is the flawless type, *in petto*, of the flawless dramatist. He possesses, in a degree, all the requisites, and they are all in perfect balance to one another. He is not a great thinker, but he is very intelligent, and keeps abreast of all the latest improvements in ideas. He is not a great psychologist, though he is a man of the world and a careful, sympathetic observer of men and women. A great humourist he is not, though he can always conceive amusing scenes and characters in comedy. Nor is he a great wit, though he has invented many smart sayings, nor a great stylist, though he writes carefully and never jars our ears. In fact (setting aside his natural qualification in art—his dramatic instinct, which is great indeed, and which has been developed by actual experience of acting), Mr Pinero is equally well armed at all points. No other born artist in dramaturgy has succeeded through so many additional qualities. Mr Oscar Wilde has succeeded chiefly through his wit, humour and mastery of words; Mr Henry Arthur Jones, through his enthusiastic sympathies, his humanity, his power of satire; Mr Louis-Parker-cum-Murray-Carson, through his humour and sentiment. Mr Pinero, on the other hand, excels in nothing, but is quite good all round; put him under a strong magnifying glass, and you will see the greatest playwright of all time. All his advantages he brought, some four years ago, to the imitation of Ibsen, and Mr Shaw was very angry with him. I myself far preferred Mr Pinero when he was working on the lines of Tom Robertson and Labiche, with both of whom he had much in common: *Sweet Lavender* and *The Magistrate* seem to me quite perfect in their way. Mr Pinero's imitation of Ibsen was less charming because it was less spontaneous. It came of that desire to do something great (? something serious) which, in England especially, overtakes and spoils so many of the most delightful writers. But, undoubtedly, *Mrs Tanqueray* and *Mrs Ebbsmith* were steps in that direction towards which Mr Shaw has always pointed the feverish forefinger of command. Alas! they were cautious steps. In imitating Ibsen, Mr Pinero had forgotten to forget all he had learnt in his unregenerate days. He had constructed both the plays more or less in his accustomed manner. They were good specimens of artistic talent, and Mr Shaw was as angry with Mr Pinero as he is pleased with Mr Heinemann. I wish Mr Shaw would reconsider his views on artistic talent. I assure him that it is not half so dangerous as he seems to think, that without it Mr Pinero would be far less delightful and no whit more progressive than he is, and that without it Ibsen himself would never have been heard of as a playwright, nor *The*

*Devil's Disciple*, which we all hope to see soon in London, have been enjoying its highly successful run in New York. I can understand Mr Shaw's desire to Ibsenise the English stage from footlights to flies, though, personally, I don't share his desire, and am not sure that it will ever be gratified. But if ever it *be* gratified, it will be so only through a long course of plays in which Ibsen's manner is imitated by competent artists. Bad imitations of Ibsen will do no good, however seriously one may take them. Such a play as *Summer Moths* will do no good at all. One should not encourage feeble work at the expense of fine work. To do so is a mistake in policy as well as in criticism. And one should not go about making other people's publishers ridiculous.

[*9 April 1898*]


## MR SHAW'S PROFESSION

I think it was Mr Street who propounded an ingenious theory that the invention of printing had made serious and philosophical plays unnecessary, that one could learn far better from books than from the stage, and that the best thing for the stage to do was to be merely comic. But I hold that there is still some justification and some use for the dramatist-with-a-purpose. Though he may no longer be able to tell us what we did not know before, he can yet impress our knowledge in us more effectively than can any mere bookman; he can make us see our knowledge at new angles, and under new and more vivid lights. Nor is direct moral purpose always a fatal obstacle, but sometimes a very valuable incentive to dramatic art. In writing *Widowers' Houses, The Philanderer,* and *Mrs Warren's Profession*, Mr Shaw was, as he admits, impelled by a direct moral purpose. *A priori*, there is no harm in that. Whether the purpose that impelled him was morally sound is not a question which I have time to discuss. Whether it was quite genuine to him is a far more important point, and I am sure that Mr Shaw is honestly firm in his convictions. Whether his convictions have helped him to write good plays, or have hindered him from doing so, is the point which most interests me and with which I propose to deal, taking *Mrs Warren's Profession* as the test case, inasmuch as I think it to be the most considerable of the three works. Mr William Archer has given us, through the *Daily Chronicle*, a long poem in which he declares this drama to be 'intellectually and dramatically one of the most remarkable plays of the age,' and Mr Cunninghame Graham, coming upon us, rather suddenly, in the character of old play-goer, vows that in his opinion it is 'the best play which has been written in the English language in this generation.' But, as I have already suggested in these columns, there are some critics so advanced as to hold that a bad play is necessarily a good play, that (need I amplify the phrase?) there must be something very fine about a dramatist who defies the canons of dramatic art. There are also those who, confounding subject with treatment, and drama itself with the Sidney Webbs, believe that a serious theme is a touchstone of dramatic ability. An unpleasant theme, seriously treated, sends them into transports. Drag in the divorce-court, and they will solemnly credit you with immense talent for the stage. Drag in a brothel, and they will never have seen so great a play as yours. Mr Shaw does not merely drag a brothel into his play, but makes it the play's basis. Let us be calm. Let us not be swept away on the strong wave of a genuine, but possibly mistaken, enthusiasm. My friends, let us consider the play as in itself it is.

The curtain rises on Miss Vivie Warren a young lady fresh from the Cambridge Mathematical Tripos, 'sensible, able, highly-educated,' and in every way an arrant survival of the day-before-yesterday's New Woman. She is about to meet her mother, a lady who has lived much on the Continent and with whom she has only a slight acquaintance. Between these two characters lies the conflict and development of the play. The principal scene is in the second act, when the daughter demands of her mother 'Who are you? What are you?' Mrs Warren betrays her ignorance of her daughter's paternity and 'buries her face in her hands.' 'Don't do that, mother; you know you don't feel it a bit,' says the girl. When Mrs Warren accuses her of having no heart, she says coolly, 'You attacked me with the conventional authority of a mother: I defended myself with the conventional superiority of a daughter. Frankly, I am not going to stand any of your nonsense,' &c. 'Here!' exclaims Mrs Warren, 'would you like to know what my circumstances were?' 'Yes,' says Vivie, 'you had better tell me. Won't you sit down?' Mrs Warren then tells the story of her fall, at great length, from the standpoint of a political economist. The daughter exclaims, 'My dear mother, you are a wonderful woman—you are stronger than all England.' Next day, in the next act, she conceives an offer of marriage from Sir George Crofts, her mother's partner in vice and in business. She rejects him. He tells her the true nature of her mother's occupation. She tries to leave the garden in which they have been talking, but he intercepts her. Frank Gardner (a youth who is in love with Vivie) has been within earshot of the interview, and now comes out with a gun. The wicked baronet declares that Vivie is the daughter (by Mrs Warren) of Frank's father. Frank raises his gun. '*Vivie seizes the muzzle and pulls it round against her breast.* VIVIE: "Fire now. You may."' He does not, and the curtain shortly falls on Vivie's determination to return to 'Honoria Fraser's chambers, 67 Chancery Lane,' where she had been staying before the commencement of the play. I must explain that Frank's father is a clergyman of the Church of England who has, coincidentally, had an early connexion with Mrs Warren. The meeting and recognition of the two brings down the curtain on the first act. Mr Shaw has drawn the clergyman as an unctuous and hypocritical person who is said to get drunk 'off' and to indulge in obscene conversation with the wicked baronet—the kind of part which Mr Harry Monkhouse might play in one of Mr Owen Hall's productions. His son, Frank, plies him throughout with a great deal of offensive and unnatural chaff. Indeed, Frank is altogether a very offensive person, and as unnatural as Vivie herself. He makes love to Mrs Warren and gets her to kiss him, whilst he is pursuing his suit with her daughter. Later, the idea that he is the daughter's step-brother does not cool his amorous ardour. 'It's exactly,' he says in the fourth act, at Honoria's chambers, 'what I felt an hour before Crofts made his revelation. In short, dear Viv, it's love's young dream.' At the close of the play, when there has been a further scene and a parting between mother and daughter, and when Frank, having learnt the nature of the mother's profession, has gone off for good, Vivie is left alone. She sits down at her desk. 'Then she goes at her work with a plunge, and soon becomes absorbed in her figures.'

I know well that, in giving a mere sketch of a play which one does not like, one is bound to do the play some injustice. I do not think that I have done any considerable injustice to *Mrs Warren's Profession*, but I should like to say at once that the play is well and forcibly written, that the idea of it is firmly gripped, and that, obviously, the scenes are ordered by one who has some instinct for stagecraft. But no amount of stage-craft, and good dialogue and philosophic grip will enable a man to write a serious play that can be anything but ridiculous, unless the man can also draw human characters. If Mr Shaw had been able to draw Vivie as a real girl, Mrs Warren as a real woman, and Frank as a real young man, he might have produced a play which would have justified even the superlatives of Mr Archer and the reminiscences of Mr Cunninghame Graham. 'No conflict: no drama,' as he himself says in one of his excellent prefaces. To this formula I would add 'No sympathy: no conflict.' Conflict of a kind there is between Vivie and her mother, but as no one could feel any sympathy for the mother, even were she real and not a mere secretion of Shawism, nor for the daughter who is a mere secretion of Shawism and more utterly unreal than the most romantic heroine across the bridges, the conflict is not of that kind which makes a play effective, but is rather such a shindy as might be waged between a phantom pot and an imaginary kettle. Maupassant's Yvette was a tragic and a moving figure because she was a real girl, to whom the discovery of her mother's shame was really horrible. Mr Shaw has declared that he thinks the scene in the second act between Vivie and her mother 'tremendously effective.' To whom, I wonder? As a matter of fact, it is not a scene at all. It is a fragment of a well-written pamphlet. Yvette tried to poison herself. 'That,' Mr Shaw would say, 'was very silly and romantic of her. My Vivie goes out into the world to make a living for herself.' But that was the intention of Mr Shaw's Vivie from the first rise of the curtain. The last fall of the curtain leaves her exactly as she was discovered. Nothing has been developed in her by the action of the play. Nothing has been developed in Mrs Warren, nothing in Frank Gardner, nothing in any of the characters. Even unreal characters *can* be developed in a play. Even real characters *must* be developed; no development: no drama. Unreal characters, undeveloped, are no good at all.

But I see that I shall not be able to complete in one article my theory of Mr Shaw as a playwright. I must resume next week.

[*14 May 1898*]

## MR SHAW'S PROFESSION—II

Last Saturday, Mr Shaw's account of his condition quite spoilt my enjoyment of the article I had written about his plays. I had not heard about his foot, and it distressed and disconcerted me, as a sentimentalist, to find myself saying unfavourable things about the work of one who was ill in bed. Were he not, happily, now convalescent, I should have to break the promise I made to my readers that I would pursue my criticism of his plays this week.

My readers may remember that I laid stress on the unrealness of the chief characters in his most ambitious play, *Mrs Warren's Profession*. Well, I cannot admit that the chief characters in his other plays are one whit more real than Vivie Warren and her friends. They are, indeed, of precisely the same type. The men are all disputative machines, ingeniously constructed, and the women, who, almost without exception, belong to the strange cult of the fountain-pen, are, if anything, rather more self-conscious than the men. I am aware that there are inhuman persons in the world, here and there. One or two inhuman characters would not be amiss in a play. But the play that is monopolised by them can never be taken seriously. Does Mr Shaw, like Mr W. S. Gilbert, wish that any of his plays shall be seriously taken? For some of them, undoubtedly, that is his ardent wish, but, until he has been re-incarnated and has thoroughly re-written them, it will not be gratified. Moral purpose is all very well for a dramatist who, like Ibsen, can express it through the tragic or comic evolutions of realised human character. To a dramatist who cannot do that, moral purpose is a disaster; it forces him to burden himself and his puppets with a load which they cannot bear, a load without which they might be quite agile, effective and amusing. Mr Shaw is not, as the truly serious dramatist must be, one who loves to study and depict men and women for their own sake, with or without moral purpose. When Mr Shaw is not morally purposeful, he is fantastic and frivolous, and it is then that his plays are good. In farce, psychological reality is not wanted—it would be out of place, and *Arms and the Man*, and *You Never Can Tell* lose nothing and gain much, whilst *Widowers' Houses* and *Mrs Warren's Profession* are ruined by the absurdity of their characters and situations. No one admires more heartily than I the keenness of

Mr Shaw's intellect and the absolute sincerity with which Mr Shaw maintains and lives up to his convictions. Nor would any one be more heartily glad than I to see more intellectual force and more moral earnestness in the serious plays that are written for the English stage. But these qualities, without that human sympathy to which in the best dramatist they are always subordinate, are thrown utterly away on serious play-writing. Mr Shaw's penetrating eye is of great use to him in satire or in criticism. He is one of those gifted observers who can always see through a brick wall. But the very fact that a man can see through a brick wall means that he cannot see the brick wall. It is because flesh and blood make no impression on the X-rays that Herr Röntgen is able to show us our bones and any latch-keys that we may have swallowed, or fish-hooks that may have entered into our hands. Flesh and blood are quite invisible to Mr Shaw. He thinks that because he cannot see them they do not exist, and that he is to be accepted as a realist. I need hardly point out to my readers that he is mistaken. To those who have read his plays I need hardly point out that, to all intents and purposes, his serious characters are just so many skeletons, which do but dance and grin and rattle their bones. I can hardly wonder that Mr Shaw has so often hesitated about allowing this or that theatrical manager to produce one of his serious plays. To produce one of them really well would be almost impossible at any ordinary theatre. There is, however, one management which might attempt and be able to achieve the task. I refer to Messrs Maskelyne and Cook.

Of Mr Shaw's philosophy I need merely say that it rests, like Plato's *Republic*, on a profound ignorance of human nature. Just as the great idealist of Athens imagined that the equality of man to man, and of woman to man, would one day be not merely recognised but also established, so does our idealist of London believe that the tactics of Fabius are the one thing needed to ensure Socialism, Women's Rights and all the rest of his touching propaganda. Let him continue to believe so, by all means. But let him not imagine that, by writing dramatic representations of men and women as (perhaps) they ought to be, he is so far advancing his cause as to make any one believe in the possibility of his characters. In a word, let him write no more plays-with-a-purpose. Let him not be beguiled by Mr Archer's contempt for *You Never Can Tell* and perfervid admiration of *Candida*. Mr Shaw, as every one knows, is a man of inexhaustible wit and humour. Such qualities Mr Archer is always ready to recognise in any writer, but he is never quite able to love them. He would rather see a man trying to be serious than succeeding in being funny. Extravagance and excess frighten him. He sees in them the constant menace to the talent of his friend, Mr Shaw, and, like a hen with a duckling, he is never free from the stress of nervous anxiety. But let him cease to recall Mr Shaw from the pond of farcical comedy. The critic's aim should be to encourage every writer to do what he can do best, what is most natural to him; not to implore him to persist in tasks which (be they never so superior) he will never accomplish. To every artist that form of art to which his own talent is best suited should seem the highest form of art. It is curious how often the artist is ignorant of his own true bent. To teach him his own true bent is the only service a critic can render him. Mr Shaw has all the qualities which go to the writing of good farces. He may try, and try again, to be serious, but his nationality will always prevent him from succeeding in the attempt. When he writes seriously, he is always Paddy *malgré lui*. A man should never be himself-despite-himself. He should be himself simply. I hope that in future Mr Shaw will be Paddy, and leave the rest to chance. If he will do that, he has a great future in English drama.

[*21 May 1898*]


## 'THE BEAUTY STONE'

*Scene*: WARDOUR STREET
*Time*: THE IMMEDIATE PAST
*Enter R.*, MR A. W. PINERO; *L.*, MR J. COMYNS CARR

*Mr C.* Give thee good morrow, gossip!
*Mr P.* Heaven save thee, merry gentleman! What do'st?
*Mr C.* Nay, but I gad me to no especial quest.
*Mr P.* Art not here in the servicement of that good knight, Sir Henry? For well I know he hath much trust of thee, and that 'twas e'en here thou didst disinter for him King Arthur's hallow'd bones.
*Mr C.* 'Twas e'en here! But th'art in misprision, natheless, of my

immediate presence. Fared I hither but for my own pleasuring, having ta'en for many yearn much delightment i' the spot.

*Mr P.* By Saint Carolo, a right goodly reason! For myself—

*Mr C.* Aye, tell me of thyself! Art still in thrall to that accursèd knave, Henrik of Norway?

*Mr P.* I' sooth, I ha' somewhat tottered i' my fealty o' late. My thought hath stray'd back to old Thomas de Robertson, my first dear liege. Hast seen my fair mummer-maiden, my last-begot?

*Mr C.* Aye, I did clap eyes on her at the Court, not many eves agone. Beshrew me, a personable wench! And hast cast off those naughty drabs—on whom a malison!—*The Second Dame Tanqueray* and *Dame Ebbsmith Of Whom All Man Wot?*

*Mr P.* That have I, gossip—'t least for a space.

*Mr C.* Then, by the finger-nails of St Luke, art thou so much the more blessèd!

*Mr P.* Methinks that I misdoubt me not of thy good wisdom.

*Mr C.* Methinks that he who would fain doubt the wisdom of a sage is not sage himself!

*Mr P.* Ha, ha, ho! Ho, ho, ho! A right shrewd jest!

*Mr C.* But, in all graveness, gossip, sith we have thus encounter'd one the other here in the very abodement of Romance herself, and sith we have naught better to do, wherefore should not we make some joint emprise?

*Mr P.* Why, by the arrows of Saint Sebastian, that will we!

*Mr C.* Thy hand on't!

*Mr P.* Let us to pen!

*Exeunt arm in arm.*

I have tried here to indicate for my readers the style in which *The Beauty Stone* is written, and the attempt has not been such a strain on me as I had expected. Indeed, it is surprising how easily this kind of English can be written, even before one has got into the swing of it. In listening to the 'original romantic musical drama' at the Savoy I was appalled by the amount of trouble which the mere writing of it must have cost its authors. I did not realise that the difficulty is in listening to that style, not in practising it. Why Mr Pinero and Mr Carr, with all their knowledge of audiences, insisted on that fearful style I do not pretend to know. It must be quite as exasperating to uneducated listeners as it is to the listeners who have some culture. It is quite unnecessary, too. The costumes, alone, immediately transport us to the period in which the action of the piece is laid. All that need have been done was to write simply and gracefully, and to avoid modern slang and colloquialisms. Would that have been a more difficult undertaking than the Wardour Street style? Perhaps. But I cannot help thinking that Mr Carr and Mr Pinero would have been wiser had they attempted it. I am sure that the indisputable dulness of their *Beauty Stone* comes, mainly, from their pseudo-archaic manner. Their primary idea for the play is rather charming. The idea of beauty as the root of all evil is not new, no doubt, nor very profound. But it is a rather charming idea, and Mr Pinero and Mr Carr seem to me to have found a good dramatic scheme for its exposition. The story of the play is pretty and simple. The scenes are nicely ordered and constructed. The crowds are well drilled and well dressed. Some of the backgrounds are quite beautiful, yet the whole thing bores one.

But I suppose there are good reasons, apart from the false literary pretensions of the libretto, for one's boredom. Like Sir Willoughby Patterne, Mr Pinero is 'not a poet.' Nor is Mr Carr. And poems written by gentlemen who are not poets are always rather depressing. Lyrics written by gentlemen who have had no experience in the difficult art of writing words for music, and sung in a theatre which one associates with Mr W. S. Gilbert, are not likely to charm the most amenable audience. The audience suffers, in much he same degree as the composer and the singers suffer, from such lyrics. Had Mr Adrian Ross been called into collaboration in the usual way, *The Beauty Stone* would be infinitely better than it is. It would be infinitely worse than it is if its gifted authors had insisted on writing their own music. Yet, really, they are quite as well qualified to write their own music as to write their own lyrics, and I hope that next time they will write neither. But is there any other reason for one's boredom? Yes, there is one very obvious reason. The libretto is deadly dull—there is not one passable joke in it. Of course, in a 'romantic musical drama' one does not expect so much fun as in a 'comic opera.' Both Mr Carr and Mr Pinero are known to possess great powers of humour, and if they had kept humour entirely out of their play, one could but have concluded that they regarded humour as inconsistent with the dignity of 'romantic musical drama.' But in *The Beauty Stone* there are many moments when laughter is wilfully courted, and at these moments one can but wonder whether Mr Pinero really wrote the exquisite farces attributed to him, and whence Mr Carr derives the delightful *mots* and repartees for which he is famous. Anything more dreary than the part of comic Devil, assigned to Mr Passmore, is almost inconceivable. Have we not had just about enough of the Devil on the stage? The part played by him is always quite inessential to the action of a piece. As a novelty, he has terribly declined: whether he be presented in a tragic light, as by the adaptors of Miss Corelli's most famous novel, or in a merely grotesque and 'thank-you-I-don't-feel-the-heat' light, as by Mr Pinero and Mr Carr, he is insufferably tedious and futile.

I am sorry that I have not found much to praise in *The Beauty Stone*. I should like it to have a long run, though I would rather not be invited to the hundredth night. I should like to see the Savoy, that charming little theatre, really popular again. In that they have not attempted to reproduce the form of the Gilbertian triumphs, but have tried a new form of their own, Mr Pinero and Mr Carr have done wisely. I think that their new form may, in the future, worked by other hands, produce a new crop of successes for Mr D'Oyly Carte. I should be rather glad to see the public leaving musical farcical-comedy in the lurch, for musical farcical-comedy destroyed both comic opera and burlesque, two forms in which I delighted. But, in the meantime, I shall continue my visits to the Gaiety and the Shaftesbury, where the shows are good of their kind, giving the Savoy my best wishes and my widest berth.

[*4 June 1898*]

## 'THE AMBASSADOR'

Neither the aristocracy nor the mob goes to the play in such numbers as would induce a London manager to cater for either of them especially; it is the middle class which vastly predominates in the classic trinity of playgoers. And to the middle-class High Life is a permanent obsession. Its own superiors have an awful, an exquisite fascination for the middle-class. At its breakfast it will linger over every sentence in the social gossip, casting but a nervous glance at the police reports. The columns which describe the doings of its own epitome at St Stephen's delight it not at all. It knows all about itself. And thus the London manager, its dependent, knows that any play whose action passes in Carlton House Terrace or St James's Square is likelier far to run well than a play of humbler venue. I share with my class-mates their fond sentiment for the 'Upper Ten'; indeed, I may say that I have a lion's share of that sentiment, for in me aristolatry is not merely natural and circumstantial but temperamental also—it is the direction to which my sense of beauty draws me. Were I admitted to the *beau monde*, the whole spell would no doubt be broken. But to me, who have never been suffered to sit down to dinner with titled persons, except at the Hotel Metropole for some public charity—to me, whose one visit to a 'Stately Home of England' was paid with other tourists when the family was not in residence—the *beau monde* seems always the finest subject-matter for literary or dramatic art. And a strong preference in subject-matter is bound to influence a critic, despite himself. I know that I cannot write quite soberly about such a play as that which Mrs Craigie has given to the St James's. The mere title of the play underlines my judgement—*The Ambassador*, the British Ambassador to Rome, spending his leave in Paris, staying with Lord Beauvedere, at 'Lady Beauvedere's residence in the Champs Elysées.' The programme, too, *nominum illustrissimorum catalogus*, moves me more deeply than a programme should. Such titles as Lord St Orbyn, Sir William Beauvedere, Sir Charles de Lorme, Lord Lavensthorpe, Lord Reggie Niton, Lady Gwendolene Marleaze, the Princess Vendramini and the Duchess of Hampshire mean very much to me and would incline me to love the play that contains them, even if that play were vulgarly written. I have seen plays in which the characters, bearing high names, might as well have been called Mr Brown, Mrs Jones, and Miss Robinson, for any distinction with which their author had endowed them. I have liked even such obvious imposture better than crude, unassuming reality. But in Mrs Craigie's play there is no imposture. The bearers of her titles behave as such, and the phases and experiences through which she puts them would be unnatural in a *milieu* less exalted. Artistically, then, Mrs Craigie is quite justified in her choice of *milieu*. Nor do I agree with those critics who have objected that the title of her play is inappropriate. I know that the Ambassador, who is the hero, does not exercise any official function in the course of the play's action. But, as Mrs Craigie presents him, he is a man whose character has been formed to a great extent by his profession, and his profession is in itself an effective foil to his actions: there is more romance in the love of an Ambassador for a young girl than there would be in that of (say) a mere Marquis. I thought that Mr Alexander played the part of the Ambassador most admirably. He is always at his best in love-scenes, and here he has two or three very beautiful love-scenes to play. But I wish he would not assume a single eye-glass for the part. It does not disguise him, if that was his object. I know that there is a tradition that a diplomat must wear an eye-glass; also that he must wear a moustache and a barbiche. Mr Alexander ought to wear all three or none at all. Personally, I think he ought to wear none at all. Playgoers are so used to his face that they do not like to see it tampered with: it belongs to the nation, as who should say. Absolute disguise, were it necessary to the part, might be tolerated, but half-measures are merely irritating. Besides, disguise is right only in the case of an actor who impersonates. An actor who does not do that is artistically justified in always wearing his own face. Mr Alexander is one of the actors whose strength lies in grafting every part they play upon their own personalities, not one of those who graft their own personalities upon their every part. Which of these two forms of acting is the truer form is an academic question which I am not going to discuss. There is much to be urged in favour of either form, and examples —both of living and of dead actors—might be quoted in favour of either form. It is enough to say that Mr Alexander is one of the personal actors. I trust, therefore, that he will (figuratively) drop his eye-glass. I thought that all the members of the cast acted well. If I were asked, off-hand, when and where I had seen a better *ingénue* than is Miss Fay Davis in this play, I might be at a loss for an answer. The part is in itself quite exquisite and enchanting, but, much as a part is, it is not everything. The reason why most *ingénues* are awful is not that their parts are always bad, but that the ordinary young lady cannot be herself on the stage before the time comes when she is no longer a young lady. All credit, then, to Miss Fay Davis for her prematurity in art. Mr H. B. Irving's acting in the part of Sir William Beauvedere I liked very much indeed, though not quite so much as I liked Mr T. P. O'Connor's criticism of it. 'I have never read Mr Meredith's *Egoist*, says Mr T. P. O'Connor, 'but it struck me that this is just what Mr Meredith meant.' I have read *The Egoist*, but, not being an Irish Member, I cannot answer for Mr Meredith. I have seen *The Ambassador*, but I cannot even answer for Mrs Craigie. However, I thought that Mr H. B. Irving gave a very clever interpretation of the part that Mrs Craigie had written. I have not always cared for Mr H. B. Irving's performances. I often think that his early reading for the Bar was bad for his dramatic talent. As a *jeune premier*, he has sometimes seemed to me too magisterial, too judicial even, in his manner. Perhaps he has rather too strong a personality for his years. Seeing him in a part such as that which he is playing now, one can but acknowledge his great intelligence: here his peculiar mannerisms, his air as of one about to assume the black cap or to inquire 'Who is Connie Gilchrist?' are by no means amiss. Miss Violet Vanbrugh and Miss Hilda Rivers and Mr Esmond are all quite effective in their parts. Mr Fred Terry does all that he can with the part of Major Lascelles —but, Heavens, what a part! Enigmatic characters are all very well in real life, but they are among the things which a dramatist must avoid. In a theatre one has no time for detective psychology. The author must make his characters reveal themselves to one. Except that he was there to do certain necessary things in the third act, one could say nothing of Major Lascelles. Mr Fred Terry is so good an actor and has so fine a presence that he is peculiarly unsuited to a shadow's part. He cannot efface himself. There he is acting—with nothing to act. There he is, with his buoyant, elastic tread, and shoulders regardless of expanse—to what purpose? A less gifted actor would not make the insignificance of the part so obvious. But I think that the part of Major Lascelles is the only point at which Mrs Craigie fails through inexperience. For the rest, she seems to have achieved through sure instinct for the stage that which most dramatists only learn from years of bitter experience. This makes her play all the fresher and more delightful. That she is witty and writes well, every one knew before. But that her wit and her literary style would lose nothing through translation to another medium, one would hardly have expected. Perhaps one over-rates the wit of her characters. When a Peer makes a joke one is apt to laugh more loudly and more readily than at jokes made by one's equals in station. Whether the aristocracy is so witty as Mr Craigie suggests I do not know. There is a kind of tradition in the middle-class that the aristocracy is dull. That is a tradition bred of jealousy, and I see no reason to suppose that the conversation of the aristocracy is inferior to that of the middle-class. Bulwer Lytton, Disraeli, and Mr Mallock have accustomed us to the witty aristocrat of fiction. In *Lady Windermere's Fan* Mr Oscar Wilde introduced the witty aristocrat to the stage. Between *Lady Windermere's Fan* and *The Ambassador* several critics have drawn comparison, and such comparison was of course inevitable. Each play was produced at the St James's, and each was a first serious essay in drama made by a writer who had gained distinction in literature, and in the one, as in the other, there is wit, style and natural instinct for the technique of drama. But the likeness of the two plays is only superficial. In Mr Wilde's dramatic work there was always a certain insolence, a disdain for his medium. He made all his characters talk as he wrote—their wit was always his wit; and their longer speeches were always prose-poems. Mrs Craigie, on the other hand, makes every one of her characters witty according to his or her temperament, and writes for them speeches which, though musical, are not unlike the speeches which people do make, now and again, in real life. Mr Wilde showed little interest in psychology, and he regarded life sometimes from the poet's standpoint, with large emotion, sometimes from the standpoint of a philosopher. But Mrs Craigie cares much for psychology, and life she regards only through a haze of pretty sentimentalism and prettier cynicism. I cannot imagine a better equipment than Mrs Craigie's for the writing of comedies. I think that Mrs. Craigie was born to write perfect little comedies. A rare distinction! I hope she will not be induced to despise her true gift, and to essay heavy tasks. I see that Mr Archer is already hinting that she ought to do something heavy. That is so like Mr Archer. It is so like most critics. Almost every critic spends his time in imploring or commanding artists to do something different from what they are doing. I do hope that Mrs Craigie will profit by the awful example of Mr Pinero, and will not fall under the spell of Mr Archer's proselytising eye. I have my misgivings. I have noted with concern that in her recent books she has shown a certain restiveness, a certain contempt for her own *métier*. How many charming talents have been spoiled by the instilled desire to do 'important' work! Some people are born to lift heavy weights. Some are born to juggle with golden balls. The lifters are far more numerous in England than are the jugglers. Mrs

Craigie is one of the few good jugglers we have. She should not try to lift heavy weights.

[*11 June 1898*]


## TWO PLAYS

Since I wrote my last article, I have seen two plays—one a farce at the Court, the other a melodrama at the Avenue, and, as I have not much to say about either of them, it is well for the length of this article that I saw both. Let me deal with them in chronological order. I do not pretend to determine their order of merit. Except, indeed, that both were received by the public with great enthusiasm, they had nothing at all in common. But I am padding. I will proceed to the farce, *His Excellency the Governor*, produced last Saturday. It is an extremely amusing farce. So much I can say with certainty, for it went, on the first night, with what is called a roar: pit and stalls were as a sea of shaking shoulders and aching sides, and the critics to the daily papers, writing in the calm hours of an English Sunday, declared that it was most amusing. Yet I cannot honestly say that it amused me. That, no doubt, was my fault, not the author's. High spirits always bewilder and depress me. Humour I like very much, but I simply cannot cope with high spirits. A 'humorous twinkle' does not compensate me for (that which it usually implies) complete lack of humour in conversation, and I consider a slap on the back to be little better than a technical assault. And *His Excellency the Governor* is (or, at least, seemed to me) essentially a play of high spirits rather than of humour. All the jokes struck me as being tentative, derived—timid sheep, bearing the brand 'G.B.S.' or 'W.S.G.,' whilst the high spirits which sent the play bouncing and rollicking along through three acts were obviously the author's own. I ought to have mentioned that the author is Mr R. Marshall, a novice, or at most a postulant, in dramaturgy. As yet, he is not expert in *technique*, but I need not bore my readers by showing him the technical faults of his play, and the important point is that he has written a play in which there is art enough to convey his own high spirits to an audience. Not every beginner can thus leap the footlights. I shall not wonder if Mr Marshall become a very successful playwright. Meanwhile, I congratulate Mr Chudleigh on having a play which is likely to run well through the rest of the season; also, on his admirable troupe of players. As the musichall singer on tour, Miss Irene Vanbrugh acted sharply and pleasantly, but she failed to be vulgar, though vulgarity was required for the part. Her refinement rather discounted the Governor's confusion at her presence, nor did there seem to be any great incongruity when a Colonial Secretary proposed to her. She ought at least to have dressed more loudly. She was dressed, so far as I could judge, in perfect taste. Perfect taste in dress at all costs is the great weakness of the modern actress—dowdiness on the one hand and loudness on the other are studiously avoided in defiance of authors' wishes. Considerations of time and space might at any rate be borne in mind by the modern actress. Why does she persist in dressing, wherever the scene be laid and at whatever hour, as though she were going out for a drive in the Park or the Bois? I am sorry to see that modern actors, also, are a prey to the distortions of perfect taste. In this play Mr Boucicault enacts with delightful humour the part of a shy little secretary who hates the company of ladies; the part is intended as a foil to that of the dashing soldier played by Mr Paul Arthur, and it was only by extreme skill in acting that Mr Boucicault was able to obscure the glories of his frock-coat, his waistcoat slip and all the rest of his incomparable costume. Mr Allan Aynesworth, luckily for him, had a part which required good clothes. Unluckily for him, it was a part which gave little in return. It was a long part, but not at all a good one. And Mr James Erskine played a short part in which Lord Salisbury himself, had he been cast for it, could hardly have made a hit.

The other play that I saw was written by Sergius Stepniak, and was acted on Tuesday afternoon at the Avenue. The size and the enthusiasm of the audience was a fine tribute to the memory of a man who worked so hard and so well for his political ideals. The play itself was rather a surprise to me. I had expected an earnest, formless exposition of views, interesting but not dramatic, and lo! I found myself listening to melodrama, not propaganda—to just such melodrama of Nihilism as was so popular in the last decade. Here and there, it is true, were scenes of interminable talk, which reminded one of the worst excesses of the Independent Theatre, but for the rest, *The Convert* was but an essay in the old, lurid convention, written with some instinct for theatrical effect. Ten or fifteen years ago, when the scent of Nihilist gunpowder was being wafted through Europe, and when knouts, knives, and the White Terror were the awful topic of our conversation, this play would have been rather impressive. I well remember how deeply I was stirred by such plays as *Lost for Russia*, *The Secret Track*, and *The Red Lamp*, with their loyalists ending in—off, and their conspirators ending in—ski. When I witnessed the arrest of innocent Olga Souravieff, in those good old days, every nerve in my body was taut on a little rack of pity and awe, and my eyes glowed like live coals when Prince Alexis Valerien, accused of faint-heartedness by treacherous Ivan Zazulick, cried out, 'Faint-hearted? What have I not sacrificed? Wealth, fame, the love of Woman, the friendship of Man —all, all, in the service of this cause, which I hold sac-a-red. Faint-hearted? Pah!' But Nihilism as a theme is now rather out of date. Nor is it yet remote enough for historical perspective. *C'est une chose d'avant-hier*, and, therefore, not stimulating. The play depressed me. At the end of the first act I went out into the street to see the daylight and breathe the fresh air—when one emerges from a *matinée* the whole town seems like some enchanted fairy-land— and I was loth to return. I wished that a droschky would come tearing down Northumberland Avenue, and that, as it drew up sharp before the theatre, the Russian Censor would spring from it, rush in and black out the three remaining acts. However I returned dutifully and saw the rest of the piece. It was, indeed, rather interesting in so far as it confirmed me in the theory that actual experience is fatal to the creative artist. No man can create a fine work of art if he choose for his subject-matter the things which he himself has done, or the things which he himself has suffered. Art is the compliment of life, and one has no genuine impulse to write of the life that one has lived—to have lived it is enough. Nor, on the other hand, can a man create a fine work of art, if he choose for his subject-matter things of which he himself knows nothing. 'Passionate observation' is as necessary as actual experience is fatal. It is only from the outside that an artist can see and show things as they are. When a man just tells his own experiences he is worthy of attention, and I have no doubt that Stepniak's reminiscences in conversation were as interesting as the narrative of Aeneas. But when a man sits down to create a work of art out of his experiences, he has to suppress his mere self, and the outcome is always a failure. Stepniak sat down to describe in dramatic form life as he had known it from within. All he could make of it was a garishly unreal melodrama of the most familiar pattern.

The performance itself was, on the whole, very good. Miss Margaret Halstan played the young heroine's part with grace and sincerity. Mr Charrington was quite capital as a newly-appointed minister. Made up like a combination-photograph of Thomas Carlyle and Mr Ruskin, Mr Laurence Irving played the chief part, Murinov, with wonderful intensity. From the moment when Murinov first opened his lips I felt sure that he was a convinced Nihilist. The more he inveighed against Nihilism, and the more he proclaimed his loyalty to the Tsar, the more certain was I that he belonged to every secret society in St Petersburg. As a matter of fact, he was but a wealthy and quite respectable merchant; but Mr Laurence Irving acted the part throughout in such a way that his final conversion to Nihilism in the last act seemed suspiciously less like a conversion than a tardy confession. However, even denying his conception of the part to be right, one could not but admire the fineness of his impersonation. Mr Laurence Irving is a young actor, and, of course, he has much to learn. The more, and the more nomadically, a young actor acts, the more, and the more quickly, he is likely to learn. Mr Laurence Irving never misses a chance of acting anywhere: he is here, there, and everywhere, sometimes taking a small part, sometimes a big one. He impresses me as a young actor who is going about his business in the right way.

[*18 June 1898*]


## 'PELLEAS AND MELISANDE,' AND SARAH

In an *entr'acte* of Maeterlinck's marvellous and lovely play, in the vestibule of the Prince of Wales's Theatre, I met a dramatic critic who shall be as nameless as one of his own very able articles. He was angrily puffing a cigarette. 'Is it life?' he asked me. 'Is it drama? It is a series of dramatic incidents put together by a competent dramatist? Is it poetry? Is it prose? Is it—,' and so forth, punctuating every question with an explosive 'No!' I make a point of always agreeing with every one—it is my substitute for good-fellowship—and so I spoke slightingly of Maeterlinck and accepted a cigarette. Gradually my friend grew calmer, and I led him on to other topics. Of what use, pray, would protest or argument have been? My friend derived no pleasure from *Pelleas and Melisande*, and I might as well have tried to solidify the smoke from the cigarette which he was so indignantly puffing as have tried to define for him the play's enchantment, its delicate and vague spell. I was spellbound and enchanted, and that was enough—why try to make a convert in *entr'acte*? Not in fifty *entr'actes*, nor by the most expert gardener of souls, can a sense of beauty be made to flourish where it has not been sown. *Pelleas and Melisande* appeals not at all to the reason, only to the sense of beauty and to the sense of mystery. The more one admires it, the less does he care to argue about it. As I listened to the story of the girl whom a huntsman found weeping in a wood and took to be his bride in his father's castle—a castle 'very old and gloomy very chilly and sunken'— I did not try nor wish to understand the things that were not made plain to me. I did but surrender myself to the story. I saw the old king sitting by his hearth, his wife full of anger that Golaud, their son, had taken a waif to his heart, and I heard him say that he himself, very old though he was, had never yet seen clearly into his own soul—how could he judge other men? And I did not try to judge Golaud according to the standards of common sense or the standards of dramatic propriety. I saw poor Melisande drop her ring into the deep fountain, and her dread became mine. I pitied her when she dared not tell Golaud that she had lost her ring. When she shrank away from the cave by the sea and dared not enter it, I was glad, for I knew in my heart that if she entered it harm would come to her. I saw her lean from her window in the tower, covering Pelleas with her dark hair. I saw her stand in the avenue, kissing him, and I knew that Golaud watched them along the distance of their shadows. The light of the setting sun came through the little window from which Melisande had leaned down laughing to her lover, and it fell on her as she lay there dying. Her baby lay beside her. Silently, as the sun sank, the servants walked into her chamber. I knew, though Golaud did not know, why they had come, and why they watched her so strangely. Suddenly they all fell on their knees. The old King bent over Melisande and touched her. He did not weep. 'She seems very small,' he murmured; 'she might be her baby's sister. . . .

She was a little, silent, mysterious creature, as we all are.' All the characters in Maeterlinck's play are 'little, silent, mysterious creatures,' timid and helpless; very real, though we see them but dimly. They are as figures on faded tapestry, moving in twilight, and yet they are all strangely real. All are like children. Even Golaud is more like a child than a man. We feel that he is 'incapable of his own distress.' When Melisande is dying, he begs her to confess to him if she ever really wronged him with her lover. 'Tell me everything,' he says, 'and I will forgive everything.' Melisande tells him that she never wronged him, and he falls back, crying, 'Now I shall never know!' We pity him as we should pity a child. Pelleas and Melisande are in love like children—they are hardly conscious of their love. They are afraid like children, knowing not of what they are afraid. And as we watch them we too become like children, wondering at shadows. I had never seen one of Maeterlinck's plays acted. I thought that to see *Pelleas and Melisande* upon the stage would set a limit to the illusion one gains from it in reading. In a way I was right. There are one or two scenes that are lovelier in imagination, but there are others which gain vastly by presentation. Perhaps I had not given Maeterlinck credit for all the theatrical power—I use the word technically—that is in him. I had not, for instance, realised the wonderfully impressive effect produced by the entry of the servants into the death-chamber, and how skilfully this effect is intensified by the preceding scene, in which we see the servants trooping out of the hall on their way to the death-chamber. Were the play not translated and acted most beautifully, its presentation would, of course, be too appalling for words. I had not known that Mr Mackail would do his work so well. The sound of the words and the choice of words were beautiful from first to last. I have heard one or two people objecting to certain colloquialisms which Mr Mackail has used. For myself, I heard no colloquialisms that jarred me, none that did not seem to me consonant with the *naïveté* of the original text. And beautifully were all the words spoken. In a play of this kind, a sense of beauty is the first thing needed by the actors and actresses. Beautiful voices are the next essential. Mrs Patrick Campbell, Mr Forbes Robertson, and Mr Martin Harvey have very beautiful voices, and their acting bore witness to their great sense of beauty. I cannot conceive a more perfect rendering of a part than was Mrs Campbell's rendering of Melisande. Mr Hearn showed himself to be worthy of the old king's part, and Mr Dodsworth, as the old servant, was almost uncannily good; he has only one speech to deliver, but if that one speech were all that the play contained I should go again to hear Mr Dodsworth deliver it. What struck me especially in the whole representation was the reverent sincerity of each performance. Every one acted with just the air of childishness, of helplessness, that was right. Indeed, the only member of the cast who seemed quite grown-up was the little girl who played the child's part. If I had my way, children would not be allowed to take parts on the stage. They cannot be themselves, and they invariably spoil with their strained, staccato utterance every scene in which they appear. It is not their fault, poor little things! it is the fault of the dramatists who write parts for them. Loth though I am to increase the many difficulties of play-writing, I must ask all dramatists to remember that for the child-actor or actress it is always bedtime.

On Monday evening I had seen *Lysiane* at the Lyric. Strange that I remember the very definite structure of M. Romain Coolus less well than I remember Maeterlinck's dream—that dim, elusive dream! Indeed, had not Madame Bernhardt herself been visible in a box at the first matinée of *Pelleas and Melisande*, and thus, in some subtle way, inwoven herself into my impressions of that play, I might have forgotten that I had seen *Lysiane* at all. Nor would that have mattered very much, for I am going to see Madame Bernhardt in some of her other plays, and in them I shall see her to far greater advantage. The scenes in *Lysiane* are but a series of hoops for Sarah to go through. Sarah rides on tip-toe round the ring of the Lyric, and through them she goes, bang, one after another, with incomparable grace, agility, and good-nature. It is, indeed, a triumph of the circus rather than of the theatre. As I saw in succession Sarah genial, Sarah sentimental, and Sarah amorous, Sarah suspicious, Sarah angry, Sarah furious, and Sarah beside herself, the 'brava!' that sprang to my lips became a murmured 'hoop-la!' To discuss the play would be absurd. At a circus one does not speculate on the quality and price of the tissue-paper spoilt by the fair rider's every percussion. To notice the actors would be absurd also. One does not, at a circus, criticise the discreet men in livery who hold up the hoops for the fair rider. I look forward to seeing Sarah in several plays—*Lysiane* is not a play—before she leaves London, and, meanwhile, I am glad to have paid my poor tribute to her transcendent powers. Some serious people are doubtless very angry about *Lysiane*, angry that an actress should be so great as to be able to subvert the laws of the theatre. Obviously, the mime should be the humble interpreter of the dramatist, and it very terrible that the dramatist does often cringe and truckle to the mime, does often rely on the mime (as in the case of M. Coolus and Sarah) for his very existence. Very terrible it is, but quite inevitable, and therefore a thing to be borne calmly. The mime is far nearer to the public than is the dramatist, and so he can dictate to the dramatist, and can extract revenge for the brevity of his own triumph. Even as the Athenians loved this or that demagogue better than the State, so does the public love this mime or that better than dramatic art. Strictly, then, Sarah should be ostracised. If the Parisians, loving her too much, ostracised her, perhaps she would live and act always in London. Really I wish that this could happen. After all, she is Sarah, *cette déesse riante et terrible*. There is none like her. She is incomparable. And a few bad plays are a reasonable price to pay for an incomparable actress.

[*25 June 1898*]


## 'RAGGED ROBIN'

The Law is not noted for good taste or kindly consideration of human feelings, but at least it does not allow the wife or husband of a prisoner to give evidence, and it is loth to subpoena any of the prisoner's near relatives. But Journalism has none of these wholesome scruples, and regards no table of affinities. I had to attend the first night at Her Majesty's as a dramatic critic, and am expected to write a dramatic criticism of *Ragged Robin*. What am I to do? To find one fault with the production would be both impious and impossible: both scandalous and unadvisable would be one word of praise. Nor can I dilate gracefully on Wessex and the early adventures of M. Richepin—have not those subjects been just exhausted by other scribes? Shall I, then, attempting continuity of policy, write of *Ragged Robin* in the manner of my predecessor—'the Dook would have had a word to say there.' I might try to parody the attack he would have written on French Alexandrines, English adaptations, apple-blossom, dialect, the Vagrancy Act, beer-drinking peasants, holly, miseltoe, and things in general. But the bow of Achilles can be drawn only by Achilles himself, and Thersites, of all men, must not trifle with it. To write my own impressions of *Ragged Robin* I refuse utterly. It would not do. Like little Susanne Laroque, at her father's trial, I can but reiterate 'I saw *nothing*! I heard *nothing*!

[*2 July 1898*]


## A POOR FARCE

I make gallant efforts against depression, and I try hard to keep my mind on the alert, but I cannot disguise the very obvious fact that these are lean years for dramatic criticism. A lustre since, when the Ibsen crusade was at its height, it must have been great fun to be a dramatic critic. A lustre since, with what enthusiasm, too, I should have fought for Maeterlinck! My respect for Ibsen's work and my love of Maeterlinck's are as great as ever, but I wish that I could get from those two masters, besides my merely aesthetic pleasure, that pleasure which, to a naturally loyal and pugnacious temper, comes with the necessity for warfare. As it is, all the battles for Ibsen and Maeterlinck have been fought, and the enemy has been routed, and the day has no burden and heat left for me. I stand in the victorious camp, wiping from my sword imaginary bloodstains, filled with a terrible, unsatisfied enthusiasm. Or, to take a humbler metaphor, I throw myself into an attitude of defence, with nothing to fight for and nobody to fight. About *Pelleas and Melisande* I wrote what I fondly imagined to be a provocative article, only to find myself in perfect harmony with the *Daily Telegraph*. Indeed, I think that the only person who persisted, this season, in denouncing Maeterlinck was our old friend Carados of the *Referee*. Mr Walkley, longing, like me, for a set-to, immediately trailed his coat, and invited Carados to tread on the tail of it. Coy Carados did but compliment Mr Walkley on its cut, and the incident closed. Thus we see that, even as one swallow does not make a summer, one Philistine does not make a controversy. Where, I would ask Mr Morton, are all the other Philistines? Have they *all* surrendered to us? Is he alone? I wish, in the interests of criticism, that he would rally some force to his side. For controversy is not merely good fun; it is an admirable tonic for the mind, forcing us, as it does, to examine our opinions, and it amplifies our aesthetic faculty by forcing us to realise our temperaments to the full. In politics, as we are always being told, even a Government of all the Talents is demoralised by a weak Opposition. Aesthetic Faculty + Talent − Philistinism : Criticism :: Patriotism + Talent − Opposition : Government. Let us hope, therefore, that the Philistines will pull themselves together. We are in need of them.

But, alas! Philistinism comes only at the heels of some new genius in art, and in dramatic art there is at present no sign of a new genius, native or alien. Oh for one who shall revolutionise English farce! At present we have to be content with such writers as Mr A. Vicarson, whose *Vicar's Dilemma* was produced last Monday evening at Terry's Theatre. I was not present, not having been invited. And I have taken no steps to see the play since. Yet, let not the strenuous reader frown on me as one who is apathetic in his instruction or in my own. I happened to see the play some months ago in a provincial town where I was staying, and, even then, when the promise of spring filled the heart with plenary indulgence to all things; even there, where there was nothing to do in the evening, and bed was the theatre's only rival, I did not hesitate to add *The Vicar's Dilemma* to the grim catalogue of plays one would rather have left unseen. Not that there was anything objectionable in this farce. It was merely oppressive, by reason of its incomparable tameness. What it was all about, I do not clearly remember. There was a choleric major in it, and a fat painter, and an amorous spinster, and Mr Fred Thorne himself played with quiet humour—with more quietness, perhaps, than humour—the part of a vicar who was always examining the bumps on the heads of his parishioners. I had a Lamb-like desire to rush on to the stage and examine the bumps of Mr Fred Thorne himself who was taking this play round the patient provinces. Mr A. Vicarson is apparently a novice. In dealing with the work of novices, we dramatic critics have a custom (due partly to kindliness, partly to the paucity of good playwrights) of saying that the young author has placed himself at one bound in the foremost rank of our playwrights, and that henceforth he is a man to be reckoned with. This is what I say of Mr A. Vicarson. But, if I might 'whisper one word in his clever ear,' I would urge him to consider that there is nothing intrinsically comic in a choleric major, or a fat painter, or an amorous spinster, or even a vicar who practises phrenology. To bring these characters on the scene is not really the same thing as to write a good farce. When the major, the painter, the spinster and the vicar, having arrived on the scene, are so developed by their author as to be amusing, then, and then only, is the farce a good one. This is a hard saying, I know, but I hope that Mr A. Vicarson, as a man to be reckoned with, will yet receive it. Since I saw the play, the cast has been strengthened by the accession of Miss Esmé Beringer and Mr Righton, and other talented artists, whom I look forward to seeing in their next impersonations. There is also a *lever de rideau*, *Meadow Sweet*, familiar to me as one of the trifles which some people call 'silly,' and others, meaning the same thing, call 'pretty.' Lest I be thought to have played this week the part of the wicked fairy who was not bidden to the christening, I hasten to urge all my readers to book seats immediately for Terry's Theatre, that subsequently they may ask themselves when and where, or whether, they ever saw so dull a farce as *The Vicar's Dilemma*, and that, having answered this question truly, they may endorse my gentle curses.

On Tuesday, by the bye, there was a *matinée* of 'Mr Wilson Barrett's great play, *The Daughters of Babylon*.' (Some plays are born great, others achieve greatness, others have greatness thrust on them.) As the performance was for a charity and its author is in Australia, I will not try to indicate in which of these three classes I should place *The Daughters of Babylon*. Enough to say that it was very well acted by an earnest company of volunteers. Miss Beatrice Wilson, whom I saw for the first time, played the heroine's part with grace, talent and conviction. Mr Jerrold Robertshaw was, I thought, very good in the part of a villain. Indeed, the whole afternoon passed for me more pleasantly than I had foreseen.

[*16 July 1898*]

## A STARTLED FAUN

Snatch a man as he lies, vacuous and dreaming, by the sea's edge, when he has scarce yet purged himself of memory in the sea's sacramental; drop him down, thump! in an apoplectic desert of dust and soot, and clap upon his head, whose coronal was erst but straw, that which will now seem heavier than one of the innumerable chimney-pots, its prototypes, in the leaden sky above him; drive him into a semi-circular den upholstered in red velvet and packed with human species, and leave him to gasp there for a hundred and forty minutes whilst certain painted bipeds, presumably human, perform behind a row of lights a certain series of merry, merry antics—do all these things to him, oh Fate, since it amuses you to do them, but don't, I beseech you, do not carry the joke so far as to ask him what he thought of the play!—

> *'Ich hab' es doch getragen*
> *Aber frage nur nicht wie*!

My opinion, as you would know, oh Fate, if you had read Mr Chalmers Mitchell's admirable article on 'Health and Brain-work' in last week's *Saturday*, will really be of no value to you at all. Mr Mitchell demonstrates that strength of body and strength of intellect are in inverse ratio to each other, and that never is a man's mind so feeble as when his body has been braced by rustication. A month ago I was a shadow with an enlarged brain, receptive as any Leyden-jar, and should doubtless have found in *Tommy Dodd*, at the Globe Theatre, an irresistable motive for my pen. But last night, sitting there in my stall, how could I be receptive? I was as one oppressed by some vague, familiar nightmare. Around me was a sea of male and female faces, most of them quite familiar to me, all of them nodding to one another like mandarins and beaming through spectacles or pince-nez—it is a curious fact that almost all first-nighters wear glasses of some kind. From an upper-box a programme fluttered down, as usual, and fell on somebody's head, making somebody very cross. When the curtain fell, half the audience stood up and began to budge about, with loud apologies for treading on the toes of the other half. And when the curtain was up, there was the usual garden, with a young lady (dressed up to the nines) in it, saying, 'So, sir, that decides me! From this day forth we shall be as strangers!' And there were men tapping one another on the chest and saying, 'Look here! You don't split on me: I don't split on you!' And there was quick music at the end of every act, and plenty of rattle and bustle, and some one came down a ladder, and some one else wanted to fire a revolver. Indeed, I am sure everything was as it should have been. The audience roared with laughter. I alone was unable to enjoy myself; my heart was far away, on the coast. My ears were as two shells, where the murmur of waves is yet lingering —how could I hear well? How could I see well through that bronze mask, my face? It was as much I could do to breathe. Let my reader, therefore, not resent my reticence about the play. At present, I am simply the young man up from the country; my mind is a seething chaos of shyness and bewilderment. I am a startled faun; be very gentle with me! Do you remember how Sulla's soldiers found in a Thessalian wood and dragged off to the Dictator's tent a creature with the face and body of a man but the hoofs and horns of a goat? Sulla questioned and examined the creature, but at length, pitying its dumb terror, ordered his men to release it, and smiled as he watched it leaping away with gestures of uncouth joy to its own wood. I am in the position of that captured faun. Though you cannot send me whence I came, do not browbeat me; give me time to acclimatise myself; let me be! My critical faculties will be in full swing, I promise you, before the Christmas holidays.

The foregoing words were written on Wednesday morning. The hours passed, night fell, and fate drove me down to the Adelphi Theatre, that I might witness the first performance of Mr Sims's new play. I was sullen enough on the way, but I 'went,' as the phrase is, 'quietly.' Resignation was setting in. Already had the roar of the traffic overcome the sea's murmur in my ears. Already was I feeling a trifle less robust, and, in due proportion, a trifle more cerebrative. Not that I was able to grasp in detail all the ingenious complications into which Mr Sims had woven his heroes and heroines, his villains of either gender. Indeed, I confess that when, in the last act ('A Riverside Cellar'), Miss Neilson grasped the arm of the worst villain and cried, 'Where are you going?' and he, setting his teeth, made answer, 'To meet the woman who was to have been the wife of the man your father murdered,' it was not so much my heart that stood still with horror as my head that reeled. Who shall say now that more brain-power might well be brought to bear on the writing of English plays? Such a play as *The Gipsy Earl* seems to me a really marvellous feat of the human intellect. To understand clearly all its involutions and convolutions were a hard task even for a person of the frailest physique: what shall one say of him who not merely understands them, but actually evolved them and developed them and solved them in the sacrosanctity of 'Opposite-the-Ducks Villa'? Driving his men thus steadfastly, his desk radiant in the dry light of intellection, Mr Sims never removes his left hand from the public's pulse, save when, now and again, he clutches at that waistcoat beneath which his own heart is so tumultuously throbbing. Perfect in him, the coalition of heart and head! Critics who sneer at melodrama as a puerile convention will do well to consider how intensely difficult a form it is. Whatever they may think of melodrama, they should regard the melodramatist with that reverence which is always owed to the indomitable. I was sorry to notice that the cheap sneers of these critics seemed to have so far corrupted the pit and gallery that there was actually a ripple of laughter when the comic man recognised the rightful Earl by an old scar on the wrist. Nor, I fancied, did the hisses sound quite so genuine as of old when the villains took their calls. Perhaps this was due to the fact that Mr Sims had made one of his villains a Yorkshireman—surely a very dangerous experiment, and a great strain on the public conscience! However, there was no doubt about the applause for the heroes and heroines and Mr Sims himself. The whole thing was evidently a great success. There was such a vast number of mimes involved in it that, were I to consider the whole cast, I suppose that even the *Saturday* itself could not contain the notices that should be written. It is enough to say that Mr Fred Terry and Miss Neilson, the two principals, were not at all afraid of their parts, and acted as well as ever.

[*3 September 1898*]

## 'THE TERMAGANT'

But why *Termagant*? Why should Messrs Parker and Carson have saddled their poor heroine with this unkind word, which her behaviour does so little to justify? 'Termagant' is a word that was often applied, like 'shrew,' or 'common scold,' to those women whose unbridled tongues landed them in the stocks or the river. The type and the mode of dealing with it are happily obsolete, although the former is supposed to survive in some fish-markets. But 'Termagant' is still a word of unpleasing significance, and Messrs P. and C. —space is precious, and collaboraters must put up with initials— would have acted wiselier in avoiding it. Their Beatrix of Moya is a trifle self-willed, a trifle capricious in her moods, but so is any ordinary girl whom fortune makes a potentate. However much she may venerate and defer to the grey-beards, her counsellors, a young queen cannot free herself from bondage to that will which is law indeed, those caprices which to thwart were treason—her own will and her own caprices. 'Very few women are not capricious,' says Disraeli in one of his novels, 'and they are always the most dangerous women of all.' For 'women' substitute 'young queens,' and the aphorism is indisputable. It is well known that our own Queen, when she first came to the throne, was not always patient of her counsellors' wisdom. It is said that she who has just been crowned in Amsterdam has moments of waywardness; yet I have no doubt that she will become, in time, as wise and beneficent a Queen as ours is, nor have I any doubt that the same prophecy would have come true in the case of Beatrix of Moya, had not that engaging creature committed suicide, for the pleasure of Messrs P. and C., on her lover's bier. At any rate, Beatrix is no more a 'termagant' than either of the real queens whom I have cited. And, even if one were to admit that the description was justified, *The Termagant* would still be a misnomer for the play. After the first act, in which she calls her suitor a 'thing' and a 'man-fish' and a 'sea-monster,' the termagancy of Beatrix evaporates. True, in the second act, she calls him a 'tailor of Salamanca,' but this is only under stress of that anger which the mildest woman feels when a man makes a fool of her. She lends her woman, Felipa, a ring with which to poison Garcia, the villain, but that is no act of termagancy, however shocking it may seem to an audience not composed of mediaeval Spaniards. She gives back to Garcia the sword he has forfeited, that he may slay with it the lover whom, on every evidence of eye and ear, she believes to be faithless. That, again, is exactly what any nice girl of that period would have done. It is not an act of termagancy at all. The authors have deliberately prepared for Beatrix a most painful misunderstanding—why should they call her a bad name because she does not immediately see through it and behave like a lamb? The fact is that there have now been so many plays acted in England and so many titles registered, that to find a title which shall be at once accurate and attractive, and shall not evoke an angry letter from some one who had, in the early seventies, produced a play with that very title at the Town Hall, Plymouth, is a task requiring more time and research than can be afforded by such busy favourites as Messrs P. and C.

I should describe the play as a very charming tragedy of intrigue. It is not a sombre tragedy in which the characters move, step by step, under the ban of inevitable destiny to their doom. Rather does doom spring out on them as they hurry through a labyrinth of ingenious complications. Felipa, whose husband is at the wars, has yielded herself to the simulated passion of Garcia. Roderigo brings with him a letter for Felipa from her husband. He makes a tryst with Felipa and gives her the letter, saying,

> 'Read here of deeper love
> Than I can word. Be this your shield, Felipa.'

Beatrix, to whom he has declared his love, overhears the speech, sees Felipa open the letter and overhears some of the passionate words contained in it. In the next act, she asks Felipa to enlighten her. Just as Felipa is about to do so, Garcia overhears her, intervenes in the nick of time, sends Felipa 'off,' and poisons the mind of Beatrix against her lover. Again, Garcia has just persuaded Felipa to give him the fatal ring, when Roderigo, having entered unnoticed, intercepts it. He supposes it to be a wedding-ring and tells Felipa that he will show it to her husband as a sure token of her death. Later, Beatrix espies it on his finger, and supposes that Felipa has given it as a love-token. Not Scribe himself ever manipulated a 'property' more prettily than Messrs P. and C. Such skill is, doubtless, comic—I use the word technically—rather than tragic, in its essence; insomuch that many people might think the austerely tragic conclusion of the play an error in art. That, however, is not my opinion. A tragic note is clearly struck in that early scene where Beatrix urges Felipa to kill Garcia rather than lose her honour, The part of Felipa herself—a very beautiful part, beautifully played by Miss Grace Warner—is tragic from the outset. Intensely tragic, too, is the scene where Beatrix is tempted to poison Roderigo with the ring but cannot steel

## 'THE TERMAGANT'

herself to the deed. The double death seemed to me, then, a quite justifiable, if not quite inevitable, 'curtain.' Altogether, it is not too much to say that I enjoyed my evening. I admired the writing of the play very much. How many dramatists would have bedevilled their dialogue with such jewels as 'marry!' and 'foresooth!' and 'tricksome popinjay' and 'naughty knave,' under the pathetic impression that they were being English! In writing a period-play all that is needed is a certain *refinement* of language, a rejection of current colloquialisms. If, as in *The Termagant*, the writer can also compass a rhythmic quality, so much the better! I was glad to note in some scenes, (especially in the last scene, where Roderigo's body is borne in), a skilful experiment in those effects which Maeterlinck gains by the iteration and variation of a phrase. There was only one discord in the writing of the play. That was the series of Wellerisms assigned to the comic servant, Nicolo. It was a very bad discord, and I writhed. Every time Mr Paulton opened his lips, I was so preoccupied in writhing that I have really no idea whether his performance was good or not. Probably it was very good. Mr Barnes looked well and acted well as a Friar; so did Mr Abingdon as Garcia. Mr C. himself played the part of Roderigo with fervour and discrimination, using his fine voice melodiously. He is, I think, one of the few mimes who, valuing elocution as in itself an art, enunciate with a sense of beauty. In Miss Nethersole's acting, sense of beauty is never apparent. But she is so very clever and so very sincere that she does attain to that truth which is, according to the *cliché*, 'beauty seen from another side.' Sincerity is the chief element of good acting, after all; to convince the audience—that is the most important thing. Personally, I confess, I would always barter conviction for enchantment. But then, I am a dilettante, as you know.

At the Vaudeville there is a very gay little piece, *Her Royal Highness*. Serious drama is the more delightful, the less one has to exert himself during the day. For him whose mind or body has been thus painfully exerted—and he is the average man in this age of stress—opera bouffe or burlesque or musical comedy is a good anodyne. Singing and dancing were the origin of drama, and perhaps they will be also its final form; certainly, they are still its most popular form. Not that *Her Royal Highness* is merely soothing; it is also most amusing. Its author has done his lyrics so deftly and displays so much of comic intention that, in the name of my Editor and colleagues, I forgive his two grenadiers their rather heterodox song about this paper. Miss Kitty Loftus plays the chief part. She has a pretty, funny, little method of her own.

[*10 September 1898*]

## MR GEORGE BANCROFT AS CASABIANCA

Mr George Bancroft's play is very dramatic, but his position is even more so: I admire him even more than I admire *Teresa*. The wreck of the good ship *Sardou*, whence all but he have fled, sinks lower and lower beneath the surface, but he, that lonely, gallant boy, stands on the burning deck with head erect and arms folded, never flinching. Though the flames envelop him and the waters compass him about, he persists, pale but undaunted, on the 'well-made' timbers of that dear old craft which he was taught to honour. He is a little hero. He is the hero of his own play.

When the curtain rose on the 'Villa Teresa, Lake of Como,' I settled down to enjoy myself. Somehow, I always feel thoroughly at home on the Lake of Como, and while two well-trained servants were giving a concise analysis of the principals' careers and characters, I indulged in pleasant anticipation of tragedy to come. Yes! for the Lake of Como, though it looks so blue and smiling on the back-cloth, always portends tragedy. It strikes the key-note of the South, where the passions are swifter, deeper, more lurid; where noblemen lay their hands on their hearts and turn up their eyes and whisper '*The Cause!*' meaning Socialism; where the frequent dagger flashes in the sunlight as it is pressed home to—but I anticipate. I was, indeed, anticipating throughout the whole performance of *Teresa*. Plays of that pattern always tempt one to look three or four scenes ahead. Given a clear brain and a little experience of the stage, one can always make a pretty accurate forecast, whose fulfilment comes as a kind of compliment to oneself and puts one in a fine good humour. Given an ornamental dagger—Teresa is given such a dagger in the first act—an Italian heroine is bound to kill somebody with it and, probably, to kill herself also. If she be engaged to an Englishman who has a bad twin-brother—Valentine Elsbrooke, Teresa's *fiancé*, has a bad twin-brother who, in the first act, casts sinister glances after the lady's-maid and talks about some girl whom he has seduced in Vienna—what more natural than that this brother should waylay her and insult her on the eve of her wedding, and that she, not knowing who he is, should stab him with the dagger? This being so, it follows that the body will be duly borne in on a bier, surrounded by picturesque policemen and brothers of the Misericordia. Valentine Elsbrooke and his father lift the pall and recognise the body They are stricken with grief. Enter Teresa. She lifts the pall. The dead man, her lover's brother, is the man she stabbed that afternoon. She utters a cry. The curtain comes down. Nothing could be more effective, except, perhaps, the scene in the next act, where she confesses to her lover. Count Caprile, Teresa's rejected suitor, tells Valentine that she saw Teresa go out closely veiled, on the eve of her wedding, and meet, in a lonely spot, some man unknown. This story might be a fabrication, or it might be easily explained by Teresa, but Valentine becomes desperate. Exit Caprile. Enter Teresa. Valentine taxes her with wantonness. She kneels to him, and begs him to hear all. He spurns her with violence, and she falls prostrate. He is ashamed of himself, and begs her to tell him all. When he hears that she unwittingly murdered his brother, who had insulted her, he tears the mourning band from his sleeve and kisses her effusively. He seems to be quite overjoyed. 'In real life,' some one next to me muttered, 'people wouldn't behave like that.' No? But in Sardou's plays they would. And *Teresa* is modelled on Sardou, not on life, as none knows better than our young friend, Casabianca. Every young artist begins with imitation of some elder artist, and one should praise or blame him according as his imitation be good or bad. I refuse to see that Mr George Bancroft is to be pooh-poohed because he has begun with an imitation of Sardou, not of Ibsen. The question is: has he imitated Sardou well? My description of the plot has been bald and fragmentary, and does no manner of justice to it. As a matter of fact, *Teresa* is a very ingenious piece of work. I do not know that it could be better of its kind. When Mr Bancroft escapes, as no doubt he will, from the burning wreck of Sardouism, he will drift or swim till he be cast ashore on that happy isle, his own temperament. And there he may do great things.

Meanwhile, his first achievement has been admirably produced at the Garrick. The costumes worn by the players are rather too modern for the atmosphere of the play—they should have been designed by Mr Percy Anderson, from the fashion-plates of 1880. But the scenery is excellent—never have I seen the Lake of Como to greater advantage—and 'the cast is a strong one.' Mr Allan Aynesworth, as the bad twin-brother, somewhat marred his performance by laughing at the end of every sentence. Perhaps he was laughing for very joy that he had at length got a part in which he had to do something more than merely look and sound pleasant. Mr Laurence Irving was intense and interesting as Count Caprile, and he looked very Italian. Mr Bourchier, as Valentine, looked very English, but he speaks the language indifferently, and I did not admire his performance—he did not seem to be doing his best. Mr Bourchier was once a distinguished member of the O.U.D.S. Is he, I wonder, qualifying for re-election? Miss Violet Vanbrugh played the heroine with much grace and power, making the most of all the situations. As the maid, no one except Miss Rosina Filippi could have been so good as Miss Gigia was.

I have also seen *The Three Musketeers* at Camberwell. I remember that when *Trilby* was produced in England a certain critic, who has earned an enviable reputation for austerity, declared that he had refrained from reading the book in order that he might be able to judge the play, impartially, as a play. That was very upright of him, and very creditable to him, but I doubt whether it was also quite sensible. *Trilby* did not pretend to be a play in itself, but rather to be an illustration, a realisation, of certain fictional creatures of which the public was enamoured, and its success or failure depended on the degree in which those creatures were realistically presented, through the new medium, to the public; insomuch that our friend might have pocketed his austerity and read the book, without scandalising any one on this side of the Tweed. When such books as *The Prisoner of Zenda* or *Under the Red Robe*, in which plot is everything and the characters are mere puppets, find their way to the footlights, there is, doubtless, some advantage for that dramatic critic who has denied himself the dubious pleasure of reading them. Though it is by reason of their many editions that they are dramatised, they gain, as plays, an independent existence, and they should be judged independently. Now, *The Three Musketeers* of Dumas is a book which every one knows and loves. Any one who dramatises it must simply aim at making his play a lively reminiscence, a lively representation, of Dumas's heroes. Mr Henry Hamilton's version, like Mr Potter's version of *Trilby*, should be judged not as a play in itself, but as a reminiscence and representation. Every one knows Porthos, Athos and D'Artagnan—they are old, familiar friends. We have all laughed with them in their taverns, sympathised with them over their love-affairs, applauded their sabre-thrusts, drawn sighs of relief at their escapes. When I say that we have all done so, you must not suppose that there are no exceptions to this rule. There are, in fact, several exceptions, and I am one of them. I have never read the book. I have often longed to while away an idle month or two in reading it, but, fearing that it might one day be dramatised, and having always had a presentiment that sooner or later I should stumble into dramatic criticism, I have refrained. And now I realise, too late, that my austerity in this case, like Mr Archer's in the other, has been but a silly error. Not having read the book, I can give no valuable opinion of the play. As a play in itself, Mr Hamilton's *Three Musketeers* is not very good—it is laborious, diffuse, jumpy. Several critics have gravely complimented Mr Hamilton on its 'literary merit.' They were impressed, doubtless, by the beauty of that speech in which Buckingham recalls to Anne of Austria their first meeting. I have not retained the whole speech, but 'Do you not remember? The *balmy* air, the *flower-enamelled* grass, the *starry* sky?' will always linger in my mind—words of strange enchantment, delicate triumphs of verbal art. Sometimes Mr Hamilton suffers his literary sense to mar the naturalness of his dialogue: 'And he, leaping on his horse, which was saddled hard by, rode away,' is not the kind of thing that people say *vivâ voce*. However, perhaps Dumas made his characters talk like that. If so, I must not complain. From the tremendous applause with which the play was received, I gathered that Mr Hamilton had really succeeded in translating the atmosphere of the book to the stage. Never was heartier enthusiasm in any theatre. Mr Waller has evidently got hold of a great success. Of his performance I speak with no less diffidence than of the play itself. I should imagine, however, that he was a very fine copy of D'Artagnan. His performance seemed to me, *à priori*, very brilliant—even more brilliant, suppler, more varied than his Hotspur. And those members of his company who were not positively good seemed to me 'abundantly adequate.' But what a pity it is that in plays whose characters bear French names there should always be such discrepance in pronunciation! In this play, as in others, every member of the cast has his or her own pet theory of pronunciation. 'D'Artagnan,' for example, is pronounced in every conceivable way, from 'D'Artanya' to 'D'Artanniong.' I think it would be well if all French names were forbidden on our stage. There would be no great difficulty in finding passable equivalents in English. For my part, if ever I dramatise *The Three Musketeers*, I shall call the heroes, quite simply, *Brown, Jones and Robinson*.

[*17 September 1898*]


## 'THE GREAT RUBY' &c.

I conceive that for people who have nothing better to do it must be great fun to write a play for Drury Lane. Last year, the management wanted Battersea Park and a diving-bell, amongst other things; this year, it wanted Lord's, a balloon, a four-in-hand, bicyclists on the road, Prince Ranjitsinhji and the Military Tournament. Mr Collins, I assume, writes these things down on a sheet of paper, which Messrs Cecil Raleigh and Henry Hamilton take to the seaside, and in due course the play is delivered. In fact, Druriolography must be very like doing *bouts-rimés*, and the ingenious result bears the same relation to drama as do *bouts-rimés* to poetry. Have Messrs Raleigh and Hamilton deduced, this year, a plausible play from Mr Collins's premisses? I do not mean a play which will be applauded —for nobody can refrain from clapping in a National Theatre—but rather a play which carries some illusion of drama: do the given scenes seem to have been evolved from the play, or does the play seem to be a mere setting for the given scenes? Is this too high a test? As a student of Druriolography, I think not. A great poem, of course, cannot be founded on *bouts-rimés*—the aim is to make a seemingly natural poem, and that aim can be attained by due ingenuity. Great drama cannot be founded on Mr Collins's lines—all that Mr Collins can hope for is a seemingly natural play, one that shall absorb his own ideas and not expose them, in all their lustrous nudity, to the public eye. And I declare that, with due ingenuity, a seemingly natural play might have been—but has not been—founded on Lord's, a balloon, &c. I admit that the task was difficult. I fancy that Mr Collins may take a sly pleasure in making his annual list as difficult as possible. Prince Ranjitsinhji may have been thrown in merely that the authors might show how far their ingenuity could really go: to turn the celebrity of a living man to dramatic account is a very hard and delicate task, with which, so far as I know, former Druriolographists have not had to cope. How far Prince Kassim Wadia is meant to be a true portrait of Prince Ranjitsinhji, I am not yet sure. He is made up exactly like him; he plays cricket for Cambridge and makes enormous scores; the India Office insists that he shall return to his native land. So far, the portrait is taken direct from life. But has the real Prince ever fallen in love with a Russian adventuress; has he helped her to steal a jewel; has he murdered a man in a balloon? If Messrs Raleigh and Hamilton know that he has done these things, their exposure of him should have been made to the police, not to the public. If he has not done these things, Messrs Raleigh and Hamilton have been guilty of a rather gross breach of good taste—for how is the public to know where the realistic part of their portrait ends and the fictional part of it begins? That the Censor did not step in and save Prince Ranjitsinhji is not extraordinary. The Censor's vagaries are a sacred institution. But I do wonder that the public has not protested against the cheapening of last year's hero. Will Mr C. B. Fry be represented as a thief and murderer next autumn? And, meanwhile, has the figure of Prince Ranjitsinhji at Madame Tussaud's been moved into the Chamber of Horrors?

I have digressed. I was saying that *The Great Ruby* is not a natural play, that the authors might have made a more ingenious solution of the problem set them by Mr Collins. But, you may argue, the public wants to see Lord's, a balloon, &c., and does not care twopence for the play's quality. Possibly; yet that is no reason why Mr Collins, to whom Drury Lane has been given as a sacred trust, should be content with trash. I am sure that Mr Collins is anxious to elevate the public with good plays. His mistake is in leaving Druriolography in the hands of Messrs Raleigh and Hamilton. Why should he not make it a public competition? Let him publish his list of scenes early in the year, fix a date on or before which all solutions must be sent in, and then select the best for his next production. That would be a very popular move. The public fritters away all its leisure in solving those little acrostics and puzzles which are the pivot of the minor press, everyone hoping to win a cottage-piano, or a sewing-machine, or even a postal-order for five-shillings, and to see his or her photograph reproduced over his or her name and address. What labour would these good people spare if the prize dangled before them were the royalties of a Druriolographist? All that very real ingenuity which they squander now on the pettiest tasks would be pressed into the service of Mr Collins. I make my suggestion in perfect seriousness. I hope that Mr Collins will make it. Think! 'The Manager of Drury Lane Theatre has pleasure in announcing that the winner of the Dramaturgic Competition for 1899 is:

Miss Hilda Parkes,
32 Lime Row,
Leamington,

whose solution will therefore be produced at Drury Lane early in September. The solutions sent in by

Mrs Albert Sprigg,
The Acacias,
Ealing,

and by

Mr Cecil Raleigh,
Playgoers' Club,

have been adjudged worthy of honourable mention.

Setting aside the play itself, I found *The Great Ruby* very good indeed. It is an admirable substitute for the cinematograph, and it has this advantage over the rival invention: it does not quiver. To watch a cinematograph is to expose one's optic nerves to an awful strain: to persist in watching it is to court blindness. At Drury Lane, however, the proscenium is quite steady, and one's eyes are safe. Whether the lives of those who sit in the two or three front rows of the stalls are equally safe, is another question. By this time, doubtless, the horses in the fourth act have become accustomed to the footlights. But on the first night the poor brutes seemed horribly nervous and unmanageable. The horse ridden by the Indian Prince, after jibbing in the middle of the stage, finally bolted off with some gallant super clinging to its bridle—greatly to my relief, for I, sitting in the second row of the stalls, had thought it quite as likely as not to take a flying leap over the orchestra, and had been wondering who would be chosen to criticise plays for this paper. Otherwise the evening passed quite smoothly and cheerfully. There was only one disappointment. In the scene at Lord's, the characters continually asked one another whether they were going that night to the Opera, and I supposed that in due course the stage would be occupied by Melba, Plançon and the De Reszkes, whilst Mrs John Wood, Mr Pateman and the rest of the company would appear in various boxes about the house. Why should not the auditorium be thus utilised in Mr Collins's scheme of realism? Perhaps next autumn . . . but I will *not* throw out any more hints to Mr Collins. Even as it is, I shall not have room to discuss *Macbeth*, the very powerful and interesting play which Mr Forbes Robertson has just produced at the Lyceum. That must be reserved for next week. But I may mention that *Little Miss Nobody*, at the Lyric, is a bright example of its kind, with many good songs and dances. Miss Kate Cutler plays the chief part in it very carefully and prettily. Mr Lionel Brough plays with such gusto as to make one forget that he was doing this kind of thing when the rest of the cast were in their cradles. But I hope that he does not mean to cut the legitimate for long. The chorus behaves vivaciously. *The Belle of New York* has evidently taught English managers the value of a vivacious chorus, and the Paris-model convention of the Gaiety will soon, I hope, be quite obsolete. The dresses at the Lyric look duly expensive. But in pieces of this kind how much better it were to make all the dresses fantastic. A chorus in Scotch tweeds is horrible. In point of realism it is a complete failure—nothing could look less like real people in the Highlands. The manager, of course, aims not at realism, but at a nice *coup d'oeil*. Then let him avoid Scotch tweeds at any rate. Never was material so unsuited to what theatrical costumiers, I am told, call 'limelight-wear.' All the Scotch dresses should have been silken. At the Prince of Wales's, where *The Royal Star* is being played, one finds a really intelligent use of costume, the aspect of a period amusingly and prettily suggested. The scheme of the play is trite and meagre, but Messrs Maurice Ordonneau and Francis Richardson, the authors, have contrived some good lyrics and jests and—the most important point—a good part for Mr Edouin, that amazing creature.

[*24 September 1898*]

## MAX, MR ARCHER, AND OTHERS

Creative power, the power to conceive ideas and to execute them, is an attribute of virility: women are denied it. In art, as in science, politics and other branches of human activity, the part taken by women may often be quite charming, but serious it never is. Neither in painting nor in writing have women ever originated. Whatever they have done in these arts has been mere work of imitation. Their aim has always been, and will always be, that their work may not betray their sex: they know that, as women, they have no *locus standi* in art. In so far as they practise art at all, they are aping virility, exceeding their natural sphere. Never does one understand so well the failure of women in art as when one sees them deliberately impersonating men upon the stage and, despite all their efforts, remaining, as they always do, utterly and obviously feminine. It often happens that men impersonate women and on the stage with great success. In gesture and manner, Mr Dan Leno talking about 'Mrs Kelly' is as feminine as anything could be. There is plenty of evidence that the actors who, in the Greek and in the Elizabethan drama, represented female characters, acquitted themselves well and produced the necessary illusion. Some of the most successful lawyers, doctors and merchants of our time won early laurels as Alcestis, or Antigone, or Electra, on the classic boards of the A.D.C. I myself have seen Mr Arthur Roberts and Mr Penley playing female parts almost as well as Mr Dan Leno is playing one now. But I have never seen an actress, young or old, in any theatre, playing a man's part with any verisimilitude. This fact is the more remarkable, in that acting is the one art in which women can rival men. Every drama must contain male and female characters, and, for a reason which I shall anon suggest, it is better that the female characters be acted by women. Thus, in theatrical art, women have a *locus standi* and can attain success. But the fact remains that, though many actors can successfully obscure their sex, no actress can ever obscure hers. The explanation is simple. Men and women are not two creatures of wholly distinct composition. A man contains in himself the whole of a women's nature, *plus* certain other qualities which make the difference between him and her. And for him to obscure these other qualities for a theatrical purpose is easier than for her to assume them. Now, in exact ratio as the man is more successful in a female character than *vice versâ*, so it is, on the whole, more pleasant to see a woman in the character of a man than a man in the character of a woman. The greater the aesthetic illusion, the more strongly does our natural sense of fitness rebel against the travesty of nature. To me, and doubtless to most people, there is something rather uncanny, not very pleasant, in (for example) Mr Dan Leno impersonating Mrs Kelly's friend. On the other hand, When Miss Millard masquerades, in *Lady Ursula*, as a youth of the last century, the effect is simply pleasing. The bounds of sex remain inviolate. In gesture, deportment and manner, Miss Millard is as feminine as ever: only the other characters in the play could possibly be deceived as to her sex. Nor, from the point of aesthetic illusion, does this greatly matter. For, like Rosalind or Mignon, Lady Ursula does but dress up as a boy, in the course of the play, and we are, at a pinch, willing to believe that the rest of the *dramatis personae* are deceived by her assumption, though we ourselves see through it so very clearly. It is only when an actress undertakes to play a male character—as Madame Bernhardt, Lorenzaccio; Mrs Bandmann-Palmer, Hamlet; Miss de Lussan, Cherubino—and tries to illude directly the audience itself, that the play materially suffers. *Lady Ursula* loses little or nothing by the femineness of Miss Millard in boy's costume, and it gains much by her gaiety in the scenes of comedy, and her tenderness in the sentimental scenes, by the general charm of her acting. Mr Herbert Waring acts, as usual, most admirably. Mr Fulton, in a smallish part, distinguishes himself by his sense of the play's period; he is, indeed, the only member of the cast who really suggests that period—the others are too obviously of this century. Personally, I would rather that Mr Percy Lyndal, Mr Cosmo Stuart and the others should play their parts in so modern a spirit as they do than that they should exploit the clumsy antics and dreary affectations with which the manners of the eighteenth century are usually parodied on the stage. Nevertheless, *Lady Ursula* would be all the better if the actors, observing Mr Fulton as their model, would import a little more 'style' into their demeanour. Also, the stage-manager might have been a little more careful about the *mise-en-scène*. In the third act, for example, though the walls, with their columns and their sconces, are Georgian enough, the sideboard and the chiffonier of imitation oak (with bevelled glass let into the panels) destroy all illusion of the period and transport us straight into the Tottenham Court Road, Also, Mr Anthony Hope might, by taking a little more trouble, have given his dialogue more of the eighteenth-century tone. In the third act, which is in every way the best act, he has managed to convey some of the florid formality of the period. But in the other acts, beyond throwing in a frequent 'egad' or 'on my life' he seems not to have attempted anything of the kind. His dialogue is pleasant enough; it is imbued with his own airy mediocrity of style, which some people might mistake for distinction. But, in the writing of a *rococo* comedy, something rather more delicate and more exquisite than that is demanded—demanded, I should say, only by a very small class of playgoers. The vast majority of playgoers neither knows or cares about literary style. The dramatic critics seem to care about it, but, with a few exceptions, not to know about it. In fact, so far as commercial success is concerned, literary style is the last thing which any dramatist need covet. *Lady Ursula* will be, commercially, a great success. Except the fourth act, it has none of those flaws on which the public set the ready finger of disapproval. Without the fourth act, it would, indeed, be a really well-constructed play. I wonder how many plays have been marred by the dramatist's insane idea that there ought always, at all costs, to be a fourth act?

I have a great esteem and admiration for Mr Archer, and I am sorry to learn, in the light of this week's *World*, that he has been fretting about me and my method of criticism. He complains publicly of me that I am in the habit of 'fabricating authorities' and 'fabricating opinions.' This is not quite just. As to my 'authorities,' Mr Archer must not suppose that every one of my quotations which he cannot immediately verify is an original composition of my own. As to my 'opinions,' I assure Mr Archer that they are all quite genuine, natural and sincere. I may often exaggerate things. I may often invent things. But that does not mean that my general opinions are not honestly held by me. Sometimes, when, as for this article, the time at my disposal is rather brief, I have no time for exaggeration and invention, and I have to serve up my opinions without the usual garnish, to serve them up as obvious, unadorned convictions. Does Mr Archer suppose that the usual garnish would make them, fundamentally, any the less real? As for Mr Archer's objections to my theory that *Macbeth*, *Hamlet* and *Romeo and Juliet* are no longer good for production, I am not at all convinced by them. He declares that 'even of those who have seen a play before, and perhaps seen it several times, practically no one retains any clear recollection of a single detail of conception or execution, intonation, emphasis or business.' Surely a very strange contention! It seems that Mr Archer himself, when he saw the new production of *Macbeth* a second time, found he had 'forgotten almost all the details of the first performance, not three weeks earlier.'

Well! every one's memory is weak in some direction. I myself cannot remember dates or proper names. Mr Archer cannot remember details of acting. But he must not imagine that the average playgoer is in similar case. He asks whether I could compare, 'even at half-a-dozen crucial points,' previous actors in the part of *Macbeth* with Mr Forbes Robertson. Certainly, I could. I have seen, in all, only three performances of *Macbeth*, and I could easily discriminate between them in many details. But I would not shrink from an even harder test. In *Hamlet* I have seen many artists, including Sir Henry Irving, Mr Wilson Barrett, Mrs Bandmann-Palmer, Mr Beerbohm Tree, Mr Nutcombe Gould and Mr Murray Carson. If Mr Archer wish—I am sure he will not wish—that I should give him a private representation, showing some of the main points in which these artists differed or agreed in treatment of (say) the 'To be or not to be' soliloquy, I shall be happy to oblige him. Possibly, my memory for acting may be abnormally developed; but I am sure that, even so, Mr Archer's memory for acting is abnormally *un*developed, and that he must not regard himself as being, in point of memory, a typical playgoer. If he inquire, he will find, I think, that most playgoers will be able to recall for his benefit many of those tricks of intonation, emphasis and so forth, which he supposes to be immediately forgotten by almost everyone in the audience.

But Mr Archer has another quaint objection to my theory. He says that 'curiosity and suspense are not indispensable factors' in drama, and he seems to deduce from that proposition that one can see a good play any number of times without any diminution of aesthetic pleasure. Of course, one's pleasure in a work of art is not limited to first sight. But I maintain that there is a limit to aesthetic receptivity, and that when one has heard about and read about a play till one knows it through and through, one cannot (even if one has never before seen it acted) derive from it any real and lively pleasure from its presentation. Even one's favourite poem or picture begins to pall when one studies it too constantly. But the poet's or painter's appeal is direct, whilst the dramatist appeals through the mime, and so appeals in a new way through every new mime? Exactly. And when one sees *Hamlet*, one thinks only of the mime. The mime overshadows the play. The proper relations between him and the dramatist are upset. And that, I maintain, is a very unsatisfactory state of things. I proposed, as a remedy, that *Hamlet* and other classics should be left in abeyance for thirty years. Mr Archer scouts that plan as impossible, and hints that, on the contrary, there ought to be a State Theatre, in which *Hamlet*, &c., shall be acted as often as they possibly can be. I am afraid that there will not be such a theatre in our time. Personally, I wish there could be, for it would be a simple means of sickening every one of *Hamlet*, &c., so thoroughly that my 'close time' for those plays would very soon become a necessity and a fact.

[*15 October 1898*]


## AN AWFUL WARNING

'The usual thing, I suppose? Nothing like the usual thing!' said Lord Twombley, the 'Cabinet Minister,' as his secretary handed him the speech he was to learn for the opening of the new street. There is in that apophthegm a profundity and truth which Mr Pinero does not usually compass. Its point was accentuated by the fact that the play in which it was spoken failed precisely because it was not the usual thing. The public likes the usual thing, and they who work under the public's eye—politicians, dramatists, policemen and such folk—can do the unusual thing only at their own peril. The further a man work from the public, and the less responsible he be to it, the greater his freedom to do what pleases him. That is why diplomacy is more progressive and more fascinating than politics, and literature or painting than the drama. Politics and drama are behind the times because of the franchise and the 'gods.' The public is always behind the times. When we speak of the 'times' we mean the ideas and actions of a small but gifted minority, which does gradually, painfully drag the public up to the position which itself has reached, though not before a newer minority has established itself still further ahead. Now, the public takes a more serious interest in politics than in the drama, studies them and understands them better, and so is in them nearer behind the times. The drama it regards—why not?—as its little diversion. It does not want to think about it, to make itself uncomfortable over so trivial a matter. It wants to enjoy itself in a quiet, vaccine manner. It wants to browse on the usual thing. So it flocked to *Sweet Lavender*, whilst it left *The Cabinet Minister* more or less severely alone. But *Mrs Tanqueray* was unusual—why was that flocked to? Only because it was thought to be improper. *Mrs Ebbsmith* failed because the public had already been bullied (by the minority) into seeing that there had been nothing so very shocking in her forerunner. If only the serio-propagandist critics had encouraged the public in believing Mr Pinero to be a wicked man, instead of showing them how good he was, the realistic drama might still be flourishing in London—might, by this time, have become the usual thing. The unusual thing can be smuggled quickly into the theatre under some false pretext, but the pretext must be kept up for some time; otherwise the public has to be converted in the ordinary way. And that is a very slow process, as I have shown. The usual thing, however, if it be done passably well, is sure to succeed on its own merits.

Till the curtain rose on the third act of *When a Man's in Love*, the play written by Messrs Anthony Hope and Edward Rose for the Court Theatre, the audience was enjoying itself thoroughly. Here, indeed, they thought was a good example of the usual thing. Messrs Hope and Rose seemed to have composed a triumph. None foresaw the sinister nature of the third act! The very surname of the two authors seemed a safeguard against sinister innovation—the one, the noblest emotion of the human heart; the other, the dear emblem of our land. The cast was a good one, the dialogue was as dolly as could be, and all the characters were ambling serenely down a beaten track such as the public loves. There was no suspicion—how could there be?—that this track led to a horrid, sheer, precipitous abyss. So far, there were only two little flaws in the production. One of these was that Miss Marion Terry, as Lady Mary Thurston, the heroine, had a rather trivial part, in which she had scope only for her charm, none for her power of acting. The other was that the cool-headed, sympathetic American was played by an American, Mr Paul Arthur, not by an Englishman, and so seemed quite unlike an

American—unlike the usual thing. True, the character of 'Captain Hilliard (late U.S. army)' had been drawn by the authors according to the strictest convention. Most of his speeches began duly with an 'I guess' or a 'See here.' He was a great hand at Poker, which he duly played, and at cocktails, which he duly mixed, on the stage. The authors had evidently meant him to be played duly with a strong twang, a sombrero and a goatee. Mr Paul Arthur, with his Cisatlantic voice and vesture, was as terrible a shock to the audience as he must have been to the authors. 'He whipped out his derringer. I whipped out mine. (*Pause*.) He rode to the cemetery. I walked behind.' Imagine that line delivered with no more of a stage-twang than you have, reader, or I.' I am glad to say that the audience bore all this, for the authors' sake, without protest, realising that the authors had splashed on the local colour with a liberal brush, and that it was not their fault if Mr Arthur wantonly washed it all out. But let me leave the painful subject of Mr Arthur. It is pleasant to turn to the first two acts of the play itself. Here was no violation of theatrical probability. Here were no idiotic surprises. Here was Lady Mary Thurston, beloved by the sympathetic American and by Percival Dekker, a nervous millionaire. She rejects the latter, declaring her deep esteem for the former. Here, too, was young and foolish Chris Athelstan, about whom Lady Mary, his cousin, is very anxious, for Chris has fallen among a set of men who cheat him at Poker, and is fast losing all his money. Hilliard tells the young man that these friends of his are sharpers. The young man is angry. In order to convince him, Hilliard devises a scheme. He will himself fleece the young man by means of a silver cigar-case which is bright enough to reflect his opponent's cards. Then he will confess the trick to the young man, who will see how foolish it is to play with elder players. Surely a very perilous and round-about scheme to achieve a very simple purpose! But no matter. Theatrically, it is the usual thing, and it secures the second act. Hilliard confides his scheme to the millionaire, giving him a letter which shall serve as evidence of his own probity. The millionaire, left alone, lights a candle and burns his rival's letter. In the next act, of course, the game takes place, the millionaire being present with another character, Lord Pitkeithly. The public loves a gambling-scene. Realistic gambling would, of course, be quite ineffective on the stage. It would not do for the gambler to play, as in real life, with a calm, inscrutable politeness. The agony of the game must be explicit. Do you remember the scene in *The Masqueraders*, where David Remon gambled for possession of the baronet's wife, and how the baronet gasped and shouted and drank deep potations of brandy, and how, when the game was over, the victorious Remon, instead of smiling and saying quietly, as he would have said in real life, 'Well, some day I must give you your revenge!' clutched his unfortunate opponent by the throat, forced him down upon the floor and half-strangled him, whilst he extorted from him a sacred oath to abide by the results of the game? Mr Ben Webster, who plays the part of Chris Athelstan, behaves in the customary manner, drinking deep potations of brandy, muttering hoarsely, snatching at the cards as they are dealt to him, and at his hair as it stands on end. The audience watches him breathlessly. Meanwhile, the millionaire silently calls Lord Pitkeithly's attention to the cigar-case. Alarums and excursions ensue. Hilliard asks the millionaire to clear him. The millionaire denies receipt of the excriminating letter, denies that Hilliard made any communication to him, Hilliard is left alone, crushed by the blow. The curtain slowly descends between him and an enraptured audience.

During the entr'acte, every one is looking forward to the last act with extreme pleasure. Every one knows what that act will be like. Lady Mary will, of course, believe Hilliard to be guilty of the hideous crime with which he has been charged. In her distress, she will transfer her esteem to the rejected millionaire. He, however, will be stricken with remorse. He will summon all the other characters, make full confession, draw Lady Mary towards Hilliard, join their hands, and, covered with glory, falter from the stage to begin a new life in a new world. The other characters will presently steal away, casting sympathetic glances at the united lovers. And then—

*Hilliard.* Dearest, we shall be very, very happy together, shall we not?

*Lady Mary.* Yes! But we must always remember *him*!

CURTAIN

During the entr'acte, all this seems to us quite inevitable. It is the usual thing and we never dream that we shall not get it. Anon, to our discomfiture and rage, we find our fond anticipations falsified in the most cynical and unseemly fashion! The curtain has hardly risen when 'the Professor,' an important comic character, is brought on, though he has not appeared in either of the preceding acts. This is a bad omen, an appalling breech of propriety. The dramatic critics around me knit their brows and toss their beards, as who should say 'The public will never stand this!' I myself shake my head, murmuring the word 'disgraceful.' But it soon becomes evident that this is no solitary indiscretion. The authors have played fast and loose with the whole act. Lady Mary firmly believes in her lover's innocence. The only difficulty is as to how he shall clear himself in the eyes of the world. Enter Frank Athelstan, a school-boy, who in the first act exhibited an automatic apparatus for taking snap-shots of people without their knowledge. He shows Hilliard a plate representing a lighted candle burning in the daylit drawing-room. From various pieces of evidence Hilliard concludes that this candle was lighted by the millionaire, and that the excriminating letter perished in its flame. The millionaire is sent for. Enter the other characters. Enter the millionaire. Lardy Mary announces that she is betrothed to Hilliard. Chris, Pitkeithly and the millionaire refuse to congratulate. The footlights are lowered, and the school-boy gives a magic-lantern entertainment—imagine! in the last act!—showing comic portraits of Chris, Athelstan, Pitkeithly and other persons of the play. Hilliard says that there is also a portrait of the millionaire, burning a letter. The millionaire is dumbfounded. Realising that the game is up, he slinks out of the room. Pitkeithly and Chris congratulate Hilliard on the happy vindication of his honour. The curtain falls just as the school-boy is taking a snap-shot of Hilliard and Lady Mary in each other's arms.

The audience is dazed. It does not hoot nor hiss. It even applauds, as from force of habit. But how significantly less loud the applause is now than it was at the end of the second act! Now it is but an empty, automatic noise; then it was the spontaneous ebullition of a thousand throats. There has been a wilful, cruel violation of the usual thing. The public is deeply wounded. The dramatic critics around me, struggling into their greatcoats, seem to have aged considerably. I myself, with a dangerous light in my eyes, elbow my way firmly to the vestibule. There I knock at the box-office and demand loudly that my order for a stall shall be returned to me in full.

MORAL

Beware of trifling with the public.

[*22 October 1898*]

## MR DAVIDSON AND HIS PLAY

I have been reading *Godfrida*, Mr John Davidson's new play, with such pleasure that I feel rather churlish in suggesting that it ought not to have been published. Had Mr Davidson published it simply to give me pleasure, I should keep my suggestion to myself; but I suspect that he had other motives as well, and so I will be quite frank. He himself has evidently foreseen that his wisdom will be called in question, for in his fantastic preface the 'Interviewer' is made to ask whether, inasmuch as people will not read a play which they have not seen, he think it wise to publish his play before it has been produced. 'I would not care,' replies the author, 'to invite an audience to witness a play which I could not invite my readers to peruse.' Ciceronian, but rather evasive! The Interviewer's doubt was, not whether the play were worth reading, but whether it ought to have been published before production. However, the question itself was evasive also. The real point is not whether the book will have a good sale. Mr Davidson is a poet of much repute, and there are many people who like to read his every book, many who will read *Godfrida*. On the other hand, there is no doubt that previous publication does mar a play's chances of successful production. The real point, therefore, is whether the publication ought not to have been delayed in the interest of the play itself as a theatrical asset. The Interviewer should have put his question conversely, as thus: 'Will not it be wise, hereafter, to produce your play, seeing that people will not go to see a modern play which they have previously read?' Mr Davidson, in his Ciceronian way, would doubtless have replied that he would not care in to invite his readers to peruse a play which he could not invite an audience to witness—or something to this (very splendid) effect. Yet do I suspect that his point of view is quite simple. I suspect him of having supposed *Godfrida* to be one of those plays which, written by literary men, are better read in the library than seen in the playhouse. (Observe that I too become Ciceronian!) He could not have made a greater mistake. *Godfrida* is a high-spirited romance of action. It is so constructed that it could be acted, with all probability of popular success, exactly as Mr Davidson has written it. Except the preface, there is nothing at all esoteric about it. One enjoys reading it because much of it is very beautifully written, but the writing is never carried to a point where it would retard or obscure the scheme. In a word, it is a play for the stage. Why have it sent thus, in the first instance, to a publisher, not to a manager, and have jeopardised its chances of production? There are two kinds of plays for which publication, not production, is the right destiny. These are, firstly, plays written without reference to the conventions of the modern theatre—plays which, like *The Cenci*, are not plays at all, but simply poems cast in an obsolete form of drama. It is obvious that only a lunatic would claim for plays of this kind any right in the modern theatre. Then, secondly, there are plays which, like *Admiral Guinea*, or *Mrs Warren's Profession*, are written with a view to the modern stage, but are, for one reason and another, dramatically worthless. *Admiral Guinea* is a piece of delicate literature, and *Mrs Warren's Profession* is a scathing fragment of political economy. No library would be complete without them. Their final form—the only form, indeed, to which they are entitled—is in a book. But no amount of sophistry will ever convert me to the belief, gravely expressed by some writers, that the dramatist of the future will find greater satisfaction in publishing his plays, than in having them produced. Dramatic writing is, essentially, writing for the stage. They who, through deficiency in dramatic instinct, cannot write well for the stage, should cast their ideas in the form of novels, or essays, or treatises, or speeches. Dramatic conventions are a necessary evil to those who write for the stage: to those who don't, they are a superfluous nuisance, to which it is foolish to submit. They hamper the writer in his work, and they mar his readers' enjoyment. *Godfrida* would be even more enjoyable in reading, were it not written directly for the stage. As it is written directly for the stage—and, though Mr Davidson may not believe me, written in such a way that it would succeed upon the stage—I regret immensely that it was sent to Mr John Lane rather than to Mr Forbes Robertson, who would be far better occupied in enacting so excellent and so live a part as Isembert than in playing spelicans, however skilfully, with the dry bones of Macbeth. I hope that I shall yet see *Godfrida* in some theatre, though I fear that Mr Davidson has, in publishing it, seriously impaired my chance of doing so. I should like to have the chance of praising, in detail, the dramatic ingenuity of its scheme. So long as it is simply a book, I will confine myself to saying that it is full of real poetry, and to imploring Mr Davidson not to let his mastery of blank-verse run away with him. I admit that fine effects can often be gained by tampering with the metre, and that no poet, in his blank-verse, ever adheres to the laws of blank-verse so strictly as does Mr Sydney Grundy in his prose. But I can conceive no excuse for such a line as—

'If it were only by being easily.'

That is not the way for a poet to sprain his iambic feet. Nor should a poet allow even the meanest of his characters to say

'Letters and gifts cease suddenly, no cause
Assigned.—I am afraid I tire you.'

'No cause assigned' is a vile phrase in anything but the report of a modern inquest. A poet can only use it out of sheer bravado. To emphasise it by splitting it into two lines is something worse than bravado. I am glad to say that Mr Davidson very rarely deflects thus from the line of beauty. I have but one other little rebuke to offer him. In publishing a play, one should describe the scenes exactly as though one were describing scenes in a book. In France, this is done by many of the younger playwrights. Mr Shaw has done it in England. Mr Davidson abides by the old convention. '*Chairs*,' he says sternly, '*on which are the hats of Ingleram, etc., are set conveniently. A spinning-wheel near the large window. A summer morning.*' That kind of tone, as of a drill-sergeant rapping out the word of command, is all very well when it is addressed to the stage-manager or property-master, who has to provide the chairs, the spinning-wheel and the summer morning. But, in addressing his irresponsible readers, a dramatist should describe every scene of his play with some measure of suavity and charm.

Last Saturday, Mr Henry Hamilton's version of *The Three Musketeers* reached the Globe Theatre, after a circuitous journey from Camberwell. As my readers may remember, I saw the play at its first production. I said then that it was badly written, but that for aught I knew the book might have been badly written also, and Mr Hamilton's style accordingly justified. Since that time, however, I have gone so far as to read the book, which is written, I find, in very decent French. Thus am I forced reluctantly to the conclusion that Mr Hamilton's style is his own, and that such coruscating jewels as 'Were it known that I were a Huguenot, it were certain death,' are cut and graven by his own hand, according to his own design. Poor dear gentlemen! However, I always admit that literary merit is unnecessary to a play's success, and I should not have again drawn attention to the appalling nature of Mr Hamilton's style had not several other critics—poor dear gentlemen!—praised it. Now that I have read the book, I hasten to say that Mr Hamilton's version of it is very ingenious and stimulating. It recalls for one all the most salient and delightful incidents of the book. A good play it is not, but the greatest genius in dramaturgy could not make of *The Three Musqueteers* a good play which would be also a full version of so vastly diffuse a book. Mr Hamilton, I take it, would not pretend that his play is good as a play: he is content to have provided a good entertainment for those who know Dumas and a passable one for those who don't. The dresses and the scenery are brand-new and exceedingly resplendent. The cast is a good one. As D'Artagnan, Mr Waller is even better, if anything, than he was at Camberwell. And Messrs Bassett Roe, Goodheart and Gurney are admirable as the three musqueteers. But the ideal impersonators of Athos, Porthos and Aramis would be—need I say?—the Sisters Levey.

[*29 October 1898*]


## MR JONES

The curtain fell, and the gods howled hideously for the author. The curtain rose, and the gods yelled cordially to the players. The curtain fell again—more howls; rose again—more yells. Vainly did Mr Maude, Mrs Maude and Mr Harrison insinuate themselves before the curtain, their upturned faces wreathed cunningly with smiles which seemed to say 'We accepted this play. We produced it. Howl at *us!*' The gods admired such chivalry, but their blood was up, and they demanded that the prime culprit, none other, should be delivered to their wrath. But Mr Jones has made a rule never to appear on a first night. So the scene was the more prolonged and embittered. Chaos, straddled on uproar, rode round the upper circles, and we, in the stalls, lingered nervously to see whether Mr Harrison would finally appear bearing the head of Mr Henry Arthur Jones on a gibus. When I left, the din was increasing. Such is modern civilisation, as observed by me in the Haymarket Theatre, last Saturday, at 11 p.m.

For my part, I consider that Mr Jones's rule is admirable, and I wish that all other dramatists would conform to it. It does not mean, as some people have supposed, that Mr Jones is indifferent to public opinion. Academically, Mr Jones might, I admit, argue that he is an artist and that, being so, he writes merely for his own pleasure. But, as a matter of fact, no artist does write merely for his own pleasure. Man is a gregarious animal, and the artist himself is, despite all that has been said to the contrary, more or less human: he has an eye to his fellows. You may be sure that if you took the most intense and single-hearted artist in literature that ever lived, and set him down, with pens, ink and paper, on a desert island, he would produce little or nothing, unless he had some reason to believe that he would ultimately be rescued; and be sure that if you came to rescue him, and if he had not been idle, he would meet you with his MS and would immediately read it to you on the beach. It is quite obvious that some men of letters care not at all for the opinion of the multitude. There are some for whom the praise of a few intelligent critics or magnanimous fellow-craftsmen is quite enough as reward and incentive. But such men as they do not write for the theatre. Dramaturgy is the one form of art which is at the mercy of the multitude. The dramatist who appeals only to a few *cognoscenti* is, to all intents, not a dramatist at all. As a dramatist, Mr Jones is not indifferent to the praise of the multitude. True, he does not, like most of his rivals, make that praise his sole objective. He does not lower himself to the public's level. On the contrary, he does his best, always hoping that the public will rise to appreciation. Sometimes the public rises. Sometimes it doesn't. It didn't on Saturday night. I suspect that Mr Jones's real motive for effacing himself at all his first nights is simply that he hates to be hooted more than he loves to be acclaimed. Such an attitude is perfectly natural, I think. When a dramatist has done his best, applause seems to him no more than his due: hooting seems to him an act of impertinent barbarity. Strictly, then, there is no reason why he should not appear only in response to applause. Nevertheless, to show himself to a delighted audience and to hide from a furious audience would be to incur the charge of cowardice. And so Mr Jones invariably keeps out of the way. I do earnestly counsel the other dramatists to do likewise. Let me appeal to them first on the ground of mere personal vanity. Frankly, when they make their bow before the curtain, they do not look their best. Either they are flushed, or they are blanched, with excitement. Hooted, they appear craven or defiant, according to their temperament, and ridiculous in either case. Cheered, they look either fatuous or shame-faced. They sidle on, they strut off, they don't know what to do with their hands, their bows are jerky and ungracious. The fact is that Englishmen have not the gift of comportment—the art of behaving suitably as the centre-piece of a great occasion is denied them. The victorious English general returns to his country in a billy-cock hat and, seeing the preparations for his welcome, asks 'What is all this fuss about?' —surely one of the poorest pieces of affectation ever perpetrated. A Frenchman could not have conquered the Sudan so cleverly as he, but at least he would have known how to behave on his return. M. Richepin recently showed an English audience how an author can bow before the curtain in a dignified and sincere manner. However, I do not advise English dramatists to model their comportment on M. Richepin's. The result of any such attempt would be ludicrous, no doubt. It is Mr Jones whom they must copy. For the real objection to the dramatist's habit of appearing is that he is, in so doing, an intruder. He is not part of the play: the play is a part of him. If, as is quite natural, he wish to hear the cheers or hisses, let him listen to them from behind the scenes. Whether he wear a beard or be clean-shaven, whether he wear three studs in his shirt or one, has nothing whatever to do with our appreciation of his play. In America, where things progress more quickly, they have already reduced the author's 'call' to absurdity. In the western states, the author of a successful play appears at the end of every act and, as often as not, whiles away the entr'acte with a speech. I myself once witnessed in one of the western cities the production of a play called *Socrates*, a four-act tragedy founded on the life of the Athenian philosopher. It was a great success. At the end of the first act, the author spoke a few formal words of thanks, hoping that what followed would 'prove acceptable.' At the end of the second act he made an emotional speech, recalling the hours he had spent in the city as a lad. At the end of the third act he spoke on local politics and concluded by calling for three cheers for the Mayor, who was sitting in a stage-box. The whole thing was very curious. No doubt it seems very ludicrous to you, reader. Yet it is only carrying our own practice a few steps further—only a difference of degree. It is a gross solecism that the author should show himself at all, and I hope that the public will be schooled to dispense with the sight of him. At first, of course, there will be a succession of such lamentable scenes as that which took place at the Haymarket. I would suggest that, in order to let the public down lightly, a magic-lantern portrait of the author might be cast on the curtain for half a minute or so, during which period the gallery could hoot or cheer to its heart's content. Gradually, the custom of the magic-lantern could be suffered to lapse. Gradually, the public would learn to praise or execrate only the play, not the playwright. Reforms must not be forced too quickly. Meanwhile, much credit is due to Mr Jones for setting a good example.

I have noticed, in the course of the last five or six years, that Mr Jones's first nights are usually stormy. That phenomenon I attribute to the fact that Mr Jones is always experimenting, learning, improving in his art. He has never been content with accomplishment in any one *genre*. He has kept himself plastic and progressive. Except in his early melodramas and in *The Liars*, which was in many respects a repetition of *Rebellious Susan*, he has never done the same thing twice. Thus, the public does not know what to expect of him, and, its wits being rather slow, such ignorance makes it uncomfortable. If Mr Jones were to write his next play on the lines of *The Manoeuvres of Jane*, he would, I prophecy, have a first night full of peace and goodwill. When the public knows what to expect and gets it, it is a good enough judge of a play. When it hoots 'the usual thing,' that is a sign that 'the usual thing' has not been well done. Its opinion of the unusual thing is, however, quite worthless. Both in treatment and in technique *The Manoeuvres of Jane* is unusual. As many of my esteemed *confrères* in criticism have been saying, 'the incidents of which it treats are not such as would generally be regarded as comic.' They mean that when a man and a young lady are stranded together during the night, the necessity that the one should marry the other is a serious situation which must not be treated lightly. Mr Jones treats it lightly. He makes his man a muff and his young lady a minx, strands them together during the night, and leaves us to laugh at the man. Mr Louis Parker recently treated a similar situation from the serious point of view. He made his man a sympathetic dreamer and his young lady a young lady. He stranded them together, neither of them knowing who the other was. Naturally, the audience took a kindly interest in their plight. But that is no reason why we should be angry with Mr Jones because he has treated the situation from a comic point of view. It is absurd to label a situation as in itself 'comic' or 'tragic.' Everything depends on treatment. If Punch were presented as a sympathetic hero, and Judy as a sympathetic heroine, we might find much to weep over in their troubled union. As it is, we laugh. Why not? Our laughter does not argue that we are heartless, or that the man who owns the figures and pulls the strings is a monster of cynicism. And so I would point out to my *confrères* that a dramatic situation is not such a simple thing as they seem to imagine, and that it is good for comedy or for tragedy according as whether the author be engaged in comic or tragic art. For the rest, I do not see why they should be angry with Mr Jones for splitting his third act into two little scenes. It is not 'the usual thing,' of course. But if it is so done as to be effective —and in this play it is quite effective—I see no reason against it. The laws of construction are not sacred. They are useful enough, but if a dramatist can gain an effect by violating them, let him violate them by all means. They were made for him, not he for them. For the rest, I thought Mr Jones's play an extremely good entertainment. Personally, I prefer his 'plays of ideas,' such as *The Crusaders*. There are several playwrights who have a lighter touch than he, but,— except in that too brief period when the genius of Mr Oscar Wilde shone, a comet, in the theatrical firmament—Mr Jones has always seemed to me the only dramatist of any intellectual force, the only dramatist with ideas. Mr Pinero is an intelligent writer, a man of engaging temperament—above all, a born artist in *technique*. But he has yet to prove himself possessed of any original, personal attitude towards life. He has yet to express ideas of his own. The trouble is that few thinkers have dramatic talent: the plays they write are dramatically impossible, whilst those gentlemen who have dramatic talent have not the gift of thought: intellectually, they are, as a class, on a level with our soldiers and sailors, tinkers and tailors. Mr Jones is an exception to this rule. I do not wish to interfere with his career. He must work it out in his own way. But I am sure that his real *métier* is in writing thoughtful plays like *The Crusaders*.

Even if *The Manoeuvres of Jane* were half so bad a play as has been supposed, it would yet be worth seeing, so admirably is it acted.

Both Miss Emery and Mr Maude always play with a keen sense of humour. In this play, both of them have full scope for displaying that rather rare quality. To see them at their best, it is always well to see them at the beginning of a 'run.' Later, when they are at home in their parts, they develop a tendency to over-act, submerging their sense of humour in mere high spirits. That is a danger that besets most comedians. It should be guarded against none the less carefully. Mr Harrison was a trifle too suave for a country squire. His manner was too archly diplomatic for the part. Miss Gertrude Kingston, always a clever artist, acted a part which would be called 'difficult' with apparent ease. She, also, has a keen sense of humour. So has Miss Rose Leclercq. When the furious father asked where, *where* was his daughter, the way she said, 'I am not quite sure,' was more than exquisite.

[*5 November 1898*]


## 'THE JEST'

Messrs Parker and Carson assure us on the authority of an old Spanish proverb that 'a tear trembles on the eyelid of every jest.' I do not doubt that their own jest is duly equipped with an eyelid and a tear. I do but protest that the actors and actresses at the Criterion did not (on the first night, at any rate) manage to coax that tear down from that eyelid. The curtain fell four times in the course of the evening, the tear not once. Every one wished the tear to fall, but it *would not* do so. For three hours every one sat wishing vainly. It was an uncomfortable, an embarrassing evening. Mr Wyndham, like all great actors, has a sympathetic personality, and to see him is to wish him well. Every one wished him to make a great hit as the tragico-romantic hero of this tragico-romantic play. He himself, conscious of the occasion, seemed to strain his every nerve towards success. He knew that he had to do something entirely different from what he had been doing with a similar company, in the same theatre, for so many years. He knew that he had to diffuse a golden haze beauty, nobility, and self-sacrifice under the eyes of an audience unaccustomed to see him do anything more sentimental than squaring his shoulders and saying to Miss Mary Moore: 'Come, come, my dear little lady! All those things that you've been saying were said in the Garden of Eden!' True, Cesare, the hero, was conceived by the authors as being by nature an airy, optimistic man of the world. In the early scenes of comedy, Mr Wyndham was, of course, admirable. But the real matter of the part was not in its comedy but in the subsequent contrast of its pathos, and when Mr Wyndham came to the pathos the audience was not less nervous than he. We shifted uneasily in our seats as when, at a public dinner, some distinguished soldier rises to make a speech. Nay, the situation was worse than that. This was no mere *mauvais quart d'heure* forced upon a great man who would forget it so soon as he had gone through with it. It was a point of ambition—a deliberate experiment, in which failure would be bitter and success proportionately sweet. I should have said rather that we were as nervous as though some perfect after-dinner speaker, anxious to enter public life, were about to address a mass-meeting on the subject of some national crisis. Well! Mr Wyndham made a gallant and splendid effort. He is so perfect an actor in his own line that he could not be bad in any other. His acting was skilful throughout the evening, but to say that it was ever great, or strong, or moving, would be more than the truth. His management of the nine-minutes' soliloquy was wonderfully skilful. Why was it not more effective? Because it was delivered in the realistic manner of the modern comedian. Had it been rolled rhythmically forth, with many gestures, postures and grimaces, it would have carried far more conviction. Mr Wyndham spoke it as though he were a real man talking to himself. Now, realistic acting is fatal to romantic plays. It shows up their unreality at once. And, try as he would, Mr Wyndham never, from first to last, got away from that realistic method in which he is unrivalled. Romantic tragedy requires one kind of method, realistic comedy another. Romantic tragedians must have one kind of temperament, realistic comedians another. The method is the result of the temperament, and temperament will not be tampered with. Mr Wyndham, I maintain, was born to excel in comedy. He has been excelling in comedy for some years, and he cannot, being a mortal, suddenly 'unlearn himself.' A Sassenach chief may, as we know, be bonnily built, he may purchase a sporran, a bonnet and kilt; stick a skean in his hose—wear an acre of stripes—but he cannot assume an affection

## 'THE JEST'

for pipes. Even so may Mr Wyndham wear an acre of chain-armour, but he cannot suddenly become a romantic actor. 'But,' some reader may murmur, 'all this is sheer fatalism. Cannot the artist carve his own destiny? It is premature to say that Mr Wyndham will never become great in romantic acting. Ten years ago, no one supposed that he would become the great comedian he now is. He was regarded then merely as a mettlesome fellow who could carry any farce through on his own shoulders.' That is so. But farce and comedy are cognate things. Their difference, like the difference between melodrama and tragedy, is one of degree, not of kind. The one is but a crude form of the other. To act in farce is an admirable training for a comedian. Most of the great comedians have previously excelled in farce, and most of the great tragedians in melodrama. But to make a great comedian excel in tragedy, or *vice versâ*, the gods must give him a new temperament—a gift which they, sticklers for precedent, do invariably withhold. Are the gods likely to make an exception in favour of Mr Wyndham? Certainly not. They have already given him such gifts as would almost justify other actors in charging them with favouritism. Mr Wyndham has made good use of their bounty, but he cannot hope to get any more out of them. Some men receive no bounty from the gods. They are helpless. Other men receive some bounty, and either waste it or use it well. But whether they use it well or waste it, the gods never reconsider their case. And no man can get bounty save from the gods. All he can do is to use what they are pleased to give him. Thus do I justify my fatalism. Were it not that every man who has used his gifts well desires straightway another set of gifts, I should see nothing very lugubrious in this philosophy. But so are things ordered that success never brings contentment. A great comedian is always making eyes at Melpomene. Mr Wyndham was bound to do so sooner or later. I trust that his infatuation will not last very long. Thalia will be ready to take him back, I am sure. Meanwhile, I must warn my reader that Mr Wyndham's performance in *The Jest* was probably far better than it seemed to me. I and most of the audience at the first night were oppressed by our knowledge of Mr Wyndham in modern comedy, and by the impossibility of forgetting what we had so often seen. Had I never seen Mr Wyndham before, I might have found more to praise in his Cesare, though even then I should not have thought it a fine piece of romantic acting. As it was, I could not gratify myself by taking pleasure in his performance. In fact, as I have said, I spent an uncomfortable evening.

Miss Mary Moore did her best, was as romantic as she could be. But she too, by instinct and habit, is a comedian, and the tear on the play's eyelid remained stationary despite her loyal efforts to bring it down. Her prime quality, sense of humour, she had to suppress. Her talent for sentimental acting did not carry her far. All her pretty little mannerisms—drooping her head on one shoulder and gazing pensively into space and chanting her words down the scale—were of no avail in the part of Fiorella. Poignant emotion was wanted for the part, and it was not forthcoming. Mr Kyrle Bellew, *né romantique* and having played romance in every quarter of the habitable globe, seemed about as much at home in the Criterion as a ritualistic curate officiating in a very low church. Besides, the part of Cosmo—'a rough soldier' he calls himself—was not suited to Mr Bellew, who never was and never will be in the very least like a rough soldier. My opinion, then, is that none of the three principal parts, on which the play (being a three-part play) entirely depends, was acted with the necessary force. Had the stress of tragic emotions been intensely rendered by the three principals, no doubt the two subsidiary, explanatory characters, the nun and the lunatic, who intervene in the play from time to time as a kind of chorus, would have come as a welcome pause in the insistent tragedy. I suspect that the artistic intention of the authors was that these two characters should afford breathing-space to an audience intolerably harrowed. As it was, both of them seemed to me superfluous intruders, if not actually bores. By the way, it is rather curious that whilst many critics have commented on the extraordinary coincidence that Cesare and Cyrano de Bergerac both indulge in self-sacrifice, not one of them has pointed out that great prominence is given to the part of a lunatic-at-large in *The Belle of New York*. It is true that the lunatic in *The Jest* kills Cesare, whilst the other one does not succeed in 'killing Mr Branson.' Nevertheless the coincidence is startling.

Of the play itself I can but speak tentatively, vaguely. Had it been acted with more fire and force, with more of the large, rotund manner necessary to tragic romance, it might have seemed to me more impressive, less artificial, than it did. I wish it had been printed and distributed among the critics. Then I could have formed a more or less sound opinion of its actual merits. As it is, the impression left on my mind is that Mr Parker and Mr Carson sat down on either side of a table and said, 'Now, let's be romantic!' *Rosemary* seemed to me, when I saw it, a work of spontaneous sentiment, *Gudgeons* one of spontaneous humour. *The Jest*, seems to me a more self-conscious affair. Is that impression wholly due to the way in which the play was acted? *The Termagant*, of which I received a copy, also seemed to me somewhat self-conscious; so that I suspect that my opinion of *The Jest* may not be a mere delusion produced by the acting of it. And I suspect that I am right in suspecting that Messrs Parker and Carson ought to write plays of sentiment and humour rather than tragico-romantic plays.

The one thing at the Criterion which really gave me great pleasure was the stage-setting. I have never seen a more beautiful scene on the stage of any theatre. It showed us a stone terrace, with a colonnade to the left and a grove of trees to the right. It was a quite simple scene, not laden with any ornamentation, and it was exquisitely designed. It made a perfect background for a play. And the grove of trees was cunningly prolonged behind the proscenium, so that there were, on that side of the stage, no wings. This made the stage seem much larger, and it gave one the illusion that the characters in the play, whenever they walked from the terrace, had really passed into a long grove of trees, beyond our sight.

[*19 November 1898*]

## DUMAS DEBASED

So soon as Christmas looms faintly from under the horizon, the waters of theatrical enterprise are frozen in the metropolis. Comes that brief interval during which the Managers close their eyelids and the hydra-heads of every Syndicate nod in coma. Then the dramatic critic finds himself dashed down from those giddy heights of obscurity in which he revolves at other times, and is confronted with the necessity of becoming a private gentleman, free to spend his evenings by his own fire-side and to doze, in the aureola of his own reading lamp, over Hazlitt's dramatic essays, or Aristotle's *Poetics*, or the latest example of those gaunt superfluities, theatrical Memoirs.

At Camberwell, however, where plays need not run longer than six nights, the waters flow still with a strong current, and the eyelids of Mr Mulholland do not droop. And thus, even now, the dramatic critic has his uses. The other night, I was summoned to a performance of *Two Little Maids from School*, which Mr Robert Buchanan and Mr Charles Marlowe have extracted from one of Dumas's comedies. As this notice can only appear on the morning of Saturday, the date of the play's last performance at the Metropole Theatre, why should I have been called in to tell the inhabitants of Camberwell whether the play were worth seeing or not? All I can do is to advise such inhabitants as have been waiting for my opinion—to advise them strongly—not to go to the Metropole on Saturday. If there be one in Camberwell who reveres Dumas, or Mr Buchanan, or British Drama, as I do, let him save his shillings for the next production in Mr Mulholland's very pretty little theatre.

I need not explain myself at any great length. The plot of the original play, *Les Demoiselles de St Cyr*, seems to have been a purely mechanical contrivance, such as Dumas loved (quite rightly) for his artificial comedies. Two men, A and B, flirt with two girls, C and D. They are entrapped into the Bastille, where A is forced to marry C, and B, D. A and B, furious, leave C and D the next morning. How to convert the formula $(C-A)+(D-B)$ into the formula $(C+A)+(D+B)$, is the problem left by the first two acts, to be solved by the last two. Needless to say, there is a masked ball; A flirts with C, B with D; C makes A jealous, and D, B; and all ends happily. Not, in itself, an enthralling story! I have no doubt that Dumas made a charming comedy of it, however. I can imagine, too, that if Mr Grundy had laid hands on the plot and translated or adapted it, the result might have been pleasing. *The Silver Key* and *The Marriage of Convenience* were no more interesting in their plot than this play; but Mr Grundy adapted them with some measure of elegance and grace and wit, with a sense of Dumas and of the plays' period, and he contrived to make of them a very pretty entertainment. In *Two Little Maids from School* there is not, so far as I could gather, one graceful or witty line, not one touch, even, of the eighteenth century. All is as dull and as common as it can be. To say that it is mediocre, would be positive flattery. The adapters do not seem to have grasped the first two principles in the adaptation of a French costume play: that the atmosphere of the period must be suggested through other modes of speech than those used by the man on the omnibus, and that the French language must be translated into English equivalents. The characters in *Two Little Maids from School* are made to talk exactly as though they were riding on omnibuses, except that their conversation is interspersed with such phrases as '*en route*,' '*à bientôt*,' '*pensionnaires*' and '*bonnes fortunes*.' From every point of view these Gallicisms are fatal. In translating French, a man's aim should be to make us forget that he is doing anything of the kind; in every word that he leaves untranslated, he does violently remind us. In translation of French for the stage, the danger is made twice as deadly by the fact that (with, perhaps, half-a-dozen exceptions) no English actors or actresses can pronounce French without giving one a shudder. It is bad enough that they should be obliged, in these adaptations, to pronounce the French names of the *dramatis personae*. In this play, for example, the name of 'Dubouloy' is consistently pronounced as 'Doobaloy' (rhyming with joy). Indeed, consistency in mispronunciation is the most that can be expected of any cast. Some casts say 'Madarm,' others 'Madamn': neither way is very pretty, but either can be borne if it is strictly adhered to throughout the evening. The cast of this play was unswerving from 'Madamn.' That, I am afraid, is almost the only compliment I can pay to the cast of this play. Miss Annie Hughes, who acted the part of D, is a clever and charming actress, and she has a sense of humour, but she did not (as she might have, despite the authors) once show the vein of artificial comedy. She chose to clown. Perhaps this choice was forced on her by the utter incompetency of the actors and actresses who were with her. The parts of A, B and C were acted, respectively, by—but I have a kindly nature, and I withhold the three names—whose bearers, I trust, will, out of gratitude for my forbearance, hasten to inscribe them on the books of some rudimentary School of Acting. It remains to say that the play was well mounted, and to regret that Mr Buchanan shows no signs of amendment. Mr Buchanan is by nature a poet and a wit, and, in literature, he has written much that is good. In drama, he seems to have no ambition to do anything but play the drunken helot for the good of the rising generation. This is a great pity, I think. There are so many drunken helots, and so few men who could, like him, have written fine plays. Had he, from the outset, chosen to use his talent honestly, instead of prostituting it to the public, he might by this time be the acknowledged master of dramaturgy in England. As it is, he can only be regarded as a very terrible example.

Looking at this article, I am struck by the fact that, for the first time since I lapsed into dramatic criticism, I have actually tried to damn a play. Hitherto, I have not found a really bad play, and so I have always been able to say more or less nice things. In one or two cases I have been quite enthusiastic. Yes, there are one or two plays which I remember as being really good. But, with the solitary exception of *Pelleas and Melisande* (which, as you know, was not written by an English dramatist), there are not any which I remember as being works of original genius, achievements of the first rank. True, I have not been a dramatic critic very long. It may be that this period of almost unrelieved mediocrity may have merely happened to coincide with my dramatic criticism, may have been an exceptional era in the history of the English stage. I am afraid that the evidence is against such a supposition. I am afraid that years come and years go, and whilst new genius crops up regularly in English literature and painting, English drama, like English music and sculpture, goes steadily on without any pre-eminent additions to its value. I do not doubt that the drama is, as we are always hearing, better than it was in the 'fifties. Tom Robertson, with his charming talent, paved the way for better things, and better things have walked along that pavement; but, having come to the end of it, they do not seem to progress. A few years ago, at the time of the Independent Theatre, one heard much of a Renascence. Ibsen was to be the regenerating influence. For a time our dramatists dallied with sexual problems. But that time has passed, and even the most strenuous evangelists of Ibsen find themselves forced to admit that native drama cannot be regenerated by the influence of any alien, however great be that alien's genius. After a few hectic months, English drama relapsed into deeper lassitude. New theatres are built, and there are always new audiences to fill them, and new plays to produce in them. But one looks in vain for the playwright who shall reveal to us some new method, set some new example, startle us violently out of our customary attitude of polite and weary approval—one looks in vain for him who shall, in a word, cause drama to progress. What is wanted is not merely a man who will write plays well according to the present conventions of dramaturgy. What is wanted is a man who will create a new dramatic form. I hope he will come in my time. There will be great fun when he comes.

[*26 November 1898*]

## ONE THING AND ANOTHER

My silence last week was due to a kind of catalepsy produced by the first night of *Cupboard Love*. I had serious thoughts of resigning my post on this *Review*, and thus severing the slightest connexion between myself and the British Drama. I felt that either I or Mr Esmond must go. Well! Mr Esmond has gone; at least, his youthful indiscretion—in mellow retrospect, it seems no worse than that—has been promptly hushed up, and I am left wondering how he ever came to commit it. I could never have supposed that the author of *The Divided Way* would do anything really stupid. However, the less said the better; and I am sure that Mr Esmond, one of the few youths who have dramaturgic instinct, will soon atone to the public by writing another very good play, and to Mr Chudleigh by giving him the right of pre-emption. When Mr Chudleigh accepted *Cupboard Love*, he must have been dazzled indeed by its author's brief but creditable past. I cannot believe that it was the best play at his disposal. Like every other manager, he must be daily bombarded with new plays, and that he, having one of the nicest little theatres in a city of more than five million inhabitants (mostly playwrights), should have had to fall back on *Cupboard Love*, because it was in itself the best of all the plays submitted to him, is an idea which even I, knowing how hard it is to write even a passable play, must refuse to entertain for one moment. I have already surrendered most of my illusions about our native talent in drama, but I must stop short of positive despair.

At Terry's—I will *not* despair!—there is a really possible farce, *The Brixton Burglary*, not adapted from the French, but actually conceived and executed by one unaided Briton. Pride in its origin enabled me to enjoy it as keenly as though it had been a very masterpiece in humour. Usually, I cannot laugh much at farces. If they are interspersed with songs and dances, I can enjoy them well enough, but mere tomfoolery does not move me. I always envy the people whom simple humour convulses, because they get so many more opportunities for laughter, that delightful function, than I can ever get. Subtle humour—and that is the only kind that convulses me—is such a very rare commodity! Perhaps 'mere tomfoolery' was a rather arbitrary description of farce. 'Primitive fun' would have been more apt, for farce's main appeal is to that primitive sense of humour which consists in laughing at unmerited misfortune. The gods and goddesses in Olympus indulged in quenchless mirth at Vulcan's lameness. In every village, the village-idiot is a source of infinite enjoyment to the inhabitants. Bullying, which is the expression of schoolboy's humour, is bound to flourish, despite masters, in every healthy school. 'But,' you may say, 'gods and goddesses, villagers and small boys, are not civilised beings. Civilisation does not laugh at unmerited suffering.' That, I suggest, depends on the kind of man who suffers. Take the case of a man who is falsely accused and dragged off to the police-station. As an abstract proposition, that produces no emotion; but let the man be a hero in melodrama, and most people will weep; let him be a comic man in farce, and most people will roar with laughter. The more suffering accumulate for the hero, the more they will weep; the more suffering accumulate for the comic man, the more they will roar. Yet the suffering represented in the one case is no greater and no less than in the other. Personally, I am so sophisticated, so over-civilised, in me the bear-baiting instinct is so dead, that I can see nothing very funny in the sufferings of even a man who is labelled comic: the more cucumber-frames he tumble through, the more band-boxes he subside into, the less cause do I see for merriment. And so I attribute my enjoyment of *The Brixton Burglary* to patriotic pride in the play's existence rather than to a love of its merits. I hasten to add that there are not literally any cucumber-frames or band-boxes in it. The sufferings of Septimus Pontifex, its hero, are chiefly mental. Mr Fred W. Sidney, its author, is evidently endowed with some talent for dramatic invention, and his plot is really ingenious—when a dramatic critic says that a plot is 'ingenious' he means that it is too involved for him to follow it at the time or to remember it afterwards. I could not follow the plot of this farce with any clearness, nor, I suspect, could the audience. But that does not matter. There were many excellent situations, and the play was excellently acted. In the part of Pontifex, Mr James Welch distinguished himself as usual, acting in exactly that vein of mock-tragic intensity which is right for such parts. Mr Barnes filled the whole stage with his broad geniality and complete experience. Mr Gottschalk, who has amusing mannerisms, played the part of a man-servant with much humour. And Miss Annie Hughes, none the worse for her sad aberration into the eighteenth century, was very delightful as Petunia Perkins. Indeed almost every member of the cast played well.

Patriotism apart, I should have liked *On and Off*, the farce at the Vaudeville, much better if it had not been an adaptation of *Le Contrôleur des Wagons-Lits*. As it was, I found the Gallicism of its idea and of its characters' names more than a little disturbing. The actors were quite obviously English in dress, manner, deportment, and it worried me to see them sitting down to *déjeuner*, to hear them talking of divorce as a trifle, and addressing one another by such names as 'Monsieur du Patty,' 'Madame Brumaire,' and 'Lizette.' I have never heard Tommy Atkins singing the Marseillaise in full uniform, but if I ever had, my sense of fitness would not, I fancy, have been more greatly outraged than it was at the Vaudeville. I wish that the characters could have been made English, the scene have been laid in England. Such a proceeding, however, would have been impossible, because the whole idea of the play is French. And so I am forced back on the regret that there is no Englishman to write for London so good a farce as M. Bisson has written for Paris. The fun of the *Contrôleur des Wagon-Lits* lay in the terrible series of sufferings in which Godfrey found himself involved as a consequence of his conjugal disloyalty. To a Parisian audience such disloyalty is not shocking; to a London audience it is. A London audience can only regard Godfrey as a reprobate for whom any amount of suffering is no more than he deserves. And, as I have already suggested, the prime pleasure which people take in farce is the pleasure of laughing at suffering which is not deserved: so soon as moral indignation is aroused, the whole essence of farce evaporates. Conscious that to play the character realistically would be to fan moral indignation to a flame, Mr Giddens cleverly refrained from making Godfrey more than a fatuous, eccentric shadow, an irresponsible abstraction. Thus the audience was more or less appeased, and was able to enjoy his quandaries almost as heartily as though he had done nothing to deserve them. Having duly applied my theory, I may as well get back to mere fact and admit that the audience enjoyed the farce immensely, and was probably quite untroubled by any of the mental reservations which I have been attributing to it. In fact, the play is a great success.

Meanwhile, there is a slight recrudescence of that 'Independent' spirit which was abroad in the early 'nineties. I was at one time inclined to ridicule that spirit. But now, as a dramatic critic, sent spinning from one theatre to another and finding them almost always under the tyranny of 'the usual thing,' I am quick to welcome any kind of experiment, good, bad or indifferent, less on the chance that it may lead to something—that chance is so remote!—than because it *is* an experiment. The 'West Theatre, Albert Hall,' does not sound inspiring, but thither I went, last Saturday, very gladly, and there I sat, whilst *Blanchette* was enacted among the faithful. A weary pagan of the Roman Empire, paying a surreptitious visit to one of those remote barns or cellars where the Early Christians worshipped, must have felt the same curiosity as I felt in the little 'West Theatre.' He may not have been—nor was I—converted; yet he, like me, must have been moved by the earnestness of the congregation, of the priests, and must have come away, as I did, with a still deeper contempt for his own gods. *Blanchette* is not a good play. Do not suppose me to mean merely that it does not conform to the red-tape conventions of the modern English theatre. I mean that it is not, in the wide sense of the word, dramatic. Its subject—a girl educated above her station—is full of dramatic possibilities; only, M. Brieux has not brought them out. What he has done, is to write a play that is closely observed from life, to create characters which, being real, would, if M. Brieux had more instinct for drama, move one very profoundly. This play has been well translated by Mr Grein and Mr Churchill, and it was, on the whole, well acted. Mrs Theodore Wright, Miss Kingsley, Mr Wood and Mr Connell were good as peasants. Miss Leonard, as the unhappy girl, acted with great intelligence and earnestness. At present, her technique is not sure enough for her to convey emotion to an audience; but *ça viendra*, no doubt.

[*17 December 1898*]

## A PLAY AND A BOOK

Last week Mr Arthur Roberts appeared and disported himself in a piece called *Milord Sir Smith* at the Comedy Theatre. It did not seem to me a good piece; but that, of course, is quite immaterial. To write a good piece for Mr Arthur Roberts would be mere waste of time; a dramatist can but abase himself and provide this comedian with what is called an opportunity. And, after all, one kind of opportunity is as good as another: everything depends on the use Mr Roberts may make of it, and one would no more praise an author for the success or blame him for the failure of a play in which Mr Roberts appears than one would praise or blame Cinquevalli's assistant according as his master succeeds or fails in balancing on his frontal bone a billiard-cue with a cannon-ball at the top. Usually, Mr Roberts triumphs. But he did not triumph on the first night of this new play. '*On ne peut pas être toujours drôle,*' and I am bound to confess that Mr Roberts's power to excite laughter was, on this occasion, less than his audience's anxiety to laugh. The audience laughed often and loudly of course, but its mirth was a tribute to Mr Roberts's past and future achievements in humour, to his record and personality, rather than to anything he said or did in the course of the evening. And it was right that the audience should laugh. Hero-worship would be a poor, graceless thing indeed if the hero were worshipped only at the exact moment when he is performing some great deed. A pretty pass if the streetsters of this city had refused to cheer Lord Kitchener because he was merely driving down to the Mansion House in a frock-coat, and not, at that moment, taking Khartoum! And, if it is only right and natural to cheer a man who did something many miles away in the presence of a few war correspondents, how much more so it is to applaud Mr Arthur Roberts whom, on the evidence of our own eyes and ears, we all know to have performed prodigies of humour in this very city. I make no doubt that by this time Mr Roberts has become very funny as 'Sir Smith,' and I wish I had not seen him on the first night. He halted and fumbled, and was altogether feeble: such flashes as he had were but flashes in a very dull pan. The worst of it was that his unwonted slowness betrayed the cheap vulgarity of his attitude towards life. He is usually so brisk, so irresistibly spontaneous, that one is dazzled into delight, and has no time to analyse the quality of his quips. That he is vulgar one knows; but he is so brilliant a creature that his vulgarity does not offend one—it is the summer-lightning of vulgarity. But, the other night, when he was slow and dull, I had the time and the power to be critical. Jokes about drinks, jokes about 'girls,' jokes about 'Johnnies'—these things I suddenly realised were his permanent apparatus in humour. I realised that all his materials were gathered in that comparatively small and none too lovely area of the world's surface which is bounded on the one hand by the Criterion Restaurant and by Romano's on the other. And I could but wonder at the genius which had hitherto used these miserable materials so brilliantly as to lull distaste. For me, *Milord Sir Smith* was redeemed only by the very admirable singing and dancing—and acting—of Miss Ada Reeve. If she sang and danced less well, I should grudge her to musical comedy, for, with a good part, she would make the fortune of a legitimate farce.

There has just been laid across my path a very large book. It is entitled *Actors of the Century*—ungallantly entitled, I think, since quite half of it is devoted to actresses. Its author, Mr Frederic Whyte, should have adopted my trick of using the word 'mimes'— useful monosyllable, covering both sexes. Except singing and needlework, acting is the only art in which women do ever rival men, and it seems rather hard that they should be ignored on the cover of this very large book. Perhaps the discourtesy can be rectified in the second edition. Meanwhile, I must congratulate Mr George Bell— for that is the name of the publisher—on having issued a book which will surely have a very great sale. As a Christmas present for the stage-struck, it is quite invaluable. Indeed, I fancy it might be used as a sovereign cure for stage-stroke, so sharply does it impress on its reader the ephemeral nature of the actor's (and actresses's) triumph. 'Into the night go one and all,' sang Mr Henley, and Mr Frederic Whyte has turned a searchlight into that darkness, has lit up for us the remote figures of the Keans, the Kembles, and many other mimes. Is not the result a little ghastly? Our forefathers worshipped these mimes so fervently that it is painful for us to realise—and Mr Whyte makes us realise so clearly—that we ourselves do not care a hoop-stick about them. Who cares about Mrs Siddons? She exists for us only as the model of Reynolds's picture at Dulwich, and it was unkind of Mr Whyte to recall that the painter, in signing his name upon the hem of her garment, declared to her that thus would his name go down to posterity. A more savage piece of irony was never uttered. Mr Whyte calls it 'a matchless compliment.' I wonder whether the 'Tragic Muse' herself took it as a compliment. I daresay she did. However, enough of Mrs Siddons and of the past! So soon as Mr Whyte comes to the drama of the 'sixties he produces a far less dispiriting effect, inasmuch as many who were mimes then are mimes now. When he comes to the drama of to-day there is real cheeriness in his pages. He seems to be an ardent playgoer, and for me it is comforting to find anybody who goes to the theatre frequently without being compelled to do so—it seems to soften the compulsion in my own case. And he is a voracious reader of dramatic criticism, much of which he thinks worth quoting in his book. How comforting for me to think that hereafter somebody may gravely copy out and enshrine in a very large book what I have just scribbled about Miss Ada Reeve! In fact, Mr Whyte is a splendid fellow. He is very modest, too. He declares that the text of his book is 'subsidiary to the illustrations.' I cannot allow that. Mr Whyte, when he is not quoting the dramatic critics, writes with much grace and discrimination. I admit that M. Beau's *cartes de visite* have a quaint charm, and that all the other portraits are well reproduced, but I refuse to regard Mr Whyte's work as subsidiary to them. M. Beau, by the way, has contributed some reminiscences of forgotten mimes—a mistake which I forgive on account of one delicious passage. 'One day,' says M. Beau, 'Robson, coming to the studio, mentioned to me that he had the burglars in his house on the previous night, and in relating the circumstance he made me feel by his earnestness what a deep impression of nervousness he experienced on the occasion. In fact, he appeared as if he was afraid they might still be in one of the adjoining rooms!' That last sentence is quite perfect. One could not have a better description of a mime's manner in private life. Of course, there are many mimes who are not particularly dramatic off the stage. But they are, I think, exceptions; most mimes are quite as dramatic off as on. Inasmuch as, when they are on, they are always figuring in dramatic situations, which in private life are very rare things; private life is to them an anti-climax. They bring with them a power of expressing various emotions, and private life affords very few occasions for exercise of that power. And so they have to be always creating situations, magnifying and empurpling the drabbest trifles, in order to keep up their spirits by manifestations of joy, wrath, scorn, despair, remorse, and so forth. And this is very bad for them. It saps in them all sense of proportion. They are so used to being wildly emotional about nothing, that they do not recognise a real crisis—a real cause for emotion—when they meet it. Diderot said that, as men, they do not on the stage feel the emotions which, as actors, they express. Why did he not go further and say that, as men, off the stage, and in a real crisis of their lives, they cannot feel the emotions which, as actors, on or off stage, they simulate. That would have been far more suggestive as a theory.

[24 December 1898]

## TWO PANTOMIMES

Full many Pantos truly there have been,
But this the best of all is, I do ween.
Each one is always better than the last,
And Mr Collins has himself surpass'd
In *Ali Baba and the Forty Thieves*.
And yet, somehow (to say so me it grieves!)
I can't with truth declare I much enjoyed it—
But don't suppose I mean *you* should avoid it!
The fault's my *own*, and, for that reason very,
I'd best *own* up and bid you all be merry!
If I myself don't like this Pantomime,
Live and let live, boys!—it is all the same!
To Drury Old, I'm certain, when you go, you—

But I have written quite enough to show you, reader, how fearfully I have been haunted by the rhyming iambics in *Ali Baba* at Drury Lane, and in *Dick Whittington* at the Adelphi. In point of rhythm my lines are perhaps superior to them, but I think I have managed to suggest the kind of order in which the words come tripping, and also the level of humour and sense above which they seldom rise. Why, I ask, have not Mr Collins and Mr Barrett discarded the old convention, and had their 'books' written in prose? Limping along in the rusty manacles of versification, their poor librettists cannot give a display, as they might otherwise, of sprinting wit or soaring fantasy. If these two managers are so deeply in love with tradition, why have they in many other respects set it quite cynically at naught? Why have they banished the two *ballerine* who used to flit and posture so formally, when I was little? That tip-toe, those raven locks, closely banded, that stiff frame of horizontal muslin, the glitter of that fixed smile—why, and to what limbo, have they been expelled? How it is that the subject of the Transformation Scene is not as, to the best of my memory, it always was in byegone years, 'The Birth of the Convolvulus,' with stolid, serried rows of girls in white slowly rising over similar rows of girls in pink? And why, before the scene is shifted, are not the lights lowered whilst 'clown and pantaloon tumble on, joppling and grimacing, seen very faintly in that indecisive twilight?' Above all, why is not the story presented to us with the old completeness and clear simplicity? At Drury Lane one finds but obscure, disjointed fragments of *Ali Baba* cast into a blaze of brute splendour and topical burlesque. The story itself has practically vanished. This must be a terrible shock for those critics who hold up their hands in horror at the dramatist's mutilation of literary masterpieces. But I am not one of those critics. A bad version of a good book does not, after all, harm literature: the book itself remains as it was. Nor, for that matter, are my susceptibilities wounded by any burlesque, however extravagant, of a famous classic. I see nothing incongruous in laughing at what one reverences. For instance, a really good parody of a classic can be written only by someone who loves, and be appreciated only by those who love, the original. However, the question here is not of parody, but of burlesque, which is another thing. *Dido in the Dumps*, an 1840 burlesque, which I read lately with some enjoyment, did not make me fume for Vergil's sake, nor did *Faust Up to Date*, nor even the late Mr Wills's version, undermine my deep admiration for Goethe's masterpiece. (True, I do not know German; but then, if it were necessary to have read all the masterpieces which one loves, reverences, and frequently extols, what a stampede there would be among the critics!) It was not, then, any feeling for the sacrosanctity of the *Arabian Nights* that caused my discontent at Drury Lane. It was merely that *Ali Baba* is such an amusing story, always so effective when it is set forth simply on the stage, that I wished to see it again on the stage, even more than I wished to be dazzled by dresses or convulsed by topical satire. Alas! the spirit of the time forbids Mr Collins to let the story be set forth in the old way. Even Mr Oscar Barrett has succumbed almost unreservedly to the new influence. In his *Cinderella*, two or three years ago, the story was set forth quite simply. I thought then (and no doubt he thought) that he had inaugurated a new era in pantomime—or rather that he had reinaugurated the old era, with certain chaste improvements. I was wrong. The experiment seems to have been abandoned, for *Dick Whittington* has been done very differently from *Cinderella*. Erst an apostle of Refinement, Mr Barrett now truckles to the 'giddy vulgar,' and his new pantomime is tarred all over — or, if you like, emblazoned—with the brush of the music-halls. A sad surrender is Mr Barrett's, and none, I am sure, deplores it so bitterly as he. For him, who in his day has sounded the depths of Refinement, it must indeed be terrible to sit nightly in the conductor's chair, face to face with so much that he despises utterly. In vain has he inserted in the 'book' quotations from what Sir Walter Besant, the Rev. Dr Lysons, and other gentlemen have written about Old London; in vain does he rest his eye on the quaint old gables and mullions which are the refined setting of his pantomime; all in vain, when his ears are incessantly assailed by sounds, his eyes by sights, which smack of nothing but the Halls. One knows that the fiddlers around him see his either profile suffused with blushes, and that, although he wields his bâton jauntily, he would turn away from the stage were he not afraid to face those for whose innate Refinement he has ceased to cater. I am quick to admit that the story of the play is better set forth at the Adelphi than at Drury Lane. So much may be accounted to Mr Barrett for righteousness. But, unfortunately, the story of *Dick Whittington* is not, in my opinion, a good subject for a pantomime. It is altogether too lugubrious a story. A youth of excellent character is falsely accused of theft. Aided by his cat, he manages to escape from confinement. He takes to the high-road, leaving behind him the tacit admission of guilt. On Highgate Hill, that depressing spot, he sinks down on a stone and dreams that he is to be Lord Mayor of London. This horrible and vulgar destiny haunts him throughout his chequered career, till, at last, it is actually fulfilled. It is a powerful story, I admit; a story that grips one with its relentless, inevitable progression. But it is too sombre, too morbid for a pantomime. After all, life is not all gloom and tragedy—there is plenty of sunshine in the world. Dame Nature is not a neurotic pessimist—she gives us happy endings as often as not. And why should the dramatist go deliberately out of his way to intensify the darker side of our human lot? One does not go to a theatre to be harrowed, but to laugh and make merry and be on good terms with things in general. Such, at least, is my view. And so, after all, perhaps it is just as well that Mr Barrett has lightened the plot of his pantomime with 'variety business.' *Ali Baba,* on the other hand, is a very cheerful and pretty romance, and I am disappointed that Mr Collins did not rely more on it.

It may be interesting to consider why in a modern pantomime the story is so deliberately neglected—is preserved, indeed, merely as a thread to connect the turns of an infinite variety show. The children of my day loved to follow the plot of a pantomime. We knew all the stories—*Jack and the Beanstalk, Blue Beard,* and the rest—and it was marvellous to have the heroes of our hearts actually incarnate before us, to see them performing there the deeds for which they were famous in the nursery. We watched them with breathless interest. Well, technically, pantomimes are still intended for children. And they are different from what they were simply because children are different also. In recent years all the conditions of childhood have been changed: children have been, so to say, 'discovered,' and are now regarded by their elders as very delightful companions. The children of my period lived all day (except for an hour or two before dinner) in the nursery. There, as also in their walks, they had only each other for companions, their nurse for mentor (and the nurse of that period was a quite simple creature, who had never been to a Board School). In fact, children were left very much more to themselves than they are now, and were, therefore, very much more childish. They were a primitive race, and their folklore—very real to them—was in the stories of *Jack the Giant Killer, Blue Beard,* and the rest, which were told to them again and again by their nurse. I doubt whether the modern nurse, fresh from the Seventh Standard, even remembers these simple tales. But if she does, that would not affect my argument. The nurse is no longer an important element in children's lives, inasmuch as children are no longer confined to the nursery, but spend most of their time in the drawing-room or dining-room—wherever their elders may be. At all hours their elders wish to be delighted or touched by their childish ways. The sad thing is, that the more time children spend with their doating elders, the more surely diminish those very qualities which are their charm. Inevitably, they become more and more sophisticated, less and less easily pleased by the things that ought to please them. The other night, at Drury Lane, I observed with interest the demeanour of three pretty little children—two girls and a boy, the oldest about nine years old—who were sitting near me in a box on the pit-tier. The antics of the huge parrot and of the horse, which would have enchanted me at their age, did not raise a smile on their faces. On the other hand, they seemed to be interested in the dancing, and when a man came on, masked in the image of Captain Dreyfus, they applauded with such vigour. The references to Mr Hooley and to the German Emperor made them laugh outright, but their attention wandered palpably whilst the story itself was proceeding; and, as soon as the harlequinade was ushered in, they rose spontaneously and looked for their wraps. Their accompanying parents, I thought, seemed rather loth to go, and cast wistful glances at the clown. They, I am sure, would have enjoyed the old-fashioned kind of pantomime as thoroughly as their children would have been bored by it. Fifteen years ago, the grown-up people who took their children to Drury Lane sat through the performance only for their children's sake, sat there with an abstracted gaze or, at most, a faint smile of tolerance. But that, of course, was before the present cult for children had been invented, before grown-up people had discovered the mine of pleasure that lies for them in the study of childish things. Now, since the new kind of pantomime is less calculated to please the modern adult than would be a revival of the old kind, how am I to account for the fact that so many grown-up people now go to Drury Lane on their own account? I suppose it is because the vogue of the Music Halls has grown so stupendously in recent years, creating a general demand. Grown-up people, going to Drury Lane, get in one evening all that they could get in two consecutive evenings spent at the Empire and at the Tivoli, and, at the same time, they are able to foster the illusion that, in watching a pantomime, they are doing something rather childish. That, I think, explains why pantomimes now have such very long runs.

[*31 December 1898*]

## R.I.P.

As a theatrical year, 1898 passed away last Saturday night, at the Royalty Theatre, very peacefully. '*A Little Ray of Sunshine!*' it gasped feebly; then, with a wan smile it turned its face to the wall, and the dramatic critics, when they knew that all was over, stole quietly, decorously, away to compose its epitaph. *Requiescat*—'let it lie.' That is quite the kindest thing we can sincerely say of 1898.

Last moments have always a melancholy interest: else should I find even less than I do find to say of *A Little Ray of Sunshine*. As a play, it seemed to me very trite and tame, though its author had cunningly sought to disarm criticism by suffusing it with a Yulish glow. When people are standing on ladders, with a trail of holly in one hand, and a hammer in the other, it cannot—so the author seems to have argued—much matter whether they say anything really amusing, and intrinsic sentiment may be dispensed with whilst Christmas carols are being sung 'off.' For my own part, I was not disarmed by these sly devices. I can imagine that in June or July they might charm me and win me over, but at this time of the year they come only as a surfeit. After laboriously filling onself with goodwill; after beaming fixedly all round, stamping imaginary snow from one's boots, rubbing one's hands to the bone, and shouting the compliments of the season till one is hoarse; after feigning intense excitement about the contents of crackers, dissembling one's dread of snap-dragon, and ruining oneself in tips; after being for a whole week, as in duty bound, hale, hearty, bluff, hopeful, greedy, tender and forgiving, one cannot gain any real pleasure from a play which has Christmas for its mainspring. *A Little Ray of Sunshine* is simply a Christmas pudding minus flame and spirit, and I doubt (though, for Mr Penley's sake, I hope) that there is a sixpence in it. The best I can say for it is that it gives Mr Penley a chance of proving, once and for all, his inability to play anything in the nature of sentiment. His voice alone—so delightful in pure farce—is enough to preclude him. To chant all words religiously on one high note is one of his most amusing tricks, but it is fatal to pathos. When, at the close of this play, he tells the story of his life, in a speech evidently charged with pathetic import, there is not a moist eye in the audience. He is a virtuoso in the grotesque, and he cannot get beyond the grotesque.

However, it is just as well that he has made his little experiment—so long as he does not repeat it.

So much for the last moments of 1898. So much for the close of an even, harmless, insignificant career. Looking back on it, I can find scarcely one occasion on which it rose above mediocrity, few on which it sank beneath that level. Stagnation was its prime attribute. Mr Jones, the most interesting figure in our tiny ring of dramatists, wrote one amusing play, but nothing worthy of his best gifts—of the gifts which distinguish him among his *confrères*. As a man of ideas, of strenuous and vivid sympathy with life, he is, I think, wasted in that line of artificial comedy to which he has been devoting himself. Mr Pinero, whose strength seems to lie, not in any great force of mind or sympathy with life, but rather in his technical skill and engaging temperament, wrote one little play which, though it appealed chiefly to members of the theatrical profession, had a *succès de crinoline* with the public. It was a pretty little thing, but how far inferior to Mr Pinero's early farces! Mr Grundy, that cynic, seems content to go down to posterity as a man who knew the French language and the British public. The glamour of mediaeval romance has been too much for Messrs Parker and Carson, whom Nature so well equipped as humourists; they have swathed themselves in heavy cloaks, and donned hats whose plumage gets into their eyes, and swords which trip them up. I implore the authors of *Rosemary* and *Gudgeons* to disrobe. Mr Esmond may now come out of the corner in which he was stood after *Cupboard Love*, beg everyone's pardon, and write a good play. There are other authors who have contributed to the year's drama, but they are not remarkable enough for me to recall their names. Stay! I had forgotten Mrs Craigie, whose *début* was a delight to me. As a student of her books, I have formed a certain opinion of what are her true gifts, and I trust she will not be beguiled from that line of artificial comedy, in which she is so excellent. I would urge her not to oversteal that line, as earnestly as I urge Mr Jones to become serious. Also, I had forgotten Mr Anthony Hope's *Lady Ursula;* but I do not know that it deserves very clear recollection. In vain do I search my memory for any work of vital originality. The past year has been utterly barren of great work, barren of any sign that great work is at hand. Of the two really fine plays that I have seen in the past year, neither has any connection with modern British drama. The author of *Julius Caesar* was an

Elizabethan; the author of *Pelleas and Melisande* is a foreigner, and a phoenix at that. Sad, that these two men should have written the only first-rate plays produced here in 1898! Both *Julius Caesar* and *Pelleas and Melisande* were successes of surprise. We are accustomed to suppose that the Shakespearean plays which we have not seen too often must be unsuitable for the stage, and it thrilled us to find in *Julius Caesar* a moving, vivid drama, and not the chilly bas-relief we had imagined it. Likewise, we, who knew M. Maeterlinck only as a mystic poet, were amazed by the intense humanity, the true drama, of *Pelleas and Melisande*. All credit to Mr Tree and Mr Robertson for their experiments! But one wishes that the best available talent in dramaturgy did not happen to be either archaic or alien. One wishes that, in the few London theatres not consecrated to dull farce or musical comedy, one could find more assurance that real drama is a fairly flourishing concern. Why is it that, whilst fine books have been published during the past year—many of them by young writers—not one fine play has been produced? In a word, why is our drama so inferior, intellectually and artistically, to our literature? Perhaps these questions are asked in every generation, in every country. Drama is always handicapped by its direct dependence on the public. Publishers are far more accessible than managers to original genius. To publish the works of a young Meredith or Pater does not bring in any immediate return in cash or prestige—probably it entails a loss at first; but there is every chance that the loss will be counterbalanced hereafter, when the public has been bullied into admiration. Meanwhile, the publisher can support himself by giving the public what it buys at once and of its own accord. But to produce a new kind of play is a very expensive proceeding. The public, having groaned on the first night, stays away on the second, and the distracted manager must either give it once more the kind of thing to which it is accustomed or pass through the bankruptcy-court; in fact, he cannot, as can the publisher, afford to wait while the public is being educated. Unlimited exchequer, and unlimited enthusiasm for art, might enable him to do so, but unfortunately he is seldom blessed with both these advantages. He fights shy, therefore, of youthful genius. When a recognised dramatist strikes out a new line, his play can be produced with some prospect of success—his name may tide it over. Such progress as is made in the theatre is mostly due to the qualms of conscience suffered by dramatists who have previously enriched themselves by pandering to the stupidity of the public. The conversion of the public is a necessary factor in dramatic progress. And thus it is that drama must always limp and lag far behind the other arts, which can advance without the public's acquiescence. Knowing that it can wreck any play which displeases it, make bankrupt any manager, terrorise any players, the public is far more confident in its opinion of plays than in its opinion of books or other works of art, and is less easily converted from its own crassness. And, undoubtedly, this dreadful state of things frightens away many men who have it in them to write fine plays. Artistic genius is a coy and timid thing—it shrinks from that personal exposure which is one of the conditions of dramatic art. Why, it argues, should it put its head in the pillory of a theatre, when there are laurel-wreaths to be won quite quietly in literature? It may long to express itself in dramatic form, but the theatre bristles with terrors for it. Ah, if only the public could be dispensed with! It cannot be. The most one can hope for is (1) some young man (or men) of artistic genius, in whom love of dramatic form is stronger than dread of the theatre, and (2) some enthusiastic person (or persons) who, with an unlimited amount of money, will lease a good theatre and devote it exclusively, for some years, to the plays of the young man (or men). There can be no doubt that, in recent years, theatrical conventions (not to be confused with dramatic conventions) have grown stronger and stronger, narrower and narrower. Playwriting is now overlaid with an agglomeration of petty difficulties not inherent in the art—large, free treatment of any theme is practically barred on the modern stage. With such a theatre and with such plays as I have suggested, one might, in course of years, educate the public, or rather make the public un-learn its present canons of taste and judgment. Once this were done, English drama would begin to show more signs of life, and . . . but I am Utopian. As yet, I see no sign of the young man (or men) with the irresistible genius for drama, nor of the wealthy person (or persons) with the beautiful enthusiasm. So perhaps I had better content myself with hoping that drama will in 1899 tread the old road a little more nimbly, a little less miserably, than it did in 1898.

[7 *January 1899*]

## AN EXQUISITE MATINÉE

As I have observed, Mediocrity—frank, flat, placid Mediocrity—is the stamp of the modern English play. There are exceptions, of course. Now and again, we find a play which leads us to conclude that its writer has more instinct for drama, more accomplishment in theatrical technique, a wider or deeper knowledge of life, a greater fund of wit or humour or imagination, or perhaps a nicer sense of verbal music, than has been granted to or acquired by the other ladies and gentlemen who disport themselves in dramaturgy. Sometimes, too, we come across a play which suggests that its writer has an even slighter share of these good qualities than have most of his or her rivals. And, for my own part, so sick am I of the drama's dead level, that I am almost as glad to see a fall beneath it as a rise above it. Is that wrong of me? Perhaps. But I doubt not, reader, that even you, were you in my place, would soon be guilty of the same cynicism: the lower the fall (even as the higher the rise), the better would you be pleased. After all, such a tendency is not really cynical. To the lover of any art it is the extremes in that art which matter. The greater his appreciation of beauty, the better qualified is he to detect beauty's absence. It is, I mean, by exercise of one and the same faculty that he finds good in one work of art and evil in another. And in either exercise of this faculty there is for him equal pleasure. Good art gives him, of course, into the bargain, another kind of pleasure—a finer, less self-conscious delight which is quite apart from his mere recognition of the work's merits. And bad work gives him no corresponding pleasure. But good work and bad work do equally stir his aesthetic sense and, in so far as they do that, they give him equal pleasure. The better the work, the worse the work, the keener his pleasure. As in the sphere of art, so in the sphere of ethics. One's moral sense is equally stirred by contemplation of the great saint or of the great scoundrel. By either one is equally interested. The ordinary humdrum citizen makes no demand on one's moral sense—he has, morally, no significance, and one is not interested in him. As in ethics, so in art, mediocrity leaves the critic quite cold. It alone can raise in him no measure of enthusiasm or indignation. And heaven deliver a man from contact with things which make no kind of impression on his soul! Anything is better than hebetation, and it is the fear of approaching hebetation that haunts me, more and more closely, in my wistful flutterings from one theatre to another. I have said enough, reader, to make you understand and condone the glow of satisfaction that suffused me during the performance of *Matches* at the Comedy Theatre. Had a deputation of the authors, the manager and my editor waited on me in one of the entr'actes, and unconditionally absolved me from the duty of sitting the play out, I should not have availed myself of my freedom. I knew that the play would never, in all probability, be acted a second time, and I was not going to miss this chance of hearing every line of it. It was unlike anything I had seen, unlike anything I shall ever see, perhaps. In point of sheer stupidity it seemed quite unique.

If it had been badly acted, my treat might have been marred—I might have supposed that there were merits in it which were obscured by its performance. But it was acted (so far as a play of this kind can be acted) exceedingly well by Miss Annie Hughes, Mrs Henry Leigh, Mr Edmund Maurice, Mr Harry Nicholls and other reliable artists, and I had the rare pleasure of seeing revealed in the clear light of their talent every inmost recess and cranny of the authors' incompetence. Nothing, in fact, was lost. Had the subject of the play been a very difficult or barren subject, I might have felt bound to give the authors credit for more talent than they had displayed. But the subject was excellent. A match-girl suddenly raised to a good social position—what better motive for a comedy? Not a novel motive, certainly; but no good motive for comedy or tragedy is novel, and, though it is not novel, the motive of a slave's sudden exaltation is as *fresh* now in London as it was at Rome in the time of Plautus. Almost impossible, one would say, to extract nothing from it! Yet the impossible was duly achieved by the joint efforts of Messrs * and §. More merciful than Mr Maurice, I will not name the anonymous authors of *Matches*. Timidity seemed to be their chief characteristic. They did not, like some dramatists, grasp their subject and go bungling merrily along with it, but walked nervously round it, avid of the slightest excuses for not handling it. The greater part of Act I. was whiled away with the humours of a gin-drinking stage-Irishwoman and a stage-coster, her son, and by the inordinate explanations and investigations of a stage-colonel, a stage-solicitor, and a stage-valet. There was nothing to show that the authors had ever taken the least interest in the life of the lower classes. However, before the curtain fell, we had so far advanced that the match-girl was proved, *prima facie*, to be a daughter of the colonel's dead comrade (those stage comrades!) and that she refused to go away without her doll. The colonel seemed to demur at the doll, but, being assured that it was a gift from the girl's mother, he turned an emotional back whilst it was wept over. The first part of Act II. was whiled away by the doubts and expostulations of the colonel's friends, whom he, for some reason, had not enlightened as to the harmlessness of the connexion between himself and the girl under his roof. Then there were one or two scenes in which the girl showed that she did not know how to shake hands, &c. &c. Then the coster and the Irishwoman were ushered in to disport themselves, and when all the characters in the play had been brought on, the colonel seated himself at a table and explained that the girl was an heiress and the daughter of his old comrade. Suddenly he began an interminable (and, to me, irresistible) account of the battle in which his old comrade fell—'we had hardly time to form squares, when they were upon us,' and so forth. The recitation being at length concluded, one of the characters —a stage-aristocrat—who had previously insulted the girl, asked her to marry him. She refused. The colonel re-entered, just about to start for the Sudan. The girl wept as he took his leave. The curtain fell after she had had another scene with the doll. Three years then elapsed, in the course of which the girl became a perfect lady. The scene was laid by the river, in order that the stage-dowager might come on after partial immersion with the stage-solicitor. There was also business with a washing-bill and with a basket of peaches, and there was another military recitation—this time by the coster who had taken the shilling and gone to the wars with the colonel. Also, the stage-aristocrat came, and tried again to force the now perfect lady to marry him. He was knocked down by the Colonel, jeered at by the Irishwoman and hustled off by the coster-soldier. Then there was the final scene between the Colonel (who duly loved his ward) and the girl (who duly loved her 'Guardy'). He proposed in the traditional way—'I want your advice. I have an old comrade who is in love with a young girl.' &c. &c. She, however, soon brought him to the point and the curtain down by presenting him with an affectionately inscribed box of matches.

I have written this brief account of the play partly as a pleasant souvenir of an afternoon which I much enjoyed; partly in the hope that it may meet the eye of the average English playwright, and cause him to review impartially, uncomfortably, his own record. 'Here,' he will say, 'was a play written without any attempt at psychology—a mere boxful of little worn-out puppets. Here was a play with a subject which the authors had never tried to see for themselves—a play that was a mere thread for the careless stringing of little worn-out scenes . . . . What of my own plays? I have acquired a certain knack, a certain accomplishment, which Messrs * and § have not. But do I aim much higher than they? Am I not content to give the puppets a touch of new paint and make them jump sprightly? Am I not satisfied so long as I contrive to manipulate the old scenes neatly, throwing in a touch or two to make them seem new? And is there not such a thing as life? And are there no men and women? And would it not be well if I began to use my eyes and my brain a little, outside the theatre?

[21 January 1899]


## PAT AND SANDY

Dreadful days are doing. Mr George Moore is prefatorially furious with Mr William Archer for not having produced Mr Edward Martyn's *Heather Field* (Duckworth and Co.) at the New Century Theatre. Mr Archer cuts in with a provocative reply. Mr Moore cuts in with a fulmineous rejoinder. He rides on the wordwind and directs the storm in the tea-cup, while the waves, 'inches high,' dash spars of wreckage against the porcelain embankment. Like the women of Mumbleshead, anguished readers of the *Daily Chronicle* balance themselves on the rim, straining their eyes tea-wards, And ah! corkily buoyant among the brown billows is seen the head of Mr A. B. Walkley.

Even were I not fulfilled, as I am, with an awful joy in the grandeur of this tempest, I should be glad that Mr Moore had splashed back into criticism. When a creative artist begins to criticise he is almost always interesting. The creative artist is, necessarily, narrow in his views of art: concentration in his own temperament and in his own method inclines him to excessive praise of any work of art which seems to echo his own ideals, and it precludes him from any wide, eclectic sympathy with other works of art—precludes him, in fact, from being a reliable critic. If he criticise frankly, with all the courage of his own prejudice, he is sure to be suggestive, nevertheless. He may make all manner of glaring blunders, but, probably, he will also strike in criticism some truth or half-truth which the professional critic would have missed, and in the glare of his very blunders we shall, at any rate, see further into his own soul. If his sally involve him in conflict with some professional critic, some just person of calm, acute temper and impaired enthusiasm, then we are sure to see sport. The collision of Mr Moore and Mr Archer is a perfect little episode in its way. It is more than a collision of critic and creative artist: as a collision of Scotchman and Irishman it is of deep interest to the ethnologist. It is a case of Pat in the kale-yard or of Sandy on the potato-patch, and when Celt meets Caledonian, ''most anything may eventuate.' Not only is Mr Moore very Irish and Mr Archer preternaturally Scotch, but Mr Archer is always at his best in controversy, and Mr Moore, beyond being a creative Irishman, is an unique, amazing creature, frank to the verge of unscrupulousness and—how shall I say it?—almost nude in his *naïveté*. From the very vagueness of his prose-style his turbulent meanings take especial force—those unfinished sentences, tapering away into three dots, seem to suggest the presence of thoughts too wild to be embodied by him . . . . Or are they breathing-spaces between the blows? . . . The crack of the shillelah echoes throughout his preface. A shrill whoop, a twirl in the air, and crack! down goes Mr George Alexander with a fractured skull. Down goes Mr Pinero. Down go Maupassant, Mr Jones, Mr James, Mr Leader, Mr —— but who shall enumerate the prone? Mr Moore, in his admiration of two young compatriots, will not allow that there is any talent save in them. Nay, so perfervid is he that he cannot bear to think that anyone save himself sees any merit in the work of these two youths, and he quaintly asserts that one of them, Mr W. B. Yeats, 'escapes the appreciation of the newspapers.' This thought's paternity is so obvious that one wonders why Mr Moore smites Mr Archer for not raving about *The Countess Cathleen*. However, crack! and down goes the Scotchman. And why (a louder crack!) did not Mr Archer produce *The Heather Field*? Then up springs Mr Archer. He grips his gude claymore and splinters the shillelah with a slick assertion that the play '*was not good enough.*' He makes a thrust and inflicts a grievous wound with the denial that Mr Moore created the Independent Theatre. Bleeding profusely, Mr Moore yet closes with Mr Archer and grounds him with a charge of betraying art to the public. Before these lines are printed, Mr Archer will be on his legs again, no doubt. But in the meanwhile, Mr Moore has certainly grounded him.

Mr Archer had declared that, if he were on the committee of an English *Théâtre Français*, he would 'ruthlessly blackball' such plays as *The Countess Cathleen* and *The Heather Field* until they 'had proved, in the experimental theatre, their power of appealing to an intelligent public.' This, as Mr Moore points out, would exclude Ibsen, whose public is exhausted by six performances. There Mr Moore 'gets home,' indeed. It is the public which, as I am always demonstrating, is responsible for the drama's inferiority to other arts, and the mission of a State-endowed theatre would be to show the public (not in a hole-and-corner-experimental fashion but with imposing circumstance) better drama than the public wants. The public stays away from the hole-and-corner-experimental theatre. But it would go to a great official theatre and be educated despite itself. Its education might be slow, but it would be quicker than it is now. Besides, the mission of a State-endowed theatre would be, not merely to educate the mob: it would also be to gratify those cultured persons who love good drama and wish to see it constantly in a worthy temple of its own, freed from its servitude to the mob. Who, as Mr Moore suggests, would care to go to the National Gallery if the pictures were chosen by *plébiscite*? The National Gallery is good because the pictures are chosen without reference to the mob's proclivities. And why should not drama, like painting, have its noble sanctuary? When Lord Rosebery made his speech about 'the predominant partner' he gave Home Rule away, inasmuch as England, which would accept Home Rule as a fact, would never believe in it as a theory. Even so does Mr Archer give away dramatic progress when he insists on the previous conversion of the public to the plays produced in a State-Theatre. Lord Rosebery's attitude was justifiable by the fact that the British public is shrewd in politics. In art the British public is—well, not shrewd, and Mr Archer, in behaving as though it were, gives away the whole position which he has hitherto maintained so ably and so finely. From the artist or art-critic to the mob there should come no compromise, and it is a melancholy thing to find Mr Archer—him 'who was young so long!'—quietly stultifying himself into popularity. It is quite right of Mr Archer not to follow Mr Moore's example of dismissing as worthless anything which does not seem to him a work of supreme genius, but, in the matter of the public's taste, my sympathies are all with Mr Moore, whom I thank for his angry superlatives.

It is curious how few people understand that the public is the drag on the drama. 'Why,' ask the *Daily Chronicle*, 'is the drama sterile?' Forthwith we find a letter from some earnest ass who signs himself 'Dramaticus,' charging the Censor and the actor-managers with the whole responsibility. (It is a safe rule that the man who, in writing to a newspaper, adopts a Latin pseudonym never talks sense. 'Paterfamilias' and 'Timeo Danaos,' 'Excelsior' and 'Audi Alteram Partem' — to what bosh they are always subscript!) The actor-manager would be delighted to produce good plays if their production did not entail bankruptcy. As it is, he has to produce bad plays, and, very naturally, he prefers a bad play with a good part for himself to a bad play without one. As for the Censor, to charge *him* with being responsible for the drama's sterility is about as sensible as it would be to blame the Lord Chamberlain because, at some Drawing Room, the presented *débutantes* were not pretty. I have no objection to 'realistic' plays and plays on sacred subjects, if they are good plays; but it is unlikely that, if the Censor's Index Expurgatorius were published annually, lovers of drama would be much depressed by its perusal. No, no! The mischief lies much deeper down than the censorship or the actor-managership. In almost every age there have been complaints of the drama's sterility, and it is always the innocent who are chastised. Thus the admirable and ingenious Canon in *Don Quixote* avers that the people would be better pleased if 'those headstrong fellows,' the actors, would consent to give them anything but trash. 'I have often,' says he, 'endeavoured to convince the actors of their mistake, that they would draw more company, and gain more credit by acting plays written according to art, than by such extravagant pieces; yet they are so attached and wedded to their own opinion that nothing will wrest it from them.' How modern that is! Only when the Canon proceeds to give as his nostrum 'the establishment of a theatrical censorship' does he seem to be at all out of date. 'All these evils would cease if some intelligent and judicious person of the Court were appointed to examine all plays before they are acted .... The writers of plays, moreover, would take more pains what they did, knowing their work must pass the rigorous examination of somebody capable of appreciating it.' How Mr Redford must blush and bridle over that passage! And what does 'Dramaticus' think of it? For my own part, I am sure that the abolition of censorship would do our drama to-day no more good than its establishment would have done Spanish drama at the beginning of the seventeenth century. Like Mr Moore and myself, 'Dramaticus' should snarl straight at the public.

Owing to the public, the theatre has sunk so low that few men of talent dare commit themselves to dramaturgy. Mr Moore trumpets Mr Martyn as a man of genius who has written a lovely play. Well! *The Heather Field* is now very deeply stained with the blood of Mr Archer and Mr Moore; else, perhaps, I should think it more beautiful than I do. Certainly, it is better and more interesting than the plays to which one is accustomed. But, for the life of me, I cannot see its transcendent peculiarities. Granted that it is based on a primal emotion which is to be found in all humanity, while *Mrs Tanqueray* was based on an emotion which is produced by certain conditions of modern society—wherein lies tthe strange beauty of its treatment? It is all very well for Mr Moore to sneer at the plot of *Mrs Tanqueray*, but is the plot of *The Heather Field* much less trite? Does Mr Martyn uplift us from the pettifogging conventions of the modern theatre and bring us face to face with the soul of humanity? Almost the whole of the second act is concerned with the schemes of the hero's wife to get her husband locked up in a lunatic asylum. She takes counsel with her friends, and on come two doctors, and the hero is 'drawn out' by them. Exit the hero. But a friend of his, suspecting the object of the doctors' visit, remains behind, and there is a long scene in which one of the doctors is persuaded not to sign a certificate, and the wife is thus foiled. The second act is, in fact, rather barren, as far as the soul of humanity is concerned. So is the third and last act, most of which is concerned with the hero's financial embarrassments and the old question of whether our old friend the mortgage is going to foreclose. I have no wish to ridicule the play. There are glimpses of merit in it. But there are not more than glimpses, and they are visible only through infrequent chinks in a common brick wall of theatricalism. Perhaps the play will seem better to me, if I see it performed in Dublin. At present, I will merely say that, as a literary play—by which term I mean a play that is well written—it has little or no merit: the writing is dull and heavy. Mr Moore seems to apply the term 'literary' to any play which interests him as drama, and to deny it to any play which does not. He denies that *Guy Domville* had literary merit, on the ground that Mr James did not understand how a play should be constructed. In order to justify this theory, Mr Moore trots out the fallacy that to think well is to write well, and to think ill is to write ill. Pooh! style is a specific talent. The poorest thinkers often have it, and it is often withheld from the finest thinkers. The most hopeless lunatic, unable to connect two links in thought, might, quite conceivably, be the author of very melodious and delightful prose-rhythms; nor do we doubt the power of Carlyle's intellect because of his numerous kakistophonousnesses. And, setting aside the question of rhythm, one knows that many fools can find the exact verbal expression for their folly, whilst many sages are 'more or less painfully inarticulate on paper.' But one need not appreciate these truths to see the absurdity of denying literary merit to *Guy Domville*.

At the Court Theatre there is a new play, of which I have not room to write this week. I am afraid Mr Moore would not see much good in it. I myself, however, enjoyed it very much.

[*28 January 1899*]

## OLLA PODRIDA

Last week, I did not leave room in which to say about *A Court Scandal* more than that I had enjoyed it. It is, as I remember, a very good entertainment. There is far more life in it than in most of the artless adaptations of artificial comedies with which London ekes out its theatrical history. The adaptors—Mr Boucicault and Mr Shillingford—have managed to bowdlerise their material without utterly destroying it, and, for that their version has several quite dramatic moments, one is inclined to forgive them the flat inelegance of their writing. The motive of the play—a young man's distress at his own youth—is, of course, quite false. A boy of nine may wish to be older than he is, but when he grows to the age of nineteen he is immensely proud of not being twenty. If the real Duc de Richelieu, at the age of nineteen, had been publicly presented by a great lady with a box of bon-bons, he would have taken it as a rather obvious compliment, handed the box round to the company, and eaten with gusto all the bon-bons that remained. The theatrical Duc de Richelieu (Mr Seymour Hicks) hangs his head, becomes husky, and behaves with such tragic intensity of humiliation and despair as to suggest that nothing less than the stage opening under his feet and forthwith swallowing him up will afford him the slightest consolation. Of course, Mr Hicks had to play the scene as it had been written, but he need not have underlined its absurdities quite so strongly. Throughout the whole play, indeed, Mr Hicks worked a little too hard—he was too exuberant, too pushful, for the eighteenth century. However, pushfulness and exuberance are good signs in a young actor, especially when, as in Mr Hicks's case, they are allied to humour and intelligence; and I should say—it is one of those vague sayings which save the critic trouble—that Mr Hicks has the root of the matter in him. The contrast between his modernity and Miss Baird's mediaevalism was rather amusing in this play of the last century, and was, I could not help thinking, rather a relief from 'the usual thing.' Miss Baird played very charmingly. Mr Beveridge was good as an Abbé, and Mr Brandon Thomas, looking wonderfully like a figure in one of the Balvadière prints, was most amusing as an old Baron. There was a host of other people in the cast, but I have mislaid my programme, and more than a week has elapsed since the first night.

Mr George Bancroft is a wise youth and industrious apprentice, who hurries slowly and has no wish to make our flesh creep by a display of precocious originality. He is still, as who should say, digging the foundations of his career, and we must not assume, just because Mr Arthur Bourchier and Mr Edward Terry have scrambled down, one after the other, into the earth-works and found in them not very much gold, that no stately edifice will be erected on them hereafter. Mr Bancroft is still, merely and frankly, a student of dramaturgy, a copyist of 'the divine masterpieces, my boy!' In *Teresa* he copied Sardou, sedulously and by no means ill. In *What will the World Say?*' he copies that writer on whose work his own parents went nap, so successfully, at the old 'Prince of Wales.' He comes forth, wearing Tom Robertson's heart on his sleeve, and keeping his own talent discreetly up it. He knows well enough that the Robertsonian manner is outmoded, but he seems to have decided that it would be a good exercise to do something in that manner, and, now that he has done it, he is trying his hand, doubtless, at something in the manner of Ibsen, or Maeterlinck, or Dion Boucicault. Fellow-critics, let him take his time—he will emerge later in his quiddity. Meanwhile, this play of his is a very creditable copy of Robertson. True, there are one or two things in it which are not to be found in Robertson: there is an American girl in it, and a dyspeptic young man, and we know that both America and dyspepsia were post-Robertsonian discoveries. But even to these two characters Mr Bancroft gives the spirit of his master. The dyspeptic young man starts for the wars, a street-organ playing 'The Girl I Left Behind Me,' and the American girl throwing him a rose from the window. And, in the last act, home comes the young man, deeply bronzed and severely wounded. He is no longer dyspeptic, and it is impossible to believe that the girl is still American—both of them have passed safely into the land of Robertson. Complete reformation before the end of the play was always one of the sacred canons of 1860 comedy. Just as the young man in this play is cured of his dyspepsia, so is his father, Mark Westoby, cured of his worldliness. In the first three acts, Mark Westoby is worldly and has dyed hair; in the last act, his hair is white and he is unworldly. I cannot help thinking that here Mr Bancroft has copied the creation of Beau Farintosh too slavishly. *Ingeniose puer, nimium ne crede colori*, and when next you show us a worldly old man, symbolise not his conversion by changing the hue of his hair—the trick is stale; rather, let him wear a wig, and then, in the last act, at his reclamation, reveal his baldness. On one very ingenious device, not known to Robertson, I must heartily congratulate Mr Bancroft. A doctor comes on in the second act and warns Mrs Westoby that her husband is suffering from 'valvular affection of the heart;' yet, when the curtain falls on the last act, Mark Westoby has not died. Thus does Mr Bancroft excite in us for his hero all the sympathy which we give only to the moribund, and yet he contrives to end the play with a village-dance and send us away quite happy. If that is not stage-craft, what is? Mr Edward Terry played the part of Mark Westoby with great energy and resource. He has, moreover, his full share of that indefinable quality which is called 'the Terry charm,' and, so long as he is on the stage, criticism is ever lulled in delight.

I went to see the new dresses for *A Greek Slave* at Daly's. I cannot say whether they are better than the old, as I had not seen the piece before. Most of the figures which crowd the stage are clad in neutral-tinted Liberty silks. This, I think, is a mistake—chronologically, because the play is dated 'about 90 A.D.,' and Mr Liberty's business is not so old-established as all that; aesthetically, because neutral tints are neutralised into nullity by so rich a background as has been given to this piece, and because, even against a severe background, they do not get across the footlights. They look very nice when one is near them in a daylit room, but are theatrically useless. I wish stage-managers would understand that a stage-crowd must, if it is to strike any real effect, be a harmony of flamboyant colours, interspersed with white and with black or, at least, very dark tones. As spectacle, the one thing I really liked in *A Greek Slave* was a dance of women in bright scarlet and women in deep purple whirling with men in leopard-skins. However, I do not wish to cavil at the production. It is pleasant to find, at Daly's, archaeological or fantastic dresses of any kind, instead of the drearily realistic modern clothes which cast a blight over most of the musical comedies. I fear that Miss Marie Tempest would differ from me in this sentiment. Evidently, she disapproves of archaeology, for, as the Blind Oracle of Memphis, she wears an evening-frock in which she might sup anywhere, after the performance, without exciting more remark than always is excited by a lady dressed in the very latest fashion. Or is the costume less a protest against the past than a hint that Egyptian Oracles used to take an unfair advantage of their less provident sisters by dressing just eighteen centuries ahead of them? Miss Tempest's singing I am not qualified to praise. But I am glad to pay my tribute to the acting of Mr Hayden Coffin. There is no living actor who understands so well as he what is meant by 'economy of means.' He expresses everything—grief, joy, jealousy, remorse, adoration—by one of two simple manoeuvres. One of these is to bend the knees, throw back the arms, press the chin into the throat, raise the eyebrows and roll up the eyes. The other is to clasp the hands before the breast, compress the lips and nod repeatedly to the footlights. I know not which is the more effective. Mr Huntley Wright is very droll, and Miss Letty Lind is delightful as ever, doing everything quite perfectly, in her gay, fragile, Lilliputian way.

[*4 February 1899*]

## OXFORD REVISITED

The loveliest of all vaudevilles, enacted in the loveliest of all cities—to have seen that is, surely, an experience worth fondling. It is well to slip, now and again, from the presence of that raucous and beetle-browed enchantress, London; thence to hurry to the Benign Mother and kneel to her as of old. If one find Shakespeare sitting at her side—Shakespeare in his gayest and most brilliant mood—why then, one's escapade will be the more refreshing. So often, and with such insistence, are the bloodthirsty and the melancholy sides of Shakespeare's nature revealed to us by the metropolitan mimes that we are apt to forget that the fellow had also a keen sense of humour, and a prettiness of conceit. All thanks, then, to the Benign Mother for reminding us, and for helping us thereby to greater delight in the most distinguished of her step-sons. I say step-sons because, in the absurd meagreness of our knowledge of Shakespeare's life, it is impossible to prove circumstantially that he was educated at Oxford. Nevertheless, no person of any real intuition can doubt for one moment that he was.

There is no more amazing and engaging masque than the *Midsummer Night's Dream*. Seeing it one cannot but regret that Shakespeare did not more often sacrifice, as herein he lightly sacrifices, his plot to tomfoolery. To imagine how much more delightful would be such plays as *Much Ado about Nothing* and *All's Well that Ends Well* if their author had 'cut' them ruthlessly and then interspersed them with fairy-scenes and clown-scenes, one need but imagine the *Midsummer Night's Dream* without its clowns and fairies. When he first conceived the play Shakespeare intended it, doubtless, to be a simple comedy—A and B in love with C, C in love with A, D in love with B. But the trite scenario and the familiar puppets palled on him, insomuch that he decided, wisely, to play the fool. He did not eliminate Lysander and Demetrius, Hermia and Helena: he sandwiched them between two wilful motives, one for his humour, the other for his poetry. He snatches us from the Court of Theseus into the Joiner's Cottage, and thence away to the Wood near Athens, and thence to the Court again—three little worlds of his, none really related to another. From one set of characters to another he boxes-and-coxes the compass with mad velocity. And the result is the most entertaining 'triple-bill' ever laid before the public. How thankful we ought to be that Shakespeare threw over the original scheme and gave us this spontaneous masterpiece in tomfoolery rather than *All in a Maze*, or *Hearts are Astray*, or whatever title he would have given to the properly completed comedy! Shakespeare fulminating, Shakespeare pontificating, has never been surpassed, but Shakespeare in his slippers has never been approached by any poet in *his*. Throughout the *Midsummer Night's Dream* we see him in his slippers—exquisitely embroidered slippers, which, in sheer gaiety and lightness of heart, he kicks up into the empyrean and catches again on the tip of his toe upturned. In English literature the great men so rarely unbend, and, when they do, it is so painfully, with such creaking of all their joints, that we wish they wouldn't. The *Midsummer Night's Dream* appeals to me as a triumph in the art of unbending. In all our literature there is not so fine a piece of 'freake or frolick, and peasant prettinesse withall.' It is quite incomparable, of its kind.

The O.U.D.S. could not have done wiselier than in producing it. The kind of play which is ruined by amateurs is that in which there are two or three very long important parts, with the rest nowhere. The plasticity and reserve and resource needed for a heavy part can be obtained only through professionalism. The amateur begins to droop and to flounder before he is even half-way through. But in a play like the *Midsummer Night's Dream*, whose weight is very evenly distributed among many characters, the amateur gets a much better chance of distinguishing himself. Besides, it is not right that a dramatic society of young men should choose any plays save those in which a goodly number of its members may disport themselves. Fun, after all, is the chief aim of such a society, and the greatest happiness of the greatest number should be its constant watchword. Therefore do I commend the choice of the O.U.D.S. this year as heartily as I should have disapproved of its choice of *Romeo and Juliet* last year. Acting with high-spirits is the prime essential to such a play as the *Midsummer Night's Dream*, and for this kind of histrionic art undergraduates are quite as well equipped as professional mimes. Climatically, Oxford (as also, indeed, Cambridge) is nothing more nor less than a malarial swamp: after a week or two of term there the healthiest mind and body sink to slackness. The elderly or middle-aged don relapses into this condition quickly, without a struggle. But the undergraduate, as having youth in him, fights gallantly against the depression, and seizes every opportunity of shouting and dancing, though inwardly he feels no real impulse to shout or dance. And thus in the portrayal of mirth he obtains a wonderful virtuosity. Smashing windows and dancing round bonfires are practices which the dons discourage, but they are, nevertheless, an admirable preparation for appearing in such a play as the *Midsummer Night's Dream*. The whole programme of the O.U.D.S. was marked by quite as great an appearance of go and gusto as it would have been if the actors had been the most experienced creatures who ever drew salaries. From no other amateur society could one have got a performance half so good. Oxford is, in a far wider sense than that which I have just suggested, an excellent training-ground for young actors. It encourages and develops all kinds of acting. That he may live at peace with the authorities, it is absolutely necessary for an undergraduate to be always simulating and dissimulating. Industry, thrift, innocence, obedience, veneration —of all these qualities, and of many others, he must try constantly to seem a paragon, lest he be fined, or gated, or sent down. In attending lectures, he will acquire (if little else) many rudiments in the technique of histrionism: to come in late without looking self-conscious, and to deliver his excuse plausibly; to sit with an expression of the deepest interest in the subject without disturbing his train of alien and trivial thoughts; to bend quickly, now and again, over his note-book and seem to be making a note; to laugh heartily at the lecturer's jokes—all these functions very surely mature him for the O.U.D.S. As a moralist, I deplore them. As a dramatic critic, I can but condone them. The other night, even those members of the cast whom I should be sorry to see plunging, hereafter, into a profession sadly overcrowded, fraught with many difficulties and disappointments, seemed to me to be acting far better than the ordinary, non-academic amateur. And there were two members of the cast—Mr H. M. M. Woodward as Puck, and Mr E. K. Talbot as Bottom—who played quite brilliantly. The agrestic jollity of the weaver could not have had a better or more truly Shakespearian interpreter than Mr Talbot. Mr Woodward, both in actual nimbleness and in imaginative humour, was a far more Puckish Puck than any of those *staccato* little girls of twelve to whom the part is generally awarded. Miss Una Cockerell had been engaged for the part of Titania, and she played it with all her own charm and intelligence. There was a well-ordered dance of fairies. The scenes, too, had been very prettily painted. But to me the setting of the piece seemed a matter of slight importance. Oxford itself, magical and matchless as ever, was for me the real background. In my sentimental vision, Theseus's Palace was the Bodleian, and the Wood near Athens was but the garden of John's, and the Weaver's Cottage one of those little cottages in St Giles's. The ripple of the Isis made incidental music to all the words. And the garland which Titania laid on the asse's nowl was woven of fritillaries, not of roses.

[ *18 February 1899* ]


## PINEROBERTSONIANA

'*Debemus in proecipuo ac perpetuo honore majores nostros habere, sed nequaquam,*' cried Cicero, in one of those bursts of common-sense which he kept usually for Atticus's private ear, '*in eam insaniam venerationis incidere ut putemus aptum nobis quidquid illi, pro suo tempore, approbaverint.*' As Cicero to the mob, so spake I to Mr Hare, when, ignoring the lapse of a generation, he revived *School* with every appurtenance of a modern play. I devoted two or three of these columns to showing him that Robertson's plays were, *as plays*, dead as door-nails, but might, properly produced, stimulate the archaeologist and touch the sentimentalist to the quick. I promised him a great success if he would produce one of Robertson's plays with the accessories of its period. Well! various eyebrows were raised, snorts emitted, heads tossed. Mr Clement Scott beat his breast and declared that the fashion in men's costume had not changed since '68. Had he backed his words by donning the clothes he had worn in that year and in them walking up Piccadilly, and had his progress been marked by no unusual incident, his case would have been more convincing, But—so far as I know—he did not embark on this adventure. Nor did the public seem unable to exist without seeing *School* in modern costume. Mr Hare, very wisely, decided to produce *Ours* with archaeological effects. I hear that the booking is excellent. Thus my advice has been taken, my prophecy fulfilled. I am much gratified by the success of the production.

As a play, *Ours* is dead. Triviality and unrealness are, I know, a great feature in most modern plays, but such triviality and such unrealness as were quite good enough for the 'sixties will not pass muster now. When we reflect that Robertson's comedies were the best in his day, and when we compare them with (say) *Lord and Lady Algy*, we see at once that we have made *some* progress after all. We see that if Robertson had been born thirty years later he would have been a better playwright than he was, and we shudder to think what Mr Carton would have been if he had belonged to the 'sixties. Such a farrago of silliness as the last (the Crimean) act of *Ours* would not be tolerated in any modern play; nor would any modern dramatist dare to play Robertson's childish tricks in technique. Even the worst modern plays are better—insomuch as they are near to life—than Robertson's. As a dramatic presentment of life, *Ours* is no good at all. But, though it tells a fatuous story and shows us no really human beings, it reflects, as every play does, the surface-manners of its period. In Mr Hare's production of *School*, the trouble was that mimes in modern dress had to behave as people who belonged to a byegone age. This incongruity annoyed the audience, and it paralysed the mimes. In *Ours*, the congruity of costume with behaviour delights the audience, and it gives the mimes a chance of acting. Mr Kerr made the greatest success. Whiskered and in vast checks, he acted better than I had ever seen him act: for the first time he showed that he could impersonate. In its essence, the part of Hugh Chalcot is a 'Fred Kerr part,' certainly; but the lapse of thirty years makes many differences, and Mr Kerr's quickness in putting himself back into the 'sixties was a proof that he could also, if he chose, play brilliantly in parts not prefixed with his own name. Mr Hare was, as usual, cameoesque. Miss Coleman, like Mr Hichens's dowager, was 'very, very Crimean,' and Miss Mabel Lewis fainted as only a Terry could. The one member of the cast who did not impress me was Mr Frank Gillmore. He did not seem to atone in intelligence for what he has yet to acquire in technique. Also, he should not have worn a little naval beard in the Crimea—the 'Crimean beard' was not at all like that.

*Sweet Lavender*, which Mr Terry has just revived, is a kind of link between the comedies of the 'sixties and those of the late 'nineties. It is an essay in Robertsonism, with some, at least, of the modern improvements. In sentiment it is as saccharine, and in plot as silly, and in characterisation almost as unreal, as any play of the Master's, but the scenes are ordered far more naturally, and the coincidences far more dexterously explained, and there are no soliloquies to speak of. The Temple laundress and her daughter—oh daughter yet more lady-like than thy lady-like mother!—and the rich banker whose adopted son loves the laundress's daughter who turns out to be also his; the news of the banker's ruin coinciding with his recognition of the laundress; the cooking, the sweeping, the dusting, the washing-up, the clearing away; the rich banker's sister who is changed suddenly from vixenishness to sweet benevolence by the loss of her fortune; the reclamation of the dipsomaniacal barrister, and the large legacy bequeathed to him, and his noble use of it—all these things are true-blue Robertsonian, of course. But Mr Pinero has manipulated them much more adroitly than Robertson could have manipulated them—so adroitly, indeed, that they are almost convincing, even now. *Sweet Lavender* is still a very pretty entertainment, and it will be still prettier ten years hence, when (as I hope) it will be revived with appropriate costumes. Humour is ever Mr Pinero's strongest point, and in none of his plays does it so gaily effervesce and overbubble as in *Sweet Lavender*: one is either smiling or laughing so long as the curtain is up—sometimes *at* the play, but, on the whole, more often *with* it. As Dick Phenyl, the tipsy but sterling barrister, Mr Edward Terry acts as well as ever. In the grotesque-pathetic style, which is the style needed for such a part, he is without any rival. And Miss Nina Boucicault plays the laundress's daughter very intelligently, and Miss Maude Millett plays the banker's niece very sensibly.

I did not see the prologue of *The Only Way* at the Lyceum. When I am forced to choose between coffee and a prologue, I take coffee. I do not blame myself. Whether one have dined ill or well, coffee is the inevitable colophon to one's meal; but who has ever seen a prologue that was not utterly superfluous to the play that followed it? Evidently, the prologue of *The Only Way* had not accomplished much, for the first two acts were little but a preparation for the last two. Ladies and gentlemen wandered about the stage, talking (in under-tones) about relationships and antecedent circumstances, slowly disposing of all those details which beset the conscientious dramatist who takes a well-known novel as his material. The effect was not inspiring, I confess. My spirits sank lower and lower. My attention wandered further and further. Sudden relief came, however, as the curtain rose on the third act.... The French Revolution in full swing, a court-house crammed with red-capped men and unsexed women, all shrieking and murmuring and shaking their fists, and taking now one side, now another. The whole act was splendidly stage-managed and was, physically, most exciting. Then came the fourth act—a charming souvenir of that scene in *The Sign of the Cross* where we saw the early Christians awaiting their turns to be devoured by the lions. Here there were *pairs de France* instead of early Christians, the guillotine instead of lions, and a Parisian mob roaring greedily instead of a Roman one. Otherwise, there was no difference, and the appeal to the emotions was, in either case, identical. Thus *The Only Way* was saved. If its first two acts could be ruthlessly revised by Mr Wilson Barrett, it might run for ever. As it is, it will probably run as long as Mr Martin Harvey's season. Mr Martin Harvey himself gave an extremely interesting performance. A more violent and ebullient method than his would have suited the part better, but he achieved much through sheer sense of the picturesque. A sense of the picturesque is very rare among actors, and without it no actor can achieve a great position. So much the better for Mr Harvey's prospects.

I had feared that Mr George Moore and *The Heather Field* would paralyse 'literary drama' for the present. But I have just received a little book which assures me that my fear was unfounded. *Excursions in Comedy*, by Mr William Toynbee (Glaisher), are plays which have real literary charm and value. In *A Prank of Cupid* and *Monsieur Methuselah* Mr Toynbee gives us the manners of the last century with a delicate fidelity that must be the outcome of great love. In all his dialogue there is wit, and a peculiar formal grace, very rare in playwrights. 'I like fastidious people,' says one of his characters; 'there are too few of them nowadays.' Certainly, Mr Toynbee is among the survivors, and I am grateful for these filagrees of his.

[*25 February 1899*]

## MORE FROM MAETERLINCK

One of the smuggest and silliest articles in Demos's creed is that 'ridicule always kills.' As a matter of fact—and none knows it better than he—it never kills. If it did, Demos himself would have been buried long ago. He knows that the deep guffaws which new genius always evokes from him are not fatal in their effect. He knows well that sooner or later, when he sees the new genius to be quite untouched by his mockery, his guffaws grow fainter and fainter, and he is left, at last, gaping blankly, humbly. But he would not for one moment acknowledge these unpleasant facts, and he cherishes fondly the pretence that he is a very dangerous fellow. In the case of Maeterlinck, he seems to be just arriving at the final stage—the guffaws have practically subsided. And the dramatic critics who used to split their sides over the 'Belgian Shakespeare' are beginning to look rather sheepish, and profess to find in Maeterlinck 'a weird charm,' or 'poetic power of no mean order,' or something else 'which it would, in our opinion, be difficult to too highly commend.' Well, well! It had to be, I suppose.

Mr Sutro's translations of *Alladine et Palomides* and *La Mort de Tintagiles*, and Mr Archer's of *Interieur*, have just been published by Messrs Duckworth. I had read the second and third of these plays in the original version, but the first, the longest, was quite new to me. According to Mr Sutro, it was written after *Pelleas and Melisande*. Practically, it is but a second version of that lovely play—an elaborated version. The thing which struck me most as I read it was what struck me when I saw *Pelleas* at the Lyceum: the amazing *dramatic* power of Maeterlinck. A great poet and fascinating thinker, he is, above all, a dramatist. The symbolism in his plays seems to me a matter of secondary import. I do not care to know why Alladine's pet lamb slips from the drawbridge into the moat; nor whether the castle with its 'corridors that wind, and wind, for no reason' is meant as a symbol of life; nor for any of those points. It is the emotional poignancy of the dialogue, of the situations, that most wins me. I can imagine no dramatic invention finer than that which I find in the conclusion of *Alladine*. Alladine herself is dying in one room, Palomides in another. In the corridor outside (which is the scene presented) stand the sisters of Palomides, and Astolaine, to whom he had been first betrothed. The voice of Alladine calls to the voice of Palomides. The lovers are dying, and they cry aloud to one another. Their voices become weaker and fainter. Presently, there is silence. The door of Palomides' room is thrown open. A nurse comes out and beckons. Astolaine and the sisters follow her into the room, weeping. The door is closed. 'Once more there is silence. Then the door of Alladine's room opens; the other nurse comes out and looks about her in the corridor; seeing no one, she goes back into the room, leaving the door open.'

Maeterlinck's wish that his characters should be represented by marionettes seems to me, I confess, a complete mistake. Mr Forbes Robertson's Golaud, Mrs Campbell's Melisande, the Pelleas of Mr Martin Harvey, were perfect refutations of his theory. His characters are utterly real and human. Racial, temporal, personal tricks they have not—these things are eliminated. They have the abstract simplicity of Greek statues, and, indeed, to the ordinary stage-characters of the English dramatist they bear much the same relation as do those Greek statues to modern wax-works. But they are not immobile nor clear-cut. They are troubled and wavering with passion, and we see them but dimly. In their very shadowiness we gain more than we lose—a mystery that makes them the more real, and an unutterable pathos. They are far too wonderful to be well impersonated by marionettes. But certainly, as it stands, *Alladine* would be a very difficult play to produce. A pet lamb which runs out of the room because it foresees spiritual danger to its mistress, and which falls subsequently from a drawbridge, could hardly be represented on the stage by any real lamb. The sagacity of real lambs is not to be relied on. And I doubt whether Mr Lauri could be induced to play the part. Altogether, there seems scant likelihood that the play will be produced at an ordinary theatre. But I have such faith in it as an acting-play that I think any kind of production would be better than none. So I have bought a toy-theatre and a box of marionettes, and this morning I have been conducting a fairly smooth rehearsal of the First Act. The scenery I am painting, unpretentiously, with my own hand, and I am afraid that the cost of the whole production will be so small as to be not worth announcing. However, I hope it may have some success. There will be matinées on Monday, Wednesday, and Friday of next week, and the proceeds will be devoted to the Gordon Memorial Fund.

I shall never allow my marionettes to perform the little melodrama which Mrs Craigie has written as a prefix to *The Ambassador*. Mr Alexander has produced it, but I shall not; for I do not wish to encourage Mrs Craigie in this kind of work. *A Repentance* is evidently designed by her to show that, despite her delicate, delightful, very feminine talent, she too can frighten us and make our blood curdle—to persuade us, in fact, that 'John Oliver Hobbes' is not the mere pseudonym we had thought it. With this end in view, she throws herself into the period of the Carlist-Christinist war and projects a lurid plot, with lurid accessories. Soldiers come tramping in and clanking out; bugle-notes are constantly being sounded; there is a mob without. The live husband of the faithful widow comes in, disguised as a monk. After a while he reveals himself. Joy! and the black velvet curtains are torn down in honour of the ἀνάγνωσις. But he has preserved his life by betraying his cause. Revulsion of his wife. Arrival of Carlists who are to arrest him as a spy. He is hustled into an inner room. His wife wounds her arm with a dagger. The Carlists find her on the floor. She says that the man they seek escaped from the window after he had inflicted the wound. They depart. The husband re-emerges, in full uniform. He vows that for her sake he will live and die a Carlist. But the Christinist soldiers are coming, by his orders, to arrest Mongero (Carlist general), and they will find *him*. They come. Challenged by the captain, he, at the pistol's mouth, declares for Don Carlos, and falls dead, with a bullet in his heart. The song of the Carlists is heard without. The widow prays.

Mrs Craigie has strung these stupendous beads on a fine thread of psychology. But the thread is not strong enough for them. It snaps, and they roll about the floor. Her analysis of the husband's mind seems to me to have considerable subtlety, but just that kind of subtlety which makes melodrama ineffective. The little hints and the frimicatorial half-shades which Mrs Craigie loves are much worse than useless when one is dealing in blood and thunder. The audience at the St James's did not know whether the hero was a fine fellow or not. Even when he fell dead, they were not quite sure. And a hero who is not utterly heroic is quite fatal to melodrama. The fact is that Mrs Craigie ought not to write melodrama. She was born to write comedies, and she must not flutter at the bars of her own delightful talent. When *The Ambassador* was produced, I did here beseech her not to go and attempt heavy drama. 'But,' said Mr Archer solemnly to her, 'man cannot live on trifle alone.' I would point out to Mrs Craigie, who seems to have been impressed by this aphorism, that though she write nothing but comedies, man will not be compelled to live on trifle alone—for that she is not the only dramatist in England; that most of the dramatic talent in England is of a heavy kind, and good comedies are very rare; that people who do one kind of thing really well should suppress their ambition to do well the things in which success can be gained only by people with quite another set of gifts. I did not see Mr Archer at the first night, and heard that he was on the Atlantic. I think the least he should have done was to stay and face the havoc wrought by his advice. Let Mrs Craigie repair the havoc by writing another comedy, forthwith.

[*4 March 1899*]

## A TRIPTYCH

In the dialogue of *The Cuckoo* at the Avenue, there is frequent use of the *double entendre*. Now, I am afraid I cannot claim, like most of my fellow-critics, to be inexpressibly shocked and disgusted whenever a *double entendre* is spoken on the stage. To me such quips seem, certainly, a rather dull form of humour, but that is because I invariably fail to grasp their second meanings. A comic character on the stage says something that to me sounds quite simple and innocuous, and behold! I find the whole audience (barring, of course, my fellow-critics, who blush and look furious) going into convulsions of helpless mirth. Long after the laughter has subsided, I sit racking my brains for the cause of it. Finally, I give it up, and find that I have lost the thread of the play. The public's love of the *double entendre* is reprehensible, but there is a fairly plausible excuse for it. In so far as the public is a playgoer, it has put its morality into commission, and it has no compunction in accepting gladly whatever has not been rejected by its own Licenser of Plays. 'Our Mr Redford,' it would argue, 'was not shocked by that joke. He would not have allowed this French play to be shown us as it was shown to the Parisians, but he felt that a few little touches of impropriety would be no more than we deserve for our kindness is allowing him to exist.' I am sure, however, that Mr Redford, like myself, is unable to detect a *double entendre*. To think of him as detecting one and not obliterating it, passionately, with a blue pencil, is a flight of imagination which I could not even attempt. I could almost as easily think of him as deriving personal enjoyment from these jokes. I doubt very much whether the playwright himself makes these jokes consciously. I am inclined to believe that from the dialogue of every kind of play many double meanings could be extracted, and that they are extracted only in plays like *The Cuckoo* because the public is trying to console itself for the loss of all those other improprieties which, it knows, must have adorned the original French version. I do hope that if ever I am able to see any of these jokes I, as a dramatic critic, shall have the satisfaction of being inexpressibly shocked and disgusted. Otherwise, I should feel obliged to retire at once from dramatic criticism, lest my colleagues be contaminated.

But for the nuisance of the *double entendre*, I enjoyed *The Cuckoo* very much indeed. Mr Brookfield is the adaptor, and the play bristles with his peculiar wit. That wit may not be of the finest kind—it is a trifle acrid, and is generally topical, superficial—but of its kind it is the very best. There are in this play lines which only Mr Brookfield could have written, and extravagant scenes which none could have so deliciously embellished. The burlesque of a public dinner, at the beginning of the second act, is the funniest thing I have seen for a long time. The whole play, indeed, for all the triteness of its plot, is very great fun. Mr Hawtrey plays the chief part. I have no doubt that by this time he is playing it with his usual composure. When I saw him in it, he seemed for the first time to show signs of effort. This was due to a severe cold—he had to struggle or be inaudible. So accustomed are we to his smooth and easy ways that we are apt to forget that he is acting all the time, and to suspect him (quite unjustly) of walking through his part. The severe cold revealed him to us in a new light. It made us conscious of his art. Mr Hawtrey should catch cold more often.

There is a rather strange play at the Comedy. A beautiful young lady, daughter of Sir Geoffrey Wildaires, a sporting baronet, shocks the County by her habit of wearing male attire, As the curtain rises, we see the hall of her father's house. There are sounds of revelry. The baronet is giving a bachelors' dinner, of which his daughter is the life and soul. Sir John Oxon enters, having just come from London to join the house-party. He has made a bet that he will seduce Miss Clorinda Wildairs. His host appears and leads him off to the dining-room. Later, the whole party adjourns to the hall, where Miss Wildairs challenges Sir John to a fencing-match, and beats him. Something decides her to give up male attire for the future. She goes to her bedroom, and presently reappears in proper evening dress. That is Act I. Some time elapses, in which Sir John wins his bet, but becomes engaged to an heiress who shall save him from bankruptcy. He comes down to Sir Geoffrey's place, in order to tell the daughter that he will not marry her. She hears about his engagement before the interview takes place. Enter Lord Dunstanwolde, an elderly man, who offers her his hand. She accepts it reluctantly. As she goes out, she encounters a young Duke, for whom she in her childhood had a kind of hero-worship. Soon we have the scene between her and Sir John. He, so far from being relieved at the calmness with which she accepts his perfidy, is furious that she does not rave and make a scene. His humiliation is complete when the elderly peer enters and announces the betrothal. The young Duke, who had also come to offer her marriage, starts and looks disappointed. That is Act II. Enough time elapses for Lady Dunstanwolde to become a widow, and for Sir John to be jilted by the heiress, and for the Duke to have met Lady Dunstanwolde in the huntingfield. Sir John insists on calling at the house, is furious that she will have nothing to do with him, heaps insults on her, and says he will prevent her from marrying the Duke by divulging her seduction. But he has no proof of that episode—not even a stage-proof. The tress of hair she once gave him was lost in a drunken bout. He is in despair. Opportunely, however, he learns where he can find the tress. He hurries off, leaving an exultant note for Lady Dunstanwolde. She reads it. That is Act III. Lady Dunstanwolde is holding a reception. The blackmailer arrives with the tress and heaps more insults on her. She takes up a hunting-crop and taps him lightly with the butt-end. He falls dead. She is overwhelmed. Pushing forward a large sofa, she conceals the body. She unlocks the door, and receives her guests with false gaiety. That is Act IV. Time enough elapses—yes! there are five Acts—for Lady Dunstanwolde to have hidden the body in a cellar, and for her sister to be dying. The sister tells how she had watched her dragging the body down the steps. While

Lady Dunstanwolde tells *her* side of the story, the Duke enters unobserved. Finally, he come 'down centre' and, enfolding Lady Dunstanwolde in his arms, declares that he would have done the same under similar circumstances. That is the play.

This *précis* does justice to the plot. But you cannot, my readers, know how dull the dialogue is, nor how grotesquely unreal are all the characters, unless—a course which I cannot honestly recommend —you book seats for the Comedy. The play is very beautifully mounted, with all scenery and costumes minutely appropriate to its period. I forgot, by the way, to indicate that its period is not 'the present.' Such indication would have been superfluous, perhaps. In writing a modern play, an author feels bound to pay some kind of attention to probability, and tries (often failing) to make his characters seem human. In writing a period-play, however, he is apt to feel that such things are of no importance. He reasons lightly thus: human beings do not now wear periwigs; *ergo*, the beings who wore periwigs were not human. And again he argues; some things were possible in the past which are not possible now; *ergo*, in the past all things were possible. I do not suppose that the lady and gentleman who are responsible for the play at the Comedy actually formulated these syllogisms to each other, but I am sure that when they read them here they will detect no fallacy. The eighteenth century is, more than any other, the period which authors consider to be susceptible of any amount of inhumanity and improbability. '*C'était une affaire bien étrange—même un peu monstrueuse—le dixhuitième!*' said Guillaume Meyer to the Goncourts. Mrs Hodgson Burnett and Mr Stephen Townsend may have had this saying in their mind when they dated their dreadful play '1701 to 1707.'

The Puritans were a harsh sect, and, however much we may admire them (with reservations) in perspective, no modern audience would tolerate a play devoted to a realistic presentment of them. The sect has long been absorbed, assimilated, by the nation. Its character has become a part of that much-advertised concern, the Anglo-Saxon race. If any playwright showed it realistically on the stage, every Anglo-Saxon would be either incredulous or indignant. Even if such a play were produced at the Crystal Palace before an audience of Nonconformists—who do, in a very faint, remote way, continue the Puritan tradition—it would probably fall quite flat. Puritanism would seem only repulsive, and it would be impossible to excite in an audience any sympathy with a really Puritan character. On the other hand, it is quite possible to write a play with a realistically Puritan element introduced for the sake of conflict or contrast. This, no doubt, is what Mr Parker meant to do when he sat down to *The Mayflower*. The play, as produced last Monday at the Metropole Theatre, Camberwell, contained only faint traces of his first intention. The Puritan father of the heroine was hardly a Puritan at all. He was a kindly, convivial, liberal-minded creature, with a taste for Shakespeare's poetry, and his objection to his daughter's marriage with Lord Gervase Carew was based merely on the ground that this worldling's father had, in byegone years, turned him out of house and home. Mr Parker's original (and better) intention was, I conceive, that the father should be a real Puritan, trying to govern his daughter according to the narrow ideals of his sect; that he should throw the whole weight of his parental authority against her marriage with anyone outside that sect. But Mr Parker, being a dramatist of genial and sentimental habit, who likes all his important characters to be also loveable, and to whom anything like Puritanism is repulsive, eliminated from the father any traces of real Puritanism and endowed him with all the worldly charms of a very dear old gentleman. This, I think, was a pity. It cheapens and weakens the dramatic conflict in *The Mayflower*. One feels that the daughter, in defying her father, is not doing anything tremendous for the sake of her lover and herself, but simply being rather unkind; and one feels that there would be—and subsequently there is—no great difficulty in reconciling the old man to the marriage. Also, one feels that, as this is a play of the Puritan period, with a majority of Puritan characters, it is a pity that all Puritanism has been so carefully kept out of it. Mr Parker intimates, in his Prologue, that he does not take his plot quite seriously, but that he has tried to give a picture of Pilgrim-Fatherism. I submit to him, in my stolid way, that a playwright who deals with a great romantic episode and wishes to convey a worthy impression of that episode, ought to take his play very seriously indeed, and that, unless he does so, he will fail to convey the worthy impression. The sailing from Plymouth Quay, the first years in the New Land, are among the fine things in history. But Mr Parker's scene at Plymouth, with its elopement and its comic sea-captain who dances a clog-dance with the waitress of the Bull Inn, seem to me a rather inadequate presentment of those days in which, as Mr Parker says in the Prologue, 'Love watched the Land till Sight was lost in Tears.' And, surely, nothing could be much more trivial than the New England scene, with the two comic married couples, and the finding of the young man in the snow. There is some very graceful writing in the play, but, for the rest, little to admire. The whole thing only goes to prove what I have often suggested: that Mr Parker ought to avoid large romantic themes. I have seen quite enough of his comedies and his romantic plays—both those which he has written with Mr Carson, and those which he has written alone—to be sure that the gods meant him to write comedies. I do not dictate to him—I do merely pressent myself to him as the gods' messenger.

[*11 March 1899*]


## 'SILET, SAPIT'

This week I have nothing to write about. I am as the cuckoo in a clock that has not been wound up. Striking-time has come round, but the folding-doors fly not open, and I cannot hop forth to coo. Mr Hare has produced *Caste*, but that is not nearly enough to set the mechanism going. I have already explained, at great length, why Tom Robertson's plays are impossible in modern costume, and (except that *Caste* in such costume seemed to me even more drearily impossible than *School*, and that in the costume of its period it might have been even more amusing than *Ours*) I have nothing to say of the production. Having whispered thus through the crack of the folding-doors, cuckoo is silent.

[*25 March 1899*]


## TWO COMEDIES

*The Gay Lord Quex* and *The Tyranny of Tears* are as unlike each other as two comedies can be. They are, indeed, antipolar in method. Mr Pinero has invented a stage-story and told it with prodigious, pyrotechnical ingenuity. Mr Haddon Chambers has taken an idea and a 'typical instance' and, in working them out, has quietly relied on their realism, without troubling himself much about situations. Both plays are amusing. Neither is quite like anything its author has done before. Mr Chambers's early work was all in the way of romance and melodrama. He proved himself to be in this way an adroit dramatist from whom much was to be expected. Never could I have suspected him of that comic spirit which he, standing against the golden background of a prolonged silence, now reveals to me. I did not suspect that he would ever take this keen interest in ordinary human character; nor that he would ever write dialogues so pointed and witty as that which he has written throughout *The Tyranny of Tears;* nor that he would ever go so far as to write a play on the basis of an idea. The idea on which he founds *The Tyranny of Tears* is not a new idea—no idea is that—but it is a rather good one. It is that no man, however much he may love and be loved by his wife, should allow all his liberty to be lost, and personality absorbed, in the process. Mr Chambers plays very brilliantly with this idea. The man and the woman created by him are quite real and likely characters, and one feels sorry for both of them. One laughs at them, nevertheless, all the time; for Mr Chambers, in his presentment of them, never swerves from the line of pure comedy. I was conscious of only one serious fault in the play, and that fault is only negative. Mr Chambers has missed one obvious chance, which, had he taken it, would have enormously strengthened his motive. Let me explain. The husband is a successful novelist; but little comes of that fact: he might as well be a lawyer, or man of any other business. True, we see him, at the opening of the play, dictating a newspaper article to his female secretary, and interrupted by the incursion of his wife into his study. Later, we see the secretary correcting the proofs of her employer's forthcoming novel. But otherwise the fact that he is a novelist is not once used to help the play. And it might have been used so easily, and with such effect. Mr Chambers ought to have presented his hero as one was in byegone days a keen artist in literature, but who, having married an extravagant woman, is compelled to turn out three or four pot-boiling romances every year. That would certainly have intensified the point of the play. Much could have been made of the hero's own contempt of his books, and his contempt of himself for writing them. As it is, except that his wife interrupts him at his work, there is no suggestion that his work, like himself, suffers from the effects of domestic tyranny. On the contrary, his genius seems to go on quite blithely, and his books seem to be all masterpieces—despite the fact that the proofs are corrected by a secretary! So I am still waiting for the comedy in which the popular pot-boiling novelist is the central figure. A better motive for a comedy could not be conceived, and I hope that whoever writes the play will plagiarise Mr Chambers's innocent little notion of secretary-corrected proofs.

As the husband, Mr Wyndham had a good part, a part evidently designed for him; and he revelled in the easiness of it, playing it with the absolute assurance of a tight-rope dancer crossing the road. Mr Kerr, too, as his friend, had the kind of part which he plays perfectly without any exertion. Miss Mary Moore was very feminine as the wife—and to be very feminine was the most important thing. And Miss Millett marred her very amusing performance as the secretary only by wearing three highly elaborate dresses; thus destroying one of the most important points in her part.

In point of stage-craft I have seen no play better than *The Gay Lord Quex*; for even Mr Pinero himself, who is unrivalled in technique, has never achieved anything technically better. In *The Profligate*, and in the other seriously didactic plays which followed it, Mr Pinero seemed to be striving after life, making a compromise between his observation of life and his love of ingenious stage devices. In *The Princess and the Butterfly* he seemed to be trying to get away altogether from the well-made play, trying to write a loose and leisurely comedy of ideas. In *The Gay Lord Quex* he has returned to his stage-craft. And I am glad that he has done so. For his ideas never were half so good, nor his observation of life half so sure, as his stage-craft. He has made many experiments in dramaturgy, passed through many phases. *The Gay Lord Quex* seems to be yet another experiment, and it is so good that I hope it is also the opening of a very long phase. As a young man, he wrote four or five quite perfect farces. I hope that now, on the threshold of that middle-age of which he wrote in *The Princess and the Butterfly*, he is resolving to write at least three or four more comedies like *The Gay Lord Quex*.

If Mr Pinero ever feel, hereafter, tempted to resume his didactic manner, let him compare this comedy of his with *The Profligate*. The main situation in both plays is identical: in both we have a man with an evil past betrothed to a young and innocent girl. The difference is that in the one play the treatment is comic, in the other didactic. And how infinitely superior the light play is to the strenuous one! When Mr Pinero was trying to be strenuous, trying to enforce something on humanity, he was always being tripped up by his own genius for stage-craft. His love of imbroglio, his juggling and manipulating, prevented him from transcribing life in any really effective way. When he should have been evolving his plot from his characters, he was inventing all manner of 'situations' for them to pose in. He was always imagining what *could*, rather than what *would*, happen—and in didactic plays the whole point is lost unless they deal only with what *would* happen. He was simply a born story-teller floundering in generalities. He fell between two stools. But here, in *The Gay Lord Quex*, he has set out to tell an amusing story for the stage, and has not troubled about anything else. He has not had to suppress his sense of humour, as in the didactic plays. He has given it full rein. And the combination of his sense of humour and his stage-craft makes the play a very delightful entertainment.

The point of the play is nothing more nor less than its third act; though such is Mr Pinero's art that the two preparatory acts, and even the concluding act, are in themselves quite amusing and exciting. The conflict lies between Lord Quex and his *fiancée's* foster-sister, who has discovered him at midnight in a Duchess's bedroom. How ingeniously the situation is led up to! Lord Quex is there, not with guilty intent, but because the Duchess, a very sentimental woman, wishes him to come and talk over the past and take a formal farewell of her. Lord Quex's *fiancée* is staying in the same house. Yet, in the second act, Mr Pinero has contrived to make Lord Quex's assent to this folly seem quite plausible. The foster-sister has overheard the Duchess making the appointment. The foster-sister is only a manicure. How then comes she to be staying in this house at Richmond? The owner of the house had been at the manicure-shop that morning, and asked her to come down and spend a happy day in the garden. It was in the garden that the manicure overheard the conversation. But how did she contrive to stay the night? The Duchess's maid had gone away. The manicure offered her services, and they were accepted. Her bedroom is near to the Duchess's. And why does she want to compromise Lord Quex? Because she knows something of his past, and is anxious to save her foster-sister from marrying him. This is the merest suggestion of all the ingenious details which are Mr Pinero's foundation for his great scene. There is no other dramatist who could have made the thing so plausible. In watching it one has the same pleasure as in watching a very skilfully played game of chess. Mr Pinero plays a kind of chess with probability, and he wins it. And his play has hardly more connexion with life than has chess itself. The characters—with one exception—are hardly more like men and women than chess-men are. They are—with this one exception—conventional stage-creatures, whose only business is to suit the situations invented by Mr Pinero.

The exception at which I have hinted is the character of Sophie Fullgarney, which is certainly quite realistic—a true and very subtle portrait of a type. The part is played by Miss Irene Vanbrugh with immense intelligence. There are very few actresses who could have so cleverly avoided exaggeration of the tone; and in the third act she plays with very real power. Mr Hare is not exactly suited to the part of Lord Quex, but he plays it artistically, and perhaps makes it seem more real than if he had been exactly suited to it. Mr Gilbert Hare plays a conventional part conventionally. As the Duchess, Miss Fortescue delivers frequent phrases in French with a pronunciation so exquisitely and elaborately pure as to make us suspect any actress we may have heard at the Comédie Française of having spoken broad Dorset.

The play deserves to succeed, because it is a perfect specimen of its kind. Its run will be considerably lengthened, however, by the riskiness of its plot and by the protest from the Bishop of Wakefield. I am not a Puritan. If we are about to have a new Restoration Drama, I, for one, shall not feel compelled to shun the Bishop of Wakefield, much as I admire his pluck in denying the sacred rights of Mr Pinero. To the plot of Mr Pinero's play I have no objection at all. But I do object to certain coarse jokes which occur in the dialogue and have absolutely nothing to do with the play. I assume that these jokes were inserted, cynically, to tickle the public and compel it to the Globe Theatre. As the play is quite sufficiently attractive in itself, and will have a good run by reason of its own merits, I think Mr Pinero may as well release Miss Vanburgh and Miss Fortescue from the unpleasant task of speaking the words to which I refer.

[*15 April 1899*]

MORE THEATRES

## BACKGROUND IN FOREGROUND

It is generally held that the most important point in the history of Greek drama was the invention of the tritagonist. That was the first step towards drama in the modern sense of the word. Thenceforth, recitation was to cede gradually to dramatic conflict. The actors, too, instead of being mere mouthpieces for poetry, became exponents of emotion, having responsibilities of their own. In the decadence, they became more important than the dramatist himself. The audience paid more attention to them than to him whose interpreter they had been; whose master, accordingly, they became. Well! and nowadays we are constantly hearing complaints that the dramatist is the slave, and not, as he should be, the sole master in theatres. Whether such complaints are well-founded, I need not discuss. The subject is a delicate one. But, as some modern dramatists do feel, rightly or wrongly, that they have a grievance in the great power and popularity of the actors, I would fain point out to them, *consolandi gratiâ*, that the actors, after all, do not invariably have everything in a theatre to themselves. There are occasions—and they seem to become more and more frequent—when the actors have little or no chance of distinguishing themselves; when their importance seems to evaporate altogether. There are plays—two of them were produced last week —wherein the actors are little more than shadows, flitting humbly about the stage without hiding the scenery against which they are cast. If the dramatist is sometimes compelled to write his play for an actor, he can, at other times, exquisitely avenge himself by writing a play for a background, for nothing but a background. So, though he may curse Æschylus for that tritagonist, he should also bless the scaffolding that gave way under the weight of Æschylus's first play. For it was because that scaffolding gave way that the Athenians demanded the building of a solid stage. And it was when the solid stage had been built that people saw the possibility of scenic effects. True, in Athens, scenic effects were never carried beyond a little conventional painting and a few simple machines. But, none the less, the marvellously elaborate spectacles of the modern theatre, the passionate glorification of background, are the outcome of a movement which owes its origin to that scaffold's collapse.

The most obvious example of the background-play is, of course, the autumnal melodrama at Drury Lane. There, quite frankly, the dramatist invents some kind of foolish story which will enable him to bring in the events and crazes of the past year. The two plays which were produced last week at the Lyceum and Her Majesty's, respectively, are, of course, on a higher plane of drama than are the plays at Drury Lane. Or I should say, rather, that they stand on the same plane, only higher on it. They are less obviously constructed with a view to spectacle. They have, at least, the semblance of drama. And so they have a semblance of superiority over the plays at Drury Lane. I can hardly, however, give them credit for more than the semblance. In the writing of *Robespierre*, M. Sardou's aim was to give a picturesque picture of a phase in the French Revolution. In the writing of *Carnac Sahib*, Mr Jones's aim was to give a picturesque picture of Anglo-India. In both cases, the story was made for the background. The background was, in both cases, the motive of the play. It follows that neither play is good.

'Give me a couple of trestles,' said the elder Dumas, 'some planks and a passion, and I will do the rest.' 'Give me,' M. Sardou seems to have said, 'an exciting period, two hundred supers and sixty-two speaking parts, and Sir Henry Irving shall do the rest.' I need hardly say that Sir Henry does quite loyally the best he can to make the play dramatic. He acts his part beautifully—how rare beauty in acting is!—and intensely. He puts all his subtlety into the part, and all his daring. All his powers he puts lavishly into it, and they are all quite wasted. The part is worthless, because the play is worthless, and Sir Henry, pouring into it the resources of histrionic genius, effects no more than the man who pours water into a sieve. In play that is not a play, no part is a part at all. In *Robespierre* nothing exists but the background. Of course, there is some kind of story—even M. Sardou has not reached in his art that culminating point when he will be able to dispense altogether with a plot. The motive is the paternal motive—father against son, son against father. A dramatic play might, of course, have been made from this motive. But M. Sardou has not sat down to write a dramatic play. If he had developed this motive at any length, or with any force, he would have obscured his background. So he just allows it to bob up occasionally, unassumingly, in the course of his play; makes of it a mere thread for the stringing of his 'stirring scenes of stirring days.' In the first act we see the lady who had been Robespierre's mistress. We have a long description of Robespierre. Robespierre comes on and is characteristic. Before the end of the act he sends men to arrest as an aristocrat the lady whom we have already seen. The first scene of the second act is the courtyard of the prison of Port-Libre. The lady is among the prisoners, but the prisoners are, of course, the important thing. Her son comes to visit her, and there is a painful but brief scene between them. The officials arrive with a list of the prisoners who are to be guillotined next day. The reading of this list occupies the rest of the act. Every prisoner has some kind of affecting business to perform as his name is read and he makes his exit. The name of the lady has not been read out. Her sons rejoices as the curtain falls. The second scene shows us the Festival of the Supreme Being. (Throughout the play, the stage-management is absolutely perfect.) There is a long procession. Robespierre comes on. He begins his oration. His son interrupts him and denounces him, and is arrested. Robespierre does not know that it is his son. So ends the second act. In the third act, Robespierre recognises his son, and learns that it is the boy's mother whose arrest he ordered. In the fourth act, he has a brief scene with the mother, who is now at liberty. Miss Ellen Terry, who plays the mother, was very nervous on the first night, and frequently forgot her words. But, as the words were of no importance, this did not much matter. The tumbrels are to pass the window on their way to the guillotine. Will the son be in one of them? As each tumbrel passes, the father and mother gaze distracted from the window. The last one passes. The son is not in it. The curtain falls.

Then comes the scene in which Robespierre sees the ghosts of his victims. The ghosts struck me as being the most material figures in the play. In the last act, the son reappears. He supposes that his mother has been executed. Someone gives him a dagger and he rushes out. Then we have the National Convention. Robespierre is denounced from the tribune. As Tallien, Mr Laurence Irving delivers a wild speech in a manner that stamps him, once and for all, as the young actor with genius. Genius is a dangerous word, and one which I have not felt compelled, hitherto, to use in my dramatic criticisms. It is also an odd quality to discover suddenly in the fifth act of a play like *Robespierre*. Nevertheless—at the risk of turning his head—I declare that Mr Laurence Irving has it. I advise those of my readers who are going to the Lyceum to watch for his performance in the last act. If (like several people who were sitting near me) they are idiots, it will make them titter. But if they have any sensibility to acting, they will, I think, agree that I have not been 'gushing' unduly. My praise of Mr Laurence Irving may sound a little inconsistent with my suggestion that in plays of this kind the actor has no real chance. It is not really inconsistent, however. The actor has no chance of moving his audience; but he can, at the same time, show them that he could move them in another play. Thus, Sir Henry Irving acted finely throughout the evening, though he could not move us to any interest in a part which was but the embarrassed shadow of a part. In like manner, his son, though I did not care twopence about what he had to say, won my admiration by his way of saying it. To resume! Robespierre tries to gain a hearing, but is howled down. He shoots himself, and the play is over. Or, to speak strictly, the spectacle is at an end. The spectacle has been superb. Anyone who regrets not having seen the French Revolution should go at once to the Lyceum. There he will see quite as much of it as is good for him. By the way, how curious it is that that orgy of prigs and cut-throats which was to result in so many eternal benefits to the human race has now absolutely no significance in the world, except as providing a background for melodramas in London!

I have no doubt that India, long after the Russians have relieved us of it, will still be used as a background by many dramatists in England. It is tremendously and obviously picturesque. Mr Jones, quite rightly, thought that much might be made of it. Having chosen it as a background, he proceeded to evolve a story that should serve as an excuse for jewels and punkahs, night attacks on insurgent tribes, beleaguered garrisons, and so forth. Unfortunately, he did not choose the right kind of story. His story would be all very well for a quiet little comedy, but it is not strong enough for the wear and tear of the lurid Anglo-Indian tableaux on which he tacked it. A colonel and his subordinate officer, both in love with a married coquette who cares for neither of them and keeps both of them in vague, bewildered suspense, encouraging now one of them, now the other, without any definite reason or purpose or result—such a motive as this would be well enough if it were developed as comedy, with fine shades, in a small theatre; but it is an ineffective accompaniment to Anglo-India in London. It seems a little subdued. It does not compel one's attention. It is drowned by the bugle notes 'without.'

Mr Jones should have chosen some strong, vivid, melodramatic story of passion. If he had made the coquette a definitely bad woman and had made her the wife of the colonel; if he had then made her the temptress of the subordinate officer, who, loving her, would nevertheless, in loyalty to her husband, his friend, reject her advances; if he had made the colonel falsely suspect his friend of scheming against his honour and had—in fact, if Mr Jones had adapted the story of Potiphar's wife, or some other story of strong, straightforward significance, I fancy that his play would have appeared much better than it does. As it is, there is practically no play at all. There are gorgeous spectacles, a great many characters, a great deal of noise. One sees Anglo-India, just as at the Lyceum one sees the French Revolution. It is an interesting place to see. But one cannot really get up any personal interest in the characters of a play which is scarcely more dramatic than was the Indian Exhibition at Earl's Court. There is a very strong cast, and Mr Tree, Mr Waller and Mrs Brown-Potter play the three principal parts for all they are worth; but the parts are worth so little, that the performers cannot make much out of them. At Her Majesty's, in fact, as at the Lyceum, the background is the beginning and end of the matter.

[*22 April 1899*]


## MR ROSE RAMPAGES

'There shall be a touch and a rustle, Affery woman,—oh such a touch and a rustle!' In these words did terrible Mr Flintwinch menace his wife, and they were recurring to me, dismally, throughout the first performance of Mr Edward Rose's new play at the St James's. Even before the curtain rose, a glance at the programme had been enough to warn me that we were in for a touch and a rustle. Firstly, 'King Henry VI. of England' was in the cast. That was a sure sign. Whenever a dramatist calls in Mrs Markham, one knows that he is going to be noisy. 'Sir Ulick Beddart (*called the Hunchback*),' 'Odo (*his brother*),' 'Sir Piers Beddart of the Vale,' and—ah yes, to be sure!—'Priests, Monks, Retainers, Soldiers, Prisoners, Courtiers, Pages, Ladies,' In fact, *Days of Old*—dreadful days a-doing, deafening days, long days! I settled down to endure them.

I beheld an armoury in a tower, full of retainers, and Mr H. B. Irving, evidently Sir Ulick, stalking about under a modest hump and looking sardonic. There was a longish scene of exposition before the noise became very great. . . . Rattle! Bump! The drawbridge had been raised. Bump! Bump! The castle was (I think) being attacked. Mr Alexander and Miss Fay Davis were alone on the stage: hero and distressed heroine. Outside, shouts, screams, clashes, bumps. The hero pulled open a trap-door, seized a torch. With the heroine, he disappeared down that secret passage which Sir Ulick (the Villain, his cousin) had thought was known to none but himself. The door of the armoury was broken down, and in rushed Sir Ulick cursing, with retainers, soldiers, and others. . . . But why, after all, should I try to describe these scenes? A pen on a piece of paper is the wrong tool for a task which one could accomplish only with a drum-stick on a big drum. Enough, to mention that the rest of the evening passed in duels and dances, suicide and murder, many rescues, many prisoners, a forced marriage, shrill alarums and cheap excursions, and all with a ceaseless accompaniment of bang-crash-bang. The play was well mounted, well received. Mr Alexander was dashing and feverishly romantic. Miss Violet Vanbrugh was spirited and graceful. The other mimes, however, were not quite so satisfactory. They did not throw off the restraint of the modern school, were penny-plain when they should have been twopence-coloured. I have already— have I not?—pointed out that the unctuous, ebullient method of the last generation is the only method in acting which suits romantic plays. Subtlety is of no use at all. Restraint is quite fatal. Shouting, stamping, strutting and rolling the eyes are essential in plays which are carefully designed for mimes to shout, stamp, strut and roll their eyes in. As the Villain, Mr H. B. Irving was far too self-contained. He should have modelled his manner on that of his hero, Judge Jeffreys. Miss Fay Davis, with her little frownings and poutings and cooings, which are so effective in modern comedy, seemed quite 'inadequate' as the heroine. Mr Arthur Royston, too, was very dry and dull. As for the comic relief, that dreadful commodity was supplied by Mr Sydney Brough, Miss Esmé Beringer and Miss Julie Opp. Doubtless, it was less their fault than Mr Rose's that they did not comically relieve me.

Everyone has limitations. One of my limitations is that I cannot enjoy plays like *In Days of Old*. It is not merely that such plays do not appeal to me: they produce in me, aesthetically, no sensation of any kind, give me no sort of illusion. Physically, I am conscious that they are noisy and that there is a great deal of movement in them, but emotionally they have for me no existence whatsoever. So it is extremely fatiguing for me to watch them. In keeping his attention fixed on anything—be it play or book, concert or exhibition of pictures—a man expends a certain amount of nervous force. If the object of his attention interest him, then he is recompensed for his outlay of nervous force by the inception of pleasure, and so, subsequently, is not conscious that he has been enduring any physical strain. If, on the other hand, he be not interested in that object on which his sense of duty yet compels him to keep his attention fixed, he is soon conscious of real and bodily fatigue. I left the St James's, last Wednesday night, really and bodily fatigued. Whether the play was good or bad of its kind, I had, and have, no means of judging. Between plays of that kind I cannot, really, differentiate. I could no more appraise one of them than 'J.F.R.' could appraise a concert given by a band of Hottentots with tom-toms. A Hottentot might have some criticism to make of such a concert, his ears being attuned to such music. 'J.F.R.' would merely have a head-ache. Likewise, a critic who is fond of romantic-historic-melodrama would have something worth saying about Mr Rose's play. Also, even if he had thought it a bad specimen, he would have left the theatre without that dreadful feeling of lassitude which weighed me down. For a critic derives aesthetic pleasure from the contemplation of good or bad work, so long as the work is of a kind he cares about and knows about. He experiences a thrill of pleasure in detecting and in notifying to himself whatever appears to him as a blemish. When I see a tragedy, or a comedy, or a farce, I feel myself on familiar ground—in a word, I am interested—whether the play be good or bad. When I see a play like *In Days of Old*, the most I can do is to sit it out. Shakespeare's historical romances I can enjoy by reason of their fine writing. The characters seem to me no better than puppets, and the situations, therefore, do not excite in me any interest; but if the blank verse be well and sonorously declaimed I can get aesthetic pleasure from the production, and am not seriously irritated by those stage-accessories of noise and glitter which Shakespeare threw in to please the groundlings. Mr Rose does not write badly, but he certainly does not write well enough to save me from being bored by his play, or to prevent the public from thoroughly enjoying it. It was near midnight before the curtain fell on the first performance, and so the public's enthusiasm had somewhat evaporated when Mr Rose made his bow. But the enthusiasm had been so great throughout the evening that I cannot doubt that the public had very thoroughly enjoyed itself. Little as I respect the public, I admit that of plays like this it is a better judge than I. Plays like this are written simply to please it. If they please it, they are good. If they do not please it, they are bad. That the modern dramatist ever sits down to write them, with artistic sense, for his own pleasure, is an idea which I simply refuse to entertain. They are commercial speculations, and have as much connexion with art as have the company-flotations in the City. . . . But I see that I am becoming dogmatic. After all, since I cannot understand how any human being can enjoy such plays, and since such plays actually are enjoyed by a number of human beings so large as to be called the British public, ought I to declare it impossible that Mr Rose should take any pleasure in writing such plays, on the mere ground that I myself should not care to be writing one? Have I not, in fact, been deducing a general law from my own limitations? Let me, by way of amends, congratulate Mr Rose on not having those horrid limitations which prevent some writers from pleasing at once the British public and themselves.

[29 *April 1899*]


## IN DUBLIN

Travelling by night always induces a vague sense of romance, even if one be not bent on so romantic an errand as was mine—to see and describe the revival of a certain form of beauty in a land that is known to be a land of tears and dreams. And so, when I saw through the dawn's mist the blurred coast of Ireland, my heart was strung to a high, vague pitch of exaltation. When I disembarked, there seemed to me a rather crude bathos in the cry of '*Express*! *Nation*! *Freeman's*!' briskly uttered by an early hawker. However, the man had a persuasive brogue, and I bought his wares. A glance down the columns reminded me sharply that I was in a land whose tears and dreams have always a supplement of wigs on the green. I should hear 'voices, voices,' no doubt, and the 'sound of a silver harp-string,' all in good time; but whoops and blows were the first sounds that came to me. Here was a furious protest from the 'Catholic students of the Royal University' against 'Mr Yeats's slanderous caricature of the Irish peasant. . . . We do not seek the goodwill of England, but we object to be made the butt of her bitter contempt.' Here was Cardinal Logue, who, 'judging by these extracts,' had 'no hesitation in saying that an Irish Catholic audience which could sit out such a play must have sadly degenerated, both in religion and patriotism.' (Pleasant, to find that Irish Cardinals and English Bishops have one habit in common, at least!) Here, too, was a vitriolic telegram from Mr Frank Hugh O'Donnell. (Strange, that Mr Yeats in luring down the Sheogue from the hill-side, had also evoked a fiery spirit from the shades of 1880!) I confess that I was altogether startled. A little play, written by a poet for no sake but that of beauty, with no aim in history or theology—and then, in a jiffy, the green covered with wigs! Dublin resounding with protests that no Irish peasant was ever so degraded as to barter his soul for bread, and that it is impious to suggest that 'the Virgin has dropped asleep' in time of famine! Well! one must take the Irish as they are —that is no hardship, for they are always loveable—and one must not be shocked to find them gratifying their eternal instinct for a shindy even over a little, delicate, remote work of art like *The Countess Cathleen*. Nor should one deduce from the present shindy that the Irish have no aesthetic sense, any more than one should see in the old custom of the 'wake' a sign that they are deficient in natural feeling.

In writing *The Countess Cathleen* and in starting the '*Irish Literary Theatre*,' Mr Yeats's aim has been to see whether beauty be not, after all, possible on the stage. Everyone who cares about the stage ought to be grateful to him, whatever the outcome of his experiment. If I were asked what were the two elements furthest to seek in the modern commercial drama, I should have my answer pat: 'truth and beauty.' I should, however, hasten to admit that there is some considerable attempt at the former element. In recent years, dramatists have been educating themselves to attain in their work, and their audiences to demand in it, a nearer approach to the realities of life and character. In that respect, there has been, is, and will be, an improvement of the ordinary drama. It is along that line that ordinary drama will progress, and I, as an habitual critic (and, in my little way, would-be reformer) of such drama, have therefore tried always to lay stress on the importance of truth. About beauty I have said nothing. To say anything about it, could have served no practical purpose; for there is no faintest effort among ordinary modern dramatists to attain any kind of beauty. In the ordinary modern theatre, beauty begins and ends with the face of the leading-lady. It is useless for a critic to try to awaken in the objects of his criticism a sense which simply does not exist in them—he need but urge them to a better use of the senses they have. 'But,' someone may object, 'truth and beauty are indivisible. You cannot have the one without the other. If Maeterlinck's characters were not true, his plays would not be beautiful. Because Ibsen's characters are real, his plays are beautiful.' That is mere pedantry. What, in exact metaphysics, are the relations of beauty and truth to each other, is a question about which I care nothing; and Keats's famous line—

'Beauty is truth,* truth beauty'§

—does not help anyone to a definite knowledge of what either really is. I use the two words in their rough and ready significance. And I maintain that the beauty of Maeterlinck's work is due, not to his capacity for creating true characters, but to his treatment of them from a standpoint of beauty; also, that Ibsen's modern plays are none the less ugly for their unerring truth. The fact is that it is impossible for an artist to create beauty if he take so ugly an age as this for his background; nay, that it is impossible even for an artist living in a beautiful age to create beauty if he take his own age for background. Athens was not ugly, nor was London in the time of Elizabeth; yet both Shakespeare and Æschylus, in quest of beauty, put their puppets into an age either fabulous or byegone. Beauty seems always something remote from the stress of common life. Though it may exist in such life, it can be conceived only as at a distance. The greater the distance, the clearlier can it be conceived. And it is for this reason that Maeterlinck billets his figures on some castle that never existed or perhaps existed 'nowhere once.' And it is for that reason, also, that Mr Yeats has laid his play 'in Ireland, and in old times.' It was inevitable that Mr Yeats should choose Ireland as the scene, even had he known that Irishmen would be so foolish as to treat the play as

* What is truth? Pilate.   § Define Beauty. M.B.

a contribution to history. But, so far as his play is concerned, I see no essential reason why the scene should have been laid anywhere really on the map. Perhaps that is because I am not an Irishman? To an Irishman, perhaps, Mr Yeats's play may seem steeped in national character. To me it seems merely a beautiful poem about some men and women.

Rather, I should have said a play about a woman. The Countess Cathleen learns that her peasants are selling to two demons their souls for bread. That she may save them, she sells all that she has, and distributes the gold. But that sacrifice is not enough. The hunger is still in the land, and still the demons are driving their bargains. At last, the Countess Cathleen gives the demons her own soul to redeem the rest. She dies. Comes an angel, telling the peasants that their lady is

> 'passing to the floor of peace,
> And Mary of the seven times wounded heart
> Has kissed her lips, and the long blessed hair
> Has fallen on her face; the Light of Lights
> Looks always on the motive, not the deed,
> The Shadow of Shadows on the deed alone.'

Logically, this conclusion of the play cannot be defended. It is also, I think, a mistake in drama. A sacrifice that turns out to be no sacrifice at all loses most of its pathos, and the beauty of the Countess Cathleen's action is inevitably cheapened for us by the knowledge that she was saved its consequence. Even in a commercial theatre it is no longer necessary for the dramatist to invent at all costs a 'happy ending.' That Mr Yeats has invented one for *The Countess Cathleen*, seems to me a matter of deep irony. However, it is the only fault I find with him. For the rest, he has written a poem of exquisite and moving beauty. I do not suggest that he is a dramatist in the sense in which Maeterlinck is a dramatist. He is so far a dramatist that he can tell things simply and clearly in dramatic form. But he is, pre-eminently, a poet; and for him words, and the ordering of words, are always the chief care and delight. His verses, more than the verses of any other modern poet, seem made to be chanted; and it is, I fancy, this peculiar vocal quality of his work, rather than any keen sense of drama, that has drawn him into writing for the stage. It is this peculiar quality, also, which differentiates *The Countess*

*Cathleen* from that intolerable thing, the ordinary 'poet's play.' Miss May Whitty as the Countess, and Miss Florence Farr as a Bard, and Miss Anna Mather as a Nurse, all delivered the verses well, giving to them the full measure of their music; and I know not when I have found in a theatre more aesthetic pleasure than I found in listening to them. I wish that the rest of the performers had been so good as these three ladies. Most of them seemed to be terrified amateurs. Yet even they, with all their nervousness and lack of skill, could not quite obscure the beauty of the verses assigned to them. Despite them, and despite the little cramped stage and the scenery which was as tawdry as it should have been dim, I was, from first to last, conscious that a beautiful play was being enacted. And I felt that I had not made a journey in vain.

I regret that I have not left space in which to write of the other play presented by the Irish Literary Theatre—Mr Martyn's *Heather Field*. Not long ago, this play was published as a book, with a preface by Mr George Moore, and was more or less vehemently disparaged by the critics. Knowing that it was to be produced later in Dublin, and knowing how hard it is to dogmatise about a play till one sees it acted, I confined myself to a very mild disparagement of it. Now that I have seen it acted, I am sorry that I disparaged it at all. It turns out to be a very powerful play indeed. For the benefit of my colleagues, I may add that it has achieved a really popular success in Dublin— a success which must be almost embarrassing to the founders of a Literary Theatre.

[*13 May 1899*]

## 'SUCH STUFF AS DREAMS ARE MADE OF'

For anyone who holds sympathy to be the very essence of good criticism it is distressing to find himself in antipathy to the kind of work he has to criticise most frequently. It distresses him to be always murmuring 'Give me something else! This is all very well in its way, and there are, I know, many people who like it. But I do not like it. Please do give me something else!' How much more, then, is he distressed if the 'something else,' when it is given, does not arouse in him any keen sense of gratitude or pleasure! I am always, more or less loudly, murmuring against the monotony of the modern commercial drama, and I am always (though I discriminate between commercial plays, seeing that some are good, and others bad, of their kind) crying out for some departure from the conventions of the modern commercial drama. Last Monday, at the St George's Hall, I had the opportunity of seeing such a departure. A classic play, adapted from the Spanish by one who was both a scholar and a poet —this was what I saw performed, And, to my intense chagrin, it did not give me any pleasure; nay, it even irritated me. I found myself wishing it were 'something else'—even a dull and vulgar musical farce. I felt as little in sympathy with the rapt scholars around me as I feel with the glossy representatives of this and that 'syndicate' who cluster so knowingly to the first-nights of musical farces. I had arrived in a glow of sympathy, and I was distressed to find myself growing colder and colder as the evening wore on. My heart stole wistfully back to Dublin. There, at least, I had seen a departure which duly kindled me. *The Countess Cathleen*! That, at least, had delighted me. It had seemed to me a live and moving play. This play—*Such Stuff as Dreams are Made Of*—seemed to me quite dead. Quite dead, I mean, as performed in the St George's Hall by the Elizabethan Stage Society. In the original, no doubt, it was a fine play. As adapted by FitzGerald, (whom Mr Poel, in his prolegomena, spells with an atheistically small g), it had seemed to me, when I read it, a fine play. I am convinced that I could enjoy a passable production of it. And thus I am driven reluctantly to consider that Mr Poel's production of it, like his spelling of its author's name, was not passable.

I know that Mr Poel's aim in founding the Elizabethan Stage Society was archaeological rather than aesthetic. His aim was not so much to produce plays delightfully as to show how they were originally produced. Well! *La Vida es Sueño* was produced in the middle of the seventeenth century, presumably without curtain or footlights, and with only one plain scene. If Mr Poel had translated the play literally, or commissioned someone else to do so, an archaeological production of it might (to archaeologists) have seemed quite justifiable. But Mr Poel took FitzGerald's version, heedless of the fact that FitzGerald, caring nothing for archaeology, had cut out the under-plot and made a free, modern version of the rest. I submit that to produce this version with every inconvenient circumstance of archaeology was a mere waste of time. If the version was to be produced at all, it should have been produced in a manner appropriate to it. It should have been produced in such a way as to make it aesthetically real to a modern audience. Or (since Mr Poel is an archaeologist it should have been produced in the manner of that medio-Victorian period in which FitzGerald lived. Not Mr Poel himself would deny that the absence of a curtain and footlights, with inappropriate scenery, militates (in modern times, at least) against aesthetic illusion. Mr Poel would admit that *Such Stuff as Dreams are Made Of* is a play which, more than most plays, requires (aesthetically) to be mounted with appropriate scenery. In the first act, the young Prince Segismund is in prison. For superstitious reasons, his father has kept him always chained in this prison, kept him ignorant of the world outside its walls. The youth is drugged and carried away to his father's palace. In the second act, we see him in the palace, dressed as becomes a King's son, in the midst of bowing courtiers. At first he fancies that he must be dreaming. Then, gradually, the reality and the reason of his new estate are explained to him. He turns on the King, cursing him bitterly for his long-drawn cruelty. The soldiers seize him. Again he is drugged, and is cast back into prison, there to imagine that the palace, and all that befel him in it, was after all a dream. I need scarcely point out that for this play two backgrounds would be better than one. I do not stickle for elaborate scenery; indeed, I much prefer simple and modest scenery. But there ought to be some definite suggestion that the palace to which the Prince is transported is not the dungeon in which he has spent his life, and no amount of good acting would help me to ignore Mr Poel's definite suggestion that the palace *is* the dungeon. If Mr Poel excuses himself on the ground that he is only an archaeologist, I can but repeat that, being so, he should have left this play alone. But stay! That is not the only answer I can make. If Mr Poel was but archaeologising what ought not to be archaeologised, why did he assign the part of the Prince to Miss Margaret Halstan? That the principal male part should be acted by a young lady—is that sound archaeology? I confess that Mr Poel bewilders me. Perhaps I had better leave archaeology out of the question, and say merely that the play, as a play, was spoilt by the selection of Miss Halston even more than by the dungeon-palace and the amateurishness of the other performers. Miss Halstan acted very gracefully, with intelligence and with sense of poetry. But the fact remained that she was a young lady masquerading in the part of a manly young man, and thereby the play was shorn of all dignity and effectually reduced to the level of comic opera. And comic opera, on a dim stage, without a curtain, without music, without dancing, in the St George's Hall, may be a powerful opiate, but is not (to put it mildly) such stuff as very bright or pleasant dreams are made of.

I had intended to write in detail, this week, about *The Heather Field*. But, since the play is to be acted in London, I postpone my remarks.

[*20 May 1899*]


## MR CARTON'S NEW PLAY

Mr Carton, through an interviewer, has lately wafted to the world his conviction that the vogue of the romantic play is over. 'The buff boot,' he says, 'is down at heel.' Else, no doubt, Mr Carton (whose foible is to be always in the fashion) would himself be wearing it. In *Liberty Hall* and in *Sunlight and Shadow* he wore (for they were still 'the wear' then) the elastic-side shoes of Tom Robertson. These, at the witching moment, he discarded for Norwegian highlows. In them he walked uneasily; but, had not the vogue of the problem-play ceased soon after the production of his *Tree of Knowledge*, he would, I am sure, have persisted. And lately he has been tripping in the patent-leathers of that up-to-date comedy which is of the very latest fashion. 'Up-to-date' is a vile phrase, but it describes well the kind of thing I mean: the kind of thing Mr Carton aimed at in *Lord and Lady Algy;* even better, the kind of thing he aims at in *Wheels within Wheels*. In respect of the fashion, Mr Carton's patent-leathers are quite perfect. They are extremely pointed, most highly varnished and—important detail!—besprent with a little mud. Whether they be the 'wear' most appropriate to Mr Carton's foot, I am not at all certain. They are more appropriate than the highlows, but the foot in them is so adaptable that one cannot safely dogmatise about it. Mr Carton is Protean. And it would be as difficult to determine his real *métier* as it would have been to say whether Proteus appeared to greatest advantage as a tiger or as a flame or as a stream of running water. Some day, perhaps, Mr Carton will cease to trouble about the public and the public's varying demands, and will write something really of his own impulse. Then, in my academic way, I shall doubtless be able to place him in the foremost rank of dramatists. At present, I can but admire his consummate agility in jumping with the cat. Other dramatists watch that animal and jump with it; but none jumps with it so quickly, so accurately, and, I may add, so gracefully, as Mr Carton.

*Rebellious Susan* created a demand for artificial comedy of 'smart' life, as distinguished from the old-fashioned 'high' life. *The Liars* and *Lord and Lady Algy* supplied some of the demand. *Wheels within Wheels* comes to supply some more of it. The play is a very adroit specimen of the artificial comedy of 'smart' life. When I call it 'artificial' I do not mean that it is unnatural or fantastic. I mean rather that it deals not with the souls of human creatures but with their behaviour in certain quandaries. Pure comedy, as much as pure tragedy, does deal with the soul. I do not complain of *Wheels within Wheels* because it is not pure comedy. I merely note the difference, in order that my readers may understand what kind of play it is. In it, so far as I could see, none of the dilemmas involve any reference to human emotion, to the sense of right or wrong, to desire or revulsion. The dilemmas are purely social: what, under such-and-such circumstances, ought Mr or Mrs So-and-So to do? The play reminds one of those 'Hard Cases' which have been appearing for so many years in *Vanity Fair*. Mr Carton propounds a cluster of them in one evening, and solves them all himself, leaving us to 'adjudge' his solutions 'correct' or 'incorrect.' Here are a few of his pretty little puzzles:

A is an attratcive widow. B, her brother, is married to C, a frivolous girl who is beloved by D. C. has confided to A that D has in his possession a foolish letter of hers and that he is using it in order to force her into an elopement. She does not wish to elope, for the Season is just beginning. What should A do?

A, says Mr Carton, should go by night to D's room, break open his safe and steal the letter. A does so. But

E, a middle-aged man of the world and a friend of D, discovers A in the act of taking the letter from the safe. He has never met her before and does not know anything about her. A appeals to his mercy, and begs him to burn the letter for her. What should E do?

E, says Mr Carton, should burn the letter. E does so. Again,

F, a man-about-town, wishes to marry A, who does not seem unwilling. He keeps a *faux ménage* which he is loth to break up. What should F do?

F should break it up. But

A overhears him talking about the *faux ménage*. She never really cared about him. What should A do?

A should dismiss him at the first opportunity. The opportunity comes later. Meanwhile,

C, not knowing that her letter has been destroyed, and supposing that her husband already suspects her, is pressed by D to join him at a country inn, *en route* for the Continent. What should C do?

C should agree to do so. But

A finds her flown and knows her destination. What should A do?

A should follow C, leaving a letter to make B, E and F think that it is with herself that D is eloping. Then

A finds C and D at the inn. She asks D to release C and to back up her (A's) strategy. But D is still anxious to elope with C. B, E and F are on their way to the inn. What should D do?

D should obey A. Finally, A and E are left alone at the inn. E asks A to marry him. What should A do?

A should accept E, and with her acceptance of him the curtain falls. For Mr Carton, and for me, and for the whole audience, the game is really quite amusing; in other words, *Wheels within Wheels* is very good of its kind. Some critics prefer one kind of thing, some another. I myself rather like this kind of thing, but even if I did not I should be in duty bound to congratulate Mr Carton on having done it neatly and well. The dialogue is always effective, and often very funny. Occasionally it is vulgar, but that is because most of the characters in the play are vulgar; and so Mr Carton is justified. In his dialogue, Mr Carton fails only when he drags in jokes that are irrelevant to the piece. I have no pedantic objection to the introduction of a joke which does not directly help the action or atmosphere of the play; but I do stipulate that such jokes shall be really good: unless they are really good, they are a nuisance. Let me give Mr Carton an instance of the kind of joke which he would have done well to omit rather than drag in. He makes two of his characters engage in irrelevant conversation about the monotonous ugliness of suburban houses. 'Yes,' says one of them, 'it is the Venetian-blind leading the blind.' Now, I presume that Mr Carton himself once made, or heard someone make, this joke, in private conversation. No doubt it raised really spontaneous laughter at the time, being itself a spontaneous incident in conversation. But there is all the difference in the world between a joke that is good merely for the moment and a joke that is so clean-cut that it will lose nothing by being printed in black and white or spoken across footlights. The former kind of joke may owe half its success to the personality of its maker, as well as to the aptness of the moment at which it is made. The latter kind has to stand on its own merit. And I submit that the joke which I have quoted (as a type of many jokes in this play) has not sufficient merit to make one pardon its irrelevance. Of modern dramatists there is, with the exception of Mr Oscar Wilde, none whose wit is in itself good enough to be welcome unless it belong to its setting. I think it were well, therefore, for modern dramatists to jest only through the characters they create, and not *in propria persona* nor for the mere sake of jesting. However, this is a side-issue. Far be it from me to disparage Mr Carton's talent. This play of his is well worth seeing. It is, on the whole, very well acted. In the part which I have called A, Miss Compton displays once more her power of suggesting that well-bred, ill-behaved good-nature which is the essence of 'smartness.' Mr Eric Lewis ambles discreetly and observantly through the part of B. As C, Miss Lena Ashwell makes a loyal effort to obscure that blunt intelligence which is peculiar to her, but her impersonation does not quite come off. Mr Thalberg, as D, has nothing to do but to repeat what he did in *The Liars*, and Mr Boucicault, as E, is rather slow and funereal in a very difficult part. Mr Bourchier (F) was admirable in the first act, acting with real observation and humour. I have never seen a better representation of the human-animal-after-dinner. In the second act, alas! Mr Bourchier began to let himself go, and in the third act he simply clowned himself off the stage. If only he would learn restraint! If only he could learn how good he was, and why he was so good, in the first act! It is a difficult question, this question of restraint. For, whilst some men on the stage ought always to be curbing themselves, there are others who ought always to be spurring themselves on. Everything depends on the personality of the man himself. Mr Bourchier is a man for whom no curb were too tight and firm. For Mr Boucicault no spur were too sharp.

[*27 May 1899*]

## PLAYWRIGHTS AND THEIR BETTERS

Dramatic critics, in their moments of leisure, seem to be somewhat perturbed about the morals of certain dramatists. They have weighed certain recent comedies in the balance, and have found them wanting in edification, wanting in refinement, prettiness and moral tone. 'Where,' they ask, recalling the worst excesses of the Restoration drama, 'where is it all to end?' And meanwhile they are not, I fear, quite sure that the authors of *The Liars*, *The Gay Lord Quex* and *Wheels within Wheels* are not very wicked men. Let me, in this moment of leisure, intervene.

Let me submit that, ere they finally convict of lewdness and levity the three prisoners at their bar, my fellow-critics should consider whether the dreadful things in the prisoners' work belong to the subject or to the treatment. I do not deny that the dreadful things are there, but I think it is important that we should determine whether they were wantonly foisted in by the prisoners, or were inherent in the matter with which the prisoners dealt, and, being inherent, were merely not omitted. If we find the dreadful things to have been foisted, let us pass an exemplary sentence. If we find them to have been inherent, the door of the dock must be flung open. Our inquiry will be the easier and quicker for that the three separate plays in the indictment have a common subject-matter: they all deal with Society as it is (or is suggested to be) in the late 'nineties. If, twenty or thirty years ago, anyone had written a play representing the Society of the time as vulgar, tricky, greedy, and immoral, we might have condemned him, off-hand, as a man of corrupted imagination. For no mere playwright, in the 'sixties or 'seventies, had any means of knowing what Society was like. Even if he had had any data, he would not have cared, nor known how, to use them; inasmuch as no one at that time had the faintest desire for a realistic presentment of life upon the stage. But there were no data at all. Society was still a remote, close, mysterious, little thing. It was a fascinating theme for romantic treatment, and as such it was treated in many plays which were not less stimulating to the public than were the novelettes of the *Family Herald*. Wherever there is any national drama, plays about the upper-class must always be popular; for the upper-class is the class that has leisure, and it is leisure that breeds comedy, tragedy and romance in the lives of human beings. In the 'sixties and 'seventies, nothing definite was known about Society, save that it was a sphere of leisure and high-sounding titles and grand manners. The rest was mere guess-work, and the guesses were all, of course, gorgeously and romantically grandiose. But, in recent years, all the conditions—both dramatic and social—have been greatly changed. On the one hand, dramatists are now trying to transcribe life, and they have infected the public with their love of realism. On the other, Society is no longer a matter for guess-work. It has torn off its veils, unbarred its doors, and rushed out into the market-place. Anyone can inspect it from every angle. It has no secrets at all. And thus it has become a theme which any dramatist can treat realistically. Mr Jones, Mr Pinero and Mr Carton have, between them, represented it as vulgar, tricky, greedy and immoral. If Society is not really so, the three dramatists have committed a very grave crime. If, however, it is really so, they have kept well within their rights. If Society is really bad, one cannot reasonably blame an artist who so represents it. Such representation cannot increase the actual evil; any moral effect that it may incidentally produce must be rather salutary than otherwise.

I need scarcely demonstrate that, in all countries, Society—a small or large number of men and women, whose aim is pleasure—always has been, is, and will be, immoral. Sometimes it has a very good moral tone, a sedate surface of rectitude. At such times, perhaps (for hypocrisy is a two-edged weapon), its average of immorality may be somewhat decreased. But that it must always be more or less immoral no sociologist could deny. We need not stop to consider whether it be at this moment more or less immoral than usual. Enough that it is immoral, and that Mr Jones, Mr Pinero and Mr Carton are therefore to be pardoned for so representing it. But 'vulgar, tricky, greedy'—are those other epithets equally well deserved? Certainly they would not be applicable to the Society of every city or of every period. The qualities they denote are not, in fact, essential attributes of every Society. So far as one can gather from memoirs, these qualities were not obvious in early-Victorian Society. However, fifty years have elapsed, and in them many new influences have arisen. Of these influences, there are three which have had a particularly strong bearing upon the condition of Society: the growth of the democratic spirit, the vast increase of wealth, the advance of Science.

The democratic spirit has taught the mob not to regard noblemen as gods. Noblemen, finding themselves no longer regarded as gods, have lost most of their self-respect. They have abandoned their old high prejudices, and are near to believing in the (quite false and fatuous) doctrine that one man is as good as another. Once the nobility began to lose faith in itself, the old idea of a small, exclusive Society was gradually abandoned. Every year Society has further and further expanded its borders, until, for a person of any social pretensions, it is as great a stigma to be out of it as it was once a glory to be in it. Meanwhile, millionaires have been invented and, in large numbers, imported to England from America, Africa, Australia, and admitted into Society without any questions asked. Most of them are quite vulgar, and their vulgarity has great results; for it is so much easier for refined people to catch vulgarity than for vulgarians to become refined. Their wealth has infected Society with a lust for wealth and for luxury; insomuch that though it is easier than ever it was to get into Society, to maintain a position there is, without endless ready money, almost impossible. Hence there has been a tremendous increase of every kind of gambling. And there is nothing—I become prosy!—so destructive of good manners and of honesty as gambling. The inventions of Science—railways, telegrams, telephones and the rest—have created, in those who can afford to use them constantly, a maniacal restlessness—a delirium which would in itself be enough to destroy all dignity in those who suffer from it. . . . I think I have said enough to demonstrate that the man who writes a play representing his betters as vulgar, greedy and tricky cannot very well be condemned as one who wantonly libels his subject or seeks to corrupt public virtue. Such an author is merely making an ordinary essay in realism. Plays about Society are always, as I have suggested, a very popular form. Such plays as *Wheels within Wheels* are the kind that will be written for the present. So my fellow-critics must compose themselves and cease to shake their fists. If, however, they cannot be happy without being angry, let them be angry with the influences which have moulded Society to its present state, not with Mr Carton and his kind.

[*3 June 1899*]

## TWO VERY DIFFERENT THINGS

I cannot imagine a wider contrast than there is between the two plays I have seen this week. The one is by a man who has obviously a feeling for drama in general and for the modern theatre in particular; who conceives life instinctivly as a sharp series of 'situations,' and mankind as a crowd of showy types; who troubles himself not at all about abstract ideas nor about intricacies of human character; whose one aim, indeed, is to tell a stage-story. Knowing all the tricks of the trade, and having a great natural store of racy humour and racy pathos, he fulfils his aim easily and admirably. But the writer of the other play is quite another kind of person. Though he has (in my sense of the word) dramatic sense, he has no sense at all for the modern theatre, and his technique, laboriously learnt of Ibsen, is a constant worry to him. His aim is to express an abstract idea through the workings of realised human character. He stumbles and fumbles and is tedious, but at length, through sheer force of sincerity, he triumphs. He triumphs in a medium for which he has no natural aptitude, and despite the lack of any by-advantages except brain-power. Of humour, for instance, he has very little, and that little is crude and heavy. He writes badly, too. His characters speak in sentences that all are a-bristle with subordinate clauses and strained metaphors—sentences that cannot be spoken naturally. I am amused to find that the poor dear dramatic critics, condemning the unnaturalness of the dialogue, have called it 'very graceful from a literary point of view,' 'pleasant to read but not to hear,' and all the rest of it. As a matter of fact, the writing has no literary quality at all: the sentences are clumsy in construction, without any rhythm, utterly dull and undistinguished. I do not suppose that the writer wished to be graceful; he wished to write naturally, and perhaps, in time, he will learn to do so. Meanwhile, his writing is the worst of all those faults in despite of which he triumphs.

The first of these two plays is *The Cowboy and the Lady*, by Mr Clyde Fitch; the second is Mr Edward Martyn's *Heather Field*. The first was produced on Monday night at the Duke of York's; the second on Tuesday afternoon at Terry's. Let me take them in chronological order.

*The Cowboy and the Lady* is called a comedy, and might as well have been called a melodrama. It is neither of these things, but oscillates between the two. Its oscillation seems to have shocked my colleagues. Personally, I am not shocked at all. The law of '*qualis ab incepto*' is an arbitrary law. It rests on the assumption that an audience, being first attuned to one kind of emotion, is upset by the later necessity of attuning itself to another. But, as a matter of fact, everything depends on the artist. A skilful dramatist can alternate and intermingle opposite elements in such a way that the audience is not upset by his transitions, and does not feel 'How can we shudder when we have just been laughing?' or 'How can we laugh when we have just dashed away the not discreditable tear?' A skilful dramatist can evolve from us various emotions without disturbing anyone except professional critics (who have their little first principles and are bound to say something or other). This, I think, is what Mr Clyde Fitch does. His comedy merges into melodrama, and out of it again, with perfect naturalness. The murder trial in the last act is full of comedy points. Thus, the prisoner-hero (expecting the answer 'no,' which will tell in his favour) asks the witness-heroine whether she loves him, and when she, after a long pause, replies 'I love you with all my heart!' he does not stagger back in a confusion of joy and horror, but beams all round the court, buttons his coat and asks the judge for leave to repeat the question. This is amusing, and yet it does not at all destroy the tensity of the situation. I suspect that this was the point in the play which most arrided Mr Fitch himself. Perhaps the whole act was written for its sake. Otherwise, I cannot help thinking that Mr Fitch would have made his last act something else than a murder-trial. A trial on the stage is simply a formal repetition of what the audience already knows. It is effective only when the audience cannot foresee the verdict. In a comedy-melodrama, one knows that the hero will finally be acquitted, and one is not much excited. Moreover, a murder-trial in Colorado seems to be a very poor unassuming kind of business. One misses that which has often made the dullest stage-trial impressive for us: the awfully measured dignity of the procedure in a French or English court. One tries in vain to think that anything very important can be decided in a bright little room furnished like a school-room, and one feels, anyway, that death would lose half its sting if sentence of it were passed by a good-humoured man in broad-cloth, seated at the teacher's desk and made up after the combined models of Brother Jonathan, Abraham

Lincoln and Uncle Sam. Here, in fact, the local colour is against the play. In the other acts, however, the local colour is of great service, and everything goes very briskly and well. The cake-walk enchanted me, and my joy was unbounded when Mr Goodwin and Miss Maxine Elliot blithely took an encore. The cake-walk alone should be enough to ensure the success of the play. The tune of the 'Honolulu Lady' is very pretty and so simple as to be a souvenir which every member of the audience can carry away with him. By the way, it was a mistake to introduce 'I lub a lubly girl, I do.' It was a pretty compliment to Mr Brandon Thomas, whose songs do doubtless re-echo across the ranches; but English people are transported by it to the back drawing-rooms in which it has been so often warbled, and not to any West wilder than Bayswater. However, that is a detail. For the rest, there is plenty of good American humour and interesting slang and strange costumes; and the word 'damn' is used so often that the critics of a town in which Mr Kipling's ballads are regarded as the supreme pinnacle of poetry have been throwing up hands of horror. Altogether, the play is a capital entertainment, and the fun of it is all the greater because half the audience, I am sure, fancies it to be an accurate representation of life as lived in the vicinity of New York City.

It is a pity that Mr Nat Goodwin has not a part in which he can show the full measure of his powers. I saw him act in America some years ago. I forget what the play was called, but his performance in it is one which I remember very clearly and fondly. The part he is acting now does not, I think, make enough demands on him: it is for him little more than child's play. It could not be acted better, but it could be acted as well by many actors far less greatly gifted than Mr Goodwin. Miss Maxine Elliott showed such intelligence and skill as would have won her a leading-ladyship even had she been but ordinarily beautiful. As cowboys, Mr Richard Stirling, Mr Burr McIntosh and others pleasantly fostered my preconceived illusions of what cowboys are like. But the most fascinating performance was Miss Gertrude Elliott's. Even if she had acted ill, she would have charmed everyone. And her acting was, to the few who care much (or, caring, know much) about the matter, a revelation as rare as it is pleasant: the revelation of a born comedian.

Master Charles Sefton, in *The Heather Field*, provided us with another revelation. Before I saw him, I had never seen a child acting.

Nobody can be on the stage what he is off it unless he can act: he has to translate his personality into stage-terms, just as he has to paint his face to preserve its colour in the glare of the footlights. Acting is a matter partly of temperament, partly of technique. Ordinary stage-children may, for all I know, have the one, but they certainly have not the other. Consequently, they do not seem like children. On the other hand, they do not seem like grown-up persons. They seem like nothing on the earth, and one feels that the earth would be an even less pleasant place than it is if it did support anything at all like them. So Master Sefton (who, acting with real art, seemed like a real child) is a person in whose career I shall take a fatherly interest. The other members of the cast . . . but I was forgetting; I have as yet only hinted at the kind of thing they had to do. When I read the play in a book, it seemed to me fairly good. When I saw it produced in Dublin, it seemed to me very good indeed. Like all really dramatic plays, it had qualities appreciable only in actual performance on a stage. When I saw it last Tuesday, it seemed to me better still. That, doubtless, was because the play depends not on incident (which becomes less exciting with every repetition) but on an idea and certain complexities of human character. In *The Heather Field* there are no incidents to speak of. Such external circumstances as there are in it are not of a stimulating kind—drainage, mortgages and so forth. The whole thing has been writtten strictly for the sake of this idea: that, as the world is constituted, dreamers are dangerous to themselves and to their dependents. And this idea is worked out through the conflict of two opposite characters—the conflict of an idealist and his practical wife. Both these characters have been drawn and developed with intense care; both are very real; and they were played, last Tuesday, by Mr Thomas Kingston and Miss May Whitty with earnestness and power. The audience seemed to share my absorption and enthusiasm; but then, it was only an experimental matinée audience. An ordinary audience would yawn and boo, for it cannot tolerate a play which has no running fire of incident, and whose climaxes are merely the moments when two conflicting characters most poignantly reveal themselves. Moreover, the ordinary audience insists on being able to sympathise, wholly and consistently, with one side of the conflict or with the other. In this play, it would be sympathising now with the dreamer, now with the wife on whom his dreams bring financial ruin. If Mr Martyn had made the wife a sweet creature whose husband showered his idealism on another woman, an ordinary audience might tolerate the play. Likewise, if he had made the wife altogether horrible, and the husband a dreamer who does not try to put his dreams into practical form. As it is, Mr Martyn has drawn a woman whose temper has been ruined by the aloofness of a husband who does not love her and wastes all his fortune on more or less madcap schemes for improving his estate. One's reason sympathises with her, one's emotion with her husband. Both sides are in the right, as (in real life) both sides always are. In fact, both the characters are typical, not faked for effect. That is why the play could never have a popular success. That is also why it interests me so very deeply. I could gladly see it several times yet. I wish some manager would put it into his evening-bill. But managers must, after all, live; and even if one of them did put it into his evening-bill, we should not, I fear, have more than one opportunity of seeing it.

[10 *June 1899*]

## NO COMMON DENOMINATOR

It must be because we live in a labour-saving age that we English are now so keen to welcome Americans both off and on the stage. They are as foreign to us (and, therefore, as surprising, amusing and instructive) as Italians or even Hottentots; yet can we study them and understand them without the galling necessity of either learning a new language or trusting to a tedious interpreter. The very fact that they use practically the same language as we use makes their contrast the more piquant, makes them the less resistible. As men and women, they see things from a standpoint antipolar to our own, yet from one which is near and clear to our vision. As mimes, they display to us an entirely new method, which we can yet appreciate and enjoy without laboriously broadening our minds. As playwrights, they have just begun to develop a national drama quite unlike ours and yet quite easily intelligible to us. *The Cowboy and the Lady* was a very fair specimen of that drama, but unfortunately it did not give Mr Nat Goodwin a chance of showing how very well he could act, and so it has been withdrawn. *An American Citizen* is its substitute. The exchange is good inasmuch as we certainly do see Mr Goodwin to far greater advantage. But there is really no comparison between the two plays. The first was a racy piece of work, done by an accomplished hand. It was trivial enough, I admit; but it was amusing, ingenious and, above all, indigenous. The second is a complicated, sprawling, inchoate concern, in which farce (good of its kind) and sentiment (bad of its kind) are alternated as abruptly and clumsily as melodrama and comedy were deftly mingled in *The Cowboy and the Lady*. The play, moreover, has (except the slang in its dialogue) no racial character: it might have been written by any of our own playwrights. I do not know whether the author, Mrs Ryley, is an American. American or English, she is a very crude dramatist. But perhaps I am applying too stern a standard? The programme tells me that her play was written specially for Mr Goodwin; and, since she has given Mr Goodwin a part which really is (so far as any part in a bad play can be) effective, perhaps I ought not to decry her talents. In any case, I hasten to assure my readers that they should see the play, in order that they may see Mr Goodwin in it. Mr Goodwin is an American of the Americans, and a comedian of the comedians. He has, too, a strain of real poetry in him, whereby on the first night he was enabled to dignify and save one of the silliest fourth acts ever written. He is irresistible, and reconciles one to "most anything.' Miss Maxine Elliott played the chief woman's part with charm and distinction, and was especially helpful to Mr Goodwin in his salvage of the last act.

Last week, Mr Murray Carson was playing at Kennington in Bulwer's *Richelieu*. I had never seen the play before, and was highly entertained by it. In its way, it is, indeed, tremendously effective. Of course it is nothing but bombast. But then, Bulwer was naturally bombastic. He was sincere in the bombastic method of his day. It is because Mr Grundy and Mr Rose are not sincere in that method, and assume it only in order to comply with what they take to be the demands of a passing (or rather, thank Heaven! past) romantic boom, that their stage-romances do so insufferably depress and fatigue me. From Bulwer one gets the real thing. And in Mr Murray Carson one finds perhaps the only young actor of any distinction who can render it at all decently. The modern school of acting is a school for subtlety and delicacy and fine shades—things which are quite fatal to bombastic plays. The average modern actor, trying to be bombastic, is a melancholy sight indeed. His whole training handicaps him. Moreover, he is obviously ashamed of himself and his performance, and his embarrassment embarrasses us. But Mr Carson is an exception. Albeit young, he has many of the attributes of the old school—an ornate manner, massive gestures and postures, rapidity of 'attack', strength and staying power; and, above all, a deep and elaborately-managed voice. All these attributes he uses to the utmost. He plunges unabashed, and grips without flinching, and expands, and resounds, and reverberates. He was, therefore, a most admirable Richelieu. I am sure that the shade of Bulwer must, at every point in his performance, have been clapping its noiseless hands in one of the stage-boxes. I myself, when Richelieu threatened to 'launch the curse of Rome' on the head of his ward's persecutor, so far forgot my duty as to applaud a little.

This week, I went again to Kennington, for it is there that Mrs Campbell has produced Professor Murray's *Carlyon Sahib*. I hope that I shall be able to revisit the play at one of the more adjacent theatres; but I doubt whether my hope will be realised. *Grierson's Way* and *The Heather Field* were given but one fleeting matinée apiece; and the presumption is that for modern tragedy there is little or no market in the metropolis. *Carlyon Sahib* is an essay in modern tragedy. The dramatic critics—that mysterious galaxy which I am so often compelled to criticise unfavourably—have been condemning it as 'morbid,' 'dreary,' 'unworthy' and so forth. For my own part, though I love comedy better than tragedy, I cannot see why the dramatic critics should be exasperated, as they are, whenever they come across a playwright who treats modern life from a standpoint not comical, farcical or melodramatic. A Shakespearean tragedy does not make them angry, though Shakespeare was far more 'morbid' than any writer in our day. Nor do they launch the curse of Fleet Street when a living dramatist writes a tragedy of some bygone time. So long as his figures wear tights or chain-armour, and talk in iambic metre, a dramatist may be as tragic (and as morbid) as he likes. Woe betide him, however, if his figures dress and talk like real, live, modern men and women! Why? Merely because the dramatic critics (and the public, whose mouthpiece they are) have not enough aesthetic sense to differentiate between art and life. So soon as modern life is realistically depicted on the stage, they are reminded of themselves and of their own private affairs. If the realistic presentment be of a pleasant kind, they feel personally cheerful. If it be unpleasant—tragic, in fact—they become personally uncomfortable. They are thinking, all the time, 'How awful! Suppose that were to happen to *me*! I do hope *I* shall never be mixed up in an affair of this sort!' Or it reminds them of some tragedy which has actually occurred in their own lives, or in the lives of those who are dear to them—'poor old Jack' or 'poor little Jill.' Of course they do not realise that it is for this reason that they detest the play. They imagine that their objections are based on aesthetic grounds, and their prattle about the 'sanity of art' is profoundly sincere. They cannot see that what is unpleasant is not necessarily unwholesome, and that the fault lies, not in the work, but in their own too sensitive egoism. So they continue, and will continue, to howl at tragedies of modern life; and *Carlyon Sahib*, in which one of the principal characters suffers from brain-disease, is howled at (despite the patient's ultimate recovery) because nobody would like to find that he himself had brain-disease, curable or otherwise. For my part, I enjoyed *Carlyon Sahib* because is is a well-written and well-constructed play, with an interesting theme. It is, I think, the first play in which we have had the problem of the great man's right to override, for the good of his country, the ordinary laws of humanity. Not that it is a problem-play! I wish it were more so. The problem is there, but it is only suggested. The great man of action, the over-rider, is there, and his antagonist, the theoretic moralist, is there, too; but though his is the title-rôle, he is not really the central figure of the play. The central figure is that of a young girl, his daughter. I would have preferred the essential conflict to be between Carlyon and the doctrinaire, and to be waged on the ground of their temperamental differences. As the play is written, the conflict is between father and daughter, on the ground of certain external and not essential circumstances. However, I do not grumble. The play is very strong, very dramatic. I shall watch the Professor's career with very real interest.

Mrs Campbell played the daughter's part not only with that sense of beauty which she brings to all her impersonations, but with an alert and strenuous power which, sometimes and, as it were, deliberately, she has withheld from them. Mr Nutcombe Gould is not well-suited as Carylon, a man who should give like 'Burly' the impression of a grosser mass of character than most men.' Mr Gould is too urbane, too polished, too pleasant, for the part.

In another column will be found an interesting letter over the signature 'M.B.' From a hurried glimpse at it, I gather that the writer, not content with the theft of my initials, has scored off me rather heavily. At least, I seem to stand convicted of insular prejudice—convicted gently, indeed, but firmly, and with chapter and verse. I wish I had time and space to defend myself forthwith. For, though I concede that to a Frenchman, and to his equivalent, French words must suggest more than to me, 'I maintain and I shall' that the French language, in its keen, quick, clean precision, must be less apt a means to the conjuring of 'purple shadows' than is this darker, slower, more massive language of ours.

[*24 June 1899*]


## THE ART WORKERS' MASQUE: AS DRAMA

I have not the pleasure of counting myself a great admirer of Mr Joseph Pennell's prose-style, nor of his method in criticism, nor of his manners. Unluckily, the first intimation that there was to be a Masque at the Guildhall came to me in the semi-official form of a more than usually blustrous article by Mr Pennell. The Masque, it seemed, was going to be the Greatest Show on Earth. Creation was going to be licked. We were all going to be made to sit up, you bet! I winced, not being a betting man. Beauty on turtleback is well enough. But Beauty under the wing of the spread-eagle . . . I found myself hoping that the Masque would be a failure. That was unreasonable of me, of course, and not generous. After all, the members of the Art Workers' Guild, quiet and modest, were going to do their best, and they had not (I suppose) dictated nor even passed the proofs of Mr Pennell's article. And yet—so wide are the eagle's wings—it was in a hostile spirit that I went, last Tuesday, to the Guildhall.

Nor did what I found there seem like to cure me of my ill-will. On a cavernous and fitfully-lit stage, the mummers were sometimes almost invisible to me. However, I saw 'D.S.M.' in the audience, and, assuming that he was come to bear the burden of visual criticism, I did not strain my eyes, and contented myself with listening to what the mummers said or sang. Alas! they were seldom audible. Mr Selwyn Image (whose name we all covet) was the Prolocutor, and it was he who had to recite most of the text. He comported himself in a dignified and scholarly way, but was not very audible. His voice drifted out in a staid, archidiaconal monotone and persistently lost itself somewhere in the defective acoustics of the hall or (as it seemed to my stricken senses) cathedral. To banish the illusion of Evensong, I opened my book of the words, briskly, found the place and followed the poetry with my eyes. It was not good poetry. The only good verses in the book were those signed by Mr Image himself. The rest were all in the way of doggerel. Those in which were described the several demons besetting London were atrociously stupid and ill-done. Perhaps because they contained many allusions which would have pained the civic mind, they were, I am glad to say, omitted. Personally, I have no objection whatever to topical allusions in a Masque. The contrivers of this Masque aimed not at a mere antiquarian revival, but at an adaptation of an old form to modern notions. By all means let there be modern satire in such work. But let it be good satire, and not such sorry twaddle as was emitted the other night. I cannot help thinking that it would have been wise to entrust the task of *writing* the Masque to persons outside the Guild. Poetry is surely an important point in a Masque, and one image does not make a singing-nest. If the poetry for this Masque had been good, it would, no doubt, have been the more charming for the fact that it was turned out (so to speak) on the premises. But that it was so turned out affords one scant consolation for the badness of its actual quality. The pity is all the greater because the main scheme of this Masque is quite attractive and deserved poetical treatment. The long sleep of Fayremonde, Spirit of Beauty, under the power of an evil dragon; her dream of the Seven Fair Cities; the coming of the knight, Trueheart, and his killing of the dragon; the awakening of Fayremonde; the saving of the hapless maid, London, from the demons of ugliness and corruption, and her final admission to the hierarchy of fair cities—all these things are, as Mr Florimel would have said, 'not unworthy of the Muse.' Had they been treated by poets, instead of by craftsmen, who knows but that they would have touched the hearts and stung the consciences of those County Councils, Vestries and Boards of Works for which Mr Walter Crane intended them as 'a hint'? Mr Crane has described this Masque as 'an endeavour to bring before the official and general public the necessity for art in all relations of life, especially in civic life.' For my own part, I have never regarded art as a necessity, nor do I quite understand why anyone should consider it more of a necessity in civic than in any other kind of life. I am, moreover, quite sure that, even if this Masque had been of such invasive power as to penetrate the hard hearts of the English people and to force all the Aldermen and Vestrymen to their knees, and to make everyone cry aloud for beauty, we should not be one inch nearer to the haven where Mr Crane would have us be. Mr Crane has always kept a sanguine eye on the future, dreaming of a time when all the streets will be white; when the British workman will be a handsome youth with long hair, attired in doublet and trunk-hose, and carrying a really well-made pickaxe across his shoulder; when the factory girl will go forth to her work in Grecian draperies covered with patterns of Mr Crane's own design. This desirable state of things is to be attained, I understand, through Socialism, through the gradual education and enrichment of the people. I would suggest to Mr Crane that he is on a wrong tack. The more power we give to the people, the further will beauty recede from us. Beautiful cities have been created by tasteful tyrants; but they have never been created by the mob, for the mob never has cared for beauty. I am not sure that, in these days when Invention (which, in the Masque, is represented as one of beauty's saviours) has made railways, bicycles, sky-signs, omnibuses and factory chimneys a necessity in men's lives, a really beautiful city is at all possible. Even a tyrant would not be able to rid London of the fell mischief worked by Invention. But the idea of London ever being helped towards beauty by or through the people of London is really too ridiculous a chimera, and Mr Crane should cease to entertain it. The English people, as being the most utilitarian in the world, is even more incapable than any other people of understanding or caring about beauty. What has been the result of that aesthetic movement which, in 1880, was created for the purpose of abolishing reps and mahogany, and of extending beauty to the mob? The walls of sitting-rooms are plastered with horrid little fans, horrid little saucers, and horrid little pieces of 'art-cretonne.' Imitation Dutch milking-pails are used as coal-scuttles, and an imitation Dutch milking-stool is offered you instead of a chair. These are the only results of that artistic renaissance. They are typical of what must always happen when artists are so foolish as to try to catch, and so unlucky as to succeed in catching, the ear of the English people. Let Mr Crane and his friends give up their idea of making London and its inhabitants beautiful. Let them realise that under the modern conditions of trade and science London is bound to become uglier and uglier. And let them realise that in the ever-increasing ugliness of life the artist will find an ever-stronger incentive to devote himself to his own beautiful works. When next they write a Masque, let its theme be that beauty must be content to be not popular.

However, the Masque itself is more important than its contrivers' ulterior purpose. The story, as I have said, is pretty. Had it been well written, well spoken and well stage-managed, I should have enjoyed it very much indeed. As it was, it bored me very much indeed, and filled me with resentment of the long distance I had come to see it. Not until the end of the evening, when all the mummers passed, in slow procession and to the tune of an agreeable march, twice round the hall, did I feel any emotion of pleasure. As the procession passed me, I was able to see well the costumes of all the mummers, the accoutrements they bore, and the symbols and the devices. All these things seemed to me charming—but that, by-the-bye, is for 'D.S.M.' to say. The sight of the mummers at close quarters inclined me kindly to them, and made me feel a brute for having scorned their efforts. After all, in every amateur performance, the appeal is *ad misericordiam*. But in most cases the appeal is made in vain: our pity is not roused. We do not realise that the performers on the stage are human beings like ourselves, doing their best to amuse us, but regard them, rather, as malignant apes, bent on boring us with unmeaning antics. I wish that at the close of every performance of amateur theatricals the players might, for their sakes, be allowed to circulate, as at the close of this Masque, among their audience. Seen closely and on our own level, they would be revealed as well-meaning, wistful men and women, and so would there be for them a happy dispulsion of all our sulks. Yes, this procession quite disarmed me, and my heart went out to all who were in it—to the little children, and to every maiden and bearded man. They were all so much in earnest, and had tried so hard, besides being so beautifully dressed up. I remembered that I myself might, if I had been asked, have been one of them. And I wished that their Masque had seemed better to me;

> Καὶ γὰρ ἐμοὶ νόος ἐστιν ἐναίσιμος, οὐδέ μοι αὐτῷ
> Θυμός ἐνι στήθεσσι σιδήρεος, ἀλλ' ἐλεήμων.

P.S. M. Coquelin is playing in *Cyrano* at the Adelphi. But I said last year all I have to say about his performance and about *Cyrano*, that brilliant play.

[*1 July 1899*]


## THE OLD PACK

A good theme were the immutability of types in every kind of commercial drama. But to be querulous of the immutability of types in farce is to be accused of taking the matter too seriously. *Egomet*, I think that nothing can be taken too seriously. I do not hold that farces ought to be stupid, and I do hold that they cannot be otherwise so long as their writers insist on trotting out the same old puppets—the same husband, the same wife, the same father-in-law, mother-in-law, house-parlour-maid and husband's friend. 'What,' you may object, 'is the matter with these puppets? Too familiar, are they? You might as well say that you cannot find any pleasure in playing whilst because the faces of the court-cards never alter. The splendid benignity with which the King of Hearts regards you; the rather sinister profile of the Knave, his son; the Queen of Diamonds, with her happy piquant smile; and she whose every lineament bears the impress of long suffering nobly borne, whom no man receives into his hand without some stirring of his heart, she, the proud, ill-fated consort of the King of Spades—the sameness of these bits of pasteboard does not make any sameness in the game you play with them. Infinite, the number of their combinations. Infinite, the skill of handling them. So, critic, be not querulous! As to whist its cards, so to farce its characters.' The analogy is ingenious enough, but false. Cards are but symbols. The personal appearance of this or that King or Queen does not really affect the game: however deep our respect and pity for the Queen of Spades, we do not scruple to profit by the King's power. But the characters in a farce are much more than symbols, and do directly affect the play's course. Thus, if the dramatist insist on a feebly unfaithful husband, a hot-tempered wife, a good-humoured father-in-law up from the country, a bitter mother-in-law, a pert house-parlour-maid and an indiscreet friend, the number of evoluble situations is, clearly, far from endless. In his latest farce,* Mr Burnand, following immemorial custom, insists on all these characters. It follows that the situations are mostly stale. But stale situations and stale characters are just what the public likes, whether in farce or in any other kind of drama. Fresh situations and fresh characters it is apt to regard as a nuisance. Mr Burnand knows this well, and has acted on his knowledge. He might (for he is, as he has so often proved in non-theatrical work, a very keen and witty observer of life) have written a farce which would not have bored me. Such a farce, however, might have bothered the public. Wisely enough, Mr Burnand prefers boring one fastidious unit to bothering the public. But, while I applaud his discretion, I must point out that he might have bored me a little less without impoverishing his manager. I am not unreasonable, really. I admit that a playwright who wished to pocket the public's money must first pocket his intelligence. I admit that, if Mr Burnand had ever brought to bear on playwriting that subtle power which made *Happy Thoughts* at once a masterpiece in English humour and a human document as valuable as any dull great man's 'Confession,' he would (at least) have had to wait many years for a reward. But why should he write his dialogue to-day exactly as he would have written it in the sixties? As a man, he is not out of touch with his fellows. When he writes anything but a play, he shows himself well primed in all the superficial facts of the late 'nineties. Nor is his reactionary manner of presenting men and women on the stage a mere concession to public taste. If it were, I would say nothing. But it is not. The public does not resent, even likes, modern versions of stale characters. Yet the stale characters in *The Lady of Ostend* (though the mimes are dressed in modern clothes) talk and behave exactly as they would have in the 'sixties. The fact that the plot of the play hinges on the existence of a cinematograph does but make their anachronism the more glaring. This distresses me. Even if I accepted the analogy of the cards, I should still qualify my position by saying that I liked the game to

* *The Lady of Ostend*, Terry's Theatre

be played with a clean pack. Mr Burnand produces an old, well-thumbed, dog's-eared pack, and shuffles it and deals it out as merrily as though it were not cohesive in its antiquity. That is so like a playwright! Writers of books or music-hall songs take some account of the outer world, trying to be more or less abreast of the time. But the playwright, not he! If he creates a servant, she shall be as illiterate as in the days when Thackeray wrote a whole volume in order to prove (to his own infinite satisfaction, and to the boredom of every-one else) what ungenteel places kitchens were. Board Schools have been invented, and there is now much fun (of a kind) to be made out of the elaborately pedantic phrases used by modern servants. But why should a playwright trouble to make it, when 'Lawks!' is still sure of a laugh? And why should not his Irish gentleman—the husband's friend in Mr Burnand's play is, as I need hardly say, an Irish gentleman—address his hostess as 'Marm' and speak of his 'discint from the kings of Oireland' and, being introduced to a girl whose photograph he has seen, say 'I have already made this young lady's acquaintance, but Nature is superior to Art'? Customs and manners change, classes merge and emerge; but that is nothing to the playwright. The stream of life flows on with an ever-changing surface; but the playwright, stolid, unheeding, squats in his old place on the bank, angling for royalties with the same old baits and landing them as successfully as ever. A placid, instructive spectacle!

Certainly, the English theatre is a curious affair, and a man might fill reams in writing a mere catalogue of the prejudices and musty conventions which make it what it is. Every time I see a new play I find some prejudice or convention which had hitherto escaped me. This play of Mr Burnand's, for instance, illustrates one strict, irrational old law which I had never realised. It is this: that only middle-class life may be taken as the background for farce. Why? Indeed, I know not. I only know that the chief part in this piece (played by Mr Weedon Grossmith) is 'Dick Whortles (General Manufacturing Agent),' and that in all farces so must it be. The upper and lower classes, might not they be treated farcically? Perhaps; but they must not be. The upper classes are not a fit subject for anything but high comedy. The lower classes are not a fit subject for anything at all. They are interesting, no doubt, to persons of low taste; but if you want to learn about them you must go to the Music Halls, which are, indeed, better suited than theatres to debased, intelligent persons like yourselves. You would like to see middle-class life treated in the vein of high comedy? It could not be done. At any rate, it must not be. You might as well ask for a high comedy about persons living before the eighteenth century. You might as well ask for another modern tragedy like *Grierson's Way*. You know, or ought to know, that tragedy dies out of the world at the end of the seventeenth century—most dramatists date its death as early as the sixteenth. You might as well ask for a farce dealing with the time of the Wars of the Roses. . . . Indeed, why should you not? Why all these arbitrary limitations? Every class, every period, is equally good game for every kind of drama. But they who made the laws of the theatre thought otherwise, in their wisdom. And those laws must be obeyed. In comparison with them, the laws of the Medes and Persians were the airiest little hints, to be taken or left.

[*8 July 1899*]


## DISCURSION

With all deference to America, I must murmur that the heart of July is hardly the moment for *El Capitan* and Mr De Wolf Hopper. Even Americans, I suspect, must prefer winter's months for the glare and blare of such a piece, and the wear and tear of so very strenuous a clown. America must deal gently with us, remembering that her civilisation is still new enough to retain strong remnants of healthy barbarism, and that she is further to the West than we, and better able to stand things. We languid Orientals cannot cope with deeds of such violence as are being done nightly at the Lyric Theatre. The coming of Mr Hopper and his legionaries has frightened us. We cower aside, murmuring those words of the Hindu Ascetic,

'Is it a god or a king that comes?
  Both are evil and both are strong;
With women and worshipping, dancing and drums,
  Carry your gods and your kings along.
Fanciful shapes of a plastic earth,
  These are the visions that weary the eye,
These we may 'scape by a luckier birth,
  Musing, and fasting, and hoping to die.'

In point of humour, Mr Hopper is neither a god nor a king; at least, an Oriental cannot accept him as such. Strong, he certainly is. He has a large physique and a large voice, is seldom off the stage, and in three hours put forth more effort than a galley of slaves in as many days. It is just by reason of the monstrous pains he takes that he fails to amuse me. His humour does not come naturally. It is the result of laborious convulsions, explosions, extortions. He never speaks but in a grotesque sing-song interspersed with grunts, groans, whines and shouts. One cannot see his face for its grimaces. Never for one instant are his limbs in repose. He shows us, as it were, over the factory of every point he makes, and the process is more than a shade fatiguing. In fact, he is not what we Orientals mean by the term 'comedian.' It is curious that American stage-humour always does seem artificial, not really spontaneous, even when it is expressed in the method opposite to Mr Hopper's. The quiet, lazy method used by most American comedians seems fraught with self-conscious challenge. There are exceptions, of course—I found a notable exception in Mr Nat Goodwin—but they do not disprove the rule. The fact is that American humour is still in its infancy. Humour is an outcome of civilisation. The Americans have invented a humour of their own, just as they have invented a constitution and are inventing an empire. A very good kind of humour it is, and a great credit to them. But, as yet, they are a little too proud of it, as of their constitution and their empire. They have not had time to take it as a matter of course. All that will come. Their comedians are, as yet, so surprised at existing that they are at too great pains to persuade us that they exist. For this reason, I cannot laugh at Mr Hopper's jests, even as I cannot laugh at Mr Mark Twain's. I admire both gentlemen as phenomena testifying to the determination of the young country which has produced them; but I can accept neither Mr Hopper as comedian nor Mr Twain as humourist. I admit their jests to be good intrinsically. But the manner in which those jests are made—manner of Hercules in his twelve labours!—prevents me from delighting in them.

Perhaps some people will think me narrow-minded. Behold how great a matter of correspondence my little spark of criticism kindled over the French language! If you think the foregoing depreciation due to mere prejudice against the American language, I advise you to write letters to my editor. I cannot, of course, promise that he will insert them. Still, the silly season is at hand, and the other great matter has burnt so fiercely that it must be almost gutted. . . . For my own part, I do not think the accusation of narrow-mindedness could be brought home to me. The American language is far more nearly allied to ours than is the French; and yet, on the night after *El Capitan*, I lost myself in admiration of M. Coquelin as Poirier. Here, as it seemed to me, was the quintessence of perfect comedy. Comic art could not be borne higher than this. A myriad of minute, meticulous touches, and yet for me no consciousness of them as touches—only the illusion of a character perfectly presented for delight and laughter and understanding. And what a relief to see Coquelin thus, himself again; not cleverly screwing and flourishing himself up to romance, but doing just what the gods have fashioned him to do better than any other of their creatures! On Saturday afternoon, Coquelin will again be Poirier, and all wise readers of mine will go to the Adelphi.

At the Comedy, *The Weather-Hen*, by Mr Berte Thomas and Mr Granville Barker. The most striking thing about this play is its difference from most of the plays written by actors. When actors write plays they are apt to rely, for their craft, on the tricks and dodges sanctified by tradition, and, for their presentment of human beings, on the puppets among which their lot has been cast. Nearer to the public than the ordinary playwright, they are better able than he to gauge the public's taste; and thus they are likely to write even greater twaddle than is written by him. But they have not acquired his talent for construction, and thus their twaddle (albeit less lifelike than his) does but bewilder the public. No one, then, is satisfied: not the public, which likes a play to be twaddle set forth in a clear, straightforward way; nor the eccentric few who like a play to be an imitation of life set forth in a clear, straightforward way. *The Weather-Hen* is quite an exception among actors' plays. Of course it does not appeal to the public, but the eccentric few find much that is good in it; for its authors have tried to study human beings, and have brought their characters together for a better purpose than the mere playing of stage-tricks, and are, moreover, in point of constructive power, as good as most professional playwrights. But what most endears them to us is their bland infringement of one of the most sacred laws in the code for dramatists: that one shall not take as the central figure a person of capricious and will-less character. It has always been held that no good drama can be built round a person who does not know his or her mind and is swayed this way or that by every gust. The authors of *The Weather-Hen* have shown this canon to be bosh. Such canons always are shown to be bosh so soon as intelligent writers disobey them.

I need not give a belated description of the plot; but I wish the authors too well not to show them, for their guidance, one point at which they have gone astray. The father of the boy who is eloping with the will-less lady arrives at his son's cottage and considers how he shall persuade his son not to compromise himself. He decides that as soon as the pair arrives supper shall be served, and that the boy shall have too much champagne. The father's view is that alcohol will accomplish what could not be accomplished by parental influence. This, too, is the view of the authors; for the boy, so soon as he is tipsy, begins to regret his escapade. In real life, of course, the effect would be quite opposite: the boy (who is nineteen years old, afraid of his father, and fond of his mother) might, in his normal state, succumb to authority; but alcohol would quickly excite him to go through with the matter. Thus, all the second part of the third act offends against reality, and one regrets that the authors did not cut it out and write it again with that realistic conscience which makes the rest of their play delightful. Throughout, the dialogue is much above the average, for (rare quality!) the characters say the sort of things which, under the circumstances, they would say in real life. But they say it in rather strained phraseology. The authors must beware of making their characters strive to appear clever. Miss Madge McIntosh played the chief part satisfactorily; and to play so difficult a part satisfactorily postulates much skill and talent. As her husband, Mr Courtenay Thorpe was far too grotesque and farcical. Mr Graham Browne was boyish as the boy, and Mr Wills, that good actor, made one wish that the butler could permeate the whole play. Mr Foss, as a reserved lover, was too stiff to be so sympathetic as the authors meant him to be. But, since the lover was an unsuccessful actor, this may have been Mr Foss's subtlety.

I have just received a circular about a 'Play-Writers' Theatre.' The circular is rather vague, as circulars should be; meant to excite curiosity rather than to satisfy it. But I gather that a play (written by a play-writer) is to be produced in September, that other plays will follow, and that anyone may send to Mr Charles Hoppe, 23

Bedford Street, E.C., the sum of two guineas, in return for which he will have a stall 'at each new production for the year.' Thirty shillings will secure him a seat in the Dress Circle; sixteen, one in the Upper Circle; and so forth. Mr Hoppe has my good wishes, and would have something more tangible if I had no hope of getting my seat for nothing; for I am quite anxious to see what his productions will be like. He promises 'certain plays not to be classified with the occasional representations of unique societies, but which offer some initial difference of subject or treatment that has been, or is, in the way of their production in the ordinary groove.' Personally, I would rather he went the way of those 'unique societies,' quite heedless of the public's conventions, and I think that subscriptions would be quicklier forthcoming if he did so. However, what he promises is better than nothing, and I look forward to seeing a final vindication of the superiority of play-writers to playwrights. The productions are, by the way, '*not* contemplated for one night only; it is intended that they shall be of a nature to warrant their continuance long enough to fairly establish the interest they are claimed to merit.' Shade of Mr Gladstone!

[*15 July 1899*]

## IBSEN, AFTER ALL

For detached spirits like myself, it is hard to feel any personal affection for a great man before the subsidence of the storms and torrents which are raised by his coming. These storms and torrents may not blind us to his greatness; they are, indeed, a sure sign that he is great. But not until they are past can we begin to feel for him that personal affection which we like to feel, and do usually succeed in feeling, for great men. True, the dulness of his enemies drives us indignant to his side; but alas! every time, the dulness of his champions drives us back again. So long as the dreary dithyrambs of Ibsen's disciples sounded in our ears; so long as persons called themselves 'Ibsenites' and expounded Ibsen through a string of hyphen-coupled substantives—'philosophy-drama,' 'world-pessimism,' 'humanity-aspiration' and other Germany-monstrosities of the kind; so long were we driven to stand aside in cold impartiality. Our judgement was not shaken, but our nerves were, and so we could not begin to be sentimental about Ibsen. About Shakespeare, and Vergil, and Goethe, we are sentimental, all of us. We do more than merely admire their work: we love them. Browning we love too. We could not have done so in the days of the Browning Society; but now Browning has emerged upon Parnassus, and there is no more of the strenuous twaddle that exasperated us. And now, too, Ibsen, though himself still lives, has passed that line beyond which prattle and fuss exist not. He is a classic now. Now, at length, we can begin to ask ourselves whether we can love him. Has he that sweetness which, born of strength, endears to us most men of genius?

I have been reading Dr Brandes's book about him.* A far less forbidding task than it sounds! Though it consists of three 'Impressions,' of which the first was written in 1867, and the second in 1882, it is quite free from the cant and jargon of controversy. It is a book of calm, broad criticism, clearly (and even wittily) expressed. There is nothing in its tone to betray that its subject was not yet a classic when it was written. It enables us to *see* Ibsen, and, seeing him, to— alas! no; somehow, not to love him. Sorrowfully, we admit that he is not attractive. We are not drawn to him, as to other great men in like case. Why is this? Browning, Renan, Newman, Turgueneff— who does not wish to have seen them 'plain'? Who would not gladly plough a furrow with Tolstoi, or eat *Hasen-Braten* with Mommsen? To Coniston, Putney, Boxhill, who is not a pilgrim *in petto*? Yet, somehow, one does not yearn to share with Ibsen that favourite corner of his in the reading-room of the Grand (is it not the Grand?) Hotel in Christiania. No! The personality of Ibsen has no magic for us. That he is great, we know well. He is greater, perhaps, than any of those other living men whom I have mentioned. Certainly, no man has better exemplified than he the methods of genius. Slow, crude, tentative beginnings; aloofness from ordinary affairs; absorption in developing his own form, so soon as he had found it; disdain of any form but that which suited himself—all these sure signs of the great artist one finds in Ibsen's life. One finds in him, also, that wrong-headedness, that incapacity for seeing life in a

*\*Ibsen and Bjornson*, translated by Jessie Muir, revised, with an introduction by William Archer. London: Heinemann, 1899

dispassionate way, which is characteristic of so many great aritists. But stay! Such narrowness is not found in the very greatest artists. Shakespeare and (no! not Mr W. B. Yeats) Goethe are the two most obvious examples of men whose greatness was so transcendent as to make them dispassionate. They saw things, of course, within the limits of their own temperaments, but their temperaments were so wide as to let them see all things clearly and, as it were, in the round. Ibsen cannot see thus, and therefore one cannot reckon him among the very greatest. He is a Titan, not a god. The gods cannot lose their tempers; the Titans cannot keep theirs. Ibsen fails of supreme greatness, because he cannot keep his temper. Throughout his life, he has been angry with the world.... Yet, that does not explain why we cannot love him. Tolstoi and Ruskin, whom we love, have always been angry with the world. But theirs has been the anger of men who love mankind despite its faults; Ibsen's, the anger of one who hates it because of its faults. 'Man,' as Dr Brandes quotes from Taine, 'is not an abortion or a monster, nor is it the mission of poetry to revolt or defame men. Our inborn human imperfection is part of the order of things, like the constant deformity of the petal in a plant; what we consider a malformation is a form; what seems to us the subversion of a law is the fulfilment of a law.' To put it more briefly, *'tout comprendre, c'est tout pardonner.'* If Tolstoi, Ruskin, and Ibsen had been greater men, they would never have been angry at all. They would have seen that there was no cause for anger, only for compassion. But Tolstoi and Ruskin, being compassionate as well as angry, have attained nearer to that supreme wisdom which pardons all, knowing all, than has Ibsen in his unmitigated wrath. Sympathy—that is what Ibsen lacks. Out of his exceeding strength no sweetness has ever come. The baseness of man has always been his theme. Noble characters he has created, but only as obvious foils to the baseness of mankind. As Diogenes sought for an honest man, not, you may be sure, that he might delight in his honesty, but that he might the more poignantly display the dishonesty of all the other citizens, so has Ibsen evolved his Rosmers and Stockmanns. And we feel that even the noble women in his plays were evolved much less from any belief in their sex than from hatred of his own. They are so many cudgels for the better cracking of men's skulls. Such, at least, is the impression one has in reading his plays. It may be just or unjust, but it is an irresistible impression.

By reason of it, we cannot love Ibsen any more than we can love Diogenes or Dean Swift.

Dr Brandes seems to me wrong in suggesting that Ibsen's hatred of mankind is due to his belief in a possible regeneration of the world. Granted, that Ibsen is a 'moral pessimist,' not a 'metaphysical pessimist,' I cannot take this as an excuse for his hatred. Tolstoi and Ruskin are only 'moral pessimists;' but they are not haters for all that. Diogenes and Dean Swift were 'metaphysical pessimists;' yet was their hatred none the less bitter. Even so, Ibsen would be none the more pleasant a person if he had no hope of bringing about that something which, in a letter to Dr Brandes, he calls 'a revolution of the spirit of mankind.' He would, however, be a wiser man and a greater artist. I do not say that he would be a *better* artist. I am not one of those who deny that good art can be produced by a man with a moral purpose. That is a mere fallacy, created to meet the elder fallacy that a moral purpose is necessary to good art. In point of fact, Ibsen could not be a better artist than he is. But a *greater* artist he might have been, if he had had no moral purpose; for the greatest men, seeing and knowing all, know that moral purpose never can effect anything. They know that, even if you do succeed in exterminating one form of (say) drunkenness or prostitution or slavery, the drunkards or prostitutes or slaves will forthwith reappear in another, if not the same, form. Thus, in the greatest art (which must be the work of the greatest men) no moral purpose ever exists. Ibsen is, as I have said, a great man. But his greatness is not of the highest order; and, as always happens, he was acclaimed chiefly for the very qualities which prevent him from being supreme. It is as a preacher, a regenerator, something with 'the larger light' (whatever that may be) that his disciples chiefly acclaimed him. They thought that he would alter the world with his intellectual ideas. True, intellectual ideas had never hitherto altered the world. Socrates left Athens just as he found it. Jesus Christ, but for his accepted divinity, would not have influenced the world for one generation; nay! can it be said that the world has ever governed itself according to the precepts of the Christian religion? Hunger, not ideas, was the cause of the French Revolution; and the three ideas tacked on to it were very soon travestied into oblivion. But Ibsen's ideas, it seemed, were going to take root. Of course, they will never do anything of the kind. Like all other ideas, they will be utterly barren of result. Let us admire Ibsen simply as an artist. He is by far the best artist in drama that has appeared in this century. All the progress which other dramatists are making, all the progress they will make for years to come, must be put to his credit. Let us, then, be vastly grateful to him as an artist. And . . . and let us even try to love him as a man, recognising what he cannot: that one ought not to be angry with anyone and ought to love everyone—even those who seem least lovable.

[ *22 July 1899* ]


## THE FLAVOUR OF THE LEES

Last Tuesday, to the Criterion; there to drain the lees in that cup whose bitter draught I have been drinking, drinking with hardly one heel-tap, since the first day of last year's September. It is said that the convict finds the last days of his imprisonment the most terrible, the hardest to bear. The near prospect of liberty narrows and darkens his cell, urging him to all manner of violence. So it is with a dramatic critic. So long as he cannot realise a close time for plays, he does his duty without murmuring. But, when the theatrical season begins to totter timely to its end, a dangerous and rebellious mood surges in him. Liberty beckons him to come forth from the shadows of the chimney-pots. He scents hay and heather and salt-water. The provocation of their wild fragrance is wafted to him along the baked, dust-fraught streets, and his feet flinch on the burning pavement, whence all but he have fled—all but he, who must needs wait to hear the ghastly conclusion of the whole matter.

A few weeks ago, perhaps *The Wild Rabbit* might have seemed to me less utterly dull and vulgar than it seemed last Tuesday. It had, also, a heavy disadvantage in that most of the mimes engaged for it were rather less than mediocre, and that it was produced, on a hot night, in that subterranean cave which by nothing but the glamour of Mr Wyndham has ever made a place to spend a happy evening in. But I am afraid that, even if *The Wild Rabbit* had been produced in the middle of the season, and well acted on the earth's level, I should not have enjoyed it much. It happens to be the kind of play which bores me in any circumstances. Do not mistake me! I have no prejudice against farce as a dramatic form; on the contrary, I love it. I have even seen, in recent years, farces which moved me to much laughter. *Charley's Aunt* was one: it had an excellent idea, excellently developed. For a similar reason, I delighted in *The Magistrate*, as I delighted in all Mr Pinero's farces. *The Importance of Being Earnest* was (in its form, at least) a farce, and I enjoyed it immensely: the stock situations of farce were used in such a way that they became new and distinguished. It is only when a farce is written without any new central idea, without wit, without humour, with nothing but a repetition of all the stock situations peppered over with as many new vulgarities as the author is original enough to invent, that I am unable to enjoy the two or three hours spent in witnessing it. Unfortunately, in the English theatre, almost all farces are of this kind. They are easy to write (being, indeed, nothing but the knockabout business of the Music Halls spun out to two or three acts), and the public likes them. No one is to blame. The public is not culpable for liking physical humour. Physical humour is the only kind of humour which is understood by primitive races, and the public, at all times and in all countries, is a primitive race. Nor are any members of the public who write farces for the public culpable for writing the sort of thing which it and they like best. My only complaint is that I myself cannot enjoy the fun. True, I can roar with laughter at things which would not twitch one muscle of the public's mouth. But these things are of a subtle kind, and subtleties are more or less rare. On the other hand, the world is so full of physical incongruities and physical accidents that I should never be dull if such things amused me. One cannot go into the street without seeing at least one fat man. Drunken men leaning against lamp-posts are, also, very common. So are men whose hats are blown off the tops of omnibuses. Fatness, intoxication, hatlessness, arouse in me only various degrees of compassion. But I see crowds of other people convulsed with laughter. Enviable creatures! Enviable, not merely because of their frequent chances for laughter, but also because theirs, after all, is the kind of humour which endures and never changes and never needs an explanation. Of subtle humour there are innumerable kinds: what amuses one subtlist may not amuse another. And what amuses him would not have amused him if he had lived in another age. What delighted the cultured Romans would have puzzled the cultured Elizabethans; and Shakespeare's favourite quips mean nothing to us. But the humour of the mob is one for all time, for all climes—a majestic, catholic, omni-unificant tradition. I wish I could share in it.

Never have I so deeply coveted a share as while I sat through *The Wild Rabbit*. But even if I could have tolerated the play itself I could not but have wondered that anyone had come to see it save under compulsion. There, despite the heat, were all the familiar first-nighters, nodding and becking, and pointing one another out to one another, in as acute a state of excitement as ever they were. What a wonderful thing it is, this love of the theatre for the theatre's sake! These people who, without being paid to do so, treat the theatre as one of the really important things in life! I like good plays, good acting. So, too, does the familiar first-nighter. But the theatre itself, with its curtain and its footlights and its O.P. side and all the rest of it, is enough to make him quite happy. And he goes to it, cannot help going to it, even while July is swooning in the sunburnt arms of August. I envy his madness. At most times it is easy enough for me to persuade myself, being paid to do so, that the theatre is the very pivot of the terrestrial globe. But there comes a time, when I cannot but despise it and detest it. There comes a scent of hay and heather and salt-water....

So, with a sigh and a slight contortion of my features, do I let the cup fall from my hand. Hollow-ringing, sped by my foot, it rolls away. It will be borne back to me, brimful? Yes! but not, at least, before September.

[ *29 July 1899* ]


## 'THE DEGENERATES'

So long and doggedly had Mr Grundy been galumphing along the primrose path of adaptation that when I first heard of this play, I supposed that it was to be a dramatic version of poor Nordau's claim to notoriety. I was curious to see what it would be like. But soon, from one paragraph and another, I learnt that it was to be 'a new and original comedy' and was to 'deal satirically with a certain section of Society.' My curiosity became intense. Evidently, Mr

Grundy was going to show us sport. He had been watching the 'certain section' from some coign of vantage, and its goings-on had terribly incensed him. He had vowed that not until he had lashed the vices of the age and purged Babylon with fire would he adapt another of Dumas's plays. And so, with thunder in his brow and lightning in his eyes, he sat down to perform his awful task. *The Degenerates*! That which other dramatists had been treating lightly, almost lovingly, he was going to reveal in all its hideousness and vileness. To that evil bull in whose flanks Jones, Pinero, Carton had nimbly planted their papered darts, he, the stalwart, the dauntless, the unerring Grundy, was about to give the *coup de grâce* . . . *The Degenerates*! An ominous, awe-inspiring title, sign of a tremendous occasion, is it not?

Mr Grundy, bowing grimly from the stage, when all was over, looked every inch the relentless accuser we had been led to expect by the title of his play. He played his part to perfection. As the matador bows over the bull which has fallen to him, so, grimly, bowed Mr Grundy to us. I did not notice that any hats or fans or cigar-cases were thrown to him, but he was quite rapturously applauded, and altogether the scene would have been very impressive and memorable but for the fact (which Mr Grundy knew as well as anyone) that all Mr Grundy had done was to write a particularly trite and silly play, foisting on part of it a little cheap satire of types which do not exist off the stage (on which they have existed from time immemorial) and giving the whole farrago a more ineptly pretentious title than any play ever had. The matador bowed grimly, and the audience, so far from tearing up the benches, was rapturous; yet the much-advertised bull had not even been trotted out! Who shall say now that the public is not to be trifled with?

I will not insult Mr Grundy's intelligence by supposing that he ever had the slightest intention of doing what his title led one to suppose he had done. If he had meant to live up to that catching title, he would, of course, have invented a plot through whose workings he could have shown us something of what he takes to be social degeneracy. He has done nothing of the kind. In the first act there are a few types which he evidently means for degenerates, but they have nothing to do with the play, and, after they have been dragged (perfunctorily, and under quite impossible circumstances) into the second act, they disappear altogether. Personally, I did not regret their disappearance. I was rather glad to think that the mimes condemned to play them would have the consolation of getting home and going to bed early. But it seems to me an act of something very like impudence to call a play after a set of characters who have nothing to do with it and are hardly seen in it. Why did not Mr Grundy call his play *The Comic Relief* at once? That, indeed, would have been far less inapposite. A drunken viscount who wonders when they are going to bring the 'lotion,' a Jew with a big nose (subject of many exquisite jests), a dyspeptic millionaire, a vulgar lady journalist—surely it is rather absurd to dignify these old puppets with any title more high-sounding than 'comic relief.' At first, I thought that perhaps Mr Grundy imagined the principal character in his play, Mrs Trevelyan, to be a degenerate. (Not that this lady is anything of the kind; she is just a healthy animal, with a passion for pleasure of all kinds—a pagan type which is bred by the dozen in any healthy community.) But Mr Grundy has written to the *Daily Telegraph* and disabused my mind of the suspicion that Mrs Trevelyan was meant to be a degenerate. If she had been so meant, she would not, according to Mr Grundy, have been permitted to appear in the last two acts. 'In the course of the second act,' says Mr Grundy, 'the cheaply cynical, the smartly sordid, and several other evil and unhappy types fade out; they cannot last. What is evil in life is cured or compensated by the ordinary processes of nature, or life could not continue. Only the characters which have in them some element of good survive,' and so forth. I am glad Mr Grundy has taken the trouble to make this explanation. I had been stupid enough to suppose that the drunken viscount, the Jew with the big nose and the other 'degenerates' had been withdrawn in the course of the second act merely because they had nothing to do with the *scène à faire* in the third act—in fact, because they were in the way. Mr Grundy has enlightened me. I see now that their withdrawal was fraught with deep moral significance. But I think Mr Grundy might have made his beautiful lesson a little clearer to my dull brain. When the curtain rose on the third act, one of the good characters might have been reading the outside sheet of *The Times* and saying 'Poor Lord Stornoway! Fancy! And Mr Marcus Mosenthal, he dead too? And —what's this?—Mr Carl Hentsch! How very sad! Oh, and Mrs Bennet-Boldero! . . . Well, well, they were all degenerates. Of course they couldn't be expected to survive.' Thus might Mr Grundy have driven home his moral, on the spot, and saved himself the painful necessity of writing an angry letter to the *Daily Telegraph*.

About the non-degenerate characters—the fit survivors of the second act—there is really not much to be said. Mrs Trevelyan has a daughter, and Lady Samaurez has a glove. The daughter comes back from a finishing-school on the Continent; the glove is embroidered with its wearer's monogram. Daughter and glove are both equally necessary to the plot, but the part played by the glove is, on the whole, the more natural of the two. Being left in the inevitable bachelor's rooms, it establishes the innocence of Mrs Trevelyan, who has been trying to save the honour of Lady Samaurez, in the inevitable way, at the expense of her own honour. Which is just what a glove would do and, indeed, generally 'does do' in plays of this description. With a yawn and a smile, then, we accept what the glove does. What the daughter does we really cannot accept. She arrives in the middle of the second act and, hey presto! makes a saint of her mother. Hitherto Mrs Trevelyan has been a lady of effulgently shady reputation, a lover of notoriety, a passionate preserver of her youth—in short, a hard, loud animal without a conscience. For years she has been dreading the moment when she must reveal a grown-up daughter. The moment comes. Had Mr Grundy any interest in human character as opposed to stage character, or any sense of comedy beyond the writing of smart dialogue, he would have revelled in this chance, and would have found in it, also, the starting-point for that noble lesson which, as he assures the *Daily Telegraph*, he was anxious to teach us. As it is, he lets the chance go by. He does not show us the embarrassment of the woman complicated by the instinct of the mother. That would have been comedy. He does not spend the rest of the play in showing the gradual triumph of the mother over the woman. That would have been comedy, and moral edification into the bargain. He brings on the daughter merely that Mrs Trevelyan may gasp in instantaneous conversion and be off to the bachelor's rooms and save her enemy, Lady Samaurez, by being discovered there, *splendide mendax*—forgive the tag, reader! it is less threadbare than the situation—after the usual dreary game of hide-and-seek in the third act. Of course, the reclaimed lady is not compromised for ever. There is the aforesaid glove: salvation of Mrs Trevelyan. Apotheosis, as usual: she marries a Duke. Thus Mrs Grundy is satisfied. So is Mr Grundy. At least, he would be, but for the stupidity of the *Daily Telegraph*, which forces him to offer the explanation reverently quoted in this article. That explanation has been quite a boon to me. I should never have guessed that Mrs Trevelyan's marriage with the Duke meant that 'only the characters which have in them some element of good survive, and it is only what is good in them that survives.' Yet that, according to Mr Grundy, is the 'one and only meaning' of the affair. 'And,' he adds, 'the pit-circle and the gallery grasped it. God bless them!' To call down a blessing on heads covering such fine brains seems to me almost superfluous.

As Mrs Trevelyan, Mrs Langtry did her best, but she has been too long away from the stage not to seem like an amateur. She had the painful incoherence of the amateur; her performance was a series of little, detached, pluckily-made efforts. Miss Lily Hanbury, as Lady Samaurez, and Mr Hawtrey, as the Duke, did what they have done a hundred times before, and did it very well. Mr Maurice had one of the worst parts ever written, and Mr Leslie Kenyon had another. And Miss Lily Grundy, as Mrs Trevelyan's daughter, was the one thing on which I can congratulate her father sincerely.

At the Strand there is an unassuming play about which, if it had been produced in the 'fifties, I might have had something to say—in the 'fifties. It is called *The Last Chapter*, and is by Mr George H. Broadhurst, and is, I repeat, unassuming. *The Silver King* is being played at the Lyceum. It has been immensely popular for seventeen years, and, as the money-standard is really the only standard by which one can test melodramas, I take it to be the best melodrama ever written. Miss Maud Jeffries and Mr T. W. Percyval do very well what used to be done by Miss Eastlake and Mr Willard, and Mr Wilson Barrett is still the hero, wearing those costumes whose strange fashion suggests a blend of Abraham Lincoln and Cornelia the mother of the Gracchi, and bringing down the house with neatness and despatch at the end of every act. At the Olympic there is an entertainment called *A Trip to Midget-Town* and performed chiefly by midgets. These little creatures are not, as I had feared they would be, painful to look at. On the contrary, they are rather nice, 'with arch baby faces and mignon forms,' like Botticelli's centaurs. And some of them act quite as well as full-grown people.

[*9 September 1899*]

## 'THE GHETTO,' AND OTHER PLAYS

It is the fashion to regard the Jews as extremely interesting people, and thus *The Ghetto*, throughout which Herr Heijermans is evidently trying to prove that they are not interesting at all, is a rather daring paradox. If the author had merely tried to prove that Jews in modern times are becoming less and less interesting, I should have welcomed his effort as making for the truth. For there is no doubt that (in England at least) they must be gradually losing those characteristics which centuries of persecution and isolation created and conserved in them. But Herr Heijermans has set forth to show that even in the Ghetto of Amsterdam, A.D. 1817, they were uninteresting; and that, surely, is to embark on a wilful perversion of historic truth. Nor does he even prove his point. For all his courage and ingenuity, the paradox does not quite come off. The milieu and the characters are fascinating in spite of him. There is an old man, Sachel, of the straitest sect, who plans that Rafael, his well-beloved son, shall marry Rebecca, Aaron's daughter. There is Rafael, full of music, full of hatred for the trickery which his father practises in his lust of wealth, full of contempt for the narrow faith in which he has been reared, and full of love for the Christian girl who is his father's servant. Here, surely, we have the makings of a most fascinating conflict—the conflict of youth and passion with the patriarchal idea; the old theme of father against son, intensified and made more poignant by the fact that it is a Jewish son against a Jewish father. Yes! all the makings of a great drama are there, and we cannot help being interested in them, even though Herr Heijermans has manipulated them in a trivial and tedious manner. We feel that the material is quite excellent, even though it has been so woefully neglected that every act is eked out with interminable staccato speeches and little irrelevant incidents. The chief mistake made by Herr Heijermans, the fault that vitiates the whole course of his play, is that Rafael has secretly married the Christian servant before the beginning of the first act. In order to get really dramatic force out of his idea, the author ought not have let Rafael even have fallen in love before the beginning. The audience ought to see him falling in love, while his father is planning his marriage with Rebecca; then, after the first revolt and defiance, the conflict between son and father would have carried the rest of the play through, naturally and impressively. As it is, the first two acts—or rather (since the second act is divided into two long scenes) the first three acts—are practically wasted. Not before the very end of the second act does the son formally make known his defiance of his father. The curtain falls on his tirade, and even in the last act no real tussle occurs between the two. Indeed, what real tussle can there be over an accomplished fact? There is only an old-fashioned game of 'keeping apart'. Rafael, for one reason or another has gone away, leaving his wife in his father's house. A week has elapsed. The father tells the girl that her husband has deserted her. She promptly throws herself into the river, and the young man, returning in the nick of time, rescues her.

'Who put her in?
Little Tommy Green.
Who pulled her out?
Little Johnny Stout.'

That is all, and it is not, I contend, an impressive conclusion. It may not be quite fair to judge Herr Heijermans by the production at the Comedy Theatre, which he has himself repudiated. In the original version, doubtless little Johnny Stout drowns himself too, and little Tommy Green is left to live a life of mourning and remorse. But even that is unsatisfactory: no inevitable solution, but only a cheap 'way out of it,' disguised as tragedy. Altogether, I do not quite see how the play came to be—my programme assures me that it is—'celebrated.' There are, after all, so many plays with good main ideas ruined by ill-treatment.

Mr Kyrle Bellew played the part of Rafael, but not even he, with all his elocution and his gift of eternal youth, was able to make Rafael anything but an insufferably tedious and long-winded prig. Mr G. S. Titheradge was quite admirable as Sachel, really seeming like a blind man—I forgot to mention that Sachel was blind. His only fault was that he had not made up his hands, whose smoothness and plumpness were in worrying contrast with his wrinkled and withered face. If the play is still running, he ought to rectify the omission. Mr Beveridge did not seem to have quite entered into the spirit of his part. As an Irish priest he is always excellent, but a Dutch Rabbi requires a slightly altered method; and Mr Beveridge had not altered his method 'at all, at all.' Mrs Brown-Potter's perpetually arched and enigmatic smile, as of one listening to something through a keyhole, and the roguish artificiality of her method in acting, did not befit the part of the Christian drudge.

At the Duke of York's there is a renewed run of *An American Citizen*, and, though the play and my opinion of it are the same as they were in the summer, Mr Nat Goodwin and Miss Maxine Elliott are such admirable comedians, so quick, sure and sympathetic, that no one need grudge a second visit, still less a first. At the Vaudeville there is a new farce, called *The Elixir of Youth* and—need I add?—adapted from the German. It is not better nor worse than most things of the kind. It contains a jealous Irish lover, a jealous French lover and a jealous English husband, all of whom are very violent and therefore (according to the public's canons) very funny. And its main motive is safe to give pleasure: an old married man coming up from the country and going out on the spree. Mr George Giddens plays this familiar old man, and it is only because the leering-senility business always seems to me the reverse of pleasant that I cannot honestly say I was delighted with his performance. Miss Ellis Jeffreys, as an actress to whom the man makes advances, played loudly and resolutely, but she did not make much of her part; she seemed to be trying hard not to be a lady, but never for one moment quite succeeding. Miss Juliette Nesville played the part of a maid with that foreign accent which English audiences mistake for 'finish,' and various other more or less popular mimes disported themselves more or less cheerfully. By far the best performance was Miss Florence Wood's. This had the true ring of broad comedy, sounded by an hereditary artist.

Mr Murray Carson is at Kennington, reviving the faded glories of the stock company. *Richard the Third*, his first item, was produced last Monday. Nothing, not even a well-chosen stock company, can make of it a good play. It is terribly diffuse and artificial, and lacks even those purple patches of poetry which Shakespeare so often wove in when he felt that he was not being dramatic. One would say that Shakespeare wrote it in a perfunctory spirit, and not because he had anything particular to write round Richard the Third, but merely that he might make an addition to the number of plays he had already written round English kings. Whatever be the explanation, the fact is indubitable: the play is very tedious indeed. Mr Murray Carson, as the King, expended a great deal of cleverness and physical force, but, though he made us admire him, he could not induce us to believe in the part. Miss Grace Warner played tamely as Lady Anne. The whole scene of the wooing is so impossible that the actress should not attempt to give her part verisimilitude. The only thing is to roll out the lines quickly and sonorously and not give the audience any time to think. Miss Warner, unfortunately, hesitated and paltered, and all was lost. Mrs Bernard Beere played sweepingly and well, in the grand manner, as Margaret, and Mrs Carson did all that could be done with the part of Elizabeth. I look forward to the next production.

[ *16 September 1899* ]

## AT DRURY LANE

It is human to err, and it is natural that we should take druriography lightly. We see it, accept it, dismiss it with a smile, and do not begin to consider it as an art-form. This loud, light-hearted, unmeaning rigmarole must (we imagine) be very easy to write. Mr Collins calls on Mr Cecil Raleigh with an alphabetical list of the scenes to be employed in next year's drama; Mr Cecil Raleigh opens a drawer and sees whether he has a plot which could be adapted to Mr Collins's demands, and, if not, he invents one.

> *Botanical Gardens, The*
> *Country-house, Baccarat-playing in a*
> *Dressmaker's Shop, A fashionable*
> *Music Hall, A well-known*
> *Royal Academy, The*
> *Swiss Mountains, The*

Such was the list Mr Collins had drawn up for the final year of the century, and one supposes that Mr Collins, in finding so many attractive scenes not yet exploited at Drury Lane, must have had a harder task than had Mr Raleigh tacking on to them enough story to satisfy an always indulgent audience. Any kind of story would do, so long as one or other of the chief characters gambled in a country house and became superintendent of a dressmaker's shop, and did something or other at the Royal Academy, in the Botanical

Gardens, in a Music Hall and on the Swiss Mountains. If any measure of verisimilitude were demanded by Mr Collins, the dramatist's might seem to us a difficult task. If the play had to be even coherent in absurdity, that task might seem to be not altogether easy. But the list of scenes is the one thing which need be respected. Any character may be dragged on any pretext into any scene, so long as the scene is one of those marked in the list. In fact, Mr Raleigh has *carte blanche* and, so far as internal evidence goes, he would seem to have taken it very blithely. One would suppose that he dashed off these enormous annual trifles—*Hearts are Trumps* is the title of his latest —with the utmost ease, with the greatest pleasure, indeed, and without expenditure of more ingenuity than is required for smoking a cigar or crossing the road. And lo! one would be quite wrong. Druriography, as practised by Mr Raleigh, is a most exigent, arduous, tremendous, nerve-destroying form of labour. I learn from one periodical, whose remarks on drama derive peculiar weight from the fact that its dramatic critic is Mr William Archer, that Mr Raleigh is compelled to live on the strictest regimen during his periods of dramaturgic creation, riding early every morning in the Park, working in strict seclusion, dining at five o'clock, supping at eleven, and all the rest of it. Nay more! the *Daily Chronicle*, which does not usually lay any particular stress on the private lives of the great modern dramatists, has been moved to reveal that Mr Cecil Raleigh is so sensitive to every breath of possible misfortune, so passionately, jealously eager to ward from his well-loved work the unseen forces which may be clustering to overwhelm it, that he will on no account finish an act on the thirteenth page of his MS. and strictly forbids dress-rehearsals on Friday. Really, this is rather touching. I am convinced that there are many people—even people who have had no experience in druriography—who could, without living on any regimen or becoming steeped in superstition, do the job better than Mr Raleigh does it, and I think Mr Collins ought to give one of them a chance. I do not say that I myself am one of these people; as a dramatic critic, I hold myself exempt from that duty of trying to write plays which seems to be laid on all other human shoulders. Nor do I pretend that the audiences at Drury Lane demand anything better than what Mr Raleigh so painfully provides for them. But there is no reason why the public's taste should limit the critic's ideal in druriography more than in any other kind of work, and I do not see why one need adopt, as do most of the critics, a merely cynical attitude about the National Theatre. By all means, let the present form be preserved; let Mr Collins make out his list, and the dramatist write round it. But let the dramatist's task be well performed. It could never be a very dignified task, but that is no reason why it should not be performed skilfully, ingeniously, plausibly. I refuse to regard Mr Raleigh as an ideal in the matter.

However, I need not carry my complaints further. I enjoyed *Hearts are Trumps* immensely; indeed, it is long since I enjoyed myself so much in a theatre. I came away feeling that they, after all, are right who hold a theatre to be a place for recreation, not for the satisfaction of high aesthetic cravings. Sunset, after all, is the signal for rest, for laughter. In the daytime one is strenuous, but in the evening one dines; and who can be strenuous after dinner? If the theatres opened their doors in the morning, there would be much more chance of that serious drama for which I so often long. As it is, I have a suspicion that I shall revisit Drury Lane at the first opportunity. I found the production quite irresistible. Not that I derived any keen delight from the realistic presentments of the Horticultural Gardens and the Royal Academy and the Swiss Mountains. These places themselves are too depressing to be otherwise in facsimile. My joy was chiefly because of the crowds with which the stage is almost always filled—those crowds of gorgeously dressed young women and of more or less gorgeously dressed young men, all so horribly awkward and uncomfortable, and looking so utterly unlike what they were meant to look like, and vainly trying to carry the thing off with a high hand. Them I could watch for ever. The way they make conversation to one another, the way they walk across the stage, the way they shake hands, ever so high in the air! But they, though themselves are a sufficient attraction, are not all that is delightful at Drury Lane. In plays of this kind, one of the most delicious phenomena is that all the characters have to conduct their private tragedies in the most public places. Under circumstances which would drive others into some remote village, they must appear at the Horticultural Gardens and other popular resorts, and confide their woes to the *habitués*. This is a condition which one accepts; it is an inevitable part of the druriographic form, and one learns to accept it quite gravely. But when Miss Violet Vanbrugh, as Lady Winifred Crosby, after ripping up an offensive portrait of her daughter in the

Academy and appealing to a serried crowd of ladies and gentlemen for sympathy in her maternal indignation, rebuked an interviewer who had called at her house to learn more of the matter, and told him in ringing accents that the system of invading the sanctity of private life was 'not honest, not wholesome, and, thank heaven, not English!'—then, I confess, my gravity gave way. Nor was it restored when Lady Winifred subsequently screamed her daughter's name in the Frivolity music hall. Indeed, the play is full of delicious absurdities. The only parts of it for which one can feel no gratitude to Mr Cecil Raleigh are the parts in which he gives rein to his humour. This is strange; for I have always heard that Mr Cecil (like Sir Walter) Raleigh is 'a fellow of much wittinesse and daringe,' loved and dreaded by members of the Playgoers' Club for his mordant comments on lectures. I cannot quite reconcile this description of him with the dialogue in this play of his. *A.* 'You're looking radiant.' *B.* I ought to be. I'm raided by creditors every morning.' —*A.* 'There ain't no flies on me.' *B.* 'I wish there were a steam-roller on you.'—*A.* 'How are you?' *B.* 'Proper!' *A.* 'That's more than your songs are.' *A.* 'They go.' *B.* 'Yes! They go too far!' These are fair examples of Mr Raleigh's lighter manner. Here —I have a terribly good memory for such things—follows an example of his more elaborate manner. *A.* 'I can't paint you with a top-hat.' *B.* 'Why not? Velasquez painted a crinoline.' *A.* 'Yes, but that's worn at the other end. A top-hat is a *capital* offence; a crinoline is only a *base* disfigurement.' And here is an example of a new kind of joke, which may be confidently recommended to dramatists at a loss: 'One sister has a bad temper, the other makes up her eyes. I call them "Crosse and Blackwell."' Is this the kind of joke that convulses the Playgoers' Club? Or does Mr Raleigh's strict regimen temporarily eclipse his humour, that refulgent orb?

There is little to be said of the performance. Miss Beatrice Ferrar was amusing as a music-hall artiste, and Mr E. Dagnall acted most admirably as a Jewish comic villain, making an old, old part quite new. Miss Violet Vanbrugh was handicapped by a very severe cold and by being naturally intelligent. The cold prevented her from speaking the lines clearly, and the intelligence made her obviously ashamed of speaking them at all.

[*23 September 1899*]

## 'KING JOHN' AND OTHER PLAYS

In a nobly vaulted chamber of Northampton Castle are set the thrones of the king and the queen mother. The portly chamberlain, wand-bearing, red-robed, stands waiting on one of the topmost steps of the great staircase. An organ sounds, and he stalks majestically down. After him skips a little jester. A long sombre procession of bowed heads and folded arms, the monks come, chanting a Mass. After them walk the courtiers. The monks pass away through the arches. The courtiers range themselves around the throne. A blast of trumpets heralds the king and the queen mother, who presently seat themselves upon the thrones. In the brief parley with Chatillon—'new diplomacy,' with a vengeance!—one feels that not the king, but the sinister and terrible old figure beside him, is the true power, ever watching, prompting, enforcing. Chatillon flings his master's defiance and is escorted from the presence-chamber. The ill-matched brothers are ushered in; the straight-limbed elder, splendidly confident and insolent; the younger, lantern-jawed and cringing, grinning with fear. At the foot of the throne, the younger whines his cause with quick, wretched gestures. The king suppresses a smile. His eyes wander to the bastard, finding in him 'perfect Richard.' 'Man and no-man' are here—an elemental situation. Sped by a blow of the jester's bladder, 'no-man' scurries out of the chamber, happy in the acquisition of his gold. The bastard is left exulting in his manhood and the glory it has brought him. . . . Under the walls of Angiers, Philip of France parleys with his enemy. The queen mother holds out her arms to little Arthur, and Constance reads in her eyes all that would befall him in England. The citizens open their gates, and on a cushion the keys of the city are presented to the two kings, who, hand in hand, pass in to hold revelry. . . Pandulpho, tremendous embodiment of the Pope's authority, comes to the two kings. John, strong in his mother's presence, receives the curse. Philip snatches his hand away from the clasp of his ally. Torn with conflicting fears, he submits himself to Rome . . . You see the two armies 'face to face, and bloody point to point.' In a corner of the dark field, fitfully lit by the flames of a distant village, you see the victorious bastard fell his arch foe and snatch from his shoulders the lion skin of King Richard... In a glade of slim beeches, John communes with the faithful, grim Hubert. The old soldier stands immovable, while his master whispers in his ear. Beyond, stands the queen mother, watching with her eyes of ill omen. Little Arthur is plucking the daisies. The king smiles down at him as he passes, and the child starts away. There are some daisies growing near the spot where the king has been whispering his behest. Lightly, he cuts the heads off them with his sword... In the crypt there is no light but from the cresset where the irons will be heated. Arthur runs in, carrying a cross-bow on his shoulder. 'Good morrow, Hubert.' 'Good morrow, little prince...' All the vassals have left their king. The jester who watched the scene from a gallery has fled too. The king takes up the orb and the sceptre, sits haggard upon his throne. Hubert comes in, and the sound of this footstep causes the king to shudder and cry out like a child. But Arthur still lives. Nothing but his death-warrant remains against the king. While the king burns this parchment on the cresset, the monks file in to their Mass. Up the stairs they go, chanting. The king smiles, and then, still standing by the cresset, folds his hands in prayer. He walks, with bowed head, up the stairs, abases himself at the altar.... It is the dusk of dawn in the orchard of Swinstead Abbey, and through the apple-trees the monks hurry noiselessly to the chapel. The dying king is borne out in a chair. He is murmuring snatches of a song. The chair is set down, and with weak hands he motions away his bearers. 'Ay, marry,' he gasps, 'now my soul hath elbow-room; it would not out at windows nor at doors. There is so hot a summer in my bosom, that all my bowels crumble up to dust.... And none of you will bid the winter come, to thrust his icy fingers in my maw.' The bastard comes in hot haste, and the king, to receive his tidings, sits upright, and is crowned for the last time. He makes no answer to the tidings. One of the courtiers touches him, ever so lightly, on the shoulder, and he falls back. The crown is taken from his head and laid on the head of the child who is now king. The bastard rings out those words in which poetry of patriotism finds the noblest expression it can ever find....

I have written down these disjointed sentences, less in order to enable my readers to imagine the production at Her Majesty's Theatre than to preserve my own impressions. Probably, I have omitted many of the important points in the play and in the show;

I have merely recorded the things which an errant memory has kept clearliest. Most of the points I have alluded to are, as you will have observed, points of 'business' and stage management. For this I make no apology. I had never seen the play acted before, and I must confess that, reading it, I had found it insufferably tedious. I had found many beautiful pieces of poetry in it, but drama had seemed to me absolutely lacking. That was because I have not much imagination. Lengths of blank verse with a few bald directions—enter A; exeunt B and D; dies; alarums and excursions; are not enough to make me *see* a thing. (And, I take it, this is the case with most of my fellow-creatures.) Therefore, when I go to a theatre and find that what bored me very much in the reading of it is a really fine play, I feel that I owe a great debt of gratitude to the management which has brought out the latent possibilities. I can imagine that a bad production of *King John* would be infinitely worse than a private reading of it. A bad production would make the play's faults the more glaring. But a good production, as at Her Majesty's, makes one forget what is bad in sheer surprise at finding so much that is good. I can say without partiality, and with complete sincerity, that I have never seen a production in which the note of beauty was so surely and incessantly struck as in this production of *King John*. As for the actual performance, there are many interesting points which, unfortunately, I cannot discuss this week. I shall write about the performance as soon as there are not so many other plays clamouring to be noticed.

Mr C. B. Fernald was, I think, tactless in calling his play *The Moonlight Blossom*. The title was obviously meant to suggest beauty, and it fails to do so. I do not say that 'blossom' is, in itself, an ugly word. I do not believe that there is such a thing as an intrinsically ugly word. Words sound ugly or beautiful according to their associations. For example, 'ermine,' which sounds very beautiful, is no more beautiful really than 'vermin,' a word which one would condemn as utterly hideous. Its sound, or the sight of it written, is delightful only because it suggests mantled queens and the finery of noblemen. In itself it is not beautiful, nor is the other word hideous. Ten years ago, doubtless, 'blossom' was a delightful word; but now, though its actual significance has not changed, it is a word to be avoided. Especially if it is preceded by another dissyllabic noun, it is a quite impossible word, a word hopelessly compromised and degraded. You may smile at my pedantry, but you cannot deny that I am right. You remember—it is one of those things which stick in the memory—that dreadful, querulous song, 'Only a pansy blossom,' which was everywhere warbled for many months and may still be heard from the lips of poor wretches who walk croaking in the side streets lest they starve. And you know the dreadful scent which is stored in automatic machines on the Underground Railway for the refreshment of stifled City men. 'Cherry blossom' and 'pansy blossom'... how could 'moonlight blossom' sound otherwise than hideous? And why was Mr Fernald so tactless? If his play had been really delightful, the title would have spoilt my pleasure. It aggravates my displeasure at a play that is as tedious as it might (had the author used his gifts rightly) have been delightful. Oh, the tedious, involved plot! I was striving vainly to understand it, whilst I might have been enjoying the background. The hero was suspected of having commited, years ago, a crime which was really committed by his half-brother and an unscrupulous widow. And there were endless machinations and botherations, only relieved by merciful pauses for symbolism and for local colour. The symbolism was pretty, though rather perfunctorily worked in. The local colour was delightful. The capture of a criminal, the duel on stilts, the little dance, made the plot seem the more intolerable when it was resumed. It would have been so easy for Mr Fernald to weave these things into a simple and pretty love story. In the love passages he shows (despite a tendency to be iambic) that he can write delicately and imaginatively. But these love passages are so bedevilled by the surrounding plot that they gave me little pleasure. I shall go to the Prince of Wales's again, taking the play as mere spectacle and letting its significance go hang. The scenery and the dresses were, indeed, fascinating. Fascinating, too, was Mrs Campbell. I know not whether she was like a real Japanese girl; if she was not, she should be taken by all Japanese girls as a model. The way she walked and the way she danced were irresistible, and the way she used her voice, like a child playing the piano with one finger, gave a peculiar, child-like charm to all the things she had to say. Mr Forbes Robertson, as the suspect hero, was a little too austere. True, the part was meant to be very sombre; but Mr Robertson put so much sombreness into his every tone and movement that I was fain to suspect him of being depressed by his part. I blame not him, but the author. There was a strong cast—Miss Rosina Filippi, Miss Eleanor Calhoun, Mr James Welch and others.

Mr Kinsey Peile is a person to be encouraged; not one to be groaned at, as at the Avenue Theatre on Saturday night. He had written a comedy which was not adapted from the French, and he had done it without a collaborator. Two good signs! And much of his dialogue was really amusing, and, though his last act fell to pieces, the rest of his play was wrought adroitly. I do not say that the future history of British drama will be the history of Mr Kinsey Peile's development; but, at least, this *Interrupted Honeymoon* proves its author to have both talent and good intentions.

*Boy Bob*, in which to see Miss Louie Freear I visited the Metropole Theatre, Camberwell, is twaddle so outrageous that not Miss Freear herself, for all her humour and sensibility, is worth seeing in it.

[*30 September 1899*]


## A MELODRAMA AND ITS MAKERS

My readers will have noted, and perhaps been bored by, my constant suggestions to this or that dramatist that he take more interest in human beings, by my constant plaints that this or that situation could not possibly occur in real life. In comedies or tragedies I do, indeed, regard imitation of reality as a quite essential thing. In farce or melodrama I am, however, no stickler. Therein, by all means let there be puppets, having any kind of customs, emotions and adventures which their wire-puller may choose for them. Therein, by all means, let the loss of a marriage certificate invalidate a marriage, and let the soldier be accompanied on his every campaign by his wife and child. Swallowing, with good-humoured relish, stage-law and stage-warfare, why should I strain at stage-science, as exemplified in *Man and his Makers*? And why should I follow my colleagues' example of demonstrating that no sane person would reject an inspiring son-in-law merely on account of a five-bottle grandfather and a drug-loving father? Such a point as that is, surely, a postulate, needing no demonstration even from critics who can find nothing better to write about. Nor does Mr Wilson Barrett's and Mr Louis N. Parker's defiance of the postulate mar any pleasure in their play.

Had these gentlemen meant their play seriously, I should have been very angry with them, no doubt. But they did not. They meant it for a melodrama; and melodrama is not, and should not be mistaken for, a serious form in art. I, for my part, go to melodramas in the hope that they will be funny, just as I go (but rather less sanguine) to farces. Sometimes they thrill me a little; more often not at all. But if they amuse me I am quite content. *Man and his Makers* does not happen to thrill me. But it is decidedly funny. It is, in fact, a play to be seen. Everyone should hear Mr Barrett, as a youth bewildered by the news that he has some hereditary taint, ask his guardian 'What is it? Is it heart-disease? It cannot be' (throwing back his arms and distending an unfathomable chest) 'it *cannot* be consump-shone?'

I suspect that if Mr Barrett had done the whole play off his own bat my evening would have been less delightful. Mr Barrett would have written it in the key of (say) *The Silver King*, with absolutely impossible characters saying absolutely impossible things. But—perhaps with a view to conciliating modern scoffers—he took Mr Parker into collaboration, knowing him to be both a student of real life and a man of literary taste. The result is strange. I have a vision of Mr Barrett magnanimously urging Mr Parker to be as literary and as psychological as if he were writing one of his own delightful comedies, and Mr Parker secretly striving with all his might to be nothing of the kind. Mr Parker must have known that his peculiar gifts would be fatal to a melodrama, that the highest high-falutin was necessary for its success. Natural writing in any melodrama immediately shows up the impossibility of the situations. If the mimes have not speeches which they can roar, the whole game of melodrama is up. And so Mr Parker did his best to be brazen. It cannot be said that he succeeded. Now and again, there are passages pitched in the proper key, but most of the writing is quite gentle and quiet. The characters talk as though they were modern human beings, living under possible circumstances. In any melodrama that would be disastrous. But in a melodrama whose plot was evidently conceived by Mr Wilson Barrett, and whose hero is impersonated by him the effect is more than disastrous— it is monstrous. For Mr Barrett is the greatest of all our melodramatists, having a keener scent for situations and a greater disregard of human nature than any of his rivals. Also, he is the greatest of our melodramatic actors, endowed with a tremendous voice, a tremendous manner, and a very fine head. Neither his voice nor his manner nor his head can be brought into any possible relation to modern life. As an Imperial Roman, as Claudian or Marcus Superbus, he seems real enough, though even then one wonders that Rome, being able to produce such a citizen, could ever have declined and fallen. But in modern dress, crowned with a straw hat, girt with a cummer-bund, he seems utterly, hopelessly unreal, or, if real, a ἅπαξ πεποιημένον, a glorious, unrelated accident. In plays like *The Silver King* this does not matter; it is, indeed, a great advantage, enabling him to banish from our minds all doubts as to the probability of any situation into which the dramatist may throw him. But in this play, where he has to say such things as any young man of the period might say, illusion flies from us at his approach. I say 'us' because I am now putting myself in the position of that compact majority which is able to take melodrama seriously. I need not add that, so far as I am concerned, I would rather see Mr Barrett in *Man and his Makers* than any other actor I can think of. To hear him declaiming, in a voice of intermittent thunder, and with a light in his eyes that never was on sea or land, the pretty little verses written in by Mr Parker! To see him receiving friends to an impromptu tea in his chambers and skipping like a little hill in quest of tea-cups and tea-spoons! His performance will always be memorable to me. The more so for being brought into such strong strong relief by the performance of Miss Lena Ashwell. One cannot imagine two histrionic methods more sharply opposed than those of Mr Barrett and Miss Ashwell. Both these mimes are quite unlike any other mime; but while Mr Barrett's strength is in being (if I may say so) superhuman—a gift which he has cultivated by every means in his power—Miss Ashwell's strength is in being simply human—a gift which she has resolutely refrained from overlaying with any of the tricks and graces of histrionic art. She does not use her voice well; she does not move gracefully across the stage; her gestures are rather uncouth. But she has power and sensibility, and the very absence of artifice from her acting gives her for some parts as great an advantage over other actresses as it gives them for other parts over her. She is the arch-realist, and in such plays as the plays of Ibsen (who demands intelligence and intensity, not any sense of beauty) there is no actress who could match her. I cannot think why she was chosen for the leading-lady's part in *Man and his Makers*. Miss Maud Jeffries should have been cast for it, not for the part she actually played.

Since I wrote the foregoing words, I have heard that the play is to be revised and reproduced next year. In these circumstances, I offer Mr Barrett and Mr Parker a suggestion. The most effective scene in the play (from the public's standpoint) is a scene which is not actually presented on the stage. I refer to the scene in which the barrister-hero breaks down in open court owing to his continued indulgence in hasheesh and opium. The public hears of this in the third act. They would, I am sure, like to *see* it. It ought to constitute the third act. The play could quite well be concluded with the scene of the hero's meeting with the heroine in St James's Park. Indeed, a riddance of the present last act would be a very good riddance. Audiences like happy endings, but they do not like a happy ending to overspread the whole of an act. Such a practice is tolerable when the characters are more or less real, especially if the scene be decked with the accessories of Christmas Eve. But melodramatic puppets cease to be interesting to anyone so soon as they have been duly extricated from their lurid difficulties. Even Christmas Eve would not have prevented the audience from yawning over them. To show them in a sunlit garden was adding insult to injury.

There is one more point on which I would advise the authors. I admit the inspired power of their scene in St James's Park, with the starving beggars on the benches listening to the waltzes wafted from an open window in Carlton House Terrace. But I am sure that the audience wanted to see the guests going to and coming from the ball. The contrast should have been driven home. A 'swell' with an eye-glass and an Inverness cape saying 'Get out of my way, fellow!' to one of the dossers, and a dowager drawing aside her skirts and saying 'Shameless creature!' to the noble-hearted Magdalen; and a few other poignant touches of that kind would have pleased the public very much.

[*14 October 1899*]

## GREEBA IN LONDON

'That's what you've done, sir; and if it's worthy of the character of an English gentleman, then God help England!' Two years ago I read *The Christian* as a book, and these words in it warned me that anon I should see it as a play. I waited eagerly for them on Monday night, confident that they would bring down the house. Surely enough, they came. But alas! though Mr Waring spoke them as they deserved to be spoken, 'not a hand' saluted them. Then I knew that the play was lost. For if it was not to succeed as melodrama how could it be saved? It could not arouse any kind of controversy in ethics or sociology. Mr Hall Caine seems to have hoped that it would. But on what grounds? There is nothing new or subversive in the idea that a beautiful young woman who goes on the music-hall stage is 'exposed to temptation,' and that a clergyman who is fond of her would like her to retire. We all know that missionaries in the East End of London do often found clubs in which destitute persons may dance and sing. When John Storm shouts to Archdeacon Wealthy that 'The boys and girls of Soho want dancing. Let's give it them. The boys and girls of Soho want singing. Let's give it them. Above all, let's give it them in our churches, lest the Devil give it them in his Hells!' we are not at all shocked or surprised. Moreover, we are delighted to see them dancing and singing under John Storm's auspices. Any interlude in Mr Caine's dialogue is cordially welcomed by us. We are grateful for the loud band which accompanies so many of Mr Caine's scenes. Sequah's loud band was not more soothing to the subjects of Sequah's forceps. But let not Mr Caine imagine that without this band we should be writhing under his indictment of our Babylon. It is his dramatic genius we should be flinching from. There are worldly clerics, as we know; but Archdeacon Wealthy is not at all like one of them. Nor is Lord Robert Ure in the last degree like one of those wicked noblemen whom we have espied in the cispontine world. In fact the greater part of Mr Caine's indictment merely displays his plenary ignorance of the persons and things he is indicting. The rest of it is a crude repetition of what nobody has even denied. We may be bored or amused by Mr Caine's fervour. But our brains are not stimulated by it. There is no food for discussion.

When *The Christian* was published as a book, one had to admit that Mr. Caine had sacrificed his claim to be regarded as a literary man. His previous novels, despite their faults, had earned him a high position. They were melodramatic and ill-written, but they showed power and intensity. Choosing a background familiar to him in real life, he told elemental stories about men and women, and made for himself a reputation among critics. In *The Christian* he succumbed deliberately to the evil influence of success. He wrote a false, garish farrago about life in London. Forgetting that the proper study of Mankind is Man (and that the proper study of Manx-kind is the Isle of Man), he wrote a chaotic, journalistic, pseudo-propagandist diatribe on the professions and institutions in a city about which he had 'crammed' some snippets of superficial information. The mob liked it; but as a man of serious pretensions in literature Mr Caine ceased to exist. Except in the eyes of the mob, he exists now only as a blower of his own trumpet and a thumper of other people's tubs. If he showed any sign of amendment, if he gave us any reason to suppose that he meant to return to his earlier manner, we might still look kindly on him. But his public utterances show him to be merely intoxicated by his ill-won success and determined to go flaunting along the lamentable path he has chosen. This dramatisation of *The Christian* is the latest incident in his progress. Whether the play will be a financial success in England I do not venture to predict. I suppose that Mr Caine's name will ensure for it a moderately long run. But it will not help to sell any unsold copies (if such there be) of the book. Judged even on the lowest plane of melodrama, the play will be found, from first to last, wanting. I admit that in melodrama one does not demand truth in the delineation of character nor probability in the situations. Nevertheless, even the silliest audience wishes to know what the characters are up to, and why they are up to it. And Mr Hall Caine does not trouble to make these points clear to the audience at the Duke of York's. Why is Lord Robert Ure so anxious for Glory Quale to be seduced by Drake? Why does he wish to turn John Storm out of his church? Why does he set the mob against John Storm? 'Because,' Mr Hall Caine will say, 'he is a wicked nobleman with a single eyeglass.' But really, that is not sufficient explanation. No audience will accept a villian who is without motive for villainy, even if he have two titles and an eyeglass in each eye. Any kind of preposterous motive will satisfy them—but a motive there must be. Again, why did John Storm wish to kill Glory Quale? 'To save her soul,' says Mr Caine. But that implies that John Storm is mad, whereas he has given the audience no reason to suppose he is not perfectly sane. In the book, if I remember rightly, he was a half-mad fanatic. Mr Caine, in the course of many pages, lashed him into a kind of frenzy which gave some kind of verisimilitude to his murderous intent. But the stage is a narrower medium? No doubt. But either Mr Caine has no skill in that medium, or the book is not one which ought to have been dramatised. Again, why does the crowd wish to kill John Storm? In the book, Mr Caine had gradually lashed the crowd into a kind of frenzy. In the play—but why should I waste space in analysing these absurdities? Mr Caine has relied, throughout, on the likelihood that the majority of his audience has read his book. He has not attempted to make of the book an in-itself-intelligible melodrama. Indeed, that would have been perhaps a futile attempt even for the most skilful dramatist. The book was so vast and inchoate a concern that it ought never to have been dramatised. As a ballet at the Empire, it might, indeed, have come out passably, with choruses attired as hospital-nurses, mashers, roughs and clergymen, and with Madame Cavallazzi as John Storm. Perhaps Mr Caine will yet adopt my suggestion. Certainly, his dialogue would lose nothing by being conducted in dumbshow. Not that Miss Millard, Mr Waring, Mr Allan Aynesworth, Mr Ben Webster, Mr Charles Fulton and the other members of the cast did less than their best for the production. Miss Millard, indeed, contrived to make Glory seem quite possible. Hers was the success of the evening. Mr Caine's was the failure. He has aimed low, but even so he has missed. He has written a thoroughly bad melodrama, tricking it out with inferior religiosity, and has left his audience quite unmoved. That's what he's done, sir; and if it's worthy of the character of a Manx novelist, then God help the Isle of Man.

I turn to Captain Marshall, whose engaging talent may be studied in *A Royal Family*, at the Court Theatre. Nothing could be prettier or more fanciful than this little play. It is not really a good play. Indeed it is, technically, a very bad one; for there is really no justification for its third act, while even the other two acts are padded with quite unnecessary scenes. The main motive—the anomaly of being both a royal personage and a human being—is such a good motive for a comedy that I wonder at Captain Marshall's recourse to other motives for keeping up the curtain. But the play has so many amusing and charming passages that one cannot but like it very much and rejoice over its revelation of what was only hinted at in *His Excellency the Governor*—a dramatist with a quite distinct temperament and manner of his own. Captain Marshall should prosper. Let him not, discouraged by his defects in technique, seek a collaborator. That would cramp his talent. It would, also, be quite unnecessary. He has obviously a true instinct for the stage; all he lacks is experience. The only excuse for taking a collaborator is that one has no instinct for the stage, and so cannot convert one's humour (or whatever it may be) into those 'royalties' which are the end of every man's desire. Meanwhile, my readers should certainly go to the Court Theatre. There they will see an exquisite performance by Miss Gertrude Elliot—that example of grace and sensibility for all the sorry *ingénues* on our side of the Atlantic. Also, they will see, and will gratefully remember, Mr Eric Lewis as a king; also, Mr Dion Boucicault, Mr Marsh Allen, Mr James Erskine, and Mr Aubrey Fitzgerald, all acting well.

[*21 October 1899*]

## TWO PLAYS

I am always a little shy of plays adapted from books. When a man dramatises one of his own novels, his natural vanity prevents him from sacrificing the many things which have to be sacrificed if the play is to be a good one. Also, his natural vanity prevents him from believing that any audience can include any creature so degraded as not to have read his book. His play, therefore, is as likely to omit many essential things as it is to include many that are quite superfluous. The result is dreadful. When a man dramatises a book not written by himself, the dangers are less great, but they are yet considerable. The dramatist is sure to be fond of the book he is working on, and loth, therefore, to hack away the things which ought to be hacked away. Also, he does not realise how few of the regular playgoers have read this—or any other—book, and so is apt to suppose that his audiences will understand the play even though it be, in itself, quite unintelligible. These rules apply to most of the adaptations I have seen; but not, I am glad to say, to Mr Grundy's version of *The Black Tulip*, at the Haymarket. Mr Grundy has well performed the inhuman task of mortifying his love for the book. Slashing, hashing, gashing, he has extracted a very decent little play, which the many who have not read the book, and the few who, reading it, have disliked it, will enjoy far more than the few who have read it and liked it. In fact, Mr Grundy is to be congratulated. I know of no person who could have done the job as well as he. (I say 'the job,' because adaptation is a job rather than an art, after all.) There are other persons who could have done it with more literary grace; for the writing is utterly undistinguished. Others, again, could have made it more amusing; for the humour is perfunctory. The trial-scene, with Dogberry and Verges and with a judge who is made to utter the old wheeze about 'instead of which,' is a terribly tedious affair. Nor is the rest of the humour more than the ordinary, traditional humour of the British stage. But, for all that, no one but Mr Grundy could have made so neat and workmanlike a use of Dumas's difficult material.

There is one point on which I would especially congratulate Mr Grundy. The part of Cornelis van Baerle, as drawn by him, is well within Mr Cyril Maude's range. Cornelis's cult for tulips is presented to the audience as an amiable, but peculiar, monomania. No hint is given to the audience that in Holland, at this period, the cult for tulips was as much a recognised national enthusiasm as (say) the old Hellenic cult for athletics or the modern English cult for athletics. A Dutchman who was not mad about tulips would have been shunned as a dangerous eccentric, even as would have been an Athenian mother who did not want her baby to grow up in the image of Pheidias's gods, or even as would be an English mother who did not hope that her baby would one day write verses in the manner of Mr Kipling. In fact, the tulip-mattoid was the normal type of Holland, and Cornelis van Baerle was a very fine fellow. But Mr Grundy, knowing that Mr Maude's talent lies in the impersonation of 'quaint' figures, has very wisely made the part a 'quaint' one, leaving the audience to regard Cornelis as no less eccentric than the men who, in our day and in our country, devote their lives to collecting stamps, or coins, or autographs, or first editions. The foolish monomaniac in love with a woman is a comedy-character, not a romantic. Consequently, Mr Cyril Maude acquits himself excellently.

Miss Emery, as Rosa, has a romantic part. She is infinitely better in romance than she is in comedy—she does not become violent. What a pity that she does not always have romantic parts written for her! For the rest, Mr Sydney Valentine is good as a gaoler; Mr Mark Kinghorne overacts the part of the villain, Boxtel; as William of Orange, Mr Harrison seems rather too amiable and accommodating, too courtly, for a King.

The conjurer, drawing from a top-hat a vast number of little cardboard boxes, has been often quoted as the classic type of productivity. '*Cedat, celerrime jam cedat*' to Mr Louis N. Parker. Assuredly, his pyramid is as nothing to the interminable procession of plays from Mr Parker's study. Out they swarm, the crisp little creatures, type-written, brown-paper-clad, all a-jostle and a-hustle. 'Faster, faster!' cries Mr Parker, clapping his hands, stamping his feet; and faster, faster, they leap the threshold. '*Allez, mes enfants!*', and off they spin to their destination, every one of them taking some theatre on the way. A gallant spectacle! yet, to the thoughtful spectator of it, not altogether cheerful. For the destination of these little creatures is —oblivion. They have their charms and even their virtues, for Mr Parker could not write a play without letting some of his great talent creep into it; but, for all that, they are sickly, unseasoned, doomed. There is no man of vitality so strenuous that he can do good work at the rate which Mr Parker has chosen. The doing of any kind of dramatic work at that rate is in itself wonderful—more wonderful, I repeat, than the hat-trick. But the conjurer has this advantage over the dramatist: that no one bothers about the quality of his cardboard boxes, whilst plays must (so to say) be passed round among the audience. Every play by Mr Parker is examined as a separate article, and the very fact that there are so many of them entails the probability that not one of them will stand the test. Art is a jealous god, and will not answer the prayers of him who kneels with a stop-watch in his suppliant hands. Even the gods in the gallery are jealous enough not to be won by such trivial sacrifices as Mr Parker has lately offered at their shrine. Playwriting is of all arts the hardest. Only by solid, patient, deliberate thought, and by the careful exercise of all the ingenuity and all the emotion he possesses, can a man construct a play that is to be considered as a work of art. Even a play which is merely to please the public cannot be wrought without a vast amount of trouble. Such a play as *Captain Birchell's Luck*, produced on Monday at Terry's Theatre, has not the slightest chance of a 'run.' As a play (in my sense of the word) it is simply appalling. Some critics might describe it as 'inoffensive'; but that were a poor compliment to Mr Parker, and I shall not pay it. Mr Parker is, by talent and temperament, an artist, with the power to do fine work. No play of his which is not good can be described as 'inoffensive.' Indifferent work by a duffer might be so described. But indifferent work by Mr Parker is offensive in a very high degree. And *Captain Birchell's Luck* is not merely indifferent: it is thoroughly bad. I am told that it was not written recently, that it is merely a revision of a play produced somewhere in the early 'nineties. That may be. But the fact that Mr Parker has suffered it to be reproduced in its present form is evidence that he thought it not unworthy of him. And it is this lack of self-pride, of self-criticism, for which, with tears in my eyes, I am venturing to chide Mr Parker.

I wish I had exhausted my space. Not having done so, I must proceed to give a few details about *Captain Birchell's Luck*, that painful theme. The main idea is a rather promising one. Captain Birchell is a drunkard. He has fallen desperately in love with a girl, and married her without telling her of his deplorable tendency. She finds him out, detests him. He is still desperately in love with her. Such is the state of things at the beginning of the first act, and it contains, obviously, the germs of an interesting play. But Mr Parker hastens to eradicate and destroy those germs with a truly scientific hand. Captain Birchell announces his intention of joining the inevitable expedition to the wilds of Africa and of either dying or coming back respectable. Why the wilds of Africa should be considered a sovereign remedy for good fellows gone wrong, I really do not know. It is one of those stage conventions which I have never been able to understand. However, Captain Birchell is a firm believer in the cure, and off he goes. Just before he starts, he finds that his wife is going to stay in the same house with an eligible young man. (Her marriage has been kept secret, by the way.) He throws some brandy into the fire, and the fire flares up as the curtain falls. In the next act, he is supposed to have perished, and duly appears with a beard and no waistcoat. He tells his father-in-law that he has 'kept straight.' It would tax one's ingenuity to conjecture how he could have done otherwise, for he narrates that he has been down with cholera at Alexandria, then down with a poisoned wound in the wilds of Africa, and then, again, down with a terrible fever. The father-in-law, however, does not trouble about the quality of this redemption. His one aim is to get rid of the Captain, in view of his daughter's chance of marrying the eligible young man. He gives him some brandy. I do not quite see how the brandy serves the father-in-law's ends. But it enables Mr Parker to bring down the curtain on a noisy tableau: the intoxicated Captain shouting and gesticulating at his wife just as her betrothal is announced. In the last act, the dramatis personae are discovered, according to custom, in somewhat reduced circumstances—all except the eligible young man, who has now succeeded (I think) to an earldom, and comes to offer Mrs Birchell guilty splendour on the Riviera. Mrs Birchell, who has gone on the stage, rejects him. She throws some hot-house flowers on the fire, one by one. Her lover retires, much chagrined, leaving the course clear for the Captain, who—delicate fellow that he is!—has been down with something at St Thomas's Hospital and has, presumably, 'kept straight.' The re-united pair are going to America, when the curtain falls. We, the audience, are left confident that the Captain will be down with something else long before the boat is signalled off Sandy Hook, and we hope that the intervals between his subsequent prostrations will be brief enough to keep him worthy of his wife's regard. But I cannot say that his history has not bored us. And I cannot congratulate his historian.

[*4 November 1899*]

## A PLEA FOR THE MIMES

But for the war, this little book\* would probably have attracted some attention and kindled some wrath. The author does not say much that is new, but he says the old things lucidly and provocatively. Sure sign that he is in earnest, his title-page bears a quotation from John Stuart Mill, and all persons who have disparaged histrionic art—from Plato to Mr Birrell—are solemnly evoked into his pages; all except Mr George Moore, whose essay on 'Mummer Worship' is carefully ignored, perhaps because it anticipated too exactly the author's attitude and manner. 'Mummer Worship'

\* *The Actor and his Art*. By Stanley Jones, Downey and Co

made a sensation. This repetition of it has made none. Not because it is less able, but simply because it has happened to coincide with a national crisis. I doubt not that the author, Mr Stanley Jones, is very glad that his book has thus fallen flat. For he was moved to write it by his indignation at the amount of interest which the English nation takes in actors, and in the hope that his pleading might induce us to diminish that interest. He saw in actors a ridiculous, dangerous obsession for the public. Now, perhaps, he realises that his fears were exaggerated, and that there are times when we forget all about actors, and are not excited by attacks on them. For his comfort, I assure him that I myself am much more interested in the war than in his book, and that I am writing about the latter merely because I am a dramatic critic, not a military expert, and because there is no new play for me to write about this week.

No one, to the best of my knowledge, has ever attempted to persuade the public that acting is the highest of the arts. Mr Stanley Jones insists that this attempt has been made, and that public taste has been degraded by it. As though public taste could be degraded! But, at least, many persons have tried to persuade the public that acting is not an art at all, and Mr Jones proceeds to trot out their prejudices. He suggests that 'the picture of a middle-aged gentleman, sitting before a glass, painting his face, may have moved many to a feeling for the mimic art other than of respect and admiration.' Why? One might as well despise literature because there are middle-aged writers who dip their pens in ink-pots, and middle-aged painters who squeeze tubes over palettes. 'But,' asks Mr Jones, 'what is the art of acting but the cultivation of the very meanest of faculties—the faculty of imitation.' And what else are the arts of literature and painting? 'We are all actors—more or less,' says Mr Jones. And we are all writers—more or less—nowadays. But has the Board School caused literature to cease as a fine art? 'The playgoer may recall performances by children among the pleasantest of his recollections of the theatre. Is there any other art of which it can be said that the mystery of it is within the comprehension of a little child?' For my own part, I can recall only one or two children whose performances were not utterly excruciating by reason of their incapacity to understand and to feel the parts they were playing. The only reason why children are sometimes allowed on the stage is that adults cannot 'make-up' as children. If they could, you may be sure that the race of child-actors would very soon cease to exist. Likewise, if middle-aged ladies could make themselves look really young, you may be sure that the young ladies who play 'ingénues' would go by the board. These young ladies act better than children, but, with very rare exceptions, they do not act at all well. They have not had time to master the technique of acting. Mr Jones wonders 'what there is in acting to be taught?' Little enough to be taught, perhaps; but very much to learn. He declares that 'the appearance on the stage of late of many young men who have been prepared for life at the public schools and the Universities' is proof that no academic training is needed. It is no proof. For these young men have not been accepted as good actors. They are obviously inexperienced, as yet. As a matter of fact, one needs no proof that academic training is unnecessary to a mime. No sensible person ever pretended that it was. But that fact does not dispose of mimetic art. That it may, as Mr Jones says, be 'picked up promiscuously,' need be accounted no shame to it. The art of literature may be picked up in that way. In cannot, indeed, be picked up in any other way. Mr Jones is more specious when he taunts the actor with being a dependent artist. No one will deny that the actor does not write his own part. But it is not fair to say that he 'is simply giving expression to ideas put into his head.' The ideas put into his head by the playwright—the typewritten words for him to speak, the stage directions, the verbal hints —are simply the material on which he has to work. Out of them he creates his part. He is, in fact, a creative artist, like any other. When he exactly realises (as, I am told, he does now and again) the dramatist's conception, he is none the less creative. When, as in the ordinary course of things, he makes the character something entirely unlike what the dramatist meant it to be, his claim to the creative spirit is still less deniable. Nor can I see any reason in Mr Jones's attempt to belittle him on the ground that he must have an audience. Mr Jones is wrong in thinking that 'a poet writes simply to please himself.' True, a poet takes his own judgment as the measure of his work, not the judgment of other people; but none the less, as a human being, he cannot write without the incentive that other people will see what he has written. Even the poems of Rossetti and Mr Robert Bridges were passed round privately, as they were written; and their subsequent publication shows that even the haughtiest, most esoteric artists have a lurking love of large audiences. Unlike poets, and like the ancient bards, actors must do their work in the presence of an audience; else it would never be known at all. This is a disadvantage, perhaps. But it is no argument against the actor.

Altogether, Mr Jones has failed to show cause why actors should not be treated with as much respect as are other artists. He has, also, failed to show that there is any tendency to worship them as demigods. There was a social craze for them in the 'eighties, but that has long passed over, and actors are no more 'sought after' than painters or poets. It is true that the public is more interested in actors than in other artists, and that the newspapers, consequently, print about actors' private affairs a great many details which are not more tedious to Mr Jones than to me. But why wonder at this state of things? Why rail at it? The public does not see writers or painters. It does see actors, and wants, therefore, to know all about them. In all ages, good actors have been interesting to the public. But there were not always newspapers. Now that there are, much 'space' is bound to be devoted to actors. But, really, Mr Jones exaggerates the amount of attention paid to them and their art, and he exaggerates the harm done by it. Does he really believe, as he suggests, that the decadence of learning at Cambridge is largely due to it? And does he really think—how one wishes he were right in thinking!—that Sir Squire Bancroft looms larger in the public gaze than Mr Rudyard Kipling? Let him purge his mind of these morbid fancies, and soften his heart towards actors, remembering the sad case of the gentleman who thought that penwipers were the cause of all the wickedness and misery in the world, and who spent his time in buying or purloining those harmless articles, with the express intention of taking them and dropping them over the edge of the world. In a word, let him cultivate a sense of proportion.

P.S. When I said that I had no play to write about this week, I forgot *The Wrong Mr Wright* (Strand Theatre). The production was not, indeed, memorable. Enough that I saw it, that the audience seemed to be amused by it, and that I seemed not to be.

[*11 November 1899*]

## MISS FLETCHER'S PLAY

The public, forgetting that some things need no demonstration, seldom misses a chance of proving that it is an ape-faced baboon. Accordingly, it hooted at the end of the second act of *The Canary*, and even made some interruptions while the last act was proceeding. I was annoyed, even disgusted, by its conduct. Hooting, even at the end of play, is, in my opinion, quite disgraceful and outrageous. If the author has written a play which does not seem to the public a good play, is that any reason why the author should be treated as an imposter and malefactor? Plays are the only works of art on which the public can stamp indirectly its approval or disapproval. What the public thinks of a play does not, artistically, matter more than what it thinks of a book or a picture. But it is too much to expect the public not to value its opinion and express it as often as it can. I merely suggest that hooting is quite superfluous. Silence would surely be a more decent, and not a less effective, expression of disapproval. I know that there are many critics who uphold the public's right to hoot, but I suspect that their attitude means, not that they have any sincere conviction in the matter, but that they delight in witnessing a brawl. Even they, however, have never contended that the public is justified in hooting before the end of a play. Interruptions are all very well at a political meeting: they give the speaker a chance of making effective retorts and so forth. But actors and actresses are tongue-tied to the dialogue of the play, and have no means of defence. The very fact that they are not responsible for the words spoken by them should prevent any brute from trying to disconcert and dishearten them at their work. Nor is my objection merely in behalf of the mimes. These interruptions are often exasperating to many persons in the audience. *The Canary* happened to be a very clever and pretty piece of work. It was original, and made demands on one's intelligence. I wanted to listen to it with both ears, and the fear that the fools who had been interrupting might, at any moment, interrupt again prevented me from doing so. In such circumstances, no critic can do justice to a play. I am quite sure that Mr Archer's opinion of *The Canary* is the result of the public's noisiness on the first night. He was distracted, and so, despite his perspicacity, he missed the point of the play. He tells us that the author had merely travestied the situations frequently found in serious plays, and that her work was in no sense a satire on life. He is, if I may say so, quite wrong. *The Canary* is a very delicate, malicious satire on a certain type of existing persons—the persons who, leading uneventful lives, try to reproduce, and do succeed in travestying, the emotions and adventures which they have found in books or plays. A really romantic nature, with romantic opportunities, is a very rare thing. Most of the romance in modern life is merely faked from books. Given a sentimental, vapid woman, with a prosaic husband and a subscription to Mudie's, you may be pretty sure that she will pose, pretend and idealise, and be on the look out for someone to pose, pretend and idealise with her. Of course, she may end by finding real emotions; but the chances are that her emotions will be conditioned by what she has read. Such a lady is Mrs Temple-Martin, in *The Canary*, and Miss Fletcher presents her flutterings with great skill and humour. Mrs Temple-Martin meets a young man who is as vapid as herself, and as indifferent to her as she is to him; thus, nothing serious occurs, and the play is kept within the bounds of farcical comedy. In real life, Mrs Temple-Martin might, of course, have met a man who would have taken advantage of her. To a clever and unscrupulous man such ladies are a fairly easy prey. But their case would have been alien to Miss Fletcher's light intent. I think, however, that Miss Fletcher might have made her play even more true and amusing if she had let the lover be a prosaic man, genuinely attracted by Mrs Temple-Martin, and without the intelligence to understand her. By making the lover a person of the same temperament as the lady, Miss Fletcher has cut the safest ground from under her feet. It is unlikely that either of the two would have gone beyond furtive flirtation, whereas is is necessary for the fun of the play that there should be, at least, some attempt at elopement. Miss Fletcher makes Mrs Temple-Martin take the initiative; but, though the result is amusing, one feels that the real Mrs Temple-Martin never would have left her husband's 'roof,' and that Miss Fletcher, in making her do so, has gone dangerously near making her not ridiculous. The lover ought certainly to have been a sane and unimaginative, but ardent, creature. The contact of the two would have made an even better motive than Miss Fletcher has chosen. I once heard of a curious incident in real life, which I commend to Miss Fletcher's attention. A rather pretty, rather silly lady met at a tea-party a distinguished soldier. She talked to him in the vein peculiar to her and to many of her kind. She said that women ought to live their own lives, that the conventions were all wrong, that life was made up of exquisite moments, that fidelity was so drab, and so on. Next day, he called. She was alone, and he went straight to the point: he said that he loved her. She rushed to the bell, screaming. The soldier seized his hat and rushed down the stairs and out of the house, under the impression that he had been lured into a blackmailer's den. Miss Fletcher might have made this incident, or something like it, the basis of her play. But I am concerned, after all, with the play as she has written it, and I find it a delicious farcical comedy. Miss Fletcher is to be congratulated on having been content to accept the limitations of her sex, to write lightly and slyly and prettily, without attempting to be grim or strong or in any way terrible. Mrs Campbell was irresistibly amusing as the heroine, playing with all the solemnity and intensity which would mark the behaviour of the real Mrs Temple-Martin. And the rest of the cast were all good, except —for once—Miss Rosina Filippi, who seemed afraid of her part.

'(*Enter* HORACE PARKER.

H.P.—It's beastly cold.'

When, in the solitude of his study, Mr Richard Ganthony, author of *A Message from Mars*, wrote these simple words, did he, I wonder, foresee that they would one day drive an audience to the verge of hysterics? Did he, in the manner of Thackeray, drop his pen and ejaculate 'By Jove! That's genius'? I doubt it. The use of 'beastly' as an adverb is common enough in our vernacular, and is not to be relied on as a lever for laughter. Nor is the idea of cold weather, in itself, very ridiculous. True, if the action of the play passed in summer, Horace Parker's line might have a kind of incongruity; but the time is mid-winter: there is 'snow without,' and Horace Parker enters in a fur coat. Would that Mr Ganthony had been, not (as announced) in America, but present at the Avenue, to see the audience rocking, and me, even me, smiling, when Horace Parker (Mr Charles Hawtrey) said that it was beastly cold! Successful dramatists (of whom Mr Ganthony is now one) are apt to be uppish. They subscribe so quickly to that old doctrine of theorists who don't go inside theatres: that the actor is but a will-less puppet, an empty vessel to be filled, a conch to be blown through. And how wrong they are! Put a good actor into a bad part, and the part will generally seem good to the public; and *vice versâ*—the dramatist is quick enough to accept that converse. Let a popular comedian come on, saying that it's beastly cold, and the result must ever be that which I noted at the Avenue. But perhaps Mr Ganthony does not need to be enlightened. I suspect that he wrote his play with (at least) one eye on Mr Hawtrey; else, surely, he would not have taken the trouble he has taken to make Scrooge a modern young man, of the type in which Mr Hawtrey excels, and to give him so many lines of the kind which Mr Hawtrey speaks so well. ('It's beastly cold' is not a fair sample of Mr Ganthony's work: his dialogue is full of very real and agreeable humour.) He would have commandeered the old Scrooge, and the old Marley's ghost, as he found them, and would have left modernity and Mr H. G. Wells severely alone. And I do not doubt that his play would have achieved a great success somewhere, for he seems to have quite a considerable talent for dramatic writing; but its success would have been paltry in comparison with that which it will now achieve at the Avenue. Here, indeed, is every symptom of a prolonged far-reaching triumph. The sentiments of forty years ago, an up-to-date setting, and Mr Hawtrey—three things which are very near to the heart of the public! The selfish young man of the period compelled by a good Spirit to distribute eighty-two pounds in the street, and to perform sundry other deeds of mercy, while 'Follow the Man from Cook's' is played by the orchestra! The good Spirit, hailing from Mars, can and does work all kinds of miracles and illusions on the stage, in the intervals of getting the community pauperised; and I need not say that Mr Hawtrey follows the Man from Maskelyne and Cook's to the goal of perfect redemption. There is also a struggling inventor, a long-lost daughter, and a ragged child who, being asked whether he is happy, says 'Happy? What's that?' In fact, I have never seen a play so obviously stamped with the scarlet seal of success. Either it will run interminably in London, in the provinces, in America, in Australasia, and, indeed, wherever men speak the language it is written in, or my name is not MAX.

[*25 November 1899*]

## BELLONA IN OXFORD STREET

They call the play at the Princess's *The Absent-Minded Beggar*, or *For Queen and Country*. The sub-title is well enough; but why drag in Mr Rudyard Kipling? He, in his turn, may drag in many members of the public, (though surely there is a gold-mine for the management which shall make its house an unique sanctuary from his poem;) but anyone who is drawn by the title will be disappointed and, perhaps, resentful. For the play has nothing to do with the pervasive creature of Mr Kipling's fancy. The hero is simply our old friend, the gently-nurtured, falsely-accused young man who enlists and takes his wife out to the war. The curtain has not been up for five minutes before we know him to be provident, chaste, thoughtful—free, in fact, from any taint of absent-mindedness. When, at the end of the first act, he is betrayed by the villain (an Afrikander) to the father of the heroine he is kissing, one feels that no one but a villain could have been so stupid as not to foresee that 'She is my wife!' would bring the curtain triumphantly down. I had some hope in the second act that we were to get, after all, a study in absent-mindedness. An acknowledged burglar came to the barracks, bent on being enlisted. His wife clung to his arm, sobbing. He shook her off very callously. I pricked up my ears. 'Better,' said the burglar, 'to die with a bullet through your heart than to finish with a rope round your neck!' After that, I gave up all hope of seeing Mr Kipling's creation across footlights. I felt that I had been brought on false pretences, and I was vexed. Mr Kipling's psychology of the private soldier interests me. I am inclined to believe that the average private soldier is as Mr Kipling represents him, and I should like to see him, with all his faults and his virtues, in the three dimensions of the stage. Even the most vividly realistic writer on paper cannot make his creations so actual, so real to us, as might a writer for the theatre. The trouble is that writers for the theatre think first of the public, then of previous plays, then (if at all) of life. And so it comes that the only plausible picture of a private soldier has been made by Mr Kipling. What a pity that Mr Arthur Shirley, author of the Princess's piece, did not make some effort to dramatise Mr Kipling's idea, and so live up to his catching title! He need not in this case have been afraid to make his hero imperfect. The public has already been educated by Mr Kipling's poem to forgive the private his imperfections, to regard them as necessary, inherent elements of his character. The lesson, the well-learnt lesson, of the poem is that one must not expect to find all the civic virtues in a good fighter; that such tendencies as gallantry and improvidence are part of his nature; that if he were in time of peace a more exemplary person he would cut less of a dash in the wars; in fact, that Nature does not let the world have it both ways, and that men who are endowed with more than the average of one quality must pay for it with a more than average lack of another. I am glad that Mr Kipling's popularity and his popular sense have enabled him to drive his lesson home, eclipsing the vogue of two poems which had, as poems, greater artistic merit than his—'Let 'em all come' and 'A little bit off the top.' By the way, it is a pity that, whereas the reciters and singers of Mr Kipling's poem are innumerable, the one man who could have rendered it quite satisfactorily has retired from active labour. The Great Macdermott—I am, alas! just old enough to remember how Great he was—has withdrawn his incomparable presence from the boards. Why was he not persuaded to return awhile? What a companion-picture to Cincinnatus at the plough: the Great Macdermott, surprised in the back-garden of his well-earned villa, and implored to place again at the service of the State that minatory forefinger of his, those polyboöphonous lungs! Mr Kipling can receive no greater tribute than that his poem has electrified the land without the help of that other Great man.... However, why should I be sneering at Mr Kipling? Reaction against him and all his works will set in soon enough. He will be not less under-rated than he has been over-rated, and then—then I shall be sorry I sneered. Besides, if Mr Kipling had not, in the past year or two, been making a guy of his Muse, he would never (not having Tennyson's extraneous gift for fusing Sunday School with Board School) have been able to make the mob caper to his piping and to force on it, incidentally, the sound moral of his latest effusion.

Thackeray, another artist whose extraneous qualities saved him from unpopularity, declares, in the twenty-sixth chapter of *Pendennis*, that he, like Warrington, is 'quite ready to protest' against the doctrine 'that men of letters, and what is called genius, are to be exempt from the prose duties of this daily, bread-winning, tax-paying life, and are not to be made to work and pay like their neighbours.'

I suspect that Mr Kipling, also, would be 'quite ready to protest.' Nor, I fancy, would Thackeray have disapproved of "The Absent-Minded Beggar" if he had heard it recited in the Cave of Harmony (or whatever the place was called). And yet, the doctrine of that poem is on all fours with the very 'doctrine' which made him and Warrington so angry. For doing good work, the man of letters or of any other art is as poorly rewarded by his country as is the soldier in time of peace, and his very power for good work—that constant abstraction and absorption without which good work cannot be done—does disable him from performing well and profitably 'the prose duties' of citizenship. He, like the soldier, is ill-balanced, lopsided. Nature has not given it him 'both ways.' He is a creature to be dealt gently with, to be forgiven many lapses, to be 'let off' many tasks which other men must be made to perform. He is, moreover, a creature to be endowed, because he cannot earn, and because his efforts to earn are the destruction of his work. This seems to you reader, as to Thackeray, a maudlin plea. Mr Kipling's parallel plea seems to you quite robust and righteous. If Mr Kipling had called the artist—and how aptly he might have called him!—an 'Absent-Minded Beggar,' and have made him the subject of an appeal to you, you would not have given a single shilling. If he had said

'When you've had your glut of *Nikola* and *Stalky* the unclean,
　When you've chucked the bones of *Dooley* to the crows,
Will you kindly drop a shilling in my little tambourine
　For a gentleman in slippers, writing Prose?'

you would doubtless have sent even *his* tambourine empty away. And yet, is the artist's lot not one for pity and homage and succour? Must not he, too, renounce and live hardly, be brave and obedient and enduring? True, all his labours he accepts willingly, because he loves them. He rejoices in his work. But so does the soldier in his. The soldier loves fighting; but does that make him less a hero? The soldier who kills twenty men is honoured by you, rightly, for his courage. But the artist may produce for his pleasure twenty masterpieces, and you take *them*—if you take them at all—as a matter of course. For him whom your charity might enable to produce masterpieces you take no thought whatsoever. (I admit that, if you did, the fund might be rather hard to administer discreetly.) And the mere notion that such a man is to be pardoned, on account

## BELLONA IN OXFORD STREET

of his power, anything which would be unpardonable in yourself—that is altogether outside the range of your comprehension. Yet Mr Kipling can open wide your hearts and your minds and your pockets for the soldier. The contrast is significant. The art of warfare still appeals to you all; the fine arts still appeal only to an embarrassed few. Do not imagine that I think a single one of the shillings for the Kipling fund misgiven, or that I admire less warmly than you those qualities of courage and endurance which your soldiers are displaying. I am as much moved as you by the glory and horror of war. But my sympathy is not bounded by my admiration of fine qualities displayed in actual violence. Art, too, has its heroes for me.

I find that I have said little about the play at the Princess's. Indeed, since it deals with the actual and present warfare in South Africa, of which the bare reports must obviously eclipse any mere theatrical version, I have little or nothing to say. To me, moreover, there is something unseemly in the act of watching a theatrical version of that terribly real thing which, done with real bloodshed, is causing agony and desolation for so many thousands of people. However, the audience, less squeamish than I, seemed to enjoy the play thoroughly. It is, perhaps, a very good military melodrama. It seemed to be well-acted, too. Mr Lawrance D'Orsay had, as usual, an idotic part; but he contrived, at one point, to show that he could act finely if ever a dramatist were to let him do something besides twist his moustache and call people 'chappies'—has anyone, I wonder, ever heard the word 'chappies' outside a theatre? Miss Lillah McCarthy played the heroine (admirably) in the old-fashioned convention. I have always held that convention to be the best for melodrama. If you say and do unnatural things, you ought, *prima facie*, to say and do them in an unnatural manner. I remember a melodrama in which the hero (Mr Terriss) was turned out of his manor-house by the villain and became a picturesque blacksmith. The villain came to the forge to gloat over the hero's fall. 'A pretty thing,' he said, 'to see the squire's son turning out new shoes!' The reply, 'Better turn out new shoes than old tenants!' has always seemed to me the type of all good lines in melodrama, and I have never been able to conceive that it could have been spoken otherwise than it was spoken by Mr Terriss. But Mr H. B. Warner, as the hero of this new play, half-convinced me that the modern convention also may be made effective. He said the wildest things in a perfectly natural way, and

I was so amazed that for the moment the things sounded to me just the kind of things I might have said myself. At the same time, he never failed to get his round of applause from the gallery. So ingenious a person must, I imagine, have a rather brilliant future.

[*2 December 1899*]

## 'CHILDREN OF THE GHETTO'

You know what happens when a well-known writer of books takes the oath and his seat in the House of Commons. The air is charged at once with deferential welcome of one who cannot fail to be an ornament to the Chamber, and with a quiet, stolid conviction that he will (and determination that he shall) be one of the most ineffectual bores in the House. It is even so when the well-known writer of books makes his *début* in the theatre. Let anyone who goes to the first night watch the dramatic critics. In their ingenuous faces he will be able to read, even before the curtain rises, every word they will scribble when the play is over. 'Mr——— has made for himself an unique place among contemporary novelists, and it is not too much to say that, as such, he appeals to as wide a public as any.' &c. &c. 'At the same time it must be borne in mind that the qualities which command success in the sphere of drama are not necessarily those which' &c. &c.

Well! there is, sometimes, something to be said for this attitude. A man endowed with real literary talent is as unlikely to acquire a talent for the tricks of the theatre as he is to acquire a House of Commons manner. Also—a more important point—he is as unlikely to possess an instinct for dramaturgy (a different thing from playing the tricks of the theatre) as he is to possess an instinct for politics or statecraft. The chances are that if he honestly try to write good plays he will be as ineffectual as Bulwer Lytton was in the House, or as Sir George Trevelyan, if he try to please the public at the expense of himself. There have been, I admit, men who could write both good plays and good books. But such cases are rare exceptions. Thus, on the whole, the dramatic critics are justified in anticipating failure for the true man of letters. Where I differ from them is in their sulky mistrust of a man merely because he is a successful author. Mr

Zangwill is a successful author, but this fact was not nearly enough to make me assume that he could not write a good play. The evidence I accumulated last Monday at the Adelphi all goes to prove that he cannot write a good play. But there was not, I suggest, any *prima facie* case against him. Mr Zangwill, despite his many books and many editions, has not, really, any claim to be regarded as a man of letters. Certainly, he has an intellect, and a personality, and a point of view. But all the books of his which I have tried to read have merely proved to me that literature is not the form through which he ought to express himself. Let me explain. There is all the difference in the world between writing and being a writer; though the inclusion of writing with reading and arithmetic in our schools' curriculum has induced a general delusion that anyone can be a writer. People think that anyone who has something to say and writes it on paper is a writer. He is not necessarily so. Writing is a means of expression, certainly; but so are painting, musical composition, dramaturgy. And the true writer must have a specific gift for writing, as has the painter for painting, the—my readers will save me the trouble of completing the sentence. Be not afraid! I am not talking about 'style,' though that is what I myself care most about. A man may be unable to find the exact words for his meaning, or, finding them, may be unable to arrange them harmoniously, and yet may possess a specific gift for literature. Not even the haters of Mr Kipling's work—and I belong to that 'acute and upright minority'—deny that Mr Kipling is a writer, a man predestined by nature to express himself in writing, a man whose soul is in his books and could not otherwise be revealed to us. Nothing irritates me more than the lately-renewed cant that literature is merely what is written by noble thinkers. Granted, that great books can only be written by great men; but emphatically denied that you need only be a great man to write great books. You may be a very great man, full of the noblest and most penetrating thoughts, full of imagination, wit and what not, and yet be utterly incapable of writing. Let us, for the sake of argument, admit that Mr Gladstone was a very great man. If his fame were to depend on his writings, would he not have been long forgotten as a most tedious mediocrity? And again, are there not many quite little men, like Horace and Charles Lamb, whose writings are immortal? Horace and Charles Lamb happened to have pleasant little natures, plus a gift for writing. Mr Gladstone had no such gift. Mr Zangwill has proved in his writings that he himself has no such gift. I am not, as you may suspect, unfair to him. I am not judging him by the coarse humours he evolved under the influence of Mr Jerome K. Jerome. I am judging him by his later *causeries*, and by his studies in Jewish life—*Dreamers of the Ghetto* and other books. Here, surely, was a man striving, plodding, floundering in a medium he never was meant for. Here was a man with ideas which, when he tried to wing them with live words, he did but bury under piles of dead words, leaving us to disinter them if we could. Here was a man with an interesting and new subject-matter, which, for all his knowledge of it, and for all his love of it, he succeeded in making tedious. *Dreamers of the Ghetto* was worth reading, though it was a bore. Many blue-books are worth reading. They are suggestive, instructive, if one is strong enough not to mind being bored by them. But the compilers of them are not literary men. Nor is he who compiled those books about the Ghetto a literary man. Had I accepted him as one, I should have expected his play to be bad—so widely different are literature and drama. As it was, I thought that possibly he might have found in dramaturgy a medium through which he could express himself well, and could make, at last, good use of his admirable subject-matter—

> 'This life that links us with purple past
> Of Babylon and Egypt, all the vast
> Enchantment of the ancient Orient,
> And yet with London and New York is blent.'

My readers must excuse me for quoting these lines from the prologue —Mr Zangwill's verse is, if anything, rather better than his prose. At any rate, these lines show one how alive Mr Zangwill is to the fascination of his theme. If he had written a play about something in which he took but slight interest, then the badness of his play would not have been positive proof that he could not write a good play. But the badness of *Children of the Ghetto* moves me to advise him not to attempt other plays. I am sorry he cannot express himself through drama any more than he can through fiction. He might turn his hand to painting, or he might give a series of public lectures, or he might compose an opera. I urge him to leave no mode of expression untried, for my belief in him makes me really sorry he should continue to be inarticulate. But in dramaturgy he can only waste his time. I do not say this because he has no sense of construction, the whole of his first act being occupied with a little incident which ought to have been merely explained by one of the characters, in a very few words, as having previously occurred. Sense of construction may be acquired. It is because Mr Zangwill has no power of making his puppets live that I advise him to leave dramaturgy alone. When the conflicts come—a conflict between a young man and the old man whose daughter he loves, a conflict between the young man and the girl—one does not care twopence about them because none of the conflicting characters has drawn one breath of life or contains one drop of blood. The young man, we know, is a millionaire and a lax Jew; the old man is a strict Rabbi; the girl accepts the hand of the young man. But that is all we know about them. Never for one moment does Mr Zangwill make them live. They are not more human than the A, B and C at the corners of a triangle in Euclid. 'Why,' soliloquises the girl, forced to choose between her lover on one hand, her faith and her father on the other, 'why is this terrible alternative forced on me?' That is Mr Zangwill's notion of a heart-cry, and it is typical of all the writing in the play. Mr Zangwill, knowing that it is the kind of thing dramatists are expected to do, devises a 'terrible alternative' for the chief character; but he cannot make the chief character express such emotion as is produced by 'terrible alternatives' in real life. He can make her see (what he sees) that she is in a dramatic position; but there his power ends; and, unfortunately, it is there that a dramatist's power begins. Many men can propound problems, contrive situations, manufacture puppets. But to live in the puppets, and so make them live for us, and so, too, make real for us the situations they appear in and the problems they illustrate—that is the test of the dramatist.

*El Capitan* did not fill me with a desire to see strenuous Mr De Wolf Hopper again. Perhaps it was for this reason that the manager of the Comedy Theatre, having invited me to the first night of *The Mystical Miss*, placed me behind a column, through which Mr Hopper was invisible. The better way would have been not to invite me at all. There are many places in which one cannot see Mr Hopper more comfortable than the little house in Panton Street, and I went to one of them soon after the curtain had risen.

[ *16 December 1899* ]

## ANCIENT AND MODERN

The dim hall of Lincoln's Inn, dimmer than ever by reason of a fog which, meaning to assert the triumph of modernity, had forced its way into those precincts, only to find itself intensifying their antique mystery and grandeur; a narrow stage at one end of the hall, backed with a dark tapestry; and, posturing thereon, cloaked and capped, and clad in a proper suit of black stripes and yellow, the ridiculous and immortal Sganarelle; and Gusman, attentive beside him. One would have said that Watteau's 'L'Amour au Théâtre Italien' was hanging before our eyes, that only the fog prevented us from distinguishing any of the familiar figures except Pantaleone and the torch-lit clown. I do not remember a more curious or distinguished effect on a stage. Costumes designed by an artist, and worn, with a sense of posture, against a dark background and on a little stage—that is an effect one never finds in the ordinary theatre. And how fascinating, to find it somewhere! Our pictorial sense never delights in huge, crowded, garishly-lit stages. Such effects may be demanded by our dramatic sense. There are plays which must be mounted 'lavishly,' with elaborate and realistic effects. Indeed, one may say that every real *play* ought to be mounted in such a way as to leave nothing to the imagination. Shakespeare wrote real plays. His aim was to produce in the spectators an absolute illusion of reality, even when he was dealing with a fantastic and unreal life. In his day the arts of building and lighting the stage, of scene-shifting, and of designing appropriate costumes, were still in a state of undevelopment; and, consequently, his plays had to be produced in the manner which the Elizabethan Stage Society has revived for them. To compare these revivals with the ordinary modern productions is to be convinced that if Shakespeare could come to life again he would give Mr Poel a wide berth, and would hurry to the nearest commercial theatre in which a play of his happened to be running. He would be the first to admit that the modern method of production is a great convenience, and to welcome everything which contributes to illusion—all the imitations of distance, of sunlight or moonlight, of trees, palaces, cottages—everything, in fact, which saves one the trouble of imagining the accessories and so enables one to be illuded by the essentials. Shakespeare's plays, as produced by the E.S.S. cannot appeal to us as drama. One may be interested in the productions as object-lessons in a branch of archaeology, but one would no more admit that they had any aesthetic value than one would desire, in taking an Elizabethan house, to have an installation of Elizabethan drainage. I repeat my admission that a dim, simple, shabby little stage, with well-dressed and well-posed figures on it, makes a far more charming picture than is to be found in the ordinary theatre; but I repeat also that such a stage is not a fit place for the performance of plays. I enjoyed immensely the E.S.S.'s production of *Don Juan*, for the simple reason that *Don Juan* is not a play. It is only a fable—a deliciously witty fable for recitation in public. It has no kind of connexion with any kind of drama. It makes no appeal to our emotions, no demand on our credulity. All we have to do is to sit, watch and listen, while the figures come on, talk to one another, express their opinions and go off again. There are no characters—only a set of puppets, the biggest of which carries a distinctive label. Consequently, there is no development, no conflict—in fine, no drama. Never for one moment does one puppet affect another; never do their wires become entangled. Don Juan is lectured by his servant, appealed to by his victim, reproached by his father, menaced by the statue; but he is not deflected one inch in any direction. And this immobility of his was not meant by Molière for a characteristic. He is immobile simply because he has no existence, except as an abstract type, and as a conch for Molière's irrelevant wit, humour, philosophy and what not. Molière was a witty and humorous philosopher—never more so, surely, than when he wrote *Don Juan*. Any recitation of this fable must be delightful. By the Elizabethans, last week, it was recited with real gusto and spirit. I hope they will give us more of Molière. If literary men would only cease cutting their fingers with the tools of dramaturgy, and would write in the convention of Molière, what a good thing it would be for all of us! The stage is not made for drama alone. There is charm in mere entertainments, as Mr George Edwardes and his kind have often proved. Of course, the public prefers music and dancing and singing to the expression of philosophic humour and literary grace. Such 'plays' as I have suggested would appeal only to a few people. But surely those few would not be too few to subsidise some little hall.

Time, that malicious harlequin, who with a sweep of his wand strikes the blossoms from the almond-tree and the tuneful pipe from the faun's lips, and the wings from the flying fairy's shoulders—Time, sworn foe to all that is fresh and sweet and dear to us, has caused Mr Jerome Klapka Jerome to become haughty. No more are we beckoned up to the two-pair-back, and told, with many a wink and homely jerk of thumb over shoulder, all about 'the slavey.' Our simple instructor has unlearnt all that he taught us, and now, thinking the genteel thoughts of a genteel fellow, writes for us stories about people with titles, and even dabbles in metaphysis. In his latest play, (*Miss Hobbs*, at the Duke of York's,) there is no 'slavey' at all. There is a lady's-maid, but even she is not really a member of the lower classes—is but a young lady who, for reasons of her own, masquerades as a maid, in clothes far more suggestive of an Arcadian shepherdess. Shall I adumbrate the plot? The young lady (Miss Hobbs) is a hater of men, and the play is the history of her conversion. She is young, pretty, without past tragedy. She has, in fact, no reason to hate men. In real life, no woman hates men unless she has reason to hate some man. Even as a woman always shirks general questions by reference to some personal question, so does she, conversely, deduce a general law from every personal experience. Thus, the man-hating woman is always one whose husband or lover has used her ill, or whose nature is such as to prevent her from having either. The conversion of such a woman would be a good motive for comedy, and an opportunity for moral-pointing. Mr Jerome—I judge by his tedious disquisitions in the third act—wishes to point a moral. I submit to him that morals can be pointed only through characters copied from life. If you make your chief character an impossibility, moralising is a mere impertinence. What one demands in fantastic comedy is humour, prettiness, technical ingenuity; and Mr Jerome supplies nothing but vulgarity, dullness, ugliness, clumsiness. I note that most of the critics found some charming qualities in *Miss Hobbs*. They do not, however, adduce any samples of these qualities. I may safely defy them to do so. Indeed, the play is contemptible throughout, and any critic who suggests that it has redeeming merits is either insincere or incompetent. A melancholy dilemma! Dramatic critics have a duty, and that duty is, not to praise a play merely because its vulgarity evokes instant cheers from the public, but to teach the public whether a play is good or bad. Some critics are on a level with the public: not they, but their editors or proprietors, are to be blamed. Other critics know better, and such of them as have praised *Miss Hobbs* are guilty of misconduct in impeding the progress of dramatic art. However, I have wandered from the plot of the play. Mr Jerome set out to show the conversion of a man-hater. Having started by making her impossible, he proceeded, consistently enough, to make her conversion also impossible. Ever since Shakespeare wrote his fantasy about Katharine and Petruchio, it has been supposed by dramatists that a man need only play the cad to make a woman fall desperately in love with him. Shakespeare worked out his paradox poetically, humorously, ingeniously. But did he, I wonder, foresee that generations would accept it as true psychology, and that dull dogs, whose only chance of doing good work is to observe things as they are, would continue to work it out dully, in the delusion that they were copying life? So much is certain; never will it be worked out more dully than by Mr Jerome. His hero makes the usual bet that he will kiss the lady. He has not seen her, but is told that she is coming to the room where he is. Hearing her approach, he hides behind a curtain. She enters, sits down to adjust her hat before a mirror. He darts out, grins over her shoulder and says 'It isn't straight yet!' She scores off him by asking if he is the piano-tuner. He wipes off the score, deftly, by asking if she is the lady's-maid. Such are the flowers of humour with which Klapka—yes! I *will* call him Klapka—decks his play and earns the gratitude of dramatic critics. Poor Miss Evelyn Millard! Poor Mr Herbert Waring! He, being a man, went boldly through with his part. He did not flinch. Chin in the air, shoulders squared, he emitted his lines with a wild pretence of cheerfulness, compelling my admiration. Miss Millard, of a less heroic sex, could not impose on any of us. She had an air of quiet reproach which was made only the more poignant by her furtive efforts to be sprightly. When, taking the hero for the husband of her friend, and thinking to unmask him by inveigling him into a flirtation, she pretended that she really was the lady's-maid, her presence of mind completely gave way. Meaning to assume cockney accent, she snatched faintly at the dialects of Somersetshire, Yorkshire, Buckinghamshire and several other counties. I did not blame her. My feeling was but of indignation that so accomplished an artist should be condemned to interpret Klapka. But again I have wandered from the plot. Nor, indeed, will I return to it, except to mention that when Miss Hobbs, having received good reasons from the hero for detesting him, has fallen madly in love with him, the final scene—the scene of avowed love—opens with the hero's exquisite assurance that when first he met her he did not *really* take her for the lady's-maid. '*I should not*,' he says, '*like you to think I was so bad a judge of faces*....' No, I will not spoil that passage with any comment. It is not necessary to annotate a *locus classicus*. Unnecessary, too, to say that at the close of a play written in this vein, loud and affectionate calls for the author are inevitable. Alas! in this case, the public had to be disappointed. Klapka was not there to take the call. I read lately in some paper that he was on the Continent, and that Count Tolstoi had invited him to pay a visit. It seems—again I quote a paragraph—that he is the only English author whom the Count reads and admires. The Count, as we know, holds that the highest art is that which gives the greatest pleasure to the greatest number of uneducated persons. And yet, there have been no paragraphs to tell us that Mr Hall Caine has been asked to stay with the Count; and we may take that as conclusive evidence that Mr Caine has not been asked. Why this hideous omission of one whose sales must, I imagine, vastly exceed Mr Jerome's? Is it possible that the Count, that prophet, knew that *The Christian* would fail on the stage, whilst *Miss Hobbs* would be the great success it is? Anyhow, it was Klapka who got the invitation. I wonder whether he accepted it. I conceive he would hardly care to stay with so ungenteel a person as the Count. But perhaps he regards anarchical views as pardonable, graceful even, in a man of title. A pleasant picture!—the Count ploughing; Klapka keeping pace with him and reading aloud the MS of *Miss Hobbs*; a series of crooked furrows testifying to the Count's rapture in the play. I do hope that, in deference to his host's real and passionate sympathy with the poor, the humble and the oppressed, Klapka skipped that passage in which he has expressed, so monumentally, his disdain of lady's-maids. 'It wouldn't have done for' the Count; the Count 'would have had a word to say there.'

[*23 December 1899*]

## TWO FARCES

You sometimes see a quite negligible play which contains, as by an accident, one quite remarkable scene; and you remember that play, accordingly, long after you have forgotten others more deserving. *The Masked Ball*, at the Criterion, though it is adapted by that skilful and amusing dramatist, Mr Clyde Fitch, is quite negligible; but I am likely to remember if for years by reason of one remarkable scene in it: a scene in which the heroine feigns drunkenness in order to score off her husband. This made a deep impression on me. I sat shuddering while it lasted. Years hence, may be, I shall still be shuddering to recall it. 'Why?' you wonder, impatiently. And I am bound to fall back on the plea of sentiment. I do not like the idea of a woman drinking too much. That, in this play, the heroine only pretends to have done so, makes no difference to me: the symptoms are the same. Logically, justly, there is nothing more repellent in the idea of a woman drinking too much than in the idea of a man doing so. My predecessor in these columns would have vindicated, irrefragably, woman's right to 'exceed' so long as man might do so with impunity. He would also have expressed his abhorence of 'excess' in man—I remember a tirade of his against Falstaff. But I, though in real life a male drunkard disgusts me, am not disgusted by a genially idealised presentment of a male drunkard. Furthermore, in real life, I am unable to be disgusted by the sight of a man temporarily excited by wine. It follows that I have no possible objection to the stage presentment of a man in that condition. I enjoyed immensely Mr Bourchier's 'Blagden' in the first act of *Wheels within Wheels*. Why, then, should poor Miss Ellaline Terriss have made me shudder a few nights ago? This question is complicated by the fact that I have seen other actresses in parts necessitating the assumption of drunkenness, and have not shuddered. There was *The Benefit of the Doubt*, and, long ago, a play called *Where's the Cat?* Neither Miss Emery nor Miss Rorke made me shudder. At least my shudders for them were aesthetic. In both those plays, the scheme demanded that the heroine should 'exceed.' The result was no more than aesthetically painful—it did not pain me for myself and for the actress personally. In this *Masked Ball* there is no reason —merely an excuse—for the scene. The play is a farce, and the scene is dragged in for the sake of laughter. But to me such scenes are no laughing-matter, are only painful. I don't mind being aesthetically pained by them. But when art does not come into the matter, then I resent them very strongly. It is possible—just possible—that if Miss Ellaline Terriss had acted the scene lightly, imaginatively, in the vein of high comedy, she might have caused me no qualms. But Miss Terriss is not an imaginative comedian, and her notion of tipsiness seems to have been founded on the manner in which Mr Charles Godfrey sings songs of revelry in the music-halls. Even in a man this crude business of lurching and leering and slurring is unpleasant. In a lady it is quite intolerable... 'Man'—'lady,' I see. I suppose I ought to have written 'woman.' But the antithesis came naturally to me, as it comes to most male writers. It is symbolical of the two standards we have for the two sexes. To drink too much may not be gentlemanly; but that does not matter. To drink too much is unladylike; and that does matter. I admit that logically, justly... but why trouble? 'Sentimentally' and 'instinctively' are far more important adverbs, far nearer to the core of civilised humanity.

It is only fair to Miss Terriss to say that she acts very prettily except in the one scene; and to the management to say that Miss Fanny Brough, Mr Seymour Hicks, and many other popular mimes are in the cast.

This is a bad time for the progress of British Drama. In the gusts of a national crisis, that poor little taper, never very bright, will not burn at all. By all means, then, let there be Old English Comedy at the Haymarket. No one—not the management, certainly—will be a penny the worse for it. It is good exercise for the mimes, amuses the public, and conciliates the habitual carpers by showing us that comedy is a quite appreciably better thing than it was when *She Stoops to Conquer* was the *dernier cri*. Ever so far be it from me to belittle Oliver Goldsmith. He was a born dramatist and man of humour. Had he been born forty years ago, he would be writing better comedies than any other man alive. But fate was unkind to him, and this his masterpiece in comedy is no better than the average farce adapted by Mr Blank from the original piece by M. Chose. Compared with the very worst of modern comedies, it were quite despicable. But such a comparison could not be made. The play is only by courtesy a comedy. According to the modern standard, it is rough-and-tumble farce, and nothing more. Labelled types go jogging through a series of complications, misunderstandings, practical jokes. But there is no idea in the play, nothing is illustrated. Nor, though every part is a character-part, are there any characters. Guffaws, loud and thoughtless, are the only things which Goldsmith tried to excite. Were he living now, his ambition would not be so limited. He would observe things, and he would think about them, and would reproduce them accurately and with some meaning. In fact, he would write comedies. The *form* of comedy did not exist in his day—he died, if I remember rightly, two or three years before *The School for Scandal* was produced. And, though we have not anyone endowed with such a combination of humour and technical instinct as was Goldsmith, we may be pardoned for patting one another on the back, and shrugging our shoulders at sight of *She Stoops to Conquer*.

I said that the play would be good exercise for the mimes. Indeed, its survival of so many years is due to the chances it has always offered to mimes. In it they can let themselves go. The more they let themselves go, the better. They do not have to think or feel, for there is nothing to feel or think about; technical experience is here all they want, a base from which to make spirited sallies and eccentric flourishes. The play must be over-acted, or not acted at all. Miss Winifred Emery's passion for over-acting makes her very burdensome in modern comedy. But she is, by reason of it, a most excellent Miss Hardcastle; all the trills and frills of method, the flouncings and bouncings, are not superfluous here, are necessary, are delightful. As Marlow, I am sorry to say, Mr Paul Arthur did not succeed in shaking off his American quietism. He tried to make the part seem possible, and so, of course, only succeeded in destroying it. There is, I hint to him, only one way in which to play the scene of the meeting with Miss Hardcastle; and that is to clown it. To give, as he does, a realistic study in the symptoms of bashfulness is as fatal as the pouring of new wine into old bottles is supposed to be—the fun of the scene, such as it is, is wasted. Mr Cyril Maude and Miss Victor were wildly, and properly, conventional as Mr and Mrs Hardcastle. Nature having intended him to play Tony Lumpkin, Mr George Giddens seconded her with all the resources of art, and deserved every echo of the applause we gave him.

[*13 January 1900*]

## AT HER MAJESTY'S

Surely, Shakespeare never achieved anything more perfect than the *Midsummer Night's Dream*. He, the weaver of wonderful brocades, not even in the noblest of his designs, the most gorgeous or sombre, the most illustriously inlaid and weighed down with jewels, ever fashioned anything whose splendour one would exchange for the fragrance of this idly-woven chaplet of little wildflowers. Idly-woven! That is the secret of its charm. The great poet never so absolutely reveals himself as in those idle moments when, laying aside the grand manner, he lolls, forgets, laughs. Smaller men may assume the grand manner, cheating us with high sounds and tremendous flourishes; it is when they come out of the giant's mantle that we see how small they are. It is when Shakespeare doffs his mantle that we see the giant's limbs, the giant rejoicing in his strength, and performing prodigious feats because he cannot help performing them. Yes! The *Midsummer Night's Dream* is the most impressive of all Shakespeare's works, because it was idly done, because it was a mere overflow of genius, a parergon thrown off by Shakespeare as lightly as a modern author would write an article on International Copyright for an American magazine. It is the most impressive of all the plays, and the loveliest, and the most lovable. I do not wonder that Mr Beerbohm Tree determined to lay hands on it.

This adventure of his was beset with many dangers, and he is to be congratulated on having evaded them. To produce *Julius Caesar* was comparatively safe and easy. The play was full of human drama, which had but to be acted for all it was worth to please everyone. *King John* was more difficult, for it was a dull play, into which humanity had to be foisted by the actors, and it was full of voids which had to be filled up with spectacular effects. But even *King John* was an easy matter in comparison with the *Midsummer Night's Dream*. Of the three separate elements in the play, the fairy element is, of course, the dominating one. The scenes of the clowns and the scenes of the lovers might be done ill without spoiling the play. But the scenes of the fairies must be done well at all costs. There must be the illusion of fairies, illusion of a true dream. And this kind of delicate illusion is hard to produce through the definite and concrete means of the stage, and may be easily destroyed by them. A poet's words, as you read them, will illude you with certain images. But those very images, materialised, may dispel all illusion. Material equivalents for the images made by words are very dangerous things to handle. They must be 'prepared' very cunningly. They must be made faint and mysterious. You remember Pater's gentle rebuke to 'painters who forget that the words of a poet, which only feebly present an image to the mind, must be lowered in key when translated into visible form.' You remember, too, Fuseli's picture of 'Titania and Bottom' in the National Gallery. That picture is a good illustration of Pater's meaning, because it is so very bad an illustration of Shakespeare's. In it all the glamour of the wood near Athens is dispelled. Even the bad light it hangs in fails to imbue it with aught of the mystery it needs. The big fairies look like pupil-teachers, and the little fairies look like freaks in a dime-museum, and Titania looks merely improper. Yet Fuseli, I think, failed less utterly than would any living painter whose work is known to me. And, if it is so hard for a painter, working in two dimensions, not to affront one's imagination, how much harder must it be for the producer of a play, working in three, with solid, live media of flesh and blood! How much greater the trouble and finer the tact, when so much more lowering and mystifying of the tone is needed! I did not suppose it possible that my imagination would not be at every turn affronted in Her Majesty's (and, since Fate has prejudiced me in Mr Tree's favour, I was wondering how I should manage to let him down easily without being altogether dishonest to myself). But my forecast was quite wrong. The production was charming. Though now and again, of course, something or other came out of key, I found myself really and truly illuded by the Wood near Athens. All the little fairies there gambolled in a spontaneous and elfin way; the tuition of them had been carried so far as to make us forget that they were real children, licensed by a Magistrate, and that 'at break of day' they were going to meet, not Oberon, but a certificated Board School teacher. They were dressed like fairies, behaved like fairies—in fact, *were* fairies, for me. The music to which they were dancing seeemd, not to have been incidentally composed by Mendelssohn, but to be the music of the birds in the enchanted wood. Oberon, too, *was* the King of the Fairies, not Miss Julia Neilson; nor did Titania strike me as being Mrs Tree. Nor did I notice Mr Hawes Craven lurking in the bosky shadows of the trees. The only real person who came on to disturb me was Miss Louie Freear. At other times, I have been very glad to see her; but, on this occasion, I resented her presence, especially as it entailed the absence of Puck—dear Puck, whom I really did want to see. Mr Robert Buchanan in these pages once declared himself to be a fairy, and perhaps Miss Freear will be writing to protest that she too is of the engaging race, and so had a right to be in the wood. But, fairy or no fairy, Miss Freear struck a false note whenever she appeared, and I think that Mr Robert Buchanan would have given a far better performance of the part. He, at least, would have shown some sense of the poetry he had to speak. Miss Freear showed none. However, she was the only discordant person in the wood. The others seemed to 'belong there.' I suppose that Mr Sidney Lee would not praise the production so warmly as I. In the elaboration of the woodland scenery he would see a further pandering to the lamentable decay of the imaginative faculty in modern audiences. But the brief performance of *Pyramus and Thisbe* would be after his own heart. When Quince comes on, bearing a board with the inscription 'THIS IS A WOOD,' Mr Sidney Lee, I can well imagine, would cease to frown and would settle down comfortably to enjoy himself. He would see, in his mind's eye, without any effort, a lovely wood ready-grown upon the stage. Even so, according to him, could the Elizabethans see things. But could they? And, if they could, must not there have been, even in those spacious days, a certain effort, a certain strain of the visual organs, the making of which must have distracted their attention from the play? Mr Sidney Lee appears to be distracted only by the actual sight of scenery. But why should he be? Surely, if the scenery is well done—that is, kept in the same relation to the figures of the players as real surroundings bear to persons in real life—there need be no distraction of the kind. If the play is good, and well acted, such scenery cannot be intrusive. On the other hand, bad or skimpy scenery is bound to bother one. It bothered the Elizabethans less than us, because they were accustomed to it. Doubtless, too, good modern scenery would be distracting (at first) to a resurrected Elizabethan, because he would never have seen anything like it. Hansom cabs and bicycles would also puzzle him. But it does not follow that, because modes of locomotion were few and primitive in his day, hansoms and bicycles ought to be abolished. They save us a great deal of time and trouble. Nor have they produced decay in our faculty of walking, though there are many occasions when they are more useful to us than our unaided feet. Even so the developments in modern scenery, which are but a means of quickening dramatic illusion, do not signify that the imagination of the race has been decaying. When the average Victorian reads the *Midsummer Night's Dream* he sees, I am sure, quite as much of a wood as was seen by the average Elizabethan. But reading a play and seeing it acted are two different things. In reading a play, you have to imagine the characters. When you see it acted, the characters are there, as large as life, before your very eyes. Surely, their surroundings ought to be there too. You must imagine either everything or nothing. The only justification for no scenery would be invisible mimes. If the Elizabethans were so imaginative as Mr Lee supposes, why did they want to see their mimes? The fact that they did want to see them suggests that they did not see scenery which was not there. However, I am quite willing to believe that Mr Lee has the faculty which he attributes to them. My contention is merely that no one else has it. And that is his contention, too. So all is well.

[*20 January 1900*]


## MR ANTHONY HOPE'S TALENT

Honour me by accepting an hypothesis. Suppose that Robert Louis Stevenson and Mr Henry James had carried friendship to the pitch of secret collaboration; suppose that the anonymous MS had been lost, and picked up by some fluent journalist, and by him translated, sentence by sentence, into the vernacular; suppose, lastly, that it were published under the pseudonym of 'Anthony Hope.' Would the imposture be transparent? Should we not all accept the book as a characteristic example of Mr Anthony Hope's talent? Some of the experts might say that it showed a 'marked advance;' others, a 'slight falling off;' but none of them, I am sure, would suspect that Mr Hope was not its author.

In Mr Hope's romances there are always the signs of a dual personality: of the exuberant schoolboy, and the nervous, modern adult. The former is all for deeds of derring-do, ''scapes,' 'emprises,' and all the rest of it. Left alone, he would range back into the remote past where such things have free play. But in the remote past there seems to be no scope for the finer shades—the little meticulous points of view and points of honour, the needle-pointed dilemmas in moral etiquette—which preoccupy the nervous, modern adult. So a compromise is made. Time, present; place, remote: Ruritania. And the compromise made by Mr Hope's two selves is that which would have been made by Stevenson and Mr James. Left alone, Stevenson went back to the eighteenth century, partly because Scotland was barbarous and romantic at that time, partly because, putting his narrative into the mouth of someone belonging to that past, he could more freely indulge his love of stately phrases and strange words. But he would have seen at once that it were unfair to drag Mr James thither. He would have agreed that the hero must be modern, but would have held out for romantic conditions in modern life. Mr James would have sighed acquiescence, and a Ruritania would have been the result. There would have been some difficulty about the hero, Stevenson stipulating for a Scotchman, Mr James for an American. An Englishman would have been the obvious solution. But an Englishman is more like an American than a Scotchman, and Stevenson would probably have demanded compensation in being allowed to do the actual *writing* of the book himself. And so the story would have been written—a story of adventure to the tune of tiny psychological scruples, a story like *The Prisoner of Zenda*, or *Rupert of Hentzau*, or *The King's Mirror*. I do not pretend that Mr Hope has all Stevenson's gusto or nearly all Mr James's delicate touch in dissection. But of the parties to a collaboration each must lose something of his own gifts; there must be a certain friction and evaporation. Mr Hope, writing alone, has shown probably to quite as much advantage as would have the other two, writing together. Except, of course, in the actual style. A book written by Stevenson would have to be very carefully paraphrased before Mr Hope could be mistaken for its author. And it is because Mr Hope has not a sensibility to words and phrases that I brought the fluent journalist into my hypothesis.

I have just expressed a doubt that Mr Hope has so much gusto as had Stevenson for romance. But that doubt does not imply that I do not prefer his romances, as romances, to Stevenson's. I hold that *Kidnapped* and the rest would, as romances, gain by being paraphrased into common, charmless, undistinguished prose. Stevenson was, far more than anything else, an essayist. In essay writing, style is everything. The essayist's aim is to bring himself home to his reader, to express himself in exact terms. Therefore, he must find exact words for his thoughts, and cadences which express the very tone of his emotions. Himself is the thing to be obtruded, and style the only means to this end. Wherever style is, there too is the author. But in a mere story, we want nothing but the story; so soon as the author comes in at the door, illusion flies out at the window. The story-teller must efface himself, therefore, and the only means to this end is the (real or seeming) absence of style—real, as in the case of (say) Scott, or seeming as in the case of (say) Maupassant, both of whom, using for their different purpose the simplest and most ordinary language, enable us to forget that they exist, and to believe that their characters were not invented, and that their incidents were true. Of course, in philosophic novels, like Meredith's, a personal and deeply-coloured style is quite essential. But remember that even Meredith, when he comes to a scene of actual passion, or to an exciting incident, is often quite direct and simple in his language. He forgets himself, lets himself go. Stevenson never could do this. He was always whittling and filing, embroidering and confectioning. He was always preoccupied with words. It follows that one is always preoccupied with *him*, not with his story. Mr Hope's invention of stories may be inferior to his, but Mr Hope has this vast advantage: that no reader gives him a moment's thought, and no reader can but be obsessed by Stevenson. Suppose that Mr Hope came to a duel-scene between hero and villain, he would describe it simply and rapidly, with just enough care to sharpen our vision. We should believe in it. But Stevenson would have let his fancy play round it, and sent such words to play round his fancy, that we should have quite lost sight of the duel through our delight in his view of it. He would have described how the moonlight ran sprightly up and down the crossed bodkins, and how the hero did, at length, with one shrewd embrocado draw a spurt of crimson that besprayed his lawn ruffles, and how the villain reeled like a toper shot from a tavern-door, and fell prone on the sodden clay, wherein, next morning, when they raised him, they found the flawless mould of his death-mask, the slick and fearful impression of distorted lineaments. All that, or words to that effect, he would have written; words fatal to the effect for whose sake they were composed; words that suggest to us, not the described scene, but Stevenson himself smiling, and thrusting aside his work, and writing to Mr Gosse to say that at last he had done something devilish good. For my own part, I am quite happy to sacrifice a story for style. I rate the essayist far higher than the romancer. I would jettison all Mr Hope's works for one of Stevenson's. I have even admitted that Mr Hope, as romancer, has less natural power than had Stevenson. But I cannot persuade myself to admit that Mr Hope's romances, as written by him, are not superior to Stevenson's. If this is a heresy, so much the better. It is only through heresies that criticism can progress.

My point, then, is that the love of words and the love of romance cannot be happily mated. Doubtless, too, the love of fine shades and the love of romance are antagonistic. But they are, as Mr Hope has proved, not irreconcilable. In *The Prisoner of Zenda* they are quite comfortably interwoven. But that book was written some years ago. As Mr Hope grows older, the schoolboy in him is likely to be elbowed out, with many apologies, by the nervous, modern man. Already, in *The King's Mirror*, one sees that the process has begun. The adventures are fewer, almost perfunctory; the niceties, more numerous and nicer. In fact, he is becoming more and more a comedian, and I trust that he will soon be able to put upon the boards as good a comedy as lies between the covers of his latest book. But at present, naturally, his talent for dramaturgy lags behind his talent for writing books, and has not kept pace with his own development. Indeed, the play which Mr Alexander produced last week at the St James's is a rather foolish affair, by no means distracting one's attention from the charming things which have been done to the theatre, during the past months, by builders and upholsterers. Mr Hope has not, on this occasion, succeeded in blending his two elements. He has allowed the schoolboy to write the first three acts, and the nervous, modern man to write the fourth. The schoolboy has brought on a great many gallant figures and written a great many stage-directions as to the shooting of revolvers; but even the gallant figures which survive into the last act have absolutely no shred of character between them. They are there, but they mean nothing more to us than so many unhit targets. The consequence is that when one of them—the hero—makes a desperate, belated effort to show that he has a mind and a heart, and to interest us in the mechanism of them, we remain incredulous and indifferent, and extend a hearty welcome to the person who presently shoots him in the back. Nor, when the scene is changed, and we see him lying on a catafalque in a *chapelle ardente*, surrounded by mourners and officers of State, do we feel more inclined to cry than we should if, at the end of a harlequinade, the clown lay in state, guarded by the policeman, and the columbine came in on the arm of the pantaloon to weep over the bier. I learn that the lying-in-state has been cut since the first night. I cannot understand how anyone with any sense of humour could have imagined that it would go down. Mr Alexander—and this brings me to the acting—has a very keen sense of humour. As Rupert, he has one or two chances of displaying it, and he takes them. For the rest, he dashes about very dashingly and agreeably, and does all that a man could do with so poor a part. Mr H. B. Irving, as the villain, is also effective, giving one the impression of a very terrible fellow. Mr Vernon repeats his success as Sapt. Miss Fay Davis, as leading lady, has been cast for the part of the Queen. This seems a pity. What is wanted for this kind of part is a 'presence' and a 'voice.' Miss Fay Davis has neither of these assets. Her prettiness and sensibility and keen intelligence are quite useless in this part, but they would have enabled her to play well the subordinate part which is played by Miss Julie Opp. Not that Miss Opp is unsatisfactory. Only, Miss Opp is playing a part which Miss Davis would play rather better, whereas she would be really successful in the part of which Miss Davis makes nothing. I hasten to admit that it will not matter a hundred years hence.

[ *10 February 1900* ]

## 'DANDY DICK'

To meet an old friend, for many years unmet, is always a rather dangerous and delicate matter, fraught with more or less disappointment and embarrassment. You see signs of age in him, and suspect that he is seeing them in you. Your heartiness has a hectic taint of fear that he has deteriorated. You grip his hand almost feverishly, as though you were going to pull him to you across a crevasse. The past! What stress you lay on that, partly in sentiment for it, partly because you guess that the present will find you with nothing in common! Even so it is when you go to see a play which you loved well years ago. You try to eliminate the interval, transmuting yourself into a former state. Passionately you sound the echoes of your old enthusiasm, but are conscious that they come from afar. You love the play: it is the same dear old play, oh! as fresh as ever it was; yet—yet, all the time, you know well, and hate yourself for knowing, that it has aged, that it has deteriorated. Of course there is this comfort, that a play cannot, like a friend, be feeling the same thing about you. At Wyndham's Theatre last Thursday, *Dandy Dick* was not looking at me and thinking 'When last I saw you, you were a merry boy in Eton collars! What has come over you?' There was something to be thankful for in that. On the other hand, I had selfish as well as sentimental reasons for hoping that the play would delight me. Again and again I have spoken of the perfect farces which Mr Pinero used to write. I have called them classics, and mourned over the inferiority of Mr Pinero's serious work. So I went determined to find *Dandy Dick* an unblurred classic.

I wonder is it a classic? Certainly, after fourteen years, it still is, on the whole, an amusing farce—a good piece of work. And the lapse of fourteen years is a terrible probation. It is more terrible, perhaps, than the lapse of a hundred years. If *Dandy Dick* be played a hundred years hence the audience will not (for example) shudder at the frequent soliloquies. For us they are excruciating, as being a bad habit of which dramatists have broken themselves. But a hundred years hence the soliloquies of Blore, the butler, will have a quaint charm, doubtless. So too, will those merely verbal quips which, throughout the play, are so annoying to us. When Sheba Jedd asks 'Are there forty pounds in the wide world?' and Salome retorts 'My heart weighs twenty!' we blush, and then turn pale. We are appalled, because we ourselves thought such quips funny—once. But our descendants will have no such sense of remorse. For them the merely verbal quips, and the soliloquies, will be nothing but amusing archaisms in form, not marring (as for us) the form itself. For us Salome and Sheba themselves come from that most revolting of all periods, the day before yesterday. Mr Gilbert set the fashion in young persons without moral scruples and with limited power to simulate them. Mr Pinero copied it. These young persons were amusing, the day before yesterday. Yesterday they became tiresome. To-day they are impossible. But who knows what may have happened ere the day after to-morrow dawns? For our descendants Sheba and Salome may be as delightful as they were for us. And the two officers, their lovers—one with a liver, the other with a drawl and an eyeglass—time may make them, too, tolerable. For us the liver and the drawl and the eyeglass are as leather and prunella. Nor do we laugh because Blore, the butler, drops his h's. Nor do we laugh at the four lovers in fancy dress, nor at the satire on 'a regular, pure, simple English evening at home.' For fancy balls have gone out of fashion, and men, when they dine out, do not any longer 'bring their music.' People don't do these things. The characters in *Dandy Dick* do them, and are supposed to be of the present day. For posterity they will belong frankly to the year 1885, and the satire embodied in them will have resumed some of its former pungency.

But I dally with details. How will the principal characters—the Dean and his racing sister—appear to posterity? At present they are more than a little crusted. This may be partly because we have, since *Dandy Dick*, seen so many comic dignitaries of the Church, and so many ladies who translate their every remark into the lingo of the stable. But, in any case, the Dean's pomposity, and Georgiana Tidman's slang, seem to us terribly overdone. 'You appear to misapprehend the precise degree of criminality which attaches to me,' says the Dean; and that is a specimen of his manner from first to last. Of course the Dean must be pompous, and, of course, everything should be exaggerated in farce. But the exaggeration of the Dean's pomposity is carried too far; it becomes actually tedious for the audience. Here again we are reminded of the lapse of time. When the play was written the Dean's speeches were not excessive. Even in the serious plays of that time all the characters talked pompously. 'Our son is older than he looks,' says one of the characters which Mr Gilbert drew quite seriously and sympathetically, 'and it is to that fact, doubtless, that your impression is referable.' That would have been considered quite natural stage-writing in the early eighties, and, accordingly, the speeches which Mr Pinero gave to his Dean were, for their time, no more than rightly exaggerated. But now that serious dramatics try to make their characters talk naturally, the permissable amount of exaggeration in farce is greatly diminished. For posterity the Dean's manner may have a charm of its own. I doubt, however, that posterity will tolerate Georgiana's slang.

Probably it will not even understand it, and the part will be irreverently rewritten in ordinary unhorsey terms. The process will be good for it. Barring her language, Georgiana is a very genial and delightful character truly drawn. The Dean, too, if you analyse him, is quite a human being. Both parts have enough vitality for survival. Both, moreover, are showy 'acting-parts.' And one must remember, in speculating on the future of *Dandy Dick*, that the plays which become classics are always the plays which give the mimes a chance. The public does not demand old plays. It is the mimes who, from time to time, insist on them. No play which has two really showy parts in it need despair of becoming a classic. *Dandy Dick* has four: the Dean, Georgiana, Blore, and Topping, the rural policeman.

I cannot say that the first three of these parts have been very well cast in the present production. Mr Alfred Bishop is always delightful, more or less; but as the Dean he is much less delightful than usual. The part does not suit him. He is too much a comedian to grasp the farce of it. Where he should be desperate he seems but mildly affronted, and where he should be richly sentimental he seems but drily introspective. Of course in the early scenes, before the fun is fast and furious, he comes off very well, and he has, throughout, the advantage of seeming more like a real Dean than any other mime could seem. Only, he is not the Dean of St Marvell's. Miss Violet Vanbrugh, as Georgiana, struggled vainly. The more she tried to be manly, the more womanly she became, and her frantic determination to be vulgar did but intensify and make more obvious her innate refinement. All hearts were touched. No one blamed her. But surely, whoever cast the play might have seen that the very qualities which make Miss Vanbrugh so valuable an actress in many parts would prevent her from doing well as Georgiana. It could not, however, have been foreseen how very bad Mr George Giddens would be as Blore. Blore is a fantastic part which makes some demand on an actor's intelligence. Mr Giddens, for some reason, ignored the demand, and did nothing at all beyond performing his familiar trick of toddling about, smiling, and wagging his head. The part of Topping was played quite perfectly by Mr Denny. Topping, as you may remember, does not appear before the third act. But when he does appear he is so delicious a creation that one forgets all about the play itself, and only prays that he may remain on the stage. Even a bad performance could not bring the part into its proper subordination.

Played by Mr Denny, it overshadows everything else. I cannot help wondering how Mr Pinero, usually a stickler for form, could have made the blunder of introducing such a character in such a way. Topping is an immortal embodiment of official stupidity. Dogberry and Bumble, compared with him, become thin and shadowy. He is the perfect expression of a type. Mr Pinero should have kept him for some other play, to be the central figure. He is the ruin of *Dandy Dick* as a work of art. But, as I have suggested, plays do not live as works of art, but as vehicles for the display of mimes. And *Dandy Dick* has all the better chance of escaping oblivion by reason of its one egregious fault in form.

[*17 February 1900*]

## AT THE ADELPHI

Mr Laurence Irving, with deft fingers, has been retrimming the bonnets of Bonnie Dundee. He has ripped off the riband of 'thrice gory tartan,' and sewn on a twist of diaphanous chiffon (*couleur de whitewash*). With dainty knots of artificial buttercups and daisies he has softened the grim outline of the original article, and with plumage of the bird of Paradise he has (in milliner's jargon) added delightful charm to the *ensemble*. Insomuch that Bonnie Dundee, *alias* John Graham of Claverhouse, *alias* Mr Robert Taber, may flaunt himself before the public without fear of being hissed. Don Juan himself, at the Prince of Wales's, is not kindlier, sweeter, more humanitarian, than he. One feels sure that at all the quiet tea-parties in Dumfries and Annandale he must have been welcomed as an exceedingly nice young man. It is quite obvious that he would not hurt a—Covenanter. In a word, he is 'sympathetic.' Thus the actor is satisfied. So is the public. So (I had almost said) are the dramatic critics. But they are not. The play being produced on Saturday night, they were enabled to dip into biographical dictionaries before writing their notices. Consequently, they have been down on Master Laurence like a thousand of bricks. He has tampered with history! He has taken a well-known character out of history and distorted him a way which would bring a blush to the ingenuous cheek of Macaulay's schoolboy! He has degraded the sacred cause of historic melodrama! Away with him! Well! I myself have been dipping into a Biographical Dictionary; but I cannot get up any great indignation against Master Laurence. If I had known enough about Claverhouse to be independent of a book of reference—if he had been to me as clear a figure as (say) Don Juan, then, of course, indignation would have come quite easy. But on the first night I had only the dimmest recollection who Claverhouse was, and I was quite ready to accept any version of him. Since I left school, Scotch History is one of the subjects which I have dropped. It always depressed me very much. I go so far as to suspect that it depresses everyone else—even Scotchmen. True, there are a few Scotchmen who piously parade a *penchant* for it. Mr Andrew Lang continues to speculate, *passim*, whether David McHob may not really have been a foster-brother of Angus McNob, and whether some of the letters ascribed to him may not really have been written by no less a person than Jamie McChittabob. But even Mr Lang strikes me less as being possessed with a passion for the light than as having contracted long ago a (quite harmless) literary habit of which he cannot break himself. However, this impression may be due merely to the saving grace of Mr Lang's Oxford manner. Possibly, some people really do care about the Scottish Jacobites. There are the members of the White Rose League: they seem to care. I remember that I had the pleasure of dining with them some years ago; and that after dinner, with some emotion, I drained a bumper to 'The Queen' without the slightest suspicion that I was committing myself to the cause of an Hungarian Princess named Marie. It was only from the subsequent speeches that I learnt what I had done, and I was so much alarmed that I lost the opportunity of picking up a little Jacobite lore. I remember vaguely that Claverhouse's name recurred several times. Had I been in a receptive mood during those speeches, I might have been indignant at the Adelphi last Saturday evening. As it was, I went quite ready to accept any version of Claverhouse which would not offend my sense of psychology and would satisfy my sense of drama. So I will write of Mr Irving's play as though it had no connexion with history.

If Mr Irving had made Claverhouse a mild man with a mild past, or a ferocious man with a past to match, I should have been quite happy. But Mr Irving's hero is a mild man with a ferocious past. His hands have been steeped in gore, but are quite immaculate now.

He is going to be married. While he waits outside the church he gives various proofs of his regeneration. A small boy (in a kilt and chestnut-coloured tights) comes on the scene. The villain strikes him. Claverhouse is very angry with the villain. He questions the child about his home—'Come! Tell us all about it!' The child tells him all about the ill treatment which he undergoes, concluding with an apostrophe—'Oh, the happy, happy people in the deep, deep grave!' Doubtless he would cap this Ethiopian sentiment with a clog-dance, did not Claverhouse cut in with an emotional announcement that henceforth he would be responsible for the child's upbringing. The child disposed of, Claverhouse gives further proof of a beautiful nature. A Covenanter, one Alexander Peden, comes on and curses him for having, in the past, brutally done to death one James Brown. Claverhouse, overcome, sinks down on a stone. Peden proceeds to threats of assassination. 'Remove that man,' says Claverhouse; 'but —*do him no violence.*' And so forth, throughout the play. Now, since Mr Irving wished to make his hero entirely sympathetic, why did he throw him against a dark and sanguinary background? Because his hero would be so much the more sympathetic? Perhaps. But when a wicked man becomes good, we demand to know how the reformation is brought about. Some kind of explanation is needed. Mr Irving does not seem equal to giving any explanation at all. Consequently, we cannot accept his Claverhouse. Why, then, did he not make his hero mild from the cradle onwards? 'Ah,' you will conjecture, if you have not seen the play, 'because he wished to bring about a terrible catastrophe: the reformed man reaping the whirlwind of crimes long ago committed—the sympathetic character paying for an unsympathetic past.' If Mr Irving had some such idea when he began the play, he very quickly jettisoned it. His hero's sufferings are brought about, not by his sins, but by the quite irrelevant machinations of the villain. The villain wants to marry the hero's wife, and there is a lady who wants to marry the hero. Innuendoes, disguises, misunderstandings, ensue. The hero's wife petitions for an annulling of the marriage. She is reconciled to her husband only on the eve of the day of his death. But why should he die at all? Why should he not live happily ever after? If Mr Irving had him assassinated by Peden, or by some other person who owed him a grudge for his past atrocities, there might be some point in his death. But Mr Irving insists that he shall die a hero's death in the

Pass of Killiecrankie. Of course, it was so that the real Claverhouse died (*see Biographical Dictionary*). But Mr Irving need not have troubled about that. Having flown so gaily in the face of history by making Claverhouse an angel on earth, he need not have stickled as to the exact means by which the angel was withdrawn to his proper sphere. One wonders why Mr Irving, in undertaking to write a Jacobite melodrama, *saw* the *Biographical Dictionary* at all. If he wanted a sympathetic hero, why not have invented one? If the name of Claverhouse had some mysterious fascination for him, by all means let him give it to his hero. But let him not hamper his conception with a mass of historic facts which he could not harmonise with it. The real Claverhouse was a savage, and Mr Irving wanted *his* Claverhouse to be a saint. The result is a kind of merman. And mermen never are convincing on the stage. But if Mr Irving had given history the go-by he could have made his hero both pleasant and possible. Nor would his play have been burdened with a motive of which, up to the last moment, we expect something or other to come.

The play is very well mounted and stage-managed. For the acting of the two principals I did not much care. The old school of acting is, as I am always pointing out, the only school of acting which suits melodrama. The moment the tone is lowered, we are reminded of the absurdity of the words and of the situations. Fustian must be delivered bombastically, and lurid situations must be gone through with a rush. Mr Robert Taber is a romantic and poetic actor of the modern school. He is excellent in the portrayal of romantic and poetic emotions, and he is always intelligent. But he has not the dash, the *brio*, the super-abundant vigour, which are essential in melodrama. The case of Miss Lena Ashwell is worse. She is not even romantic or poetic, is merely realistic. She has no tricks, no graces, no power of exaggeration. For the best kind of modern play she is invaluable. For this kind she is disastrous: she shows up the absurdities in no time. Miss Suzanne Sheldon, on the other hand, enters thoroughly into the spirit of the thing: as Anna La Riva, she does all that is required of her, and more. So does Mr Fulton, as the villain. His stride, and his Satanic smile, are quite admirable. He has, also, the art of infusing deadly significance into the simplest phrases. When he says to an accomplice 'Mind your own business!' he says it thus: 'MIND' (short pause) 'your *OWN*' (long pause) 'business!' This little speech, accompanied by the

Satanic smile and by a terrific toss of the cloak, thus really thrills the audience. At any rate, it thrilled me.

[*17 March 1900*]


## AT THE LYCEUM

Mr Benson 'continues to continue,' and still the wonder grows how one small head holds all the parts he knows. He himself, I am sure, would deprecate the enthusiasm to which his encyclopaedic memory moves us. I suspect that when he reads what the newspapers say of his productions he skips any mention there may be of his own acting, and is eager merely to see whether Shakespeare has got a good notice. I picture him coming down to rehearsal every Friday morning in the highest spirits, and saying to his business-manager 'Isn't it splendid?' 'Isn't what splendid?' asks the business-manager. 'Why! *The Daily Telegraph*!' cries Mr Benson, whipping out from his overcoat the current issue. 'Haven't you seen it? Look! This beautiful play'—'this stirring drama'—'passages in which the immortal bard seems to surpass even himself'—'the universal, we had almost said the superhuman, range of his genius. Ah, you see, they're beginning to appreciate him! I haven't been working in vain all these years. He has an awfully good notice in *The Times*, too. Here it is,' &c. &c. In fact, Mr Benson has the temperament neither of the mime nor of the commercial speculator. He is a man with a mission, a man devoted to a mission which leaves him no time for personal vanity and blinds his eye to the main chance. This sacred and all engrossing mission is to propagate the worship of Shakespeare. Hitherto, he has carried it on mostly in the provinces. Through the breach at the Lyceum he has, at length, invaded the metropolis, and has put to shame those sceptics who, arguing that provincial minds were ever readier than metropolitan minds to be improved, predicted that his tenure of the Lyceum would not be prosperous at all. These sceptics had declared that only 'stars' and gorgeous scenery would reconcile the frivolous metropolis to classic drama, and that Shakespeare in homespun would be given a very cold shoulder. But I was not one of those sceptics. Not I! knowing well that London contained thousands of simple, earnest folk whose dearest ambition was to have their minds improved—more than enough thousands of them to insure Mr Benson against fiasco; I know they would 'flock' to the Lyceum, week after week, every one of them carrying the Clarendon Press edition of the play to be performed, and would sit religiously through the performance, rarely raising their eyes from the text, and utilising the entr'actes by reading up the pithy 'notes' of Dr A. or Professor B. They would not, I knew, enjoy themselves: but then, they would not go to enjoy themselves: they would go to be edified. It is quite extraordinary how few people seem to have realised what a void there is for edifying drama. Mr William Archer, for many years, has complained bitterly that in Germany the number of Shakespearean plays enacted is far greater than it is in England; and his voice has always been regarded by most people (including himself) as the voice of one crying in the wilderness. Yet lo! Mr Benson's season succeeds from its outset, and, to the consternation of all dramatic critics, is to be prolonged far beyond its original limit. Mind-improvement, which was merely a wistful ambition, becomes a fierce passion. Subscriptions pour in. The Clarendon Press drives a tremendous trade, and the soul of Mr Benson is uplifed. The Lyceum's atmosphere becomes, week by week, more and more like that of a mission-house; insomuch that I should not wonder if Sir Henry Irving, returning, found that the very walls had turned to corrugated iron.

I admire zealotry in any form, and am glad when it pays. I am glad Mr Benson is succeeding so well in London. But I do not pretend that I find any overpowering joy in the mere thought that so many plays of Shakespeare are being given in so short a time. I care not a brass farthing that the public's mind is being improved. If such improvement were likely to make the public more tolerant than it is of serious modern work, I should be very glad indeed; for then there would be more chance of progress for modern drama. But the public is going to the Lyceum for moral reasons, as I have suggested, and not for aesthetic reasons. Its visits will not quicken in it any love of fine dramatic art. Indeed, the effect will be rather the reverse: having sat out the whole of Shakespeare, the public will feel less than ever inclined to weary itself by listening to the work of serious persons who have not the good fortune to be named Shakespeare. And as to my own personal inclinations, I repeat that I have no desire for the more frequent performance of Shakespeare's plays. Of *Hamlet*,

*Othello, Romeo and Juliet,* (and other plays which, as they attract 'stars,' are often produced,) I have already seen more than enough to last me for a lifetime: much as I love them, I do not wish to see them again. Such enchanting plays as *The Tempest,* which I have never seen, or as others which I have seen but seldom, I look forward to seeing under Mr Benson's auspices. But I do not want to see Shakespeare's inferior plays merely because they are Shakespeare's. Of course, even in his worst plays there are wonderful passages. There are wonderful passages in *Richard III,* in *Henry V.* But my pleasure in them does not counterbalance my boredom in seeing *Richard III* and *Henry V.* Such plays as these are the mere hack-work of genius, and had better far be neglected. Shakespeare must have groaned over them himself not less bitterly than do his discriminating admirers to-day. One can imagine him sighing as he plied his quill—'"*Another* part of the field!" Heaven send it be less melancholy than the first!' One can fancy the tired smile he wore as he wrote:

> 'Where is the Earl of Wiltshire? where is Bagot?
> What is become of Bushy? where is Green?'

And oh! there are hundreds of such lines in every one of his historical plays. In *Richard II,* which Mr Benson was playing till last Thursday, there is a quite painful number of them. But *Richard II,* as a whole, is triumphantly redeemed by the character of the king. So soon as he gets to the king, Shakespeare is at his best, and thoroughly enjoying himself. But the early scenes, how frigid and uninspired they are! With how contemptuous a finger the poet pulls his puppets! One cannot resist the feeling that Shakespeare never really wanted to write historical plays at all. Sometimes, as in the case of *Richard II,* he found by the way means of inspiration. But how wearily all the historical plays open! One can imagine how different John of Gaunt's farewell to Bolingbroke would have been if the two characters had been created by the poet, and named by him, for one of his imaginative dramas. The old father, stricken with sorrow for the banishment of his son, would not then have indulged in such pretty-fantastical word-spinning as this:

> 'Suppose the singing birds musicians,
> The grass whereon thou tread'st the presence strew'd,
> The flowers fair ladies, and thy steps no more
> Than a delightful measure or a dance.'

Shakespeare was obviously bored throughout this scene, and tried to console himself by turning it (as he could always turn anything) 'to favour and to prettiness.' But he must have been angry with himself for not treating the scene properly, or he would never have mortified himself by concluding it with the appalling couplet

> 'Where'er I wander, boast of this I can,
> Though banish'd, yet a trueborn Englishman.'

Let us be thankful that in the character of the king he found something to call forth the resources of his genius. From the 'scene before Flint Castle' to the end of the play, we have a masterpiece in psychology—an analysis of that weak and morbid, yet never quite ignoble, temperament which Shakespeare seemed to understand better, and to delight in more, than any other. My enjoyment of *Richard II* was increased by the impression that Mr Benson was acting much better than he had acted in the other plays—showing, above all, just that quality of imagination which one had thought was utterly denied him.

Of his Malvolio, the less said the better. Indeed, the whole production of *Twelfth Night* (which I have seen since I wrote this article) is lamentably undistinguished, except for the Sir Toby of Mr Weir and the Sir Andrew of Mr Swete. Mr Weir, by the way, was excellent also as the gardener in *Richard II*. He is a true comedian.

[*24 March 1900*]

## 'THE MAN OF FORTY'

Mr Walter Frith has not inherited his father's talent for telling a plain story plainly. Had he become a painter—and who knows but that he, too, 'tossed up'?—he would have produced nothing in the manner of 'The Road to Ruin.' Whatever may be said against his father's work, no one could dare to argue that it was obscure or not exactly what it pretended to be. 'The Derby Day' was obviously the day of the Derby: not Christmas Day, nor Maundy Thursday, nor the first Monday in August. 'The Railway Station' could not have

## 'THE MAN OF FORTY'

been called 'The Cottage' or 'The Cathedral' or anything but what it was called; and 'Coming of Age in the Olden Time' showed us a young man in the act of attaining his majority in a time unmistakably olden. Even so *The Man of Forty* showed us a man slightly bald at the temples, sitting before the fire, with carpet-slippers on his feet and a reading-lamp at his side, sentimentally transfixed by the entry of a young lady in white muslin. At least, that is what we should have had if the title had occurred to the father instead of to the son. The father would have done something relevant: the son does not. The father would have been straightforward: the son is implected with a passion for putting his public on false scents, and comes forth, the merry rogue! equipped for dramaturgy with nothing but a sackful of red herrings.

Herring number one is, as I have suggested, the title of his play. When a dramatist fixes in his title the exact age of his hero, one supposes that in some way the hero's age matters. This *Man of Forty*, one fondly supposes, will get some crucial advantage or disadvantage from his age: things will happen to him, and be felt by him, otherwise than they could if he were either young or old, and on these things the play will hinge. Not a bit of it! *The Man with Grey Eyes* or *The Man in Patent-Leather Boots* would have been quite as apt a title as that which Mr Frith has chosen. To prove this to my readers, let me adumbrate the plot. Mr Fanshawe is a rich and rather frivolous widower, and an M.P. He is in love with a woman whose husband disappeared four years ago and has not been seen since. He has a secretary. He has a daughter. Now, the secretary is a good man, but he has a wicked brother who is physically identical with him. The daughter has just returned from South Africa. On board she has met and fallen in love with one who happens to be the secretary's wicked brother. Worse remains behind, for the secretary's wicked brother happens to be the long-lost husband of the lady whom Mr Fanshawe loves. The first act closes with the recognition of husband and wife. In the second act, the wicked brother has a love-scene with the daughter, and complains of heart-trouble. He forces his wife not to reveal his identity, and suborns evidence for Mr Fanshawe that her husband is dead. In the third act Mr Fanshawe learns (1) that the secretary's wicked brother is secretly engaged to be married to Miss Fanshawe, (2) that he is also the long-lost husband. He has a scene with the scoundrel, who dies duly of heart-trouble. Six months elapse. Mr Fanshawe forgives the widow for having deceived him, and Miss Fanshawe pairs off with a young man who has won the V.C. and has always loved her. All this may be very amusing, but what, in heaven's name, has it to do with the age of forty? Mr Fanshawe's age effects his actions no more than does his seat in the House of Commons, and Mr Frith, as a matter of fact, lays very little stress on it even in the preliminary dialogue. Why, then, have dragged it into the title? Perhaps to give the play a nice veneer of sentimental comedy, a *locus standi* (or rather, *currendi*) on this side of the bridges, and to give Mr Alexander a chance of seeming to repeat the kind of thing he did in *The Ambassador* and *The Princess and the Butterfly*. Or, perhaps, merely to gratify the author's extraordinary delight in misleading the public at any cost. That is, on the whole, the likelier motive. At any rate, it is only charitable to suppose so. Judged as a series of practical jokes or mystifications, Mr Frith's play is a really ingenious piece of work. Judged as a play, it would only prove that its author had not acquired the rudiments of his craft. So I prefer to assume that its absurdities are dragged into it for mischief's sake—are, in fact, so many herrings across the scent. And thus I can proceed to enumerate them without seeming ill-natured.

Herring number one I have displayed already. Herring number two is the exact resemblance of the secretary to his wicked brother. We know these 'doubles' of old, and we know that in most plays they have some effect beyond saving the manager a salary. Accordingly, we are all attention when the secretary dilates on his brother's likeness to himself, and we are thrilled when the brother enters. Something is sure to happen. The wicked one will do something for which the good one will suffer, or the good one will . . . but let Mr Frith tell his own story—which is that nothing at all comes of the likeness. The nearest approach to something is just before the final fall of the curtain. The lady whom Mr Fanshawe loves is playing the piano, dreamily, up centre. The lights are low, as is right in a sentimental fourth act. Miss Fanshawe is in the arms of the V.C. Enter the secretary. She shrieks. The lights are turned up. She sees her mistake. Apologies, smiles, and everyone is satisfied—everyone on the stage, *bien entendu*: the audience is as much disappointed as Mr Frith meant it to be. 'Why,' wonders the audience, 'should there have been this elaborate double, if nothing was to come of it?' And

Mr Frith rubs his hands gleefully, and preens himself on the hoax. By the way, what a chance he missed in letting the wicked brother die of heart-trouble! Having, in the second act, elaborately prepared his audience for the death, why did he not let the fellow survive? That would have been splendid. Of course, it would have prevented a happy ending to the play; but really no one cares how such plays as this are ended, so long as they *are* ended. In any case the wicked brother need not to have succumbed to his heart-trouble: he might have shot himself, or died of consumption, and so fooled the audience once again. Curious that Mr Frith overlooked this herring! Herring number three is a Mrs Portman. She is tired of her husband, and secretly enamoured of Mr Fanshawe. In the first act, she received from Mr Fanshawe a cheque to meet a gambling debt. Surely she is going to affect the plot of the play. Not a bit of it! So soon as she declares her love, Mr Fanshawe shows her the door. She reappears only to be reconciled with her husband. In a comedy of manners, she and her husband would be passable figures. But in a melodrama, (even though it be, like *The Man of Forty*, a comic melodrama), they are mere herrings. Yet another potent herring is 'Raymond Barker, M.P.,' who, in the second act, urges Mr Fanshawe to take seriously to political life and to join a kind of Fourth Party which is being formed. One imagines that something is going to come of this. Mr Fanshawe will be at the House at the very moment when there happens that vital something which he might, had he been at home, have prevented; or perhaps ... and again Mr Frith has the laugh of us: nothing happens. Still he is not satisfied, the incorrigible creature! He must needs make Mr Fanshawe give to his daughter the ring which had been worn by her mother, telling her that she must give it to the man who shall win her heart, and threatening that if she give it to an unworthy suitor he will be inclined to tear it away 'as a Christian would tear away the symbol of his faith if he saw it hung as a trophy on the breast of some hideous monster!' 'Oh, papa,' says the girl, 'why can't you always be serious?' Now, surely, that ring is going to play an important part in the imbroglio. Surely, we shall see Mr Fanshawe tearing it off the finger of the wicked brother, or ... yet when he hears, subsequently, to whom the ring has been given, he remarks coldly that of course he has nothing more to say. The ring reappears ultimately, for the finger of the V.C.; and that is all that comes of the ring. Again, great stress is laid on the fact that

Miss Fanshawe is endowed with certain spiritualistic powers, and ... but I am tired of following up all these herrings. Suffice it that Mr Frith has had his practical joke, and that it has 'come off.' How soon his play will do likewise depends on the number of playgoers who enjoy having practical jokes played on them.

As for the performance at the St James's, I am not one of those experts whom good acting compensates for a bad play. No doubt, Mr Alexander was very good as Mr Fanshawe, and Mr H. B. Irving as the two brothers. But as the parts were wholly puerile, I should have been as well pleased to see them played by small boys: for me histrionic talent was wasted on them. Miss Julie Opp, Miss Granville, and Miss Fay Davis, for a similar reason, made no impression on me. On the other hand, Miss Carlotta Addison, Miss Esmé Beringer and Mrs Maesmore Morris had so little to do that I had hardly time to connect them with the play, and accordingly was able to take pleasure in the way they did it.

[*31 March 1900*]


## ACTING GOOD AND EVIL

I was so engrossed here, last week, in trampling on Mr Walter Frith that I forgot to bow to Sheridan, whose *Rivals*, that delicate evergreen, I had just been seeing at the Haymarket Theatre. Let me hasten to my amends. I had seen the play often before, but never nearly so well produced and cast. Hitherto I had been unable to revel in it really, being distracted by inappropriate scenery and mimes. Well! here, at last, was a real illusion of the North Parade. In the book-shop, at whose door the little salesman stood snuffing the evening air, *Peregrine Pickle* and *Mrs Chapone*, one fancied, really were brand-new stock. The lamplighter hobbled by, and one felt that for years he had gone a nightly round of 'that Resort where Virtue treads with Genius, and Wit is not dissociated from Decorum.' One breathed the very air of 'the genteel, delicious Province.' Nor did the mimes make havoc of the local and temporal colour achieved so nicely in the setting. There was a merciful absence of that inane ambling and swaying on tiptoe, that flourishing of hats, and waving of finger-tips, which most mimes seem to regard as constituting an eighteenth-century manner. Every mime here behaved like a human being—a being with a manner rather more elaborate than yours or mine, but still quite human. I hope this innovation will be taken as a precedent at large. There is really no evidence that people in the eighteenth century were always dancing minuets; still less, that they were always trying to turn somersaults, and making fools of themselves generally. Indeed, it is probable that their deportment, for all its greater elaborateness, tended more than ours to an effect of repose. In Goldsmith's farces, the traditional method of clowning the eighteenth century is quite permissible, even desirable. In farce, (whose aim is not at reality, but at mere fun,) let the mimes be as funny as they can be: amble and sway, flourish and wave, to their hearts' content. But in comedy let them curb themselves, *behave* themselves, like the admirable company at the Haymarket. So shall *The Rivals* give me pleasure, when, in due course, it is revived elsewhere. That it is still acted so frequently is due, of course, not to its deserts in art and in wit, but to the irresistible chances found by mimes in the parts of Sir Anthony, and the Captain, and Bob Acres. The public, I infer, loves the play especially because of Mrs Malaprop. Every speech uttered by that lady sends the public into convulsions of mirth. For me, she is the one blot on the play. The kind of mechanical, verbal humour for which she is a vehicle exasperates me to distraction. If I spoke of her botanical, vernal humour I should not expect anyone to be amused, and it vexes me to think that Sheridan expected people to be amused by such devices. But Sheridan knew his public, and knew that when Mrs Malaprop, in the first act, said 'supercilious' and meant 'superfluous,' and, in the second act, meant 'superfluous' and said 'superstitious,' the public would be so gratified at its own erudition and quick perception that it would almost roll off its seat. *Punch*, for many years, made a similar appeal through 'Mrs Ramsbotham;' also through 'Jeames' and the 'City Waiter.' To me such appeals are made in vain, and I resent them proportionately as I admire their maker's ordinary work. When ever I think of Thackeray, I am chilled by his responsibility for *The Yellowplush Papers*, and whenever I see *The Rivals* Mrs Malaprop almost drives me out of the theatre. At the Haymarket last Tuesday, Mrs Calvert somewhat appeased me by playing the part in a manner suggestive that she was not less bored by it than I was. And Miss Winifred

Emery glorified my evening by being quite perfect as Lydia Languish. For me, Lydia is the salt of the play. She is the flawless incarnation of a type, and no lapse of years can hurt her, and the play which hinges on her vagaries will be a classic always. She existed before Caxton, and when Mudie's Library is dust she will still be flourishing. The novels which turned her head in *The Rivals* are forgotten now, or remembered only because her head was turned by them. They have been swept away, but she remains quite modern—so modern that, in *The Canary*, most modern of all recent comedies, she turned up in the flimsiest disguise and seemed quite topical. We call her Lydia Languish, but she is really incarnate girlhood—one of the eternal verities, and not the least delightful of them. Since writing for her this tribute, I find that Mr William Archer drily dismisses her as 'a poor part.' Of course, from the standpoint of 'the profession,' she *is* a poor part. She makes no rough-and-ready appeal to the audience. She is a creature subtly variated, not a formal stage-figure with a label. To understand her you must observe her with careful and alert sympathy. You cannot be sure what she will do or say at any given moment. Always she is taking you by surprise, and then making you wonder why you were surprised at all. In a word, she is *natural*. I do not say that in real life there are no hard-and-fast figures; but I suggest that they are rare: most of us are more or less fluid and ambiguous. But to be fluid and ambiguous on the stage is to be not a 'showy' part. If a part is to be 'showy' it must be such that the audience will grasp it at once, foreseeing all its possibilities from the first. Sir Anthony is an example of such a part. From first to last, he is 'heavy father,' and his every outburst comes as a happy fulfilment of the public's anticipation, and comes, accordingly, welcome and applauded. It makes no demand on the public's intelligence, none on that of the actor, who has but to use himself lustily to be sure of a triumph. Heavy father, juvenile lead, villain, *ingénue*, and the rest—these are the 'showy' parts (if they are strongly worked out by the dramatist). Had Sheridan elaborated in Lydia a mere *ingénue* of the theatre, instead of a soaring human girl, she would not be, as she is, despised by the 'profession.' It is natural enough that actresses are shy of such a part, but I wonder that Mr Archer, who will never (surely) be called on to play it, and who usually concentrates his mind on dramatic art, leaving histrionism to its own devices, should have let slip this obvious opportunity, by me taken, of doing homage to a masterpiece by the way. All the greater credit seems due to Miss Winifred Emery. She rose to the part, and did not, as she so often does, rise too high. She foisted no glosses of histrionism on the obvious passages, gave them for no more than they were worth; and where interpretation was needed she interpreted with exquisite sensibility and skill. In fact, she was the very Lydia, 'innocently wild and bashfully irresolute'—that, and no more. I cannot conceive a better performance of the part. Mr Cyril Maude was amusing as Bob Acres, but he seemed to me to over-act the duel-scene. Of course, this particular scene was meant by Sheridan for mere farce, and Bob was meant to be merely ridiculous. But in the present generation, which duels not, Bob's reluctance seems entirely sensible and sympathetic. The best way for an actor to treat it in would be, I think, the way of serious comedy. At any rate, the experiment might be made.

The gods, I fear, are anxious to destroy Mr F. R. Benson. By no less sinister supposition can I account for the fact that he has been appearing as Antony, and allowing Mrs Benson to appear as Cleopatra. There is no ordinary reason why he should have done this. It is not explained away by his anxiety to leave no Shakespearean play unacted. He has in his company at least one actor who might have been good as Antony, and no actress in his company (except, perhaps, Miss Kitty Loftus) who would not have been a more plausible Cleopatra than Mrs Benson. Personally, I do not care to see such a play on the stage unless the two chief parts are filled in such a way as to satisfy my definite ideal of them. There is a score of ideal Hamlets, of ideal Lady Macbeths. But Antony and Cleopatra are 'fixed' for me. They must be superb figures, both. Through the mists of their tragic and stupendous passion, they must loom over me, as it were, rather more than life-size. They must be 'such a mutual pair' as they are boasted, lest they be blown away by a mere puff of ridicule. Cleopatra must have a hand 'that kings have lipp'd, and trembled kissing.' She must be one who has held all mankind in thrall, one for whom Actium were well lost. And Antony must be one who would lose it for her; and she, again, one who for love of him would press the asp to her breast, fondling it, as a mother her child. In other words, both must be tremendous embodiments—noble monsters—of tragic passion. If Antony looks and talks like Robert Elsmere, the whole game is up. It was even so that Mr Benson looked and talked. For Mrs Benson's performance I can find no simile. Suffice it to say that the shadow of an automaton would have been more welcome. Yet, apparently, Mr Benson supposed that he and Mrs Benson would 'muddle through' all right; else, the play (since it had to be done) would have been cast otherwise. Clearly, he is on the Olympian black-list.

[*7 April 1900*]


## 'SAMSON AGONISTES' AND 'ZAZA'

Doubtless, Milton meant *Samson Agonistes* to be really dramatic; so, doubtless, Mr Belasco means *Zaza*; but each failed utterly of his purpose. Thus the two plays of which I have to say something this week have one fundamental quality in common—the quality of not being plays. However, parallels are notoriously so hard to pursue, and the superficial divergencies in this case are so wide and many, that I prefer to deal with these two plays separately. Let me, then, take them in order of merit.

*Samson Agonistes*—do I see Mr Belasco's brow darken?—was produced very creditably by the Elizabethan Stage Society. Seeing that Milton was the pre-eminent sounder of what is perhaps the dominant note in the English character, I had often wondered that no English enthusiast had even gone so far as to attempt this tribute to his ashes. For there is little doubt that Milton himself wished *Samson Agonistes* to be enacted. True, in his preface, he speaks of 'the stage, to which this work never was intended;' but he says nothing to imply that it ought to be kept from the stage, and one may assume that he would have liked it to be used as one of those 'set and solemn panurgies in theatres' which he had recommended to the civil magistrates as means of grace for a paganised public. Yet it was not until a century had elapsed after his death that anyone even mooted its production. In the latter part of the eighteenth century Bishop Atterbury proposed to have it produced at Westminster, and he is said to have asked Mr Pope to superintend the rehearsals; but one does not hear that anything came of this pious plan. To Mr Poel, a man of sterner stuff, was left the glory of leading the van—and, I am afraid, of bringing up the rear, for one cannot suppose that the play will be acted again, at least in our time. It has none of the qualities which make production tolerable to more than a very few even in the inner ring of the faithful. I admit that I, for my part, enjoyed it very much indeed, and came away from it moved and impressed. But then, I am able to sit and listen to declamation of mere poetry, for any number of hours, without being bored. And this is a taste which is very curious and rare, for, while the general public, of course, cannot stand mere poetry under any circumstances, literary creatures mostly prefer to read it to themselves. I am one of the few literary creatures who cannot with pleasure read it to myself: I prefer that it be read aloud or recited to me by someone alse. For this reason, I always cultivate the acquaintance of people who like reading things aloud, and I go as often as I can to 'recitals' in this or that little hall. It was in such a spirit that I went to hear *Samson Agonistes*. The play, I knew, had no dramatic quality whatsoever. It has often been compared with the work of the Greek dramatists, and it is, of course, cast in the form created by them, and modelled on their manner. Particularly, as Mr Gosse has somewhere said, it is founded on the *Prometheus Vinctus*. So far as the grand manner is concerned, it is worthy of the comparison. But in point of dramatic quality no such comparison could well be made. The unending anguish of Prometheus, the despair and discord of the heart-cries wrung from him, the doomed struggles in which his soul seems to rend asunder his body, and his body his soul—these things are essential drama for us, even though they were first revealed to us in a 'construe.' Interesting, admirable, edifying, correct, is Samson's attitude of submission, but it never for one instant touches drama. Nor is there in this play any organic life, any progress; the *personae* come on, speak, go off, without swelling or expediting the volume of the idea. There are so many scenes, so many choruses, and then the play is over. All is quite static and marmoreal. For him who can appreciate poetry in his study the play can gain nothing by the visual method of the stage. There is no intrinsic reason why Milton should have cast his theme in dramatic, rather than in epic, form. Strange that the dramatic form, for which vocation is so painfully rare, is the form which, more or less, sooner or later, attracts and involves every man who can write anything at all! Milton told how he, as a young man, rusticated from Cambridge, was for a time stage-struck. He confided to Charles Diodati his enthusiasm for the '*garrula scena*,' and the '*sinuosi pompa theatri*,' &c. &c.; and his *Samson* suggests to us that he was stage-struck even in those mature days when he came to regard the contemporary theatre as an abomination to be scourged. And *Samson* was only one of fifty or sixty subjects he had jotted down for dramatic treatment. That he chose it from the rest was due of course to its autobiographical appeal—the blindness, the isolation, the bitterness for time past. It is as a piece of autobiography that his play lives—as autobiography set forth in magnificent verse. As drama it is still-born. Yet I am glad that it was cast in dramatic form, for else I should not have had the opportunity of hearing it under Mr Poel's auspices, and of enjoying it far more than I ever had at home. Mr F. Rawson Buckley spoke the part of Samson exactly in the right manner, making no attempt at any kind of dramatic emphasis, but insisting carefully on the rhythm. The Chorus, too, was managed skilfully. The ten women and three men who were in it passed listlessly to and fro, crossing and re-crossing one another, now one taking up the chant, now another, and all moving and chanting in a solemn and monotonous manner which became almost uncannily impressive.

*Zaza* is an absurdity within an absurdity. It is absurd, in the first place, to suppose that you can make a play by merely writing a part in which a celebrated actress may run through her favourite tricks and by setting up a number of little dummy parts round it. When a dramatist subverts the nature of things by making himself the humble interpreter of an actress, he ceases, forthwith, to be a dramatist. Also, he does a grave disservice to the actress; but as she is always very anxious that he should do it, and as the doing of it is almost always very lucrative, his eagerness for the job is not unnatural. There are many people who delight to see the celebrated actress disporting herself in a part specially made for her. I can understand their taste, though I do not share it myself. I can understand that Madame Réjane must have played the part of Zaza quite perfectly, though I personally, who care for mimes only as media, do not regret not having seen her in it. Such plays as *Zaza* are all the more objectionable when they are translated into another language for the benefit of other actresses who do not at all resemble the actresses for whose benefit they were orginally faked up. I called *Zaza* an absurdity within an absurdity because Mrs Leslie Carter is not at all like Réjane. She is a very capable, even powerful, actress, but she has little instinct for comedy, and the part which fits Réjane like a glove does not fit her. The glove, if I may say so, splits loudly at every seam. Loudness is, indeed, the chief feature of her performance; every point is exaggerated and underlined, every scene is over-acted. On the first night at the Garrick, Mrs Carter over-acted to such a degree that at the end of the fourth act she had ten or eleven 'recalls.' Quite apart from the obvious fact that she has established herself as a favourite, the play will, I suspect, run through the season. In New York it had, I believe, a kind of *succès d'esclandre*, and, though it is said to have been toned down for London, it contains enough mild libidinosity to get itself talked about and booked for. Commercially, its one drawback is that it is much too long. In Paris and New York they dine earlier than we, and are allowed to sup later. I would suggest some of the inoffensive scenes should be cut.

[*21 April 1900*]


## MR CARTON'S PLAY

'AHLSHWYWATISHTRFUSHEDSHINTRESHTEDOFFER' says Mr Dion Boucicault as the drunken earl to his contemptuous countess; then striking the kitchen table, he pauses for her and us to interpret him as meaning 'I'll show you what it is to refuse a disinterested offer,' and to admire his unflinching realism. But is it realism? I admit that it must be very difficult to do, and must have needed infinite rehearsal; but to accept it as realism I refuse flatly. There is no reason to suppose that the aristocrat in his cups speaks otherwise than the ordinary man in his. If Mr Boucicault wishes us to believe that anyone ever behaved as he does (how laboriously!) throughout this scene in the second act of the new play at the Criterion, let him adduce his evidence and get the management to print it as a foot-note to the programme. But a theatrical performance which has to be annotated into credibility is an error in art. Besides, Mr Boucicault must know well enough that no man under the influence of what he calls 'wshky' or of any other stimulant ever talked in the least as he suggests. He cannot have passed through life without seeing a Bacchanal here and there. Why, then, have sought his inspiration in the legends under Charles

Keene's drawings? That would have been well enough had he wished his performance to be taken as farce (though even then he ought not to have caricatured the manner of those legends into unintelligibility). The popular idea of the drunkard was created by Charles Keene, and in a farcical part an actor may reproduce it to his heart's content. But Mr Carton meant this to be a tragic, realistic part; and as such (at first) Mr Boucicault plays it. In the first act, where the earl comes on sober, his voice, and his walk, and the movements of his hands, all are copied elaborately from the dipsomaniac in real life. One would suppose that when he came on drunk the note of realism would be preserved. One would expect him to enunciate with that careful division of his words which is remarkable in every drunken man one has ever met. But no! Mr Boucicault steps on to the stage out of the back-numbers of *Punch*, and proceeds to make ridiculous, not merely his work in the first act, but also the play which Mr Carton has endeavoured to make serious. Now, to make the play ridiculous, to turn it into farce, is (as I shall suggest) to confer really a great benefit on the author; but why did not Mr Boucicault do this from the outset?

Of course, Mr Carton wished the part to be played in a tragic way. Written as he wrote it, it could hardly be played otherwise by a literal-minded actor. But why did Mr Carton write it thus? Why did he foist this sinister figure into a farce? For, strictly, the play is a farce. A countess masquerading as cook in a rural vicarage, mixing a salad on the lawn, refusing offers of marriage from the vicar, the butler, and the inevitable captain, hiding the vicar in the larder and the captain in the broom-cupboard, is not a character whom you expect to meet anywhere but in a mere farce. And I suspect that Mr Carton, not quite knowing what new thing to do for the Criterion, disempigeonholed a scenario which in his early youth he had made for a sentimental farce. But '*possumus puerilem togam, nequimus aetatem, resumere*,' and Mr Carton cannot be altogether giddy nowadays. In the first place, he has acquired a love of comedy, and a reputation for writing it well. In the second place, he has acquired the habit (a habit for which I cannot help being grateful to him) of writing his comedies round Miss Compton. This lady is a comedian, and would be quite lost in the kind of rough-and-tumble part which (as I conceive) Mr Carton had originally intended. I take it that in the original version the countess who became a cook and fell in love with the captain was to be a farcical widow, with no more than the ordinary attributes of all other farcical widows. Obviously, Miss Compton could not play such a part as that. At all costs, the part had to be brought into the key of comedy—into that particular key of comedy in which Miss Compton excels. 'But,' wondered Mr Carton, 'how is this to be done?... Happy thought! Comedy is as much graver than farce as it is lighter than tragedy. Therefore, farce + tragedy = comedy.' And so he proceeded blithely to turn the widow into a (collusively) divorced wife of a brutal and malignant dipsomaniac. 'There,' he cried to Miss Compton, 'is a thorough-going comedy part for you!' And she, reading it, and finding that the character and speech of the countess had been (despite her history) assimilated to those of Lady Algy and the rest, was delighted to appear in the play.

Now, I revel in Miss Compton's acting. In her limited range (to which, thank heaven! she so resolutely limits herself) she gives me perhaps keener pleasure than any other actress. I can imagine that she may not delight everyone. A strong fixed personality being the basis of her art, her appeal cannot be universal. But to me her lazy air of good-fellowship, and her drawl, and her broad vowels, the rudeness of her blank gaze into space, and the suddenness of her rare smile—all these things, to me, are quite irresistible. I could revel for ever in the monotony of them. I should be the last to urge Mr Carton not to spend his life in showing them off. By all means let him dot a recurring decimal over *Lady Algy*. Let him, with variations, repeat that comedy till doomsday. But this *Lady Huntworth's Experiment* is an experiment which must not be repeated, and ought never to have been made. Mr Carton has no right to waste his coming talent on the tragic adulteration of farce. Of course, as I have often said, farce with touches of extraneous comedy is much more tolerable than farce without them. But farce with a background of tragedy is really too monstrous. So long as Mr Boucicault kept up the tragic note sounded by Mr Carton, I was simply bored: the farce destroyed him, and he destroyed the farce. But as soon as he began to hide the sinister significance of his part under (unintentionally) farcical behaviour, I began to like the play immensely, finding it full of quite delicious touches in character and in dialogue. Indeed, it is long since I have so much enjoyed myself in a theatre. But that only aggravates my grudge against Mr Carton for not having written a proper comedy, and so allowing me to enjoy myself unreservedly throughout a whole evening.

There is some very good acting in the play, besides Miss Compton's. Mr Arthur Bourchier has exactly the kind of part that suits him. He has done it a score of times already, and the ease he has acquired in doing it is not marred by any slackening in his determination to do it well. Mr Eric Lewis, as the vicar, is as amusing as ever. But the chief delight of the evening is provided by an actress whom (so far as I know) I have not seen before. She is called Miss Polly Emery, and she plays the part of a parlourmaid. The part itself is conventional enough, but she plays it with absolute originality. We have seen this 'Keziah' many times in real life—or, at least, Miss Emery makes us believe that we have—but never on the stage. By the way, what a pity it is that no dramatist will condescend to draw servants except incidentally and from a farcical standpoint! Why should not someone devote a whole play to the serious portrayal of them? It is quite possible to collect 'documents' about their life; Mr George Moore did it when he wrote *Esther Waters*. Why do the dramatists confine themselves to collecting 'documents' about the upper classes? The peculiar conditions under which servants live, and by which their characters are shaped, are quite as interesting and dramatic as the conditions of 'high life.' The very fact that they have not yet been exploited should incline the dramatists towards them. I hope it will. The setting of a new fashion in subject-matter might do much to redeem our drama.

*An American Beauty*, at the Shaftesbury, was mercilessly long on the first night. Considering that it, or something very like it, had already been running in New York, I cannot see why it should have been tried on London in so interminable a form. Doubtless, it has been 'cut' now, and anyone who (like myself) delighted in *The Belle of New York* will delight not less in it. The critics have been complaining that it has no coherent story. Of course it hasn't. That is the charm of it. It is a mere vehicle for songs and dances, which are, I take it, the only things any sane person wants in a musical piece.

[*5 May 1900*]

## LORD HOPETOUN'S UNSTRENGTHENED HANDS

'Lord Hugh Cecil (Greenwich) deprecated a division, and was speaking at midnight when the debate stood adjourned.' Thus ended that historic discussion which followed the rising of Mr S. Smith (Flintshire) 'to call attention to the low class of plays now exhibited in some of the theatres of this country, and to move: "That this House . . . growing tendency . . . demoralising character . . . stricter supervision . . . interest of the public and"' all the rest of it. Unversed in the sinuous and elusive forms of our Senate, I supposed at first that 'adjourned' implied 'to be resumed.' I am told that I was wrong. It seems that our senators have exhausted their talent for dramatic criticism, and dare not formulate in academic judgment their airy impressions. Thalia and Melpomene will not, after all, be summoned to the Bar of the House. I am very sorry for Lord Hopetoun. He, in private conversation with Sir Matthew White Ridley, seems to have hinted 'that a debate on the subject, and an expression of opinion by that House that there were certain things that might be checked with advantage, would greatly strengthen his hands.' The language of a Lord Chamberlain, filtered through a Home Secretary, cannot be so definitely expressive as one would wish. But it is easy to form some rough idea of what was in Lord Hopetoun's mind. He disapproved of some of the plays which he had been advised by the Censor to license, but he felt that if he had not licensed them the public would have been very angry. For the future, he wished not to license plays of which he disapproved; but he had no wish to expose himself unarmed to execration. If the elected representatives of the public would but say that the public had been degrading itself, then he would be able to do his duty—with little or no discomfort. But, if a man be not strong enough to stand alone, he should rely on any support rather than that of the House of Commons, which is notoriously unkind. The debate about drama cropped up (thanks to Mr S. Smith), but it did more harm than good to the cause at Lord Hopetoun's heart. Mr S. Smith, who had never entered a playhouse, desired that the power of licensing should be given to the London County Council. Mr T. P. O'Connor made an impassioned appeal for more 'realism' on the stage. Mr Gibson Bowles made some senatorial jokes. Mr Birrell disapproved of any kind of Censorship. And so on, till the debate was allowed to end in its own smoke. A sad evening for Lord Hopetoun, who (I assume) was in the Peers' Gallery, clasping, in an agony of suspense, those hands which he had brought there to be strengthened.

I should have supposed that one man, at least, would stand by the Lord Chamberlain in his hour of need, and that this one man would be the Censor. But no! Mr Redford, it seems, is at Brighton, and there he has been saying to the reporter of a daily paper things which must add much to his chief's embarrassment. Mr Redford pooh-poohs the notion that the public ever delights in anything which could harm it. 'Three plays,' he admits, 'may be considered more or less risky, and they are *The Gay Lord Quex*, *Nurse*, and *Zaza*. First comes *The Gay Lord Quex*. Are not the denunciations of it answered by the course of the play itself? It was written by the greatest of living dramatists, Mr Pinero, produced by the most famous of comedians, Mr Hare, and it scored the greatest success of the season.' I will not insult Mr Redford by assuming that he really believes Mr Pinero to be the greatest of living dramatists, nor by assuming that he means (as his words imply) that he would probably, in the exercise of his duty, be harder on a play written and produced by obscure persons than on a play written and produced by popular, influential persons. What he means is that the long run of *The Gay Lord Quex* justifies him in having licensed it. In the case of *Nurse*, which has not been such a success, he cannot use this triumphant argument; he falls back, rather gamely, on his opinion that it would not 'in any degree demoralise any person who witnessed it.' But of *Zaza*, again, he says 'its success shows that I was justified in passing it.' If *Zaza* and *The Gay Lord Quex* had been failures, Mr Redford would not have been so sure that they were quite wholesome. And yet, surely, he knows as well as anyone else that the unusual success of both these plays is due chiefly to the fact that they have been attacked on the score of impropriety. However, I will assume that he does not know what everyone else knows. I can believe anything of a man who, existing as an official for no reason but that the public is believed to be incapable of looking after its own morals, blandly argues that the public's approval of a play is proof that he was right in licensing it. If Mr Redford really thinks that the public knows exactly what plays are good for it, he ought, for honesty's sake, to resign his office immediately. If, on the other hand, he has not this touching faith in the public, his defence of himself is unworthy of one to whose judgment the work of sane artists is submitted, and he ought to be asked to resign by the person or persons responsible for his appointment. He was appointed merely to advise the Lord Chamberlain whether this and that play ought, on grounds of morality and expediency, to be licensed; he was not appointed to speculate whether this and that play were likely to have long runs.

It is not only Mr Redford who embarrasses Lord Hopetoun with his real, or feigned, belief in the probity of the public. Mr S. Smith himself is a subscriber to the faith. 'He was no believer'—I quote, as before, from *The Times*—'in the judgments of experts.' True, he said that 'he founded himself very much on the views of the best dramatic critics, among whom there was a concensus of opinion that great deterioration had taken place of late years in the character of the English drama.' But this seems to have been a mere aberration, since one of the two dramatic critics on whom Mr S. Smith professed to have founded himself very much is a man who is always proclaiming, in and out of season, that the English drama is steadily progressing, and that the only way for it to go on progressing is along those very lines which Mr S. Smith seems to abominate. Probably, Mr S. Smith has never read more of that critic's work that the few lines which he quoted. In any case, it is not to the critics, nor to the Lord Chamberlain, nor to the Censor, that Mr S. Smith looks for the salvation of the drama; 'he believes rather in the average common sense and average morality of the ordinary householder.' He regards the public as a blameless body, which wicked playwrights are trying to debauch. He trembles to think that these villains may succeed in their fell purpose. 'Was it not certain that the same effects would follow in London as in Paris—that a decadent drama and what always accompanied it, a decadent literature, would produce a decadent nation?' The touch about 'Paris' is delightful, but even more delightful, more thoroughly worthy of the place in which it was spoken, the suggestion that a decadent drama is the cause, and not the effect, of a decadent nation. 'Was it not,' Mr S. Smith might have said (perhaps he did; the report is not verbatim), 'certain that, unless something were done—aye! and done quickly, and done without flinching—was it not, one might almost say, inevitable that the tail would wag the dog?' Of course, there is not really any decadence in our drama. There is now, as in all times, a certain amount of what is called impropriety, which, as in all times, the public rather likes. It is in order to keep that impropriety within reasonable limits that the licensing-system exists. The Lord Chamberlain thinks that the system is not working well, and, though I do not agree with him, I am sincerely touched by his desire to have his hands strengthened in the House of Commons. Might he not, in his discomfiture, try to strengthen them himself?

I have written on this subject because there is really nothing to write about Mr Brookfield's play at the Comedy Theatre. Mr Brookfield is an actor, and one expects a certain degree of staginess in his plays; but from Mr Brookfield, even as a cynic, one does not expect anything so cynically stagy as *Kenyon's Widow*.

Of Duse I shall write when I have seen her whole repertoire.

[ *19 May 1900* ]

## A MIGNIARD PLAY

If you, like Lady Betty Fanglestar, be 'craving an elegant, light dissipation for a summer's afternoon,' you ought certainly to visit the Royalty Theatre; for there they are playing *The Fantasticks*, quite the prettiest and wittiest little thing in the town.

You may remember that I was very angry when Mr Wyndham produced *Cyrano de Bergerac* in an English version. I gave my reasons why that play should never have been transported, why it was bound to be absurd in any version but the original. Doubtless, now that Mrs Campbell has produced another of M. Rostand's plays in a similar manner, signs of a similar indignation are expected of me. Alas! I cannot show them. *The Fantasticks* at the Royalty delights me not less than *Cyrano* bored me at the Criterion, and my pen is a-quiver to write praise. Lest you think me inconsistent in my views, or suspect me of being in the pay of one theatre and not of another, I must proceed to draw certain distinctions between the two cases. Of course, I would rather see *The Fantasticks* in M. Rostand's French than in Miss Fletcher's English: translation, however good, must spoil much of its curious delicacy and elegance; but I have good reason to prefer seeing it in Miss Fletcher's English to not seeing it at all. To Mr Stuart Ogilvie and Mr Louis Parker, though they did not translate *Cyrano* badly, I was not grateful, because either of them could have evolved from his own head quite as good a romantic drama as the best imaginable translation of *Cyrano*. In England we have plenty of writers who can originate romantic drama quite decently, and it is sheer waste of time for them to be grovelling in alien soil. But in England we have no one who can—no one, at least, who does—write plays in the way of elegant and delicate fantasy. In an English theatre, the nearest approach that can be made to that kind of play is through a good translation. Miss Fletcher has made quite a good translation of *Les Romanesques*, and I am accordingly grateful to her. But my distinction between the two cases is not merely that translation of romance is superfluous, and that translation of elegant fantasy is desirable; I suggest also that *Les Romanesques* is, in itself, much more fit than *Cyrano* for translation. Cyrano was a local French type, unintelligible to the English mind. Nor was he a realisation of the type; he was a poet's inspired idealisation of it, and, shorn of M. Rostand's verses, would have seemed even to Frenchmen nothing but a rather unpleasant lunatic. What folly, then, to make an English prose version of him! But Percinet and Sylvette, of *Les Romanesques*, are not at all unreal; if they expressed their sentiments, not in verse, but in prose, they would be less charming, but they would still carry conviction. And they are not local types; they belong to any province of any country. There was no reason why Miss Fletcher should not lay hands on them.

The idea which M. Rostand shows through them is an idea to which no place, no time, were more appropriate than another. It is simply the idea that aesthetic romance is a sorry basis for a married life, that lovers who trust to it will be estranged when, as sooner or later they must, they begin to find each other out. It is, in its essence, just such a satire as Mr Bernard Shaw himself might have written— did write, indeed, in *Arms and the Man;* but it is infinitely more effective, in that it is written by one who himself loves romance, and understands it, and knows the power of it. What could be more perfect, for truth and prettiness, than the stolen scene between Percinet and Sylvette across the wall of the two gardens? They have met often thus, revelling in the secrecy, in the thought of the fearful things which would happen if either's father (sworn foe to the other's father) were to find them there. Their minds are filled with the history of Romeo and Juliet, and their love is built on it. Suddenly, it occurs to Sylvette that they ought to be formally engaged:

> 'Puisque nous aimons, il faut nous fiancer.
> PERCINET. C'est à quoi justement je venais de penser.
> SYLVETTE. Dernier des Bergamin, c'est à toi que se lie
> La dernière des Pasquinot!
> PERCINET. Noble folie!
> SYLVETTE. On parlera de nous dans les âges futurs!
> PERCINET. Oh! trop tendres enfants de deux pères trop durs!

Percinet hears a footstep in the garden. They both drop down from either side the wall. Bergamin, Percinet's father, comes and upraids his son loitering so often by the wall which divides his garden from that of Pasquin, his sworn foe. A little later, in the other garden, Pasquin comes and chides his daughter for the like offence. Sylvette runs away. He climbs up, and peeps over the wall. Bergamin is there, and climbs up to meet him. They embrace. Indeed, they are the best of old friends. Their avowed feud is a mere strategy to secure what is at their hearts: that Percinet and Sylvette shall fall in love with each other. They chuckle together over the progress of the affair. Pasquin has hit on a plan for bringing the betrothal about at once, with a public reconciliation between themselves. A Bravo, named Straforel, is at hand. He is a professional abductor, and does business on very reasonable terms. He is to abduct Sylvette that very evening, to be caught in the act by Percinet, to offer a desperate resistance, to be overcome in single combat. Then both the fathers will appear, and Pasquin, overcome with gratitude will give his Andromeda to her rescuer... The moon rises. Cloaked and masked, with a company of minions and minstrels, Straforel creeps into the garden. The minstrels group themselves picturesquely, and play softly on their flutes. The minions hold torches in the shadow. A closed chair is borne by negroes... All happens well. Straforel, prostrate on the ground, furtively stretches up to Bergamin the point of his sword, on which is transfixed a piece of paper. Bergamin reads the paper. His face lengthens. It is the bill... The lovers learn the true history of the rape. So! they are hero and heroine no longer. They quarrel, and they part. Percinet, furious, rushes away, in quest of actual adventures, actual loves... Straforel, (payment of whose bill depends on the marriage,) disguises himself as a nobleman, makes romantic love to Sylvette. He terrifies her with a passionate recital of all the glorious discomforts which she will suffer when she flies with him. She shrinks away, pining for anything prosaic... Percinet, scarred and tattered prodigal, comes slinking home. Sylvette runs to meet him. They are both wiser now. They can love each other without the circumstances of romantic sorrow and joy.

The figures are real enough, as you see. But they speak in poetry, and move in a sophisticated scheme, in a series of conventions. What happens to them is natural, but the way in which it happens to them is artificial always. What they do and say is natural, but they say and do it in the manner of poetic artifice. And so, of course, the chief requisite in the performance of the play is style. The mimes must express themselves and comport themselves exquisitely; anything like realism would mar the effect which M. Rostand aimed at. Mrs Campbell, I thought, was rather too intense as Percinet; she let her sense of drama run away with her sense of mere prettiness. Miss Winifred Fraser, as Sylvette, was more Watteauesque, played with less emotion, and so played (in the circumstances) better. Mr Gerald du Maurier, as the Bravo, did his best to be fantastic, but did not succeed in being more than boisterous. And Mr E. W. Garden and Mr George Arliss, as the fathers, showed no signs of understanding that they were not engaged for a rough-and-tumble farce. But, of course, it were very hard to cast well a play which is of a kind never written in this country. And, perhaps, one is the readier to forgive mistaken mimes in a play whose charm no amount of bad acting could obscure. *The Fantasticks*, I repeat, is the prettiest and wittiest little play in the town. By all means, go to it.

[*2 June 1900*]

## 'RIP VAN WINKLE'

'*Personne n'est toujours sublime.*' Mr Beerbohm Tree must not be expected to produce no work but Shakespeare's. He cannot devote perpetually himself and his theatre to that reverent service. Now and again, being but human, he needs a little rest and recreation. Who shall grudge it him? After his live and lovely productions of *King John* and *A Midsummer Night's Dream*, who shall deny that he has earned the right to put on *Rip Van Winkle* before he passes to some other play by the Bard.

Not I, at any rate. True, as one who happens to be keen on the progress of British drama, I would rather that Mr Tree had found diversion in some new and original play by a modern author. Dion Boucicault may have been very good of his kind, very good for the 'sixties; but it seems a pity to bother about keeping his memory green at the expense of playwrights who are working in the 'noughts (if I may so call the present decade). In any case, a revival of Boucicault's version of the 'Rip' legend can keep green no memory but that of the simple public, to which erst that version seemed a very beautiful play. From the commercial standpoint, doubtless, Rip is still a name to conjure with. But from the standpoint of art, it is merely a name to punctuate—R.I.P. None, I am sure, knows this better than Mr Tree himself. Why, then, did he disentomb Rip, instead of trotting out some new and vital play? Perhaps you come to the conclusion that he is not, like me, really enthusiastic for the progress of British drama. If so, you are wrong, I think. Mr Tree's preference is probably due to the fact that Her Majesty's is a very large theatre. It was often suggested against Sir Henry Irving that he neglected modern drama at the Lyceum; but the fact that he produced few modern plays was no proof that he would not have liked to produce many. I suggest, it meant merely that the Lyceum was a very large theatre. Such a theatre as the Lyceum or Her Majesty's requires very large plays—plays, I mean, with broad and sweeping motives, and with plenty of spectacle. Comedy, a thing of little delicate lights and shades, is impossible on the stage of such a theatre. To succeed there, plays must be tragedies, romances or melodramas. Unfortunately, the best of our modern playwrights are tending more and more towards comedy. Mr Jones, Mr Pinero, Mr Carton, Mr Parker, Messrs Parker and Carson, Mr Grundy, Mr Haddon Chambers and Mr Esmond do not run to tragedy, romance or melodrama; they find in comedy the natural outlet for their talents. Mr Esmond, I admit, has written one admirable tragedy, *Grierson's Way*. But that was a realistic tragedy, dealing with modern life in a Chelsea flat (where there was little opportunity for spectacle,) and it was altogether in a minor key. It would have been impossible on the stage of a large theatre, unless Grierson and his wife had been made a King and Queen, and cast into another century where they could have behaved violently, and installed in a palace where there was plenty of room for crowds. In fact, tragedy of modern life is impossible in a large theatre. But I digress. My point is that our best playwrights are writers of comedy, and that, since comedy is impossible in a large theatre, it is the Zeitgeist, and not Sir Henry Irving or Mr Tree, that must be blamed for the neglect of modern dramaturgy at the Lyceum and Her Majesty's. If there arose a modern writer of pictorial tragedy, or romance, be sure that you would see his work at both these theatres. Be sure that you would see there any good pictorial tragedy or romance that might be written by Mr Jones, or Mr Pinero, or one of the rest. But could these gentlemen write such plays well? Could they, with the best will in the world, transform their whole method for the sake of bringing grist to these large mills? You remember *Carnac Sahib*? In writing that play Mr Jones had evidently grasped the necessities involved. He had provided a large, picturesque background—palaces, temples, what not?—and had made a liberal use of the British army. Also, he had tried to make lurid the love of his two men for his married lady. But he had tried in vain. The years which he had devoted—so well devoted—to comedy had sapped all the lurid instincts of his early youth. The motive of *Carnac Sahib* never rose above, or sank below, the level of modern comedy. It was useless, therefore, to Her Majesty's. Yet I doubt not that Mr Tree, who is reputed sanguine, would again be willing to commission Mr Jones or any other famous writer of comedies to write a tragedy or romance for his theatre. It is, I suspect, the playwrights themselves who are shy. Perhaps the day will come when one of them will pluck up his courage. But I suspect that the successful modern play at Her Majesty's, when we do see it, will have been written by someone whose name we do not know. Of them whose names we do know, Mr Bernard Shaw is the only one who has written a play with enough spectacle to meet the requirements. I understand that in his unpublished *Caesar and Cleopatra* a certain number of elephants is quite indispensible to the scheme, and that fifty of them would not be too many. But then, I understand also that the play is a comedy. And so I can exclude Mr Tree from my recent condemnation of the London managers who still fight shy of Mr Shaw's work.

That Mr Tree regards *Rip* as an interlude in his policy, not as a part of it, is proved by the fact that he has not had the play overhauled and brought up to date—a task which (say) Mr Parker could have performed very easily and prettily. True, it is said that there are certain differences between the play as written by Boucicault and the play as produced at Her Majesty's. But they cannot be essential differences; they do not make the play less old-fashioned than it was. The first and second villains are still there, in all their redolence of the 'sixties, with their plot to do Rip out of his inheritance. The first villain is still angry that Rip's wife would not marry him, and is still anxious to marry the second villain to Rip's daughter; and all the rest of it. The foiling of their 'sixtiesque designs is still the dénouement of the play: Rip comes down from the mountain, produces a document, establishes his claim to the property. The villains go off cowering and snarling, menaced by the heroic young sailor who loves Rip's daughter. Rip and his wife fall into each other's arms. Rip is at last a landed proprietor. Curtain. Of course, in the 'sixties, Rip's accession to wealth would have been held to increase greatly the happiness of the ending. Nowadays, it merely spoils the sentiment of his return and his reconciliation. The whole intrigue about the property seems to be out of place; it has nothing to do with the idea of the play; it is mere padding. The play would be immensely more effective if the intrigue were cut out, and if the time thus saved were devoted to some development of the main idea. It is absurd to bring Rip down from the mountain, after twenty years' sleep, merely that he may gradually recognise and be recognised by his relations, and may finish up with a little bit of foiling. It is sheer waste of an idea. The twenty years' sleep is an interesting idea, and something vital ought to come of it. Rip's body has grown old, but his mind is exactly what it was when he was a young man. However great his love for his wife and daughter and his neighbours, there is a gulf between his heart and their hearts—a gulf of twenty years. Will that gulf ever be bridged? That is the point that a modern dramatist would insist on. In fact, the play begins to be really interesting just when the curtain falls. We want to know whether Rip can make himself one with his old world, or whether he will wander back, wistfully, up the mountainside, praying that his next sleep be unbroken. Obviously, the whole play ought to begin exactly where it ends—the rest could be given in a prologue. But perhaps, in that case, it would be rather too like *Le Chemineau*, which Mr Tree produced not long ago. And perhaps I am making an unnecessary fuss. After all, the main point is that Mr

'RIP VAN WINKLE'

Tree has appeared in the historic part of Rip—a part which, however had its setting, is really fascinating, and gives him many chances of displaying his powers of humour, and pathos, and imagination. I have seen no previous Rips, and so cannot offer you a comparative criticism. Other reasons prevent me from telling elaborately that which is yet the truth; that I admired and enjoyed his performance, scene by scene. Miss Lily Hanbury humanised the shrew-wife with much intelligence and power. Mr McLeay played with his usual intensity as first villain. The peasants' dresses were curious and amusing. The scenery was quite beautiful. It had been painted by Mr Fred Storey, on whom the gods seem to have lavished an alarming variety of gifts.

[9 *June 1900*]

## DEMOS'S MIRROR

The tardy sun will have no difficulty in scorching the life out of such plays as have survived in London the excitement of the war in South Africa. The pallid, exhausted managers are all summoning up strength for one final effort—to close their doors, through which no one passes. Yet, night after torrid night, the Music Halls are packed with uproarious humanity. There is not—there never is—any need for the manager of any Music Hall to close his doors, except during the interval spent by him in the enlargement of his premises. The public, now as ever, tilts over his treasury an inexhaustible cornucopia. His not to offer a wistful lure, but merely to prevent the place from being overcrowded. And the cause of this queer difference? You need not seek far for it. The entertainments in Music Halls have grown, feature for feature, from the public's taste. They are things which the public itself has created for its own pleasure; they know no laws of being but those which the public gives them. Drama, on the other hand, is an art, and bound by an art's traditional laws. It may try to attract the public, to obey the public's laws rather than its own, to be an entertainment rather than an art. (The modern commercial necessity for it to do or be so is the reason why it is so tragically inferior to the other arts.) But it never can succeed completely in its effort. Try as they may to debase themselves, dramatists never can quite put away the last vestige of their self-respect. They are working in an art-form, and they would not, even if they could, forget *all* that is due to it. A still small voice is always urging them to save, for art's sake, *something* from the havoc to which, for sake of cash, their material is destined. No play ever belongs wholly to the public. And the public, unconsciously knowing this, leaves drama to fall more or less violently between the two stools on which the dramatists enthrone it, and flocks to the Halls. There the poets and the mimes have no secondary allegiance. Every 'turn' there has but one aim: to please the public in the quickest and most obvious way. If (as not often happens) a 'turn' fail to do this, out it goes, an awful example. There is no nonsense about the Halls, no pretence. The mirror is held up, and in it the face of Demos is reflected, whole and unblurred. Thus, for those who, like myself, have the misfortune to hate humbug, a Hall is preferable to a theatre. It has an air of honesty and freshness not to be found in a theatre. It is nearer to life. The average song, maybe, does not distort life less than the ordinary play; but, at least, it distorts life exactly as the public likes to see life distorted. It shows us, in fact, what are the tastes and sentiments of the public. It is an always trustworthy document. And, in this sense, it is near to life.

An intelligent foreigner will learn more about the soul of the English people in one visit to (say) the Tivoli than in a hundred excursions to this or that 'typical' locality. He will find in the Tivoli a perfect microcosm, enabling him to leave England next morning with all the materials for a really accurate and exhaustive book about us. His first and most obvious impression will be that we lack sense of beauty. He will see Mr Dan Leno, Mr George Robey, Mr Harry Randall and all the other most popular male 'artistes' coming on, one after the other, in the guise of unwashed drunkards. Seedy frock-coats, battered and greasy top-hats, broken and amorphous boots, crimson noses, wigs of sparse lank hair—these and all the other invariable details will be a revelation to him. At first, perhaps, he will find reason for them in the quality of the characters impersonated. But then he will see that even the performers who do not impersonate at all, but merely tell stories or sing songs at large, are dressed in a similar way. He will contrast them with the trim creatures who, in scarlet swallow-tails and black knee-breeches, illustrate nightly the convention of the *café chantant*. He will remember that in France even the impersonators of low-class types are never unpleasant to the eye, never grotesque in an ugly way, never aiming the illusion of uncleanliness. The French people have a sense of beauty in costume, as in all the other details of life. The poor are not less seemly clad than the rich, having found and accepted a convention which makes beauty cheap. The *ouvrière*—the coster girl! But the foreigner need not go nearer to Whitechapel than the Tivoli to understand that not only have we no sense of beauty, but that we revel in ugliness for its own sake. 'Nay!' you exclaim. 'But he will admit that we have a great sense of beauty, when he finds that most of the female artistes are chosen for their good looks rather than for their talent, and that they come upon the stage attired in satins and diamonds and everything else that can accentuate the handsomeness of their limbs and faces.' Granting (insincerely) that the costume of the 'serio' is not always hideous, garish and absurd, I reply that your objection is off the point. Every 'average sensual man' exercises a sense of beauty in regard to women; and the fact that he admires handsome women and likes to see them showing themselves off in handsome dresses does not imply that he has any sense of beauty whatever in any other connection. Show to the 'average (English) sensual man' anything hideous, except a woman, and he will not be at all put out. Indeed, if the thing is but hideous enough, he will be very much pleased by it. He is, for example, very much pleased by the comedian's seedy frock-coat and crimson nose.

The intelligent foreigner, pursuing his investigations, will be struck by the ugliness of the humour not less than by that of its purveyors. He will find that most of the jokes are made about ugly things. I need not give examples; that would be familiar to anyone who has frequented Halls. I do not, of course, refer to indecent things. There is very little indecency in the Halls; but the love of ugly details of life is ever rampant, and will strengthen the conclusions of our intelligent foreigner. Another thing which will instruct him is that, whereas in France the comic impersonator usually comes on in high spirits, in England he almost invariably comes on in the depth of gloom or in a paroxysm of resentment. In France, something pleasant has happened to him, and he proceeds to sing his song about it gaily. In England, he has some tale of sordid woe to unfold: the upstairs lodger has assaulted him, or he has just been expelled from a public-house, or his wife has left him. In both cases, the aim and the result are laughter. But, in the striking difference of means, our intelligent foreigner will find, rightly, a proof that despondency is as much the normal state of existence in England as is cheerfulness in France. In England we make our own sufferings tolerable by laughing at other people's; in France personal gaiety is increased by sympathising with the personal gaiety of others. Yet another point of interest to our visitor will be the enormous amount of attention paid to drink. Hardly a song that has not at least a passing reference to inebriation; many that have that state as an exclusive subject. Again, perfectly legitimate conclusions will be drawn.

Indeed, there is not one peculiarity of our race, good or bad, that is not well illustrated in the Music Halls. Were I to attempt a full list I should far exceed my space. I must content myself with one further instance. Hypocrisy! Where would you find that quality of ours more obvious than at the Tivoli and such resorts? Part of the Englishman's pleasure, like the Frenchman's, is strictly sensual. Handsome women, dressed in such a way that the fewest possible number of their good points shall be missed, come upon the stage and sing songs. As I suggest, they do not often sing well, or wittily, or wisely; but that does not matter: the 'average sensual man,' of whom the audience is composed, is not there to admire their art, but to have a good look at them. In France, the situation is frankly accepted. The women sing songs in accord with it. But this would never do in England. A touch of 'verbal impropriety' is permitted, now and again, to a male comedian, or to a plain female comedian. But the pretty female comedian must never sing anything that is not purely patriotic, or sentimental, or infantile; else the audience would be outraged by being reminded what it is there for. A few years ago, I heard Mdlle Anna Held singing in London a rather suggestive song, whose refrain was 'For I have such a way with me, a way with me, a way with me.' The audience was obviously distracted between horror and joy. Joy got the upper hand; the applause was fairly loud, yet with a note of resentment in it. Mdlle Held stood bowing her acknowledgements, and then sang an encore verse. Suddenly a voice from the gallery cried, 'Yes! *Away* with you!' The situation was saved. Puritanism had triumphed. The audience was able to applaud the encore-verse, whole-heartedly, on pretext of applauding that wrathful voice. At the Tivoli, lately, there was a 'sketch' which exactly illustrated how far an English audience likes things to go.

It was called *Rose Ponpon*—the name of 'an infamous woman.' Soon after the curtain rose, a woman appeared, cloaked and bonneted as a hospital nurse. She threw off her covering—behold Rose Ponpon in all her attractive vileness! She was not really vile, however; she had reformed, become a hospital nurse, worked miracles of tenderness and endurance, and only revealed herself in the old light 'in order to save the life of the man she loved.' She continued to reveal herself in that light throughout the 'sketch,' to the delight of the audience. Finally, of course, she resumed her cloak and bonnet.

Well! though I dislike hypocrisy, I have no doubt that it is a very valuable asset for a nation. National licence means national decay. Human nature being what it is, true virtue is not generally possible. The next best thing to virtue is that active form of respect for virtue which is called hypocrisy. A bad day for England when she no longer practises it! On that day her downfall will begin. Happily, there are, at present, no signs of its advent. Hypocrisy reigns supreme in the places which truliest reflect the nation's spirit. It is our duty, however, to keep our eyes constantly directed towards those places, in order that we may detect the first signs of vicious frankness. Considering the vast importance of Music Halls as indices of national character, I cannot understand why every newspaper does not keep a Music Hall critic. The dramatic critic, that mere luxury, might well be jettisoned.

[*21 July 1900*]

## DRAMA OF THIS YEAR

Comes the end of July. At this time, before crushing my trusty quill under heel, usually I look back and write a review of the past 'theatrical season.' This year, I can do no such thing. I am engaged here not as a creative artist, but as a critic, as one who deals with materials ready-made. I do not feel called upon to invent what does not exist. No past 'theatrical season:' no review of it by me.

The theatres have been open, of course. Some interesting plays have been revived. Shakespeare has flourished. So has Sheridan. Many uninteresting plays have been revived by the managers who were originally responsible for them. But a season of revivals is no season at all. Here and there, certainly, one has seen a new play. But I do not, unluckily, recall any new plays that have been interesting.... Yes, there was *Lady Huntsworth's Experiment*... and of course, *You Never Can Tell*. For the rest, no echo comes to me but of my own footsteps. The long corridor lies dark and empty behind me. May the door of the next one, when it opens, show me a bright vista of entrancing revelations!

Two plays by a young poet are to be produced in the course of the next season. It will be interesting to see whether Mr Tree and Mr Alexander succeed in persuading the public that Mr Stephen Phillips is, like Shakespeare, so edifying that he must, in spite of his poetry, be accorded a respectfully rapt hearing. In any case, one will be glad to see new poetic drama actually on the stage. Not that we are likely to have a general renascence of it. In these times, poetic drama can but be a happy survival, a beautiful little backwater remote from the main current of the stream. That main current, as I have often said, is of realistic modern comedy and tragedy. Regret it as you may, modern realism is the only direction in which our drama can really progress. And in that direction it had been slowly progressing till the South African dam stopped it; and in that direction, when the dam is removed, it will again be progressing slowly. But for the public, the progress would be quick enough. If only the dramatists could banish the public from their minds, we might have already a fine drama of the modern realistic kind. The dramatists have been doing the best they could, having regard to the necessity of luring the public along with them. Every decade has brought us perceptibly nearer to something fine. I calculate that in sixty years, at the present rate of progress, we ought really to be in the midst of that something fine. Meanwhile, though the public is being slowly educated in serious drama—for 'though,' on second thoughts, read 'because'—it is becoming more and more fond of music-halls and musical farces. If it would only become so fond of them that it would utterly abstain from patronage of drama, and so necessitate a drastic revolution in the commercial system which clogs the modern dramatist's every footstep, then I should not have to bide my sixty long years. A mere decade would be needed for the dramatist to realise the new conditions—to realise that he was free, like the painter, to do his best work for his own pleasure and for the pleasure of a few patrons. You doubt whether any patrons would be forthcoming? But a taste for good drama is not more rare than a taste for good pictures. The reason why subsidies are not now offered for any theatre is that no one is imaginative enough to conceive, in the present state of drama, the existence of a drama worth subsidising. So soon as our dramatists were rid of the public's yoke, they would be able to prove, in their new MSS, that such a drama did actually exist. Subsidies would forthcome then, quickly enough. Good dramatists would be able to live by doing good work. The better their work, the larger their income. Of course, that income would never be so large as the income they now make by doing half-good work. But then they would not be selling their self-respect with their work.

I wrote nothing last week about *Madame Delphine*, a little play by Mrs T. P. O'Connor, privately produced at Wyndham's Theatre. My silence was not due to defective admiration, but to an idea that I, dramatic critic, had been admitted to the theatre rather to receive a foretaste of the things which will happen when Mrs O'Connor becomes a professional dramatist than to criticise her first guarded flight among her friends. However, now that I have seen notices of the play in various public journals, I hasten to insert my belated little sprig of laurel in Mrs O'Connor's wreath. I hope there will be many more plays like *Madame Delphine*, equally deft and well written. Mrs O'Connor ought certainly not to let slip that future which she proves herself to possess. As the play was privately produced, adverse criticism would be out of place, though favourable criticism, as I am glad to find, is in place. If I did not sincerely like the play, I should preserve my silence. Likewise, if I did not think it had been acted well by its cast of volunteers, I should say nothing about them. Fortunately, they acted very well indeed—with one exception—and I may waft them my compliments. But there was the one exception, and I care not what laws of good taste I trample on in calling attention to it. I stand in a peculiar relation to Mr Laurence Irving. I have described him, here in these columns, very solemnly and fervidly, as a genius. I have made myself a kind of Godfather to him, and I must not let him run wild. I must, at any cost of good manners, not allow him to labour under the impression that I did not think his impersonation of an old French priest in *Madame Delphine* the most appallingly bad piece of acting I had ever seen. Indeed, his performance confirmed me, more than ever, in my opinion that he is a genius. To act so badly as all that postulates a power almost supernatural. Had I never seen Mr Laurence Irving before, I should have exclaimed 'Here is one whom the gods have endowed with a gift vouchsafed to none other of their creatures. Never let me see him again!' Having seen him act amazingly well in other plays, I conclude my outburst with a hope that I shall see him again as soon as possible, wildly wondering whether he will be on the heights or in the depths. To describe what I saw of those depths is quite beyond my power in writing. I am not Dante. But my impression was not the less awful because it is incommunicable. He who should have been a benign, quiet, tender old creature with a French accent, a mere spectator of the play's action, became a croaking, grunting, shrieking, raving lunatic with an accent for which every nation in Europe had been held in fee, and with the combined gestures of a windmill, an octopus, and a monkey-on-a-stick—horrific gestures which, even what the gesticulator himself had nothing to say, were continuously employed in order to explain to the audience the true meaning of what the other mimes were saying.... Those poor other mimes! For their sake, for mine, for his own, for all sakes, let Mr Irving cultivate a sense of proportion and restraint, a sense of the when and the when not, of the how and the how far. To make really tremendous failures is one of the sure signs of genius. Nevertheless, genius should try hard not to make them.

It seems that my article in last week's number of this Review produced an effect of inconsistency. At any rate, five separate readers of it, polite strangers, have written to me, complaining that in the first paragraph I credited the Music Hall with 'an air of honesty and freshness not to be found in the theatre,' whereas in the last paragraph I twitted it with the fact that that 'Hypocrisy reigns supreme' over it. I hasten to answer these signals of distress. Let my five correspondents read the article again, more carefully, and they will find that there is no real contradiction in the collated passages. The Music Hall is honest, because, as I said, it makes its appeal straight to Demos without any side-reference to art. It is a 'trustworthy document' of Demos's soul. Now, as I also demonstrated, Demos in England is a hypocrite. Therefore the Music Hall provides entertainments in strict accordance to the various pretences which he likes to keep up. It panders to the disingenuous tyrant—panders frankly, and with all its might. But the theatre panders both to Demos and to art. Serving two masters, it betrays (and is found out by) both of them. But the Music Hall is honest (and thrives) because it has only one allegiance; nor is its honest single-heartedness less apparent because its master seems to you and me contemptible. 'Paula Tanqueray' is a less honest creation than 'Rose Ponpon,' even as half a lie is worse than a lie whole.

[*28 July 1900*]


## THE ST JAMES'S THEATRE

Exile has always been treated by the poets as in itself a dreadfully pathetic affair. Yet (I have often thought) the real bitterness of exile is the return from it. No doubt there is some pain in the severance of home-ties and friendships, the sudden rupture of life-long habits. But this wrench, like the dentist's, is soon over, and has salutary results. It is not long before the exile begins to realise how narrow his life has been, and to congratulate himself on the happy release from that vicious circle. Day by day of his new irrestrictible career, in contact with strange men and strange cities, his soul shoots up and expands like a well-tended tree in sunlight, and puts forth fragrant blossoms, and bears marvellous fruits. He is doing that which, as now he sees, he had never done in the old days: he is *living*. In the multiplicity of experience, he forgets utterly that one little fleck on the world's surface which he had childishly regarded as the world itself. Suddenly, one fine morning, comes a messenger, bringing him his pardon, bidding him return. Ere the exile has time to send this impertinent fellow about his business, he is overwhelmed by a tide of that sentimentality to which we are all liable, and on it he is swept home. It is then, and not till then, that he needs the poet's pity. It is there, in his old environment, that he savours the veritable wormwood. All, all are there, the old familiar faces, with precisely the same expressions as when last he saw them; and the old familiar hands fumbling away at the same tasks; and the old familiar tongues still wagging to the tune of the same shibboleths. Nothing has changed. Nothing has grown. The exile shudders and grimaces. To think that he could ever have existed in such an atmosphere of stale vegetables! 'Faugh!' he says. And that is the last word (if you can call it a word) uttered by him before he sickens and dies.

Even more bitter, because it is compulsory, is the return from that voluntary exile which we call a holiday. When we have been dallying with strange territories, listening to strange tongues and seeing strange sights, improving our minds and strengthening our bodies, how horrible to be clutched up by Fate's bony fingers and dropped back into the fetid and familiar city we had fled from, with a strict injunction to remain there till the moon shall have waxed and waned eleven times! To breathe this breathless air under these chimney-pots in these narrow streets, and to hear the organs still grinding out 'The Absent-Minded Beggar,' and to find the newspapers still talking about our policy in China, and chronicling the sentimental journeys of General Buller, and casting doubts on the accuracy of some passage in some book which Mr Andrew Lang has written about Bonnie Prince Charlie! A month ago these affairs might have stirred me. But that month (for the gods have a trick of compensation) seemed to me to last a full year. My mind acquired, in that illusive interval, a new focus. At present, I am seeing things in a large way, in a cosmopolitan way. I see how little anything here matters. And, if I detect the insignificance of the real things which are agitating my brethren (and will soon be agitating me), how much more am I painfully alive to the absurdity of bestowing a moment's thought on unreal things invented by Mr Sydney Grundy! Picture me as standing here with a pair of scales. In one of them I have placed Life. Comes Mr George Alexander and places in the other, with an air of modest confidence, Mr Sydney Grundy.... That is what it is to be a dramatic critic in the first week of September.

Picture me, whose eye is still focussed for infinite and sun-bright plains, gazing across a row of footlights in King Street, St James's, while beauteous 'Isabel Holroyd' (Miss Julie Opp) tells ardent young 'Philip Graham' (Mr Marsh Allen) that his suit is hopeless, that she loves another; picture me, whose ears are still attuned to torrents in glens and waves on shores, listening while 'George Carlyon, Q.C.' (Mr George Alexander) comes suavely forward in dress clothes and pays an elaborate compliment about 'your charming sex, Miss Holroyd.' A month ago these things would have come as matters of course. Now they exasperate me. Mr Alexander's black-rimmed eyeglass, the pink rose in Miss Opp's hair, seem to be specially and malignantly designed to madden me. I sit dreading the moment when (as always happens in a crowded after-dinner scene of the stage) one of the characters suggests a game of billiards in order to clear the way for an important dialogue. The moment comes. 'Sir Jacob Holroyd, M.P.' (Mr W. H. Vernon) is left alone with 'George Carlyon, Q.C.' With a horrible clairvoyance, I seem to have foreseen every syllable that falls from their lips. Sir Jacob thinks that so rising a man as Mr Carlyon ought to have a seat in Parliament, and Mr Carlyon says 'You have a daughter,' and, as soon as that matter is settled, in runs Miss Opp, clapping her hands and crying 'Only think, Papa, Jimmy gave Mr Baxter fifty in one hundred, and he ran out on the first break!' Thus the first act draws to its close, and I begin to speculate about the four others. 'Act II.,' I see on my programme, 'the next afternoon at Mrs Floyd's, Park Village East.' 'Gipsy Floyd—Miss Fay Davis.' Evidently, Carlyon has an 'entanglement.' He has indeed. And one soon sees how he will be finally freed of it. 'James Antrobus' (Mr H. V. Esmond) comes in and speaks incidentally of those noxious drugs 'which women take to *cure* a headache or a heartache, instead of *bearing* it.' A few moments later (note the dreary skill of the playwright!) he takes up a small phial from the table and asks what is in it. Mrs Floyd replies that it is for her headaches, and Mr Antrobus throws it into the fireplace. The matter then drops, and I am left wishing I could telescope the time that must elapse before Mrs Floyd takes her overdose. Part of that time, I know, will be occupied by a meeting between the two women, the wife and the cast-off mistress. 'Am I addressing Mrs Floyd?' Isabel Carlyon will say. 'That is my name,' will be the answer, given with a pathetic dignity. How the meeting will be brought about I do not profess to know; nor do I care; and I am sure I shall be infinitely depressed by the ingenuity with which Mr Grundy will contrive to bring it about. In due course, the *scène à faire* is gone through. Mrs Carlyon does not know that it is her husband who deserted Mrs Floyd. She has come to patronise the unfortunate woman, not to upbraid her. It is only when she hears her husband's 'voice off' that the horrible truth dawns on her. This is what is called 'a strong situation,' and I give Mr Grundy due credit for having found a pretext on which to bring Mr and Mrs Carlyon together under Mrs Floyd's roof. All I protest is that it is too early in September for me to be edified by skilful pulling of wires. I suspect that if Mr Grundy had treated his theme in a really human way, I should have written of him ungraciously. But he has done nothing of the sort. As usual, his one aim has been at 'situations.' And this latest play of his is all the more irritating because its theme is really worthy of serious treatment. A really interesting play might have been written about a man who had, in his youth, formed an 'unfortunate connection,' and who was confronted, after ten years, with the alternative of deserting the woman or sacrificing a brilliant career. There one would have had a real problem. But Mr Grundy carefully cut the ground from under his own feet. With an eye on leading-ladydom he made the man's mistress a creature of the most exquisite refinement and the sweetest temper. The man might have married her at any moment without jeopardising his chances of worldly success. The whole play is radically absurd, because the man and woman would, in real life, have been married years ago. Even admitting the possibility of their not having taken this step, one cannot accept the manner in which Mr Grundy brings about their parting. Carlyon, being still loved by the woman, could not (in real life) make the rupture without being rather brutal. But Mr Grundy had his eye on leading-mandom, and was determined to have no brutality. Accordingly, Carlyon comes to see Mrs Floyd and is hoodwinked by her into a belief that she herself has ceased to care for him, and that her one anxiety is as to the sum of money he intends to settle on her. The man who could not tell when the woman with whom he had been living for ten years was making a martyr of herself must have been an exceptionally arrant fool. Carlyon, even had he not been a Lord Chancellor in embryo, would have seen through the game in no time. But Mr Grundy assumed that leading-men prefer to impersonate fools rather than brutes, and made Carlyon dash out of the room exclaiming 'To think that for such a woman I might have sacrificed my life!' All these sacrifices of truth (as it is understood by me) to effect (as it is understood by mimes) are pardonable in the case of trivial stage-themes. But they ought not to be made by a playwright who ventures to tackle a really decent stage-theme. Finally, I would conjure Mr Grundy, when next he attempts a serious play, not to interlard it with comic relief. If he cannot rid himself of that old-fashioned habit, let him, at least, spare the elderly clergyman who goes to a music-hall and has his watch stolen. That figure may have been funny a few decades ago, but is so no longer.

Miss Fay Davis played the part of Mrs Floyd very nicely, but in the later scenes was too obviously influenced by Duse. I do not suggest to her that such an influence is a bad one; on the contrary, I can imagine that it might be very profitable to her in certain plays —the *Antigone*, for instance, and the *Electra*. But I do suggest to her that the simplicity and rigidity of Duse's method is not suited to such plays as *A Debt of Honour*. Mr George Alexander and Miss Julie Opp played with more of a flourish, and Miss Fay Davis would do well to imitate them.

[*8 September 1900*]


## CAESAR AND CROMWELL

The revival of *Julius Caesar* at Her Majesty's is a boon and a blessing to those who, like myself, have come back to London as giants refreshed—giants with no stomach for those sickly little saccharine drugs which are all that our dispensing dramatists will make up for us. Last week I wrote petulantly. Mr Sydney Grundy, smugly handing across his counter the old dose so neatly wrapped up and so neatly sealed, was too much for my patience. I had to dash his little bottle down these columns and break it, as much for his good as for the relief of my own feelings. But this week my good-humour is restored. I have found in the theatre something really to be admired, something all the more welcome because it differs so utterly from anything else that the theatre affords. *Julius Caesar* is a ἅπαξ πεπονημένον, unrelated to anything else done by the writer of it or done by any other writer. It is a man's play, with no use of women as subject-matter, and no appeal to them as audience. Its mainspring in drama is the impassioned comradeship between two men of opposite temper, and its idea—how finely developed!—is the vanity of idealism in practical affairs. No one has ever used the poetry of friendship so finely as Shakespeare has used it in the 'Tent-scene;' and no one has ever satirised the public to such bitter effect as he has satirised it in that 'Forum-scene,' when the cheap man of the world easily upsets, by one cheap appeal to sentimentality and greed, the noble calculations of Marcus Brutus. The play ranges between a sphere where the appeal is merely intellectual, and a sphere where emotion is strictly divorced from sex. It deals only with men, and with those abstractions which men alone really care for and understand. And yet, observe! it is a great success, is greatly applauded. Till Mr Tree produced it, two or three years ago, it had long been imprisoned in the library; 'for,' said the theatrical theorists, 'no play can succeed without a strong love-interest.' Mr Tree deserves some credit for having refuted these serried croakers, for having asserted the right of men (and their desire) to find sometimes in the theatre food meant only for the masculine palate and digestion. I do not suggest that the audiences at Her Majesty's are exclusively composed of men, or that the women do not applaud; all I say is that the women can derive no more real enjoyment from seeing *Julius Caesar* than they can from listening to the conversation in a smoking-room, or than men can from listening to the conversation in a boudoir. The play succeeds simply by reason of its appeal to men, and the fact of its success makes me hopeful that we may have other plays written in a similar scheme. Only in the theatre—the short-sighted, hard-of-hearing theatre—lingers the tradition that men and women can have no separate existence. From modern civilization the tradition has long vanished; every large house has its smoking-room and its library, as opposed to its drawing-room and its boudoir; and every little house contrives some equivalent barriers. Even in the dining-room, that common territory of the sexes, the last mouthful is the signal for separation; the women sweep out to their chiffons, and the men settle down to their first principles. As in life, so in books. Novelists have begun to take the liberty of not always dealing with the love of a man for a maid. The lust for money, religious doubt, ambition in politics—these, and many other matters foreign to women, are becoming quite fashionable among our writers of fiction. And yet, since Shakespeare made his experiment, no play has been written without an eye to sex. May Shakespeare, with Mr Tree's help, now gain a few imitators in this line.

It is a pity that the poet, by force of habit, called his play by the name of the (historically) most eminent figure in it. *Brutus and Cassius* he should have called it, or, perhaps, *The Way of the People*. Either of these titles would have signified a strong point, whereas *The Life and Death of Julius Caesar* merely underlines the initial failure to make Caesar live. Caesar, in fact, is the one blot on the play, and I wonder that Shakespeare did not recognise the fiasco. There is an obvious reason why we cannot accept Caesar as he is here presented. He appears merely as a subordinate figure, with very little time to disport himself on the stage. Our notion of the real Caesar is a notion of such awe, he looms so largely over us, that we could not possibly be illuded by a stage-figure of him unless it were a central and dominant figure, elaborately created. Also, we think of Caesar always as a man of enormous power, a conqueror, a bender of wills; whereas here he is presented as a purely passive figure in the hands of Fate and of a few men who disliked him. Historically this presentment of him is right enough; but dramatically it is no good at all. Had Shakespeare shown him to us first in all the majesty of his will, then the coming of his doom would move us. We should echo the warnings of Calpurnia, and, with the soothsayer, clutch at his toga as he passes to the Senate. But, as we hardly see him except under the immediate shadow of his doom, our imagination is unstirred: we do not see Caesar, but only a stage-puppet, a transparent ghost. The actor who undertakes this part is not to be envied, except for his courage. In the revival at Her Majesty's Mr Murray Carson undertakes it. He does his very best to make the puppet live and to solidify the phantom. Complete success were impossible. But that is not Mr Carson's fault; it is Shakespeare's, and Caesar's. All that can be done Mr Carson does, using his fine voice subtly, and showing much of that rare quality among mimes, imagination, in his rendering of some few really magnificent lines which Shakespeare wrote into the part. Besides Mr Carson, there are several other changes in the cast. Mr Beveridge is Casca, and plays excellently, with all Casca's geniality and with very little of his own brogue. Mr Robert Taber is Cassius, and his conception of the part tallies closely with that of the late Mr Franklin McLeay; a better conception could not be. Mrs Tree plays picturesquely as Calpurnia. Miss Lena Ashwell, as Portia, makes much of that little and lovely speech in which Shakespeare has embodied the whole of the *Doll's House* philosophy. Miss Ashwell (if only someone would give her the chance) would be quite perfect in such parts as that of Nora; her intelligence and her sincerity are unrivalled by any other actress. But for such parts as Portia she lacks the requisite sense of beauty. She has not the grand manner of one who boasted herself 'Cato's daughter.' 'Tell me your counsels,' she pleads earnestly, 'I will not disclose 'em.' In a modern play this would not matter; we should be thinking only of Miss Ashwell's sincerity and intelligence. But in poetic tragedy the mimes must sacrifice to the Graces, just a little; and they must remember that to the Graces no sacrifice of a *th* is at all acceptable. Miss Ruby Ray, as the boy Lucius, is incarnate girlhood, and plays with a graceful and glowing coquetry which enchants us. One would much rather see her as Lucius than not at all. At the same time, one would rather not see her as Lucius.

At the Globe Theatre is a play called *Colonel Cromwell*. The authors of it have approached the Great Protector in a wiser spirit than Shakespeare approached Caesar: they have been careful to make him the central figure of their play. It is also to their credit that they have not involved him (as most playwrights involve their great historical figures) in some impossible love affair, but have had the courage to attempt a presentment of Cromwell in his public capacity —a warrior and a schemer. Unfortunately, they avoided one pitfall only to tumble into another. They have made Cromwell an ass—a fine, chivalrous, sterling, sympathetic ass, but still an ass. My own private notion of Cromwell is that he was, at least, a very clever man; and by the sharp conflict between that notion and the notion here set forth dramatic illusion is frightened quite away. Even if the authors of the play had not provoked this unfortunate conflict, and had given me a truly convincing figure, my illusion would have been banished by the persistency with which the dramatis personae refer to the hero as 'the Colonel.' Verbal associations are very mysterious things, but they are none the less very powerful; and it is a fact that for me (and probably for large proportion of the play-going public) 'the Colonel,' spoken *tout court*, suggests nothing but a genial American, with a big white moustache and a big green cigar, telling very long and amusing stories after dinner. That Cromwell was indeed a Colonel I do not deny. My objection is made merely on the ground of literary tact, and it would have been quite a serious objection if this 'Colonel Cromwell' had been a figure which anyone could take seriously. Mr Charles Cartwright appears as the Colonel, and the aptitude of his natural method to the impersonation of a truly convincing Cromwell makes me all the more sorry that the authors (of whom, by the way, he is one) have not done more than write a silly little melodrama round him. As I have just suggested, I have a great respect for Mr Cartwright as an actor. He has weight and power, and he never forces a situation. But I trust that he will not always, as he did the other night, let his passion for elocution run away with him. To be distinct is a great thing, no doubt; but an actor ought not to let every word fall with a dull thud before he emits the next. This is what Mr Cartwright did throughout the second and third acts. In the first act, curiously enough, he had gone to the other extreme, and thrown correct punctuation to the winds. 'My Lord,' he cried, 'welcome to our house, Mother. This is my Lord Charlton our Guest,' and so forth. These tricks are distressing, when a fine actor plays them.

[ *15 September 1900* ]

## FARCE FOR MERRIE ENGLAND

Nothing seems to me more dismal than humour unadorned, humour by itself. In the expression of an intellect, or of a sense of beauty, or even of a point of view, let there, by all means, be a strong flavour of humour: the stronger the better. By such pervasive flavour are intellect and sense of beauty and strong moral purpose made the more palatable. But at the flavour itself, 'neat,' my gorge rises and revolts; I am as one called on to make his meal off a condiment. The whole secret of humour is for me in contrast, in incongruity. Except in union with some form of high seriousness humour does not exist for me.

Thus you will understand that I have no toleration for what is called 'the funny man.' I do not, however, deny that many people like him very much. To most people (for the true sense of humour is given only to a minority) 'the funny man' is one of the luxuries (or necessities, perhaps) of life. And the demand for him is readily supplied. In social life he is ubiquitous: almost every household contains a sample of him. In journalism, too, he is never far to seek. He has his 'column' here, and his 'page' there; and bookstalls groan under the weight of little papers exclusively consecrated to the somersaults he is turning in words and in line. Naturally, you would expect to find him actively working that unique mine of lucre, the theatre. You would think to pass him squatting nightly outside the stage-door, grinning over enormous pans of ore. Why should you be disappointed? Why is he not there? In a word, why are there no British farces?

The British public makes as constant a demand for farces as for comic papers. I can sympathise with this demand (though, by reason of a peculiarity confessed at the outset, I cannot share it), and I wish it were met. It was not really met by the American farces which were lately in vogue at the Strand Theatre. American fun is more nearly akin to British fun than is that of any other nation; but there is still a wide gulf between the two; and fun, like fruit, is the worse for a crossed Atlantic. Nevertheless, the policy of importation from America is much better than that elder policy which Messrs A. and S. Gatti (under the spirited supervision of Mr Charles Frohman, an American) have revived at the Vaudeville Theatre—that elder and utterly idiotic policy of importation from France. American fun behind British footlights is as much better than French fun as would be British fun than American. Why does not our prancing native breed of 'funny men' save us, at least, from the leavings of the Palais Royal?

Of course, the explanation is in that simple fact which explains so many mysteries of our drama: that most of our theatres are managed by the blind and the deaf. By all means, let the afflicted classes have as many special chances of diversion as a Christian community can afford them. But let these diversions be such as will not inflict actual discomfort on all the other classes. Let the theatres be managed by men who have, if not eyes to see for themselves, then at least ears to hear from other people. If, by some subtle means of communication, one could appeal to the present class of managers, and ask them why they persisted in having their farces adapted from the French, they would reply that it was because that had always been the custom; and, if they could be called to account for this custom, they would account for it by the proposition that no one in England could write a really good farce. Forty years ago, indeed, that proposition had been true enough. *Punch* had not yet produced its crop of imitators and thus created a general demand for fun and a consequent supply of 'funny men' in all walks of life. Drama, moreover, did not exist here. Not only for farce, but also for tragedy, comedy and melodrama, London had to hold Paris in fee. But now that the three other forms have become naturalised, why should the first not be allowed to come in with them? How, by the way, were the managers induced to realise that there were British writers capable of those three other forms? Obviously, by the importunities of those British writers. Thus it seems that I have exaggerated the degree in which managers are afflicted. It seems that they *can* see and hear if only they be enough bullied. The true reason for the continuance of French farces seems to be that the ordinary routine of 'the funny man' is in itself so arduous as to unfit him for the exertion of bullying fools out of their folly.

Meanwhile *Self and Lady*, the farce at the Vaudeville, is a type of the abortions to which Merrie England is accustomed. It differs from the rest only by reason of the fact that M. Pierre Decourcelles, the author, has not yet presented a version of it in Paris. Thus British playgoers may console themselves with the hope that the addition of impropriety will make it funny, instead of mortifying themselves with the knowledge that the elimination of impropriety has made it dull. Things past, even when they were never ours, fill us with melancholy; whereas we rejoice vaguely in things to be, even though we are to have no share in them. Thus it may be that *Self and Lady* will succeed better than most plays of its kind. I do not know whether anyone, seeing these plays, really takes any aesthetic pleasure in 'spotting' from internal evidence the passages where the impropriety came in or, (as here,) is to come in. In any case, such an aesthetic pleasure seems to me of a poor kind; and it is, unfortunately, the only one which these plays can pretend to afford. In fact, I have no patience with these plays. The public laughs at them, certainly; but it would laugh at anything called a farce. It does not, however, laugh heartily. Only once, throughout the whole first night of *Self and Lady*, was there a really spontaneous and full-bodied roar of laughter; and that was when there was a genuinely funny sentence spoken from the stage. 'You are an actor!' says someone to a pathetic and melodramatically-dressed man who has been telling some rigmarole. The man throws up his arms and folds them across his breast, murmuring 'At last!' That is good, crude, straightforward, indigenous fun. The audience rose at it, then gradually subsided into their attitude of genial toleration. Not once again had it any reason for rising. The blanks left for the impropriety of the French version were filled in by those 'wheezes' which are tried persistently on this generation because they failed to amuse either the last generation or the last but one: ' "Who are you?" 'Huret.' 'Huret? The Devil!' 'No, not the Devil." ' &c., &c. One character distinguished himself by drawing away a chair on which another was about to sit; another, by tripping over the door-mat; another, by accidentally squirting the water out of a siphon. I refuse to see why these immemorial things should be done, why those immemorial things should be said, in the theatre. Any 'funny man,' picked up at a hazard out of the street, could very quickly invent any number of funny lines to be spoken, and any amount of funny 'business' to be done; and thus would the unhappy mimes be saved from looking foolish, and the unhappy public from being insulted. And it would not be at all difficult to find in London some 'funny men' who could construct really funny farces. Might not the attempt be made? Messrs Gatti are probably too deep-sunk in traditions to make it of their own accord. But Mr Frohman has lived mostly in America. Let *him* make it, and so justify his intrusion.

It is too late in the day (nor have I space wherein) to dilate on *English Nell* at the Prince of Wales's. But I may as well express my pleasure in the apocalypse of a new and true comedian, Miss Marie Tempest.

[22 *September 1900*]


## A HINT TO THE DRURIOCRACY

'Yes,' slowly replied one of Mr Cecil Raleigh's Cabinet Ministers to a lobbyist eager to know whether there were any news from the East, 'we have news—very *great* news, very *wonderful*, very *satisfactory*!' The last adjective sounded to me, at the moment, rather bathetic, and lowered my opinion of Mr Raleigh's literary sense. Whatsoever is great and wonderful must, I felt, be satisfactory as a matter of course. But reflection brought me round to Mr Raleigh's side. *The Price of Peace* itself is very great, very wonderful, and not (I venture to think) satisfactory at all. Nothing could be finer than the background, more delicious than the bare situations. A bride rejecting her bridegroom at the altar of Westminster Abbey, a Prime Minister confessing at the table of the House of Commons that he has murdered a Russian diplomat, and going one better than Chatham by dying before anyone can conduct him into the lobby—these things, and many other things in this melodrama, leave nothing to be desired. But they are not presented in the right spirit. What no one will take seriously ought not to be presented as serious matter. What will amuse everyone ought to be made more amusing by humorous treatment. To Drury Lane we all go to be impressed by the scenery and amused by the play; none of us goes to be thrilled by the play. Impressed by the scenery we all are. Amused we all are by the play. But our smiles would be laughs if Mr Raleigh had but the courage of his material—the tact for it, rather. It cannot be argued that Mr Raleigh, under guidance, would be incapable of using his material aright. He is known to be a humorist. He, I am sure, smiles in writing his plays not less than we in witnessing them. Why will he not allow that smile to shine through them? Why does he persist in writing as though he were engaged in serious melo-dramaturgy?

The recent annals of the Adelphi Theatre prove that the taste for serious melodrama is obsolescent. The metropolis, at least, has become too sophisticated for the blond hero and the dark villain of that dear old form, cheering the one and hissing the other only in a perfunctory way, for old sakes' sake, with no belief in either of them. If the metropolis cares little now for serious melodrama, how much less can it care for the kind of melodrama which never (save for the manner of its authors) had any vestige of seriousness about it! The form invented by the late Sir Augustus Harris and perpetuated by Mr Arthur Collins is simply this: half a dozen backgrounds representing fashionable or popular scenes, *plus* some motive for throwing some Adelphic characters against them. Obviously, this form excludes the probability of a good melodrama. It is conceivable that with infinite ingenuity and good luck a good melodrama might be written in it. But the fact remains that no one ever has written in it a play which could cheat the audience into forgetting that the scenery was the dominant matter. Nor is it likely that any melodramatist ever will be ingenious and lucky enough to do the trick. But suppose that such a monster were to arise and do the trick, and suppose that meanwhile a taste for serious melodrama had revived in London, would the audience at Drury Lane get an aesthetic illusion? It would not. The essence of melodrama is improbability. An unsophisticated audience will accept the improbable as possible, will be illuded, if the background is not definitely related to common life. An ancestral home, or a village street, or a hillside, or the vasty deep, is an accommodating place where all sorts of things may happen without being laughed at. But such places as 'Niagara' and Westminster Abbey and the House of Commons set sharp limits to receptivity. An audience knows so well what really happens in them that any lurid incidents cast into them by the melodramatist become at once ridiculous. Thus, even if a good serious melodrama were by hook or crook written in the Drurian mode, it would not be worth while. I hope I have said enough to discourage Mr Raleigh from making another forlorn attempt. Mr Collins may say to him 'Pay no attention! I am perfectly satisfied with these plays of yours. Go on in the same way every year of your life!' It is, indeed, quite true that these plays are vastly successful, by reason of their setting. But my point is that they would be even more successful if Mr Raleigh would take his humour in both hands, and make them avowedly funny.

I do not know whether Mr Raleigh has ever read Robert Louis Stevenson's *New Arabian Nights*. If he has not done so, he must. In that delicious book he will find the means of his salvation. He will find there something very like his own work, with a great difference from it. He will find the most preposterous and unheard-of things happening in the very heart of London as we know it: robberies, conspiracies, murders, lovers' meetings, flights, rapes— all the stuff of melodrama scattered blithely broadcast around the railings of Leicester Square. All the scenes are described in a manner of most minute realism. Melodrama has here as realistic a background as at Drury Lane. But here it is not merely diverting: it is excruciatingly funny, for every page is lit up by the irony of the writer. The smile shines through, and how lustily we rejoice in every fresh adventure! Nay! the frank absurdity of everything, the fact that no appeal is made to reason, enables us to believe that everything actually happens. Prince Florizel is for us a real figure *quia impossibilis*, and we hold our breath in the mysterious mansion while he goes forth into the dawn-lit garden to kill in single combat the President of the Suicide Club. We are bursting with laughter, and yet we are really frightened. When Mr Raleigh's Prime Minister shoots the Russian diplomat we are merely conscious that Lord Salisbury would do nothing of the kind: we are not moved, because Mr Raleigh wishes us to be moved. But if Mr Raleigh would be frankly extravagant, making his characters speak some such fantastic language as is spoken by Stevenson's, then we should really be thrilled even in our roars of laughter. Mr Raleigh could not of course reproduce the queer beauty of that language; but he might at least be comically high-flown. Would that Stevenson himself were alive to dramatise one of his own extravagant tales for Drury Lane! I fancy he would have delighted in the task. *The Dynamiter* would be quite irresistible under Mr Collins's auspices, with a realistic reproduction of the outrage of Red Lion Court, in which, as Zero pathetically boasted, 'a child was injured.' Yes! I wish the author of *The Dynamiter* were here to make Drury Lane delightful in the autumn; more especially because then Drury Lane might be made delightful in the winter, too, by the author of the *Child's Garden of Verses*.

Mr Jones's new play at the Duke of York's Theatre requires much more space than is left to me; I will write about it next week. Meanwhile, let me reply to a long and interesting letter which you will find (or will have found) in another column. 'H.H.,' with delightful ingenuity, tries to show that the moral drawn by me from *Julius Caesar*—the vanity of idealism in practical affairs—was never pointed by Shakespeare himself, for that his Brutus was not an idealist but a self-seeking humbug. For the real Brutus I hold no brief. He may deserve all the unkind things said of him by Mommsen and 'H.H.' But I must defend, warmly, the Brutus of Shakespeare. Had the poet, like 'H.H.' and myself, read his Mommsen, his Brutus might have been a sorry figure. But the poet had not done this, and I cannot swallow the attempt to show that he made up in instinct for his lack in erudition. I cannot swallow the suggestion that Brutus was won over by the ignoble arguments of Cassius. There is nothing in Shakespeare's dialogue to support such a theory. Cassius, in a rough and ready way, uses the kind of arguments that would appeal to himself. He betrays his own character, not that of his friend. Brutus lets him talk himself out. 'How I have thought of this and of these times,' he says, 'I shall recount hereafter,' and hints an approval of Cassius's policy. He has already arrived independently, along his own lines, at the same conclusion as his friend. 'But,' 'H.H.' would argue, 'his own lines were those of "jealousy, envy, and ambition." He took a high moral attitude throughout the conspiracy because he was a hypocrite.' Very well. Then how would the dramatist show him to be a hypocrite? Obviously, by making him reveal his true self in soliloquy. This is how Shakespeare makes Brutus soliloquise in the next act:

'It must be by his death: and, for my part,
I know no personal cause to spurn at him,
But for the general.' &c. &c.

'Ah,' the irrepresssible 'H.H.' would say, 'that is Shakespeare's subtlety. Brutus is such a hypocrite that even for himself he will not doff the mask of righteousness.' But that kind of subtlety would defeat its own end. Shakespeare knew his business in drama, and must have known that, if he made a man profess both in public and in private the noblest motives, the audience would accept that man at his own valuation, unless, of course, his actions belied these motives, or unless some other person in the play showed him up. And Brutus does nothing to belie his professed motives, nothing inconsistent with the theory that he was a tyrannicide merely for Rome's sake. And nobody attempts to show him up. On the contrary, he is held up throughout as 'the good boy of the class.' Just before the fall of the curtain, his arch-enemy declares him to have been 'the noblest Roman of them all,' the one conspirator who acted not 'in envy of great Caesar,' but 'in a general honest thought,' and all the rest of it. Shakespeare would not, I think, have written this speech at the very end of his play unless he had meant it to embody what he himself took to be the true judgement on Brutus. No, with all deference, I must continue to believe that Shakespeare believed in Brutus as an honest idealist. As for Antony, my description of him is scarcely combated by 'H.H.' He loved Caesar, certainly, and was anxious to avenge him. But he was very careful that the avenging process should not compromise himself. He was prepared to face either way. Being a man of the world, knowing the temper of the people, he played off immediate self-interest against the idea of liberty. He knew how little ideas count in politics. And it is in his triumph that I still find the moral of the play. 'H.H.' finds the moral elsewhere. I do not object. A masterpiece can be seen rightly from many aspects. I have merely tried to justify my own aspect.

[*29 September 1900*]

# THIS INIMPEDIBLE MR JONES

I know not which is the quainter phenomenon: the persistency of the dramatic critics, as a class, in belittling Mr Jones, or the continued success of Mr Jones in dwarfing before the public those rivals whom the dramatic critics delight to honour. Mr Jones, according to the scribes, is not a good playwright; and yet, obviously, he is the most successful playwright of his time. Of course, the scribes might reconcile these two facts by asserting that public favour is no criterion of merit in art. But that would be to cut the ground from beneath their feet; inasmuch as (I speak of them as a class) they regard the public as a sage court of appeal in dramatic cases, and themselves as loving interpreters of the public taste. And so they must use some other means of persuading themselves that he who puts their backs up writes bad plays. Necessity is the mother of invention, and they found the means on the hundredth night of *The Manoeuvres of Jane*. They explained, unanimously, that this poor rigmarole had been saved by the genius of the mimes engaged for it. Confronted with *The Lackey's Carnival* and with the likelihood that it would have as unconscionable a run as *The Manoeuvres of Jane*, they again rushed into ecstasies over the acting: the play was poor stuff throughout but it was possible that the brilliant interpretation of it might &c. And they have just repeated the trick over *Mrs Dane's Defence*. 'Mr Jones,' says the most typical of the critics, 'has fitted up a kind of framework, and Mr Wyndham, with the members of his company, has filled in the living figures with such success that a drama of extraordinary thinness in construction and in the quality of its story becomes at once a success through the quality of its acting.' Doubtless, the critic of the *Daily Telegraph* knows as well as I that the most a playwright can do is to 'fit up a kind of framework,' and that a play is good or bad according as the framework is of a right or wrong kind. But his implication is obvious: Mr Wyndham and Miss Lena Ashwell deserve the credit of having saved Mr Jones, and had their parts been acted by inferior mimes the play would have been nowhere. I should be the last to deny the value of Mr Wyndham's acting, or of Miss Ashwell's. I intend to pay each of them a flaming tribute before I conclude this article. I know that the tensity of our emotion in watching the third act of *Mrs Dane's Defence* was due partly to the fineness of the acting. But I protest that it is unfair (or would be unfair, were it not so ludicrous) to withhold praise from the man who conceived that third act and wrote that dialogue which the two mimes so finely interpret for him. Anyone with any sense for the theatre must know that the scene between Mrs Dane and Sir Daniel Carteret would be tremendous even in the hands of two duffers. It is an 'actor-proof scene,' in the sense that it could only be more or less tremendous in proportion to the ability of its exponents. Had any other dramatist written it, how differently it would have fared at the critics' hands! Had Mr Pinero written it, what a marketful of flowers would have thrown across the shoulders of Mr Wyndham and Miss Ashwell at the feet of 'our premier dramatist'! But then Mr Pinero has never got himself disliked by the critics. For he is not a personal force, he stands for no ideas. His amiable lack of courage and originality (combined with his great technical ability and his humour) have won him his exaltation at the critics' hands. He is still dubbed 'our premier dramatist,' and will continue to be so dubbed, although Mr Jones is now (after many years of learning) his equal in technique, and has as much sureness and neatness in expressing through the medium of drama what is in his head as has Mr Pinero in expressing what is in the heads of other people. What Lord Rosebery is in politics, that is Mr Pinero in drama: each is a leader by reason of his not leading. When Lord Rosebery tried to lead his party, he was by his party hustled out of public life. If he tried to lead again, the process would probably be repeated. If Mr Pinero had ever tried to lead, he would have been hounded down by a pack of furious critics. He would no longer have been dubbed 'our premier dramatist.' His weakness is his strength. Mr Jones's strength is his weakness. He must expect no laurels from the critics as a class. But he may find consolation in the rare coincidence that he, whose plays have on the average longer runs and catch the public more surely than the plays of other men, is also the dramatist most admired by the few folk who take a serious interest in dramatic art.

'Of extraordinary thinness in construction and in the quality of its story.' In other words, a simple play, evolving itself quite naturally through the conflict of a few characters who are placed in certain simple circumstances. Not a machine-play, compact of little wheel-like characters, for the out-grinding of situations. Mr Jones has used his ingenuity not in twisting up and smoothing out a series of complications beyond the power of Life, but in contriving certain complications in which Life might easily keep pace with him. In form, the play is a comedy, with a tragic interlude. This interlude is the great point of the play. It may be that Mr Jones wrote the rest of the play for its sake. But it matters not whether Mr Jones acted on this principle or not. A dramatist is quite justified in writing a play for the sake of a scene, so long as he leads up to the scene in a natural and plausible manner. And in *Mrs Dane's Defence* there is nothing to betray a hunt for effect. The great scene comes inevitably out of what has gone before, and what has gone before was a natural procession of events. Nor is what comes after the great scene a mere perfunctory winding-up. It is an anticlimax of the right kind. The results of the great scene are dubious when the curtain rises on the fourth act. The characters have still to find their way out. And Mr Jones leaves them to find it out for themselves, leaves them to do what they would do in real life. The way they find is, as we are convinced when it is shown to us, the only way which they, being what they are and being placed in these circumstances, could find. There is no straining after effect, no suicide committed with a view to giving the audience an extra thrill. None of the characters is of a suicidal tendency, and accordingly none of them commits suicide. They make the best of a bad job, and the curtain falls on a convincing comedy.

But, even if the setting of the great scene were wrought ill, Mr Jones would still have to be congratulated on a triumph. He would still have done what no one else has yet done: given us in the theatre that peculiar kind of emotion which is sometimes to be felt in a law-court. Law-courts are dull enough places at most times, though one finds in the dullest little suit more entertainment than in the average play. But there are times when the law-courts afford one the most intense and intolerable emotion. To see a clever witness, whose whole future depends on his ability to maintain unshaken some story which (you are sure) he has invented; to hear him (or her) cross-examined by a master in the horrible art; to watch that long-drawn contest between mind and mind, that duel of stealthy approaches and stealthy evasions, of sudden thrusts parried, and of blows driven home—I know not any excitement so fearful as comes to me in these moments. It is often said that no false story, however ably planned, can withstand the onslaught of a first-rate cross-examiner. But this is not true. I remember hearing the late Mr Hurlbert cross-examined for two whole days on a story which was well known to be false, cross-examined mercilessly by the late Mr Candy. He never tripped once. Preposterous and impossible as his story was to common-sense, it could not be shaken legally. The verdict had to be given in his favour. But usually, of course, the desperate skill of a witness at bay gradually breaks down before the cold professional skill of the lawyer. The witness begins to hesitate. He contradicts himself. Asked to reconcile the contradiction, he is silent. You hear the rustle and the sigh that are called 'sensation' by the reporters. You see the Judge turn and glance ominously over his spectacles. Your sympathy is all for the wretched creature in the witness-box, and yet all the time you are aware of a keen intellectual delight in the process by which he is being ruined. Well! it is that dual emotion which Mr Jones has enabled us to feel for the first time in a theatre. When Sir Daniel Carteret is putting his questions to Mrs Dane, we hold our breath, while one side of our nature is bleeding for the woman, and the other rejoicing in Sir Daniel's skill. What will be his next question? Ah, she betrayed herself then! No, she has extricated herself.... Never, save in the crisis of a *cause célèbre*, was such intense silence and stillness as during this scene. Every now and then, after some point elicited, there was the rustle and the sigh which I know so well elsewhere. Of course, the issues in a law-court are real, here they are fictional. But one's interest in a law-suit (unless one be a litigant or a friend of the litigants) is merely aesthetic. I vow that not I nor anyone ever was more moved aesthetically in a law-court than at Wyndham's Theatre last Tuesday. I cannot pay Mr Jones a higher compliment than that.

He, I am sure, will be eager to give a share of the compliment to Mr Wyndham and Miss Ashwell. Let him do so, by all means. Miss Ashwell (whom I delight to see, at length, in a part worthy of her) was quite wonderful as the distracted witness. I shall remember those hunted eyes, those pauses, those quick faint answers, that wild hysteria of her breakdown which after the long ordeal came to us all as a physical relief. And Mr Wyndham, too, was immensely skilful in his combination of the professional lawyer with the prospective father-in-law. He has never done anything better. So fine were the two chief performances that it were absurd to enumerate the rest. Enough that they were satisfactory.

Melodrama, the celebrated art-form, died last Saturday evening at the Lyceum Theatre. As I lately announced, it had long been ailing. At the Adelphi Theatre, the home of its greatest triumphs, it had been lying in a state of piteous collapse; but no one foresaw that its removal to the Lyceum would prove fatal; there was great hope, indeed, that the change of scene would bring about a turn for the better. The end came very suddenly. Universal sympathy will be extended to Messrs F. Latham and Seymour Hicks. They, and Mr Comyns Carr, the eminent specialist, have the consolation of knowing that all was done that could be done by skill and devotion. Indeed (metaphor be dropped), it was because *Auld Lang Syne* was a remarkably good melodrama, fraught with topical emotion, remarkably well acted, remarkably well mounted, that its failure to impress the audience was so signal a proof that there is no longer (at least, in London) any use for melodrama. Had it been a poor play, poorly acted and mounted, the unmannerly 'guying' of its last two acts would have proved nothing. In the actual circumstances, the 'guying' proved conclusively that London audiences can no longer be coaxed even into a sentimental toleration of this form which enthralled them a few years ago. Managers will have to recognise the change that has come over the public. Mr Seymour Hicks, gliding deprecatorily from the footlights under a shower of playful groans, evidently recognised the change. Even Mr Comyns Carr, leading him firmly back and upturning to the gallery 'the front of Jove himself,' must, in his heart, have known that the game of melodrama was up. I think I know the reason of the change that has come over the public; 'but that is another' article. Enough that the change has come, and that all old playgoers who keep warm corners in their hearts for the old hero and heroine and villain must lose no time in booking seats for the Lyceum. After the run of this piece, these figures will be (in London) no more. Their knell was tolled in the titters of last Saturday evening. Melancholy music! all the more melancholy because it was suspended during the appearances of the comic man. Yes! even the comic man will have to go. 'Him too hath Time betrayed unto Death.' Let the indignation of him and his comrades as they fly down to the shades be tempered by us with a tear or two.

[*13 October 1900*]

## ADVICE TO OLD PLAYGOERS

Time is often accused of dealing hardlier with women than with men. The imputation is unfair. Time has an equally cruel 'sinch' for either sex. The tragedy of woman, that her face changes with the progress of the years, is not less bitter than the tragedy of man, that with the progress of the years his mind changes not at all. That tragedy which gradually unfolds itself on the surface of a woman's mirror is well balanced by this tragedy which passes in the cells of a man's brain. Nay! the very fact that we hear so little about the man's tragedy, so much about the woman's, seems to imply that the man's is the more bitter of the two. The worst tragedies are those which cannot be endured save in silence; and this is one of them. Now will I, over whose head have passed not yet so many lustres as to make me personally sensitive, venture to break that deep silence, to obtrude my sympathy with old age generally, and to give some wholesome advice to old playgoers in particular. I shall not be thanked, perhaps, by the recipients; but I have a purpose, and will risk ingratitude for its sake.

Let the old playgoers not try to cover their position. That which they know so well in their hearts let them confess with their lips, and let them cap confession with good works. Let them, for the good of the community, confess unflinchingly that the very fact that they are old playgoers robs of all weight their opinions on current drama, and let them cease henceforth from their efforts to hinder that drama's progress.

Time flies (let them confess), and under its wings the world changes. New men spring up, bearing witness to new gods, new ideas, discoveries of all kinds. Always the world is changing, always the races of man are progressing, or going retrograde, through troubled air, under shifting lights, mysteriously. And every man who is born into the world moves with the world during the first period of his life. He grows, he sees, he absorbs until he is replete. Repletion, incapacity for fresh notions, the end of youth, may come sooner or later according to the nature and circumstances of the man himself. But it does always come, for every man to whom ironic Fate grants 'a goodly span' of life. For every 'spared' one of us, sooner or later, life becomes as a book on the lap of a blind man, or, say rather, as a book which man had but begun to read when blindness fell upon his eyelids. And the poor fellow sits there trying to persuade himself, by proclaiming to others, that there was nothing left for him to read. Some of these others are convinced that he is right, and become blind themselves. Others, pitying him, do not contradict him. Others, again, take the book gently from his lap, and read to him from the point at which he ceased. And the blind man shakes his head, and stops them, and declares that what they are reading is sheer twaddle. He is loud in his surprise at the sudden falling-off of the author, and he harks back to the brilliant chapters which he read with his own eyes. Them he mumbles, word for word, fired with a strange enthusiasm. In the rosy haze of memory, they seem to him now even more beautiful than in the white glow of the first perusal. And we who have not read them, flick back the leaves and run our eyes over them, and find them extraordinarily stupid, and tell him so, brutally. A violent scene ensues between us, and we leave him to sit alone in his blindness. He sits there, and the tears fall from his sightless eyes, for he knows well, by some instinct of his heart, that we are right and that he is wrong, that what we have read to him is finer than what he read with his own eyes, and that he hates the continuation only because we have eyes for the reading of it, whilst he has not.

This metaphor (of which I am heartily sick) holds good, of course, only for periods and places in which the movement is really progressive. There are periods and places of retrogression, and in these the protests of the blind man are quite sincere—and salutary. But London and the year 1900 A.D. are not a place and period of retrogression, so far as I (dramatic critic) am concerned. Whatever may be happening to politics, literature, music, painting, in drama there is a very obviously progressive movement. In the halcyon days of our old playgoers drama touched its nadir. Practically, it did not exist. Clear proof of this is afforded by the almost unbroken silence preserved about it by our old playgoers. Now and again, they let slip the name of Sheridan Knowles, or Bulwer, or H. J. Byron; but the whole flood of their garrulousness is stored for the mimes of their day—the genius displayed by this or that member of this or that vast family beginning with a K., in this or that Shakespearian revival. There were no playwrights in that period. Playwrights only began to crop up in the 'eighties. Till that decade dawned, the mimes had

had all the glory to themselves. This unhealthy state of things is now being remedied, slowly and surely. Our drama is not yet very much to boast of; but it is better than nothing, and its superiority to nothing is being annually increased. Our playwrights are pressing nearer and nearer to life, and are, moreover, becoming less and less coy of ideas. In a word, they are progressing. And thus by their outcries against modern drama our old playgoers make themselves ridiculous. But my wish to hush them down is inspired not merely by the sentiment that age ought to be venerable, but by the fact that they have, unfortunately, a very real power for mischief. Some of the morning papers (and it is by the morning papers that the public is most affected) still employ old playgoers as dramatic critics. Others, again, employ gentlemen who have not even that bad qualification, and who attend theatres simply in the spirit of reporters, with a view to reeling off half-a-column or so of the kind of verbiage which gives them least trouble. The kind of verbiage which gives them least trouble is the kind of verbiage which has been poured forth again and again. To say new things postulates thought, and so these writers follow the line of least resistance by copying exactly the manner of the old playgoers. They stolidly range themselves against any progressive movement in drama. Thus the public is misled, and the progressive movement is seriously retarded. But, if the old playgoers would only realise that they were writing nonsense, and would make modest way for the younger generation of thoughtful persons, then the mere reporters would be deprived of the example and the excuse which now they find in them, and would begin to model themselves on the superior young men. The result would be a palpable acceleration of our progress in an art which, alas! cannot, under modern conditions, progress without conversion of the public.

Therefore, I earnestly entreat the race of old playgoers to efface itself. Those who merely talk are not so directly mischievous as those who also write. But the fact that they do talk, and talk loudly, encourages the writers to persevere. If they were silent, these writers would be more likely to let the pens drop from their hands. Of course, there are exceptions among old playgoers—men whom I delight to honour. Nothing is more attractive (is anything more rare?) than a man who, despite many years, has kept his mind malleable and elastic, who is able to understand, and eager to welcome, new developments in the things which he loved when he was young. Among the old playgoers who are also dramatic critics there is one such reverend signor. But one critic of *The Globe* does not make a summer, does not mitigate the bleak winter of his contemporaries. It is in the hope of making his example efficacious that I have been composing my precept. After all, what does my precept amount to? Merely an appeal for a little modesty. One hears much of the arrogance of youth; yet youth is not really arrogant, being ever ready to submit to new masters. A far more plausible charge can be preferred against the bumptiousness of eld. They are the real arrogants—the old men who declare that what themselves have learnt is all that is worth knowing, who boast that they were active and mature at a time when we young men were in swaddling-clothes —as though that fact were not in itself a *prima facie* vindication of our opinions against theirs. I do not ask Nestor to surrender his ideals. Let him cherish them as fondly as he will. Only let him be modest enough to perceive that we cannot be expected to bow down to them, that we have acquired a new and better set, and are on the look-out for a newer and still better. Let him cease to interfere with our ideals, knowing well that in them is our salvation. If he will promise to do this, I will promise that I, hereafter, will not irritate my juniors by declaring that Mr Jones was the last of the good dramatists.... Should I succeed, hereafter, in not breaking my promise? I wonder. I have my doubts.

[*20 October 1900*]

## 'STYLE' AND THE STAGE

Writing, like talking, is the art of expressing thoughts in words. (Shade of Mr Barlow) But there is, necessarily, a vast difference between the oral and the scriptural use of words. When we talk, we have for our ministers not words only, but also gesture, play of feature, modulation of the voice's tone, and regulation of its pace, whereby we may subtly temper or accentuate the words themselves, and fit them, be they never so carelessly chosen, exactly to our meaning. When we write, we have nothing but words, words, with those little summary and meagre things whose hard office is to ape the infinitely variable pauses of the human voice. In some cases, we have also handwriting, in which there is a kind of implicit expressiveness. When, as in letters to our friends, handwriting is the form in which we shall be read, we can, certainly, well express our meaning with less care in the choice of words, can afford to be more colloquial. Letter-writing has a half-way place between conversation and writing for print. It is an art in itself. It may be killed gradually by perversion of that loathsome engine, the type-writer. A typewritten letter composed in an epistolary style means little to him who receives it. Without the handwriting of our correspondent, we cannot (as otherwise, more or less, we can) see him and hear his voice. The correspondent must express himself as carefully as though he were writing for print. At present, the barbarians who type-write their letters (alas! the number of them is increasing annually) have not realised this necessity. They dash off their letters blithely and carelessly, in the old manner, with no suspicion that the result is a kind of bald offence to its recipient. Perhaps, when they realise that true expression through a type-writer entails an elaborate literary style, they will be less loud in their joy over the easiness of the actual manipulation. Perhaps they will go back to pens and ink-pots. Else, the art of letter-writing is obsolescent, for certainly the type-writers must soon realise that the old style does not survive their machinations, and that to persist in it is absurd.

But I have digressed. My concern is with the inequality between the means in talking and the means in writing. The writer has to balance this inequality. He has to produce through printed words the same effect as that which he would produce through spoken words. In short, he must have a style. Not only has he to condense and give form to the matter of his expression, that it may be effective through the medium of print: also he must translate into his phrases his oral manner, reproduce some clear idea of his own personality, his gestures, his inflections, his pauses. To accomplish this difficult process is to have a style. Without a style writing is nothing. Few men have it. None can acquire it. It is a gift bestowed by Nature. It can be cultivated—cannot be too constantly cultivated—by him on whom Nature has bestowed it. But no toil will win it for him to whom Nature has denied it. By dint of practice, certainly, most men of intelligence can acquire style in the old, narrow sense of the word. They can learn to formulate well their matter, to give it close expression and logical sequence and good grammar. They can use prose according to the ideal of the eighteenth century without more trouble than is involved in the learning of any other common trick. They can express meanings easily enough in an impersonal, general way. But to do that is only one fraction of style, as style is understood now. The leader-writers of the daily newspapers, even, have that half at their finger-tips. Would they, on that account, pretend themselves to be stylists? The old journalism, which is the manner of Polyphemus on the Delphic tripod, and the new journalism, which is the manner of 'Arry garbed and coifed after the fashion of Cassandra, are for us equally remote from true style. For in recent years we have discovered that true style is essentially a personal matter, a medium through which a man expresses truth as he himself sees it, and emotions as he himself feels them; that it is, in fact, not a mere spy-hole to things in general, but a spy-hole to things as they are reflected in the soul of the writer. Thus is style in the modern sense a far more complex thing than style in the eighteenth century's sense. To express through printed words all the little side-lights of thought and fine shades of meaning that are in him is the task of the modern stylist; and the tricks and formalities which must be gone through in accomplishing that task carry him further and further away from his ordinary manner in colloquy. It is that very manner which he is trying to reproduce; but the only medium for its reproduction lies leagues away from it. Modern prose style is further removed from colloquialism than was the prose style of the eighteenth century, for this paradoxical reason: that colloquialism is its model.

In dramaturgy, you will perceive, there is a deep pitfall for modern stylists. Most of them are quite aware of the danger, and refrain from writing plays. Occasionally, however, one of them does write a play and walks straight into the pitfall. Mr Henry James did so a few years ago. The characters in *Guy Domville* were made to speak precisely that curious and intricate language through which Mr James reveals himself to us in his books. When Mr James makes the characters in his books speak this language, the result is a trifle disconcerting, and we tolerate it only because Mr James is a more interesting character than any character that even he, finely creative though he is, could project for us. But to hear that language spoken by mimes is quite intolerable. The language becomes mere gibberish. Dialogue spoken on the stage must be composed in a natural and un-literary manner. Every character in an acted play has a voice, has gestures and tricks of face; he must say the kind of things that he would say in real life, and not the kind of things that he would write if he were a modern stylist addressing the public through print. But here I must make two qualifications. One of them is that my dislike of the dialogue in *Guy Domville* does not imply that a dramatist is better without style. On the contrary, the more style he have the better. Only it must be style of a particular kind—the style that selects the most characteristic and pregnant phrases for every character in every situation. In other words, every character must be made to say always what he might say in real life, whilst he must (owing to the conditions of drama) be prevented from saying a great many other things which he might say in real life without adding to the effect of the speech selected by the dramatist. Style, in dialogue, is thus a matter of compression from real life, of translation never. Never? There comes in the other qualification that I premised. In poetic drama the mimes must, of course, express themselves beautifully and unnaturally. The stylist may let himself go there, may be (objectively) a stylist to his heart's content, inasmuch as our illusion is not wooed from the plane of realism. And there is another non-realistic form in which the stylist may give us (objective) style— the form of farce. It is only in the (for us moderns) more important forms of realistic tragedy and comedy that he must curb himself. In poetic drama style is essential. In farces it is an added grace, an intensification of the fun. To be able to make an absurd and absurdly-situated character express himself in terms of exquisite, elaborate gravity is a very valuable power for the farce-writer, and ought to be tended by him lovingly. Robert Louis Stevenson was a master in the art, as I recalled a few weeks ago, regretting that he was not alive to use it in Drury Lane melodrama. You remember the scene between Mrs Vandeleur and her husband when the Rajah's diamond was missing? ' "Madam," said the General, "you might have paved the gutter with your own trash; you might have made debts fifty times the sum you mention; you might have robbed me of my mother's coronet and ring; and Nature might have still so far prevailed that I could have forgiven you at last. But, Madam, you have taken the Rajah's Diamond—the Eye of Light, as the Orientals poetically termed it—the Pride of Kashgar! You have taken from me the Rajah's Diamond," he cried, raising his hands, "and all, Madam, is at an end between us!" "Believe me, General Vandeleur," she replied, "that is one of the most agreeable speeches that I ever heard from your lips; and since we are to be ruined, I could almost welcome the change, if it delivers me from you. You have told me often enough that I married you for your money; let me tell you now that I always bitterly repented the bargain; and if you were still marriageable and had a diamond bigger than your head, I should counsel even my maid against a union so uninviting and disastrous,"' &c. &c. In that immortal scene we have the emotions of rage and horror, contempt and defiance, beautifying expressed in terms of a fantastic style, and it is the contrast between the speeches and the characters that makes the scene immortally delicious. I should love to see it on the stage. Mr Gilbert is the only dramatist who has contrived on the stage a similar effect. Many other dramatists have tried to do so—Mr Pinero, for example—but they had not the requisite combination of literary sense with sense of humour. Captain Marshall, in *The Noble Lord*, which was produced last Thursday at the Criterion Theatre, has also made the attempt, but he again has not enough literary sense to bring it off. Someone else must try. I am surprised to see that Mr Archer, in commenting on the formality of the speeches in Captain Marshall's play, declares that 'such speeches are totally ineffective and burdensome because they spring neither from the character nor (from) the situation.' This is a queer view, surely. The speeches are tedious because they are composed in the style of a leader-writer; not because they are dramatically inappropriate. If they had the grave fantastic grace of Stevenson's speeches their very inappropriateness would make them irresistible. Mr Archer ought to distinguish between farce and realistic comedy.

As for the play itself, there is little to be said of it. The idea is good: a lady loved by the Prime Minister, the Leader of the Opposition, and the Leader of the Irish Party. But Captain Marshall, having conceived the idea, rested on his laurels and made little or nothing of it. There are one or two funny situations in the course of the play, but they are not worked out. The whole thing is spasmodic, perfunctory, and not strong enough to bear the dead weight which Captain Marshall has shovelled on to it—the dreadful dead weight of a satire on the forgotten Women's Rights Movement. There are, however, many good jokes and some very bad epigrams in the play, most of them uttered by Mrs Calvert, to the rolling delight of everyone. In virtue of them, and of her, and of the many other popular mimes engaged, the play will succeed, perhaps.

[*27 October 1900*]

## ENTER MR FRANK HARRIS

To what shall I liken this entry? I need a staggering metaphor. Mr Meredith, only he, could find one for me—one of those monstrous blossoms which he uproots from gardens so remote. His wit would fly off in quest, Puck-like, putting 'a girdle round about the earth,' and anon the far-fetched herb would be to hand. None but he could provide the necessary article. Inalienable is his genius for metaphors which, seeming, at first flash, merely far-fetched, are truly, as one sees a moment later, fitted with minute precision to their purposes. For ordinary occasions ordinary metaphors will serve. But now and again one envies Mr Meredith his inspiration. Vainly I have quested, since the first night of *Mr and Mrs Daventry*, for a metaphor adequate. I return crestfallen. I can but offer to you the obvious old figure which I had rejected—the bull in the china-shop. This poor beast has been overworked so shamefully, for so many years, by so many drovers, that now, perhaps, he scarcely signifies a surprising and destructive energy. But he is all I can offer. Horns to the floor, hoofs in the air, tail a-whirl, the unkindly creature charges furiously hither and thither, and snap! crash! bang! into flying smithereens goes the crockery of dramatic laws and conventions, while the public lies quailing under the counter.

A noble, uncomfortable sight! Never did a dramatist play such havoc with what one is accustomed to hold sacred as does the author of what Mrs Campbell has dared to produce at the Royalty Theatre. The first act of the play contains nothing relevant at all, except a few meagre hints of character to come. The curtain falls on a soliloquy in which these hints are recapitulated. A soliloquy is bad enough (to modern ears) even when it tells us something we did not know. But a soliloquy for the summing-up of our knowledge! Mr Harris revels in such soliloquies. At the end of the second act, Mrs Campbell is again explaining to us what we perfectly understand. Can it be that Mr Harris has a sentiment for the rococo? No, obviously, he does but wish, in his wantonness, to wound us. He stands there, ταυρηδὸν ὑποβλέψας, determined to have his horns through all our sacred prejudices, be they ancient or modern. We have a modern prejudice against irrelevant comic servants, in serious plays? 'Very well then,' snorts Mr Harris, with an ominous glare in his eyes. And forthwith he throws into his second act a comic English cook, into his third act a comic Irish valet, into his fourth act a comic German waiter. We expect the great excitement of a play to be kept till we are near the end of the third act? Accordingly, Mr Harris drops his climax plump into the middle of his second act. When a good, unhappily-married lady is loved by a good man, we expect that he, not she, shall press for the elopement? Accordingly, Mrs Daventry presses for the elopement, quite of her own accord. When the good lover is told by his valet that the bad husband has arrived unexpectedly, and asks the lady to retire to an inner room till her husband shall have taken his leave, we expect some variation on the 'screen scene'? Nothing of the sort, accordingly, happens. The husband, in due course, takes his leave. The lady emerges and resumes the thread of her discourse. When the runaway pair is living in guilty comfort at Monte Carlo, and the bad husband wishes to put a bullet through the head of his supplanter, we do not expect him to put the bullet through his own head? Of course not. So he proceeds to do it.

You will observe that the prejudices gored by Mr Harris are of two kinds; some are technical, others psychological. Some of our technical prejudices he ought, I think, to have spared. There is a real and sound objection to soliloquies, for example: they are unnatural, they spoil illusion. Sometimes it must be very difficult for a dramatist to avoid them; but he must learn to overcome the difficulty whenever it occurs. To do so is an essential point in dramaturgy. I am no over-rater of technique. I would far rather see a play by an interesting man of letters who has not mastered the tricks of stagecraft than a play by a man who has done nothing else. I would willingly sacrifice the whole life-work of (say) Mr Sydney Grundy for *Mr and Mrs Daventry*. I regret very much that the tricks of stagecraft are so many and so difficult that many interesting men of letters are by them frightened away from dramaturgy. If modern drama were a loose and fluid form, like the Elizabethan drama, we should have a far finer class of playwrights. But the fact remains that modern drama is a very close and precise form, and that modern plays cannot be well written except with closeness and precision. These qualities can be acquired, through patient practice, by any man who has a natural sense of drama. No one who knows Mr Harris as a writer of short stories (or, for that matter, as an editor) will deny his natural sense of drama. No one who has read 'Elder Conklin' and other little perfect works will deny that he is a master in the exigent art of the *conte*. The *conte* has its peculiar, necessary tricks, its artistic conventions, as Mr Harris would admit—tricks that must be acquired, conventions that are binding. I suggest to him that dramaturgy has some similar tricks and conventions. Let him not despise them. Let him not, when he writes his next play, go in for— especially not go out of his way to go in for—soliloquies. Let him eschew comic servants, who do but impede the action and set our emotions out of tune. (Let him imagine what would have been the effect of comic servants in 'Elder Conklin'!) Let him begin his play at the beginning of the first act, as strictly as he begins his every story at its first line. Let him postpone his great scene to the end of the third... no! my pen was running away with me. In putting his great scene into the middle of his second act, Mr Harris has flouted a convention which is not essential to drama. He was quite right to flout it, and I applaud his courage. I do but regret that he did not go even further back, that it was not into the middle of his first act that he put his great scene. I call it the 'great scene' because it is undoubtedly the most exciting. Taken by itself, it has all the appearance of a *scène-à-faire*. But, taken in relation to the rest of the play, it is merely a preparation, a means to an end. It is a circumstantial crisis, easily 'led-up to,' necessary in the production of certain psychological crises. It puts the two chief characters to the test, reveals them to each other and to us, and from it their future relations are evolved. Mrs Daventry is a witness to the misbehaviour of her husband, and subsequently leaves him on account of it. In the meantime, she shields him from a scandal, and he is won over to her by the pride which makes her shield him, and by the pluck and resource with which she does it. On this scene the whole play hinges. And that fact is, by the way, the scene's justification against the furious onslaughts on its decency. That so stalwart a vexillary of public prudery as the critic of the *Daily Telegraph* should cry out against it, was, of course, inevitable. To him all things are impure. With him one does not argue. But Mr Walkley, whose gay banner bears 'common-sense' for its legend, has professed himself terribly shocked, and I cannot help asking why. If nothing came of the scene, if it were dragged in without any relevance to character, then, no doubt, we might be shocked to our hearts' content. But, as the scene is an integral part of a serious drama, we ought not to call attention to such blushes as may mantle to our cheeks at the sight of a married man in a darkened room kissing a lady who is not his wife and locking the door of the room into which they have stolen. Such blushes may be creditable to us as men; but surely we ought not, as serious critics of serious art, to be proud of them. Pressed to a logical conclusion, Mr Walkley would have to deny a dramatist's right to present, in any circumstances, or even to hint at, anything but the domestic virtues. That is a position from which he would certainly be averse. He must forgive me for calling attention to the momentary eclipse of his common-sense. Were not that orb so steadily radiant at other times, I should have said nothing.

The character of Mr Daventry is admirably drawn. It sets Mr Harris very far above the level of ordinary dramatists, and does much to atone for his faults in technique. I know no other stage-study of the apolaustic 'barbarian' than can match it. The man is not heartless, but merely heavy and unimaginative. All his faults spring from his circumstances and his absolute lack of imagination. Having married a sensitive girl, he kills her ideals not because he would not respect them if he could understand them, but simply because they are unintelligible to him. She shrinks into herself, and he becomes bored. 'You're looking a bit pasty, Hilda,' he complains, 'you ought to brisk about more.' He turns with relief to an intelligible lady, one of his own type. His lips are eager for *'les verres épais du cabaret brutal,'* some less brittle vessel. Under the shock of his wife's salvation of him from an unpleasant scene with the lady's husband, he veers heavily round. At first, he merely bursts out laughing. 'By Jove, Hilda, how you scored! You scored all along the line!' But gradually the force of the incident penetrated his pachydermatous soul. His sluggish imagination is stirred at last. He conceives a canine admiration and adoration of his wife. Nothing can cure him of it. Her flight inflames it. He makes clumsy efforts to induce her to return to him. He cannot imagine how she can stand not being respectable. 'You, of *all* women,' he cries, unimaginative to the last.

Told by her that she is quite happy with her lover and still hates the sight of her husband, and that she is going to have a child, he abandons his intention of shooting the lover. He shoots himself. The critics all exclaim that this is an unlikely action. It is not so. It is subtly right. He shoots himself because he cannot bear the idea that his wife should live with a man who is not her husband. By suicide he opens for her the way to matrimony. Stupid to the last, he regards that as her salvation. The good that has been aroused in him culminates in an act of blundering self-sacrifice. He dies from lack of imagination. His death is as characteristic of him as is his every other action. Mr Harris is to be congratulated on a perfect essay in psychology. There are many other good things in the play. But the character of Daventry is the dominating feature of it, putting all the others into the shade. *Mr Daventry* the play should have been called, simply.

Mr Fred Kerr was perfect in the part. The heavy face, heavy gait, heavy voice of the 'barbarian' were exactly rendered, and the heavy bad manners of one who, by accident of birth, had never had to defer to anyone, and who had not enough imagination, not enough sympathy, to make himself pleasant to anyone without definite reason for doing so. Mrs Campbell, too, was very good as Mrs Daventry. But she need not have been quite so *souffrante* at the beginning of the last act. Mrs Daventry, being with the man whom she loved, ought to have effloresced a little. That, obviously, was the author's intention. Mrs Campbell gave one the impression that Mrs Daventry was as miserable as she had ever been. The moral was excellent, no doubt, for the audience; but aesthetically it was amiss. Mr Gerald du Maurier, too, as the lover, need not have been quite so deeply sunk in melancholy calm. He might have managed a bright smile or two, now and again. He might have gesticulated, just a little. His immobility distressed me. Restraint is an admirable thing in acting, but it should not be the kind of restraint that is enforced by a straitwaistcoat.

[*3 November 1900*]

## 'HEROD'

Seeming to me beautiful as poetry, beautiful and terribly powerful as drama, this tragedy does not 'invite' my criticism. Like all great work, it gives me a distaste for the duty of taking a pen and therewith fishing out of an inkpot a record of such emotions as I may have gained from it, such opinions of it as I may hold. The only things worth writing about are the only things one does not care to write about—not, anyhow, on the hebdomadal spree. 'The adventures of the soul among masterpieces'? Oh yes, doubtless; yet the soul is shy of the reporter, however eager be the public. The soul comes back to its home stealthily, loth to be 'interviewed,' even though 'proofs will be submitted' to it. True aesthetic pleasure is inarticulate. What wish have I to explain to myself, to anyone, *why*, or *how*, or *to what degree*, Herod is beautiful; to decide whether the author be a classic or a romantic; to doubt whether this or that scene be 'dramatically effective,' this or that motive 'made clear,' this or that line 'musical'? Why should I put myself out to this solemn fuss of criticism? Presumably, because it is my business to do so.

Lest I seem to gush over *Herod*, let me confess that I did not, by any means, go determined to praise it. Many critics had already staked their reputations on Mr Phillips's genius; but I was not one of them; I was not standing or falling by Mr Phillips. Indeed, I was somewhat prejudiced against his work. I had had the misfortune to read *Paolo and Francesca* after, not before, its boom. It is a fact that, when a figure is set upon a pedestal, the higher be the pedestal the smaller does the figure appear to our eyes. One instance of this law in optics is Lord Nelson in Trafalgar Square. Another was Mr Phillips immediately after the publication of *Paolo and Francesca*. If the sailor-hero were on our own level, we could better appreciate his magnitude. If the star-touching sublimity of Mr Phillips had not been proclaimed to me so vociferously, *Paolo and Francesca* (such is human weakness) would have impressed me more. Nelson, after all, has only one column. Mr Phillips had columns and columns, in all the newspapers, and there were all the critics, of all ages and denominations, turning ecstatic somersaults around the plinths. Apart from the natural reaction caused by such antics, one is quite well justified in doubting genius that is, at its outset, so widely welcomed. Genius implies strangeness, a gift of new things—in fact, originality. Accordingly, it must always be distrusted at first. The history of all the arts proves this rule. Nor could I find in *Paolo and Francesca* the additional proof of an exception. It seemed to me very delicate, very smooth, wholly derivative. It might have been the work of a beautiful, etherialised sixth-form boy with an instinct for the stage. It was exquisitely tactful, could give no offence to anyone. Such tact is not a good sign in a young man: what young genius has ever been tactful? Original power, in its first outburst, may have any quality, except tact. Here, in *Paolo and Francesca* was a happy blend of drama and poetry. To that extent, the play was new for us. But had either the poetry or the drama any strong new note in it? I found none, neither strength nor newness. Possibly, that was my fault. My love and knowledge of literature is less for poetry than for prose. Nor have I the particular kind of imagination which enables one to judge surely of drama from printed pages. Had I seen *Paolo and Francesca* acted, it might have overwhelmed me. But *Alexandro aliter visum*. Having now seen the second play acted, I am quite prepared to be overwhelmed anon by the first. I merely say that my reading of the first left me cold—kindly but frosty, and with no passionate anticipation of the second. Indeed, I expected that the second would be inferior. I could not imagine Mr Phillips going beyond a wistful austerity, whether in poetry or in drama. *Paolo and Francesca* was a theme well enough suited to such treatment; but how would a fiery-coloured theme fare under it? What would become of Herod, magnificent monster? I waited, and wondered.

Well! I am not sure that in *Paolo and Francesca* the concord between the poetry and drama was not more perfect than it is in *Herod*. But that is because Mr Phillips, as a dramatist, has risen so grandly to his new theme. His drama is so fiery-coloured, so intense, the characters so largely projected, the action so relentlessly progresses from scene to scene, always accumulating strength, till, at last, the final drops of pity and awe are wrung from us, that only the greatest of dramatic poets could accompany it with verse quite worthy of it. Tremendous sonority and depth and swiftness, tremendous images, are needed for its perfect expression. Merely having twice seen the play, not possessing a copy of it, I cannot well substantiate my suggestion that Mr Phillips is, throughout the play, lyric rather than tragically dramatic in his expression. Such, nevertheless, is my suggestion, and perhaps, when the play is published, I shall be able to follow it up. (I leave, meanwhile, due margin for the fact that modern dramatic training does not include the delivery of blank verse, and that full justice is not done to Mr Phillips's lines by more than a few of the mimes at Her Majesty's.) Of course, the connexion between matter and manner is a very subtle one. The two things are hard to disentangle. Expression of tragically dramatic emotions is sure to be, in a degree, tragically dramatic. But still, if we venture to compare the expression in Shakespeare's tragedies with the expression in Mr Phillips's *Herod*, we shall find that, whereas the latter is seldom tragically dramatic except in virtue of its matter, the former is so, invariably, in itself. In Shakespeare there is never any loss by friction. The words and rhythms are as great as the thoughts, and the full measure of the thoughts comes upon us with immediate percussion. Listening to Mr Phillips's lines is like watching a fiery waving torch through a thin clear sheet of ice that never quite melts, or that melts only at moments and then freezes again. The ice is very thin, very clear, has a beauty of its own, and lends, even, a peculiar beauty to our vision of the torch. Still, one wishes it away. As for the merely technical aspect of Mr Phillips's verse, the prosody, that I leave to the experts, of whom I am not one. Enough for me that the verse sounded always musical. Often it was murdered by the mimes (first murderess: Miss Maud Jeffries); but then, it was beautiful in death. When it was well delivered, one was never (as in all other modern poetic plays) conscious that it was an artificial mode. It came to us (having come likewise to Mr Phillips) as a natural language, not as a feat in translation. There were but two moments when I was jarred. Any reminder of the common language of life makes one uncomfortable in listening to poetry. Such a line as 'The multitude of labourers thrown from work' is bad because 'thrown out of work' is familiar slang to us. 'The multitude of men thrown out of work' would be bad enough, as recalling the daily newspaper. 'Thrown from work' is worse, for it not only recalls the daily newspaper, but also shows us Mr Phillips forcing the daily newspaper to be metrical. I suggest 'The multitude of unused labourers' as one of many loopholes. My other objection is to

> 'By day a cloud,
> By night a pillared fire.'

Here, of course, the phrase recalled is not slang. If 'a pillar of cloud by day and a pillar of fire by night' happened to scan, Mr Phillips might use it without doing any damage. But his metrical version of it is objectionable because the phrase is so familiar to us that any change in it gives us, inartistically, a jump, and sets us thinking of the tricks played with the Psalms, long ago, by the present Duke of Argyll. The worst of the matter is that the words occur in the final speech of the play. At this of all solemn moments, we should have thoughts for none but Herod, not even for the Duke of Argyll.

So much for *Herod* as poetry. I must defer the consideration of *Herod* as dramaturgy until next week.

[*10 November 1900*]


## 'HEROD' AS DRAMATURGY

The prime point to Mr Phillips's honour is that he has given us in Herod himself a finely convincing figure. He has not merely conceived a lover and labelled him with the name of an eminent character in history. That is the lamentable way of most dramatists, but not his. He convinces us, by adduction of dramatic evidence, that this is indeed Herod the Great. He does not say 'You may take it from me that my hero is the great statesman or warrior whose name is familiar to you all; and now let's get on to the love-interest.' With the dramatist's instinct, he knows that this little trick is bound not to come off, never has come off, never will; and that if a dramatist wish to obtain leverage with the name of a great historical figure he must make the figure show on the stage something of the greatness which we suppose it to have shown in real life. Accordingly, he shows to us not merely Herod the lover, but Herod the statesman, the tyrant, the man of grandiose ambitions and achievements. We see Herod, under the shock of Antony's death, determining on his policy, brushing aside the unimaginative cunning of the advice offered by his Chief Councillor. Forth he will go to be face to face with Caesar himself, and will either have his will of Caesar or defy him with war. Forth he goes, the imaginative brain of Judaea, leaving to his ministers 'whom to corrupt, and whom to kill, and whom to magnify,' while he is at the higher task. He returns, and we hear how he has secured his sovereignty. Even as he has wrestled against Rome, we see him wrestling against his own citizens of Jerusalem. And we see him bend these maddened citizens to his will, even as he bended Rome—Rome, whose mysterious, unseen power we are feeling throughout the play, as it were midway between Herod and Jehovah. The armed mob dares not strike him, subdued by his not idle boast that he is Judaea itself—'these veins are rivers, and these arteries are roads.' Yes, here before us is indeed Herod the Great. And it is because of this conviction, because we see in him a man fulfilled with power and with the lust for power, that the tragedy strikes deeply into us. For the motive of the tragedy, the pervading motive of it, is the conflict between Herod the king and Herod the lover, his passion for policy and his passion for Mariamne. Always these two passions are at war. Now one, now the other, triumphs. Again and again does Herod the lover triumph over Herod the king. And by our knowledge of the king's passion we measure how great must be the strength of his love for Mariamne, how awful his severance from her. 'Witness at least,' he cries to Mariamne's unheeding ears, 'that never woman was so loved as thou, that never man from the beginning loved as I.' And again the boast seems to us not idle. His love being thus realised by us, we realise, also, how deep must be that love and mourning for her murdered brother which enables Mariamne to withstand it, and prefer death to it. The whole tragedy is great because Herod himself is great. It is because the poet has had the power to create a great figure that his drama becomes sublime. Other dramatic poets might create a love-passion as finely as Mr Phillips. But could they create a great figure as its receptacle? The inquiry is rather futile, Mr Phillips being the only dramatic poet we have.

Out of the conflict he has chosen for his tragedy, out of the interplication of 'policy and passion', Mr Phillips draws his cumulative series of tragically ironic scenes. The boy Aristobulus, Mariamne's brother, must die, lest Herod be cast from his throne. As he passes out from the palace, Herod stops him and asks where he is going. He is going to bathe in the lake. Are there no treacherous weeds that will drag him down? No, he is a strong swimmer. He is going to swim, and to float, float 'with his eyes skyward.' Herod looks into his eyes, looks away—those eyes 'are so like to Mariamne's.' The boy passes out, and the faithful Sohemus, who is to do what 'the treacherous weeds' will not do, follows him. Mariamne appears from the door of her chamber, and calls her husband to her. At sunset he will be on his journey; let him come to her and be with her now. Herod approaches her, slowly. They go out in each other's arms. The sun sinks lower. Somewhere the brother of Mariamne is bathing. Through the empty hall of the palace pass certain maidens. They pass to the balustrade of the terrace. They are languid from the heat of the long day. A little breeze is stirring, cool and scented, from the west. The maidens talk of this breeze. They sing for gladness of it, and, singing, disappear. The silence deepens. From her chamber comes the queen, with the king, her lover. She tells him that it is because he is so terrible and strong and merciless that she loves him so well. She had never loved him so well as on that day when he slew the assembled Sanhedrin. She bids him lift her from the ground and sway her to and fro. Sohemus passes them, on his way from the lake. 'Bend back my head,' she cries, 'and look down in my eyes.' He looks, and knows that somewhere those other eyes, 'so like to Mariamne's,' are turned, like hers, skyward. From the distance comes a faint sound of wailing . . . The bier is borne into the palace . . . Mariamne, kneeling over it, can scarcely bid her husband farewell, when he sets forth to meet Caesar.

I have tried to give some vague notion of the power with which these scenes are ordered, of the ways in which the tragic irony is accumulated. I will now pause to make my one objection to Mr Phillips's conduct of his theme. When Herod has gone, Gadias, the Chief Councillor, passes by the bier, and says 'Perhaps 'twas for the best. Had he lived he might have been a public peril,' or words to that effect. Mariamne immediately suspects. She then forces a full confession from Sohemus. This method of discovery is not dramatically convincing. Gadius would never have been guilty of the indiscretion foisted upon him by Mr Phillips; nor would Sohemus have betrayed his master, who had chosen him for his dog-like devotion. At any rate, their behaviour strains credulity. The nature of the discovery is out of key with the rest of the play, and savours too much of a tricky dramatist pulling wires for puppets. Mariamne has to know that Herod is the murderer of her brother. Confronted with this necessity, why did not Mr Phillips let Herod himself confess? Then, instead of a complicated accident, we should have had a true and terrible development in the play's scheme. What could be more dramatically right than that Herod, when Mariamne unburdens herself of her admiration for his strength and mercilessness, should unburden his own remorseful soul of its secret, sure that the revelation would not rob him of her, sure that he could quickly overbear her first horror. Mr Phillips may object that I am rewriting his play? Not at all. I merely suggest a change of detail, which would not affect the true course of the play itself. The act would end with the departure of Herod, appalled by Mariamne's revulsion, but sure that she would forgive him before his return. The beginning of the next act would be practically unchanged. Mariamne would rise, as now, to meet Herod, 'like a black pine amid the bending corn,' and he would recount to his court, ever looking at her, his triumph over Caesar. He would be unable to conceive that she was still steeled against him. The irony of the scene would be even more poignant than it is now. Then would come a scene between the two, very slightly altered from its present form. Thenceforth the play would be exactly the same as it is now. Stay! Herod's jealousy of Sohemus, the motive which goads him finally to the murder of Mariamne, would have to be jettisoned. And really, this deothelloisation would in itself be an improvement. It would knit the action still more closely to the idea, and make the tragedy more complete, if Herod (despairing, as now, of Mariamne's love) were to have her murdered solely for the sake of his sovereignty. Her refusal to discontinue her inflammatory visits to the tomb of Aristobulus ought to be the occasion for her end. I do not suggest that Mr Phillips, even with Mr Tree's concurrence, should alter the play in its course at Her Majesty's. But, in view of later editions of his forthcoming book, he might turn my suggestions over in his mind.

I wish I had space in which to record the sequence of the scenes in the second act. I have never seen anything more powerful in its irony than the close of the second act,—Mariamne lying dead yonder in her chamber, and Herod striding up the steps to tell her of the territories which Caesar has ceded to him—'Hippo-Samaria, and Gadara, and high-walled Joppa'—all these new territories which are for her alone. I wish I had space in which to follow the gradations of the perfect last act. Herod, crowned with ashes, sits on his throne. He is weak as a little child. His physician stands over him, watching. His courtiers stand around him, trying to win back for Judaea the brain that made it mighty. One feels a kind of dull pressure in the air—the pressure of so many minds all willing Herod back to sanity. The architects come to him with the plans of the new city. He has still his love of power, his love of beauty. But these passions burst out into impossible desires, into mad blasphemies. And through them both runs the one great passion which has destroyed him—the passion for Mariamne. Again and again he sends messengers to her, beseeching her to come. The messengers return, tell him she is coming indeed. He knows in his heart that Mariamne is dead, yet will he not believe that she is dead. Only by not believing that, can he live and be a king. She sleeps? But her breasts moved? The messenger must swear that he saw the moving of the breasts.... She spoke? No, they need not repeat her words. He could so well imagine.... As he begins to lose his power of deceiving himself, he loses his control of himself. The singing-boy runs to the steps of the throne and sings him into silence. Again the king cries out, wildly, for Mariamne. He strides down, and the dancing-women scatter before him. The Physician orders the bearers to bring forth the queen. Herod kisses the queen's lips. Shrinking back to his throne he 'is stricken, and in catalepsy bound.' Trumpets sound, Roman messengers march in and announce that Arabia has been ceded to him by Caesar. The final irony is consummated. Herod stands, unconscious, in the zenith of his power. He, whose mother bore him 'neath a wild moon by a wintry sea,' has fulfilled his appointed fate. By his greatness he has fallen. The conflict of such great passions as were in him was too fierce a conflict to be waged in the frail body of a mortal man. That is the meaning of this tragedy.

As Mariamne, Miss Maud Jeffries seemed to me too modern, not broad enough in her method. She looked very beautiful, however, and that was a strong point in her favour. Mariamne is one of the parts for which no actress, however fine, could be cast, unless she were also beautiful. It is, therefore, not an easy part to cast. I fancy Miss Jeffries was the best lady available. Miss Bateman played the part of Herod's mother, and was not so impressive as usual. She showed a tendency to be eccentric. Miss Calhoun, on the other hand, was admirable as Herod's sister, playing with a breadth of manner and a real sense for blank verse—qualities which one does not expect from actresses of the new school. As Gadius, Mr Somerset, also, delivered his lines well, but was inclined to be rather too amusing. The part of Aristobulus demands little but youth and simplicity of demeanour, both of which were well supplied by Mr Norman Tharp. The accident of consanguinity debars me from praising him who is Herod.

At Terry's Theatre Miss Loie Fuller is dancing; also a foreign troupe is performing in dumb show. I saw this dual affair when it was at the Coronet Theatre, a week or two ago. Madame Charlotte Wiehe, leader of the mutes, cut a very gay and graceful figure, and did not, as do most artists in *mimique,* act on the principle that gestures were given us as a means of concealing our thoughts. Miss Fuller's art had become even more elaborate and startling than it was. But I am no convert to it. If the stage were filled with a hundred Miss Fullers, all working together, all in uniformly whirled and illumined veils, the effect would please me, no doubt. In a ballet, one forgets the human units. But the solitary dancer on the stage must have personal importance. One wishes her to dance beautifully, to express her soul in movement, to *be* something. Merely mechanical tricks, however skilfully played, will not atone to us for personal nullity. Miss Fuller seems to me null, and so I can snatch no pleasure from her skill in the art of manipulating layers of gauze, none from the limelighter's taste in tinting them. I sit in wonder, but that is all. Astray from the Lowther Arcade into a kaleidoscope, a doll would not less enrapture me.

[*17 November 1900*]

## AESCHYLUS MADE RIDICULOUS

I do hope that Cambridge, despite the ignorant or insincere eulogies that have been raining on it from the daily press, feels heartily ashamed of its stupid, tawdry perversion of the *Agamemnon.*

I hoist no pedantic standard. I do not suggest that without strict archaeological accuracy Greek tragedies cannot be finely presented. I see no reason why the *Agamemnon* should not be impressive in an ordinary modern theatre. It could not, certainly, be so deeply impressive thus as in a theatre like that for which is was written. The primitive, elemental largeness of Aeschylus harmonises with sky and sunlight better than with footlights and an ornamental ceiling. In the overt theatre of Bradfield, where we saw the *Agamemnon* last summer, the original spell of the tragedy seemed to fall on us in all its fulness; our hearts were opened to the full measure of the theme, and to all the poet's music. In a modern theatre there must needs be some sense of incongruity between the tragedy and its surroundings, however reverently the tragedy be produced, however ably rendered. And therefore, I think, the committee of fourteen dons responsible for the Greek play at Cambridge would have been wiser not to project the *Agamemnon* this year, not to challenge so direct a comparison with Bradfield. They should have produced some other play—why not the *Choephoroe*?

But this is a mere 'aside.' My main objection is, not to the fact that the play has been produced, but to the very vile manner of its production. Duly allowing for the large number of cooks engaged in making the broth, and for the kind of saucepan they had to make it in, I maintain that the concoction need not have been disgusting. Disgusting it was, to anyone who has any love for Aeschylus. Surely, (one would have thought,) the fourteen committee-men would have had one common aim in producing a tragedy of Aeschylus, however much they might have differed as to the means whereby that aim was to be accomplished: surely, they would have agreed that a large, chaste, abstract simplicity must be the keynote of the production. On the contrary, they seem to have determined that the affair must be as elaborately realistic as possible. Aeschylus, they seem to have thought, must be brought up to date. He must be mounted as Shakespeare is mounted, as M. Rostand, as Mr Stephen Phillips. Here was their primary error. Shakespeare may be—ought to be, as I think—elaborately mounted; for he wrote with romantic realism for a stage which was already struggling (even without his guidance) towards elaboration of scenic effect. The romantic realism of his method could not, in his day, find its full expression on the stage. We, after the lapse of three centuries, are finding its full expression. But Aeschylus is quite another matter; there was no romantic realism about *him*. He was, from first to last, a classic idealist, and he was perfectly content that his art should be conditioned by such arbitrary means as were at his disposal. So soon as we expand those means, we do that which is discordant from his art, and fatal to it. So soon as we introduce 'scenic effects,' his severity becomes baldness, his abstract figures—those statues!—become shadows, his supernal poetry becomes bombast. Yes! elaboration of scenery is fatal to him. At Cambridge there was not merely elaboration: there was ugly elaboration. The palace of Agamemnon was strangely like the Alhambra Palace of Varieties, Leicester Square. It may have been, as it professed to be, archaeologically like a Greek palace. The Greeks did paint their buildings, and may have made them as hideous as the Cambridge scene-painters had made this one. There is little or no evidence as to the manner in which scene-painting was done by the Greeks; and it is right to assume that the σκήνη for a royal palace was not, in Aeschylus's day, a tawdrily realistic affair which would have contradicted the whole spirit of his writing, but rather a chastely simple affair in accord to that spirit. It is right, also, to assume that the carpet spread for Agamemnon's entry was not the kind of grandiose article which one is liable to behold through plate-glass in the Tottenham Court Road—not the kind of article which has commended itself to the committee of fourteen. Before I pass from the visual aspect of the production, I must ask why the crowd which accompanied Agamemnon should have been dressed like the figures in the Scriptural chromo-lithographs, which are still to be found in some seaside lodgings? 'Abraham in red, offering up Isaac in blue' is not the best source of inspiration for the costumiers of a Greek tragedy, and is objectionable on grounds beyond the essential difference between Hebraism and Hellenism. I must also ask why the altar of Dionysus was made to look like a font in time of harvest-festival, piled up with pears, apples, grapes, melons and bananas. I had always understood that this altar, in the Greek theatre, was crowned simply by a sacrificial flame. Cambridge may have some authority for its display of the fruiterer's best; if it has, I shall be glad to know what the authority is. But probably the display was made without reference to archaeology; probably, the fourteen dons thought it would strike a cheerful note. Though ugly, it was decidedly cheerful, and so, perhaps, from the standpoint of the committee, it was justified. Cheerfulness, a cosy, modern cheerfulness, seems to have been their aim throughout. The fact that they did not achieve their aim is due to the impossibility of making Greek tragedy cheerful. This ancient form cannot produce an effect similar to that which is produced by (say) comic opera, even though it may be robbed so cunningly of its dignity as to make it no more impressive than comic opera. Nothing could have been less impressive than the *Agamemnon* at Cambridge, and yet nothing could have been more dreary. Even if the committee had had the courage to do their work thoroughly, even if they had engaged Mr Lionel Monckton to intersperse 'additional numbers' in Sir Hubert Parry's cheerful music, and had composed the chorus of pretty girls, not of grey-bearded undergraduates, their production would have disappointed them by exhilarating no one. Aeschylus must be taken as he is, or left.

The acting was in key with the rest of the production. The elaborately realistic and cheerful setting was matched by elaborately realistic and cheerful acting. None of the actors seemed to have the slightest inkling that Aeschylus was simply a tragic poet, creating, not real characters, but abstract figures, who were to express in a grand manner certain tragic emotions. Even Mr J. F. Crace (Cassandra), though he did strike the note of tragedy, never struck the right note of it. He was acting all the time, acting realistically, instead of merely giving forth, solemnly, for all it was worth, the poetry which Aeschylus had put into his lips. But, certainly, he acted well, according to his lights, and I hope to see him hereafter in a modern tragedy. The other actors I am not anxious to see again. With the exception of Mr F. H. Lucas, who, as Clytaemnestra, showed that he might do very well in modern comedy, none of them seemed to me to show any talent of any kind. Agamemnon, the Herald, Aegisthus, the Choregus—in point of sheer dufferdom, there was nothing to choose between them. However, that is no great matter. One does not expect undergraduates to be good actors. What one does expect in a Greek tragedy at a university is, that the mimes shall show some signs of having been coaxed towards a proper conception of their parts by the scholars who are responsible for the production. These mimes showed no such signs. And, seeing how the scholars themselves had conceived the production of the play, I can only assume that the mode of the mimes' performances was well in accord to the scholars' wishes.

The whole thing was discreditable to what is, after Oxford, the most distinguished of our Universities. To an Oxonian even Cambridge may seem a bad second, but it is indubitably a second. Being so, it ought to keep jealous guard over its reputation, ought to do nothing which would shock an intelligent foreigner. Wherefore, I do hope that any guilty qualms which its travesty of the *Agamemnon* may have caused in its conscience, will not have been lulled by the congratulations it has had from anonymous critics, of whom those that are not its own pious *alumni* must have read the name of Aeschylus for the first time when they received their tickets for the performance. Let Cambridge be sure that my criticism represents the view of everyone who has seen its *Agamemnon* with a competent and disinterested eye. Let it make a discreet effort next time. Its special devotion is, we know, to science and mathematics rather than to the classics. But that is no excuse for desperation. Oxford does not confuse alkalies with alkaloids, nor maintain that $2+2=5$. Nor need Cambridge make hopeless hash of a Greek tragedy.

[*24 November 1900*]

## TWO PLAYS

If I really had the cause of British drama so deeply at heart as I sometimes seem to have it, 'This,' I should be crying, with the sob of one into whose soul the iron had entered, 'has been the blackest week of my life!' For I have beheld, within that period, a pathetic failure to do well that which ought to be done, and a grinning triumph in doing well that which ought not to be done. I know not which sensation was the more lamentable—the sensation of being bored by Mrs Craigie's modern psychological comedy, or the sensation of being stimulated by Captain Marshall's unscrupulous scheme for bringing Tom Robertson up to date. True, my principles have not been affected. My contempt for the art of the 'sixties, and my belief in the art of the 'noughts, are as strong as ever they were. I am, moreover, as sure as ever I was, that to be on the side of the 'noughts is to be on the winning side. But this conviction does only make it more exasperating for me to behold meanwhile, on the one hand, virtue floundering and unrewarded, and, on the other, unrighteousness flourishing like a green bay-tree, with the critic of the *Daily Telegraph* cooing lustily in the branches.

In Mrs Craigie I take always an especial interest. She, as dramatist, and I, as dramatic critic, saw the light simultaneously; and our connascence has inspired me with a sentimental wish that she should do great things. Do not mistake my use of the epithet 'great.' I remember that in my criticism of her first play I struck the keynote of common-sense (which has, I hope, vibrated through all my criticisms) by advising her not to attempt 'great' work. Other critics were urging her to the highest flights of ambition. I, divining certain limitations which are set to the talent of women in general, and of 'John Oliver Hobbes' in particular, urged her to follow sedulously the fashion she had set for herself in *The Ambassador*. Fearing that she would wish now to be profound, and knowing that the only work of women which can be taken seriously is their superficial work, I cautioned Mrs Craigie against probing far beneath the surface. I implored her to be always light. She has fulfilled 'more than my prayer.' She has not merely remained light: she has become imponderable. Let her not suspect me of complaining that *The Wisdom of the Wise* has no such effective little situations as abounded in *The Ambassador*. On the contrary, I applaud her desire to write a purely psychological comedy, a comedy evolving itself, through collation of certain persons with well-defined and various characters, into expression of an idea—in fact, a *modern* comedy. That was a fine desire, and the psychology in *The Ambassador* was (of course, without pretence to depth) sharp and delicate enough to justify her in expecting to achieve it. But she has not achieved it, alas! Her failure is not due to any weakness in the basic idea of the comedy. The idea itself—the idea of the mischief that may be wrought by putting a young wife on guard against her husband—is quite excellent. It is not a new idea; but no good idea is the less good for antiquity, or the less capable of being well worked out in a new manner. It is exactly the kind of idea which, remembering her peculiar talent, I should have expected Mrs Craigie to make the most of. Why, then, is her comedy so dull? The dialogue is as delightful as ever, showering off its innumerable little bright sparks of wittiness and prettiness. But the characters who speak it! They do not exist. They are the vaguest puppets, there to work out the basic idea, precisely through jigging of their joints; they are not human characters to illustrate the idea in a human manner. Their antics are tolerable, and seem even like human movements, so long as the idea is in process of expression. But this period is very brief. When the curtain falls on the first act, the whole idea has been worked out. The husband and wife understand each other perfectly, and any complications that ensue are merely factitious. The remaining two-thirds of the play are but a device for keeping the audience in their places until strikes the hour when the carriages will be ready in King Street. Without the idea, the puppets cease to exist for us. Without its mouthpieces, even the dialogue bores us. Nothing remains but the furniture, and the pretty frocks, and the subtly aristocratic names of the dramatis personae. The whole thing degenerates into an *édition de luxe* of M.A.P.

Since the first night, Mrs Craigie has written a good-humoured letter to the *Pall Mall Gazette*,—explaining her reason for appearing before the curtain to take her call; 'As I had given the public my very best—the result of two years of care, thought, and observation—I felt I had no reason to slink away like a thief in the night.' Exactly. But the point is, why should Mrs Craigie, having tried conscienciously to do her best, expose herself to the risk of being treated as though she really were 'a thief'? Why should she pander to the stupid rowdyism of certain self-important brutes? 'Because,' Mrs Craigie might answer, 'I have, on previous occasions, given these same brutes the opportunity of applauding me.' That would be quite logical. A dramatist who personally courts applause for success must also court execration for failure. But to court execration for failure is an undignified proceeding; therefore it is unwise to court applause for success. Mrs Craigie, having satisfied her conscience by letting herself be 'booed at,' can now make a fresh start. She need have no compunction in evading such demonstrations henceforth, and should have no regret in evading demonstrations to the contrary. I trust that she (and every other dramatist) will join Mr Henry Arthur Jones in his determination to be invisible, and so keep the public in its place, and teach it manners.

I am sure there are many successes in store for Mrs Craigie. I am glad that, in the letter from which I have quoted, she declares that she is not going to alter her 'method of work' or her 'point of view.' This I take to mean that she is not going to be deflected from the strait path of modern psychological comedy. I know that she has the power to do well the good thing which, on this occasion, she has done ill. I know she has the talent for sound construction and sharp characterisation, and that this talent will out, as it outed, so signally, in *The Ambassador*. It was just this talent for sound construction which seemed to me to be lacking in Captain Marshall. His early plays, especially *A Royal Family*, struck me as the work of a man who was destined to write good comedies of observation, if only he could acquire a specific knack for dramaturgy. Here, I felt, was a man creeping along the right path; he would never turn aside from that path, and he might, sooner or later, be walking upright on it. I watched him with a kindly eye. Conceive my astonishment when I found him, last Tuesday evening, striding with the gait of an athletic giant—along the path of damnation. No recent play has shown so utter a lack of artistic conscience as *The Second in Command*. The unblushing effrontery of the thing staggers me. With a muscular sweep of his arm, Captain Marshall has thrown life to the winds, and has taken a flying leap into the saccharine kingdom of Tom Robertson. There, with his own strong hands, he has builded a palace of sugar-lumps, and has installed in it as many of 'John Strange Winter's' soldier-heroes as he could lay hands on, and round about it he has laid out a garden of flowery speeches and coincidences in full bloom. The whole thing has been done so well, so firmly, so boldly, that I defy the most sensible of modern playgoers not to admire it, not to be (despite himself) exhilarated by it. The story, the impossible, intercomplicated story, is carried through with such skill that it seems quite possible and quite clear. In the quality of its stage-craft, the play really is prodigious. Do you wonder that the house rose at it? Do you wonder that the soul of the critic of the *Daily Telegraph*, starved by the 'extraordinary thinness' of *Mrs Dane's Defence, Herod*, &c. &c., revived under it as a parched rose revives under the fall of long-pent rain from heaven? Can you wonder that he revelled so deliriously in what he calls the 'web of fruitful misunderstandings begotten of the pecuniary embarrassments of an only brother'? For the sake of him, I hope Captain Marshall will continue to use his newly-acquired technique in the cause of old-fashioned drama, will never do anything but beget these fruitful webs. But, for his own sake, I hope the gallant Captain will return to the path on which he first ventured forth. The amount of money that will, meanwhile, accrue to him from *The Second in Command* will be more than enough to enable him to regard with equanimity a long series of 'noble failures.' Assuredly, this ignoble triumph will pack the Haymarket for many months—to say nothing of theatres in the provinces, and in America, and in other parts of the world. Out of evil, then, good may come. Some good has already come in the manifestation of Miss Sybil Carlisle as a far more gifted actress than we had had the chance of supposing her to be, and in the renewed manifestation of Mr Cyril Maude's delightful art.

[*1 December 1900*]

## A SATIRE ON ROMANTIC DRAMA

Last week we had to record two regrettable occurrences at the seat of dramatic war. That daring and unscrupulous commander, Captain Marshall, after his successful operations at the Criterion, had appeared with incredible rapidity in the neighbourhood of the Haymarket, and had forced Messrs Harrison and Maude unconditionally to surrender. It would be premature to speculate on the reasons which prompted these two gallant managers to give over to the forces of old-fashioned drama a theatre which we had supposed to be well provided against any such necessity. Far be it from us to hastily condemn. We, who sit at home, propping our blotting-pads against the cushions of our arm-chairs, must bear in mind that those who are nobly risking their money in theatrical management, and incurring the various dangers and hardships inseparable from that pursuit, often are compelled by causes of which we know nothing to take measures which are at first sight unintelligible. But the loss of the Haymarket, whether or not it was inevitable, is none the less humiliating to our pride, or the less eminently calculated signally to encourage the rapidly dwindling forces of the enemy. Marshall's occupation seems to be completely effective, and his vast supplies of sugar and spice and all things nice will probably enable him to hold his own for some months. There is reason to fear that the box-office is being besieged. The other occurrence which I had to record—the serious check experienced by Hobbes's Light Horse in the St James's district—was even more regrettable. We had felt such confidence in, and had founded such high hopes on, this spirited little arm of our service that we could hardly credit the news that it had failed in the execution of its duty. Far be if from us &c. &c. It is pleasant now to turn to the brighter side of things. Last week we were so preoccupied with regrettable occurrences that we had no time to comment on the recent engagement in which the 'cape-and-sword' commando were completely routed and cut to pieces by . . . but how am I to express Mr L. N. Parker in terms of militancy? His second name, I am told, is Napoleon; but that does not help me. Let me drop metaphor and plainly say how glad I (disliking, as I do, that empty, dull, noisy, insincere business of 'cape-and-sword') to find the audience at the Duke of York's entering well into the spirit of

Mr Parker's satire, laughing merrily at all his points. For the laughter assured me that the 'cape-and-sword' nuisance was over, at least for the present. In France ridicule does not kill, because to the inhabitants laughter is a natural function: they can laugh at a thing without losing their respect for it. In England ridicule seldom kills, because the inhabitants can seldom be made to see a joke. But whenever they do see a joke, then does their laughter signify that they will no longer respect the thing at whose expense the joke has been cut. I rejoiced, accordingly, in the reception of *The Swashbuckler*. A superficial person might say that Mr Parker's method had been to take all the stock-incidents of the neo-romantic hacks, and to cast into them, as hero, a wholly absurd creature, who should act as a leaven to the whole, making the stock-incidents not less absurd than himself. That is one way of describing Mr Parker's method. Another, a better, is to say that he has made his hero a plausible human being, who is bound to show up the inherent absurdity of the stock-incidents by his contrast with them. Consistent absurdity may carry conviction; but the game is up so soon as one serious element is introduced. It is by the introduction of this element into absurdity that satire works. Burlesque works, conversely, by the introduction of an absurd element into serious matters. Mr Parker proves himself a good satirist, and he is to be thanked for added graces of humour and fancy which make his play not less delightful than salutary. The entertainment has other added graces, in the way of pretty scenery, well-designed dresses, good acting. Mr Waring, as the hero, obviously revels in the chance of being something more than a caped monster with a sword, and of showing us that his painfully dry, bombastic performance in *Under the Red Robe* was not his own fault. And Miss Millard, as heroine, achieves with much grace her second, preliminary canter for the part of Rosalind.

I am sorry I can say nothing valuable about the dramatic version of *Marmion* presented last Saturday by the Elizabethan Stage Society. Unavoidable circumstances prevented me from reaching the scene of entertainment before one half of the play was over; and the intensity of the subscribers, who had come in full force and occupied every seat except one seat at the back of a very high and remote gallery, prevented me from forming even a half-opinion. It is only fair, then, to assume that the version was admirable and admirably performed. On the initial question, whether or not *Marmion* was worth so much trouble, I will keep my counsel. I am glad Mr Poel has brought his interesting and eager little Society from abeyance, and I look forward to its activity in the future.

The death of Mr Oscar Wilde extinguishes a hope that the broken series of his plays might be resumed. The hope was never, indeed, very strong. Despite the number of his books and plays, Mr Wilde was not, I think, what one calls a born writer. His writing seemed always to be rather an overflow of intellectual and temperamental energy than an inevitable, absorbing function. That he never concentrated himself on any one form of literature is a proof that the art of writing never really took hold of him. He experimented in all forms, his natural genius winning for him, lightly, in every one of them, the success which for most men is won only by a reverent concentration. His native energy having been sapped by a long term of imprisonment, the chance that he would write again was very small. His main motive for writing was lost. He would not, as would the born writer, be likely to find consolation in his art. *The Ballad of Reading Gaol*, though it showed that he had not lost his power of writing, was no presage of industry. Obviously, it was written by him with a definite external purpose, not from mere love and necessity of writing. Still, while he lived, there was always the off-chance that he might again essay that art-form which had been the latest to attract him. Somehow, the theatre seems to be fraught with a unique fascination. Modern dramaturgy is the most difficult of the arts, and its rewards (I do not mean its really commercial rewards) seem to be proportionate to its difficulties. To it, but for his downfall, even Mr Wilde might have devoted himself. But for his death, he might possibly have returned to it. And thus his death is, in a lesser degree than his downfall, a great loss to the drama of our day. His work was distinct from that of most other playwrights in that he was a man who had achieved success outside the theatre. He was not a mere maker of plays. Taking up dramaturgy when he was no longer a young man, taking it up as a kind of afterthought, he brought to it a knowledge of the world which the life-long playwright seldom possesses. But this was only one point in his advantage. He came as a thinker, a weaver of ideas, and as a wit, and as the master of a literary style. It was, I think, in respect of literary style that his plays were most remarkable. In his books this style was perhaps rather too facile, too rhetorical in its grace. Walter Pater, in one of his few book-reviews, said that in Mr Wilde's work there was always 'the quality of a good talker.' This seems to me a very acute criticism. Mr Wilde's writing suffered by too close a likeness to the flow of speech. But it was this very likeness that gave him in dramatic dialogue as great an advantage over more careful and finer literary stylists as he had over ordinary playwrights with no pretence to style. The dialogue in his plays struck the right mean between literary style and ordinary talk. It was at once beautiful and natural, as dialogue should always be. With this and other advantages, he brought to dramaturgy as keen a sense for the theatre as was possessed by any of his rivals, except Mr Pinero. Theatrical construction, sense of theatrical effects, were his by instinct. I notice that one of the newspapers says that his plays were 'devoid of consideration as drama,' and suggests that he had little or no talent for construction. Such criticism as this merely shows that what Ben Jonson called 'the dull ass's hoof' must have its backward fling. In point of fact, Mr Wilde's instinct for construction was so strong as to be a disadvantage. The very ease of his manipulations tempted him to trickiness, tempted him to accept current conventions which, if he had had to puzzle things out laboriously and haltingly, he would surely have discarded, finding for himself a simpler and more honest technique. His three serious comedies were marred by staginess. In *An Ideal Husband* the staginess was most apparent, least so in *A Woman of No Importance*. In the latter play, Mr Wilde allowed the psychological idea to work itself out almost unmolested, and the play was, in my opinion, by far the most truly dramatic of his plays. It was along these lines that we, in the early 'nineties, hoped Mr Wilde would ultimately work. But, even if he had confined his genius to the glorification of conventional drama, we should have had much reason to be grateful to him. His conventional comedies were as superior to the conventional comedies of other men as was *The Importance of Being Earnest* to the every-day farces whose scheme was so frankly accepted in it. At the moment of Mr Wilde's downfall, it was natural that the public sentiment should be one of repulsion. But later, when he was released from prison, they remembered that he had at least suffered the full penalty. And now that he is dead, they will realise also, fully, what was for them involved in his downfall, how lamentable the loss to dramatic literature.

[*8 December 1900*]

## 'CAPTAIN BRASSBOUND'S CONVERSION'

It may be that my neighbours 'D.S.M.' and 'J.F.R.' will from this number of the *Saturday Review* launch retrospects at the history of their two spheres in the past century. But do not demand 'British Drama: 1800–1900' from *me*. In the year of grace 2000, if I am alive and in full possession of my faculties, I shall possibly find need to be retrospicient. I find no need now. This expiring century, except in its last decade, made no attempt to produce a drama for us. Throughout its first ninety years it gave us many mimes, many theatres, nothing else. I might compose a catalogue of its mimes and theatres; but how dull that would be, and how superfluous! I might recall some events of the past decade; but they are fresh enough in your memories. Besides, to a practical art-critic, art's present and future are much more important than its past. Let me, then, even in the last article this century will get from me, devote myself to a play which the semi-private and wholly admirable Stage Society produced, a few days ago, at the Criterion.

It is not a good play, this *Captain Brassbound's Conversion*. It is not, never could be, effective on the stage. It is in no danger of becoming a classic and being called *The Captain* by affectionate mimes. Like all Mr Bernard Shaw's plays, it is a good entertainment, full of thought and fun; but it is not, as are some of them, dramatic. It jumps too much. It has no continuity of manner. Farce, comedy, melodrama, and other forms less easily labelled, play hide-and-seek through it, none of them ever catching another. All of them are distinct from one another, and all of them have innumerable turns. Had I the script of the play and a different coloured pencil for every different form that is exploited in it, every page would be like a kaleidoscope. It might be rather pretty. But the stage is one thing, the study another. Mr Shaw's kaleidoscope method does not do for the stage. In point of dramatic art, it is a pity that Mr Shaw is master of so many forms—so many more forms, Polonius, than are dreamt of in your category! Or, rather, it is a pity that he is sometimes bent on showing them all off separately within a couple of hours. When he fuses them, the result is all right. In *The Devil's Disciple* there was a true fusion of melodramatical with farcical, farcical with comedical, comedical with Shaw-Historical, Shaw-Historical with

335

Shaw-Philosophical-Propagandistical-Demoniacal-Angelical. Innumerable other -icals were there, but they were all fused well into unity. In *You Never Can Tell*, again, there was sufficient fusion. Here every -ical performs *pas seul*.

Our author might say 'Pooh! I am a realist. I give you life as it is. Men and women are diverse creatures. There are all kinds of people existing, side by side. Nor are they consistent even in themselves. They are ridiculous at one moment, respectable at another. In an honest play there can be no harmony of form. You stick up for harmony? Pooh!' This, or something like it, is what our author probably *would* say. The prime tenet in his creed, as you all know, is that he is a realist. Of course, as you all know, he is nothing of the sort. He is an idealist—idealist to the core, but cursed with a sense of humour. His plays are presentments of life as he thinks it ought to be, life as logic. So keen always is his hunger for logic in life that the wish becomes the proud father of the thought. He does quite honestly believe that logic, not passion, is the pivot on which the world goes round. So he has no compunction in depriving his characters of emotions. He differentiates them (not as human beings are differentiated, by the quantity and quality of their emotions, but) by the quantity and quality of their logical powers. His heroes and heroines, as Mr Walkley has said, are they who can, in the twinkling of an eye, see through a false syllogism. His villains and villainesses are they who can't, they to whom the fallacy has to be explained, with admirable patience and lucidity, by the heroes and heroines whom he worships as passionately as (say) the late Mr Pettitt worshipped his. Mr Shaw, in fact, is a very rampant idealist. But he has also a very strong sense of humour. He cannot help making even his heroes and heroines ridiculous. Nor does this process (being natural to him, and inevitable) diminish his idealistic reverence. Nor does it induce in him a doubt of his unflinching realism. Well! Far be it from me to induce in him that poisonous doubt. His mind and his attitude are far too delightful for me to wish to alter them. The one suggestion I was going to make to him is this: that in a play, as in every other work of art, there must be unity of form. Life may be comic, tragic, melodramatic, &c., &c., in a series of snippets. But life is long, art is short. Life need not select, art must. A play even, more than any other work of art, must be *qualis ab incepto*. For a play is meant to be seen in a theatre, not to be studied in a study.

## 'CAPTAIN BRASSBOUND'S CONVERSION'

If I had here my coloured script of *Captain Brassbound's Conversion*, I might, reading it very slowly, with many pauses and efforts, be able to attune myself to every passage of it. But a play has no business to rely on the appeal it would make through its script—plain or coloured. A play's proper appeal is to an audience. And no audience, however quick-witted, can appreciate a play which can only be appreciated through constant changes in the key of receptivity. Mr Shaw's dialogue jumps out of one key, without warning, while the audience is still in another key. The audience proceeds to jump after it, only to find that the dialogue has already jumped elsewhere. The chase is hot. It is great fun, in its way—exciting, exhilarating, good mental exercise. But it is not aesthetic pleasure. Without unity of impression there can be no aesthetic pleasure. And it is at the production of aesthetic pleasure that plays should aim. Mr Shaw, I know, would say' Pooh!' to that law. I have laid it down merely because it is true, not with any hope of inducing him to respect it always. I have no faith in the reformatory powers of criticism —especially when Mr Shaw is the criminal. For my part, I am quite willing to accept Mr Shaw exactly as he is. But then I delight in 'personality.' The public does not delight in it as I do. And so we admirers of Mr Shaw's work must not wonder that *Captain Brassbound's Conversion* was not produced publicly and in the odour of commercialism, but semi-privately by the Stage Society. There are several of Mr Shaw's plays which might well be produced publicly in the Metropolis—plays which would be very great successes. But *The Captain*, I venture to think, is not one of them. Without unity no play can 'draw the public.' Without unity no play can seem to me good. Thus, once in a way, I find a point in common between the public and myself.

There is no lack of unity in the dramatic version of *Struwwelpeter* made for the Garrick Theatre by Messrs Philip Carr and Nigel Playfair. Reading preliminary announcements, I had anticipated that the various and separate moral tragedies contained in that classic book were to be staged as a pantomime, and I had wondered on what thread they would be strung. Messrs Carr and Playfair, however, have eschewed the pantomime form. They have done the trick by concentrating under one roof, or rather in one garden, most of those familiar children whom Hoffman diffused over Frankfort. Fidgety Phil is no longer an only child. The lives of his Papa and Mamma are afflicted by other offspring—Augustus, the refuser of soup, Shock-Headed Peter himself, and Foolish Harriet. The members of this family, between them, manage to reproduce on the stage all their own exploits and most of the exploits attributed to their rivals. Thus, it is they who mock the blackamoor and are dipped in the ink. It is Phil who sucks his thumb and is pursued by the Long Tall Tailor. It is Peter who is wafted to the clouds by his umbrella. Papa himself is Agrippa, and the tailor, and other ministers of vengeance. The only incidents denied us are the incidents of which Little Johnny Head-in-Air and Cruel Frederick were the respective heroes. Otherwise, *tout est là, rien ne manque*. The adaptors must be complimented on the ingenuity and reverence with which they have done their work. In one instance they have even improved on their original. When Papa has solemnly dipped the three boys in the ink, he sends them into the house to be washed. Mamma comes out presently, complaining of the trouble she has been put to. 'And they tell me,' she says to Papa, 'that it was *you* who dipped them in the ink. But of course that cannot be.' Papa, bribing Harriet not to betray him, is a tragic instance of the evil that may result from even the noblest forms of zeal. I wonder what Hoffmann, that out-and-out champion of adults, would have thought of this interpolation. I suspect he would have been pained, also, by the modern tenderness with which the collaborators have mitigated the doom which befell the various children of his fancy. That Harriet should not really be burnt, that Augustus should regain his former bulk, that the sucked thumbs should not really be cut off—all these concessions to modern taste would, I fancy, have revolted him. However, the play is quite delightful, and deserves to prosper. Precedes it a mawkish and ill-written affair called *The Man Who Stole the Castle*.

[*29 December 1900*]

## SHAKESPEARE IN TWO DIRECTIONS

It has been the fashion of the past few years, and is still the fashion, to clamour for sight of all the plays that Shakespeare wrote. That any one of them should not be seen somewhere or other, now and again, across footlights, is held to be an insult to the national poet's memory. I do not profess to take this view. On the contrary, I am inclined to think that the less good of Shakespeare's plays ought, for Shakespeare's sake, and for sake of the reverence we owe him, not to be pulled off shelves into theatres. They do not increase his reputation: rather, they detract from it. To scholars and artists they are interesting, as the hack-work of genius. But to the majority of people (to impress whom, it is argued, they ought to be produced) they are but a means of persuasion that Shakespeare is over-rated. Therefore, I should prefer that they were left on those shelves, from which scholars and artists are able, and other people are unlikely, to take them down for study. 'But then,' you might argue, 'we should be driven back on a constant repetition of the best plays.' Well! no one has argued more persistently than I that we have seen *Hamlet* and certain other masterpieces so often that they have become stale and unprofitable as drama, so often that they are mere vehicles for rival expositions in the art of acting. Nor do I evacuate this well-held ground. My answer to your argument is that there is no reason why Shakespeare should be acted at all seasons. To have a glut of him is not necessary to the national salvation. Certainly, it were well that we should be kept always in touch with his best work. But his best work should not be laid before us so often as to rob us of the capacity for being freshly affected by it. And his second-best and third-best work should not be laid before us at all. We ought all to love him, and those frantic idolaters who would fain force him down our throats are making the task rather difficult. They are doing a disservice to their idol. They have succeeded in persuading the public that the more it sees of Shakespeare the more its mind will be improved. Accordingly the public goes, and goes, to see Shakespeare. It sees in him a vast and necessary means of edification. But, one may safely hazard, the more it sees of him the further it recedes from aesthetic delight in him. The more often it sees *Hamlet* the less does the play mean to it. Nor can it see such plays as *Henry V* and *The Taming of the Shrew* without feeling, aesthetically, (not, of course, morally) that Shakespeare was not so great a man as we make him out.

At the Lyceum, *Henry V* is running; at the Comedy, Mr Benson has just produced *The Taming of the Shrew*. It is quite safe to say that neither of these plays would have been set before us on its own merits. Had either of them been written by any other Elizabethan, it would have languished on the shelf, where languish so many Elizabethan plays much worthier than they to be set upon the stage. Each of them is but the hack-work of genius. Here and there, in the facile rhetoric and braggadocio of the one, you have passages of authentic poetry, of emotion nobly inspired; here and there, in the crude rough-and-tumble and the long-drawn verbal japing of the other, you have passages of strong and dancing humour. But in neither of them is the proportion of true to false, of delightful to tedious, great enough to console me for the knowledge that the public is sitting through them and seeing in them reason for supposing Shakespeare's supremacy to be due rather to the vague edification that is to be derived from him than to consummate genius in art.

However, there the public sits, having paid its money, and I am not likely to deter managers from their task of providing this vague edification which the public has been taught to demand of them. Since the second-rate and the third-rate plays of Shakespeare will continue to be produced, let me consider merely what is the best manner of producing them. Or rather, I should say, *which* is the better manner; for these are but two. One is to produce them with pomp and circumstance, with all accessories of beautiful dresses and scenery, elaborate stage-management, appropriate music, accomplished and carefully-selected mimes. It is in this, the modern manner, that *Henry V* has been produced by Mr Lewis Waller and Mr William Mollison. The other manner, the old-fashioned manner, applied by Mr Benson to *The Taming of the Shrew*, is to give the play, quite simply, for what it is worth. I say advisedly 'what it is worth.' For, certainly, such a play as *The Taming of the Shrew* does not in itself deserve any great outlay of money or taste. Nor such plays as *Henry V*. Nevertheless, I prefer them to be rewarded beyond their deserts. Shakespeare's good plays, which do deserve a great outlay of money and taste, are (if you do not know them too well) delightful under any conditions. Good conditions merely heighten the degree of one's pleasure. But Shakespeare's bad plays can be made tolerable only by beautiful production and performance. If the production and performance be beautiful enough, they become delightful. This was the case with *King John* at Her Majesty's. It is also, I think, the case with *Henry V* at the Lyceum. I remember Mr Benson, last year, produced this same play at this same theatre. I found it insufferably tedious. Now that it is beautifully mounted and acted, I enjoy it very much indeed. At least, I enjoy the mounting and the acting. My enjoyment of them does not make me cease to regret that they are not applied to worthier material.

To the part of Henry V Mr Waller is as well-suited as was Mr Benson ill-suited. Mr Waller is not a supple nor highly imaginative actor; but he has immense *verve* and virility; he bears himself gallantly, and he has humour; he has, above all, an incomparably fine voice, and an elocution which wrings the full value out of every syllable. His innumerable long speeches in this play stir one in virtue of their delivery. The rest of the mimes support him well, especially Miss Lily Hanbury. She, as the Chorus, has most of the purple patches of poetry that are in the play. Mr Benson, I think, omitted the Chorus from his production. It is, in point of fact, the one thing quite worth retention.

Mr Waller, I fancy, would be a good Petruchio. Mr Benson is not. Nor is Mrs Benson a good Katharina. Such charm as can be extracted from the story of Petruchio's wooing can be extracted only if Petruchio seems a sanguine gallant, and Katharina a hoyden whose roughness is but on the surface of a sweet and womanly disposition. Mrs Benson makes Katharina a shrew to the core, a malevolent being whose manners are but the outward sign of a thoroughly hysterical temperament. Even admitting Mrs Benson's conception of the part, I should object that her expression of it was inartistic. In comedy, unpleasant things must be pleasantly unpleasant. They must not be carried to the point of making one personally uncomfortable. Mrs Benson's manner of threatening Bianca with a pin was such raw realism that one felt inclined to cry 'Don't.' And the prolonged shriek which she uttered when Petruchio held her in his arms was such that the shriek of an express train passing through a station would have seemed musical by contrast. But my main point of objection is that Katharina ought to be represented as being in herself a charming creature, worthy to be tamed. If she had been a shrew and nothing else, Petruchio would not have tolerated her for one moment. In any case, no Katharina—Shakespeare's or Mrs Benson's—would have been tamed by such a Petruchio as Mr Benson's. All the while this Petruchio was trying to dominate his bride, Sydney Smith's phrase about 'being preached at by wild curates' was recurring to me. Mr Benson's conception of the part was good enough. But Nature, and his habit of intoning his words, prevented him from being possible in it. From first to last, he was a wild curate, and nothing more. Though some members of the company were good in their parts, the performance, as a whole, lacked the gusto that one finds in most of the Bensonian shows. However, I am glad to see the company again, and to know that I shall have to see it often in the immediate future. Habits are stronger than principles. Deeply though I disapprove of a stock-company devoted to Shakespeare, it exerts on me, despite myself, a kind of cosy fascination. Mistaken and mischievous though Mr Benson seems to me in his policy, I cannot help wishing him well. As a fanatic, he compels me to like him, to respect him. *'C'est bien beau, cet amour qui ne se fane jamais. Moi, je ne le comprends pas. Mais c'est beau.'*

[5 *January 1901*]

## 'THE MERCHANT OF VENICE'

The higher you rate Shakespeare, the more deeply must you deplore his habit of taking his plots *là où il les trouvait*. It is no excuse for him to say that the Elizabethan public wanted him to confine himself to the stupid stories with which it was familiar, and that, unless he had obeyed it, he could never have caught its ear. For a second-rate dramatist that excuse were valid enough. But Shakespeare was not a second-rate dramatist. With his transcendent power, he could have imposed on his time anything, however new, and unexpected, and unwanted. That he chose the line of lesser resistance, taking for his material whatever would tickle those groundlings for whom he, as a great artist, had so great a contempt, is a fact that must lower him, as a man, in our esteem. Nor is it sound criticism to say that, since he was always prodigal of his genius, never sparing one tittle of his poetry, his sense of character, and his sense of dramatic effect, it matters little on what foundation he was working. This is an attitude struck by many of his critics. 'If,' say they, 'the result was a series of perfect masterpieces in poetry and drama, we need not complain about the method by which it was obtained.' The answer to that is simple: Shakespeare did not produce a series of perfect masterpieces. Throughout the fabric of his work you will find much that is tawdry, irrational, otiose—much that is, however shy you may be of admitting that it is, tedious. And these cankers are, plainly, the result of his plagiaristic method. A transcendent poet may, as Shakespeare did, glorify with transcendent poetry, and so make immortal, stupid stories conceived by stupid writers as a quick means of catching a stupid public. He may, if he be, like Shakespeare, a great dramatist and seer of hearts, insinuate into these stories a great deal of true drama, of true life. But he cannot purge them of their general stupidity. In so far as he adheres to that in which stupidity is inherent, he is writing stupid plays, and is wasting his genius. Conceive, if you can, that the twentieth century will evolve for us as great a dramatic poet as Shakespeare. And then, if you can, conceive that this gentleman will be so weak or so modest as to found his plays on the farces of the late Mr H. J. Byron, and on the melodramas of the late Mr Pettitt, and on the romantic dramas of the late Mr Wills and the present Mr Henry Hamilton. And then conceive (what is quite inconceivable) that this will not be a pity, and that all the critics will not say 'We cannot but hold it to be matter for regret that Mr ——, instead of inventing for himself (and who is potentially more inventive than he?) stories in which his unexampled powers of eloquence, of wit and humour and pathos, of characterisation, and of dramatic effect, would have their full dramatic scope, still persists in taking ready-made material of an inferior kind, which, if we may be permitted to say so, cannot but cramp his genius and render it less effective than it would otherwise, in our opinion, be. It may seem presumptuous in us to hint' &c., &c. It may seem presumptuous in me to make a similar hint in reference to Shakespeare. Nevertheless, I make it.

*The Merchant of Venice*, which I have just seen under the auspices of Mr Benson at the Comedy Theatre, is a particularly sad instance of the way in which Shakespeare wasted so much of his time. What would one not give for the play which Shakespeare might have written about a persecuted but obdurate usurer? And yet how lightly one would forego the privilege of witnessing *The Merchant of Venice*! Indeed, but for the purple patches of poetry in it, and but for the character of Shylock, which betrays to us the mastery of its delineator whenever its delineator dared to deviate from *The Iew and Ptolome* into his own genius, one would much rather not see the play at all. It is doubly tedious, being founded not only on *The Jew and Ptolome* but also on that old legend of 'the caskets.' Thus, besides the eternal double couple of comic lovers going through their frigid Elizabethan complications, we have the terribly tedious exposure of 'the greediness of worldly choosers.' In its original literary form this moral legend was delightful enough. (Those of my readers who care to acquaint themselves with it may do so by dipping into Joannis Damasceni *Opera*, pp. 824, 825, ed. Basil, 1575.) But for purposes of drama it is quite impossible, in any variation whatever. A suitor is confronted with three caskets; the first is of gold, the second of silver, the third of lead; one of them contains the portrait of the lady for whose hand he is suing, and if he 'spots' it his suit shall be granted. After some hesitation, he chooses the gold casket. Well! in a written legend you would accept this idea readily enough. But when you see across footlights, in a play meant to be realistic, a man of flesh and blood communing with himself before the caskets, the illusion is gone. You simply think him a fool to doubt for one moment that the portrait is in the leaden casket, and when, like the Prince of Morocco, he selects the gold one...! 'Inconsistencies,' says an eminent editor of Shakespeare, 'vanish when (they are) "*oculis subjecta fidelibus*;" and the Prince of Morocco and the Prince of Aragon become as real personages as Antonio or Bassanio, when they appear in flesh and blood on the stage.' This, of course, is the exact reverse of the truth. The actor who is cast for the Prince of Morocco is to be sincerely pitied. The better he acts, the more tediously futile is the effect. Mr Oscar Asche, who is the Prince in the production at the Comedy, is a very good actor, and thus the futility of the effect passes all bounds. Miss Calhoun, who plays Portia, is also to be pitied for her share in this 'casket-scene.' By dint of hard clowning, or of very exquisitely fantastic comedy, an actress might carry the thing off, to some extent. But Miss Calhoun is not a fantastic comedian, and she is too good an actress to be capable of clowning. She cannot fall below her own level of dignified sincerity; she cannot help being real. Portia being but the conventionally unreal minx not only in this scene but also throughout the rest of the play (except when she masquerades as lawyer), Miss Calhoun has my heart-felt sympathy. She has the additional consolation of looking very distinguished—Venice incarnate, one might say—in her robe of white embroidered with gold roses and black roses, and with large corals at her throat, and a trellis of pearls woven into her towered-up hair.

## 'THE MERCHANT OF VENICE'

As I have suggested, the character of Shylock does in some measure redeem the piece. One can see that Shakespeare, had he not clogged himself with *The Iew and Ptolome*, would have made of him a fine creation, and would have written round him a fine play. As it was, Shakespeare fell between two stools. The groundlings of his day must have been mystified by the dignity, by the righteous indignation, by the human pathos, which he foisted into Shylock's character; whilst, on the other hand, his desire to please the groundlings by adhering to the scheme of the original play, and the consequent necessity for making Shylock a blood-thirsty old savage, must have prevented him, as it prevents you and me, from gaining any personal satisfaction from his work. That Shakespeare himself sympathised with Shyloock no thoughtful critic can have any doubt. Only, he had not the courage of his sympathy; or, rather, the form of his play prevented him from showing it except furtively, at odd moments. The result is that Shylock is neither fish, flesh, nor good red herring. He is inconsistent, not in the Aristotelian sense of consistently-inconsistent. He wobbles, not as a human wobbler, but as a puppet pulled by two showmen on bad terms with each other. He is a fine figure and a bogey alternatively. His speeches are mutually destructive. You cannot reconcile his various aspects. Accordingly, the part is not an easy one to play. To make it effective, an actor must slur and blur one side of it or the other. Which side is slurred and blurred depends on the fashion of the time. Among the Elizabethans, who thought the Jews merely absurd and remote monsters, the part of Shylock was played in a spirit of grotesque farce. In later times, when the Jews began to make their power definitely felt in England, and were feared and hated as a coming terror, Shylock became a melodramatic villain. Nowadays, when we all have a very great admiration and sympathy for the Jews (the admiration and sympathy which is always given to people who have us in their power). Shylock has become a romantically pathetic hero. It is on those lines that Mr Benson, after the manner of Sir Henry Irving, is now playing him —and playing him, it seems to me, very well indeed. He puts into his performance much more of imagination, and much less of angularity, than is his wont.

[*19 January 1901*]

## 'TWELFTH NIGHT'

What would one think if Mr Haddon Chambers had called his new comedy (of which I shall write next week) *February 6th*, or *Anything Else That May Occur To You*? Yet that were a precise modern equivalent to Shakespeare's title *Twelfth Night, or What You Will*. So perfunctory and formless an affair was *Twelfth Night*, and so contemptuous of it its maker, that he called it merely by the date of its production, giving leave to anyone else to re-christen it if he thought it worth the trouble. A few years later, it actually was produced as *Malvolio, tout court*. The Elizabethans, evidently, perceived that the character of Malvolio was, for all its slightness, by far the most interesting feature of it. And their opinion has been upheld by posterity. Malvolio is alive and attractive because he sprang from Shakespeare's own brain. Sir Toby, too, and Sir Andrew, and Maria, are, in their lesser degrees, genuine creations. But the rest of the characters (except, indeed, the Duke, who is remarkable, extraneously, as a study in aesthetic sensuousness) are merely steppers in one of those familiar quadrilles of which Shakespeare was not less sick than we are. The main plot of the play was, as usual, 'lifted' from elsewhere—from Venice, to be exact. And Shakespeare, on this occasion, took even less pride than usual in his booty. Various discrepancies of time and place in the scheme of the play testify to the hurry in which this *Twelfth Night* was knocked off. Of course, there are many lovely and immortal passages of poetry in it. Shakespeare radiated such passages whatever his theme; he could not help himself. But not all the exquisite things that Viola has to say could prevent the main plot from appalling even the gentlest reader with its tedious and frigid artificiality. If only Shakespeare had taken himself more seriously, our dramatic literature would have been as much the richer as it would have been the poorer had he never existed at all. If, in his comedies, he had given the go-by to the farcical inventions of fifth-rate playwrights, and had relied on his own transcendent genius, how much happier we should all be! Imagine what a splendid play he might have written if he had made Malvolio specifically the central figure! That he was as much interested in Malvolio as in Shylock, as indifferent to Viola as to Portia, nobody with the slightest artistic instinct can have any doubt.

It is amazing that he should have cast Malvolio, as he cast Shylock, into a deliquium of extraneous nonsense. Artistic conscience and artistic genius usually go hand in hand. Shakespeare, who had more genius than any other writer that ever lived, seems to have been without the faintest rudiment of a conscience. He is immortal despite himself. That he, with his methods of working, should yet cut the most impressive figure in the world's literature, is the most striking testimony to the miraculousness of his gifts. What pedestal would be exalted enough for him, what eyes unshaded could gaze up at him, what syndicate of intellects and temperaments could measure him, if he had possessed as much of the artistic conscience as is possessed by any of the Toms or Dicks or Harrys whose names are printed in the theatrical advertisements to-day?

*Twelfth Night*, I suggest, is in some degree redeemed by its accessory characters. The play is worth seeing across footlights, for sake of them. If the figures in the quadrille—Orsino and Viola, Sebastian and Olivia—be acted by mimes who look nice, and move gracefully, and make the most of the words allotted to them, rendering the music musically, then even they become tolerable. You are able to forget the frigid convention of the quadrille, steeping yourself in the verbal poetry. Of such plays as *The Tempest*, which Shakespeare wrote for his own pleasure, and in which the drama is throughout exquisitely consonant with the poetry, indifferent or even positively bad interpretations are worth seeing. Them nothing can mar utterly. But plays like *Twelfth Night*, which consist mainly of hack-work, should be interpreted with real charm and ability, or not interpreted at all. It were well also that they should be shown to us against beautiful backgrounds. With those critics who rail against beautiful backgrounds I concur so far as to admit that the really good Shakespearean plays are tolerable even when they are skimpily produced. But such pills as *King John* and *Henry V*, as *The Merchant of Venice* and *The Taming of the Shrew*, ought to be gilded as richly as possible. This metaphor is unfortunate, perhaps. It implies that I crave gorgeous display; whereas, of course, I crave merely beauty, which is quite another thing. I maintain that Shakespeare's masterpieces are not at all degraded by a setting of beauty, that they deserve such setting, and by it are made more beautiful, and that anyone who by it is distracted from their own intrinsic beauty betrays in himself a lack of visual sense. Visual beauty is complementary to beauty of sound and thought. Some people have no taste for it, just as others have no ear for music. To them, no doubt, an effect of visual beauty, being unintelligible, is an obstacle, a distraction. But they should not make a virtue of their defect, even though they cannot hope to remedy the defect 'by taking thought.' At any rate, they should not try to deduce and impose from it a general law in the aesthetics of drama. However, I admit readily that Shakespeare's masterpieces, skimpily produced, are well worth seeing. What I protest is that his inferior plays ought to be done elaborately or not at all. One ground on which the pedants base their objection to scenic elaboration is that the expense involves long runs, and that accordingly the public does not get constant chances of paying fresh homage to the bard. To this argument the answer is simple: the public does not go to Shakespearean plays unless they are elaborately produced. At least, it does not go to such plays as *King John*, &c. If we consider the edification of the public, we find this elaboration of scenery to be indispensable. And if we take a broadly aesthetic view of the matter, we come to the same conclusion. And so, in either case, we cannot but plump for the modern mode.

At Her Majesty's Theatre is an excellent production and performance of *Twelfth Night*. The garden of Olivia, in which most of the figures of the quadrille are gone through, is a very lovely Elizabethan-Illyrian garden, lying at the foot of an infinite staircase of green grass, and from it, in the distance, a little arched bridge leads to a lovely park whose trees loom blue through the haze of summer. And the dancers in the quadrille perform their evolutions with grace and skill. True, Miss Maud Jeffries, who is Olivia, does not appreciate the beauty of blank verse so well as the audience appreciates the beauty of her appearance; she speaks her lines, indeed, as though they were bad prose. But a new-comer, Miss Brayton, who is Viola, acts delightfully, and masquerades as the page in a spruce and mettlesome way that is most refreshing after the mincing coyness of other actresses in similar case. She has a quaint humour, too, and a pretty voice which she uses in strict accord to metre. As Sebastian, Mr Quartermaine has the advantage of looking really like her twin-brother. He, too, speaks his lines musically. And Mr Taber, as the Duke, strikes just the right note of delicate sensuousness. Thus the quadrille becomes tolerable.

The Clown is a kind of link between the merely conventional and the properly Shakespearean characters in the play. With his jibes and his warning, he pervades the whole scheme. It was an excellent idea that he, at the fall of the curtain, should be on the stage, blowing a trill on his secular flute, when the other characters have trooped off to the sound of marriage-bells. 'After all,' he seems to pipe, 'what does it all amount to?' just as Shakespeare threw in that *What you will*. Both as actor and as singer, Mr Courtice Pounds is an admirable Clown, infusing always a touch of sinistry into his mirth. Mr Lionel Brough and Mr Norman Forbes are well matched against each other as Sir Toby and Sir Andrew—a contrast of the fruity with the scrannel grotesque. The drinking-bout is done by them in thoroughly Shakespearean fashion. At the end of it comes an effect which Shakespeare did not, perhaps, adumbrate in his stage-directions, but which rounds it off very prettily. As the two topers reel off to bed, the uncanny dawn peers at them through the windows. The Clown wanders on, humming a snatch of the tune he has sung to them. He looks at the empty bowl of sack and the overturned tankards, smiles, shrugs his shoulders, yawns, lies down before the embers of the fire, goes to sleep. Down the stairs, warily, with a night-cap on his head and a sword in his hand, comes Malvolio, awakened and fearful of danger. He peers around, lunging with his sword at the harmless furniture. One thinks of Don Quixote and 'the notable adventure of the wine-skins.' Satisfied, he retraces his footsteps up the staircase. A cock crows, and, as the curtain falls, one is aware of a whole slumbering household, and of the mystery of an actual dawn. Pedants might cavil at such imaginative glosses in a production of Shakespeare. To me the question is simply whether the imagination be of a good or bad kind. In this instance the imagination seems to me distinctly good.

The analogy between Malvolio and Don Quixote occurs inevitably. For both men were of lofty bearing, cursed with an exaggerated sense of their missions, and in both of them this sense was used by irreverent creatures to entice them into ludicrous plights. But the analogy does not go further than that. I cannot subscribe to Charles Lamb's ingenious paradox that Malvolio was in himself a fine fellow, whose dignified bearing had solid basis in a dignified nature. Malvolio does not, indeed, at the beginning of the play, say anything which would contradict this theory. But that is due to Shakespeare's slap-dash technique. Shakespeare's real opinion of Malvolio is shown in the words which he puts into the mouth of Olivia: 'O, you are sick of self-love,' &c. Malvolio is meant to be an egomaniac—a state quite inconsistent with true dignity. He is intrinsically absurd. This, evidently, is the view of Mr Tree, whose dignity throughout is of an absurdly foppish and fantastical kind. So much for Mr Tree's conception of the part. As for his execution of it, I think I can safely say ... but I must not break a certain self-imposed rule with which my readers are already familiar.

[*9 February 1901*]

## METROPOLITAN, TRANSMARINE, AND TRANSPONTINE

I was rather nervous about *The Awakening*. Through *The Tyranny of Tears* (and through that only) I had conceived such a respect for Mr Haddon Chambers that I was appalled by the possibility that he had backslidden to his early manner. However, I soon breathed freely. All was well, 'lights burning bright,' and so forth. *The Awakening* is, indeed, a very good sample of modern dramaturgy. Its author shows a keen interest in the surface-manners of contemporary life, and in the intricacies of human character. And, primarily, as in *The Tyranny of Tears*, he uses his innate sense of the theatre, not for striking out unscrupulously theatrical effects, but for creating effects of real life across footlights. Of 'good situations' his play has no lack, but they are situations that arise naturally from the opposition of various well-observed and well-projected characters, placed in likely circumstances. The characters are not mere little bits of wood—not mere little chessmen, with conventional shapes and appointed moves, played by one whose eyes are blindfolded to life, and whose one purpose is to stagger us with his skill. They are live creatures, with free wills; they move, instead of being moved. Thus they satisfy what is, for me, the prime test of good modern drama. And the play in which they move is to me as much more fascinating than (say) *The Gay Lord Quex* as is life than chess.

Only at one point does it seem to me that Mr Chambers is guilty of staginess. And that is when, in the first act, the young girl pays a midnight visit to the rooms of the sporadically-amorous man with whom she is in love. This visit, which Mr Chambers tries by various means to make plausible, remains quite implausible. One feels that the girl's sole reason for coming is that she may be duly seen by us, and may acquaint us duly with her antecedents, before the second act begins. There are many ways in which Mr Chambers could have let her do this duty without trampling on likelihood. One way would have been to make the first act pass in the afternoon instead of in the evening. Why did not Mr Chambers do this? My conjecture is that he had, in his first (written or unwritten) scenario intended the girl to have been previously seduced by the man, that (for commercial reasons) he changed his mind, and that he would not, however, take the trouble to re-model the details in order to harmonise them with the general change in his conception. Assuming that I have guessed aright, I deem it a pity that he would not take this trouble. Or, rather, I deem it a pity that he changed his main conception of the girl's history. If (as were quite probable, in the given circumstances) the girl had been 'deceived' in the technical as well as in the literal sense of the word, her subsequent scene with the newly-widowed woman who has been for some time the man's mistress would be far more poignant in its conflict. However, it does not greatly matter. By changing his main conception Mr Chambers has done no real mischief. The conflict of the two women is, as it stands, a quite natural conflict, and gives very poignant emotion to the audience. The point is merely that the emotion might have been still more poignant, if Mr Chambers had adhered to his original scheme. And remember! I may be (and probably am) quite mistaken in assuming that he did not do so.

Miss Fay Davis plays the girl's part very—what shall I say? There is no recognised adverb that expresses the exact degree and kind of praise that I would bestow—very faydavisically, let me say. That is, she displays her usual charm of manner, and, as soon as it is needed, her usual power. Perhaps it is because both the power and the charm are peculiarly her own, and so make a very sharp impression every time one sees them, that one feels as if one had been seeing them rather often. The part of the amorist, played by Mr Alexander, is drawn with much sympathy. Every man, good or bad, sympathises with himself. No dramatist can draw a character truly unless he project himself inside it—unless he become, imaginatively, the character itself. Accordingly, no character, good or bad, can be drawn without sympathy. It is just this quality which has made the amorist of this play live, and distinguishes him from the stage's ordinary dummy of a Lothario, drawn disapprovingly from without. The part is played very attractively by Mr Alexander, whom, nevertheless, I should like to see again in those strenuous parts which suit him much better than parts in modern comedy. Miss Gertrude Kingston is admirable as the newly-made widow. Possibly she does not extract for it from the audience so much sympathy as the author put into it; on the other hand, she brings to it exactly the outward manner which it needs, and which no other actress could have brought to it. All the subordinate parts are drawn with unusual care and vividness, and are, with one exception, well cast. The exception is the part of a stupid smart young man. In it Mr H. B. Irving, with his brow and gait and manner reflecting all the more serious intellectual aspects of the Augustan era and the Renaissance and the Romantic Movement of 1830, provides endless fun for young and old.

'It's a wonderful invention!' exclaims the Duchesse de Reville, as she turns up the gas in the conservatory. The words are as illuminative as her action. *Le Monde où l'on s'ennuie*, of which an English version appeared last Tuesday afternoon at the Strand Theatre, was written in that dark age when gas was still regarded as a luxury. Seeing it played by mimes in the costumes of 1901 A.D., one is apt to forget its period, and is consequently irritated by its manner. This naïve exposition at the outset, these naïve devices of intercepted letters and overheard conversations, this stiff symmetry of action and of character, come upon one with much the same effect as they would from a comedy of to-day. But the Duchesse's tribute to gas sends one for a moment straight back into the proper period. A pity that the translators, Miss Martia Leonard and Mr J. T. Grein, did not so far tamper with the original as to make the Duchesse praise gas frequently throughout the play. But the best way would have been to treat the play frankly as a costume-play. In substance, as in technique, it belongs definitely to the time in which it was written. Pailleron is, for practical purposes, as remote from us as Molière, and *Les Précieuses Ridicules* would seem no more queer to us in modern garb than does this later satire of similar things. Every comedy of manners belongs definitely to its own time, and should be treated accordingly. Be it never so masterly, no comedy of manners can but oppress one if it be dragged visually up to date. I am sure that Miss

Leonard and Mr Grein will concur with me. Probably, the only reason why they did not put their mimes into costume was the very good reason that the play was for one performance only. As there is a law of time in these matters, so is there also a law of space. Almost every play belongs definitely to the country of its author. The only modern plays that can be translated without serious hurt are the plays of Maeterlinck, whose spirit and method have no nationality at all. Even Ibsen, despite the universality of his themes, suffers, inasmuch as his creatures are Norwegians in Norway. How much more so the ordinary dramatist, who reflects his locality and nothing outside it! How weird to see Anglo-Saxon mimes, as I saw them last Tuesday, trying to get into the impregnable skins of Parisian characters, trying to echo with Anglo-Saxon lips things unspeakable in any language but French! Free trade in art is a pretty catchword, a pretty ideal. But alas! however wide we may open the door to foreign merchandise, Nature steps in and imposes a tariff of very heavy duties. However, far be it from me to seem ungrateful to the two enterprising translators, or not appreciative of the mimes' endeavours. As Mr Grein is one of the two or three dramatic critics who care and know about histrionic art, naturally one found in the cast several of those admirable mimes to whom managers prefer mimes not admirable at all. The Duchesse was played by Miss Susie Vaughan, Bellac by Mr Courtenay Thorpe, Susanne by Miss Nina Bouicault. These three comedians have in their little fingers, respectively, enough talent to make one wonder why they are not fixtures in the best theatres.

Mr Martin Harvey, with upturned eyes, and wearing ever that etherially mystic smile, is proceeding steadily on his sentimental journey from bad to worse. 'Halt!' cry I to him. For is it not a thousand pities that so important a young mime as he should persist in wasting his gifts on quite worthless plays? *The Only Way* was a dull melodrama, which 'ran' by reason of Mr Harvey's glamour. *Don Juan's Last Wager* was such poor stuff that even Mr Harvey could not underpin it for more than a very few weeks. *A Cigarette-Maker's Romance* (produced last Monday at the Court Theatre) is such pitiably old-fashioned balderdash that only the author's invisibility, *plus* a very adroit and glamourous little speech by Mr Harvey, saved my sense of decorum from being outraged by an ugly demonstration at the end of the evening. On merely commercial grounds,

I do strongly advise Mr Harvey to reform. That he himself, being obviously an artistic and intelligent person, liked the play which he has produced, I cannot persuade myself to believe (though he *did* dare to describe it as 'beautiful' in his speech). But from the fact that he has produced it I assume that he supposed that it would be a success. And, unless I am very much mistaken, it won't be. Thirty years ago, in the more remote parts of the provinces, it might have had some measure of success. But in London, and in the present century, the public really has no use for it. Mr Harvey will perceive that I am speaking quite objectively. Past, I do assure him, is that era when even the provincial public would have been thrilled by so silly a villain as Anton Skariatine, or convulsed by such primitive fun as comes of a female servant tumbling downstairs with a tray of dishes and sprawling across the stage, or moved by such maudlin clap-trap as has been infused for Mr Harvey into this clumsily-made melodrama. To truckle to the present taste of the public is the quickest way of making money, no doubt. But to truckle to what may once have been its taste, but long since ceased to be so, is very bad policy indeed—'it isn't business.' A man of Mr Harvey's glamour may lure the public back to a position from which it has progressed, but he cannot keep it there long. For the sake of his box-office Mr Harvey ought to bestir himself and catch the public up, taking care not to outstrip it. But 'there is a greater thing on earth than riches. With it the poor man is wealthy; without it the rich man is poor; beggars may possess it; it is not to be bought by kings.' This quotation I quote from the programme, for which Mr Harvey, showing his sincerity in its sentiment, does not charge sixpence. I suggest that a greater thing than riches is an artistic conscience at rest. Why should not Mr Harvey soothe his artistic conscience by outstripping the public? He would not find the adventure disastrous to his exchequer. He would, indeed, find it much more remunerative than his present policy can ever be. Attracted by the glamour of a personality, the public will always, sooner or later, lumber forward to the point where the personality has pitched itself, and will there abide faithfully until the personality moves on further and beckons to it. That is how drama progresses. That is how Mr Harvey himself might progress. At present he is letting the grass grow under his feet; or rather he is roving the desert. And very soon he will not be able to suppress by the light of his handsome eye the demands of his followers for some refreshment. His followers will leave him to eremetise, an awful example. I urge Mr Harvey to use his gifts aright, to lead forward instead of luring backward. He must cultivate *ambition*; else will he find his reputation as evanescent as the smoke from those cigarettes of which, on the first night, three were presented, with his compliments, to every male member of the audience. I am smoking one of those cigarettes at this moment, thus showing, perhaps, a certain disregard for the finer niceties of behaviour. I hasten to atone by affirming that it is a very good cigarette. Mr Harvey is at liberty to make whatever use of this testimonial he may think fit. But might he not raise his standard in drama to the level of his standard in tobacco?

[ *16 February 1901* ]


## MELODRAMA AND THE SEVENTH STANDARD

If theatrical speculators would but keep an eye on modern English history, the pressure in Portugal Street would be lightened somewhat. On the public they depend, yet make no study of the public's condition. They persist in offering exactly the same kind of drama as pleased the public twenty years ago, and, not realising the effects of the Board School, come to smash without the solace of guessing why. Let them lift their eyes from their pathetic ledgers, and look around, and gauge the vast change that has been wrought in the proletariat by twenty years of compulsory education. Let them analyse Hooliganism. Let them analyse the dearth of good domestic servants. They will find that these two phenomena result from discontent with the dulness and sordidness of that state of life to which boys and girls in the lower class are still called by poverty. Why this discontent? Because these boys' and girls' wits have been sharpened; because they have capabilities for which we have devised no outlet; because they are too intelligent for the only kind of work we can give them. How to dispose of them politically, without abrogating the Act of '72, seems to me the hardest problem that confronts you and your statesmen. How to cater for them intellectually, is a problem that has been solved, for the present, by Mr Harmsworth and other seers. By assuring them that a drop of lemon-juice contains 150,000,000 infusoria, and that the Tsar of Russia has 527 pairs of boots, and that Talleyrand, being told that one must live, replied 'I do not see the necessity,' and that rheumatism may be avoided by wearing a small bag of camphor and anise-seed next the skin, and that if all the lamp-posts in London were joined together longitudinally they would form a line extending from Charing Cross to Edinburgh Castle, you slake their thirst for knowledge without demanding of them that mental concentration which, as yet, they are too unsettled to afford. But editors are always ahead of theatrical managers, and it has not yet been discovered that the kind of melodrama which appealed to an utterly uneducated public must be intolerable to one that is fresh from the Seventh Standard. Managers merely wonder why melodrama is a failure, why even in the remote provinces musical comedy succeeds while melodrama fails miserably. They imagine that it is because there is something wrong with the individual melodramas, and proceed to produce others in the hope that at them the public will rise. It never occurs to these managers that the State has sophisticated the public out of its joy in villains and rhodomontade, and, moreover, that the public does not care to concentrate its mind during three hours on any one thing. Musical comedy succeeds through its analogy to 'snippet-literature.' If it were informative, as well as bright and disjointed, it would succeed even more splendidly than it does. Meanwhile, the old melodrama is as dead as a door-nail. The proletariat eschews it for its stupidity and for its unity, even as it now eschews the tales in the *Family Herald*. The only melodramas that are not disasters are those of Mr Cecil Raleigh and Mr Wilson Barrett. Mr Raleigh's succeed because he, with Sir Augustus Harris, created a form in which the snippet*ismus* is allowed for; Mr Barrett's because he saw that the absence of religious teaching in Board Schools would create a class hungry for religion in its mature years. But Mr Raleigh, Sir Augustus, and Mr Barrett are the only melodramapolists to whom has come a glimmer of the new needs. The other authors and managers are still doddering blindly around in the belief that what was sauce for the wild goose of the last generation must be sauce for the overstuffed gander of this.

*Est locus*, as the Latin poets used to say—a place called Church Street, turning off the Edgware Road. There, with a kind of devious dignity, stands a little theatre. It is called the West London, and is controlled by Mr William Bailey and Mr William Bailey, junr, and I had heard of it as a stronghold of melodrama. Thither, with gaily adventurous companions, I went one night this week, to see what I might see. And there I saw 'the new and original drama entitled *Under False Colours* by Myles Wallerton and Francis Gilbert.' My main motive for the excursion was merely human: a wish to be amused. But I had also, incidentally, the motive of a dramatic critic: a wish to study the attitude of the audience towards unadulterated melodrama. My main wish was not wholly fulfilled. As I was not there by invitation, as I had not gone to pronounce judgment on the play, nor to treat it as a work of art, my sense of humour fell into abeyance. Nonsense is ridiculous to me only when I am expected to regard it as sense. And thus, when the curtain rose, I slipped at once from my mood of humorous contempt into a mood of indulgence, and therefrom I slipped soon into a mood of simple receptivity. Taking the play for what it was worth, I took it for all it was worth, and was as excited by it as though I had been one of the extinct carles for whom its form was invented. I went to scoff, and remained to pray that the villain might not succeed in his nefarious attempt to crush the heroine to death in a cider-press. When my prayer was answered at the fall of the curtain, when virtue had triumphed and villainy had recoiled on its own head, I went out into the air feeling that for once I had spent a thoroughly sincere and enjoyable evening. That the melodrama was very good of its kind I do not, in cold blood, care to maintain. It had that fatal drawback: the impersonation of hero and villain by one actor. The knowledge that hero and villain can never meet, and so can never directly conflict with each other, must always detract much from excitement. In this instance, moreover, the actor who doubled the part—Mr Arthur Bearne, to wit, and a very good actor indeed—made no attempt to differentiate his appearance and voice according to his dual duties. And thus it was not always child's-play to be quite sure whether he were being noble or vile. However, the point is that I always *wished* to be quite sure. I was loth to miss one point in his heroism. When he, as hero, was gagged and thrown down a precipice by two minions, and when, in consequence of the fall, he entirely forgot who he was, and so was in danger of losing his birthright, my heart bled for him profusely. Yet, only the other day, the similar lapse of memory suffered by Count Skariatine in *A Cigarette-Maker's*

*Romance* left me quite untouched. Such is the difference between going to criticise a play that is meant to be taken as art, and going to be amused by a play that has no pretension but to please the public.

To please the public! That phrase brings me to my secondary motive for going to the West London. As often as I could distract myself from the play, I did observe the demeanour of the audience. And it was just as I had expected—frosty and apathetic. The quality of the applause showed that the audience had no share in my enthusiasm. 'Not a hand' greeted the speech in which the female villain extrolled the wonderful power of love—'that ponderous, irresistible force which sweeps all away—the hero and the coward, the idiot and the Master of Arts.' The antithesis between an idiot and a Master of Arts, implying the latter to be the embodiment of all that is finest in human wisdom and culture, may be a trifle crude. But the whole speech—of which I can quote only this fragment—was as fine a piece of stirring melodramatic prose as ever was declaimed across footlights, and its cold reception were enough to convince any melodramatist that the game, even in Church Street, is up. If further proof had been needed, it would have been found in the titters which punctuated some of the most serious scenes in the play. When the villain meets the heroine for the first time after his attempt to kill her (by landing her on a rock in mid-ocean, pushing the boat off, lassoing her and dragging her down into the waves), he excuses himself by saying simply 'Circumstances over which I have no control compelled me, Mercedes, to take this step.' To me, in my receptivity, this seemed a very good excuse—one which any heroine might accept. But there were titters from the audience. To an audience drawn from the lower class, such a theatre as the West London is a serious matter. They go to it for illusion, as their parents went before them. They do not go to it, as I went, for mere fun. They do not, like me, condescend to it from a pinnacle; and so they have not my chance of being illuded. They go with all their wits about them, as their parents went before them. But their parents' wits had not been sharpened by the Board School. What was good enough for their parents is not good enough for them. Nor, I repeat, have they the power of concentration which a melodrama demands. Theatrical managers should realise these facts.

I do not go so far as to declare that melodrama, as a dramatic form, is henceforth impossible. Melodrama, I fancy, satisfies an eternal craving in mankind. When (or if) we solve the problem of what is to be done with the educated lower class, and so restore to it the stability which has been taken from it, the educated lower class will be able to appreciate something better than snippets, and will read books. Likewise, it will enjoy continuous plays as much as it now enjoys musical comedies. Only, the melodramas will have to be of a sensible, intellectual kind. So much for the future. 'In the present,' wails the melodramapolist, 'is there no hope for me?' None; unless, perhaps, ... Conceive a villain who wishes, not to crush the heroine in the cider-press, but to prove to her that a drop of lemon-juice does *not* contain 150,000,000 infusoria; and conceive that he is triumphantly foiled in this attempt by the hero.... That way, maybe, salvation lies.

[*23 March 1901*]

## 'HAMLET' IN PANTON STREET

Unkind chance prevented me from seeing the one performance of Mr Zangwill's play, *The Revolted Daughter*. Thus, lacking imagination, I must confine myself to Mr Benson's production of *Hamlet*, which I *did* see, on Thursday evening. I am sorry. Granting that *Hamlet is* a masterpiece, and assuming, for sake of argument, that *The Revolted Daughter* is not, I maintain that the production of any new play by any live writer is an event more important than *Hamlet* for the million-and-one-th time of asking. But let me be quite honest. Let me confess that my sense of proportion does not always control my preferences, and that I should be even more sorry not to have seen again the Elizabethan play than I am to have missed altogether the Edwardian. Lately I was analysing here the peculiar charm of the Benson company—the subtle pleasure of seeing the same mimes again and again, at brief intervals, in the same place. *Hamlet* is fraught for us with a similar fascination. For we have seen it times out of number. We know it scene by scene—nay! line by line. We know it 'backwards.' It has become an integral part of us. It is implicated in our very fibres. To see *Hamlet* is one of our natural functions, one of our needs. How restful the play is, in its hold on us, how intimate and cosy! Nowhere, I protest, have I such a sense of home as in the Castle of Elsinore. Whenever the curtain rises on that 'Room of State,' I seem to recognise every brick in those low arches and squat columns, every fold in those arrases of neutral-coloured serge. Comes the slow procession one knows so well: the wimpled young ladies of the Court, with whom the blond-wigged young gentlemen converse in gestures as they range themselves before the throne. Comes Hamlet, moody and sable, and sinks into the curvated chair. Comes Polonius walking backwards, swinging his wand. Majestically, Claudius and Gertrude dispose themselves on the throne. 'Though yet of Hamlet our dear brother's death...,' as who should say 'When the wicked man....' The words strike a mysterious chord in all of us. Years have obtunded for us their actual meaning, but have given them a fast grip on our subconscious souls. Throughout the whole play we are entranced. Those fatuous young friends of Hamlet, and fatuous old friends of ours, Rosencrantz and Guildenstern—who is not kindled at the familiar sight of them? And then the players, and the grave-diggers, and the interminable oath scene on 'a more remote Part of the Platform,' and the closet-scene and the mad-scene, and the burial-scene—who does not delight in them and in the lovely speeches and phrases that spring out of them? To me, every time I hear it, the language in *Hamlet* seems lovelier, comes with a new thrill. But words are one thing, action is another. Words are mellowed by repetition, but action is thereby made void. As drama, *Hamlet* has no power to affect me at all. The familiarity for which I love it prevents me from getting any dramatic sensation out of it. I am too much at home in Elsinore. I seem to have stayed there so often, to have written so many letters on its note-paper, helped the son of the house so often with his theatricals, talked so cordially about him to his *fiancée*, tried so sympathetically to reassure his mother as to his sanity, been so very sorry when he was called away to England. I take the whole play, fondly, as a matter of course. Indeed, I doubt that to me, to anyone in this age of the world, *Hamlet* can ever have made any true appeal as drama. In modern times dramaturgy has become a strict art-form. A play has to be a concise exposition and development of a theme, and to be consistent in its manner throughout. Else it confuses us, does not hold our attention, does not illude us. But to Shakespeare dramaturgy was a go-as-you-please affair, in which any amount of time might be spent in divagations from the main theme, and in which one manner of treatment might be alternated with another, and in which the characters might, from time to time, and without warning, become the mere mouthpiece of the author. On most of Shakespeare's plays there is a certain impression of unity. But this is because most of his plays were written quickly, without time for elaboration. Usually, he let his genius gallop lightly over the ready-made material, glorifying it, but leaving it, essentially, much as it was before. On *Hamlet*, expending, as we know he did, a long period of creation, he had time to graft a vast amount of himself. He put almost 'all that he knew' into the play. And the result is for us rather a variety entertainment than a drama. The melodramatic matter on which he was working is robbed of all sequence and significance by the elaborated psychology of the principal character. Conversely, the history of Hamlet's soul loses for us its dramatic force through the incongruous melodramatic scenes which interrupt it. And, even if we could disentangle the psychology from the melodrama, we could not disentangle Hamlet from Shakespeare. As Mr Walkley has pointed out, some of Hamlet's speeches are mere interludes, not merely irrelevant to his character, but actually inconsistent with it. In these it is not Hamlet that speaks, but Shakespeare. And, since Hamlet is obviously unreal at some points, how could we accept him without suspicion at others? There is not one of his soliloquies that would not tease us with the problem of how far he was speaking from his own heart. In fact, he would fail to illude us even if we could dissociate him from the melodrama. There were but one way in which *Hamlet* could be made a really dramatic play. And that were to cut down the part of Hamlet so drastically as to reduce him to the level of a mere puppet in the melodramatic action; in fact, to do to Hamlet what always is done to Claudius. The experiment might be made. Of course, it never will be made by an actor-manager. Hamlet is too 'fat' a part for that. Nor, of course, will it ever be made by anyone with any sensibility to poetry. But I wonder that it has never been made in any of the theatres controlled by theatrical syndicates. The result might be very lucrative indeed.

Perhaps, after all, the ordinary way of producing *Hamlet* is the safest way. Though no one with any power of analysing his own emotions would pretend that this play appeals to him as drama, everyone likes to see it, because everyone, consciously or not, shares my delight in its familiarity. Of course, there is the additional excitement of seeing what sort of reading A will take of Hamlet, and how B will succeed as Ophelia, or C as Polonius. In the case of the Bensons, this excitement is lacking. We have all seen them in their several parts. Our interest in the performance is merely the affectionate desire to renew impressions. It may seem like excess of affection to record such impressions. Enough to say that the Benson company acquits itself at the Comedy this year exactly as it acquitted itself (in the unabridged version) last year at the Lyceum. But if I contented myself with that sufficient phrase my article would look skimpy. So let me aver that Mr Benson's temperament and style fully justify him in casting himself for the part of Hamlet. He is not a very poetical Hamlet. He is thoughtful rather than imaginative, and his bearing is distinguished rather than beautiful. Nor does he ever seem able to express fully as an actor what he knows and feels as a scholar. His voice, his face, his limbs, are not safe and ready vehicles for transmission of what is in him. In fact, he is a made actor, not a born actor. His gestures are always of that crudely literal kind which mars rather than illuminates the words spoken. When he says 'The time is out of joint,' he shakes his arms in front of him, as though to imply that he feels it in his own joints. When he says 'There is nothing evil, but *thinking* makes it so,' he taps his forehead with his forefinger. And these two instances of his method might be multiplied infinitely. No gesture at all were better than gesture of this mechanical kind. Another drawback is his elocution. His voice itself is very pleasant, though its modulations do not answer readily to his meaning. But his manner of pronouncing his words, and of arranging the pauses between them, often makes him almost unintelligible. In his first scene with the Ghost, well as I know every line, I had the greatest difficulty in following him. Probably this fantastic delivery of his is due to the vast number of times he has played the various parts in his repertory. When we do a thing very often we begin to take it as a matter of course, to slur it, and at the same time to twist it. Thus our signatures are always quite different from the rest of our handwriting, and much less legible. Thus, also, the crier of wares in the street utters a jargon which defies you to guess what his wares are. Thus, also, the curate taking a Church service, and the toast-master, bidding you charge your glasses &c., have fantastic tricks of voice quite unrelated to their manner in ordinary life. And

Mr Benson's elocution must surely be attributed to the same cause as theirs. However, when all is said, Mr Benson's Hamlet is a very laudable performance. Though it is not full of beauty, it is done with a sense of beauty, and with loving care and thought. I hope to see it again next year. Coming now to the other members of the cast.... But no. I can say now, without appearance of skimping, merely that the other members of the cast were as last year.

[*30 March 1901*]


## MR LYALL SWETE IN TWO PLAYS

Just now Mr E. Lyall Swete is very much on my mind—a pleasant burden. I saw him again and again in Mr Benson's series of productions, and I am inclined to blame myself for not having 'spotted' and trumpeted him then. That he was a born actor I did realise, soon enough. But he is much more than that. Born actors are not so very uncommon. There are many men who can express themselves, easily and satisfactorily, through the medium of histrionic art. But, for the most part, themselves are not interesting creatures: they are not rich in thought or in passion. Consequently, their technical talent does not carry them far when they are cast for important parts. There are, conversely, a few actors who are well endowed in point of intellect or emotion or of both, but who cannot, unfortunately, act. (Mr Benson himself is an example of the intellectual actor *minus* the specific vocation to the stage.) The great actor is he who can (1) bring great power of thought and of feeling to a part, and (2) communicate the result, readily and without loss, to the folks across the footlights. This combination of gifts is rare. Great actors are rare, accordingly. At first sight of so rare a bird one ought to make a considerable fuss. That Mr Lyall Swete is a great actor I am convinced. Why, then, has my fuss about him been postponed to this moment? The explanation of my backwardness is more than a trifle humiliating. It is—it must be—that I have not the true *flair* for acting. Had I that true *flair*, I must surely have disengaged Mr Swete from his Bensonian colleagues, and have guessed the infinite possibilities of him. I should have not have been blinded by the fact that in a stock-company great acting is not encouraged and is not possible. I should have remembered that Mr Swete, playing more or less small parts in a round of Shakespearean drama, was bound by the laws of good-fellowship to subordinate himself to the *ensemble*. I should have remembered, further, that these parts are so clogged with tradition that, had he tried to take an unfair advantage of his colleagues by putting into them his whole heart and mind, he would probably have failed in the attempt. Realising all these reservations, I should have divined in Mr Swete the peeps of authentic greatness. I beg your pardon, and his, for having done nothing of the sort. In mitigation of your contempt, and his, I may plead that, lamentable as it is not to perceive greatness through a veil, it is far more lamentable not to perceive it when no veil intervenes. With the latter kind of impercipiency not a few of the dramatic critics are afflicted. But not I. I can recognise great acting when I see it. I recognised it quickly enough in the Strand Theatre last Monday, under the auspices of the Stage Society, when Mr Swete appeared as John Vockerat in Hauptmann's *Lonely Lives*.

The way had been paved for this apocalypse on the previous Friday, when I had seen Mr Swete as the Reverend Mr William Collins in Miss Rosina Filippi's clever adaptation of *Pride and Prejudice*. I had much admired his creation of the part. It was a creation in more than the technical sense of the word. The Mr Collins of our dreams—the smug, pedantic, sly, silly Mr Collins—was incarnate to our eyes. The character had been thought out to its recesses, and was projected with the sure sobriety of perfect humour. I perceived in Mr Swete a great character-actor. That he was also a great actor I did not perceive till I saw him in that great part, John Vockerat. I say 'a great part,' meaning that the character is drawn by the author as a highly vitalised and complex human being, and drawn so elaborately as to dominate the whole play. To understand the character postulates far more intelligence than the ordinary actor possesses. To present it in all its many-sidedness, in all its swift transitions from mood to mood, without losing the consistency that underlies it, and to retain for it our sympathies throughout, is a feat that only a great actor could compass. It is a part that has to be thought deeply, to be felt deeply, to be presented with a quickly alternating mastery of comic and tragic method. It is a great part by reason of its great difficulties. And all these difficulties Mr Swete had overcome. He had fused thought, passion, technique, into one perfect whole, so that we gained a perfect illusion. He did not seem to be acting: he *was* the man. That is a *cliché*, I know; but you must accept it; it is one of those *clichés* which are occasionally indispensable—one of those compliments which cannot be turned otherwise. If there be any other way of expressing the kind of praise I would bestow, I cannot find it. I am so unaccustomed to panegyric that I must needs lisp it in common terms. The task of dramatic criticism has estranged me from any mood but of mild approval or mild disgust. Thus I am rather at a loss when I try to make the welkin ring. Also I feel rather ashamed of myself for the effort. I trust, however, that for you my enthusiasm may derive a certain weight from its rarity, and that its clumsiness may seem a seal to its sincerity. I fear no possible misunderstanding from anyone who, like me, saw Mr Swete's performance last Monday. Any such person must agree with me that Mr Swete is on a plane far and away above any of the young actors who permanently grace the metropolis. It is a thousand pities that we cannot keep him with us. Mr Benson ought to make us a present of him. If Mr Benson's generosity does not go so far, he ought, at least, to have refrained from giving Mr Swete an *exeat*. To dangle before our eyes a pearl of such price and not to let us wear it, is an act of wanton unkindness.

Though *Lonely Lives* and *The Bennets* (as Miss Filippi calls her version of *Pride and Prejudice*) are as different, superficially, as two plays could be, they have one fundamental point in common: neither makes any pretence to what is called dramatic action; each depends solely on exposition of human character. That the mere conjunction of various persons may, without leading to 'situations,' be theatrically effective is a truth which has been gradually dawning on the dullest of us. Nevertheless, Miss Filippi must be given credit for audacity in having collaborated with the shade of the incomparable Miss Jane. No one had dreamed of doing so before her. For Miss Jane was accounted a leisurely subtlist, who made her effects little by little, ever so gently and imperceptibly. To preserve aught of those effects for us in the narrow compass of a play was a task that seemed impossible: dramatic congestion would surely produce a mere void. But Miss Filippi perceived, and we perceive now, that the slightness of Miss Jane's stories gives the dramatist of them time to develop the characters quite elaborately, and that the quality of Miss Jane's dialogue is so direct and exact that whole passages of it may cross footlights and be to us not less effective than they are on the printed page. This was a great discovery. But if it had been made by a duffer the result would have been lamentable. Miss Filippi has shown great skill in her selection of the passages which she found in *Pride and Prejudice,* and in the structure of the frame which she has made for them. That she has not eschewed such technical errors as soliloquies and 'over-hearings,' matters little enough to me. In a play of modern times such errors distress me. But in a play that harks back to the early part of last century they strike no discord: they seem to belong to the period. What really matters is that Miss Filippi has preserved the atmosphere of the book, and that the characters are sharply and accurately outlined. True, some of the atmosphere evaporated at the Court Theatre, and not all the characters were satisfactory. But that was due to the exigencies of a special *matinée,* and to the difficulties of keeping square pegs out of round holes. Miss Winifred Mayo had not the vivacity and subtlety required for Elizabeth Bennet; Mr Harcourt Williams had not the dignity for Darcy; Miss Elsie Chester was merely farcical as Lady Catherine; and so forth. But the parts themselves, discernible through the mimes, were very creditable to Miss Filippi. She herself, by the way, was delightful as Mrs Bennet. To be able to act delightfully in a first production of one's own play seems to me, however, scarcely human—a feat not to be encouraged.

My enthusiasm for Mr Swete was so long-winded that I am forced to postpone my remarks about Hauptmann.

[ *6 April 1901* ]

## 'CORIOLANUS' AND OTHER PLAYS

Let it be taken as read that I have a profound admiration for the genius of Sir Henry Irving. My sentiment being what it is, and Sir Henry, alas! being seldom now at the Lyceum, I would rather see him there in a bad play that gave him a chance either of being himself or of making an effective impersonation than in a good play that was not so accommodating. That *Coriolanus* is a bad play we all agree. That is contains one fine and interesting part we all agree. Played by an appropriate actor, this part would justify to me the play's production—except during Sir Henry's tenancy of the Lyceum. No profundity of admiration can cheat me into the notion that of the appropriate actors Sir Henry is one. On the contrary, Love, ever acutely perspicacious through that bandage which has earned him a false epithet, reveals to me Sir Henry as an actor who cannot 'touch' the part of Coriolanus, nay! as one who never could have 'touched' it at any moment in his career. By the defects of those very qualities which I love would Sir Henry have always been debarred. It is no mere matter of age. It is not merely that Sir Henry's noble face and subtle voice are no longer the face and voice of a vigorous man in the prime of life. It is a question of innate temperament. Coriolanus, fine soldier, was a very stupid man. All the egomaniacal pride that obsessed him came directly from narrowness, from lack of imagination—from stupidity, in short. And, just as the soldier is the one type of man that never could have been reconciled by us with Sir Henry's outward bearing, so the one human quality with which Sir Henry never could have harmonised his soul is straightforward stupidity. As a schemer (in the large sense of the word) Sir Henry, with his obviously active intellect, is seen at his best. As a passive, stubborn monster, with the strength and insentience of a rock, he is seen at his very worst; indeed, *he* is not seen at all; nor is the monster. I know two or three actors who could impersonate this monster quite admirably, declaiming its speeches for all they are worth. Sir Henry, to the best of my knowledge, never has been able to declaim. Beauty of diction he has often compassed, and he compasses it, now and again, as Coriolanus, but at the expense of the part's whole significance. To take the speeches of Coriolanus with a rush—to 'spout' them—is the only legitimate method. To break them up, and to inject vocal subtleties into them, is to make them absurd. Coriolanus, as interpreted by Sir Henry, is a character wasted. And—this is to me a far more lamentable matter—Sir Henry, interpreting Coriolanus, wastes himself. Not the beauty of the whole production did one whit appease me for the loss. Nor, certainly, did the sight of Miss Ellen Terry as Volumnia. Indeed, Miss Terry was not less disastrously wasted than Sir Henry. She is always, whatever she do, the merry, bonny, English creature with the surface of Æstheticism—always reminds me of a Christmas-tree decorated by a Pre-Raphaelite. To see her thus when she ought to have been a typical ancient Roman matron, was rather more than I could bear. I understand that there may be some revivals later at the Lyceum. With this consolation I pass on.

Throw some tepid water on the strained and sodden tea-leaves in the teapot of yesterday's drama; pour out; sugar well with sentimentality; milk well with human kindness. Such is the best-known means of refreshing the public. But Mr Basil Hood knows a recipe worth two of that. He has emptied the sugar-basin into that teapot, dissolving the ingredients with a half-a-pint or so of his own salt tears. Need I say that this brew, dispensed at the Vaudeville, was sucked down by the public in an ecstasy of gulps. Never, I vow, was beverage so subtly concocted to its taste. *Sweet and Twenty* the play is called, and I may mention, in tribute to Mr Hood's acumen, that in every act there is a heart-broken adieu—a going through mists of tears to begin a new life in a new world, that the scene is laid at the vicarage of the Hon. and Rev. James Floyd, and that the action has a running accompaniment of hymn tunes, texts, flowing metaphors, and puns. The Vicar's sons, Eustace and Douglas, both love Joan. Douglas, who is going to sea, and wishes to prepare the audience for his subsequent dismissal *inebrietatis causa* from the Navy, bids his old nurse bring a bottle of champagne into the garden. The old nurse retires, and it strikes him that Eustace and he ought to seal 'the bond of brotherhood.' Perceiving a touch of surliness in Eustace's manner, he says 'There is a shadow between us.' 'It is Joan's shadow,' pipes a little boy, who has entered unobserved; 'isn't it long? She was crying just now when she played "For those in Peril on the Sea."' 'Joan's shadow!' says Douglas hoarsely. 'Out of the mouth of babes,' says Eustace. The champagne and the rest of the characters are brought on, and Douglas, trying to smile through the tears that *will* well up, makes rather a long speech, not forgetting to let the glass fall from his hand as signal for the curtain to fall too.... Through the French window into the Morning Room darts Douglas. From the fact that his coat collar is turned up to his ears we know at once that he has already been court-martialled for being drunk (and, from Mr Seymour Hicks's interpretation of the lighter passages in the first act, we guess that he must have been very disorderly as well). Scene with the old nurse, scene with Eustace, tears that *will* well up. A shade too painful were a scene with the father, on whom, as minister of the Established Church *and* son of a Peer of the Realm, his son's disgrace would fall with double impact; and so, with the merciful instinct of the born dramatist, Mr Hood lets the news be broken 'off' to the Hon. and Rev. James Floyd. But there is a drenching scene with Joan, and drenching scenes there are all round, ere Douglas again sets out for foreign climes.... Eustace, who is technically a villain, tells Joan that Douglas in Australia has again back-slidden. Joan's tears *will* well up. But who comes here? Who but the old nurse, able to foil the villain and restore Douglas to his place in Joan's esteem—nay! to restore him to her arms: Douglas has returned, is even now &c., &c. Enter Douglas. Mutual happy tears that *will* well up. Exit Douglas. This time it is Eustace's turn to begin a new life in a new world. He hints as much to Joan, significantly toying with a loaded pistol which he has taken away from the little boy, and which, he mentions casually, he is going to fire off in the garden. Joan seems to guess, with uncanny shrewdness, the billet of that bullet. She suggests that if Eustace go away for some time all will have been forgiven when he comes back, and then smilingly allows him to go off with the pistol. In comes Douglas. Bang! Ah! what is that? Joan shows signs of swooning. Douglas rushes to the French window. Eustace is quite all right. Curtain.... Of such a play description is better than criticism. Such a play cannot, indeed, be criticised. But a description of it is useful, as giving a peep into the minds of Mr Hood and the public—minds unfathomable. Useful it may be, also, as a kind of paper-pattern from which young dramatists who want to be immediately rich should cut their cloth.

I go so seldom to musical comedies that I have no standard by which to judge them authoritatively. Most of the people whom I consulted at the Duke of York's last Tuesday evening told me that *The Girl From Up There* was not good. To me, in my unenlightenment, it had seemed very good indeed. I, personally, do not care a brass farthing for continuous dramatic interest in such pieces. To most of the critics it seems to be a fetish. But how in the name of wonder can any sane creature wish to follow the fortunes of the dramatis personae? What does it matter what these dancers and singers are supposed to be up to so long as they dance and sing well? In fact I take these pieces, as I think they ought to be taken, merely as a music-hall entertainment. As such, this American piece gave me very great pleasure. The stoppages for the story were mercifully few and brief, and the rest had as much jollity and élan as any glutton could ask for. Here, as in *The Belle of New York*, the chorus with its trained mobility, its scrupulous grace and overwhelming heartiness, seemed positively a tonic for Europe. And Miss Edna May, though she betrays not yet any specific talent (except, no doubt, for vocalisation, of which I know nothing), has kept intact the charm of her personality—has quite as pretty and original a way with her as ever.

I see that the Oxford University Dramatic Society is to give *Much Ado about Nothing* on 20–25 of next month.

[*27 April 1901*]


## ANSTEY VERSUS THE MIDDLE-CLASS

The foyer of the theatre, like the lobby of the House, has its peculiar quidnuncs, whose minds seem to be worked on one string. In the entr'actes of a first night there is always a concensus among these bustlers. They dart up to one another, saying the same thing simultaneously, neither listening to his interlocutor. The catchword is bandied from lip to lip. Everyone thinks he has said something original, and proceeds to say it again in unison with everyone else. 'But is it a *play*?' seemed to be the correct thing to say on the first night of *The Man from Blankley's*. The question was asked vigorously all round. Awful emphasis was laid on the word 'play.' To give the noun its due value, the inquisitor usually brought his right hand sharply down on the palm of his left; then, not waiting for an answer, he rushed away to ask someone else. 'Is it a *play*?' rang round the foyer, rang through the corridors, rang up and down the stairs. The quidnuncs seemed to be in very grave doubt whether they ought to have come, and whether, having come, they ought to return to their seats. Personally, I was not infected by their agitation. If what is being done on the stage gives me pleasure, I care not a hang whether it be a play or not. *The Man from Blankley's* was giving very great pleasure to me—to everyone, not excepting the quidnuncs. If it had happened not to be a play, I should not have savoured poison in the fair cup. Indeed, have I not often suggested that plays which are not plays are sometimes quite admirable entertainments, and that there is no reason at all why the stage should be reserved exclusively for drama proper? Molière's *Don Juan*, for example, is not a play; it is nothing but a witty and diffusely philosophic presentation of a type. But that is no reason why it should not have the advantage of that sharp, direct means of communication which the stage alone can give it. The only difficulty in the way of such a play's production is that the public has been taught to expect drama and nothing but drama in the theatre, and is apt to set up a howl of dismay when it does not get what it supposes to be the indispensable thing. Probably the public would howl at *Don Juan*. Yet *Don Juan* —I saw it played once—is a wholly delicious entertainment. If it were a play it would be not more delicious to me. If *The Man from Blankley's* were not a play it would be not less delicious to me. Yes! you see, it *is* a play. The right answer to the quidnuncs' question was a simple affirmative. Had they waited to hear it, they might have lulled their consciences.

Strictly, in point of form, *The Man from Blankley's* is an ordinary farce. It hinges on an absurd misunderstanding which results from an absurd coincidence, and it ends with the clearing-up of the misunderstanding. But it is a farce of a peculiar kind. Though there is the fine thread of a story through it from end to end, the thread is only visible at long intervals. No madcap situations are evolved from the misunderstanding. The story is left to take care of itself (and does so) throughout nine-tenths of the play, while the author devotes himself to mere presentment of 'manners.' Mr Anstey is interested in the characters rather than in what befalls them. He has tried to make them real, and the story is a mere excuse for them. Thus the play is, in spirit, the reverse of farce, where the characters are mere symbolic bladders to be buffeted this way and that. Essentially, it is a comedy. The class from which Mr Anstey has drawn his characters is what may roughly be called the middle-class, and I believe one of the reasons for the great success of the play is the delight of the public in a comedy which spares it for once the unctuous list of titles that it knows so well, (the Duchess of Coombe, those Ladies Agatha and Mary Arlane, that Lord Reggie Taverton, and *toute cette boutique là*,) and lets see on the stage, for once, a lot of really ugly mimes in ugly dresses among ugly furniture saying ugly things. The whole thing comes with a sudden gust of sincerity. The riot of ugliness seems so much more real, so much more accurately copied, than the riot of those good-looking, overdressed mimes epigrammatising among Maple's best. To them, indeed, life gives no analogy. The 'high-life' of the stage is but a glossy invention, made, without imaginative grace, after furtive peeps through key-holes. Thank heaven for a playwright who is content to use for his art a milieu which he has been able to inspect constantly at first hand! In Mr Anstey's play the characters speak an authentic language. Every sentence in the dialogue is a synthesis of things that have been said, that are being said, in real life. Sometimes, certainly, Mr Anstey caricatures the manner of speech. But the caricature is always a true one—based on observed fact, and scientifically distorted. It is never mere burlesque. And most of the dialogue is realism unadulterated. The bore who says 'Ah! now there I join issue with you' and proceeds to do so; the host who, when the ladies have left the table, presses wine on his guests with the remark 'Why what abstemious chaps you all are!' the guest who says at parting 'Well! the most delightful evenings must come to a close, and we have a train to catch at the Royal Oak'—one knows them all, or feels that one knows them all, so intimately. It is, indeed, in virtue rather of what his characters say than of what they do, or of what they are, that Mr Anstey excites one's grateful admiration. As every student of his *Voces Populi* knows well, he has a subtle ear for the peculiarities of dialect. His is that sly appreciation of the fine superficial shades which is more often bestowed on a woman than on a man. Were he an unknown writer I should suspect 'F. Anstey' of being a bashful pseudonym. His play is full of that subtle malice which nothing on the surface can elude. It is a series of pin-pricks. With every line of the dialogue another little pungent dart is planted in the stout hide of the middle-class. It is banderillero's work, perfectly done. The business of more serious attack is beyond Mr Anstey's range. He does not pretend to it. Concerning himself, exquisitely, with what the middle-class says, with what it does and is, he skips with light heart and light fingers to the Book of Snobs, from which he snatches for us a random impression. Thus there is rather a jostle of periods in the play. The characters are of Thackeray's date, (behaving with a touch of Dickensish extravaganza,) though they speak the words of contemporary life. The aftermath of antique fashion appears even in the details of the play. For instance, at no modern dinner-party such as is depicted in this play could there be any doubt of the propriety of smoking after dinner. The objection to such a course is a mere echo of the

Thackeray period. In the mounting of the play, also, there are a few lapses in point of temporal accuracy. For instance, the wall of the drawing-room which is the scene of the second act is papered with a chintz-like pattern of bold poppies. In Thackeray's time, maybe, such a paper would have been chosen by the kind of people with whom Mr Anstey deals. Nowadays they would, without doubt, choose some dingy aesthetic muddle from Morris's assortment. The charm of old-fashioned sunny patterns—the charm of chintz—is not recognised by them now. Its recognition is confined to a few people of taste, to the very antithesis of the kind of household represented at the Prince of Wales's. However, I do not wish to carp. The sum of the production and of the play is altogether delightful. The performance, too, is very good. Mr Hawtrey, as the 'Barbarian' among 'Philistines', does perfectly the little he has to do. Miss Jessie Bateman, as a governess, gives a very pretty performance. Miss Fanny Brough, as the hostess, is perhaps a little too farcical: a less stridently and sweepingly capable actress might have been more in the proper key. But all the other characters are sharply and amusingly represented, with obvious appreciation of the author's intent. I trust that other playwrights will soon be following the lead which has been given. The middle-class is a rich mine, and these samples of ore displayed by Mr Anstey must surely provoke the greed of everyone who can write plays. No one can rival Mr Anstey in the art of maliciously minute observation; but there are many other methods by which the middle-class may be treated in drama. There is the sympathetic method, which has never been tried. And there is the philosophic method, which Matthew Arnold, as essayist, used with such delightful results. I hope to see on the stage examples of both these methods in the near future. Meanwhile, decidedly, the Prince of Wales's is a place to go to.

I am sorry I cannot say so much for the Garrick. There were in the whole of *The Queen's Double* only three points that gave me any pleasure; and these were points of literary, not dramatic, interest. One was when Marie Antoinette assured Louis Seize that she loved him still 'despite the iceberg which you have built between us.' The second was when she said to a man who had expressed the intention of throwing himself into the Seine, 'Take your bath, Monsieur, by all means; but do not lay it at my door.' The third was when somebody else said, 'So! the fly returns to the spider's web. Stars shine propitious!' The rest of the play seemed to me very dull indeed. Miss Janette Steer, in a double-role, was intelligent, but woefully stiff and uninspired.

[*4 May 1901*]


## THREE PLAYS

Art, competing with life as an attraction, ought not to give its adversary the least advantage in the game. When, for instance, we have been lured from the sunshine of a real afternoon into a theatre, a very long entr'acte is apt to be dangerous. Even though spell of illusion be not utterly broken by the interval, we, sampling the sunshine at leisure, wonder how the dim footlights could have made truants of us. Wondering, we are apt not to return to our seats. Last Monday, at the Garrick Theatre, the Stage Society appointed a gap of twenty-five minutes between the second and third acts of *The Pillars of Society*. I regard that as a bit of sheer bravado. After preening oneself in the gold haze of spring, to be expected to dip back into a dim sarcophagus upholstered in velvet and filled with a crowd of intelligent people! Sickening is the idea of the velvet. Even more so, the idea of the intelligent crowd. A crowd of stupid people is all very well: one is used to it. But an obviously and feverishly intelligent crowd is an unnatural, an intolerable nuisance, from which Heaven defend me! I ask, does any man, in these circumstances, return to his seat and see the play through? I answer this rhetorical question by recording that *I* did. But I regard the fact of my return as a very signal tribute to Ibsen's genius for dramaturgy and to his inalienable power of filling us at the moment with a kind of intellectual excitement for which, analysing it later, we may or may not discover adequate cause. *The Pillars of Society*, the earliest play of his final period, is interesting rather as a story than as a philosophic reflection of life. Ibsen here is, first and foremost, the rattling good playwright. Why this strong, ingenious, rattling good play of his has never been produced by a commercial manager, is a mystery that I cannot fathom. Thought, of course, (with propagandism) comes into the play; but it is wholly subordinate to the conceived story. Hatred of idealism and respectability, hatred of

Man and love of Woman, and all the rest of Ibsen's 'fads,' may be found in it, but never for one moment do they make or mar the story itself. Thus they would not incommode the public. As an attack on social institutions the play is quite negligible. It ought to have been called, not *The Pillars of Society*, but *The Skeleton in the Cupboard*. Consul Bernick is essentially the man with a guilty secret and a predisposition to villainy. Ibsen, by presenting him as an average type of the class that he wished (incidentally) to attack, made nonsense of his incidental motive. But this matters little. The man is projected with great vitality, and is (except as the pretended type) a very impressive figure. Nor is it so much on what he is as on what happens that the excitement of the play depends. Will the noble young man who became his scapegoat unmask him now in all his hideousness to the world? Will his attempt to murder this young man be crowned with success? Will his little boy, whom he dearly loves, be drowned? Oh no, no! Do not harrow us too much! Let there be a happy ending! And there is. The young man is saved; so is the little boy; and the wicked man (this is the one impossible thing that Ibsen makes him do) atones for his sins by confessing them to his fellow-citizens, and so inaugurates his perfect reformation. Superior persons may sneer at the play (especially its last act) as melodrama; but it is melodrama of the very best kind. It is a hustle of ingenious and exciting chances around strongly and truly delineated characters, and the comic relief (of which there is much) is real straightforward fun. The public would take to it like a duck to water. Perhaps Mr Asche, who produced it for the Stage Society, and played very powerfully the part of Bernick, will one day give the public this chance. The whole performance last Monday was very good all round, the cast including Miss Annie Webster, Mr Albert Gran and many other very capable persons. The only important fault to be found was that all the men were much too smartly dressed. Mr Charles Quartermaine, as Rorlund the schoolmaster, was the one exception. He wore a frock-suit of rusty black, with a small black bow topping a long expanse of shirt-front. That, I am sure, is how Ibsen means all his men to be dressed. It is a uniform, to be worn unquestioningly by his interpreters.

There are two farces to which I ought to have called your attention last week: *The Night of the Party* at the Avenue, and *A Woman in the Case* at the Court. There is not much to choose between them as farces; but, if one must be taken and the other left, I think the former should be taken. For in it Mr Weedon Grossmith, its author, has a very good part, which he plays to admiration; whereas in the other Mr George R. Sims and Mr Leonard Merrick have not given a chance to any of the many popular mimes engaged. It is quite worth your while to see Mr Grossmith's study of the eternal lackey-type. There is one moment at which, in his dual responsibility, he achieves greatness. This is when he is standing at the window, with his back turned to us, watching his master get into a hansom *en route* for Euston. He is muttering a good riddance, unpacking his heart of long-pent disrespect and rebellion. Suddenly his shoulders droop, his neck takes an exquisite inclination, he smiles (we know it by the curve of his cheek), and 'Good-bye, Sir, good-bye!' he murmurs. His master's glance up at the window has renewed the broken spell, changing not merely the man's physical aspect, but bringing to his nervous lips what he knows to be beyond ear-shot. The whole thing takes place in a moment (would it could be described in one!), but it is a moment of such poignant truth that it would redeem a play that had no other virtue. So long as Mr Grossmith is on the stage his play seems full of virtues. The rest of the cast is negligible. It has been recruited I know not whence. But that none of it shows particular talent is rather a blessing. For if such talent were shown we could only regret that it was wasted. It is, as I have suggested, the prodigal waste of talent that prevents one from bearing with equanimity the farce at the Court. Here is not a single part that has anything in it. Here are merely the stock dummies for 'complications.' Played by mimes who know no better they would pass muster. But we resent them as played by mimes who do know infinitely better. Mr Kerr and Miss Kingston play the two central parts, and at every moment we are jarred. We hear the spades of their intelligence grating against that stony surface which is all that the authors have allotted for them to dig. These two comedians should accept the situation frankly, saying to themselves 'We are here to play the fool. Let us play it, and not attempt any other part.' Miss Esmé Beringer is wiser than they in this respect. She does not remind us (even though she may not make us forget) that she is thrown away. Cast for a dummy-part, she plays it as stagily and emptily as she can. Mr W. H. Denny, too, manages to be more unlike a German Baron, and more in accord with the author's intention, than I should have conceived possible. To hear him 'agzebt ze egsblanation' and so forth, is a lesson in the proper method for such a part. But it is a lesson which any duffer could have taught us equally well. Mr James Erskine, too, impersonating an Officer and a Gentleman, contrives, by dint of twirling his moustache as though he were working a machine, and of talking as though he had a bunch of grapes in his mouth, to be quite unlike any Officer or Gentleman seen by him off the stage, and so keeps well within the stage-convention. But one regrets that he is not in a play where he could use in the interest of art the advantages which he has had as a private person. As for Miss Carlotta Addison, her case is even worse. She does not even do what is required of her. Playing the inevitable dowager who tries to bully her daughter into a loveless union, she lavishes on the part all those sweet, tender, translucent qualities of womanliness for which the dramatic critics have been praising her for so many years that now she cannot, for the life of her, suggest any qualities inferior. Another misfit is Mr R. C. Herz as an Eton boy. If Eton kept her pupils till they had reached the age of thirty (which is, roughly, the age suggested by Mr Herz's appearance) Mr Herz as an Eton boy might be all very well. But as this reform in the rules of the school is not likely to be made before Mr Herz reaches the age of Methuselah, I urge Mr Herz to discard the ambition of appearing as an Eton boy, even though (as in *Peril*, and in this play) the dramatic critics seem to think him satisfactory.

[*18 May 1901*]

## PHILLIPS AND PHILISTINISM

Poor Mr Stephen Phillips, heavy with resentment and alarm, has been unbosoming himself in one of those 'Real Conversations recorded by William Archer' for the *Pall Mall Magazine*. The distress of a poet is necessarily a tragic affair; but, when it is recorded thus, the purgation of us through pity and awe is so drastic that we shall not soon be able to feel sorry or afraid about anything else. The large and marmoreal severity of the manner in which Mr Archer really converses—a manner fallen straight into by whomsoever he really converses with—is an ideal medium for the transmission of tragic emotion. Month by month I have been reading these immortal dialogues with cumulative rapture, with cumulative homage to Mr Archer. That in ordinary circumstances Mrs Craigie and Mr Hardy, Mr Pinero and Mr Phillips all talk like books, I have very good reason to doubt. That they all talk like the same book, is obviously impossible. And yet, mark you! when they come within Mr Archer's sphere of influence, there is not a pin to choose between them: one after another leaps heavily upon the pillion of the high wooden horse whose saddle Mr Archer, with open note-book, is uprightly bestriding. The solemnity of them! The length, the solid construction of the sentences that mount from their lips! The aptness of their quotations from the Hundred Best Books! The little coy amenities that sparkle up now and then, and do but illuminate by their giggling contrast the awful impressiveness of the whole! The perfect temper on either side—'Ah! there you have the very gist of my complaint,' 'There you are at the root of the matter,' 'Ah yes, that is of enormous importance,' 'Granted with all my heart.' What overwhelms us in these dialogues is not so much what is said as the way in which it is said. It is the manner, rather than the matter, that makes admiration compulsory. We feel that if Dr Johnson had chronicled for us, reverently, with all the classicism of his prose-style, the conversations of Boswell with Mrs Thrale and other estimable creatures, the result might have been approximate—not quite equal, indeed, but approximate—to these monthly treats which Mr Archer provides for us. It is true that in certain English versions of Ibsen's plays we find the characters talking somewhat as do Mr Archer and his interlocutors. But there is not in all literature another possible analogue. We feel that Landor's 'imaginary' effects are, in comparison with Mr Archer's 'real' effects, flimsy. The elastic graces of Plato seem positively vulgar. As for the dialogues of real life—we are ashamed of ourselves. There would be an ugly rush to La Trappe, but for the hope that flutters faintly in every breast, the little pale hope that faintly whispers 'Some day, some distant day, the eye of Mr Archer may fall on me, and by the dry light of its incomparable majesty enable me, even me also, to talk as nice as him!'

'Twas in 'the Smoking Room of the —— Club' that Mr Archer opened his note-book and drew Mr Phillips nobly out. I do not seek to penetrate the mystery of the '——.' (Enough that it is evidently a club unhampered by the usual rule against transaction of business by members within its precincts.) But I like to think of the scene as it was enacted—the two men face to face: *Herod's* author, profoundly agitated, gripping tightly the arms of his arm-chair, Mr Archer sitting on the extreme edge of another arm-chair, plying his pencil to record the words that flow from the poet's lips, and constantly interrupting the stream with words of his own, which he takes down, not less faithfully than he takes down the poet's, even as they are being uttered. A 'real conversation' in the making! What a beacon in the mirk of current history! You may be sure that the beacon is espied by the other occupants of the Smoking Room. They are watching it discreetly from behind their newspapers. They cannot overhear the conversation, for it is conducted in hoarse whispers, but they can see the interplay of the light that flashes now from the poet's, now from the critic's, handsome eyes, and the flush and pallor that alternately o'erspread the well-modelled cheeks of each. Would that we, too, had been privileged to observe these phenomena! We can but imagine them, and insert in our copies of the *Pall Mall Magazine* the stage-directions which Mr Archer meanly omits. 'Mr Phillips. Yes, yes; *Herod* was very well treated on the whole, and I have no reason to complain of the acceptance it has met with.' Here, instinctively, we add '(*removes right hand from breast of buttoned frock-coat and waves it gracefully on level with shoulder*).' Again, 'W. A. Complain, indeed! Why it was a triumph,' &c. Between 'indeed!' and 'why' we insert '(*throws up both hands, dropping pencil and note-book, which he stoops quickly to recover. Then, more soberly,*).' These passages occur in the earlier part of the interview, before Messrs Archer and Phillips have worked themselves up to a full sense of solemnity—before they have got their long wind, as it were. It is Mr Phillips who first strikes the deeper note: 'Tell me, Archer, is there no hope of awakening the editors of newspapers to the monstrous injustice and absurdity of the way in which they treat the drama? I said I had no reason to complain of the reception of *Herod*, but I withdraw the remark. Of one paper I had reason to complain, and do and shall complain . . . because of the manifest unreason involved in its policy, and the deadening effect it must necessarily have on all imaginative effort. You know, of course, the paper I mean—' 'When,' said W. A., 'hostility to the higher drama is in question, there can be no doubt what paper you have in mind. I hope it accorded you the honour of its contumely.' One would have thought that W. A.'s tone here was grave enough for anyone. It wasn't, though, for Master Stephen. 'It is all very well,' said he (*frowning*), 'to treat the thing lightly, but it is a serious matter for the future of the drama.' And W. A., that fribble, sat corrected, while the poet proceeded to formulate his indignation against the critic of the *Daily Telegraph*. If *Herod* had been ruined commercially by this critic, Mr Phillips's grievance might have been perceptible. But, as he repeatedly demonstates, no such disaster happened. The play was a great success. The *Daily Telegraph* did no harm. Then why give that paper a belated advertisement? 'Because of the manifest unreason involved in its policy.' But Mr Phillips is a poet, not a newspaper proprietor. I suspect that Sir Edward Lawson knows better than Mr Phillips what kind of a critic is right for the *Daily Telegraph*. The critic engaged by him does not, assuredly, write like a clever man, or like a well-educated man, still less like a man of refinement. But if he cannot corrupt the public, why make a fuss about him? 'If,' says Mr Archer, 'you succeed in realising your ideal, if you go on producing vital drama, never fear but that the British genius will accommodate itself to the accomplished fact.' Exactly. And the critic of the *Daily Telegraph*, seeing which way the wind blows, will probably accommodate himself also. In any case, let Mr Phillips stick to the business of dramatic poetry—to his own business, and not bother his head whether his plays be unanimously praised or not. If one bad notice in one widely circulated newspaper is enough to deaden 'imaginative effort' in him, his imaginative talent must have very shallow roots. But he moans that he is not moaning for himself merely: he 'can't help thinking of the other and bigger men that will come after. Just consider the disastrous effect such criticism might have on a man of much finer talent than mine—disastrous in proportion to the delicacy of his talent. Let Mr Phillips be soothed. The finer the talent, the less likely it is to be snuffed out by obloquy, and, on Mr Phillips's own showing, the amount of obloquy which greets good work in modern times is happily negligible in proportion to the amount of praise. If anything, it is the praise which is the dangerous factor for the modern artist. But the finer the talent, the less likely it is to be killed by kindness. Because Mr Phillips's talent strikes me as remarkably fine, I am sure that he will not be undone by the eulogies which we have (almost) all poured over him. For the same reason, I am sure that he will not wither away because one or two dolts don't give him his due. In fact, I have no fear at all for his future. But he has, I think, somewhat marred his present by this tirade in the *Pall Mall Magazine*. To buffet the air—even when one does so under the auspices of Mr Archer, and in the Smoking Room of the —— Club—is always undignified and absurd.

[*25 May 1901*]

## SEVERAL THEATRES

Except that it contains two parts which may be very effectively acted, *Mariana*, in English, is not of the stuff that one raves about. Indeed, if its author's name were, not Echegaray, but Smith or Jones, I should loudly decry it. I should say that it was tedious in the first two acts, and melodramatic in the last two. I should urge Mr Smith to study his craft and to observe life, or I should proclaim my failure to understand why Henry Arthur had jeopardised his high position by giving us a play so immeasurably beneath the level of his recent work. Towards Echegaray, however, I must take up a more respectful attitude. I must assume that, in the original version, the caterpillaresque progression of the first two acts is atoned for by a superlative grace of language which Mr James Monteith Graham, the adapter, has not (despite many excellent qualities that his style shows) been able to transmit for our delight. I must assume, also, that Echegaray, a Spaniard, knows more about Spaniards than I do, and that in Spain they do the things which he would have us believe them to do. If an Englishman had created the characters in this play, I should twit him with having played the old trick of saddling them with exotic names merely in order to enable them to behave impossibly without destroying the illusion of possibility. I should suggest, for instance, that no woman in the wide world would make it a point of honour that her lover should stay at her side and leave his dying father unvisited. But, since it is Echegaray who makes a woman do this, and since all I know of Spain is what it looks like on the map, I am quite ready to believe that in Spain sexual passion is so much stronger than in more northerly latitudes that filial devotion is treated as impertinent for daring to co-exist with it. That proposition I accept readily. Having accepted it, however, I find myself in immediate difficulties. For filial devotion is the very fulcrum of the play. When Mariana was a little girl, her mother was seduced by a man who turns out to have been the father of Montoya, the man with whom now Mariana is in love. This discovery having been made, the heroine, still loving the man passionately, marries somebody else, in order that she may escape contamination. Well! let us, for a moment, set aside stage-convention; let us discard those dodges by which in the theatre life can be twisted to afford exciting scenes. Let us suppose Mariana's situation to have occurred, not in the theatre, but in real life. What would have happened? Loving Montoya so intensely as she did, she would have married him in spite of all. She would not have allowed the shadow of filial piety to stand between her and the passionate reality of her love. That her lover was not the son of someone who had never wronged her mother, would have seemed to her a horrible pity. But the fact would have remained that he was he, and that she was she; and in comparison with that salient fact everything else would have gone to the wall. Even in England, where sexual passion is evidently a less lurid affair than in southern countries, a woman in love with a man would not be diverted by such a discovery as that which is made by Echegaray's heroine. It is only the English dramatists (the situation is common enough in English melodrama) who try to persuade us that she would be diverted. In lurid Spain how much less possible would such diversion be! Yet Echegaray asks us to believe in it. How can we do so? Only by assuming that in Spain, as in China, the filial passion is a more real and potent passion than any other. But Echegaray's Mariana has already in the first act shown us how lightly the Spaniards esteem filial passion in proportion to sexual passion. Thus we behold the sharp horns of a dilemma. Either Spain is not like China (in which case the whole play is impossible and must be treated as mere melodrama) or Spain is like China (in which case Mariana, showing herself to be an unnatural monster in the first act, behaves quite incredibly in the last two, and thus reduces the play to mere melodrama). It matters not on which horn we impale ourselves. Either compels us to regard as mere melodrama this work of a distinguished and much-lauded foreigner, whose very name we are afraid to pronounce. This is a painful pass to which I have brought you—I, who set out to be so respectful to Echegaray.

However, the fact remains that Mariana and Montoya are fine vehicles for an actor and actress. Mrs Campbell, as Mariana, acts so well that the evening passes off very pleasantly indeed. In the early scenes she is so full of humour and *espièglerie*, and in the later scenes so directly and forcefully tragic, that we long to see her again as Juliet. At the time when she played Juliet, she was passing through an unfortunate phase. Neither gaiety nor any passion of love or grief would she express. Everything was reduced to a convention of wistful and listless gloom. The convention was very beautiful in its way. In it Melisande was born, and it lives for us immortally. But it smothered poor Juliet at birth. Mariana has, I believe, been compared with Juliet, and not found wanting, by a certain enthusiast. That, of course, is absurd. Nevertheless, the qualities through which Mrs Campbell makes Mariana live are precisely the qualities through wilful suppression of which she prevented Juliet from living. And I hope that anon I shall see her as Juliet again. Only I do protest to her, in her capacity of actress-manager, that I do *not* want to see Mr Titheradge as Romeo. His Montoya is a terrible phenomenon. Never again let him be lured from the line he excels in—the line of quiet, modern, drab, Anglo-Saxon emotion —into the line of lurid young Latin lovership.

I suppose that a time may come when I shall be weary of Mr Wyndham as *raisonneur* for Mr Jones, weary of his beneficent influence on ladies who are wavering about their marriage-vows, weary of that tender spot which, throughout his long and distinguished career in this or that profession, he has kept in his heart for the woman he loved 'once,' weary even of the fascinating manner in which he now meets half-way some other woman who has succumbed to his breezy spell. And I suppose that a time may come when I shall be weary of Miss Compton as the straightforwardly dishonest smart woman in Mr Carton's comedies, weary of her lazy, massive way of basking in her own good-humour, weary of her drawl and her smile and her leisurely alertness, altogether weary of her. But, certainly, neither of these times has come yet. And thus, since Mr Wyndham and Miss Compton are the centre-pieces of *The Case of Rebellious Susan* and *Wheels within Wheels* respectively, both Wyndham's Theatre and the Criterion Theatre may be confidently recommended by me. (I am so easily bored in theatres that I cannot believe that anything which doesn't bore me there can bore anyone else.) Both the plays are as amusing as ever they were, and in both there is much good acting besides that of the principals. It is a pity that Miss Mary Moore cannot be in two places at once, and so play the wayward wife at the Criterion. Miss Alice de Winton is too undulating, and too contortive of voice and face, to befit a part that is meant to be human.

Shakespeare is far from being at his best in *Much Ado About Nothing*, but Oxford was at its very best last week, with the candles of its vast horse-chestnuts still alight and unashamed by the imperious sun, and with its lilac and laburnum still a-wave to mock the staid gravity and greyness of its walls. So I am glad that I went up to see the production of the O.U.D.S. Many *longeurs* may be forgiven to a play which calls one to a scene of such continuous beauty. As a whole, the performance of the O.U.D.S. this year was comfortably up to the usual standard. Mr H. M. Tennent (Wadham) was spirited and elastic as Benedick, and Mr G. P. Langton (also of that college) had digested well the traditions for Dogberry. The other undergraduates played their parts very decently, none taking unfair advantage of another by suggesting to any metropolitan fogeys who might happen to be there the suspicion that he was loaded with genius. Miss Janet Alexander acted prettily as Beatrice, and Miss May Martyn was strikingly good as Hero. I suspect that both these ladies are professional actresses, or, at least, amateurs who have had much experience. They were really rather too good to be in the picture. This contrast between the sexes is often palpable in the productions of the O.U.D.S. Would it not be better artistically—besides being in itself a pretty act of local chivalry—if Somerville and Lady Margaret Hall were allowed hereafter to give yearly of their nymphs?

[*1 June 1901*]


## MAINLY ABOUT MIMES

The fashion in acting changes always according to the fashion in dramaturgy. Twenty years ago, when the current drama was composed of melodrama on the one hand and farce on the other, the leading mimes played accordingly. In the past ten years melodrama and farce have been ousted by realistic comedy. That is, the dramatists who count for anything at all devote themselves to realistic comedy. Mr Pinero, (unhappily, as I think) abandoning farce, and Mr Jones (happily, as none will deny) purging himself of melodrama, have converged to the same point of endeavour, whereat, also, Mr Haddon Chambers, Mr Carton and the rest have come from their several directions. No respectable person (except Mr Shaw) will have anything to do with either of the two forms that were but lately predominant. As a result of these changes, we have what is called the modern school of acting—the school of quiet and subtle effects—in fine, the comedic school. It is significant that the most characteristic actor in this kind is Mr Wyndham, who himself was for many years the high-priest of farce. Conversely, it is a queer trick of fate that Mr Tree, who was one of the earliest 'modern' actors, is now debarred from subtleties by the size of his theatre. Her Majesty's is too big for modern comedy, and thus, devoted to poetic drama, it is apart from the main current of modern dramaturgy. It is an up-standing rock in the stream. The existence of such a theatre ensures that some of the general histrionic talent will ever be diverted from modern comedy. Nevertheless, one may say that the typical actors of the moment, and of the moments to come, are Mr Wyndham, Mr Kerr, Mr Boyne, and Mr Hawtrey, and that on them the young aspirants are modelling themselves.

Unfortunately, acting is so much easier an art than dramaturgy, that we have not enough modern comedies 'to go round'—to keep our modern comedians worthily employed. Modern dramatists are not numerous enough to meet the demand which their supply has created. Two or three weeks ago, for instance, I was complaining that Mr Kerr had thrown himself away on a farcical part, and had spoilt the part (not that this mattered much) by playing it comedically. Now that at the Court Theatre *A Woman in the Case* has made way for *Women are so Serious*, my grievance is removed. Mr Kerr has a delightful comedic part, and he plays it perfectly. But this relief is cancelled for me by the distress of seeing Mr Leonard Boyne at the Great Queen Street Theatre playing a merely farcical part. True, this part is amusingly farcical, whereas Mr Kerr's previous part was very dully so; but that only makes the matter worse: not merely is Mr Boyne's talent for comedy thrown away, but the situations which are ruined by his gentle, slow, elaborate realism would be really funny if they were taken by a rough and ready farcifier. *Women are so Serious*, which has been very skilfully adapted by Mr Brandon Thomas from *Celles qu'on Respecte*, is, in strict point of form, perhaps, rather a farce than a comedy. But the central part in it (the part of a philanderer) has been developed with a realistic sense of character, and accordingly Mr Kerr has his chance. *A Lady from Texas*, composed by Mrs T. P. O'Connor, is so strange an affair that one cannot classify it offhand as anything in particular; but this is certain: the central part (again, the part of a philanderer) is sheerly farcical, and must be played at top-speed. Mr Boyne, purring his leisurely way through the part, spoils all the fun. His method is too inveterate in him to be cast off. He could not play the part better then he does play it. On the other hand, nobody could play it worse. Through whose weird error in judgment was he cast for it? Why was not that sound farcifier, Mr Giddens, procured? Perhaps because he was already engaged at the Court. But that was only an additional good reason for the acquisition of him. He goes far to destroy the charm of *Women are so Serious*. Though that play be strictly a farce, Mr Kerr is so pervasive from the primary base of his comedic part, and so exquisitely authoritative, that he brings it all into the key of comedy. In that key Mr Giddens is a thumping discord. Unlike Mr Wyndham, he has not been able to accommodate himself to the changed spirit of the age. He survives as the embodiment of bursting and bounding farcicality. As such he is incomparably good, and he is proportionately noxious in the atmosphere at the Court. Indeed, hardly one of the performers there is really in the comedic key. (This fact makes it the greater tribute to Mr Kerr's power that our main impression is of a comedy.) Miss Ellis Jeffreys is too metallically go-ahead in her part. Her acting is, as always, brilliant, and would be exactly right but for the predominating presence of Mr Kerr. In relation to that presence, it jars. Miss Jeffreys ought to have said to herself at rehearsal 'Either Mr Kerr's method, or mine, must go,' and straightway to have let go her own. She is evidently young, and so would have had no difficulty in striking out a new line, even though she might not at first be so successful in comedy as she has been hitherto in farce. Miss Constance Collier acted wrongly in quite another way. Cast for the part of a girl who has been jilted by the philanderer, she was so bent on being powerfully pathetic, and so successful in her aim, that only by a hair's breadth was Mr Kerr able to save the play from tumbling straight into the black abyss of tragedy. Mr Herbert Standing, again, as a taciturn Major in the regular army, marred his scenes by comporting himself only like a sergeant of police. Except Mr Kerr, Mr R. C. Herz and Miss Mabel Terry-Lewis were the only players who really pleased me: the one, because he showed acute sense of character as a valet; the other, because of the grace that is her birthright—a grace so airy and unerring that even when she stumbled over a mat the quick forward-and-backward movement was a poem in itself.

Mrs O'Connor, as I conceive, set out to write a serious comedy. To make doubly sure of achievement, she bound herself to two separate motives of a serious kind: firstly (a well-worn motive) the wife whose husband, loving her, yet neglects her for affairs of State, and finally is made to realise his unwisdom; secondly (a fresher motive), the American woman, with all her superficial faults and fundamental virtues, cast into the effete society of England. But sense of fun came and played skittles with the good intentions of Mrs O'Connor. Mrs O'Fish-Withers became a wild stage-caricature of vulgarity and minxishness, quite unlike anyone that ever came out of the wildest West; insomuch that only at odd moments—as when the Duke says he likes her because she is 'good,' and she solemnly declares herself to be the truest friend he ever had—do we divine what Mrs O'Connor had patriotically intended her to be. Also, though the relation between Lord and Lady Walter Bective is serious enough in itself, we are quite unable to take it seriously, because the lover of Lady Walter, like most of the other characters, is merely farcical. Of the serious things that one cannot take seriously dulness is compounded. Thus Lord and Lady Walter are both awful bores. Mr Charles Cartwright and Miss Cynthia Brooke evidently feel their position acutely. The latter, being very pretty and feminine, manages to slur matters over to some extent. The former, being merely a powerful melodramatic actor, and not even having in his composition one ounce of that comedic sense which would have enabled a man to play the part effectively in less unfavourable circumstances, behaves with so grim an air of suppressed wrath as to suggest that only fear of the law restrains him from murdering everyone on both sides of the footlights. Never have I seen so frightening a person as Mr Cartwright's Lord Walter. In him all the 'villains' that ever perished in fifth acts are re-incarnate. We feel that it is sheer devilry, not national emergency, that has impelled him, as Chancellor of the Exchequer, to put a shilling on the income-tax. When he smiles to his wife and murmurs 'This is our second honeymoon,' we stretch out our hands to save her from him. Throughout, Mr Cartwright uses his fine voice in a way that irresistibly reminds us of the Abbé Bruneau playing the organ to drown the dying moans of his latest victim. As all the other members of the cast (except Mr Marsh Allen, and Miss Cheatham, who plays the chief part rather funnily) are either frankly incompetent or miscast, Mrs O'Connor, obviously, need not attribute to the performance much of whatever success may come to her wayward little play.

[*8 June 1901*]

## A BIBLIOMANTIC VIEW OF THE STAGE

When, from his abstracted sphere, a plain scholar or man of letters denounces the modern theatre, the plain dramatic critic is always very angry. As a pied dramatic critic, knowing and caring rather more about books than about plays, I, personally, am not put out by these jeremiads. I have enough sympathy with their spirit to enjoy calmly the fun of them. The latest of them we owe to Professor Walter Raleigh. It was delivered (in a weekly) a fortnight ago, when pressure of other things prevented me from speaking of it; but its echoes are still insistent in my ears, and I cannot but pay my tardy tribute to it. It is a particularly complete and delicious sample of its kind. There is (in form, at least) no vagueness about it. The Professor declares the theatre to be bad, explains how it is bad, and why it is bad, and the means by which it may yet be saved. He is very thorough, in form.

Roughly, of course, I admit that the theatre is bad. But I cannot admit that its badness is quite of that kind which the Professor suggests. I go to the theatre. That he, lucky man, does not go, is internally evident in his essay. According to him, the two forms that flourish now on the stage are 'burlesque' and 'charade'. The former is a bad shot. Let me assure the Professor (I call him so, not as a term of reproach, but for brevity's sake) that 'burlesque' breathed its last rather more than ten years ago, and that no one has attempted to revive it. 'Charade' is luckier: the word does well describe such plays as the modern imitations of Tom Robertson, and these are, undoubtedly, at this moment, the most lucrative form of drama. But there are other forms that flourish also. The Professor asks where he is to find 'high comedy, appealing to the intellect, tickling the young, not asking to be punctuated throughout by sentiments of approval or disapproval'. If he had playgone during the past few years, he would have found several plays of this kind—not perhaps very good of their kind, but still coming well within the Professor's definition. Also, we have had more than a few good comedies that appealed to our moral sense. The Professor seems to imply that any such appeal is outrageous and inartistic. I dissent from him. To rule out a comedy because it has a moral appeal is as absurd as to rule out a comedy because it hasn't. Both forms have an equal right to exist. In England the moral comedy has the much better chance of existing. I dissent from the Professor's off-hand description of us as a nation of humourists. To say that we are a nation of moralists would be nearer the mark. And I believe that the moral comedy is the form that has the greatest future in our drama. That is the form that we critics ought to foster. At present it is (usually) overlaid with sentimentality, smothered in sugar. Our business is to coax it into realism. But the Professor won't have realism at any price. He speaks scornfully of characters which 'seem to have walked on the stage by mistake and are behaving as anyone might behave in a suburban drawing-room.' There speaks the man who does not playgo. In what theatre has anyone caught the atmosphere of a suburban drawing-room? Across what footlights has been wafted the scent of those wax-flowers? The trick has never been attempted. One of the curses of modern drama ... but I must not stray into that eternal subject. The Professor does but touch on comedy. It is the dearth of poetic tragedy that absorbs him and makes him desperate. Mr Phillips he ignores. To Mr Phillips himself, already smothered in academic laurels, this must be a surprise, a relief. Nor need I blame the Professor for his omission. *Herod*, as I have maintained, was a mere 'side-show.' Roughly, the modern drama is indeed destitute of poetic tragedy.

For this disaster the Professor seeks a reason, and finds it, as you will have guessed, in the actor-managers. Them he compares with speculative builders, who 'think poorly of architecture'. Is the comparison happy? Except in some world of academic phantasy, was there ever an actor who thought poorly of drama? Of course not. There are, however, many playwrights who think poorly of actors. It is through this fact that the Professor professes to elucidate the dearth of poetic drama. According to him, there is no tragidramaturgy because there are no tragic actors. I agree with much that he says against the manner in which Elizabethan tragedy is acted. For sake of peace and quiet, I will assume that we have indeed no tragic actors. But I cannot acquit the Professor of having harnessed the horse behind the cart. If a man has it in him to write poetic tragedy, he will write it; it will out, willy-nilly. Does the Professor really mean that if we had good tragic actors, we should have good poetic tragedies? According to him, we have no high comedies. Yet even he can have no hearsay whereon to deny the existence of Mr Wyndham and many other mimes who are born to excel in high comedy. How does he explain the discrepancy? The only possible explanation is that actors do not produce dramatists. Dramatists, in point of fact, produce actors. There are no actors for modern tragedy because there is no modern tragedy for them to play. The reason why there is no modern tragedy is that the intellectual spirit of the age is against those qualities through which poetic tragedy is evolved. That spirit is favourable to realistic comedy. And the reason why realistic comedy does not progress at greater speed is that the theatre is so conducted that it cannot get along without the ever-laggart public. The Professor, merciless to actors, is very kind to this same public. Because there is a public for good books, he holds the public is guiltless in the matter of drama. But to make a book successful, is needed a number of buyers infinitesimal in comparison with the numbers of playgoers necessary to the success of a play. Even the Professor lets slip an admission that some actor-managers are 'not hostile to art—if their public will have it'. Exactly. They are bound to wait on the public. The public is the villain of every piece that is produced.

The Professor, however, is so sanguine as to hope that the public would support the remedy which he proposes. The remedy is that certain men who have never written plays should now proceed to do so, that they should then secure a theatre and train amateurs to interpret their work. That good plays will be forthcoming he has no doubt at all. He avers that the sticks of stage-craft may be easily picked up. Certainly, the theatrist is made, not born. But the dramatist must simply be born. And to be born with dramatic imagination is not necessarily (as the Professor supposes) to be a born dramatist. The Professor, irrefutably, cites Browning as having had dramatic imagination. But Browning was not a dramatist, and never would have been. His failure to write good plays was not due to mere ignorance of technique. It was due to the fact that dramatic form paralysed him. He had no sense for it. The Professor also cites Trollope. He might cite many other novelists. But to do so would merely drive home the inherent difference between dramatic imagination in books and dramatic imagination in plays. But, assuming that true dramatists leapt up on every side in answer to the Professor's call, the theatre to which they rallied would not be rallied to by the public. It would have to be run privately, like the Elizabethan Stage Society.

In wishing this phantom luck, let me express a hope that my tone in this article has not been tainted with any air of disrespect towards one whom indeed I respect highly. The Professor, though truculent in spirit, is in tone scrupulously urbane, towards the stage. That his spirit has a right to be truculent I admit fully. Modern drama is a poor thing in comparison with the Elizabethan drama of which he is a student. It is as yet, indeed, an infant art. My point is that the Professor has not studied that infant. What would he think of a doctor who, being a specialist in the diseases of adults, gravely diagnosed the case of an ailing infant whose cradle-side he had not visited? What, moreover, would he think of the family-practitioner who, fresh from that cradle-side, listened patiently to, and argued lengthily with, that eminent but inappropriate and unscrupulous specialist? What must he think of me for writing this article?

[6 *July 1901*]


## PHÈDRE AND MASCARILLE

Obviously, the ideal pleasure to be sought in a theatre is a perfect play perfectly acted. London, however, is not the capital of Utopia, and we must needs be content with what we can get. *Phèdre* I take to be a perfect play of its kind; but for its kind we, here and now, care nothing at all. For us it exists merely as a vehicle for acting—for the performance of the title-part, the other parts being, according to the form of the play, mere feeders. If this part be played perfectly, we have a pleasant evening and no right or wish to grumble. *Les Précieuses Ridicules* I take to be a perfect play, of a kind that appeals to us here and now. The principal part in it, Mascarille, could not be played perfectly except by a very great comedian. In this sinful world great comedians (unless, of course, they are English, or unless they are present members of the Théâtre Français) always follow 'the star-system'. Thus the choice is usually between seeing the play decently acted all round, or perfectly acted in its principal part, with 'the rest nowhere'. In *Phèdre* Racine himself set the rest nowhere; there (even his contemporary compatriots would have said) let them remain. But in *Les Précieuses* Molière set the rest in more or less important positions. When they are ousted from these positions, the play loses much of its point and savour. We, caring for the play, resent such loss. But, if we are philosophers, we set in the balance against it the joy of seeing a perfect Mascarille. We are content to take the play as a mere vehicle for him, taking it for its own sake in the printed copies that we read by our own hearths.

As a feast for lovers of acting, there is not likely to be in our time anything better than the recent 'bill' at Her Majesty's: Sarah as Phèdre, Coquelin as Mascarille. Such is the power of Sarah that she almost makes us forget the obsoleteness of Racine. So perfect is her art that we forget how little the play means to us. We are caught back, as it were, into the Hôtel de Bourgogne, into an age when Attic tragedy lost none of its effect through being confectioned exquisitely in pink and white sugar. We forget the clash of the astricted grandeur in theme and form with the delicate minuetishness of the poet's manner. By reason of Sarah we forget Racine. Throught the poetry of her own passion Sarah lifts us out of the mazes of Versailles into the court of Phaedra herself. Save for her we have no thoughts at all, and the play thus becomes for us evocative of real pity and awe. Altogether, a signal triumph of histrionism over dramaturgy.

There is nothing modish about *Les Précieuses*. It is as fresh and vital as on the night when it was produced in the Petit Bourbon. Its satire is as modern as the satire of Aristophanes—one cannot pay it a greater compliment than that. In every age of civilised society there must always be exactly those phenomena which Molière set himself to ridicule. There must always be 'movements' which, beginning admirably as a protest against vulgarity and as a striving towards fineness of thought and conduct, degenerate lamentably into mere excesses of unmeaning affectation. The theme of *Les Précieuses* is immortal, universal; and the play itself is the perfect type of its kind. Never was satire more swift and deadly than in this juxtaposition of the transcendental exquisites with the absurd rogue of a lacquey. No wonder that at the impact of such a battering-ram the walls of the Hôtel Rambouillet tottered and crumbled to the ground. Some critics, not very sapient, have argued that Molière was attacking merely the vulgar imitators of aristocratic preciosity. Such a theory is obviously false. The two *précieuses* here, Magdelon and Cathos, belong to the *bourgeoisie* merely because Molière, the upholsterer's son, just promoted into the suffrance of the Court, would not have dared to attack in a direct manner persons of noble rank and great influence. By professing to attack mere *bourgeoises*, he managed to make the satire not merely safe so far as he was concerned but also more effective against the true *précieuses*. He got a double juxtaposition by these means: not merely the two *précieuses* in the play cheek by jowl with Mascarille, but also all the *précieuses* of the Hôtel Rambouillet cheek by jowl with their base imitators. You may remember a ballade, in which Mr Henley attacked the contemporary aesthetes, with the refrain 'In fact, my form's the bloomin' utter'. There the aesthetes were made ridiculous by association with the lowest forms of cockneyism. But no one with any sense of satire would imagine that Mr Henley was attacking such members of the lower class as strove to be 'greenery-yallery'. He was attacking the originators: they alone were worth attacking. Similarly, Molière was attacking the Hôtel Rambouillet itself. Reading the play we revel in its point. When we see it acted, with Coquelin as Mascarille, the point is somewhat obscured. If the other characters were as perfectly played, then all would be well. But that is not a practical hypothesis. When Coquelin appears, the play is put out of joint by his genius. We forget the motive and meaning of the play, merely revelling in that figure of stupendous vulgarity, those leers, those frowns, those ogles, that gay, unscrupulous, unredeemed lowness of soul. When the curtain falls, our one feeling is of regret that there will be no more Coquelin for us this evening. Another triumph of histrionism over dramaturgy! More signal than Sarah's triumph, because here the play itself is a live thing. It is also less justifiable, because this is not a one-part play. However, Coquelin is cheap at any price. We can even forgive him for deliberately cutting out the final scene in which Gorgibus, upbraiding his daughter and niece, rounds the play off and points its moral: '*Allez vous cacher, vilaines; allez vous cacher pour jamais. Et vous, qui êtes cause de leur folie, sottes billevesées, pernicieux amusements des esprits oisifs, romans, vers, chansons, sonnets et sonnettes, puissiez-vous être à tous les diables!*'

Miss Winifred Emery's accession to the part of heroine in *The Second in Command* is pleasant as a sign of her complete recovery from her illness, but it is not an improvement to the play. To me, at least, Miss Sybil Carlisle was far preferable. A pretty little impossible part ought to be played prettily, and no more. So soon as it is played in grim and forceful earnest, we forget everything but its impossibility. Miss Emery had not been on the stage for three minutes (two of which we spent in her 'reception') before we began to feel that her performance was going to be a sore trial. Those eloquent eyes and lips, that affecting voice, that strong and haunting personality! All these redoubtable engines of art brought to bear on poor little What's-her-name, the heroine! When a nut is to be cracked, why drag in a Nasmyth hammer?—especially if the hammer is not a machine under our control, but a live human being, rejoicing in its strength, and quite unable to refrain from crushing husk and kernel out of existence. Since the first night, Mr Cyril Maude, as the stupid Major, has assumed a lisp—*th* for *s*. I know that in the time whose spirit informs this play a lisp was a symbol of stupidity in general, and of soldierly stupidity in particular. A lisp, therefore, is here artistically right. But there are lisps and lisps. *Th* for *s* is kakophonous and distracting. *W* for *r* is less unpleasant. Besides, it is more traditional. During the rest of the run (which, apparently, will be concurrent with his life-time) Mr Maude might adopt it. His present trick really does get on one's nerves. It makes his performance positively resistible.

[*13 July 1901*]

## IN A MUSIC HALL

August impends, and in London the number of theatres capable of keeping their doors open (or rather ajar) does not run nearly into two figures. The heat wave rolls over us, submerging ruthlessly the last faint semblance of theatrical enterprise. Yet on the crest of that wave, glad and buoyant, ride the managers of the Music Halls. To them not one of the four seasons is less kindly than another. Though the imprisoned mercury be seeking an outlet through the top of the thermometer, for them comes little or no decline in the receipts of their box offices. The bulk of the British public, apparently, would rather die of asphyxiation in a Music Hall than just manage to breathe elsewhere. Is it not strange?

Provided with an apparatus for artificial respiration, I ventured one night this week into the Hall which (as Wordsworth would have said) from Oxford has borrowed its name. The place did not seem so sprucely gorgeous as usual. A sign of failure? On the contrary, a sign of overbounding success. The interior of the building was being overhauled, redecorated. In the passages one saw stripped and excavated walls. The staircases seemed strangely bare. All sorts of improvements were evidently in progress. Yet the entertainment was going on as usual. When, at this time of year, a theatre is ripe for repairs and redecoration, usually the manager is only too glad of the excuse for closing it; seeing that the cost of even the most drastic repairs and most sumptuous redecoration is slight in comparison with the cost of keeping the theatre open. But in a Music Hall the conditions are altogether different. A Music Hall will be frequented by the public, in any circumstances, so long as the doors are not barred. And so, when it has to be overhauled, the workmen have to clear out every evening. At all hours of the night and day they are working, except during the few hours of the entertainment. Such is the present state of things at the Oxford. One could not have a more signal proof of the triumph of Music Halls.

What is the secret of that triumph? Partly, the fact that in Music Halls the public may, and in theatres may not, drink and smoke. England is a bibulous nation. Matthew Arnold, determining what exactly were the respective ideals of the Barbarians, the Philistines and the lower class, stated that the ideal of the lower class was 'beer,' *tout court*; and, to the best of my knowledge, no one has ever tried to controvert his statement. Since the time of *Culture and Anarchy* various changes have crept into our national mode of living. One of them is that the Barbarians drink between meals much more than they used to. The Philistines, snobbishly, have followed suit; insomuch that the amount of beer drunk by the lower class hardly preponderates now over the amount of spirits and mineral water consumed at odd moments by the other two classes. This system of 'pegs' is due, of course, to the necessity for some artificial stimulant that shall enable people to keep pace with the nerve-destroying high pressure of modern life. The enormous increase in the habit of smoking is due to the same cause. It is not however the cause, but the fact, that concerns me here. The fact is that nowadays everyone smokes, and smokes more or less excessively. Whereas the habit used to be considered a wicked and obnoxious pastime, to be indulged in on the sly, now it is everywhere accepted and encouraged as a matter of course—everywhere except in the theatres. Managers of theatres (blind, in this as in most other matters, to the spirit of the time), think that a smoking audience would derogate from the proper dignity of dramatic art. They are still under the sway of that period when no gentleman was suffered to smoke except in some remote 'den' consecrated to the vice, or in the conservatory, where the fumes were supposed to affright plantivorous insects. They are still slumbering in that crinolined age when young ladies cried 'Oh, you horrid creature!' to a gentleman who betrayed the scent of what was then called 'the fragrant weed', and when a vow not to smoke was one of the inevitable preliminaries to marriage. Managers of theatres ought really to rouse themselves from their lethargy and adapt the rules of their theatres to the spirit of the time. Neither drinking between meals nor smoking incessantly is a good habit. But the moral and physical salvation of England is not part of these managers' scheme. What they wish to do is to make the legitimate drama pay. And it never will pay so long as in the theatres the public is forbidden to do what it may do anywhere else.

However, even if theatres were smoked in and drunk in, they never would really rival the success of Music Halls. Legitimate drama, as I suggested a year ago in these columns, is (even at its lowest) a form of art, and to the public any form of art is something in the nature of an imposition; whereas the entertainments in Music

Halls are the exact and joyous result of the public's own taste. 'Turn' by 'turn', these entertainments have grown up with reference to nothing but the public's own needs and aspirations. There is no compromise, no friction, between the form and the audience. The audience is the maker of the form, the form is the symbol of the audience. And thus a Music Hall offers always a great chance to any student of humanity at large. Such a man (even if, unlike myself, he cannot enjoy the entertainment as in itself it is) will always, when he leaves a Music Hall, feel that he has been spending a highly instructive evening.

The band was playing loudly as I entered the Oxford, every brazen instrument seeming to intensify the terrific heat; but over and above it all, from the triply-brazen lungs of one who wore a torrid suit of black and white checks, and who had one Union Jack tied round his hat and another round his walking-stick, were wafted to me these words:

*On Coronation Day, Coronation Day, we'll have a spree and Jubilee, singing hip-hip-hip-hooray! On Coronation Day, Coronation Day, drinking whisky, wine, and sherry, won't we all be jolly merry on Coronation Day?*

Were to-morrow the day in question, and were the evening tolerably cool, the singer (Mr Bignell) could not stamp around the stage in a more perfervid ecstasy of anticipation, nor could the audience be more obviously infected by his rapture. Coronation Day! To you or me, how remote, how negligible as yet! To think that the great heart of the public is already thumping at the thought of it! To think that Demos can see it clearly across the intervening span of more than three hundred other days, and can calculate how gloriously drunk he will get on it! Nowhere but in a Music Hall could one find this lurid side-light. Luridly pathetic? It is. But for me, at least, the pathos of it is obscured by delight in the 'document' . . . Who is this loathsome object? this seedy scaramouch, lank-haired, red-nosed? At mere sight of him the audience rocks with laughter. 'Mr T. E. Dunville—The Funny Man.' Me his make-up disgusts merely. Unsightliness in itself never makes me smile; only, as a student, I am glad of the reminder that it invariably splits the sides of the public. I do but note the fact now: some day I must try to elucidate it. Ugliness of appearance, ugliness of manner, ugliness of jokes—such is the panoply of Mr Dunville. Hark how the audience chokes with laughter! Now he is reading them a sheaf of telegrams. One of them purports to come from a general 'at the front': *No truth in report that De Wet has lost his reason: he never had any.* Loud and prolonged cheers—another side-light to make one gasp. You and I wince at a depreciation of a person who has been persistently scoring off our gallant soldiers. To the British public, because he is not a Briton, he is still merely ridiculous. Sheer stupidity enables them to treat as mere guys true bogeys; and hence that admirable self-control which has been the envy of foreign nations throughout the war. I wish I had space in which to go through the other songs *seriatim*. Not one of them, believe me, but cast its own lurid sidelight.

[*20 July 1901*]


## 'EVERYMAN'

What, I wonder, would have been the feelings of poor Mr George Alexander Redford, the Censor, had he strayed last Saturday into the sunny grey quadrangle of the Charterhouse? To ban any introduction of sacred figures into stage-plays is one of the primal functions of his great office. His, night and day, to mount guard over the chained Bible which theatrical *entrepreneurs* would fain rape to their lairs. Alas that he can be circumvented! Alas that his court-sword glances vainly off one who is armoured in 'private subscription'! Such an antagonist is Mr William Poel, who has been giving us *Everyman*. In this play appears a white-bearded, gold-haloed figure named 'Adonai'—the Creator of the universe. According to the tenets of our Censorshop, could profanity further go? Yet the whole performance was 'under the patronage of H.R.H. Princess Louise, Duchess of Argyll and'—as though to leave no stone unturned against poor, bewildered, excoriated Mr Redford—'the Right Hon. the Lord Mayor'. Nor was that all. 'The Proceeds, after paying expenses, will be given to the Queen Victoria Memorial Fund.' Worse still: many clergymen were present, *complaisants*. Foremost among them was Dr Haig Brown, having seen fit to lend for this performance those dear precincts which now, in the fulness of time, felicitiously, he rules again. It may be that he, in the dim past, counted among his pupils a child named George Alexander Redford. Let us hope it was so. It would crown the irony of the situation.

That no one orally protested against Mr Poel's production, is explicable in the light of two facts: the stage had been rigged in the open air, not behind footlights, and the cast was of anonymous amateurs. There is, undoubtedly, a strong national prejudice against contact of the Bible with the drama; but it is based on survival of the old Puritanical feeling that a theatre is a devil-haunted place which never can have any pretension to respectability, and on the (quite intelligible) difficulty in reconciling with a sacred figure any worldly, well-known, well-interviewed mime who may impersonate it. Had 'Adonai' been impersonated by (say) Sir Henry Irving, and had the Lyceum been the venue, most of us would have been (quite intelligibly) shocked. For we know so much about Sir Henry's career, and the fact that his career is so extremely creditable as it is to a mortal man would make little difference to us. Also, we associate the Lyceum hardly less with the late Mr Wills and his compeers than with Shakespeare. But when, under the dome of Heaven, 'Adonai' is impersonated by someone unknown and unnamed, nobody is made uncomfortable. The only person to chafe at such a spectacle is Mr Redford, who, in virtue of his office, were bound to be horrified by any manager who wished to produce it even *al fresco*, and with an anonymous cast, under those commercial conditions which would bring it within the Censor's jurisdiction. I, for my part, belong to that minority of persons who hope to see, under commercial conditions, in actual theatres (though always with anonymous casts), plays dealing with sacred themes. Not that I am one of those who are greatly indignant that such a sight is withheld at present. No responsive chord in me was struck, the other day, when Mr Martin Harvey complained bitterly that he had been forbidden to produce a very beautiful play founded on Holy Writ. Having seen several other plays which Mr Harvey had considered beautiful, and had been allowed to produce, I heaved my first sigh of relief at the existence of the Censor. I am in no hurry. I do not cry out for sacred plays in the theatre so long as the theatre is in its present state of abjection. But the theatre is slowly raising itself. I believe that this process will continue, and that, a few years before the time when I shall have fulfilled the allotted span of human life, dramatists in England will have risen to a level with those other artists, who, with impunity and without offence, take any subject-matter that arrides them. I believe that the theatres will have become, at its best, something more than a machine to retard the digestion of one's dinner. Perhaps I am too sanguine. It is a dramatic critic's duty to be so.

The spirit of the age is to secern conduct from faith, and probably the sacred plays of the future will not be primarily didactic. Implicit morals they will have, doubtless, like most other works of dramatic art; but their direct intention will be, I conceive, merely aesthetic treatment of the infinite materials that exist in the Old and the New Testaments. *Everyman* is primarily didactic, and its lesson is so sound that after the lapse of four centuries it is still impressive. But for us, of course, its main appeal is to the mere sense of curiosity. We regard it mainly as an instance of the manner in which virtue was inculcated from the stage in the early sixteenth century. As such, this artless little play touches and fascinates us. 'Adonai' and 'Dethe' and an 'Aungell' are the only supernatural figures in it; the rest are typical human beings, or types of this or that human quality. The idea of the play is derived from a Buddhist parable in that archaic romance of *Baarlam and Jehoshaphat*, with which I am accidentally familiar through Mr Douglas Ainslie's recent book *John of Damascus*. Mr Ainslie, in that poem of delicate fancy and curious erudition, paraphrases the parable very charmingly; and his paraphrase, coinciding closely with *Everyman*, shows how little our Catholic moralist diverged from the alien original. Everyman, beckoned by Dethe, entreats Felaship to support him on his way. Felaship deserts him. Kynrede, too, turns his back. Goodes mocks at him. The only one who will bear him in company is Good-dedes, who (I quote Mr Ainslie's version)

> 'disarms
> Our cruel enemies which wait
> To accuse us at the dreadful gate
> And claim the utmost of their due,
> Which he will pay for me, for you,
> Forgetting as true friend forgets
> That from his store he pays our debts.'

From Mr Ainslie's version I gather that the Buddhist parable ceases with the promise of Good-dedes to intercede for Everyman.

In the Morality we are carried several steps further. We have the actual pilgrimage of Everyman, and his ascent to Heaven, 'with other matters pertinent to this history'. By Mr Poel the very difficult task of stage-managing the play had been accomplished most skilfully. To avoid ridiculous effects in so naive a concretion of abstract things is almost impossible; and I pay a high compliment to Mr Poel's tact when I vow that at scarcely one point in the performance had I the slightest inclination to smile. One of the few faults to be found was that the costumes (imitated from Flemish tapestries of the play's own period) were too fire-new for the occasion. Flamboyant colouring was right, of course; but there should not have been that flamboyance of newness which diverts one's mind from the wearers to the costumiers. In ordinary theatres one is often offended by the aggressive newness of the mime's clothes; but there, by reason of the artificial light, that fatal newness is considerably toned down. In an overt theatre, under the rays of the all-searching and all-revealing sun, the newness is dreadfully obvious. The stage-manager ought to implore all the mimes to wear their costumes, night and day, for at least a week before the first performance. Failure to reckon with the difference between natural and artificial light was also the reason why the face of Dethe looked not at all like a skull and very like the face of a half-bleached nigger. The black mark round each of his eyes and down his nose might have passed for hollows if there had been merely light from below. Circumambient light made smudges of them. By the way, why was Dethe allowed to assume a strong Scotch accent and to trot comically instead of walking? Is there any evidence to show that in these plays Dethe, like the Devil, was treated as a comic character? If so, I think the evidence might well have been disregarded. On the other hand, I think it was wrong of Mr Poel to fly so violently in the face of archaeology as to cast a lady for the part of Everyman. However, the lady played in the right key of simplicity. Indeed, (such is the greater quickness and adaptability of the female sex) all the best performances in this unusual play were given by ladies. Knowledge, above all, and the Messenger were admirably played.

[*27 July 1901*]

## TWO PADDED PLAYS

A loiterer in other climes, I am not yet abreast of London's theatrical season. I have seen only two samples of it—Mr Esmond's play at the Comedy, and Mr Carton's at the Criterion. Neither of them, alas! pleases me. But each of them, belike, is rather better than it seems to me, or, at least, would have seemed to me better two months ago. Unless he be a true dramatomaniac, it is very dangerous for the critic of theatres to take even a brief holiday. From even the briefest contact with actual life he comes back impatient of the life behind the foot-lights. He is no longer able to make to theatrical art those due concessions which, by subtle force of habit, he had been making quite readily. Even the noblest play will give him the fidgets. He will not surrender himself to any illusion. All art will strike him as mere artifice, as a fuss about nothing. His body will be conscientiously in its stall, but his soul will be petulantly aloof, marvelling to find the same old games still going on, marvelling still more to find human beings still able to take some semblance of interest in the results of them. Therefore Mr Carton and Mr Esmond need not be driven to suicide by my disapproval of their latest achievements. At the same time, I assure them that these achievements have sensibly diminished my own will-to-live.

Unable to derive pleasure from these two plays, or to believe that anyone else in the audience could really do so, and yet desperately anxious to look on the bright side of things, I fall to hoping that perhaps their authors enjoyed the writing of them. In a lately reprinted essay on Amiel, Walter Pater wrote of 'that criticism which is in itself a kind of construction, or creation, as it penetrates, through the given literary or artistic product, into the mental and inner constitution of the producer'. Let me apply such criticism to *When We Were Twenty-One* and to *The Undercurrent*; let me make a dash for the mental and inner constitutions of Mr Esmond and Mr Carton. Perhaps I shall find that these gentlemen may have revelled in their work.

The chief note of Mr Esmond's latest play is sentimentalism—a luxuriant, uproarious sentimentalism. Not one scene could have been written but by a true sentimentalist, and, since it is the nature of the sentimentalist to enjoy the function of sentimentality, it follows that

Mr Esmond must have relished keenly the process of his work. Bitter though that work is to me, I like to think of Mr Esmond at his desk, smiling, beaming, with the complete works of Dickens and Thackeray piled around his comfortable chair (an exact model, doubtless, of the empty one at Gad's Hill). A reading-lamp sheds its cosy radiance on his scenario, for, though the day is yet young, the curtains are drawn carefully across the windows, lest some glimpse of the outer modern world intrude to tempt him from his affectionate smatterings of the two great novelists of the past generation. Dick! Yes, the hero, of course, must be called Dick. He mustn't be young, because then he wouldn't be able to go through the play duly unconscious that the heroine is in love with him. And he mustn't be old, because then the heroine couldn't fall in love with him. He must be just middle-aged—the darling age of all sentimentalists. And he must be very absent-minded. He must leave half-burnt cigars on the polished oak-table. 'Ah, Dick, Dick, you sinner', murmurs Mr Esmond, 'where *do* you expect to go to? No, no, old chap, I was only joking. Those half-burnt cigars are symbols of a heart in the right place, and the audience will take them as such. And don't be ashamed of your shabby clothes, Dick. The audience will respect you for them. They are shabby because you are saving up that some-one else may live in luxury. You are sacrificing yourself for someone. Heavens! Before all comes right at last, what sacrifices you will have had to make! You shall have a ward to make them for—the son of a dear dead comrade, bequeathed to you as a sacred trust. It shall be the dream of your life that this ward and the heroine shall be man and wife—yes! though you yourself love her fondly, passionately. And the unworthy ward shall get into 'an entanglement' from which you shall try, in the most fatuous way possible, to disentangle him. But don't be afraid, Dick! You shall marry your girl right enough, and my word! how touching shall be your joy in the sudden revelation that she has loved you 'from the first'! And as for the son of your dear dead comrade, just you leave him to me. There shall be grit in that lad, after all. He shan't go to the bad. 'There is always a war somewhere' he shall exclaim, as many another stage-lad has exclaimed before him, marching out with a firm tread to make himself worthy of you and of his father, whom Heaven bless. Yes! Mr Esmond must have immensely enjoyed the mapping-out of this play. It seems, however, that when he came to the actual writing he found there was not quite enough to fill an evening bill. But there is for the artist an awful joy in tackling difficulties, and Mr Esmond's heart must have leapt when he had the happy inspiration of multiplying Dick by four in order to swell the play to its proper length. Four Dicks! Think of it! Four dear middle-aged cronies, who were boys together and are still always together, and always trying to do what is best for the ward, except when they are talking over old times. One of them is 'commonly called Waddles'. Another is described as 'the Soldier Man'. Bless their hearts, how their tongues do wag, while they sit playing whist and drinking whisky as sentimentalists should. 'I say, Dick, old boy, do you remember that day in Bulloin (Boulogne)?' 'Do I remember that day!' 'That night!' 'Ah, that was a night!' 'Waddles don't remember it, not he! Didn't even remember it next morning, did you, old boy?' 'Shut up, Soldier Man. I'm a respectable citizen now.' 'So am I—worse luck! So are we all. Ah, those days! Well, well, well! Shove that decanter across, will you? Thanks. Gentlemen, pray charge your glasses! I give you "the old days".' 'The old days, the old days!' In some such manner as this the old cronies maunder on. They do not amuse me. They do not touch me. I am glad that Mr Esmond likes them, but I do trust that in his next play he will not reproduce them or any equivalent for them. I trust that he will once more deign to write a realistic play. I am not an out-and-out stickler for realism. I can admire fantasy. If Mr Esmond had no talent for realistic work, or if his fantasies were charming, I should let him go his way unmolested. But his fantasies are always a blend of mawkish sentimentality and crude humour, whereas in *Grierson's Way*, an attempt to deal honestly with a grim side of life, he gave us really admirable work. Let him cleanse himself and hark back to the manner of that play. Meanwhile, let him be grateful to Mr Nat Goodwin and to Miss Maxine Elliot, who interpret him with a charm he does not deserve.

Examining *The Undercurrent*, I have not the solace of belief that Mr Carton can have been happy when he wrote it. It is, obviously, the work of a witty man, and of a man with an instinct for dramatic construction. Even if Mr Carton had written nothing else, this play would stamp him as a person to be reckoned with. And it is because I regard him as a person to be reckoned with that I am sure that he cannot have felt any pleasure in this play. Having got his main idea for the plot, he, like Mr Esmond, found that he could not make enough of it to occupy a whole evening-performance. Consequently, like Mr Esmond, he proceeded to pad. Unlike Mr Esmond, he did not find a congenial means of padding. Mr Carton has no talent for melodrama, and his lack of such talent is glaringly illustrated by his failure to endow with any trace of verisimilitude the adventuress whom he drags in, or to extract from the situation in which he places her an ounce of dramatic force. As Mr Carton must have foreseen, the adventuress falls completely flat. That he took any malicious pleasure in this doomed creation I refuse to believe. I pay him the compliment of averring that he must, also, have been deeply depressed by the other means which he found for expanding his play. People in a country-house rehearsing for amateur theatricals, and finally stumbling on dressed as Puritans and Cavaliers, may have been a funny enough motive many years ago. But all the fun, such as it was, has long since been extracted from them. To-day they are merely depressing. No one, I am sure, would be more depressed by them than Mr Carton. They must have terribly intensified the fatigue which beset him when he wrote the play. That he was fatigued from the outset I deduce from his inability to make his central idea sufficient for an evening. The central idea is not a startling one—indeed, it is of the same kind as Mr Esmond's, and hardly less hackneyed; but it is just the kind of idea from which, at his best, Mr Carton would easily have got enough to make a charming comedy without any excrescences. Countess Zechyadi, the principal character, is quite delightful, as far as she goes, but Mr Carton should have made much more of her. I retract. Since Hymen has induced Jove to decree that Miss Compton must always play the chief part in every play written by Mr Carton, the part of Countess Zechyadi ought to have been made much less of. For in it Miss Compton is as hopelessly bad as the French accent which she assumes for it. 'On ze day zat my friend marry, I zay to 'im "Bong Voyaj"' is one of many passages that have bitten into my memory. But no system of phonetic spelling can do full justice to Miss Compton's pronunciation. Nothing has ever been heard like it. And then the solid Britannicism of her voice, face, figure, manner! If she came upon the stage helmeted and tridented, with a lion and a unicorn frisking around her skirts, she could seem less continental. Miss Violet Vanbrugh is to be pitied for having to play the absurd adventuress: it must be dreadful to waste so much earnestness night after night. Remarkable is the quietness with which Mr Bourchier plays the principal man's part. Someone has evidently converted him to 'restraint'. At present his restraint is rather like that of an arrested motor-car. One seems to hear strange snorts and to feel terrible vibrations. But that, doubtless, is a mere nervous fancy.

[*21 September 1901*]


## PARLOUR MELODRAMA

Now that children enjoy such unbridled licence, what were known as 'parlour-games' are quite obsolete, I suppose. They belong to the period when little girls and boys were forbidden to 'tear their clothes and make a noise'—functions which the elders of this generation sentimentally encourage them to perform. Unmitigated forms of football, cricket, croquet and other games are now, I fancy, welcomed by these elders at all times and in all places, even in the drawing-room after dinner. In my day there were more strict canons of behaviour. We had to amuse ourselves quietly, and tidily, or not at all. To supply a happy compromise between young England's innate love of outdoor games indoors and middle-aged England's desire for peace and quietness, parlour games came into fashion. They were simple affairs. A table-cloth was removed, a few diminutive properties were set up, and forthwith one was playing some national game. The joy was a chastened one, with many drawbacks. That article common to all games, the ball, was for ever overleaping the bounds of the table, and having to be searched for, feverishly, under remote furniture, and under a running fire of complaints from the disturbed elders; and when, at length, it was retrieved, such spirit as had come into the game had gone out of it, and was hardly recovered before the ball was lost again. Not that any real ardour was ever aroused in us. When you had to handle the willow betwixt finger and thumb, before stumps not larger than matches and attached to a small green stand, or when you had to kick off a football with a finger-nail instead of a foot, and to ward it away from a goal-post that was always succumbing to your elbow, I defy you to have experienced in any high degree those hot and healthy passions which it is the glory of British pastimes to arouse. And then the 'Rules'! In the apparatus of every parlour-game was included a code of rules which gave us constant agony. The verbiage of them was so formidably involved that more than our poor childish power of exegesis was needed to afford us a glimpse of what they were driving at. The various interpretations we made of them, or pretended to have made of them, led to many whispered quarrels, which, as the evening wore on, culminated in shrill altercations and caused us to be sent summarily to bed. Altogether, these parlour-games were a most depressing and demoralising institution, and I am convinced that some of our battles in South Africa two years ago were lost on the drawing-room tables of Belgravia and Bayswater. However, it is not that conviction which has impelled me to speak here of parlour-games. It is merely a play written by Mr Isaac Henderson, and produced last week at Wyndham's Theatre. Of Mr Henderson's childhood I know nothing, but from his dramaturgic methods I deduce that it must have been largely devoted to parlour-games. The child is father to the man, and no one who had not been a confirmed parlour-game-player in his day could have so ingeniously, and so dispiritingly, adapted a noisy, rough-and-tumble melodrama to the requirements of a little troupe of quiet comedians in a little theatre.

Once upon a time there lived in Rome a very wicked Italian, who was called Signor d'Orelli. He wore the points of his moustache waxed up towards his flashing eyes, and, after seducing a married peasant-girl in his native land, came to England, wormed his way into the best society, and there proceeded to lay snares for the young, lovely and virtuous Lady Lumley. She, after the manner of her kind, came to his rooms, at midnight. So did the husband, after the manner of his. And somewhere in the background was one without whom the villain had reckoned—one Giuseppe, originally the husband of the aforesaid peasant-girl, later the grinder of an organ, hissing 'vendetta' through his flashing teeth, and now valet to Lord Lumley, and still on the vendetta-path. These, I take it, were the elements in Mr Henderson's first mental draft of his play. And it is probable that from them, in the ordinary course of things, there would have been evolved a stirring melodrama. But a strange thing happened to Mr Henderson when he had got thus far. Something, perhaps the knowledge that melodrama was no longer so popular as it had been in London, or perhaps an exclusive admiration for the art of Mr Wyndham, impelled him to change his tactics. He pitched his scheme in the comedic key, toned it down and made it 'psychological' and all that. Lord Lumley, instead of being merely a hero, became a neglectful husband, absorbed in scientific inventions, and this change opened up the way, not only for Mr Wyndham's comedic power, but also for interesting discussions as to the proper relations between wives and husbands. The villain himself became a famous Italian novelist, whose misdeeds, as we infer, are due rather to the vanity of the artistic temperament than to mere villainhood. Indeed, in the whole play, the vengeful organ-grinder is the only figure whom Mr Henderson left frankly melodramatic. A sailor and his lass, who, as I conceive, were originally to have supplied that comic relief which in true melodrama gives our blood time to curdle between the essential episodes, were turned into figures of highest comedy—Commander Lord Ronalds and Mrs Ruth Thornton: their names speak for them. In the last act the villain does not fall stabbed to the heart by the organ-grinder; on the contrary, he gets off with a very good start. The heroine does not fall into the orating hero's arms as the curtain falls; on the contrary, they go into the next room to enjoy a good dinner. And the title of the play is not *Through Darkest Waters* or *Even Unto Death*, but *The Mummy and the Humming Bird*. Everything that could have been done by Mr Henderson was done to bring the play within the accustomed range of Mr Wyndham, of Mr Wyndham's company, and of Wyndham's Theatre. The attempt has succeeded in so far that Mr Wyndham accepted the play and produced it, evidently thinking it was comedic enough for his self-respect. It has succeeded in so far that the play held spellbound the majority of the audience on the first night. But it has not succeeded in so far that the play can appeal to such sophisticated persons as you, reader, or me. You or I can be trusted to enjoy a naked and unashamed melodrama. Our pleasure in that kind is dual: we are thrilled now and again despite ourselves, and throughout we are tickled by the absurdities. Blood and thunder, by all means, for us. But the blood must be red and the thunder loud. When we see not a drop of the one, when we hear but faint claps of the other at a genteel distance, we are neither thrilled nor amused. We are merely bored. If Mr Henderson thought to propitiate us by the elements of comedy in his play, he was too sanguine. We can take no pleasure in comedy that alternates with melodrama. The two things are mutually murderous. Not only does the one put us out of key for the other without putting us into key for itself, but also it is impossible that when they are mixed up either should be decently good of its kind. Mr Henderson, who perhaps has a real talent for one or the other, or for both, should devote himself to one of them, or to both separately. At present he has fallen between two stools.

Such is the view taken by you and me, the sophisticated. But, as I have said, the unsophisticated majority was delighted with this play on its first night. At the end of every act the curtain was raised again and again, to the tune of deepest-throated enthusiasm. Yet, when at the end of the play the author appeared to take his reward personally, there was the usual outburst of angry caterwauling. The mental workings of the gallery are certainly strange. Why suddenly turn and rend a man in whose work you have been revelling for the past three hours? The anomaly recalls to me from my school-days a certain form-master who was a most amiable, easy-going creature throughout term-time, but who at the end of every term sent in a most vindictive report of his every pupil. 'Makes no effort to compensate for natural lack of ability, sloth being his one apparent aim'; 'His progress both in work and in manners has been in a backward direction, and lamentably rapid'; 'Idle, impertinent and, not infrequently, underhand'—such were his descriptions of even the most industrious and intelligent and innocent of his charges, to whom he had never once spoken a harsh word. In most cases, the personality of a man as expressed in his writings is quite different from his real self, nor is it always easy to accommodate style to facts; thus the inconsistency in this form-master might have been explained on the supposition that he had a strong literary bent towards invective, and that his pen ran away with him. But how to explain the similar inconsistency of illiterate first-nighters? The old instinct of savagery, the old joy of inflicting pain for pain's sake, may account for it: bears being now protected by law, dramatists are baited in their stead. A safer explanation is that the public, being now half-educated, knows enough to be sure that whatever gives it really keen pleasure must be very sorry stuff. Intellectually, then, these caterwaulings are a sign of grace. But they are very bad form, and ought to be discontinued. The drunkard does not yell curses at the publican whose liquor has pleasantly inebriated him. If he does, he ought not to.

[*19 October 1901*]

## LUCK AMONG THEATRES

Literature and musical composition are the only arts in which brain-power and temperament are equally needful. Brain-power without corresponding temperament will make a journalist, but not a writer. And it will make one of those musical Professors about whom my neighbour, J. F. R., is so constantly unkind. Conversely, temperament without corresponding brain-power will not enable a man to string together even a few sentences or bars to any purpose. The two qualities must be there, proportionate to each other. On the other hand, I do not think that my other neighbour, D. S. M., will demur to my presumption that a man whose brain-power lags ever so far behind his temperament may become a very fine painter. Certainly he will not be shocked when I apply that rule to the mime. Nor will anyone else be shocked, except perhaps the mime himself, that touchiest of human creatures, whom let me hasten to assure that I mean him no disparagement whatever. Acting is one of the fine arts. It is, though appearances are against it, a creative art. I respect it fully. But I protest that, though there is plenty of scope for brain-power in the practice of it, temperament is the essential thing. There is nothing to prevent a man of rich temperament and slight brain-power from excelling in histrionic art. The proof of this assertion is in the fact that mimes, as a class, are by anyone who has come much into contact with them held to be at once the most emotional and the least intellectual of all classes. They can laugh and cry, in quick alternation, or even simultaneously, for the slightest causes, and their laughter is never hollow, and their tears, if you analysed them, would yield a precipitate of authentic salt; but they do not often say anything worth hearing. What they do say is said always clearly, forcibly, effectively; but say it later to yourself, and you will have to admit that it was the manner, not the matter, that so deeply impressed you. Of course, there are exceptions. There are among mimes men who can think as well as feel, men who can reason acutely, projecting and developing ideas, and all the rest of it. But they merely prove the rule. The art of acting attracts to itself the emotional rather than the intellectual natures, and the practice of it expands the heart more than the brain.

The ordinary plain citizen is apt to mistrust mimes. He thinks they are not sincere. He is wrong. The mime is always perfectly sincere. His sympathies are yours without reservation; but so easily moved are they as to be equally without reservation anyone else's. His heart goes out always to the nearest person. That person becomes 'a part' to him. He finds himself inside the part, and proceeds to play it for all it's worth. Thus he may be you at one moment, and at the next your most hated enemy. Sooner or later, such changes bring confusion to plain citizens, and a mis-reading of the mime's nature, and a fear of his company. Thus, in this age as in all others, mimes are a somewhat sequestered race—mutual comminglers, takers-in of one another's washing. Accordingly, all their natural tendencies gain strength. And one of the natural tendencies of emotional and illogical natures is a tendency towards every kind of superstition.

The whole theatrical profession is honeycombed with superstition. Nowhere so devoutly as on the stage is faith put in black cats, horseshoes, and similar tomfoolery. But the ordinary superstitions are not enough for the mimes, who supplement them, as you know, with a host of superstitions peculiar to their own calling. Most of these have been handed down from antiquity, but every generation adds to their number; insomuch that nowadays the difficulty of infusing any spirit into a rehearsal is intensified by every mime's fear that at any moment he may, by some little act of commission or omission, imperil the play's chances 'on the night'. But superstitions are not confined to rehearsal. One of the more general of them is the belief, firmly held, that certain actors and actresses bring financial disaster to any play in which they appear. There are at this moment some well-known mimes of whom it is said, and said truly, that during the past ten years they have not appeared in one successful production. It is remarkable that without exception these mimes are, in point of artistic skill, among the foremost in their profession. I do not mean that it is for that reason that baleful qualities are attributed to them. Personally they are not unpopular, and none of their brethren would wish to do them a wanton harm. I mention their pre-eminence merely because in that lies (according to my rationalist lights) a likelier explanation of the failures with which their names are connected. I mean that whenever they appear they play everyone else off the stage, thus upsetting the balance of the whole production and spoiling the public's pleasure. Another superstition, equally fixed, is that certain theatres are lucky, and that in others some kind of black magic prevents anything from succeeding. For the practical purpose of conversion, it is, of course, useless to assail with reason beliefs that are founded on unreason: the only thing is to suggest a contrary set of beliefs that have the same basis. Nevertheless idly and for my own pleasure, I may as well bring a little reason to bear on the notion of good and bad luck among theatres.

It is true that theatres often have long spells of success or failure; but such spells can always be accounted for in a quite prosaic manner. Management of a theatre is not a game of chance. It is, rather, a very difficult game of skill, from which the element of chance is almost entirely barred. It is a most solid form of business. Any attempt to treat it as a giddy speculation is the shortest of cuts to Portugal Street. I can think of hardly one form in which bad or good luck can visit the manager of a theatre. Of course, his theatre may be burnt down in the middle of a successful run. But even that disaster may be almost surely avoided by compliance with the requirements of the County Council, and it may, at least, be minimised by proper insurance. Of course, too, the manager may receive from an unknown writer a play which will take the town by storm. But that is a contingency so remote that it may be dismissed altogether. Successful plays are written only by well-known writers, who have passed through a probation of failure. The prime secret of success in management (I am speaking of commercial success, of course) is to keep in touch with these writers, and to select from their work what is likeliest to please the public. It is true that into this part of the business some element of chance seems to enter. You or I, inexpert, would not always care to prophesy from a type-written copy of a play whether it would succeed or fail. But when we have seen the play acted publicly we are never in doubt as to the reason why the public likes it or dislikes it. In the production certain things that were latent have emerged. And the manager likeliest to succeed is he to whom is patent from the outset what we can but subsequently discern. This prophetic power is partly a natural *flair*, and partly a science, based on experience and calculation. It has been carried to its highest pitch in recent times by the managers of the Haymarket Theatre. If you went to Messrs Harrison and Maude and asked them to reveal the secret of their extraordinary financial success, would they, do you suppose, say that it was luck? If they had failed they would no doubt say that fate had been against them. But, such is human vanity, we do not talk of fate when we succeed: we own up to being very clever fellows. That is what Messrs Harrison and Maude would do, no doubt, if you cross-examined them. At any rate, Mr Maude would say very gratifying things about Mr Harrison, and Mr Harrison would make no secret of his admiration for Mr Maude. Between them it would leak out that *Under the Red Robe* was produced because at that time the public was keen on cape-and-sword plays, and *The Little Minister* to meet the demand for kailyardery which had not yet been exploited on the stage, and *The Second in Command* to cope with the war-fever. Further, you would learn that inasmuch as these plays were all solidly constructed, and cheery in either a sensational or in a sentimental manner, and all contained suitable parts for Mr Maude and his wife, the management knew perfectly well before the actual productions that they would be a great success. You would learn that the success of the theatre was due partly to the charm of Mr Maude's and Miss Emery's personality, accentuated for the public by the fact that they were man and wife, and partly to the charm of the theatre itself as a building, and to its central position, and partly, again, to the care with which for every part in every play some clever and fashionable mime was selected, and partly ... But I need not enumerate all the other reasons you would get from Messrs Harrison and Maude. One kind of reason you would not get—the fatalistic kind.

That, however, is the only kind you would get from the manager of a not prosperous theatre. You would have to discover for yourself the causes of failure. Nor would you, in most cases, find the task a hard one. Take the case of the Court Theatre, which (I hope I am not libellous) has not in recent years been a by-word for continuous success. What are the causes? Firstly, I suppose, that the theatre is so far from the other theatres: to go to it breaks one's sense of custom. Secondly, there has not been a great theatrical star to compel people to come. Thirdly, there has been no continuous policy of any kind. Fourthly, the public being ovine, every failure detracts from the chance of the next production, just as every success would improve that chance.

Apparently, the idea of the present management is that the Court Theatre has got into so parlous a state that human enterprise cannot uplift it, and that the only thing is to wait for a turn of luck. I cannot believe that anyone was simple enough to suppose that the present programme could, without some direct intervention of Providence, lead to commercial success. It consists of a triple bill. The first item, a farce by Mr Gerald du Maurier and Mr S. O. N. Frere, is amusing, but it lasts only half an hour, and the rest of the evening is filled with 'a light Olio Entertainment', which may be Olio but certainly is not light, and with an unspeakably tiresome little burlesque of comic opera as it may have been thirty or forty years ago. I have never in a theatre been offered a flimsier excuse for keeping the doors open.

[26 October 1901]

## TWO PLAYS, PROFESSIONAL AND AMATEUR

From a talented writer who has not hitherto tried dramaturgy a better play may be expected than from a talented writer who has written plays only. By 'a better play' I mean, of course, not a play that is technically better, but one that savours less of those stale traditions which beset the theatre. Light is likelier to be cast from without than from within. The saviour of our drama would be a middle-aged man who, after spending his youth in assimilating the outer world, suddenly discovered in himself a born dramatist. Alas! that kind of belated *trouvaille* seems to be impossible. The born dramatist takes to the theatre as soon (relatively) as a duck takes to the water. Straight down to the fascinating little pond he waddles, to spend the rest of his life in swimming round and round it, and feeding and thriving on the weed that covers it. Others there are who discover the pond only after they have learnt something of the dry land we live on, but they are the non-aquatic creatures—they cannot swim. When, after a fascinated and shivering pause, they dive in with a terrific splash, they either sink solidly to the bottom and there end their days, or scramble out as best they can, to be 'restored' by kind friends and warned never to be so foolish again. But anyhow they do make their splash. The duckweed does part under their impact. The water does bubble up. I, loafing on the bank, do get some sort of a thrill. In other words, I prefer the amateur dramatist to the professional. I prefer ill-given glimpses of

## TWO PLAYS, PROFESSIONAL AND AMATEUR

real life to well-contrived panoramas of a life that does not exist. I prefer for example *The Likeness of the Night* to *The Sentimentalist*. Both plays are equally well-meant. Mr Esmond, I am sure, set out to give us a sincere story, but his slight knowledge and love of life were quickly overborne by his very great knowledge and love of the theatre and all its dear little old tricks and dodges. Mrs Clifford, likewise, set out to give us a sincere story, but partly through her ignorance of the means by which real life can be without damage translated into drama, she failed to make her story seem true as a whole. Neither play, then, is satisfactory. But Mrs Clifford, for all her floundering, does manage to get some real human character into hers. Mr Esmond gets none into his.

But stay! I wrong him. The prologue to *The Sentimentalist* more than passes muster. I will not make him and myself ridiculous by comparing it with any of the great scenes of 'first love' in literature. It would seem but a scrannel tune if you tried it after the 'Diversion on a Penny Whistle'. But, so far as I am concerned with modern English drama, I believe that there is no other first-love-scene conceived with such imaginative truth. If only Mr Esmond had not ventured beyond his prologue! In the twenty-three years that elapse between it and the rest of the play he goes hopelessly to the bad. Scarcely has the curtain risen when we realise that we have to deal with a hardened and irreclaimable sinner of the lowest theatrical order. Reading these words, Mr Esmond may suspect me of confusing him with Evan Griffin, the hero of his play. True, this hero, who in the prologue was a young poet, has become in the interval a demon of worldly wickedness. But it is Mr Esmond, not he, that I blame for his perversion. Had Evan been a creature in real life, with a real will of his own, he would have remained quite respectable despite the fact that he had been jilted by the girl whom he loved. He would have been much embittered by her faithlessness. He would have raved and sulked, and would have written in immature verse furious diatribes against the female sex. In course of time (say, when he attained his majority) he would have realised that it was hardly fair to suppose that the girl who had tricked him was typical of her entire sex. He would have taken a broader view of life, and would have begun to enjoy himself. Sooner or later, he would have fallen in love again *pour le bon motif*. By that time he would have altogether forgotten and forgiven his first love. Of course, it is just possible that he might not have done so; but as he was a poet, (and as poets are amorous and consequently forgetful, and as they are very quick to forgive anyone for anything that has quickened their experience and been by them moulded into the form of their art,) the chances are a hundred to one that he would have done so. At any rate, one may be quite sure that he would not have taken his jilting as the signal for entering on a career of dismal, painstaking villainy. He would not during the next twenty-three years have gone about the world betraying every possible woman under the impression that she was only too anxious to betray him if she got the chance. When, at length, he met again the lady who had jilted him he would not have glared at her and exclaimed 'You have robbed me of my respect for women and of my belief in love', for she would not have robbed him of anything of the kind. In a word, he would not, in real life, have become a transpontine villain. That he does so on the stage it is not his fault, poor fellow! but his creator's. It is Mr Esmond who is the real villain of *The Sentimentalist*. It is he, not his creature, that we ought to hiss. Unfortunately, the sins of the creators are visited on their creatures, and we all lose interest in poor Evan Griffin as soon as we know that he has been forced into that ridiculous stage-convention which ordains that a man who is crossed in love must go to the bad even though he had not the slightest previous tendency thereto. One must admit that this convention does not belong to the stage only. It is still accepted by many writers of books. Even Lucas Malet accepts it for Sir Richard Calmady. The fact that his jilting is due to his physical deformity makes it credible that he should have rushed off to the Continent (always, in these cases, the Continent!) with a view to profligacy. But that he should have become suddenly so dead to all his own self that he could ignore and nearly break the heart of his mother, to whom, throughout the rest of his life, he had been passionately devoted, is as incredible as that he, having duly become a monster of viciousness, should have been torn with agonies of remorse and self-loathing because he had not rejected the advances of an obviously 'improper' married woman for whom he had a real passion, and whose husband he had never even seen. Sir Richard, as a villain, is a melodramatic figment. So is Evan Griffin. Some of the dramatic critics, thinking powerfully, have come to the conclusion that the scene in which Evan, purified by love for the daughter of his jiltress, murders the Duke, her bridegroom, is not quite probable. What do they want? What is such a figure as Evan there for, if not to thrill us with a murder? If the murder be really thrilling, as it is in this case, we have no right to complain. Evan's poisoned heart is quite uninteresting; but Evan's poisoned serpent is very great fun indeed. The doomed Duke is admirably played by Mr C. W. Somerset, who, in expressing the emotion of terror, has no rival on the stage. Mr Lewis Waller, who has no rival in expressing grim determination, was an admirable murderer. In the prologue he was duly boyish and natural, and Miss Miriam Clements was duly girlish.

I have lavished so much space on *The Sentimentalist* that about *The Likeness of the Night* I must leave unsaid much that I meant to say. I should like to have praised in detail the drawing of the three chief characters. Especially well conceived is the dull, stiff, literal-minded English lady who, loving her husband romantically, has not the *technique* for expressing to him her love, and succeeds only in boring him to distraction. This Mrs Archerson is a character that lives indeed, quite apart from Mrs Kendal's superb impersonation of it. Only in the end does it become unreal. It is a pity that Mrs Kendal cannot gloss that part of it into verisimilitude. Mrs Archerson's unreality begins only when we have seen the last of her across the footlights. The knowledge of her husband's love for another woman never would have caused her to commit suicide even in so dreary a place as Gibraltar. The suicide is a piece of stage-convention at which Mrs Clifford must have clutched because she was not sufficiently sure of herself as a dramatist to feel that she could bring the play to a conclusion that should be natural without being tame. But, even if we accept the suicide, we cannot believe that Mrs Archerson, dying (literally) to secure her husband's happiness, would have left for him a letter to make him unhappy by announcing her heroic intention. Here Mrs Clifford seems to have fallen a victim, not to lack of technique, but to that belief in the inevitability of moral retribution which is widely held even by people who do not write for the stage. To propagate that belief, she should have allowed Mrs Archerson's letter to reach her husband punctually. Then, doubtless, he, being a very decent man in his way, would have felt himself permanently cut off from the woman whom he loved. But the letter is accidentally delayed. It arrives some time after Mr Archerson's second marriage. Of course, it comes as a most unpleasant shock to the husband and wife, and natural (for the moment) is their notion that it will keep them for ever apart. But anyone else can see that it will do nothing of the sort. Anyone except, presumably, Mrs Clifford, who rings down the curtain as though this fleeting emotion were the conclusion of the whole matter—the triumphant proof that the second Mrs Archerson had all along been right in her theory that no amount of natural passion can save us from lasting unhappiness as a consequence of infringing the social code. Mrs Clifford might have adduced a more specious proof of the doctrine of moral retribution, and given a more logical end to her play, if she had made the Archersons discover that their mutual passion, which had thriven on the forbidden fruit of intrigue, was not strong enough to thrive on the plain regimen of matrimony. However, much must be forgiven to a writer who during three acts of a play has shown us three really human characters. Mrs Kendal I have already called superb. If you care to search the dictionary for still stronger epithets, you may write them between these lines, with my full sanction. Mrs Tree, as the second wife, gave a very brilliant and touching performance. And Mr Kendal was as accomplished as ever.

[*9 November 1901*]


## OUGHT THEATRES TO BE RASED?

*Beyond Human Power* has evoked duly the screams I had expected—the piercing screams of them who think that we should exclude from the theatre anything that smacks of spirituality, anything how remotely soever connected with sacred subjects. There is no doubt that this prejudice is held by the majority of people in England. I could respect it (though I could not endorse it) if it were based on a sentiment that religion is so delicate a subject that to speak or think of it anywhere except on consecrated ground, and on Sunday, is a flagrant breach of good taste. But that sentiment is not generally held. Painters, composers of music, writers of books are all chartered to deal with sacred subjects—nay! are very practically encouraged to do so. The clumsiest and most undistinguished of these artists may, and do, earn most gorgeous incomes if they do but work on sacred themes. Alone among the arts, drama is warned off these themes. Why this peculiar snub? Perhaps I were more accurate in saying that it is not drama, but the theatre that is snubbed. For in every decade the number of tourist tickets issued here for Oberammergau is equalled only by the amount of 'edification' which is supposed to be derivable from that famous undertaking in drama. A performance in the open air is one thing, a performance in a theatre is another. The open air is respectable, quite above suspicion. The theatre, on the contrary, is a place of evil fame, a very sink of iniquity, and dear haunt of devils. Shall we lure into that polluted atmosphere anything that we hold more or less sacred? No! a thousand times no! Such, evidently, is the popular sentiment. Those who believe that the English are a consistently moral race might deduce that we hate the theatre. In point of fact, even among the straitest of our sects, the number of people who hate the theatre is now quite infinitesimal. Nine out of ten English adults love the theatre fondly. And, oddly enough, it is ever the most passionately fond lovers of it who shriek loudliest about its inherent vileness, its glaring unworthiness to be mixed up with aught that is reverend.

The most obvious example need hardly be named. You will guess at once who has been most frantically offended by Bjornson's play, and in whose best manner is bemoaned the 'introduction of the name of the "Divine Master" in the Coulisses'. Do not impute to me the error of treating Mr Scott seriously as a critic of drama. As such (at any rate, since I came to years of discretion) Mr Scott has always been negligible. He was (if he will pardon my anticipation of his retort) criticising plays when I was in swaddling-clothes; and I am quite ready to assume that in that period he really did take an intelligent interest in plays, and really did good work by fighting for the acceptance of a dramatic ideal higher than the ideal held by most of his contemporaries; but on this graceful assumption must be superimposed the clumsy bulk of a regret that never since I learned to read, and used this accomplishment on his copious output, has he written about drama one sentence which seemed to me fraught with the sense of understanding what is not stupid, or with the taste for appreciating what is not common, in dramatic art. I am glad to qualify this qualification. Full though they are of nonsense and bad taste, Mr Scott's writings have always seemed to me worth more than the work of most of his colleagues rolled together. For

Mr Scott is a personality, a definite and unmistakable personality; and in all kinds of writing it is this which is of most account. I care little whether the personality be admirable or otherwise; my demand is that it be genuine and distinct. As revealing a distinct and genuine creature, Mr Scott's work has always pleased me. Further, his enthusiasm for good acting I have always admired. Despite his occasional tendency to hail geese as swans, and swans as geese, I have always regarded him as a man more genuinely affected by good and bad acting than anyone else outside the histrionic profession, and better able to give clear, sound reasons for his preferences. I am amused to find in the article from which I have already quoted an assertion that 'we come [to the theatre] to see acting first, and plays afterwards'. That is delightful. Mr Scott should not have hedged by adding 'at any rate, we require the scope for the player's art, in the play'. He should have had the full courage of his self-betrayal. Acting first, plays afterwards—that principle has been the secret of his strength, not less than of his weakness. A man in whom such a principle is implanted cannot, of course, be taken more seriously as a critic of plays than can one who walks to the theatre on his head, not on his heels, and looks at the stage with his boot-laces, not with his eyes. Nevertheless, in his love of the theatre, and in his conviction that the theatre is so vile an institution as to be the one place in which 'the name of the "Divine Master"' cannot be spoken without profanity, Mr Scott typifies the vast majority of his fellow-citizens, and is so far to be taken seriously. To him, therefore, as representative of the rest, I make a solemn appeal. He is not what is called a thinker, and an appeal in the form of an intellectual idea would be wasted on him. But a man of strong moral sense he is, and I put it to him, on grounds of morality: can he, being what he is, and knowing what plague-spots theatres are on the fair face of our civilisation, reconcile with his conscience his habit of creeping, night after night, to the play? Ought he not to mortify himself, ruthlessly eradicating this illicit taste? Ought he not to strive with all his might and main to eradicate it from others? Ought he to rest till every theatre in London and in the provinces is rased to the ground? And would not the load off his conscience more than compensate him for the sacrifice of a pleasant sin? Would he not, in fact, be truly happier than he is now?

It is a common trick of the man who knows he is not so good as he should be to drown the accusations of his conscience by accusing other men of naughtiness. Perhaps this consciousness of wickedness in going to the theatre is the reason which impelled Mr Scott to charge the keepers of Mrs Campbell's box-office with telling a falsehood—two falsehoods, indeed—on the afternoon of Saturday, 9th inst. 'First, that there was not a spare seat or corner in the house. Secondly, that money was freely turned away.' Mr Scott managed to secure 'an excellent seat immediately in the very front row of the dress-circle for 7s. 6d.'. And he assures us that he found 'dozens and dozens of empty seats' around him. This statement, unchecked, certainly makes a black case against the keepers of Mrs Campbell's box-office. But fortunately I can check it somewhat. I, too, was at the *matinée* of Saturday, 9th inst., and was surprised (considering the nature of the performance) to see not a single seat vacant. I do not ask you to doubt Mr Scott's good faith. But I suggest to Mr Scott that perhaps he, not having 'booked' a seat, arrived early, and that the seats then vacant were merely awaiting people who had 'booked' them, and who, unnoticed by him, arrived later. This is, at least, a plausible hypothesis, leaving unimpugned both Mr Scott's veracity and my own. But the keepers of Mrs Campbell's box-office are still cowering under the horrid suspicion of having had one vacant seat of which they at first denied possession. Let us be charitable to them, too. Let us credit them either with an oversight or with a praiseworthy desire to save Mr Scott, despite himself, from going into a place which his better nature must have told him he ought to shun. And, finally, let Mr Scott, if go to theatres he must and will, express merely his opinions of the players and (secondly) of the plays. To make assertions about audiences is not always a very safe or profitable game, as he has reason to know.

[*23 November 1901*]

## TWO OF THE CHRISTMAS PLAYS

In my last article I dilated on the vast advantage held by the inexpert over the expert critic. But, curiously enough, though the public is far more easily impressed and persuaded by a critic who comes fresh and ignorant to a subject than by one who is jadedly sound on it, there is a general prejudice against the amateur in creative art. I use the term 'amateur' as implying not necessarily a futile dabbler but one whose main business and sources of income lie outside the creative art which he practises. Such a man may, of course, do very fine work; indeed, the very fact that he is not dependent on his art for his lucre gives him a distinct advantage. Nevertheless, in the eyes of the public (among whom I am, for this occasion only, compelled to reckon myself) his work will always be suspect. He will have to war at the outset against a shrewd suspicion that he is a mere futile dabbler. In Captain Marshall I find an obvious instance of this law. It is true that he, by persistence in dramaturgy, and by the gradual dissemination of the knowledge that 'Captain' is a mere survival of a past estate, has at last forced himself into the esteem of critics and public. But at his *début*, and during the first few years that followed his *début*, we would none of him. We admitted that he had a pretty fancy and so forth, but we were shocked by his utter incompetence in the art of writing plays. Doubtless, his early plays were not so capably constructed as *The Second in Command*, but when we read them now or see them revived we are bound to admit that they were very much better than we thought them. The plain substitution of 'Robert' for 'Captain' would have saved us one mistake. 'Captain' was a peculiarly unfortunate label; for (owing to I know not what accumulative action of novels, comic papers, farces and the like) it suggests always a kind of dashing stupidity—a lisp, a monocle, and other things incongruous with the dignity of art. 'Colonel' (thanks, mainly, to Thackeray) suggests in itself a kind of ripe and simple dignity, a loftiness and honesty of purpose, which would in some degree counteract for a dramatist the disadvantage of being labelled with it. Of course, any military title, or title of any other profession, has this advantage for a dramatist, that it saves him from having any holes picked in such parts of his play as bear reference to the things of his profession. If *Carnac Sahib* had been written not by Mr Henry Arthur but by Captain Jones, *tout court*, we should never have had from the press that unexpected outburst of technical military lore. The dramatic critics would have been afraid to pit their lore against a real live soldier's. They would never have dared to hint that the soldiers of the Theatre Marshall say or do anything that would not inevitably be said or done in an actual mess-room. Yet officers in the service have been heard to proclaim that the notion which Captain Marshall gives us of themselves is as untruly roseate as was untruly black the notion which (in happily past days) Mr Kipling gave us of the men under their command. Similarly, if a plumber took to dramaturgy, and wrote plays with a strong plumbing interest in them, we should not be so rash as to complain that his flushings and trappings did not carry conviction, or that his pipes and cisterns did not for one moment hold water. His technical knowledge of plumbing we should accept as infallible. On the other hand we should be mercilessly down on his views of life, his conceptions of the souls of men and women, his technical knowledge of dramaturgy. We should pick maliciously as many wanton holes in his work as ever he had picked in our own property. We should not give him credit for any sane convictions based on observation of the world. Were he a pessimist, we should merely commiserate with him as one who, having throughout his life grovelled in dark and unclean recesses, could not possibly be otherwise. An optimist, he would be twitted with his folly in supposing that human hearts could be soldered to soundness as easily as can metal tubes. We should hint unanimously that the last act of his play was quite superfluous—that he had, in fact, been 'making a job of it', and that the public would be careful not to employ him again. Luckily for themselves, plumbers derive no distinctive titles from their trade. They can, therefore, at any moment, become playwrights without any special handicap to success. For aught I know, some of the most prominent of our successful playwrights may be plumbers in the background. But the aspiring playwright whose regular profession has prefixed his name with a title should drop that title, like a glowing cinder, lest it for ever brand him. Conceive another case. Conceive that a County Court Judge suddenly took it into his head to become a dramatist. And conceive him as not docking surreptitiously his name of its prefix, but making his bow to the public with all the majesty of the law at his back. What would happen? . . . Nay, what *has* happened? A specific instance is better than an hypothesis, and I was foregetting that in the course of this very week had been produced at the Prince of Wales's Theatre a play written by a County Court Judge. *Katawampus* is the play's name, and Judge Parry the author's.

England contains many County Court Judges, and these, doubtless, are of various kinds—the just and the unjust, the acute and the stupid, the grave and the facetious. Alas! so unevenly do the reporters of the press distribute their favours, it is only the facetious County Court Judges of whose existence I am ever reminded. And of that existence I am not willingly reminded; for it seems to me that of all the bad jokes made daily throught the land the worst, the the feeblest and most degrading are made by these County Court Judges. Thus against County Court Judges, generically, I have a strong prejudice, and I was was completely under the influence of this prejudice when I went to see *Katawampus*. I expected that the jokes in it would all be bad jokes. Such a presumption is fatal. If you expect a joke to be bad, bad it seems. If it does *not* seem wholly bad, you imagine that you are the victim of an illusion, and then you are the angrier with the joke and with its maker. Thus I did not at all enjoy *Katawampus*. Every joke in it appeared to me a dry verbal quibble, instinct with that peculiar puerility of which the Judges in County Courts, more perfectly than the Judges in any other Courts, have mastered the secret. The invention of the whole play struck me as tame and forced; and I doubt not that, despite the loud enthusiasm of friends in the theatre, this was how *Katawampus* struck the majority of the audience. 'County Court humour', we murmured to ourselves. And we were the less willing to reconsider our verdict because he whom we were judging was one who, for aught we knew, might hereafter be judging us. Authority is always unpopular, and when it happens to approach us as suppliants it appeals to deaf ears. Why, moreover, should we be just to a man, who in his own Court, would probably be too much absorbed in thoughts about 'Brownies' and other ingredients of romance to render anything but a hollow semblance of justice to us? So, though Mr Courtice Pounds as a beneficent Cave Man was not less lively than he had been as Feste, and though there were in the cast many little girls and boys who romped about the stage very prettily, and though Miss May Cranfield gave a wonderfully natural impersonation of a child, and though, in fine, the whole production was as well done as it could be, 'Away with Judge Parry!' was my unspoken watchword throughout the afternoon.

Reflection came in the evening. The strength of my disapproval brought its proper reaction. I was determined to inquire whether I had not been unduly harsh. I had recourse to a 'book of the words' which had been thrust, free of charge, into my ungracious hands.

My reading of it convinced me that I had indeed been unduly harsh. Now and again, it is true, I came on a passage of true judical humour. 'As by the rules of the House a boy may speak who has nothing to say, I do not see why a boy should not speak who has nothing to wear'—that is an unmistakable specimen of the dreadful authentic brand. There is a good deal of that dry, precise, mathematical jocularity which Courts foster, and which (as is probably the case here) is also fostered by a too close acquaintance with the works of Lewis Carroll—the only man who ever did or ever will make tolerable that kind of jocularity. But, with all due deductions, in the study I found *Katawampus* very much better than I had found it in the theatre. It has quite an agreeable humour of its own, a pretty and distinctive fancy. Had it been presented as the work of mere 'Edward A.' Parry I should have liked it from the outset, not knowing what 'Edward A.' Parry was. Now that I do know, I strongly urge Judge Parry to sit down and invent for himself some impenetrable pseudonym before he makes (and I trust he will make soon) his next venture. To come shamelessly before us *in puris judicialibus* was fair neither to himself nor to his collaborator. By the way, I had forgotten to mention that he had a collaborator—Mr Louis Calvert, whose cunning hand is evident also in the stage-management of the play.

At the Royalty Theatre is a play entitled *The Swineherd and the Princess*. There is not much to say about it except that in it Mr Herz is tremendously industrious and well-meaning in the part of a comic king (suggesting to me constantly the efforts of a grown-up relation to prevent an impromptu charade from boring the little ones for whose doubtful benefit it has been begun), and that Miss Decima Moore is a good principal boy in it, and that Miss Phyllis Broughton dances in it with all her well-remembered grace.

[*28 December 1901*]


# AN ANOMALY IN THEATRICAL ETHICS

In all South Kensington there exists not a more interesting couple than Mr and Mrs William Blank. Their real surname I must withhold from you, for obvious reasons. But any of you who happen to know them will not be slow to identify them from the brief account that follows. It is not that they seem in themselves, at first sight, so very unlike other people. They are ideally happy together, beyond measure mutually devoted and sympathetic and dependent; but such an estate is not, after all, so rare as to compel wonder. They have no eccentricities to speak of. They look and behave quite like their neighbours. What differentiates them in the eyes of their old friends, is the strange past that lies behind them—the strange ordeal through which fate decreed that they should come to the commonplace bliss of their present. Shortly before his marriage, young Mr Blank had inherited from his father a substantial fortune. He did not have to 'do' anything, and so did nothing. He was simply a husband and (for there was one child) a father. Seeing so much of his wife and child, he began to weary of them, became distant in his manner, and in his heart eager for diversions not domestic. In this dangerous period of his life, there happened to be living next door to him an elderly gentleman named Dash. These two had formed a neighbourly friendship. Mr Dash's influence was, alas! wholly for evil. Himself, despite his age, a man of low principles and unedifying practices, he did both by precept and by example foster and ingeminate the ignoble side of his young friend's character. Insomuch that, one day, as Mrs Blank was coming downstairs, she oversaw her husband kissing the brainless but not uncomely person who was her maid. Mrs Blank was a proud woman, and did not let her husband know that she had seen him thus. But she was also a woman agile in resource, and she determined that she would win back his love. She had a mother—an invalid, living in Asteriskshire, N.B. She had also a twin-sister, whom her husband had never seen, who was exactly like her, and who was expected to arrive very soon on a visit. Of the existence of these two relatives Mrs Blank made a strategic use. She told her husband that she was off to Asteriskshire, and that if her sister arrived before her return he must do his best to amuse her—take her to the play, and so forth. She added that she should not take her maid with her. There was a subdued sparkle in the eyes of Mr Blank, as he stood on his doorstep, watching his wife and her luggage out of sight. Uninterrupted now, he pursued his adventure with the maid. But interruption came with the morrow. The twin-sister arrived. Except that her hair was lighter in tint than her sister's, and that she was somewhat better dressed, there was not one apparent particle of difference between the two. At first, Mr

## AN ANOMALY IN THEATRICAL ETHICS

Blank could hardly believe that the new-comer was not really his wife. Gradually, he was reassured, and then, finding that the newcomer was sprightlier, more coquettish, more irresponsible than her married sister, he fell desperately in love with her and began to snub the maid. One night, after dinner, he wrung from his sister-in-law a confession that she, too, was desperately in love—that in him, her brother-in-law, she had found at last that perfect knight whose vague image had so deliciously sustained her, from her school-days onwards. Flattered and overjoyed, Mr Blank proposed that he should be admitted to her bedroom. She replied that on the morrow he would find her amenable. Thereupon, deaf to his objection that on the morrow Mrs Blank was expected to come home, she retired to her bedroom, the lock of whose door Mr Blank tried, unsuccessfully, to pick with a pocket-knife. On the morrow, punctually, Mrs Blank arrived. Or rather, Mr Blank thought she had arrived. In point of fact, she had been in the house all the time, flirting with Mr Blank. She had, it is true, spent one night away from her home, but that adjacently, at the Kensington Palace Hotel. Next day, having had her hair peroxidised, and having bought ready-made a few new frocks, she had come straight home. The person who now really arrived was her twin-sister. As you may imagine, Mr Blank took some time to unravel the situation, and Mrs Blank enjoyed vastly his discomfiture. She did not, however, upbraid him. She was not really angry with him. Her main sentiment was of triumph in the recapture of her husband's heart. Before the sounding of the dinner-gong, she and he were on such a footing as never had they been since their honeymoon had waned. And on that footing they have remained ever since. Now do you wonder that the Blanks seem to me an interesting couple.

Their story, as here set forth veraciously and in detail, is not an altogether pleasant story—in fact it is about as loathsome as mind of man could invent. I think I see the face of Mr Redford, our Censor, if to him such a comedy were submitted. Suppose that it killed Mr Redford, and that in the subsequent brief interregnum, some manager (driven mad by the bereavement) produced it. What would happen? I shudder to conceive. I shudder to think of the grim silence throughout the four acts, the outburst of deep-throated caterwauling at their close. I shudder to conceive what the 'notices' would be next morning. 'Never within our recollection . . . a grave mistake... a disgrace... hard to understand how any manager could have seen fit... not even on the Parisian stage are such secrets of the alcove... things which may exist, but which, thank Heaven! ... festering sores... dissecting-room... morbid, unhealthy, unclean'... And yet, and yet, was not this very play, *The Twin Sister*, produced last Wednesday evening, under the auspices of Charles Frohman (with whom was Mr Redford), and was it not by the audience applauded rapturously from start to finish, and I—have I not scanned vainly the morning-papers for one faint word of protest against the kind of drama by it exemplified? There is a canon among dramatic critics that uncleanness comes from the North, as surely as wisdom from the East. Neither Herr Fulda, the play's author, nor Mr Louis Parker, its translator, is a Scandinavian; and possibly this fact may have lulled the critics into security, and saved them from understanding what the play was about. Yet no! The critics tell the story of the play clearly, exhaustively. They have understood it well enough. What has so obtunded their moral sense that they are not howling with pain?

The answer to this question will throw an interesting light on the inner workings of the critics, and on the inner workings of playgoers in general, and of Mr Redford in particular; it may also be useful to young dramatists, as showing them how far they may with impunity go if they do but go clad in the right accoutrements. Though the story of Herr Fulda's play is precisely the story which I have told in this article, there is a certain difference between the manner of my narration and the manner of Herr Fulda's. Mr and Mrs Blank are by Herr Fulda called Orlando and Giuditta Della Torre, and Mr Dash comes out as Count Andrea Parabosco. The drawing-room of the house in South Kensington is converted into the Loggia of a villa near Padua. The period is cinque-cento, the costume strictly according to the Umbrian School, the conversion strictly iambic. And these differences make all the difference. Of a modern play an audience takes a personal view. If the characters in a modern play are realistically weak and wicked, if the theme is unpleasant, the audience is made uncomfortable and flies into a huff. Such a play is regarded as a personal insult. 'I am *not* like that', mutters almost every member of the audience: 'and my friends are not like that. If they are, so much the worse. I don't like this play at all. It is most unwholesome'. Thus is resented any touch on a seamy side of modern life. The seamy-side dramatist is always a very solemn person, shocked by what he sees, and calling attention to it only that he may point some good moral. Therefore, though shunned, he is not lynched. Lynched he would be, assuredly, if he did his work with a grin, making light of wickedness, making wickedness attractive and triumphant. And yet Herr Fulda and Mr Parker, whose play is written throughout in a vein of blithe comedy, with interludes of screaming farce, and with no moral except that of the green bay-tree, are winning golden opinions all round at the Duke of York's Theatre.

It remains to be said that the dresses in this play are delightful in their accuracy of form and colour—and fabric, for all I know. The Loggia, however, is a chaotic horror, and looks as if all the members of Mr Frohman's trust had come over to paint it co-operatively. The acting was very good all round. Mr H. B. Irving, as Mr Blank, acted with a strenuousness of passion which is remarkable in anyone belonging to the younger school of mimes. Also, he has acquired now the geniality and humanity which one used to miss in him. Mr Norman Forbes, that inventor of grotesquely humorous antics which, being inimitable, need not be patented, was quite delightful as Mr Dash. And Miss Lily Brayton did much with the part of Mrs Blank, in her capable and quaintly astringent way.

I have seen the revival of *The Wilderness* at the James's, and must leave my readers to repeat to themselves what I said about it when first I saw it.

[4 *January 1902*]


## MR GRUNDY IN TWO SAMPLES

'What, then, did Mr Grundy mean?' At the close of the first night at the Haymarket, in answer to loud calls for the author, he appeared duly, was not received with due unanimity, held up his hand, fixed the house with an unflinching gaze, and, when the malcontents had at length been fascinated to silence, remarked sternly and simply that the authors of the play were Messieurs Scribe and Legouvé, and immediately withdrew himself from the public eye. The malcontents blushed, fumbled tremulously for their hats, and crawled out into the night. Nothing quite so impressive had been seen since the days of Coriolanus. Envious of the man who had, at a moment's notice, been able to produce so terrific an impression, the dramatic critics have meanly striven to distort against Mr Grundy the obvious meaning and purpose of his words. They have twitted him with trying to shift a responsibility which he ought to have accepted. But to suggest that he meant 'Don't boo at me: boo at two deceased foreigners' is to suggest that he is at once a coward and a fool—a coward for not being able to stand up against a harmless mob, a fool for imagining that anyone would acquit him of responsibility inasmuch as he had adapted freely into modern English form a play written many years ago in French. Now, whatever may be objected to Mr Grundy's talent, Mr Grundy is neither a coward nor a fool. He is, indeed, of a rather unwisely pugnacious habit, as he has proved in many letters to the newspapers. And his work is always, quite clearly, the work of a clever man. So much, then, for the critics' ungenerous theory of his speech. What is the true interpretation? Obviously, that Mr Grundy meant 'Take care. Don't make fools of yourselves. You will be sorry to-morrow morning. At this moment you don't think *Frocks and Frills* a good play. But it is founded on *Les Doigts de Fée*, which was written by those immortal masters Scribe and Legouvé. And so it *must* be a good play. Now are you sorry you booed? I am. When last a play of mine was produced in this theatre, I wrote to the *Daily Telegraph* and called down on you a divine blessing for your acumen in having applauded that which the critics were so crass as to disparage. I am sorry you have sunk thus in my esteem. Next Saturday evening you will have the chance of rising in it again. Another adaptation of mine is being produced on that evening at the Criterion. See that you return to your senses between then and now. Good-night.' Mr Grundy, being (orally) a man of few words, did not say all this. But I am sure he meant it. My interpretation, acquitting him of cowardice and stupidity, convicts him, I regret to say, of being old-fashioned. But then, I regret to say, Mr Grundy *is* very old-fashioned, and an interpretation which did not square with that fact could not possibly be correct. Mr Grundy still stands rigidly in that period when England was so destitute of native dramatists that adaptation from the French was the best—the only—policy, and when M. Scribe and M. Sardou were upheld as heaven-sent geniuses who had brought dramatic art to its highest pitch of perfection. That period is past for us. For Mr Grundy it is in the glorious and immediate present. Now and again he has written an original play. But, despite success, he has always forthwith relapsed into adaptation of work done by byegone Frenchmen, evidently deeming such adaptation the safest and wisest course that poor little humble English dramatists can pursue. And thus it has come about that Mr Grundy is no longer one of the dramatists to be reckoned with. Formerly, I well remember, he used to be bracketed with Mr Jones and Mr Pinero as one of the three considerable men in modern English dramaturgy. His name has long since dropped out of the bracket, or is included in it only when many other names are included. No one denies that he shows very great skill in his work. No one pretends that he shows less skill than he used to show. Indeed, his structural ingenuity seems to be growing ever neater. He is still progressing. But his progress is in a direction which has ceased to interest any serious critic. If a man is walking backwards, his deportment (unless he be a courtier) really does not matter. The art of a retrograde dramatist may be ever so fine, but it is not the less negligible. At this time of day, who can pretend to take any interest in a boxfull of little puppets all dismembered by Time and Distance, and furbished up to look like living Englishmen and Englishwomen by a man who, in jumping at such a job, shows how very little he can care for the life around him, and how very little, consequently, he can know about it? A literal translation of such a play as *Les Doigts de Fée* might be amusing—an amusing sample of a past and alien mode. But Heaven—or, at least, as much of it as Messrs Harrison and Maude hope to occupy hereafter—protect us from any attempt to make such a play seem real to us! *Frocks and Frills* is scrupulously up-to-date. '*C'est le dernier mode*!' quaintly exclaims Victorine, the French maid, when her mistress dons a frock that has just come from the dressmaker's. And throughout the play everything is '*au dernier mode*', as Victorine would say. The frocks, the furniture, the slang, all are of the latest moment, and there is a peer who presides over a company of which he knows nothing, and —so on, and so on: you know the kind of thing. And it is this very kind of thing which at once accentuates the exotic antiquity of the puppets and robs them of any historical or ethnological interest. They are not English, and they are not French; not modern, and not ancient. In fact, they are nothing at all. No one working on Mr

Grundy's lines could create anything at all. Nullity of result matters not in the case of a talentless writer. In the case of so talented a writer as Mr Grundy it is reprehensible. Little wonder that the first-night audience reprehended it. I wish I could believe that Mr Grundy's hide was pervious to this loud rebuke. If *Frocks and Frills* were a dead failure, perhaps his dead conscience would be stirred to life. Alas! the production is stamped with the scarlet seal of success. The glittering expensiveness of the dresses, the popularity and expensiveness of the mimes engaged, and, above all, the popularity of th Haymarket Theatre itself, conspire to make certain a long run. Barren fig-trees will flourish like green bay-trees if they be but planted between the boards of the Haymarket Theatre. When, many months hence, Mr Grundy finds himself still culling big ripe cheques from the withered branches, he will be a more than ever devout believer in the immortality of Messieurs Scribe and Legouvé. Perhaps, in his heart of hearts, he will ascribe even to himself some little measure of the play's success. For he is, after all, human (though anyone who knows him only through his work will be inclined to doubt me).

Of the mimes, Mr Allan Aynesworth acts as airily and agreeably as ever. (The smoothness of my accidental alliteration well suggests the manner of his performance.) But I should like for once to see him in a part that would call forth some of that intelligence, as well as all that agreeable airiness, with which he is endowed. Mr Eric Lewis gives another of his exquisite little performances, his power of humorous observation coaxing into reality the most conventional of parts. Miss Grace Lane acts very cleverly, on the model of Mrs Kendal, and Miss Ellis Jeffreys, whose artificiality is apt to be irksome—apt to nullify her humour—in other parts, delightfully impersonates a lady with an artificial manner. Mr Cyril Maude, as a young man with a stammer, scores a great success, and will doubtless lengthen the play's run as appreciably as he lengthens its duration every evening.

Mr Grundy's other sample, *A Pair of Spectacles*, though it too, of course, is an adaptation of an old French play, seems to me much less spectral than *Frocks and Frills*. The little play does not pretend to be a representation of life: it is frankly a fable, a fairy-story. Such a character as Benjamin Goldfinch never existed anywhere. Consequently, he has as much right to exist here as anywhere else, and now as at any other time. One does not feel that he is a foreign antique faked up to seem like a modern Englishman. One accepts him because he always was impossible, and because his impossibility was always of a charming kind. In matter, the play does not date at all. In manner it dates considerably. Its constant soliloquies, and its catchwords, and the naivete with which all its i's are dotted for us, and its t's crossed, keep us mindful that many long years have elapsed since first we saw it—make us even exaggerate the number of those years. When Gregory Goldfinch says 'Meet me at Temple Bar', and his son replies 'You mean the Griffin. Temple Bar was pulled down long ago', we are surprised into murmuring '*Had* Temple Bar been pulled down yet?' We are tempted to think that the dialogue has been mis-spoken, that Gregory Goldfinch ought to say 'Meet me at the Griffin', and the son to reply 'There is no such thing as the Griffin. Perhaps you mean Temple Bar?' And yet how fresh we found the play's manner twelve years ago! In us those twelve years seem to have made so little difference—to have passed over us so quickly, touching us so lightly. Can they have been working on us as relentlessly as on this play? Mr Hare and Mr Groves, as the two brothers, embolden us to answer 'no' to this melancholy question. Each, in his own way, is as perfect as in the old days.

[*11 January 1902*]


## 'ULYSSES'

Forewarned that Mr Stephen Phillips had been dramatising *The Odyssey*, and that his version was about to be produced at Her Majesty's Theatre, I set myself a short examination paper. There were only two questions in it:

I. Define the difference between epic and drama.
II. What do you know of (α) Homer, (β) Mr Stephen Phillips?

I adopted this plan because I have always, even in my school-days, loved *The Odyssey*. We all keep jealous guard over the things we love. We resent that anyone should take them and pull them about and display them to us in any form but the form in which we have known them. We are always apt to be unjust to any such intruder, calling him 'bungler', however skilful he be, and 'vandal', however reverent. When a man dramatises a story that we love, we do not pause to consider whether the differences between the scheme of his version and that of the original have been made wantonly by him, or were necessitated by differences between dramatic and literary form. We set down to his outrageous vanity any differences in spirit between the old and the new, leaving no margin for possible and probable differences, not to be bridged, between the spirit of the originator and the adapter. Well! Though I wished Mr Phillips had let Homer be—wished he had not construed that occasional nod as an invitation to himself—I was determined that I would do strict justice to his work. I would not demand of him the whole *Odyssey* and nothing but *The Odyssey*. Before visiting Her Majesty's, I would try to ascertain how much of *The Odyssey* it was reasonable to expect, and how much of Homer's spirit in proportion to Mr Phillips's. So I set myself that brief paper, wrote out my answers within the class's space of three hours, read them through, and, had I not disqualified myself for cribbing, should have received an '$a+$' for each.

These answers had a twofold effect on me: they strengthened my regret that Mr Phillips had taken Homer in hand, and they insured me against the captiousness begotten of deep disappointment. I knew that whereas Homer, having twenty-four books to bless himself with, could take his time, making vast circuits, and retracing at will his own footsteps, Mr Phillips had to compress everything into a small compass. Everything? No, that would be beyond human power. A few of the innumerable things—a tiny residue—would be all he could manage. He would not be able to produce any of that vast and cumulative effect which is one of the secrets of Homer's charm—that sense of many full and continuous years, with nothing in them hidden from us. He could not send his hero over seas and lands, through inexhaustible experiences. We should but see his hero here or there, doing or suffering this or that. Even as in the well-known advertisement the prairie-ox is to the tin of beef-extract, so must Homer's Odysseus be to the Ulysses (why not Odysseus?) of Mr Phillips. Of course, I reflected, Mr Phillips's extract need not be inanimate. But its life would probably be quite different from that of the original creature. Epic shows us the hero as hero, as leader of men, lover, schemer, toiler, conqueror. Drama (modern drama, at any rate) taking the line of least resistance, shows us the hero as lover mainly, and only incidentally, or by inference, as leader of men, &c., &c. Thus it was likely that the interest of Mr Phillips's play would be centred on (that which, indeed, is technically the central point of *The Odyssey*) the home-coming to Penelope. How about Calypso, Circe, Nausicaa? We could not hope for them all. Circe might be ruled out at once, on the practical ground that, though real actors might pass for warriors, real swine on the stage could not possibly pass for anything but real swine. Nor would a performing dog be passable as Argus: Argus must be jettisoned. Also the Cyclops, who would create an atmosphere of Jack the Giant-Killer. And Hades—that, again, could not possibly be realised. And . . . well! You see that my answer to the first of the two questions had made me pretty modest in my expectations. My answer to the second was equally contractive. I had not written down what was known about the two poets personally: the one was too obscure, the other too illustrious. But I had analysed the work of each, and a comparison of the two analyses did not betray a single point at which the spirit of the younger poet converged with that of the elder. There seemed to be nothing but sharp contrast—contrast between antiquity and modernity, between Pagan faith and sceptical Christianity, between naïveté and cleverness, between barbarism and hyper-sensitiveness, between overwhelming creativeness and carefully nursed artistry, and between so forth and so on.

Having thus prepared myself, I was able to enjoy and to admire *Ulysses* very much indeed. And you, reader, thus prepared by me, will be able to do likewise. In *Herod* Mr Phillips proved his possession of an authentic gift for dramaturgy, and this later play, in its technical scheme, seems to me as good a version as anyone could make of *The Odyssey*. It opens, as it should, in Olympus. The gods in council are determining the hero's fate. We are translated to Ithaca. We see the suitors in their insolence, and Telemachus in his distress, and Penelope in her guileful patience. Next, we see the hero himself, bound by the spell of Calypso (in whom, very skilfully, Mr Phillips has incorporated Circe, thus throwing in a pleasant little surprise for us, without spoiling the shape of his play). Next, as Zeus has ordained, Ulysses descends into Hades. This is another, a still more pleasant, surprise for us. We had not reckoned with the imaginative resources of Her Majesty's. Mr Phillips had. The seemingly impossible is achieved: the aspect of the Homeris Hades is realised for us, impressively, on the stage. Ulysses, having held converse with the twittering ghosts, sails for Ithaca, where, by an adroit process of selection and congestion, all the principal events of the home-coming are pressed into two dramatic scenes. But, though the play is thus admirable in construction, it has one glaringly bad defect in treatment, which I had not anticipated, and for which I can find no excuse at all. It is, as I have said, right that the play should open in Olympus. The reason for this, of course, is that *The Odyssey* is a fatalistic poem, in which the hero, for all his bravery and steadfastness and cunning, can achieve nothing at all without the help of Athene and the sanction of Zeus. The essence of modern drama is free will. All its interest is based on the theory that the characters have power to act of their own volition—to make or to mar their own lives. But to apply this theory to a play founded on *The Odyssey* would be gross anachronism. Mr Phillips has not been guilty of it. But he has done something worse. He has retained the gods and all their interfering potency, but, as if to conciliate modern notions, he has presented them to us in a deliberately ridiculous light. Zeus, though he duly wields his thunderbolts, is shown up as a vain old man—the butt of the lesser deities. Hermes is described by Ulysses as 'a most garrulous god'. Even Poseidon is made ridiculous. And what is the result? Not that Ulysses seems to be cutting a more considerable figure on the earth, but that, on the contrary, we despise him for being governed and directed by a handful of creatures for whom no one—not even he—feels anything but contempt. If Mr Phillips could not take the gods seriously, he had better not have taken them at all. But it is absurd to suppose that he could not take them seriously. For the rest, Mr Phillips seems to have left nothing undone that he could do, to make his play worthy of its theme.

As Penelope, Miss Lily Hanbury speaks her lines with a fine sense of their rhythm, and Miss Constance Collier does likewise as Athene. Mr Fulton, not content with having been the Duke of Wellington and Julius Caesar, appears as Zeus, and with his impressive voice and face tries to make the part seem like what it ought to be. Mr Oscar Asche and Mr Gerald Lawrence are well-cast for the parts of Antinous and Telemachus. And, in the title-part, Mr Tree is duly δῖος and πολύμητις.

[*8 February 1902*]

MORE THEATRES

## THE LYRIC, THE GARRICK, AND THE O.U.D.S.

I am grateful to Mrs Madeline Lucette Ryley for having written *Mice and Men*, and to Mr Forbes Robertson for having produced it at the Lyric Theatre. It is a play which I have long awaited—so long awaited that I had begun to fear it never would be vouchsafed. For years I have been sneering at every sentimental play that has been produced, and thus (I fear) alienating the majority of you, my readers. Doubtless, you have come to regard me as a creature with a heart of stone, as a ruthless brute, quite impervious to any soft appeal, quite incapable of delight in the presentment of aught but what is grim and terrible. And I, all the while, have known my heart to be really an up-welling spring of the most limpid sentiment, undiscovered only because no dramatist had come by with a divining rod. All the while, I have been beset with an ardent, unsatisfied desire for the bread and butter, the buttercups and daisies, of drama—for fresh butter, nicely spread on new bread nicely cut, for field-flowers really a-growing and a-blowing. Waxen imitations of field-flowers, set under domes of dusty glass on mats of gaudy wool, hunks of stale bread supporting lumps of rancid butter—these things are not what I wanted, and these things are what I was always being put off with. At length, Mrs Ryley has given me the things I did want, and with them the chance of disproving myself a monster. You who have misjudged me, behold me now dancing with all the grace of true joy among the real buttercups and daisies, and swallowing the good bread and butter like a hungry, healthy child.

The apocalypse will be the more startling and convincing for that the scheme of *Mice and Men* is not merely compact of sentiment and sentimentality, but is also compact of them in their most conventional forms. The middle-aged doctrinaire who was once crossed in love, but who has at length decided that it is his duty to marry and beget an heir—what playgoer does not know him? What playgoer does not know that he will, in a cold and calculating way, select from the lower class some healthy and very young girl who, after she has been educated for a certain number of years according to an ideal system, will be in a position to marry him and in due course supply him with a paragon worthy to carry on the traditions of his family? Who does not know that he will, after the due lapse of years, realise that he loves his intended bride madly, devotedly? Who does not know that, when at length he makes his proposal to her, he will make it so delicately that she will imagine that he is asking her to marry his scapegrace nephew—the young and joyous soldier, who is her ideal, even as she is his? And who does not foresee the end—the middle-aged doctrinaire, cloaked and hatted, faltering slowly down the garden path, opening the wicket, and turning, ere he utterly effaces himself, an almost happy smile towards the house—the house that was to have been his and hers—from which are wafted the strains of 'My love is like a red, red rose', sung as a duet by the two young people? This is a story that must have been exploited in a score of sentimental books and sentimental plays. In real life, of course, it would be impossible. Granting the premisses, one would find that the result would be exactly the opposite of that which is here evolved. Even though the girl might not (as she probably would) conceive a romantic love for her benefactor, it is quite certain that the man would ultimately abandon his cut-and-dried scheme of matrimony, finding that the few years' training, despite its superficial effects, had brought the girl not a whit nearer to him in spirit than in age. He would realise, if he still wanted a bride at all, that he wanted a kind of bride very different from this one. If he had a scapegrace nephew who was in love with her, he would make a handsome settlement, and think himself very well rid of an encumbrance. But these objections to *Mice and Men* are made by me merely in cold blood: I had no glimmer of them during the play's procedure. I surrendered myself whole-heartedly, taking the play for all it was worth, smiling and sighing and brushing away tears with the best of them. Why? Because the costumes were of the eighteenth century, and so the challenge to reality was not so sharp? No. I vow that *Sweet and Twenty* in modern costume did not disgust me more, did not seem to me more disgustingly ridiculous, than any of those sentimental costume-plays which Mr Martin Harvey has thrust on my notice. The reason why I was able to enjoy the sentiment and sentimentality of this play is simply that Mrs Ryley has a genuine talent for sentimental comedy. Though her characters and their motives are conventional and unreal, she has imagination enough to believe in them, and so transfuses that power into me. The Freeman Willses and Basil Hoods are so obviously insincere. They are so obviously faking up the emotion, piling falseness on falseness. They are so obviously making asses of themselves in order to make money. If they had any sense of humour they would not be capable of this deliberate process. But sense of humour has been denied them. It has not been denied to Mrs Ryley. It prevents her from ever becoming maudlin in her sincerity, as they become in their insincerity. She gives us never that horrible, cloying stickiness of sentiment through which the Hoods and Willses have (presumably) enriched themselves. Her sentiment is always airy and wholesome. Moreover, she can write. What a relief, after that illiterate slush to which the Willses and Hoods have accustomed us, to find dialogue that is really like human speech, yet terser and more distinguished than human speech! Even by mere reason of its literary style, *Mice and Men* is delightful, and rare among plays. But the chief ingredient of its delightful rarity is that it is a fairy-story conceived in a sincere spirit—a fairy-story in which I can believe.

Mr Forbes Robertson evidently believed in it, too. For in the production of it he has to efface and sacrifice himself almost as completely as does the hero whom he impersonates. The sacrifice is not made in vain. For through it we have that desired thing which has been withheld from us—a full revelation of Miss Gertrude Elliott's exquisite little genius for drawing tears and laughter. Anyone with a sense for acting must have realised, when Miss Elliott made her début in England, that here was a real artist, a something quite distinct from a mere real leading lady. But hitherto we have known her worth only through the glimpses of it. Here is the full worth itself. Let no one miss this chance of appreciating it, and let no one cease to hope that the Peggy in this play will one day be the Perdita in another.

*Pilkerton's Peerage*, Mr Anthony Hope's new play at the Garrick Theatre, would have been better if it had been rather a serious study of the coronet-hunting millionaire than a slap-dash satire of him. Let us have slap-dash satire, by all means; only, Mr Hope is not the man to do it really well, and he has, in his later books, proved himself to be very good at serious and minute delineation of character. In a slap-dash satirical play, which caricatures men and things, making them what they are not so that we may realise something of what they are, we demand a broadly amusing method of treatment. Mr Hope cannot compass that. Pilkerton and the rest of the characters are duly exaggerated in outline, but they are not amusingly filled in. The filling-in is too reticent, too delicate, too realistic. The dialogue is witty in a minor key when it ought to be full of rollicking high-spirits. We want to be roaring with laughter, and therefore cannot even smile (as elsewhere we could) at the wit. Mr Jerrold Robertshaw, as Pilkerton, intensifies our discomfort by taking his part in the grimmest earnest. Sir Henry Irving's Beckett was a trifle light as air in comparison with Mr Robertshaw's Pilkerton, though the two creations have, superficially, many points in common. Mr Edmund Maurice, as a Prime Minister, and Mr Bourchier and Mr Esmond as his secretaries, are more light-hearted and accordingly more appropriate. Miss Eva Moore is not good as a frivolous woman of the world, nor is Mrs Maesmore Morris good as a naive daughter of the millionaire. Either would have been good in the other's part.

The *Two Gentlemen of Verona* is an ideal play for a company of amateurs: no one in the cast has a long part, and so no one can come saliently to grief; and everyone in the cast has scope in which may be made a nice little success. Therefore, the O.U.D.S. needs no excuse for having this year repeated the choice which it made but nine years ago. This year, undeniably, the greatest success was made by the anonymous impersonator of Crab—a Skye terrier which, in ease of deportment and in alert resourcefulness, could give points to any performing dog that ever was seen on the stage of the Palace Theatre. This triumph of the amateur over the professional seemed to hearten the human members of the cast. Perhaps because he, as Launce, was most nearly in touch with Crab, (or perhaps because my judgment is affected by his title) the second prize must be awarded to Lord Tiverton (New College). Mr R. K. Cox (Hertford) was excellent as Speed. As the 'Two Gentlemen' Mr J. F. G. Gilliat (University) and Mr E. Kenworthy-Browne (Balliol) contrived to seem as though they were hardly at all ashamed of having to seem romantic. Any student of undergraduates as actors will admit that this was an almost unparalleled feat.

[*15 February 1902*]

## A TRIPLE BILL

I deem it a pity that fashion tempts every dramatist among us to make of his every dramatic idea a play whose performance shall occupy a period of two-and-a-half or three hours. There are, assuredly, some dramatic ideas which cannot be fully developed in a briefer period, and which would lag superfluous beyond that period. For such ideas the fashionable span is the right span. But there are other ideas so large as to be hurt by this imposed time-limit. And there are others, again, so small that the virtue goes out of them by reason of their propounders' determination to stretch them out to the popular length. I have seen between dinner and supper plays which ought to have lasted at least eight hours, and others which, though actually constructed as bridges to bear one from coffee to consommé, ought to have lasted not more than eight minutes. The dramatic form, like all other art-forms, ought to be kept in a state of elasticity. Books are of all lengths. Statues are of all sizes. Canvases are made to measure what you please by what you will. To take an analogy from life, a man can buy gloves of any size between 'sevens' and 'eights-and-three-quarters'. If none of these sizes be precisely right, he can have special sheaths made for his hands. This is as it should be. It would be intolerable, even in these somewhat democratic times if all citizens were compelled by a sumptuary law to wear some one size of gloves. The argument against such a law is obvious: hands are of various sizes. Yet not less obvious is it that dramatic ideas are of various sizes. Away, then, with the iniquitous system whereby these ideas are expected to yield as much as, and no more than, a certain fixed quantity of amusement and instruction! Let Procrustes no longer dominate our drama. Let dramatic ideas be suffered to make their own beds and lie on them, comfortably filling them, without torture by rack or hatchet.

The flesh, alas! is always outmatched in its eternal conflict with the spirit. I must admit that I am not, except in theory, keen to see an eight hours' play. But a play of eight minutes or thereabouts—they are quite another matter, with nothing to disembolden me in my outcry for them. I welcome any attempt to break away from the modern three hours' form, and to present brief plays of various duration. I welcome, therefore, the triple bill which was presented last Saturday, under Mrs Tree's auspices, at Wyndham's Theatre. Two of the plays are adaptations from the French, one of them is home-made. I should be glad if they were all home-made, and well made at home; but that would be expecting too much. Under the present conditions in England, only the despicable dramatists write short plays—'curtain-raisers', as we call them. In France, where the prejudice does not exist, decent dramatists write short plays whenever they feel inclined to do so. Through adaptation and production of their work is the sole means of persuading our own decent dramatists to do likewise. Had Mrs Tree laid hands on home-growths only, she would but have intensified the conviction that short plays are beneath the dignity of decent dramatists. It must have been to make more lurid the lamentable contrast between France and England, in this matter of short plays, that she decided to begin her programme with an English specimen. She could not have found for this purpose a more lurid specimen than *Irish Assurance*. I need not describe it in detail: you will know the kind of thing it is when I say that one of those tearful retrospectors who 'do' the theatres for most of the morning papers hails it as 'Boyle Bernard's capital old farce *His Last Legs*, now rechristened'. It is a one-part play, and I regret that Mr Leonard Boyne plays this one part. For he, with his brogue and blarney, his *élan* and sure art, plays it so delightfully that he somewhat obscures for us the international lesson which Mrs Tree meant to inculcate.

Luckily, the next item is a good one-part play, splendidly performed by Mr Charles Warner; and thus Mrs Tree's lesson is driven home, after all. Had this play been performed badly, the reverse of the lesson would have been taught. For, whilst a good actor can reconcile us to a bad one-part play, a bad actor can make a good one-part play intolerable. But, though the power of acting is thus stronger in practice than jealous theorists would like it to be, we do not derive equal pleasure from a bad play well acted and a good play well acted. We plump, immediately, for the latter. *Au Téléphone*, or *Heard at the Telephone*, as the adaptation of it is called, is a good play inasmuch as it is founded on a new idea, and gives us the illusion of absolute reality, and thrills us to terror. The new idea is the use of the telephone as material for drama. The situation evolved is briefly this: at a distance of so many miles as to make him incapable of interference, a man knows that his wife and child are being murdered. He can hear their cries, knows exactly what is happening to them; but (Science having thus conquered Space for our ears and lungs, but not yet for the rest of our bodies) he can only stand still, and listen, and advise, and go mad. Such is the situation, evolved and prepared with perfect verisimilitude. One cannot but be thrilled by it, as played by Mr Warner. The thing is terrific; 'but is it art?' Most of the critics seem to think that it is not art. 'Suffering', to quote a typical protest, 'should overtake people owing to faults in their character with which we can sympathise'. It *should*, no doubt; but the fact remains that, in real life, it doesn't. I agree that the most interesting kind of tragic drama is that in which fate seems to be acting, not blindly, but with wide-eyed reason. But I cannot see that it is inartistic to reproduce on the stage one of those too frequent occasions when fate makes a fool of itself, committing this or that uncalled-for brutality. Of course, if such an incident as this incident of the telephone were used as the solution of some tragedy of human character, I should object to it as irrelevant and inartistic. But, standing thus by itself, it seems to me quite legitimate, as being quite relevant to human life, and as not being one of those irrelevant things which, like the torture-scene in *La Tosca* or *The Sign of the Cross*, are *disgustingly* horrible, and therefore unfit to be enacted on the stage. Of course, if a man asserted that this play disgusted as well as thrilled him, then, if I believed him, I should admit his right to protest vigorously against it. But I should not believe him. Disgust here is as impossible as terror is inevitable.

In *L'Enigme*, as they played it in Paris, the one weak point was that a young man went out and shot himself in order to shield his mistress, whereas he could, obviously, have shielded her much better by continuing to live. Unfortunately, in *Caesar's Wife*, the English version which concludes the triple bill at Wyndham's, this weak point is made weaker. For good reasons the relations between Vivarce and Léonore had to be made strictly platonic; and thus the suicide of Vivarce, just credible in *L'Enigme* on the assumption that he was a fool, becomes in *Caesar's Wife* quite incredible on any assumption at all. However, the English public is by this time accustomed to judge Parisian successes by the spirit rather than by the letter, and so is not, I dare say, seriously inconvenienced by the change made for its good. On the first night, a more serious drawback was that Mrs Tree was unable to appear. Much of the play's point is lost if Léonore and her sister-in-law, Giselle, be not women of the same mould and manner. Between the method and aspect of Mrs Tree and Miss Fay Davis there is a certain superficial resemblance. But Miss Lena Ashwell, who played Mrs Tree's part, is as unlike to Miss Fay Davis as one actress can be to another. The play's point, to which I have referred, is that almost to the last moment the audience cannot guess of which of the two women Vivarce is the lover. Of course, M. Hervieu is an inveterate preacher, and this play is used partly for a vehicle for his doctrine of live-and-let-live, &c., &c. But primarily, as is shown by the title he gave to it, he wrote it as a puzzle—a goad to curiosity. Everything that Léonore and Giselle say or do is consistent both with guilt and with innocence. From first to last, our suspicions are kept oscillating from the one woman to the other. This is a new sensation in drama, and except to evoke this sensation the play would never have been written. But among the stock-in-trade of our critics is a precious theory that never, in any circumstances whatever, must an audience be mystified. And it is delightful, as a revelation of crass stupidity, to find many of the critics gravely pointing out to M. Hervieu that he has not succeeded in letting the audience into his secret. One of these sages, after enumerating M. Hervieu's red herrings, complains that 'it is hardly just of him, therefore, to expect the audience to be more knowing' than the characters in the play. Thus is dramatic criticism written, for the most part. And yet there are in London many quite sane and needy persons, unemployed; and this is supposed to be an age of fierce competition.

[ *8 March 1902* ]

## A TRAGEDY AND A CURTAIN-RAISER

'Poetic drama is the highest form of drama, and we needs must try to love the highest when we see it. Nor must we miss any opportunity of seeing it. It is for our good. Duty calls. Let us not hold back. Courage! Forward! On!'

Such, I take it, is the mental attitude of the public towards Shakespeare and Mr Stephen Phillips. If playgoers were swayed merely by the base appetite for pleasure, there would never be, I fancy, more

## A TRAGEDY AND A CURTAIN-RAISER

than five or six persons in the auditorium of any theatre whose bill consisted of a poetic play. Even supposing that all these enthusiasts had paid for their seats, the effect on the management would be depressing. Poetic drama would have to languish in cupboards. This would be a pity. For is it not the highest form of drama? Luckily, the British public is nothing if not conscientious. So strongly does the Puritan instinct survive in it that it is irresistibly attracted towards whatever casts a gloom over it. It loves to suffer. Only through suffering does its spirit find peace and pride. In the music-halls it is happy, and, since, for it, the idea of happiness is hopelessly entangled with the idea of wickedness, it must impose on itself some kind of penance for its hall-goings. Shakespeare, hitherto, has been the only obvious penance open to it. But now, at length, has arisen another poet whom the managers are not unwilling to inflict on it. Mr Stephen Phillips has arisen. The public is very glad and grateful. If you have passed lately through the Haymarket, between the hours of six and seven p.m., you will have observed, outside the portals that lead to the pit and gallery of Her Majesty's Theatre, a long and serried queue of men and women, all barefooted and wearing hair-shirts. There is now, daily, a similar congress in King Street. For, on the sixth instant of this month, Mr George Alexander, cruel only to be kind, produced *Paolo and Francesca*, which, as all the world knows, is an essay in the highest form of drama.

It was a great occasion. The house looked very brilliant. Everyone appeared in a brand-new hair-shirt. The applause, from first to last, was ecstatic. Deep-sounding waves of rapture swept the auditorium from corner to corner. Delight surged to delirium, as in those strange rites whereat, in honour of some harsh deity, the prancing heathen maim themselves, madly glorying in their paroxysms of pain. Certainly, it was a great occasion. I was glad, next morning, to see that most of the dramatic critics had risen to it. I wish I could rise to it now. I wish I could rush, with reverent war-whoop, into a synthesis and analysis of all the impressions which *Paolo and Francesca*, as a piece of literature, left on me. But, somehow, my lungs and limbs fail me. I feel that I am too late. Not only during the past week, but also during the past year or two, so very much has been written about Mr Phillips's first dramatic work that I can find no new praise to deck it withal. Moreover, I myself, in these very columns, some little time ago, incidentally set forth my opinion of it. My opinion came to this: that the play was charming and delicate, and that it could not be too cordially welcomed; but that it was not fraught with the kind of original and simple beauty which bowls me (personally) over, and leaves me gasping; that it could never, for example, be mentioned in the same breath with such a work of original genius as that in which Maeterlinck treated the same subject —*Pelleas and Melisande*. And practically, that opinion is now the same as it was then. I will not re-inflict it on you in detail. Merely will I 'oblige' with a note or two about the production.

It is curious that no one, however expert, can, in reading a play, predict exactly how it will strike him in performance. One can say, roughly, that a play is utterly undramatic, and unfit for the stage, or that it is dramatic, and will come out well on the stage. But exactly how well it will come out remains a secret—till after the event. *Paolo and Francesca* is dramatic in a very high degree. The action is well-knit, it rises and falls to its climax in a thoroughly professional way. It is (I speak, of course, only for those who, like myself, are not aesthetically impervious to poetic drama) always interesting and exciting, except in the incidental scenes which Mr Phillips has introduced in order to brighten things up. These scenes are quite intolerable. They were bad enough between the covers of the book; but they are much worse on the stage. And the fact that they are so proves that Mr Phillips has written an even better play than we had imagined. We resent irrelevancy in proportion to our admiration for the main work. Mr Phillips has absolutely no talent for humour. He has so many other talents to display that I wonder why he should insist on displaying his lack of this one. The jocular soldiers in this play are even worse than the jocular gods in *Ulysses*. They ought to be cut mercilessly out. They are there, I suppose, because Shakespeare was addicted to comic relief. But that is really no excuse for them. Shakespeare had a very keen sense of humour, even though, after the lapse of three centuries, his jokes appeal less to the humorous than to the antiquarian sense in us. And, moreover, though Shakespeare's comic relief is interesting, we cannot but wish that he had not inserted it. It is a jarring interruption to ears attuned to tragedy. Time has taught us that in dramatic art one form should not be mixed up with another. If Mr Phillips were writing a modern tragedy, he would not be afraid of being serious throughout it. He would not dream of 'spatchcocking' into it scenes of irrelevant frivolity. Even Shakespeare, we may assume, thus 'spatchcocked' in order to propitiate the groundlings. 'Merrie England' would never have come to a theatre to be bored throughout a performance. The clown-scenes were so many sops, unwillingly thrown to them. But the Puritan movement has relieved our tragic dramatists of the necessity for such sop-throwing. Nay! I assure Mr Phillips that the bulk of his audiences must resent from its own point of view not less keenly than I do from mine his insistence on comic relief. They are not amused by the jokes, but they know that they are expected to laugh; and the mere thought of direct enjoyment strikes a discord in their mood.

I am not sure that the public, in its eagerness to mortify itself, would not rather have seen the play mounted according to the stern ideals of Mr Sidney Lee and the Elizabethan Stage Society, and acted by a company of amateurs. However, the love of beautiful sights that are not gaudily beautiful is not implanted in any great portion of the public; and in this production at the St James's the beauty of the backgrounds is of a sombre kind. The hall of the castle of Giovanni Malatesta in hung with dim tapestries, and even in Francesca's garden the roses are pale in the twilight of dawn. From first to last, there is no hint of the Lord Mayor's Show, or of the ballet at the Empire, or of the facade of the Alhambra, or of any of those things which minister truly to the lust of the public's eye, and, as for the performance, four years of observation have taught me that the only thing which the public really admires in a tragic mime is his or her capacity for making a great noise. Any mime who, at an important point of a tragedy, makes a great noise may always rely on a round of applause as soon as the great noise has subsided. It matters not that the noise be kakophonous, or be inappropriate, or that the maker of it be a duffer, without any rudimentary knowledge of his or her art; sheer lung-power, violently exercised, is all that is wanted. No, not quite all. Grimaces and violent contortions of the body must be added. At the St James's, fortunately, the mimes do not, with one exception, perform these dear tricks. Except by Miss Elizabeth Robins, who plays the part of Lucrezia, no passions are torn to tatters. For her, as an interpreter of strenuous emotion in modern realistic plays, I have an abiding admiration. But I am determined to forget her impersonation of Lucrezia as soon as a somewhat retentive memory will let me do so. Such shoutings, such stridings up and down and across the stage, such slappings of other people on the chest for sake of emphasising this or that point, such contractions and contortions as never were on land or sea! I longed for one brief interval of repose, of dignity. It was as much as I could do not to cry 'Hush! Sit down! Count twenty, and *then* speak!' I suppose that Miss Robins's over-acting was due to fear of an accusation of being 'modern'. Yet the real difference between the old and the new schools of acting lies less in the fact that the old mimes were tremendously ebullient than in the fact that they cared more than their successors for the beauty and dignity of port and gesture and elocution. I dare say that Miss Robins has toned down her performance since the first night, her own judgment being no longer obscured by fear that the stupid critics would call her 'Ibsenish'. Mr Alexander was powerful as Giovanni. It is always good to see him in some forthright part that demands power rather than subtlety. The parts of Paolo and of Francesca are parts for which suitable personalities are essential, and more important than anything else. Mr Henry Ainley, drawn from the inexhaustible company of Mr Benson, was exactly the right person to be Paolo. And Miss Evelyn Millard, though she did not play quite so simply and childishly as one could have wished, was as good a Francesca as could have been secured in this world of compromises.

*Worldham M.P.*, which precedes *Mlle Mars* at the Imperial Theatre, is not like most curtain-raisers. It is, at least, an effort to do something good. And though Mr Lewis Waller (as an unscrupulous financier, who suddenly blows out his brains because somebody else's ancestor had blown out his) has not a deeply impressive part, he plays it with exemplary fervour.

[*15 March 1902*]


## AN INDISCREET PLAY

Perpend. *Scene*: The hall of a country-house. *Time*: Midnight, or thereabouts. *Persons*: Prince and Princesse de Chalençon; he, French; she, English; both young. *Circumstances*: The Princess has just ordered out of the house a certain married lady, with whom, (there is good reason to believe) the Prince has arranged an elopement. Urged by a somewhat tedious uncle to 'win him, win him, win him', the Princess means to win the Prince. She is a resourceful person, with an elaborate and elastic method. First, she asks him to compliment her on her appearance. He does so, but coldly. Trying, then, the paternal instinct in him, she suggests a visit to the cradle-side of their child. He accepts the suggestion, but coldly. As they are starting cradlewards, the Princess perceives a brougham waiting outside. The Prince admits that he is going to drive in it to the station, thence to accompany the other lady to London. The Princess sends a telegram, withholding its contents from the inquisitive Prince. (In it she asks the other lady's husband to meet the train at the terminus.) She then declares that she will travel with her husband and the other lady. He demurs. She sulks, and kicks off one of her slippers. He restores it, but coldly. She kicks off the other. He restores that, but, again, coldly. She tells him that there is still half an hour to spare. He resigns himself. She tries to kill his purpose with ridicule, laughing loudly, prophesying pneumonia, advising him to put on his thickest tweed suit, and to have a foot-warmer in the brougham. He smiles, but coldly, and is not deflected. He offers to kiss her before he says good-bye. She shudders, and exclaims 'How dare you?' four times. Quickly recovering herself, she offers him a brandy-and-soda, a stirrup-cup, and a cigar. He stipulates for a mild cigar. She insists that it shall be a strong one. He lights a cigarette. She has a happy thought. Wouldn't he like to see her in her 'new negligée'? He assents, but coldly. Her maid is in an adjacent room, and will help her to put it on. But would not he himself take her maid's place? He refuses, politely. Very well, then: she will be back in a minute. The Prince walks about in a state of intense irritation. The Princess, 'off', calls out to him a well-known quotation from Robert Burns, and suggests that she too, if he whistle, will come to him. Presently she comes, telling him to keep his eyes shut till she permit him to open them. The lightly-clad apparition has not its due effect. The Prince praises it, but coldly. The Princess breaks down, passionately imploring him not to leave her. The Prince, at length, succumbs. A moment later, learning from her the contents of the mysterious telegram, he hardens his heart, orders the carriage, and drives off.

Such is the *scène-à-faire* in Mr Henry Arthur Jones's new play at the Duke of York's Theatre. No playgoer will assert that it is, as drama, a monotonous scene. On the contrary, no playgoer will deny that it is, from first to last, an ingeniously contrived excitement. Throughout it, one is anxious to know what will happen—'what will happen next' would be the more exact phrase. Nor, given the characters and the circumstances, will anyone maintain, in cold blood, that such a scene would be impossible in real life. If you take it (and by most of the critics such things always are taken) as ethical teaching, then, of course, there is nothing at all to be said for it. But I see no reason for confusing Mr Jones with the Princess's somewhat tedious uncle. Mr Jones does not subscribe, or wish to convert us, to the doctrine that a young wife, neglected by her husband, should bar no means of attracting his attention. He does not wish her to exploit herself, persistently, as preferable to a rival whom her husband openly persists in regarding as preferable to herself. But life does not always proceed exactly along such lines as Mr Jones, or any other one of us, would lay down for it. And Mr Jones, as a dramatist, has the right to represent life as it is. It is quite possible that some woman might behave as Mr Jones's Princess behaves. True, most women would not behave so. The behaviour is not typical. But a dramatist, in his search for material, must not be confined to typical instances. He has the right to draw his material from any corner, however devious, so it be a corner of the real world. Mr Jones had a perfect right to show us on the stage a young wife behaving in the shameless (and stupid) manner which I have described. Yet do I deplore and condemn the whole of that elaborate scene.

Perhaps my description of it jarred on you? I meant it to do so. I meant it to jar on you exactly as the original thing had jarred on me. I let flow just such an undercurrent of facetiousness as had been let flow by Mr Jones, in order that you might the quicklier sympathise with my dislike of *The Princess' Nose*, and with my objection to it as a work of art. The verriest skimmer through the articles I have written about the stage will not accuse me of having ranged myself among the fools who think that dramatists ought to keep their hands off unpleasant themes. The prettiness or ugliness of its theme makes no earthly difference to my pleasure in a play. Only, if the theme be ugly, I maintain that it must be handled in a special manner. It must be handled seriously, or not at all. In art there must be adjustment of manner to matter. An artist may treat as a laughing-matter anything that would make us laugh in real life. But anything that would pain or revolt us must be treated by him in grim earnest. There must be no chuckles from him, howsoever subdued, and no winks, how sly however. Else are we surely offended. I defy anyone not to be offended by the situation which Mr Jones had set before us, inasmuch as Mr Jones so obviously, and unaccountably, has meant us to be amused. If the scene stood by itself, as a little one-act play, it would be bad enough, by reason of its comic vein. But it is worse in relation to what precedes and follows it. For there we have not merely comedy, but fantastic farce. The explanation of the play's title is that the nose of the Princess, when she was at school, was red. Her rival, who was also her school-fellow, still twits her with this reminiscence. The solution of the play is that the rival is thrown out of her carriage against a motor and breaks her nose. I need neither commend nor disparage this invention: enough that it is an invention, and that it sets the whole work on a plane of fantasy. Some of the characters, moreover, are in themselves merely fantastic. There is a Mr Eglinton-Pyne, an altogether farcical character, who makes love to the Princess, assuming that his detection of her husband's infidelity will incline her towards himself. In the course of the scene which I have described, the Princess informs the Prince that someone has made love to her, and that, if she is deserted, she may go desperately far. I have said enough to show the fantasy of the surroundings of the scene. And it is this fantasy, even more than the comic treatment of the scene itself, which stirs distaste. For by us, in the theatre, the scene cannot be dissociated, however different it be, from its setting. And in a fantasy there is no excuse, no room, for anything that is unpleasant. Patient fidelity to life is the necesssary justification for showing us an unpleasant thing. If a man set out to invent, to embroider, his work must be all delightful. He must show us only things which are prettier, daintier, more amusing, than the things among which we live. We resent as wanton the display of a thing that is horrible. It may be, in itself, a true thing. But our minds have been set in a direction away from truth. Our ears are agog for fantasy. Everything has for them a fantastic sound. Thus, if a true thing be horrible, we murmur 'Why invent such horrors?' Rightly or wrongly, the playwright gets himself disliked. Wrongly, in that he was innocent of actual morbidness; rightly in that he had made a blunder in art.

I have now, I hope, justified the title of this article. Mr Jones's new play is an indiscretion, not only in the common sense of the word, as giving a chance to the detractors of our ablest playwright. It is an indiscretion, also, in the strict and literal sense—a failure to separate two things (in this case, realistic drama and fantastic drama) which ought to be kept apart.

It is admirably acted, however. Miss Irene Vanbrugh, as the Princess, is everything by turns, and nothing ill. Mr H. B. Irving, also, being as good a modern Frenchman as he has just been an Italian of the middle ages. Miss Gertrude Kingston plays with her usual aplomb and humour. Mr Cosmo Stuart cleverly caricatures his caricature of a part, and Miss Ethelwyn Arthur-Jones is quite delightful in a quite possible little part. But who is Mr Lennox Pawle? Why have I not often seen this ingenious and authoritative comedian?

[22 March 1902]

## DRURY LANE, AND WYNDHAM'S

It were beyond my ingenuity to prove *Ben Hur* a good play. I should shrink even from the task of proving it a bad or an indifferent play. It is not, from any obvious point of view, a play at all. However, it is an enormous success. For, though it panders not to the dramatic instinct. it satisfies fully, and in a new and startling way, three other instincts which are, perhaps, more strongly rooted in our populace.

Firstly, the sporting instinct. For this there is a chariot-race, with real chariots and real horses, which, if you look straight at them, really do seem to be rushing across the stage. The illusion is very cleverly contrived. To me, personally. it does not give any special delight. If I want to see a race, I prefer to see a real race. There is, in my opinion, a place for everything. There is a place for galloping horses, and a place for men and women quietly walking and talking. There is a race-course, and there is the stage of a theatre. I do not like the two places to be confused. If I were at Newmarket, and that the course had been cleared merely in order that Mr Arthur Collins might thereon 'present Klaw and Erlanger's stupendous production of *Ben Hur*', I should lodge a complaint with the Stewards. Conversely, at Drury Lane, I wished the horses away and asleep in distant stables. But the public does not share my views of local propriety. It loves nothing so well as to see something, which might be done quite easily in one place, being done despite terrific obstacles in another. The fact that the thing can always be done much better in the one place than it ever could be done in the other subtracts nothing at all from the public's innocent pleasure. Ingenuity against the nature of things: that is what most surely tickles the average Englishman. He likes to see a real race on a race-course. But an artificial race across a stage transports him, at one bound, into the seventh heaven.

Then, secondly, there is *Ben Hur's* appeal to the religious instinct. Throughout the play are many references to the Founder of our faith, and in one scene we have the actual representation of a miracle. Two lepers kneel down; a powerful flash-light is turned on them from above: presently, they rise from their knees, cleansed. This mode of representation is to me, certainly, unimpressive. But I do not go so far as to call it objectionable. I have always maintained that from drama sacred subjects should no more be excluded than from literature, or from painting, or from other art forms. Holding this view, I cannot object to a form of religious drama merely on the plea that it seems to me cheap and ludicrous. Temperaments and tastes differ. What touches religious emotion in one man leaves another man quite cold. Some of us are unaffected by the crude tract or gaudy chromolithograph which really does edify our neighbours. But we do not therefore brand such a tract or chromolithograph as an offence against piety. Its meaning we know to be reverent, and its effect we know to be, in many cases, edifying. Such a production as *Everyman*, given to us by the Elizabethan Stage Society, touches religious emotion in you or me, making no friction against our aesthetic sensibilities. But let us remember that it would produce little or no effect on the inaesthetic multitude, for whom, not less than for us, the Christian religion was founded. We have no more right to protest against the scene of the lepers in *Ben Hur* than would the inaesthetic multitude have to protest against *Everyman*, or against the Madonnas of Botticelli, or against the writings of John Henry Newman. Different kinds of religious art edify different kinds of people. And there, it seems to me, is an end of the matter.

The third appeal of *Ben Hur* is to the instinct of loyalty. Not long ago, I was considering here the well-known fact that an increase in the booking for a theatre follows, as the night the day, a visit paid to that theatre by a member of the royal family. That the King should visit Drury Lane and witness the performance of *Ben Hur* was no improbable or strange contingency. But, by a flash of genius in the management, the visit has been invested with a peculiar and compelling glamour. On the morrow of the visit, it was known in every corner of His Majesty's dominions that a special royal box had been constructed in the centre of the pit, and that from this coign of vantage His Majesty had graciously watched the procedure of the chariots and horses. Did ever the work of mortal playwright receive such an advertisement as that? Mr Matthew Arnold, who, in his day, suggested that we use royalty too frequently as a means of pushing this or that ware without inquiring whether it were a ware worthy of 'our *best* self', might, were he living at this hour, have been tempted to smile and be unkind. But Mr Arnold was notoriously superfine, and England hath no need of him. If royal boxes in the future be hastily constructed in the gallery, or even suspended from the ceiling, according to the nature of the production, we shall have no right at all to cavil. If there be any possible objection to them, let it be made not by us, but by their august occupants. Meanwhile *Ben Hur* will be irresistibly magnetic attraction.

Some weeks ago, I read that the author of the forthcoming play at Wyndham's Theatre was a very well-known novelist. Later, when his name was revealed, I chid myself for a grovelling ignorance. My self-respect returned after fruitless efforts to find anyone who *had* heard of Mr J. Dudley Morgan. I conjectured that the name was a pseudonym, taken as a shade against that light which beats yet more fiercely and impertinently on the playwright than on the novelist. The play itself presently confirmed the conjectures. I would wager that Mr J. Dudley Morgan is a lady.

One reason for my belief is that the heroine of the play is a lady who writes clever novels. I know no instance of such a heroine in a play or book written by a man. A clever man (and does not the writing of any book or play postulate some degree of cleverness?) does not like the notion of a lady novelist. He does not necessarily choose as heroine a pretty and helpless doll. A woman may be brave and energetic, even plain, without alienating his sympathy. But cleverness he resents in her, and a talent for writing he resents especially, as a trespass on his own ground. It never occurs to him to make her his heroine. If he trust himself to speak of her at all, he treats her as a butt for mere satire. This balance of injustice is redressed, however, by the self-same quality which has caused it—the quality of egoism. When a lady writes a play or a book, her natural instinct is to make a writer her heroine, And so, as soon as the author of *The End of a Story* revealed to us the cottage of Miss Eleanor Murray, the successful novelist—a little cottage at Stratford-on-Avon, with many tokens of its owner's love for flowers, and birds, and music—I knew that if, subsequently, the author were called forth, the apparition would be feminine. Unluckily, when the curtain fell, the audience did not insist on any apparition, and so my evidence is merely circumstantial.

My case, however, does not rest merely on the presentment of the heroine. It is upheld also by the general quality of the play. The main idea of the play is that the blameless daughter of a woman who has led an irregular life is unfit for marriage with a decent man. Mr Wyndham, as emotional raisonneur, propounds this idea, and but for its acceptance there were no material for the play. Even the mother herself is induced to accept it, and consequently to commit suicide. By this rash act, apparently, the taint of irrespectability is purged away from the daughter, and a happy ending is secured. This kind of tritely false and stagey tale, you argue, is as likely to be conceived by a male as by a female novice in dramaturgy. True; the novice of either sex is almost always reactionary. But the male novice is always clumsy in his technique, whereas the female, in virtue of her quicker adaptability, will set forth her ready-made materials in quite presentable form. *The End of a Story*, though not a masterpiece of skill, is decidedly neat and well put together. Such technical competence could not have been acquired by a man without years of practice. And he, in the lapse of those years, would have developed some originality, some sincerity of observation. Clearly, then, this play cannot have written by a man. I hope that the lady who wrote it will, when she comes to years of keener discretion, write a really interesting play. The trouble is that women, however nimble their aptitude for dramaturgy, do so seldom reach the stage of seeing, or thinking, or feeling, for themselves. . . . But I must not risk a charge of exemplifying that ungracious jealousy which I have attributed to other penmen.

Mr Wyndham, Miss Mary Moore, and Mr Alfred Bishop play as delightfully as ever in their several manners. But the signal thing in the production is the return of Mrs Bernard Beere to the stage. It is well to be reminded how fine an actress she is.

[ *19 April 1902* ]

## TWO ANTIQUE NOVELTIES IN DRAMA

A fashion paper for critics (why is there no such publication?) would tell us that the very latest mode is Optimism—Optimism in the very brightest colours and of the very amplest 'make'. This fashion for the coming Spring and Summer was set by (or, at least, finds its most ardent follower in) Mr G. K. Chesterton, that excited and exciting novice, *quem honoris causa nomino*. At the cradle-side of that infant Hercules, current Life and Literature appear not as a pair of horrid snakes to be grappled with and strangled, but as two dear, kind, good snakes to be kissed, and to be romped with, and to have a lusty admiration lisped and crowed over them from the tips of their tails to the tips of their tongues. Watching the roseate little Herculean contours rolling so blissfully among the coils, I cannot but wonder, with a sigh, what sort of dramatic critic Mr Chesterton would be. Would he be able to make a pet of our Drama? I suppose so. Even Mr Archer, born a judical pessimist, now mildly fondles in his bosom that same snake which, in his hot youth, he was so assiduously scotching. How he overcame those feelings of repulsion, how first the glow of this almost paternal tenderness for the monster came and suffused him, I cannot, for the life of me, conjecture. I can only envy him the mysterious soul-process which made him take that reptile to his bosom and brought that beautiful light into his eyes. For myself, I try hard to be an Optimist. Sometimes I almost persuade myself, through assuring you, that the stage is in rather a good way, that steady progress is being made, that the auguries for the future are very propitious. And then up, invariably, crops some grotesque and appalling fact to hit the poor little pretence on the head.

I wish I could hush up the grotesque and appalling fact of last Saturday. But it has already been fully reported in the Press, and my only course is to point for you its full significance. For your quicker grasp of this full significance, I offer you an hypothesis.

## TWO ANTIQUE NOVELTIES IN DRAMA

Suppose (a golden dream!) that the publication of books were as difficult and infrequent an affair as the production of plays. Suppose, in other words, that a publisher could produce, at most, only two or three books in one season. And then suppose that one of the most powerful and respected and popular publishing-firms announced in its advertisements as 'now ready' a new edition of some crude and stupid version which had been made of a German masterpiece, twenty years ago, by an inferior amateur in poetry. Suppose, too, that another firm, of not less repute, announced simultaneously a new edition of a novel published about forty years ago, and written by a novelist whom, even in his heyday, no discreet critic would have called great. Now tell me what, in such a case, would be your feelings? Would you not be ashamed, downcast, at the thought that the national faculty for literature had sunk so low that the best of our publishers had found no new MSS which could, even with their advantage of novelty, compete as books with even the inferior output of the past? And, if you care, as I presume you do care, for drama as well as for literature, were you not likewise ashamed and downcast, and had you not exactly similar cause to be ashamed and downcast, last Saturday evening, when (after *Caste* had been revived in the afternoon, without one word of explanation or apology, at the Haymarket Theatre), *Faust* was revived, unblushingly, at the Lyceum Theatre?

The late W. G. Wills, author of this *Faust*, was a salient figure in his time, and still is interesting as a type of that ineffectually artistic Bohemianism which was so common in the seventies and now is so very rare. I remember seeing him, very many years ago, on the King's Road at Brighton—a very old and bent man, white-bearded, with a snuff-coloured cape hanging from his shoulders, and a wide black sombrero shading his eyes. One of my elders and betters presented me to him, and he spoke to me kindly and playfully. All who knew him bear witness to his very generous, simple, lovable nature, to the originality and distinction of his mind, and to his keen instinct for the fine arts. It is a pity not to leave that picture as it is; but criticism —especially criticism in posterity—must concern itself with results rather than with intentions. Mr Wills had, besides his truly artistic instincts, a measure of executive ability. For instance, he painted many pictures. All that is known of them now is that they were very bad. In Mr Henry James's 'Madonna of the Future', the old painter was pathetic, as being one who, with an exquisite knowledge and love of his art, and with all a painter's instincts, had so little executive ability that he never could begin to paint the picture of his dreams. He died before a blank canvas. The case of Mr Wills seems to me even more pathetic. He had executive ability, but of a bad kind. His hand was free enough, but only to distort his pre-conceptions, only to multiply daubs. There is this decent mitigation of the pathos: that his pictures are not hunted out and re-varnished and exhibited. I wish that Sir Henry Irving, in similar piety, had let lie the prompt-copy of *Faust* in its shroud of cobwebs. Mr Wills, I doubt not, reverenced Goethe's work, and was wont to say eloquent and illuminative things about it. But alas! so soon as he laid his executive hands on it, how piteously it fared! Faust became a walking-gentleman—an operatic tenor with nothing to sing. Margaret became a self-conscious doll, made to soliloquise.

> 'I wonder will my happy, simple life
> Ever be dreamful and disturbed'

exactly in the manner of the 'serio-comic' artiste who sings

> 'I've just come up from the country
> And I don't yet know what's what'.

And Mephistopheles suffered a second fall, down into the region of the lower comic papers. Certainly, this version of *Faust* is an altogether dreadful affair, and I cannot pass too quickly from it to its interpretation. Mr H. B. Stanford does nothing to redeem the title-part from its insignificance. Mr Laurence Irving, on the other hand, does too much to redeem the part of Valentine; he is really too Titanic; the whole terrestrial globe—to say nothing of the stage at the Lyceum—seems to 'give' under him. He has great gifts, as I have testified in the past; but he has still much to learn from his father—lessons of restraint, dignity, and so forth. How Sir Henry contrives to be dignified as Mr Wills's Mephistopheles I do not profess to explain. I only know that he does invest the part with dignity, and with that air of magnetic mystery which is one of the peculiar secrets of his being. As Margaret, Miss Cecilia Loftus, though, now and again, she recalled for us her old days by imitation of Miss Ellen Terry, showed that she had learnt quite enough technique to go on with, and that she had kept all that charm of personality to which, eight years ago, London succumbed. In her own modest way, she did for Margaret what Sir Henry did for Mephistopheles.

The pill of *Caste* might, at least, have been gilded for us. Appropriate costumes and scenery would have been some solace for the play's revival. *Ours* is a far sillier play; yet, when Mr Hare produced it in the proper way, it became quite a fascinating entertainment, whereas *Caste*, which he dressed up to date, was quite uninteresting except as a vehicle for acting. Even in regard to acting, it is important that the clothes of the period be worn. Eccles, Sam Gerridge and Polly are human characters, as true to nature now as in the 'sixties; but on the surface they are quite out of date. Their language and behaviour are not those of low life in the twentieth century. Their interpreters must switch themselves off into the past; and how can they do this properly in clothes which tie them to the present? We should smile if we could see an actor of the eighteenth century playing Julius Caesar in a periwig; yet really that sight were not one whit more absurd than the present sight at the Haymarket. It were less absurd, indeed. For the actor of the eighteenth century, having no knowledge of archaeology, would not be distracted by the absurdity of his costume. Whereas, in these researchful times, the embarrassment of the misclad actor is painfully obvious. Allowing for the self-consciousness induced by anachronism, I think the performance at the Haymarket is very good all round. Mr Maude is not genial as Eccles—too bent on a minute study of mere drunkenness and senility; but Miss Marie Tempest as Polly, and Mr Giddens as Sam, are very jolly and spontaneous. All the other parts, both those which are dummies and those which are dull caricatures, are honoured far beyond their deserts.

[*3 May 1902*]

## THE THRESHOLD OF A THEATRE

If Aristotle were alive, and had dropped his republican heresies, he would define the virtue of loyalty to the throne as a mean between the extremes of seditiousness and flunkeyism. Had he, moreover, been a guest at the recent banquet in Burlington House, or had he read a report of it, he might have been tempted to think that

England, receding from the former extreme (to which, so lately as thirty years ago, she had been stumbling), had not unconsciously overstepped the mean. In walking briskly backwards there is always the danger of going too far, and Aristotle would, I think, have found in the coupling of the toast of Literature with the name of Sir Donald Mackenzie Wallace reason to suppose that we had gone rather too far. 'Who', I mused, over the report of this toast, 'is Sir Donald Mackenzie Wallace?' Off-hand, I should have guessed his name to be that of some eminent surgeon. 'But', I reflected, 'the books written by eminent surgeons are not classified as literature'. And then suddenly I remembered that there was a book about the recent voyage of the Prince and Princess of Wales, and that Sir Donald Mackenzie Wallace was its author. I do not profess to have been surprised, but pained I was, to think that at what is, after all, the most distinguished of all annual gatherings of variously eminent men, the finest of our arts should have been answered for by a gentleman who had nothing to do with it. Living are twenty writers, at least, of whom any one might have risen to his feet without making the toast ridiculous and himself ridiculous. There are three or four writers of whom any one would have shed on the occasion a great lustre, being more than worthy of his task. Strange that these persons should have been ignored in favour of a person whose one apparent claim was that he had been by Royalty chosen to do, and that he had done, very decently, a bit of official hack-work! It is well that Royalty should grace with its presence, and with its voice, a symposium of painters. But if mere attachment to the Prince of Wales's suite is supposed by these painters to make of a word-stringer a pre-eminent man of letters, why were not those of the Prince's equerries who happen to have been in the Army or Navy called on to respond to the toast of the United Services? Such equerries have, at any rate, been real soldiers, real sailors, in however humble a way; whereas no sane person will assert that Sir Donald Mackenzie Wallace ever has been, in however humble a way, a man of letters. Let Mr Spencer Wilkinson and those others who feel that we do not, as a nation, take questions of national defence at all seriously, extract such comfort as may be for them in this inconsistency. And let anyone who deplores our indifference to literature find cause for mirth, rather than for wrath, in the quaint farce of Sir Donald's glory.

One would have supposed that, in the circumstances, this sponsor for literature would emit warily a few vague platitudes of optimism and then resume his seat. That, I think, would have been the best course. Sir Donald took another. Boldly he bemoaned the absence of 'giants' from modern literature. 'Where', he inquired, 'are the Scotts, the Byrons, the Keatses, the Tom Moores, or, to come down to more recent days, the Thackerays, the Dickenses, the Tennysons, the Brownings of our degenerate age?' Surely that artless intercalation of 'the Tom Moores' is as neat a give-away as ever fell from the lips of exalted incapacity. And, in the lifetime of Mr George Meredith (I name but him, not because no one else, in other ways of literature, could be mentioned in the same breath with him, but in order to make my point briefly), is it not almost as neat another give-away to complain that we have no 'giants', and are 'wandering in a wilderness of mediocrity'? Mr Meredith is a poet, a thinker, a wit, an all-round creator, of such force and dimensions that 'the Dickenses' seem clowns beside him, and 'the Thackerays' pantaloons. Perhaps Sir Donald does not know Mr Meredith's books? Perhaps he does? Either horn of the dilemma impales him equally well. He might escape, narrowly, with the plea that he had ignored Mr Meredith as belonging already to a past generation, and with the contention that in the present generation there is no writer whose proportions can be matched with his. It is, indeed, quite true that the stock of *great* writers seems to have been exhausted among us. ('Seems' I say because every generation is apt to belittle its great men. But I fancy that my precaution in this matter is superfluous.) At the same time, there is a wretched lack of perception in accusing the present age of 'mediocrity' in its writers. You apply the term 'mediocre' to a man who performs his task only half as well as it might be performed. For example, Mrs Humphry Ward is mediocre, because she, working on a large scale, lacks the requisite degree of inspiration, and therefore writes dull books. We have many writers who fail as she does, and many more who fail on smaller scales. But one judges the literature of an age not by its failures, but by its successes. And we have now in England a quite considerable number of writers—poets, essayists, novelists—who, not being great, and being wise enough not to work on great scales, constantly attain to something very like perfection in what they set themselves to do. It is in the light of these writers that this age's literature must be judged. Accordingly, this is not an age of 'mediocrity' in literature. For these writers are not 'mediocrities'. They are little masters. Accordingly, this is an age of good, but not great, literary art. Had Sir Donald said something to this effect, the impertinence of his saying anything at all would have been somewhat mitigated.

The most salient instance of a writer who could not be called a 'great' writer, and could not be called a 'mediocre' writer, is Mr Henry James, that perfect master of a small method, and, accordingly, that perfect type of the modern artist in literature. Manywise very like unto him, in the younger generation, appears Mr G. S. Street. Both writers, in their outlook on life, have the same fastidious coyness, the same unwillingness to stray beyond a certain highly-civilised radius, the same fear of penetrating into the passions of those who revolve in that radius, the same way of looking askance at a definite event in that radius, as though it were a rather vulgar thing, to be hushed up, even to be denied. Like Mr James, Mr Street is chiefly a student of that portion of life which may be called 'manners'. He confines his gaze to the manifestations of the vaguer, lighter griefs and joys which befall such mankind as he admits into his ken; and his gaze, like Mr James's, is a finely meticulous register; and his brain, like Mr James's, receives and studies the record of his eyes in a spirit of grave irony. Each writer is essentially a critic, detached, standing aside to watch, an outsider seeing 'most of the game'—of as much of the game, that is, as he cares to see. Each is content to observe human life as the average man observes animal life through the bars of the Zoological Gardens. Each, accordingly, is an untrammelled artist, having no moral purpose to serve or to be served by. Each accepts all that he sees without any wish to protest against it, even as the visitor to the Zoological Gardens will accept quite calmly this or that interesting convention which the animals obey, because he is not one of the animals. Each has the same sense of humour, the same smile. There is, however, this difference between them: Mr James is a cosmopolite, while Mr Street is an Englishman, who came early under the influence of Mr Henley, that patriot. Accordingly, Mr Street, studying English life, has moments when he imagines himself on the other side of those bars, in with those other animals, and then his absorbed patriotism leads him to accept everything as being for the best in that best of all possible cages. He becomes, as Mr James never becomes, genial. And sometimes his geniality overflows into actual and very delightful farce.

In one of these interludes he wrote a play, *Miss Bramshott's Engagement*, which has just been produced, as curtain-raiser, at the Prince of Wales's Theatre. I wish it had been produced there a little earlier, for then Sir Edward Poynter might by its princely venue have been moved to couple his toast of literature with the name of Mr Street. I wish, too, that I had not lingered here so long, talking at large, on the threshold of the theatre. For now I have not time to do justice to Mr Street's play. Enough that it is conceived in his most amusing manner, and executed with a deftness which makes me confident that the stage will know more of him anon. So, when you go to the Prince of Wales's, go early. I am afraid I cannot counsel you to stay late. *The President*, the main item of the programme, is a feeble show, not redeemed even by Mr Hawtrey's art.

[ *10 May 1902* ]

## MISS SYRETT'S PLAY

It is Whitsuntide. You, reader, who have just subsided comfortably into a railway-carriage, pray drop this *Review* as soon as the engine whistles its way out of the terminus, and look out of the window, steadfastly, until the green fields appear.... Now, what have you seen? Mile after mile of little squalid houses huddled beneath the line, most of them having narrow, walled-in strips of mud—gardens —in which ragged and dingy linen hangs out to dry. And beyond those houses, an inginite panorama of wretched chimney-pots and roofs, topping, presumably, houses which are counterparts of those immediately beneath you. An infiinite panorama of meanness, ugliness, hopeless and helpless poverty.... And now, if the sight suggests nothing to you, resume forthwith your reading of this *Review*. But it is probable that you are lost in a vague pity and wonder—a vague pity for all those fellow-creatures, and a vague wonder how and why on earth they continue to exist, quietly, and without obvious rebellion, as though such existence were worthy to be continued. You have read, now and again, of some hideous act of violence wreaked on some human symbol of things as they are. And you have agreed with the general comments that the wretch who did the deed must undoubtedly be a lunatic. But, in your present mood, you may be inclined to question whether you can reconcile with sanity the patient endurance of the majority. How is it, you may be wondering, that these myriads of creatures, starved and stunted, deprived of all semblance of joy in life, do not feel themselves goaded irresistibly to uprise, and to defy and overturn the injustice of society, to assert and win for themselves, as men of like passions with ourselves, those rights from which they are now precluded by mere accident of birth? And perhaps, casting about you, you will come to my own conclusion that it is stupidity, a lack of imagination, which staves off such an upheaval. These unfortunate fellow-creatures have not enough imagination to be envious of us, cannot conceive for themselves another life than that which they are leading, and so, though they are not happy, are content—content to be miserable. A little more alertness of mind in them, and then—the deluge? You remember, with a start, that we are educating their children, compulsorily. Themselves are slow and stupid, but their children are becoming daily sharper-witted. When all these children shall have grown up, having a keen sense of values, being able to differentiate between the injustice of Nature and the injustice of Man, knowing themselves to be not brutes born beneath our level, but fellow-beings whom we keep down....

At present, luckily for our peace, the spirit of intelligent revolt is to be found only in the breasts of those well-bred and well-educated young women who by poverty are compelled to spend their lives in some kind of unattractive drudgery, and are thus just cut off from that kind of easy and pleasant life which, but for their poverty, would have been theirs. Too fastidious to associate on equal terms with the class with which they are in contect, and too poor and too busy to associate on any terms with their own class (even if their own class encouraged them at all to do so), they are peculiarly stranded, thrown back on themselves and on the contemplation of their wretched present and future. Having little or no chance of marriage, they know that they will probably go down to their graves without ever getting off the miserable path which they are treading. Between them and their graves lies one long, bleak, steep vista of drudgery. There is no apparent escape for them except in a defiance of that moral code to which instinctively they cling. In such a life as theirs, in such bitterness as that life must foster in them, what material for a modern dramatist! But Mr Pinero, Mr Grundy, and their kind, will none of it. They, after due consideration, point out to us that only among the leisured classes are possible those spiritual complications which are the stuff of drama: the squalid or dowdy toilers have no time for such nonsense. And so it is but one bashful novice in dramaturgy, Miss Netta Syrett, who has ventured to try to make something out of the kind of life which I have described. Nor, needless to say, has her play been produced by any manager as a possible 'commercial asset'. But for a casual jest made by Mr George Alexander to amuse the Playgoers' Club, and by that Club's committee turned to serious and unexpected account, *The Finding of Nancy* would never, probably, have been produced at all. All thanks, therefore, to the committee of the Playgoers' Club. For I do not hesitate to say that in my time there has been nothing on the stage so interesting, so impressive, so poignant, as the first act of Miss Syrett's play. The three following acts were not, in my opinion, nearly up to the mark which Miss Syrett had set for herself; but that first act, in its simple strength, is enough to make her in my eyes a more important person than a score of ordinary fashionable dramatists rolled into one.

Nancy Thistleton, type-writer; Isabel Ferris, teacher in an art-school; both of them well brought up, young, pretty, penniless beyond their earnings, and almost friendless. To the room of Nancy comes Isabel, neither having seen the other for some months. They have tea and compare notes. Isabel is a meek, acquiescent creature, who sadly accepts things as they are. Nancy is high-spirited, romantic, angry that things are not as they ought to be. She is appalled by the facts of her life, of her friend's life, of the lives led by hundreds of girls like them. Deliberately she enumerates these facts, sums them up, and passes on them the judgment of her heart's despair. Her friend can plead nothing in extenuation; she is bewildered at hearing spoken what she knows to be the very truth; she can only entreat Nancy to acquiesce as she does, not to do anything wrong. She knows that there is a man, a journalist, who often comes to Nancy's rooms, gives her little presents, takes her to theatres. Has he offered to marry her? No, he is a married man. Isabel is troubled. Nancy reassures her: she will do nothing wrong; but why should she give up seeing this man? He loves her, she likes him. He is the one friend she has—the one ray of light in her life. Isabel argues, persuades her that it is wrong and dangerous to see him. Nancy promises, at length, to see him no more. But fate decrees otherwise. The man comes, and she sees him. He has been offered an appointment in Vienna. It is his duty to accept it. He longs to refuse it, to stay here in London. Only, he will not stay as a mere friend; he loves her too much for that. Her whole nature shrinks from his proposal. She is not angry, she understands; but he must go. The door closes after him, and down she sits before her type-writer. She strikes a few keys, and then, with a sob, rushes to the door, calling her lover back.

That is a rough outline of the first act, which, as filled in by Miss Syrett with dialogue of amazing force and naturalness, gives one the impression (so rare in the theatre) of something that really matters, something that is in direct relation to a general reality. I wish Miss Syrett had left that scene to stand by itself—a *tranche de la vie*. Of course it would not have been quite satisfying. We should have wanted to know what happened after this prelude to a new life. But it would have been much better than knowing what, according to Miss Syrett, actually did happen. Doubtless, in her heart, Miss Syrett was anxious to keep her drama on the plane of simple and significant sincerity in which she had begun it. Only she succumbed to the base fear of being thought not to know anything about 'the requirements of the stage'. And so off she whisked her three characters to the Riviera, and there commingled them with a whole crowd of other, mostly irrelevant, characters, and invented a great many possible but not inevitable circumstances, and let up to a mild *coup de théâtre* for the close of the third act, and a conventional happy ending for the last act, *et patati et patata*. Mixed up with these devices there is still plenty of good work, especially at the beginning of the second act. But the general impression is of a decline into theatricals. It is not my business to re-write Miss Syrett's last three acts for her. But I may, without impertinence, suggest to her that, if she ever re-write them for herself, she will find plenty of the right material in a conflict of Nancy's natural respect for the moral code and her delight in her emancipation from the life she had been leading. This would be a conflict similar to that which occurs in *Evelyn Innes*; and its close would, perhaps, have to be similar to the close of that one. But no matter. In any art, only a weakling need fear to do what has been done before. And Miss Syrett is no weakling except when she tries, as in the last three acts, to beat the weaklings on their own ground.

Miss Lilian Braithwaite, who appeared as Nancy, ought to be very grateful to Miss Syrett, and Miss Syrett ought to reciprocate the emotion. Miss Braithwaite's whole performance was admirable in its simple and sincere power. The part of Isabel fell to Miss Madge McIntosh, another actress who has intelligence and sensibility as well as charm. Mr Aubrey Smith, in manner and costume, was more like a cavalry officer than an obscure journalist. He came amiss in the milieu of the play. But he did his best.

[ *17 May 1902* ]


## MR HAWTREY, RECURRING

I should like to make a collection of those dear cant-phrases without which no leading article is complete, nor any serious conversation in a club. I should give one of the places of honour to 'This is an age of specialism'. It is such a very great favourite of all our oracles and owls, for it has so very impressively the air of being a curious and profound *aperçu*, and is all the time a vapid platitude, committing its enunciator to nothing. For what does it mean? This: that in our age the man who has the best chance of success is he who devotes himself to one kind of work. If you think for a moment, you will see that this would be equally true of any other age in the world's history. As in the age of Mr Chamberlain, so in the age of Pericles or Chaucer or whom you will, a baker who merely baked must have baked, on the whole, better than the baker who also shod horses; and a smith who merely shod horses must have shod them, on the whole, better than the smith who lightly oscillated between anvil and oven. Accordingly, the mere baker and the mere smith must have earned, in the long run, more silver than the baker-smith and the smith-baker. As in the trades, so in the arts. Only more so. For no man is a born smith or a born baker, whereas men may be born writers, or born painters, or born to excel in some other art. Thus, by confining himself to one art, a man is not only likelier than the pluralist to master that art's technique, but he shows also that he has a strong natural bent in the direction of that art. Accordingly, people are more likely to believe in him and to patronise his wares. Furthermore, if he confine himself to one of the many forms of his art—one of the many species in the genus by him chosen, then he will show that he has a strong natural bent for that one form or species; and thus the number of his competitors before the public will be appreciably reduced. Furthermore, if he do this one thing always in the same manner, then he will show that he has a vital personality to express. For it is only the colourless, derivative person who is able to hop from manner to manner. The person who really exists on his own account, the person whom we call a personality, may develop his manner, but he cannot change it. And in art it is personality which is of greatest account, whether you look from the artistic or from the commercial standpoint.

Look, from the commercial standpoint, at the art of acting. In this art the predominance of personality is not greater than in the other arts, but it is more obvious, inasmuch as the actor uses his personality in a direct way, through his own limbs and face and voice (usually without serious attempt to disguise them), instead of using it through such abstract media as painted canvas or printed pages. Enumerate the highly successful actors on the English stage, and you will find that the baker's dozen is composed almost entirely of actors who are immediately and definitely recognisable as themselves—actors who are for ever doing the same kind of thing in the same kind of way. The kind of thing that any one of them is always doing may not be a great kind of thing; and his way of doing it may not be a great kind of way. But that does not matter. His way of doing it is his own way, separate from the way of anyone else. His mere name conjures up a definite image, definite memories and anticipations. He is, in fact, a personality. And therefore he is a successful actor. You might argue, academically—and I am sure that you would, if you were a dramatist—that actors ought to be able to merge themselves utterly in various parts, and to adapt their methods to all those various forms of drama which Polonius rolled over his tongue. Also, it is quite true that we have at this moment one or two highly successful English actors who do 'impersonate' all kinds of different characters, and who do launch out from comedy into tragedy, thence into melodrama, thence into farce, and so forth, in a bewildering cycle. At first sight, this happy possession of ours seems to be an argument against the necessary connection between personality and success. But it is not really so. Our one or two versatile actors have succeeded, not by reason of their versatility, but in despite of it.

They have succeeded, like the rest, in virtue of personality. Born with that gift, they cannot conceal it, much as they may wish to. They can 'impersonate' only in the sense that they can impose themselves on this or that character so strongly and so ingeniously that it surrenders itself wholly to them, becomes inseparable from them. They are still specialising in self; and the public, if it could truly formulate its pleasure, would say, not 'This actor *is* this character', but 'This character *is* this actor'. Genuine versatility in acting is precluded by personality. There are on the stage many scores of really versatile actors. And very useful they are for the filling-up of casts in which suitable personalities cannot be found for all the parts. But they do not draw large salaries. They get no rounds of applause. They come on, they go off, unobtrusive helpers, now in one theatre, now in another. They grow unobtrusively old, and to the last they can, at a pinch, undertake juvenile parts, and acquit themselves creditably. When they die, there is an unobtruisve paragraph about them in the *Era*. Neither in life nor in death do they get anything like their deserts. But then, all round, the world is full of such injustice. What we are born with counts for so much more than what we can acquire. What we can do matters so much less than what we are. All the world's a stage, and all the applause is for the players who happen to be blest with personality.

Than Mr Charles Hawtrey I know not (in my own province) a more lustrous example of this law. No one with a sense of verbal values would call him a 'great' actor. No portents can have marked his nativity. No divine flame can ever have hovered about his brow. The Elements cannot claim the credit of having composed him. His soul is not comic. He is not more than life-sized. He is of the earth earthy, of this island insular, of the west end of this metropolis occidentally metropolitan. He has never thrilled us to terror or to pity, never laid a spell on our imagination, never touched the chords of our hearts. Nor could he ever perform any of these noble tricks, even if he tried till crack of doom. But, happily, he never has tried, never will try. He is content to be himself, and his self is a very peculiar and delightful affair. What playgoer does not know it— that large, neat, sleek, amiable, imperturbable presence; that vacant smile; that vacant stare; that purr; in fine, that baffling blend of a cat and a baby and a man of the world? How much is summed up for us in the dissyllable 'Hawtrey'! He never plays any part but one

—a 'Hawtrey part'. But, through long practice, how exquisitely he plays it! No piece in which he plays it, however bad the piece be, is foredoomed to failure. And a piece that has any merit at all is almost certain to be a triumph by reason of him.

The play in which he is now appearing at the Prince of Wales's was written by Mr George Arliss, and is entitled *There and Back*. It is, as its name suggests, a farce of the conventional kind. Two husbands going away for a holiday, two wives remaining at home, a lady of doubtful reputation intervening, secret change of husbands' plans, complications, disclosures, lying explanations, reconciliations: you know the kind of thing. But, though the scheme is trite, the management of the story is quite ingenious in its details, and there is a great deal of real and fresh fun in the dialogue and in the 'business'. Mr Arliss has done very well what he set out to do, and deserves his luck in having secured Mr Hawtrey for the part of one of the two husbands. It is a pity that Mr Hawtrey could not secure another Mr Hawtrey for the part of the other husband. In farce-writing the old trick of reduplicating a character is quite justifiable: it intensifies the fun, even as the reduplication of a beautiful object in a room intensifies that beauty, making us realise it (we know not why) more clearly. But it is essential that both the doubles should be played by actors with some affinity to each other. In no possible respect is there any affinity between Mr Hawtrey and Mr Arthur Williams. In his own way, Mr Williams is an admirable actor; but his method wars against Mr Hawtrey's, and Mr Hawtrey's wars against his. Each detracts from the other what he ought to add. This fault cannot be found with Miss Helen Macbeth and Miss Henrietta Watson, who play (delightfully) the two wives. Miss Beatrice Ferrar, as the intervening lady, repeats the fatiguing little failure that she made in a similar part a few weeks ago.

[*31 May 1902*]


## A NEW PLAY AND AN OLD

Experience has taught me that the theatrical performance given in aid of this or that deserving charity is very seldom a deserving thing in itself. Its common form is a tedious, incoherent medley of snippets, a scratch-rally of eminent mimes in a hurry and obscure mimes in a panic. The ordinary member of the public, doubtless, can sit it out in patience, buoyed up by the consciousness of having paid a high price for his seat. But the critic, not having disbursed a penny, is apt to judge the affair on its own merits, and to snatch the earliest chance of folding his programme and stealing silently away. The performance given last Saturday night at the Garrick Theatre in aid of the Queen's Fund for Soldiers and Sailors was an agreeable exception to the rule. True, it began with a concert which—stay! that is not my province. But after nine o'clock (when Sir Squire Bancroft had read Mr Owen Seaman's very graceful ode to the Queen—a set of ceremonial verses which had the rare advantage of a subject inspiring sentiments apart from flunkeyism) the programme consisted of one carefully prepared item: *The Bishop's Move*, a new comedy in three acts, written by Mrs Craigie and Mr Murray Carson. I presume that Mr Carson contrived the plot, and that Mrs Graigie wrote the dialogue. I commend Mr Carson, heartily, for not having succumbed to the fear of being twitted with an inadequate share in the collaboration. He might, doubtless, had he cared to do so, have invented the scenario of a strong, ambitious, complicated drama, full of passion and incident. This would have won him many compliments from the average critic, and many condolences on Mrs Craigie's failure to do justice to it. For Mrs Craigie would, undoubtedly, have done justice to it. Knowing that, and knowing the line in which Mrs Craigie excels, he gracefully effaced himself, adumbrating the slightest, simplest trifle of a plot—a mere fine-spun cobweb in the air. And the result is a quite delightful and distinguished little comedy, for which, in strict justice, both collaborators deserve equal praise. Mrs Craigie's talent is essentially and exquisitely feminine. She has not the strength and grip for doing good work on a large scale. But for work on a small scale her neatness and lightness of hand are quite invaluable. When she handles high philosophy, she is apt to be rather dull. When she goes for large passions, she is apt to seem rather tame. But when she is content with the artistic limitations of her sex, when she confines herself to little light things, there is not in England a lady whose work can be compared with hers. None has so subtle a sense for the airier emotions of her fellow men and women, none so quick a sympathy for what is nice in them, none so delicate a way of satirising what is not nice in them, none so dainty and ingratiating a wit, none so sure a choice of appropriate words, and so sure an ear for pretty cadences of words. She is not, being a woman, a great creative artist, but she does happen to be a very exquisite artist, capable of very exquisite effects when she does the right kind of work. In *The Bishop's Move* she started with a scheme exactly suited to her talent—a scheme, I hope, after her own heart. Behold the Abbey of Veyle, and the Bishop of Rance, and his young nephew, Mr Francis Hericourt, wavering in his decision to enter the priesthood, for that he is under the spell of the enchanting Duchess of Quenten, whose wealth, if she marry again, will pass to the Abbey. The Duchess herself is fascinated by Mr Hericourt, though she is senior by a decade, and thinks him rather stupid. She is not at all sure that she would not marry him, much as she dislikes the prospect of poverty. Miss Barbara Arreton also adores this young man. She is his equal in age and in intelligence. He is half in love with her, despite his devotion to the Duchess. Such are Mrs Craigie's materials. At first I supposed that the Duchess was merely pretending to be in love with the young man, that she was luring him away from the Abbey merely for Miss Arreton's sake. I supposed that the Bishop's move was directed to making her marry the young man, and so securing her fortune for the Church. This would have made a stronger conflict, undoubtedly. But, for that reason, it would not have suited Mrs Craigie's talent so well as the conflict which actually occurs—the Bishop, won over to Miss Arreton's side, trying, in the interest of human happiness against the interest of the Church, to make the Duchess hand the young man over to the girl who loves him more than she does, and whom he loves (unconsciously) more than he loves her. This is just the right kind of slender framework for Mrs Craigie's embroideries. I wish I had space in which to describe the many little ingenious touches of which the play is composed. I must content myself with one example. The Bishop has just wrung from the Duchess an admission that she does not think his nephew a brilliant boy: he has not much to say for himself, and what he does say is rather commonplace. Presently, little Miss Arreton comes in. She has been for a walk with the Bishop's nephew. 'And what did you talk about?' asks the Duchess 'Oh', replies the girl, '*I* didn't talk at all. I only listened. I never do anything but listen when I am with him'. 'Really? And what does he talk to you about?' 'Oh everything, everything. He is so extraordinarily clever. He has such a wonderful insight into character' &c. &c. Thus is the Duchess made to feel the disparity of years between herself and him. What could be more prettily ironic than this scene, more tenderly humorous, truer to reality? And in such scenes as this the whole play abounds. The critics have generally condemned it as 'too thin'. As usual! 'These slices of bread-and-butter are quite uneatable. They are not beef-steaks.'

Neither Mr Bourchier, as the Bishop, nor Miss Violet Vanbrugh, as the Duchess, showed a nice appreciation of the difference between beef-steaks and bread-and-butter. Miss Vanbrugh did with all her might and main what ought to have been touched so lightly. She behaved so strenuously that she had to assume a forced laugh, all the while, lest we should fancy that the play was a tragedy. Such compromises are rather distressing. The part of the Bishop is a part requiring a light touch, with much grace and dignity of demeanour. It is not a horse-collar to be grinned through. But as such, alas! it was handled by Mr Bourchier. Mr H. B. Warner chose to make the young man seem rather sillier and feebler than the authors can have meant him to be. Indeed, the one really good performance was given by Miss Jessie Bateman, as the *ingénue*. This had the charm of real sensibility, real understanding, so rare among actresses who still look girlish.

Take it all round, I suppose *The Merry Wives of Windsor* is the wretchedest bit of hack-work ever done by a great writer, and by us condoned for the sake of the love we bear him. If this jumble of a play, in whose facile coarseness can be discerned hardly one gleam of genuine humour, was really written to please Queen Elizabeth, let us hope that Shakespeare underrated the taste of that remarkable woman. Else will its revival hardly seem to us a felicitous way of celebrating the coronation of one of her successors. However, in this production at Her Majesty's the acting, not the play, is the thing. Mr Tree's Falstaff is as prodigious a feat of impersonation as ever. It is difficult for us, to whom Mr Tree's personality is so familiar through photographs in the illustrated papers, to accept him as a perfect Falstaff. But that difficulty is due to the inelasticity of our imaginations. If we project ourselves into the state of knowing nothing whatsoever about Mr Tree as he is, we get, I think, the true impression of a fat mind in a fat body. Mr Kemble, as Doctor Caius, and Mr Lionel Brough, as the Host of the Garter, are as fruity and authoritative as ever. And Mrs Tree once more is charming as Anne Page, though she infuses into the part a pathos which would have startled the author. But of course the great feature of the production is the sensational juxtaposition of Mrs Kendal and Miss Ellen Terry as Mistress Page and Mistress Ford. A greater contrast could hardly be conceived. On the one hand, Miss Terry, with her exuberant, sun-bright charm, her spontaneous jollity, and, above all, her long training in Shakespearean plays; on the other hand, Mrs Kendal, with her neat, trim, delightfully prosaic method, her quick, quiet, unadorned realism. It is needless to say which of these two, in a play of this kind, plays the other off the stage. Mrs Kendal is too pre-eminent an artist in modern comedy, and modern tragi-comedy, not to fail in Shakespearean farce. To redress the balance, Miss Terry ought to appear with her in a modern play.

[*14 June 1902*]

## CRAWFORD VERSUS DANTE

'And all this has been to her but as the sound of lyres and flutes, and lives only in the delicacy with which it has moulded the changing lineaments...' These are the familiar words that form themselves annually on the tip of my tongue, while Sarah Bernhardt, with radiant eyes upturned, and deprecant palms outstretched, stands to receive the British salvoes in honour of her *rentrée*. For surely Mona Lisa is not more remarkable a lady than she, does not bear lightlier a graver load of manifold experiences. Nay! Time has been stealthily corrupting the canvas of Leonardo, drawing over it a network of delicate cracks, rubbing away the first magic bloom of the colours as Vasari knew them. But Time has not ventured to lay hands on Sarah. He grovels before her, ever crowning anew the already monstrous pile of gifts that he has laid before her, and exacting of her nothing in return. She really is a most marvellous creature—more of a myth, one might say, than of a human being. Her 'lineaments' are, like Mona Lisa's, ever 'changing', are ever being 'moulded' by her manifold experience, in so far that in one year she is plump, in another comparatively slim. But, slim or plump, she is never older by so much as an hour since the previous year. If anything, she is an hour or two younger. And if Mr Marion Crawford, in his passion for historical accuracy, had betrothed Francesca to Giovanni at the age of nine, Sarah, you may be sure, would have looked the part quite passably. As it is, Mr Crawford does not vouchsafe us the heroine before she is seventeen years old. A Zoilean might object that Sarah looks sixteen. But we can disregard that missing year. What really does trouble us—or, at least, would trouble us if Mr Crawford's play were a salvable affair—is that after the prologue fourteen years are supposed to elapse, and thus Sarah looks a full fifteen years younger than Francesca is supposed to be. Though by her art in acting she contrives to suggest the manner of a woman of thirty, our illusion is badly hampered by her appearance. Signora Duse has inspired much awe through her contempt for the art of making-up. But Sarah ought to be above such bravado. She ought, when a part needs it, to simulate the ravages which Time leaves unmade on her.

A stolid maturity of passion is the keynote thumped by Mr Crawford in his re-creation of Paolo and Francesca. M. Pierre Magnier, who plays Paolo, is enabled by his temperament and physique to accept and preserve this keynote. And if Sarah were in similar case, and if Mr Crawford's keynote seemed to me a proper one, *Francesca da Rimini* would seem to me quite a good entertainment—a play somewhat trite and vulgar in tone, but cleverly worked out, and provided with several thrilling moments. But alas! I, like everyone else whose opinion is or is not worth having, am obstinately convinced that Mr Crawford ought to have thumped quite another keynote— the keynote of young and etherealised passion. Not that I have been yearning for yet another dramatic incarnation of 'the two most memorable spirits that floated past Dante'. D'Annunzio has given us their hearts' passion, Maeterlinck (changing but their names) has given us their souls' pathos, Mr Stephen Phillips has given us their elegant and wistful winsomeness. If we had much more of them, just at present, they might get on our nerves. Therefore it is as well that they have not been trotted forth for us at the Garrick Theatre. But it is not at all well that they have been taken, and turned inside out, and trotted forth in a metamorphic state of grim, prosaic ugliness. We do not need the true Paolo and Francesca again, but still less do we need two other persons of the same names. The one pair would fatigue us, but would still illude us; the other revolts us, nor do we believe in it for one instant. Mr Crawford, doubtless, would demur to the epithet 'true' as applied to Dante's, not to his own, creatures. And I am not going to fly in the face of history (as learnt from Mr Crawford's interesting preface and notes) by denying that there once lived in Italy a lady named Francesca da Rimini, and a gentleman named Paolo Malatesta, whose lives and characters have been grossly distorted by Dante and drawn with some measure of accuracy by Mr Crawford. Yet will I not transpose the epithet 'true' from the place I put it in. For who cares a wooden hoop what sort of people Paolo and Francesca were 'when they were at home', or what sort of love they really had for each other? They simply don't exist for us. They never did exist, except for the scandalmongers of their period. But there is a very real and fiery existence for those two figments, Paolo and Francesca according to Dante. Them we accept, them we love (within reason), in them we believe with all our hearts. And there is a rude shock in store for anyone who, ignoring Dante —'*Diabolo Dante Dedi*': Mr Crawford is welcome to this weird paraphrase of a famous motto—comes airily assuming that we shall not reject with scorn his revised version of the twain.

One phrase in that last sentence is not quite happy. Mr Crawford is not a man to be conceived as 'airily assuming' anything. He is painfully conscientious in the collection and verification of data. It seems that, before writing this play, he made a thorough examination of the castle in which Paolo and Francesca met their doom, and that he even succeeded in identifying beyond a doubt the very room in which that doom was met. Submissive to a famous precedent, 'upstairs and downstairs and in my lady's chamber' wandered Mr Marion Crawford, wasting that which his exemplar had not to waste —shoe-leather. If he had proceeded to put into his play the whole truth, as evolved by his various researches, and nothing but that truth, then perhaps the waste would seem to me to have been made good. If he had been frankly and consistently archaeological, then might his play, though giving no aesthetic pleasure to anyone, have had some value for students. And I suspect that this is the line which Mr Crawford, better versed in mediaeval Italy that in modern dramaturgy, would have preferred to take. But '*j'ai usé la liberté du dramaturge*', he says in apology for not showing us Paolo swinging to and fro, with his doublet caught by the hinge of an unfriendly trapdoor. Furthermore, Mr Crawford wishes it to be distinctly understood that he has had regard only to the exigencies of drama, and has not attempted to make an historic study. So that this new version of Paolo and Francesca is not a really trustworthy version for the dry-as-dust. What, then, is it? Merely a painful fall between two stools, to serve as a warning for those about to write plays round obscure episodes which have been transformed and immortalised by poetic genius. So salutary a warning deserves permanence. But I fear that *Francesca da Rimini* is doomed to very speedy oblivion. Nor can we be justly blamed for trying to forget this stodgy and sordid creation, which, though it is so unreal to us, does tend to mar the preconception which destroys it. It is unlucky for Mr Crawford that his play was not produced some four years ago; for then these very columns would have been resounding with a paean in his honour. But I fancy that 'G.B.S.' is the one and only person to whom Paolo, as a stout, middle-aged father of a family, stricken down untimely in the fourteenth year of his intrigue with Francesca, would appear as a reason for enthusiasm.

M. Magnier, as I have hinted, was an ideal interpreter of this part, whilst its fellow was toned down (though not made tolerable) by youth and beauty and poetic utterance. Mlle de Bray made Concordia, the daughter of Francesca, appear almost as young as her mother. And Giovanni was played with a more than Latin ebullience by M. de Max.

[*21 June 1902*]


## THE CASE OF 'MONNA VANNA'

Had Mr Redford, on the point of banning Maeterlinck's latest play, guessed how garish an advertisement he was preparing for his already too-well-advertised insipience, he would surely (unless he is implected with a passion for notoriety at all costs) have allowed M. Lugné Poe to produce the play, with a blessing, in the ordinary manner. As it was, the play, accursed, saw English light only in a remote hall, under the auspices of a 'society' trumped up for the occasion. This embarrassment was in itself no great matter. Tiny is the public for such things as *Monna Vanna*, and probably the number of people who saw the performance in the remote hall approximates quite closely to the number of people who would have seen it in a central theatre. But there is a larger, and more serious, aspect of the affair. Mr Archer, that keen student of the censorship, thinks that the prohibition of such plays as *Oedipus Rex* and *The Cenci* and *Monna Vanna* is ridiculous 'but not practically important', for that it does not retard 'the development of the English drama'. I agree with Mr Archer that it is the modern native drama that matters most. One of my constant tenets in dramatic criticism has been that a live English dog is for us a more considerable beast than a dead English lion or a live lion from overseas. But I hasten to dissent from Mr Archer's idea that the prohibition of *Monna Vanna* is an accident quite negligible in relation to our native drama. It is, on the contrary, an event of very sinister significance.

For some time past there have been rumours, trustworthy rumours, that the censorship of plays is to be exercised more severely than it has been exercised hitherto. We are told that certain modern English playwrights have, in the eyes of high authorities, been going too far and ought to be pulled back and kept back. You remember Lord Hopetoun's piteous appeal to the Commons to strengthen his hands—an appeal which the Commons unkindly neglected. Lord Hopetoun has ceased to superintend the superintendent of our drama; but his successor is said to be not less averse than he from any serious play to which the maiden of bashful sixteen would not be taken as a matter of course. Indeed it is since Lord Clarendon's succession that the aforesaid rumours have become persistent. Of course, we have had, under his régime, *The Girl from Maxim's* and other not quite decent frivolities. But they do not count. It is, I understand, against attempts to deal seriously wih 'questions of sex' that the official face is set. *Iris* was such an attempt, but its triumphant slipping through Stable Yard is explicable thus: it was an attempt made by Mr Pinero, to be exhibited at the Garrick Theatre. As Mr Archer says, 'a play which has the prestige of a popular author and an established management behind it' is fairly safe from the censorship. The official mind hates a scene, carefully avoids a hornet's nest. And a swarming, stinging scene there would have been for the official who directly molested 'our premier dramatist'. But there are indirect means of molestation. It is sometimes quite possible to frighten a man out of doing that which, if he did it, you would be afraid to reject. It is quite possible to frighten Mr Pinero and his

## THE CASE OF 'MONNA VANNA'

fellows out of dealing seriously with the facts of life, by making them believe you have made a hard and fast rule against such impertinences. Sit heavily on the prostrate weak, casting stern glances around you, and down on their knees will fall the upright strong. And therefore, lately, M. Hervieu, that poor immigrant, was so heavily sat upon that his play was squeezed out of recognition. And therefore, last week, that other alien, M. Maeterlinck, was actually suffocated. *Pour encourager les autres*!

In this latter stratagem the censorship has signally over-reached itself. It would be interesting, of course, and the precedent of Elia tempts us, to 'examine the bumps' of the gentleman directly responsible for this stratagem. But no passion for phrenology, however keen, would justify us in demanding Mr Redford's head on a charger—or on a saucer, which would be, I fancy, the more proportionate vehicle. After all, the general policy in the licensing of plays is not attributable to Mr Redford, a mere underling. All that he can do is to misuse the general instructions, and to endanger the general policy, of his superiors. The Lord Chamberlain is not expected to keep pace with modern dramatic literature. Such details as that are, naturally, delegated to Mr Redford. And Mr Redford seems to have been labouring under the delusion that Maeterlinck would be as safe a victim to tackle as was M. Hervieu before him—a mere 'foreign devil' against whom the door could be closed without any fear of public protest. He does not seem to have realised that Maeterlinck is one of the greatest of living writers, and is certainly the most loveable writer of his age, and that in England he has a devoted following of influential persons, quick to scrutinise very narrowly the grounds on which any work of his may be debarred from public performance, and to protest very loudly if those grounds have any flaw in them. It is not part of the Lord Chamberlain's duty to read the plays for which is craved the right of public production. That is, obviously, the duty of 'the Reader'. And even Mr Redford, had he read *Monna Vanna* with due care, would have discerned that its moral delicacy could not be denied, or for a moment doubted, even by such prudes as are monomaniacs in prudery. Indeed, the play's artistic fault is its deficiency in sensual passion—a fault which you must have found for yourself if you have read or seen the play, and which you may have divined from merely reading the accounts given by the critics of the daily press. Sensuality there is, doubtless, in the passion of Guido Colonna for Monna Vanna; but the fact that the former is the latter's husband immediately disposes of any conventional objection to the play on this score. The passion of Prinzivalle for Monna Vanna turns out to be merely spiritual; and it is because the play, unlike the previous plays of Maeterlinck, is to be judged on the plane of romantic actuality, and because, given the characters and the circumstances, Prinzivalle's passion would not, assuredly, have been altogether spiritual, that *Monna Vanna* seems to me unsatisfactory in point of art. '*Mais nous parlons ici*', says Monna Vanna, '*comme si nous etions dans une île déserte*'; and that is a shrewd criticism of the play. The characters talk entrancingly, with all the authentic Maeterlinckian magic of thought and metaphor; but only entrancing creatures on a desert island would talk thus, feel thus. So long as Maeterlinck stranded the action of his plays on desert islands in 'faëry seas forlorn', such talk and such sentiments were exquisitely right. But now that he has transported his creatures into the hurly-burly of the habitable globe, their talk and their sentiments strike me, for the first time, as slightly ridiculous. True, Guido Colonna is a man of flesh and blood, suitable to the venue of the play. But Prinzivalle is merely Pelleas or another of those childlike phantoms, tricked out in the costume of a condottiere of the fifteenth century. The victorious sword wielded by him in the cause of Florence is, one feels, only a dummy sword. The passion he has for Monna Vanna is only an idyllic fancy learnt by him from Maeterlinck. '*Je ne suis qu'un pauvre homme qui regard un instant le but même do sa vie ... Je suis un malheureux qui ne demande rien, qui ne sait même plus ce qu'il faut demander.*' It is thus that love is made by Maeterlinck's dashing warrior. But the over-refinement, the etherealisation, from which the play suffers robs Mr Redford of all possible means of justifying his objection. I go so far as to say that he cannot have had any sincere objection to the play (unless, of course, he skipped through it in a couple of minutes). The only plausible explanation of his action is that he saw that the main motive of the play was the love of a man for a married woman, and guessed that the author of the play was a Russian or a Norwegian or something of the sort, and that therefore a wholesome example might be set without any fear of protest and with every prospect of a commendatory smile from the Lord Chamberlain. Alas for these brave hopes! Up crop Mr Swinburne and Mr Meredith and many others, loud in protest. Up crops every dramatic critic, loud in protest. Many persons there are who know nothing about Maeterlinck in general and *Monna Vanna* in particular; but they are all, by sheer force of example, loud in protest. And thus, since public opinion is the one thing that frightens the official mind, the hands of the censorship are weakened and, inferentially, the backs of the native dramatists are stiffened by the very device that was to bow them. As Mr Redford must be in sore need of a kind word just now, let me express to him my gratitude for this very salutary state of things.

[*28 June 1902*]


## A NON-THEATRICAL CRITICISM

To be so passionately absorbed in one's own usual work as to be quite heedless of some vast and sudden upheaval which violently agitates every other soul in the neighbourhood—is not that a nobly impressive state to be in? Archimedes, poring over a problem, though Syracuse has fallen, and the soldiers of Marcellus stand round him with drawn swords; Fragonard, suavely putting the last touches to one picture, and meditating the scheme of another, and of another, never for an instant less exquisitely and frivolously aloof by reason of the gutters running red for the Rights of Man; Goethe, for all his patriotism, quite unable to resent the Napoleonic invasion of his fatherland, so dear to him in his library are the many shelves sustaining French literature—by such examples as these, taken here at random from the roll of greatness, can any heart be not touched to a wondering reverence?

But suppose that these men had not been engaged in great work. Suppose that Archimedes had been doing for his pleasure a simple sum in rule of three. Would you not impute to him an irritating lack of sense of proportion? Would you blame the centurion for dealing that blow which for ever stopped the working of his brain? Suppose, again, that Fragonard had been engaged on a series of hack illustrations. Would you not respect him the more if he had looked out of the window and taken an intelligent interest in the Revolution? Suppose, again, that Goethe had taken for his province not the whole world of human culture, but some such little hole and corner as is the British Theatre to-day. Would you not think he ought to have been shot as a traitor for writing that letter to Eckermann? Detachment from lurid circumstance is a fine thing only if the occupation of the detached person be a fine thing in itself. Only thus, indeed, is such detachment possible. You may say that it is my duty, my despicable duty, to write here every week about the British Theatre as though that institution were all in all to me. But the fact is that I cannot, with the best will in the world, oblige you. When as now, the nation is moved by some affair of national importance, I, too, am moved. The British Theatre dwindles and is dimmed for me. I try to write about it as though it still monopolised my horizon. But the effort is painful. It is also absurd. It is also disingenuous. Why should I make it? Why should I tell you at great length about M. Coquelin and Cyrano de Bergerac? Enough that the one is again impersonating the other, at the Garrick Theatre, and that whereas the nose of the true Cyrano is an excrescence, tragically conflicting with Cyrano's heart, the nose of Coquelin-Cyrano seems to be an integral part, even a felicitous symbol, of Coquelin-Cyrano. Why should I again analyse the charm of Madame Charlotte Wiehe in *La Main* and *L'Homme aux Poupées*? Let me, this week, practise the art of dramatic criticism on fresher and larger materials. Let me write around that real drama which, during the past two weeks, has been holding all of us in spell.

Fate has one very salient advantage over her human rivals in dramaturgy. The man who writes a play is bound to preserve certain laws of logic. He must rationalise his episodes. He must not elaborately lead up to a definite and foreseen climax, and then, of a sudden, without warning or explanation, fob us off with an anti-climax. Fate may do this with impunity—nay! may create a tremendous effect by doing it. Whereas at a tragic anti-climax in a play we gasp and then laugh, a tragic anti-climax in life leaves us merely gasping, gasping in proportion to its magnitude. Man is a rational being, Fate is not. But Man is at Fate's mercy, nevertheless; and it is when Fate most insolently flaunts over him her unreason that he is most profoundly impressed by his bondage. Never in my time, certainly, never perhaps in the memory of any living person, has Fate delivered so signal a stroke—'played so silly a trick' one would say, were she human—as when she brought to naught the ceremony that was to be solemnised last week. All those myriads of pounds spent, all those multifarious myriads of human energies and interests concentrated—vainly. A whole vast city disguised in its aspect, and filled as it has never been filled before, and knowing itself to be for the moment the cynosure of the world—a confident, ecstatic city, seething with excitement over one man; and that one man suddenly laid low; and the whole fabric of things falling, in an instant, with him. This is not a place for a full analysis of this tragic peripety. But the immediate effect on the audience and on the critics is a point which may be profitably considered by me.

It has been generally remarked that the behaviour of the populace left nothing to be desired. And this remark has gone unchallenged. It does not, however, tally with my own experience. Against the good-feeling of the populace I make no imputation. But their behaviour, so far as it came under my notice, was not ideal from the first. The news of the King's dangerous illness was known all over London soon after noon on Tuesday, the 24th. The street in which I live is a turning out of one of the most typical thoroughfares of London. From 11 o'clock p.m. to about 2 o'clock next morning, this thoroughfare (at least, the part of it near my street) resounded with those peculiar noises which were heard in London after the successes of our army in South Africa. When the noises began, I could hardly believe my ears. As they persisted, I tried to account for them, hoping that philosophy might lead the way to charity. Nor was I disappointed in my hope. It often happens, I reflected, that I catch myself thinking a previous thought, or re-experiencing an emotion, despite something which has meanwhile befallen to make that thought or emotion irrelevant or absurd. This is particularly often the case when the thought or emotion had become habitual before the occurrence of the event which routed it. For instance, if a man looks forward passionately to something which is to happen a long time hence, and which eventually he knows not to be going to happen after all, he will often catch himself again in the act of pleasant anticipation. Well, I reflected, in this peculiarity of the human brain must be the explanation of the mafficking on the first night of the King's illness. I remembered the song which I heard so long as a year ago, in one of the music halls, and which I quoted wonderingly in these columns: 'Won't we all be jolly merry, drinking whiskey, wine and sherry, on Coronation Day?' For a whole year this determination had been dominant in the popular mind. And now even the shock of the sudden bulletin had not been strong enough to stem the accumulated impetus. They were not heartless, these people. They did not mean to be indecorous. They simply did not realise what had happened.... But, after all, it is one thing to forget a simple fact, quite another not to be able to understand it in the first instance. And what a sombre reflection it is for a playgoer that the drama's laws are given by these very dolts who, so far from being likely to catch a delicate nuance in a play, cannot grasp a glaring fact that confronts them in real life. I was glad not to hear those sounds of mafficking next day. Evidently, the news had been assimilated. Only one belated reveller did I see. This was in the afternoon. A street-organ was being played opposite to my door. Hard by, on the pavement, was a middle-aged man, poor, weather-beaten, but respectably dressed, and perfectly sober, dancing all by himself, in correct time, to the tune of 'Coronation Day'. I shall not soon forget him.

So much for the audience. As for the critics—the leader-writers and the reporters of the daily press—they, as a class, seem to me to have even less distinguished themselves. The concoction of obviously false details is bad enough. But even worse is the wholesale hysteria by which the national tragedy has been vulgarised. By their coarse piling-up of the agony, the newspapers have made even our genuine emotion seem suspect. 'From the highest pinnacle of joy', writes a popular and influential *causeur*, 'we have been hurled to the deepest abyss of gloom'. That is a fair sample of the cant with which we have been deluged. What was really the sensation of the average Englishman when he heard the bad news? Firstly, and chiefly, personal disappointment that there was to be no show, and (in many cases) annoyance at the loss of money laid out. Secondly, a loyal hope that the King would recover. Thirdly, an aesthetic realisation of the whole tragedy, hardly more painful to him that the realisation of a vivid tragedy in fiction or in past history. This may not be an agreeable analysis. But it is a true one. And it is more wholesome, and less really offensive, than all the others which have been made for us. National tragedies cannot affect us as do our own personal tragedies, as do the tragedies of those who are near and dear to us. What use is there in pretending that they can?

[*5 July 1902*]

## 'HAMLET' AND 'THE HEDONISTS'

Yet once again we are in the Castle of Elsinore! Heigh-ho! What, I wonder, should we think of the dear old place if we were visiting it for the first time—watching for the very first time in our lives the doings of its dear old denizens? I suppose we should be breathless, knowing, indeed, what was going to happen next, but never having *seen* that next thing happen. I suppose, in other words, that the play would give us the illusion of drama. I, for my part, was illuded at first sight of it; but that was long before I came to years of discretion. I should like to see it in company with some uninitiated adult, and to watch its effect on him. But where is such an one to be found? If there be a recent convert from the straitest sect of the Nonconformists, let him communicate with me. I will pay gladly for both tickets. I fancy that even for him, though he might receive the play itself as a play, the words spoken by the characters would be a grave obstacle to illusion. For is not every passage compact of phrases which have passed into current speech—phrases which are quoted every day without consciousness of their source, and in senses utterly different from Shakespeare's? In *Hamlet* a character can hardly make the most trivial remark, without switching our minds on to some quite irrelevant matter in modern life. His meaning may be no more than that he is going out on the battlements; but his actual words—have we not just been reading an article in which they were applied, in quite another sense, to Mr Arthur Balfour, or to the problem of alien immigration, or to Henley Regatta? Another obstacle to illusion—I speak now not for my Nonconformist convert, but for those who, like myself, are more or less connected with the theatre— is that in *Hamlet* every scene reminds us of at least one amusing (or not amusing) story told about this or that blunder made by this or that mime. On rushes Laertes, sword in hand, and forthwith we remember that the late John Blank, who was playing the part in Manchester, many years ago, somehow lost his footing, &c. &c. Queen Gertrude snatches the goblet, and up rises the ghost of the late Miss Clara Dash, who, at Sadler's Wells, one night, somehow managed to &c. &c. No, assuredly, we must not dream of going to *Hamlet* for dramatic illusion. Why then do we go to it always so eagerly? Just because we have gone so often before. We go to be fascinated by its familiarity, its intimate renewal of past experiences. The more often we go to it, the more irresistible does it become. But, ostensibly, we go to study the interpretation of the title-part. Mr Forbes Robertson, who is now appearing as the Prince, for a limited number of afternoons, at the Lyric Theatre, is not a new interpreter. But I have had no previous opportunity of praising him. Bear with me, therefore, even though I do but repeat praises bestowed by others.

'The air bites shrewdly; it is very cold.' Thus speaks Hamlet, emerging upon the platform of the castle, to await the ghost of his father. It is not a profound remark, but the tradition is to speak it in a hollow voice, mysteriously, ruminantly, in order that our nerves may be strung up to concert-pitch for the things impending. Not so does Mr Forbes Robertson speak it, but briskly, with a peevish emphasis on the 'very'. One feels that Hamlet expected the weather to be cold, but that so low a temperature as this seems to him really excessive, considering the time of year. Also, one feels that he is not really vexed—rather, that he wishes to make conversation for the benefit of Marcellus and Horatio, and so employs the method which we ourselves employ, in real similar cases, every day of our lives. We feel that the remark is a real remark made by a real man. (For sake of convenience, I speak as though dramatic illusion were possible.) The keynote thus struck is the keynote of Mr Robertson's performance from first to last. In the difference between his manner and the manner of all other Hamlets in commenting on the weather, you have the whole essential difference between his Hamlet and the Hamlet of anyone else. Every other Hamlet has been a mysterious and abstract figure—not a man, but an incarnation (successful or otherwise) of a human soul, or of all human souls. Mr Robertson, realistically, shows us a man—a pleasant, high-souled young man, placed in distressing circumstances, and behaving just as one would expect such a person in such case to behave. He shows us, for the first time, Hamlet as a quite definite and intelligible being. I do not profess to say whether this be really the right reading of the part or not. I am inclined to think that Shakespeare himself would have preferred the ordinary classico-romantic performance. Shakespeare lingered so long over the creation of Hamlet, putting into him so prodigally much of poetry and of passion, together with so many philosophic irrelevancies, that Hamlet may have seemed to him, as he has seemed to us, less a single man than a conglomeration of men innumerable, a vast and shadowy symbol of all the mysteries of life itself. Mr Robertson's quick and slick simplification of the whole matter is, certainly, a shock for us. We cannot help resenting it, just at first. But soon, despite ourselves, we are forgiving it and admiring it. Mr Robertson may not be giving us the ideal Hamlet of Shakespeare; but he is giving us a Hamlet which is quite perfect on its own plane, whereas, on that other plane, who of us has seen a Hamlet that came anywhere near perfection? In face, and in voice, and in manner, Mr Robertson is a heaven-born Hamlet. And even though there be in the soul of the part a something which evades and defies the keen intelligence he has brought to bear on it, we cannot be too cordially grateful to him. Mr Ian Robertson, as the King, has the advantage of family likeness to Hamlet. But he is too wilfully agreeable to be impressive in so sinister a part. On the other hand, Miss Gertrude Elliott's agreeableness in the part of Ophelia is a great relief from the ugly and inappropriate antics and noises to which most leading ladies treat us.

Adrian Harley was said by his creator to be 'an Epicurean whom Epicurus would have scourged out of his garden'. I have always doubted the justice of this criticism. The bent of Adrian, after all, was ever to those negative and tranquil pleasures which in the garden of Epicurus were esteemed so highly. His fleshliness was swayed by a fastidious intellect. There was nothing gross in him. Finding him, at length, incapable of setting comradeship above self, Epicurus might have asked 'the wise youth' to leave the garden. But he would have opened the gate regretfully, and might even have called the disciple back. On the other hand, there can be no doubt that Mr Rosenstein, the chief character in Mrs Ashton Jonson's play *The Hedonists*, would have been scourged out of the garden in less than no time. He would even have been scourged from Cyrene by Aristippus, so conspicuously is he lacking in that intellectual culture and that moral self-control which even Aristippus deemed necessary —culture, to enable a man to select the right pleasures; self-control, to prevent him from selecting too many of them. Mr Rosenstein talks a great deal about hedonism, and seems to regard himself (and to be regarded by his creator) as an authentic type of the school. But examine his credentials. He is a stock-broker, living in Park Lane. Well! there is no inherent reason why a stock-broker, living in Park Lane, should not be a hedonist, though the chances are a hundred to one that he will be something very different. Apart from his profession and his residence, what sort of person is Mr Rosenstein? What does he do? He sends the true lover of a poor but virtuous young lady to South Africa, and then cuts in with an offer of guilty splendour. The young lady has an invalid father, and she wavers. She attends an evening party in Park Lane. Mr Rosenstein is furiously angry with a medical practitioner who follows her with the news that the invalid father is dying. He thinks it disgraceful that enjoyment should be spoilt for so trifling a cause. Next day, he visits the young lady, is repulsed by her, threatens her with legal proceedings (for that a sixpenny-stamp makes a telegraphed promise a legal contract), insults her in the presence of the true lover, is knocked down by the true lover, and exit, mumbling vengeance. In fact, our dear old friend the villain across the bridges! He is all very well in his way, but why, why drag in hedonism? Hooliganism were quite as appropriate a term. When next Mrs Ashton Jonson devotes her quite remarkable instinct for stage-tricks, and her quite remarkable ignorance of human life and human nature, to the service of British drama, let her not, I beseech, try to mystify us by another pretentious title. The throwing of such dust in our eyes merely sets up irritation: it does not blind us into an illusion that there is some important thing on view.

[*12 July 1902*]

## 'CHANCE THE IDOL'

'*Vivent les vacances!*' cried the hero of a delightful comedy of which I wrote here in the last days of July; and, at the time, my heart, a-pant for cooling streams, meekly echoed his sentiment. But last Tuesday evening, when, before my sun-cleared eyes, the curtain rose from the stage of Wyndham's Theatre, I was hent by the annual spirit of revolt, and '*A bas les vacances!*' was the murmur that would out. After tasting life itself, after knocking up against nature and mankind and so forth, it is a bitter thing to be forced back on that familiar, but for a while forgotten, imitation of life and nature and mankind and so forth which constitutes theatrical art. The whole thing seems so unnecessary, so unsuccessful. In the course of eleven months, compulsory playgoing dims one's ken of men and women as they are: one accepts the stage's simulacra of them, quite amenably, as being an excellent imitation of the real thing—nay! as being the real thing itself. But after a rest, how brief soever, one *sees* and, seeing, sighs. The mimes seem like nothing in heaven or on the earth. One suspects them of having been cast up mysteriously from the water under the earth, and one longs to return them to their native element and be rid of their painful wrigglings and gaspings. Men and women? They? Let us not insult humanity by listening to so preposterous a notion. Voice, face, port, gesture, all betray them as quite inhuman. Look, for present example, at Miss Kate Serjeantson striding and shouting, with an unmeaning stare, through the part of a grande dame. Is *she* real? And Mr Graham Browne, rolling his eyes and coaxing his voice up and down—does he pass muster as a young soldier? And Mr H. V. Esmond—show me the human being who ever cocked an eyebrow so significantly, or smiled with so poignant a sweetness, at nothing in particular, or drew sighs so deep, interspersed with backward glances so piercing, whenever he had to leave a room. Had the production at Wyndham's Theatre been made but a brief month ago, doubtless Mr Esmond and Mr Graham Browne and Miss Sergeantson would have not at all bewildered and distressed me. As it was, the one person in the cast who gave me any illusion was Miss Lena Ashwell. She alone managed to walk and talk and look like a real person. To be able to perform these tricks is not the whole secret of acting, and Miss Ashwell's distinction does not rest on that power alone. Still, that is the power for which, after a holiday, one is most grateful to her, and which one most keenly misses in the work of her fellows.

Hitherto, whenever I have returned from a holiday, it has been my lot to be confronted with the work of some ultra-mechanical playwright. Two years running, I remember, I stumbled straight into the toils of Mr Sydney Grundy. This year Fate has shown mercy in decreeing for me a play by Mr Henry Arthur Jones. He, of all our regular professional playwrights, is the one whose view of life is least restricted by the conventions of the theatre. Like other playwrights, sometimes he succeeds and sometimes he fails; but neither his successes nor his failures are ever discreditable to him, as those of the rest are apt to be to them; for always he makes a fresh effort to tackle honestly some interesting theme in the real world that exists 'off'. He is always alert and courageous. He never lets himself rest, never takes the line of least resistance, never takes any line in a way that can be foreseen exactly by an old playgoer. Hence the hard suspicious eye with which he is regarded by the majority of the critics, and hence their invariable eagerness to underline his failures and to explain away his successes. In this latest play, *Chance the Idol*, Mr Jones has shown his courage in two ways. He has flown in the face of two accepted shibboleths—one that you cannot make interesting or effective on the stage a character that is always vacillating from point to point; the other that you cannot get any truly dramatic stuff out of the theme of gambling.

The vacillation character presented by Mr Jones is that of a seducer. According to the immemorial tradition of the stage a seducer must be one of two kinds: either he must spurn his victim, loading her with as many intolerable insults as he can muster, and making himself quite unworthy of the name of gentleman, &c., &c., or he must have his better nature stirred by her appeals and secure a special licence. Cyril Ryves, seducer of Ellen Farndon, conforms with neither of these two rules. He is much stirred by the appeals, and is genuinely anxious, as he reiterates, 'to do the right thing'. Only, the facts remain that he has gambled away all the money he might have married on, and that Miss Farndon is not a lady, and that he is no longer in love with her, much as he respects her, and that his people are strongly opposed to the notion of his making himself unhappy for life by making an honest woman of her instead of marrying an attractive heiress who is at hand. So he goes on floundering between his desire to live up to his own sentiments and his inability to do so in the face of difficulties. He is not a hero, as you see. On the other hand, he is equally not a villain. He is, accordingly, much more like a human being than is the seducer to whom playwrights have accustomed us. He is, indeed, one of the truest, and most interesting, and most amusing, characters ever projected by Mr Jones. That he does not 'come off' on the stage of Wyndham's Theatre is not the fault of Mr Jones, but of the aforesaid Mr Graham Browne, who plays him with no more intelligence than would suffice for the part of a quite ordinary *jeune premier*. The part of Cyril Ryves is, of course, a very difficult one. When you see a strong-minded woman pursuing a weak-minded man who tries to escape from her, you are very ready to wonder what on earth she can see in him. It is the business of the actor who plays that man's part to prevent you from wondering. He must have, besides intelligence, some magic of personality. Mr Graham Browne may have a hidden mine of intelligence. But I vow he has no magic of personality whatsoever. I think it a pity that Mr Esmond, who has some of that magic, and whose acting is always much more real in young than in old parts, was not allowed to appear as Cyril Ryves.

Gambling as a dramatic motive is pooh-poohed on the ground that in drama the characters must be exercising free will, whereas gamblers absolutely surrender themselves to inscrutable Fate. This is a specious argument, but it does not dispose of Mr Jones's play. Certainly, you could get no dramatic interest out of the career of a real gambler—a man who sits down to play simply for the sake of the excitement, and whose winnings mean to him nothing more than the prolonging of his operations. This kind of man surrenders his free will entirely, and so is not dramatic. But gambling for some desperate purpose is quite another matter. The reason why in this play Ellen Farndon gambles is not that she is a born gambler, but that she hopes to win thereby enough money to pay her seducer's debts and to induce him to marry her. She gambles because otherwise there is no chance of respectability for herself and her baby. Though, of course, like all people who are gambling, she becomes a prey to various forms of superstition, she is not at all mad. It is all very well for Mr Walkley to say that 'drama is the struggle of a conscious will against obstacles, and there is no conscious will in disease'; but the point is that Ellen Farndon has a conscious will, which is all the while struggling against a definite obstacle, the chances in favour of the bank at roulette and trente-et-quarante. Hysterical she may be, from time to time, but she is no more mad than (let us say) Hamlet, and no less capable than he of inspiring in us that true sympathy which, as Mr Walkley very rightly says, can be inspired only by the sane. Nor is her campaign at the tables made uninteresting by our sure knowledge that she will be beggared at last. So long as there is a real struggle between will and destiny it matters little in drama whether the result be or be not a foregone conclusion. A woman with her whole life at stake, and against her the blind, remorseless logic of the tables—surely it is but pedantry to say there is no dramatic conflict here. Setting theory aside, I protest that Mr Jones has written a play by which you will be much excited.

He is fortunate in once more having Miss Lena Ashwell to play the principal part. I have already praised her way of seeming like a real person. In some parts—in any Shakespearean part—this very realism, this utter refusal to compromise with beauty, is rather a drawback. Even here, as Ellen Farndon, she need not, I think, say 'Congratulate me!' when she comes from winning at the tables. But that is a trifle. In a part of this kind, beauty may go hang. What we demand is sincerity and the power of expressing a series of strong and various emotions. On Tuesday night Miss Ashwell supplied this demand more fully, I think, than ever before. The steadfastness of those eyes, the quaver in that voice, were more harrowing than words can say. She even eclipsed the memory of Mrs Dane. I congratulate her.

[*13 September 1902*]


'WHAT WOULD A GENTLEMAN DO?'

The philosopher in every age has been annoyed by the vague way in which words are used in common speech by his fellow-beings. 'You say this and you say that', he snaps; 'but what do you *mean* by this? And kindly define that.' And his fellow-beings, as he expected, stammer after a long pause that by 'this' they mean—well! 'this', and by 'that' just 'that'. And the philosopher is left to demonstrate, triumphant but not listened to, what his fellow-beings really do mean, or rather what in his opinion they ought to mean. There is, I think, something to be said for their indifference to his demonstration. Their rough and ready use of words is, on the whole, quite good enough for all practical purposes of intercourse, and any serious attempt to rummage under the surface of their own vocabulary would involve them in something worse than a waste of time: horrid confusion would supervene. No one would know what anyone else was driving at, or even what he himself was driving at. Everyone, in fact, would be a philosopher, with all the vices of remoteness and obscurity and aimlessness peculiar to philosophy, and the world really could not go on. Men know what they mean by (for example) the term 'justice', simply because they don't know what they mean by it, having never given ear to Plato or any of those others who have tried so laboriously to tell them. However, though the philosopher is useless (and might be worse than useless) in trying to elucidate such terms as 'justice', which have a fixed and permanent signification for mankind, he has his humble use in dealing with terms which are used in different senses by different persons, or whose common usage varies in one generation and another. Take for instance the term 'gentleman'. There is a fashionable tendency to use it as connoting various moral qualities—truthfulness, courage, consideration for the feelings of others, disdain to do a mean action, and so forth. Most people, on the other hand, still use it in a merely aesthetic sense, to suggest a dignified port, an urbane and easy demeanour, a correct pronunciation of words, a knowledge of what to do and what not to do in the lighter emergencies of life. Here, you see, is a real danger of confusion, and an excuse for the philosopher to interfere. Borrowing for a moment his cap, I should urge that the aesthetic is the right sense in which to say 'gentleman', and that those who (in the morbid modern fear of being thought snobbish) are using it in the other sense should cease to do so, substituting some such term as 'good man' or 'spotless knight'. By doing so they would make for clarity. It is always a dangerous and reprehensible thing to tamper with the traditional meaning of a word in one's own language. And the traditional meaning of 'gentleman' has nothing at all to do with morality. 'When Adam delved and Eve span, who was then the gentleman?' would become a very pointless question if the modern use of 'gentleman' were to become inveterate in us. For, according to that use, Adam at the fall had so very obviously ceased to be a gentleman. It would be a pity if we lost the couplet's old true meaning, that 'it takes three generations' to polish a man's manners, and that there can have been no master of deportment before Irad.

I suspect that Irad himself was rather a rough diamond. For the gentleman, like the poet, must be both born and made; and, even supposing that he can be born in a simple and primitive community, he cannot be made except through that artifice and tradition which come only of a complex civilisation. Gentility (another word which has been prostituted by our fear of snobbishness) is the result of an instinct inherited and elaborately trained in the heir's elastic youth. You might send a street-arab to the best of our public schools, and you might send to a board school Mr Kipling's 'son of a belted earl'; and in neither case would the subsequent adult be a gentleman.

Breeding and rearing are equally essential. In the ordinary way, of course, it does not much matter to a man whether he be a gentleman or not: either he is one, or he isn't; and in whichever sphere he happen to find himself he has other and more important things to think about. But sometimes it happens that the fact of not being a gentleman is the primary obsession to a man's mind. Take the case of a man, ill-bred and ill-reared, who by recent accident of wealth finds himself cast among his superiors in rank. If he have modesty and good sense enough to recognise that these people are his superiors not only in rank but also in the graces of life, and if he be sensitive enough not to be content with their perfect willingness to take him as he is for the sake of his riches, and if his health be so sound as to be no distraction, his whole life will be overshadowed by the regret that he is not a gentleman. This is his tragedy. Moreover, if he be still fairly young, and a man of spirit, he will strive, in the face of fate, to become a gentleman. This, whether we ourselves be gentlemen or not, is one of our comedies. In every age, wherever there has been a complex social life, this fore-doomed effort towards self-gentilification has been one of the favourite themes of the comic dramatist. More than one masterpiece has been made of it. In England and in this generation it has been tried several times, but not with mastery. And doubtless it is that tempting void which lured Mr Gilbert Dayle (not alas! into itself, but) into the writing of *What Would a Gentleman Do?*, a play now being acted at the Apollo Theatre.

I fancy that Mr Dayle, but for the aforesaid dubiety of the term 'gentleman', might have written a fairly amusing play. But, instead of taking the word in its aesthetic sense, and sticking to that, he took both senses in a half-hearted way; and the result is very incoherent. The early scenes, where we see the young parvenu feverishly turning the leaves of a manual of etiquette, are quite funny as farce; if the play were developed on this plane, all would be well. But presently 'gentleman' looms up in the moral significance, bringing a cloud of dulness with it. The parvenu has paid a debt of honour for a young man of whose sister he is enamoured. The young man drops the cheque, and it is picked up by the sister, who feels herself accordingly compelled to accept the parvenu's offer of marriage, though she cannot stand the sight of him and is desperately in love with someone else. The parvenu, later, overhears her explaining why she

## 'WHAT WOULD A GENTLEMAN DO?'

has accepted him. He releases her from her engagement and she is duly betrothed to the other man. The parvenu learns that the other man has been guilty of a certain very wicked action, which, if revealed, would debar him from the society of decent men and women. What does the parvenu proceed to do? He proceeds to accuse himself publicly of having committed the very wicked action, and is, I suppose, quite fully recompensed by the knowledge that the girl who is all in all to him will presently be led to the altar by the man who actually had committed the very wicked action and who had blandly allowed him to incriminate himself. That is a kind of self-sacrifice familiar to all playgoers; and apparently Mr Dayle thinks very highly of it, for does he not (entitling the act in which it occurs 'What a Gentleman Would Do') suggest it to be the very acme of gentlemanly behaviour? If Mr Dayle had satirically shown to us the parvenu behaving in this idiotic and unscrupulous manner under the delusion that it was the only right manner for polite society, then I should have found the satire amusing, though a trifle far-fetched. But as Mr Dayle is terribly in earnest, and claims for his hero an exemplary moral rectitude, the only thing to do is to condole with the poor gentleman on his complete lack of moral sense, and to urge that if ever again he happen on a subject which seems to him equally susceptible of moral and aesthetic treatment, he must not for an instant hesitate as to which is the right treatment for him to apply.

The part of the parvenu is, as I have hinted, a farcical part, until it becomes melodramatic. But Mr Louis Bradfield, doubtless oppressed by the strange dignity of having no song and dance, and by fears that the critics would accuse him of not being able to shake off old habits, was very evidently determined to be comedic at all costs. Thus some of the fun evaporated, the rest being saved by Mr Bradfield's frequent involuntary lapses into genial farce. To play so stupid a part as has been assigned to Mr Frank Mills must be a sad infliction; but I think Mr Mills might make more effort to dissimulate his broken spirit. Let him profit by the brave example of Miss Nina Boucicault, who manages to seem, with equally little reason for being, quite cheerful.

[*27 September 1902*]

## THE TRIUMPH OF THE 'VARIETY SHOW'

The overwhelming triumph won by a certain new form of journalism rouses in the breasts of literary men much sorrow and anger, many sighs and sneers about 'an age of snippets'. How, wonder these gentlemen, did this age come into being, and what will be its dread duration? And they assume that it is all the fault of the School Board—a half-educated nation wolfing the only kind of stuff it can yet assimilate. And they assume that there is a good time coming, when the nation, wholly educated, soundly digestive, will settle down in all its leisure moments to a solid and continuous study of the higher forms of literature. I should like to share the fond hope. But I cannot. It seems to me that the mischief lies far deeper than the indicters of 'an age of snippets' have yet probed, far wider that they have yet surveyed. The craving for snippets is not a disease peculiar to the class of persons turned out by board schools. Nearly all other classes in this country and at this time suffer from it. Except among those few persons whose business in life is to read books and to write about them, you will find that same impatience of continuous study which literary men ascribe to the lower and lower-middle classes in particular. Nay! you will find that the literary men themselves read books much less and write about them much more than did their predecessors in slower and quieter days. Slower and quieter days!—there, surely, we touch the root of the whole mischief. Quite apart from the fact that the bent for concentrated study must always have been a rather rare bent, even in the days when there were no snippets for man's beguilement, it is quite obvious that in an age when the struggle for life has become so much keener than it ever was before, and demands of the strugglers so much more obstinate concentration on the complete art of struggling, to take literature as something more than a means of recreation for fagged brains—more than a box of pink pills for pale people—cannot be at all a strong or general tendency. It might be argued that the very concentration made necessary by modern competition would naturally be kept up, by force of habit, in leisure moments. But the theory of 'change of work' is not one in which anybody really believes—anybody, that is, who has ever done any work. Moreover, the modern concentration on the struggle for life is a peculiar kind of concentration: it is snippety in itself.

## THE TRIUMPH OF THE 'VARIETY SHOW'

Railways, twopenny tubes, telegrams, telephones, and all those other devices by which Science, with her helpful smile, has complicated and bedevilled the erst simple lot of mankind, all tend to cut up life into snippets. The more 'strenuous' a life be made, the jerkier must it become, and the more confirmed a victim to snippetitis he who lives it. And, as 'strenuousness' is like to go on being intensified till mankind ceases prematurely under the strain of it, we, superior persons, may as well make up our minds that snippet-literature 'has come' (in its maker's phrase) 'to stay', and that our best policy is to grin and bear it. After all, we don't have to read it. And whenever we do of our accord read a little of it we cannot but be interested in it as an index to the needs, a peep into the souls, of the greater number of our fellow-beings. We are, moreover, in our heart of hearts, conscious of an unholy charm in it. And there suffuses us suddenly a faint glow of kinship with all those others—a queer sensation, unacknowledged, but not, I think, unpleasant.

Snippet-literature is not the isolated phenomenon which it has been treated as being by my brethren. A necessary result of modern conditions at large, it has its counterparts in many directions. Reading is but one of the forms of recreation in which humanity indulges, and all the other forms are falling equally under the snippet-sway. Take, for example, the form with which I deal here, week by week—the recreation that consists in sitting for three hours, after nightfall, staring across a row of footlights. As the penny weekly magazines are to literature, so are the music halls to drama: snippets there, 'turns' here, to perform precisely the same function of catching your attention for one thing and switching it on to another before you know where you are. Nor is the triumph of the penny weekly magazine more signal that the triumph of the music hall. I will not go into statistics: they take up too much space, and are said to mislead the persons to whom they are not altogether unintelligible. Sufficient the obvious fact that the music hall is the place to which the public gives its constant and spontaneous support. The theatre still survives, precariously. But it is not really wanted, and in course of time it will become the private hobby of a handful of persons whom wealth secures from 'strenuousness' and who happen also to have souls above horse-racing. And then, by the way, there will be a chance of something like respectable drama. Emancipation from mob-law is drama's crying need. Its present thralldom may not be the reason, but is at least a very plausible excuse, for the lamentable figure it cuts beside its fellow-arts. Meanwhile, the theatre, trying to cater for the many, has not for the few even the charm of reflecting what the many want. The music hall, on the other hand, has this further thing in common with the weekly penny magazine, that it does reveal to one, convincingly, the secret of the public's taste. One refers to it eagerly, as to its analogue, for instruction. Alas! it is only instruction that one gains. For such amusement—and so for such happy sense of kinship —as you and I cull from the penny weekly magazine, we look vainly in the music hall. The variety show, despite its name and aim, has ever this unifying principle, that in all its variegations it is portentously and preposterously dull.

One evening last week, in a studious mood, I went to the Empire. Perhaps the unrelieved gloom in which my studies were conducted was not due wholly to the character of the entertainment itself. Miss Elfie Fay, the eleventh item on the programme, is in herself, I believe, a very bright and amusing artist. But my faith is not founded on revelation. It rests on hearsay. At the Empire she seemed to me—well, I had no impression of her at all. A vast stage is a fit venue for vast crowds; but alas for the solitary performer reduced to the insignificance of a gnat in a landscape! Even four gnats do not 'tell' much in a landscape. All that I could gather of 'The Manhattan Comedy Four' was that, even on a miniature stage, they would have been insufferably tedious. Imagine four men, with elaborately hideous disguises, singing sentimental part-songs for several minutes! Yet I am told that this is quite a common form of entertainment. These two items which I have mentioned were practically the only items whose direct appeal was for laughter. Yet the rest seemed to me scarcely less gloom-inspiring. 'Animated Pictures'—what a misnomer for a series of quivering cold grey photographs, recording in a ghostly manner the past processions of which one is so heartily sick—ghosts of lifeguardsmen cantering interminably past, with glimpses of ghosts of carriages containing invisible ghosts of illustrious personages! And who would have supposed that the last had not yet been of that affair called 'the serpentine dance'? Yet here it still was at the Empire, gaudier and more pretentious than ever. And here was a lady, styled 'Illusionist', performing tricks that would not have illuded the youngest and least blasé attendant at a juvenile party. And here was a trio of gymnasts. Gymnasts! Why should able-

# THE TRIUMPH OF THE 'VARIETY SHOW'

bodied men thus devote their limbs and lives to the performance of feats which can serve no practical purpose, when they might be making themselves really useful as railway porters, or as steeplejacks, or in some other manly and sensible vocation? These gymnasts, at any rate, are well paid for their folly, and make fools of themselves voluntarily. But you have not even this thought to comfort you when the performing dogs make their bows. To any lover of dogs, what could be more exasperating than the sight of a dog dancing about in the costume of a ballet-dancer, or making arithmetical calculations on a blackboard? One is assured that in training dogs to do such things no cruelty is used. But that does not answer the objection against the unnatural stupidity of making them do such things at all. And then the ballet! Imagine a ballet run on Board School lines, with painstaking tableaux of scenes in the lives of the various Kings Edward—Carnarvon Castle, the Seige of Calais, and so forth! A portrait of the present King was being upheld by enthusiastic coryphees, amidst tremendous plaudits, as I left the building.

Throughout the evening, for every item, the plaudits had been tremendous. The packed audience had been enjoying itself uproariously from first to last. It is said that the English nation takes its pleasures sadly. That is not true. The sadness is in the pleasures themselves.

[ *18 October 1902* ]


## 'MY LADY VIRTUE'

We, living in a civilised state of society, are constantly suggesting to one another what is false, and suppressing what is true, and even telling downright lies. Otherwise, civilised society would cease to exist. To most of us, from time to time, occurs the wish that we could be always quite fair and square and above-board, and the wish is promptly succeeded by a sense of horror at what would happen if we were, and by hasty self-justifications for being what we are. Suppose, for example, we forbade our servants to say 'not at home' to any visitors except when we were actually out of doors. We should not like our privacy to be always at anyone's mercy. If everyone were to be always shown straight in, life would become intolerable. Therefore a plain refusal and dismissal would be the formula. How would our friends take it? Very much amiss. And, though most of us have friends whom we could well spare, we are loth to be altogether friendless. Besides, we are highly civilised, and accordingly loth to alienate even the undesirable by causing them actual pain. And so our servants must continue to fib for us, on the tacit understanding that we take the blame in the next world. Likewise, in those thousand and one other common emergencies of life, where the choice is between a slight dishonesty and an all-round unpleasantness, we prefer, on the whole, to be slightly dishonest. And I think our preference is right. Of course, if strict honesty in all things were the general rule of the community, then there would be no excuse for the disingenuous person; for honesty would cause no pain to anyone. But, while civilisation endures, such never will be the general rule. And there is this further point: disingenuousness, being the general rule, is hardly disingenuous at all. Truths which we expect to be suppressed for us are easily perceptible, and untruths which we expect to be suggested are easily seen through. The common lies of civilised life are, in fact, more ornamental than useful. For instance —to revert to the not-at-home problem—we do not always, when we hand a visiting-card across a threshold, believe literally that our friend is out and about. We may believe firmly that he is at home. But if we were told that he was at home and inaccessible we should be affronted as by an unfriendly act. Told that he is out, we respect his wish for privacy, and scent no slight cast by him on ourselves, no reason to suppose that he would not generally be quite glad to see us. The truth, the whole truth, and nothing but the truth, can be told and stomached only by savages. Such, I take it, is the conscious or unconscious opinion of the ordinary modern person. But there are, here and there, some extraordinary persons, whose moral consciences are of so fine a fibre, and whose human sympathies are so undeveloped, that they shrink from telling an untruth, or pardoning an untruth told to them, in any circumstances whatsoever. It is difficult for us to like them, but easy to admire them, and easy, too, to pity them inasmuch as they must suffer, in the long run, as much inconvenience as they cause. And we are glad of them, inasmuch as it is amusing (at a safe distance) to watch them. One of them is the central figure of Mr Esmond's new comedy *My Lady Virtue*, at the

Garrick Theatre; and, though we should shun her in real life, she is quite delightful on the stage.

Lady Ernestone (thus has Mr Esmond punningly entitled her) is no noisy propagandist. She is very modest of her priggishness. It has to be dragged out of her through severe cross-examination by the minor characters in the first act. Indeed, she is one of those prigs—the worse kind—who do not know that they are prigs. 'Am I', she objects, 'a prig because I have convictions? I don't blame other people for not having convictions. That is not their fault. It is their good fortune'. Observe that she does not welcome her virtuousness as a delightful thing in itself. Rather does it seem to her a burden under which she must stagger bravely along. She feels that she spreads discomfort around her, and she wishes she didn't; but it is her *métier*, and she must stick to it. What other people call tact, she calls deceit; and she suggests, modestly but withal firmly, that if ever her life came to some great crisis where all might be saved by a little tact, without harming anyone, she would be as resolutely tactless as ever. Thus is the curiosity of the audience whetted. What sort of crisis will her life come to? In what kind of ruin will she involve herself for the sake of a principle? Will she cut so noble and pathetic a figure that her present priggishness will be all forgotten and forgiven? We suspect that she will. But Mr Esmond has a little surprise in store for us. Lady Ernestone does not, in her goodness of heart, get herself into trouble—not she! All she does is to try to wreck the career of two other persons. One of these persons is Sir George, her husband; the other, Mrs Bramley Burville, her neighbour. Sir George, before his marriage, had loved Mrs Burville before hers, and had written passionate letters to her. He was abroad when she married, and, imagining her to be still a maiden, he wrote to her another passionate letter. The correspondence ceased as soon as he heard of the wedding. Mrs Burville, being romantic, kept his final letter, Unluckily, it was dated, and she was careless, and her husband, into whose hands it fell, was hard-up and very unscrupulous. Here is the situation. Mr Burville comes to call on Sir George, bringing with him a pocket-book in which he has placed the compromising letter. He demands in exchange for it the sum of two thousand pounds. Otherwise, he will immediately file a petition for divorce. He looks rather a fool when he finds that the letter is not in the pocket-book after all. As a matter of fact, the letter is at this moment in the possession of

Lady Ernestone, having been stolen back by Mrs Burville and by her mischievously sent to pain the wife of her former lover. Enter Lady Ernestone, holding the letter in her hand, and presently exit Mr Burville, very grateful to her for voluntarily restoring it to him. What was the motive of her generosity? Her love of truth before all things. But where does truth come in? If she had thought that Mrs Burville had committed adultery with her husband, then there might have been a high moral reason for exposing her to the glare of the divorce court. Considering that she herself was the wife of the prospective co-respondent, who would therefore have been unable to marry the respondent in case the decree were granted, and considering that the prospective petitioner was an out-and-out scoundrel, this high and dry enthusiasm in the cause of truth and of the people who enjoy reading the newspaper reports of 'scandals in high life' would have seemed somewhat unintelligible. Still, it would have been right enough from Lady Ernestone's standpoint. As she knew her husband and Mrs Burville to be innocent, there was absolutely no excuse or reason for getting them into trouble. She simply made a fool of herself. The contrast between the height of her principles and the depth of her folly provides a screamingly funny scene. But I do not think the fun is quite legitimate. We ought to have had some previous inkling that Lady Ernestone was mentally deficient; and this inkling was not vouchsafed by Mr Esmond. So sudden an aberration as hers may be pathologically right, but it is dramatically wrong in the case of a character in which we are expected to take serious interest. Mr Esmond seems to have realised at this point that no one in the audience could again take Lady Ernestone seriously. Her bland astonishment at her husband's displeasure is in the best manner of farce. She had thought he would be delighted. 'He is angry', she complains, 'and I had so wanted him to be kind to me this evening'. To secure his kindness, she abandons her muddle-headed service of the truth, and goes off to Mr Burville's flat in pursuit of the letter. The letter has already been burnt, and the only result of her visit is that she is seen, by an ill-natured gossip, in Mr Burville's arms There, with that flippant moral, the play should have ended. But Mr Esmond seems to have thought that we might, after all, have again begun to take serious interest in Lady Ernestone. And so there is a last act, in which she is freed of any suspicion of scandal in the eyes of her friends. This is a pity.

'MY LADY VIRTUE'

Lady Ernestone being the central figure in the play, I have taken her as the main theme of this article. I wish I had space in which to deal with the other figures. They come off far better. Indeed, I think that the characters of Mr and Mrs Burville are quite the best thing Mr Esmond has yet done. Both are drawn with a subtlety and truth that are quite delightful; and they are well realised by Mr and Mrs Bourchier. Than Miss Eva Moore some larger and more majestic actress is needed, I think, to bring out all the fun of Lady Ernestone.

[*1 November 1902*]


MRS HUMPHRY WARD'S PLAY

It is indeed an ailing household into which Mrs Humphry Ward ushers us. Blue, blue the sky that glows over the Alban hills and is mirrored by the Alban Lake. Fair, fair the Villa which the Manistys have taken. Yet hush! Tread very lightly up the steps. Knock very lightly on the door. Miss Manisty cannot see us: 'she is suffering', says the butler, 'from one of her headaches'. Poor dear lady! She always is invisible. Her headaches are chronic; but subtly, as an unseen presence, she pervades the play, wafting the scent of the sal volatile across the footlights . . . Could we see Miss Eleanor Burgoyne? We are shocked when we do see her. She is worn to a shadow. She has become a literary 'ghost' used by her cousin Edward for his horrid book about modern Italy. What a brute Edward is! He knows that Eleanor was sent here for complete rest. Why cannot he write his own books? She presses her hand to her forehead. She assures us that there is nothing wrong with her. Poor dear lady! We wish she would not be so bright and uncomplaining. We have not forgotten that her life was despaired of last autumn... Here comes Edward himself. We will take him aside and speak strongly to him. Our resolve is shaken: poor dear fellow! he seems terribly nervous and run-down... Who is this? Miss Lucy Foster, a young friend from America. Another 'ghost'? Ah no! All a-flush with health and independence. It is just going to do our hearts good to look at her when we are called aside and presented to a livid and bodeful lady in deep mourning—Miss Alice Manisty, Edward's sister. We are very uncomfortable. The eye of the poor lady roves in a manner which we do not at all like. We have a train to catch ... A week later we call again. The young American, even she! has now become a poor dear lady. Pallor, langour, a touch of fever, and offerings of quinine from Eleanor, who is now more poor-dear-ladylike than ever, and needs for herself, surely, every drop of quinine that may be in the Villa. How is Miss Alice? A stupid question!—we might have *known* she had crossed the border-line at a bound. She is upstairs, locked into her bedroom. Her maid is with her—a Scotchwoman, we learn, a most capable person, absolutely to be relied on. We are cheered by the notion of this Scotchwoman. We like to think that there is on the premises one person hale and hearty. We should be glad to set eyes on her. Ah! Eleanor has some instructions to give her. She appears. She is very pale. Her hand passes across her brow. Eleanor, always thinking of others, presently dismisses her, imploring her to rest. . . At whatever hour we go to the Villa (built on clay-soil perhaps), we find the same wan congress of invalids, every one of them invariably a trifle worse than at our previous visit.

Really, there is no inherent reason why in this play any of the characters (except Eleanor) should be unwell. That Mrs Ward has thus wantonly afflicted all the feminine creatures of her fancy is the more regrettable for that her own talent is not in itself tonic. Having not a manner that radiates vitality, she should eschew matter which is 'below par'. We all admire her books, for the fine spirit which inspires them, for the thoughtfulness and the drab sense of beauty that we find in them; but not even if we were all on the literary staff of *The Times* could we lay our hands on our hearts and declare Mrs Ward to be a great creative genius. She invents, but she never projects; holds, but never grips; enlightens, but does she ever illuminate? Her characters and incidents are always well conceived, well described, and impress us with a sense of reality, but never with a very vivid sense of reality. We remember them, but not clearly and for ever. Nay! reading one of Mrs Ward's novels we can always, at any moment, lay it aside for an indefinite period. We are never in a hurry to finish it. Nor does Mrs Ward herself ever seem to have been in a hurry to finish it. The true creator in fiction always gives us the sense of speed. Mrs Ward is rather a critic, an essayist, working ably in another medium. Hers is the leisurely method of the true essayist, and it is that which both gives to her books the charm they have and denies them the power they need. But on a play the leisurely method is an influence for evil alone. In drama everything must be sharp, swift, salient. There must be none of those lingerings and divagations which are essential to an essay and pardonable in a novel. Things must go steaming full speed ahead, not less necessarily if they be things of the soul than if they be things of actual circumstance. And Mrs Ward cannot make things do that. Here, in *Eleanor*, there is dramatic progress of a kind; but it is slow, slow. The characters talk, talk. Admirable is their conversation. Mrs Ward has at least this advantage over the ordinary playwright, that she gives to her dialogue a careful beauty of phrase and cadence; and over the extraordinary playwright—the literary amateur—she has this other advantage, that her dialogue sounds (though it is not) like the ordinary language of real human beings. She is, in fact, one of the few persons who have solved the secret of what dialogue ought to be. But the wool here is not proportionate to the cry. The characters talk round and round their theme, and boredom casts over all its inky shadow. When Eleanor is dying, Manisty becomes longer-winded than ever. Wishing to explain to her some rather abstruse point in his development, 'I must use', he says, 'an image'. Relenting, he asks if she is fatigued. One longs for her to say 'Well, as I am dying, I think we might skip the image'. But she is patient to the last. And out flows a prettily-wrought précis of the Platonic metaphor of the cave. Eleanor's death comes as a merciful release for us all. It does at least make Manisty laconic. I am sorry to say that in the whole play the only thing that does not pall is a whole act which ought to have been omitted. In the book, so far as I remember, Alice Manisty's attempt on the life of Lucy Foster was not artistically absurd. It was just a little useful incident in a long story. But here, occupying one fourth of a psychological play, its 'value' changes. It becomes a slab of inappropriate melodrama. True, it has its use in the scheme of the play. It hastens Manisty's passion for Lucy Foster. But this should have been done by some simpler and more consonant means. The second act, as it stands, mars an otherwise artistic failure.

Even were she a born dramatist, Mrs Ward could hardly have made *Eleanor* effective on the stage. When a woman is breaking her heart for love of a man, we are (unreasonably, perhaps, but inevitably) irritated and unsympathetic unless we ourselves can detect in the man some flavour of fineness. Manisty, in Mrs Ward's book, was not morally a fine person. He was, indeed, a weak and vain egoist. But he was also a man of genius. Mrs Ward succeeded in persuading us of that. We felt (except when they verbally quoted) that Manisty's books were great books. And so we understood and sympathised with Eleanor's devotion. But it is practically impossible to convince an audience in a theatre that one of the characters is a great writer. In the theatre we are so suspicious. We take nothing on trust. We must see and hear all. It is not enough that one of the minor characters shall take up a book from a side-table and say that it is a work of genius. We want that book to be read aloud, in order that we may judge for ourselves. But that would be undramatic, even if the book were a work of authentic genius, specially written by a too zealous property-man, and not merely *Bradshaw's Guide* bound in brocade. And thus the writer of genius is never a serviceable figure in drama. If Manisty were shorn of the defects common to most writers of genius, he might here pass muster as Eleanor's demi-god. As it is, we see in him only a vacillating fraud of a man, and Eleanor seems to us only a fool for her pains in adoring him. And without a truly pathetic Eleanor what can the poor play do?

'The Terry charm' is a mysterious thing, putting logical criticism to rout. I am forced to admit that Eleanor, as played by Miss Marion Terry, was pathos incarnate, To cover my confusion, let me suggest that the tears drawn by Miss Terry were the tears that will sometimes come at the sight of mere beauty—beauty, in this case, of every pose and gesture, of every modulation of the voice. Mrs Ward was as unlucky in her hero as she was lucky in her heroine. We were not merely unconvinced of Manisty's genius: a noodle confronted us. Miss Robins played the mad woman with all the power and imagination that are hers, and seemed to have exorcised that demon of harsh violence which possessed her in *Paolo and Francesca*. Miss Braithwaite, in the part of Lucy Foster, was as charming when she remembered the American accent as when she forgot it. Mr Leslie Faber was excellent as an attaché, and was not abashed (a triumph for a young actor) by having to make love emotionally. The moral of Mr Bernard Fox's impersonation of a priest was that it is useless to be made up as Cardinal Newman if you walk and talk in the manner of Uriah Heep. Miss Rosina Filippi, as Madame Variani, played with merry ease the kind of part for which she is indispensable. I should have mentioned Madame Variani before. She stands saliently out from among the other women. She is not unwell.

[ *8 November 1902* ]


## 'LYRE AND LANCET'

Were this an agony column—a column in which one pays to write little about things which matter much, and not a column in which one is paid to write much about things which matter little—I might go so far as to insert in it the following words: 'F.A. Return to earlier manner and all shall be forgiven. MAX.' Situated as I am, I must go further, amplifying the ample.

Emphasis is a great help in such cases, and I say emphatically that *Lyre and Lancet*, the new play by Mr Anstey, produced at the Royalty Theatre, will not do at all. From the author of *The Man from Blankley's* one has the right to demand something infinitely better. In Mr Anstey, as a writer, are two main ingredients: observation, imagination. None has a keener ear than his for the superficial oddities of human converse and character as exemplified by the people whom he has studied. These oddities he catches very neatly for us, and preserves them for us in a spirit of gentle malice. He is not a satirist. His malice does not go deep enough for that. He merely hears, and remembers, and laughs, and makes us laugh with him. Such is the one side of Mr Anstey's equipment. The other side is his power of fantastic realism—his power of combining ludicrously the humdrum with the impossible. The Pagan statue comes to life in the Chelsea studio, the outer semblance of Mr and Master Bultitude is transmuted, the authentic genie surges voluminous from the neck of a brass bottle bought in Wardour Street; and not only are we tickled by the stark anomaly itself, and by the ingenious multitude of anomalies that follow, but also we are illuminated by an implicit and accidental criticism of life and character. Not Apollo in Picardy himself, nor any of the gods in exile, drew for us sharplier the contrast between the new world and the old than did Mr Anstey's absurd *Tinted Venus*. Pater and Heine were conscious teachers, and Mr Anstey came but as a careless jester; but its form gave to his jest an inevitable significance. Likewise in *Vice Versa*.

Never have we seen so far into the soul of an affluent respectable, middle-aged merchant as through the boyish body of Mr. Bultitude; nor was the generic schoolboy ever so intelligible to us as when Master Bultitude became his own father. Nothing is so instructive as contrast. Things which are misty on their own plane become on another suddenly clear and obvious. In virtue of his very frivolity Mr Anstey is a teacher, and from his romantic inventions more food for thought can be extracted than from a whole libraryful of solemnly realistic and didactic fiction. Well! Either of Mr Anstey's two powers is suitable to the stage. The first he used triumphantly in *The Man from Blankley's*. During the whole three acts nothing at all happened. There was merely a group of eccentric types making conversation. But, from first to last, so truly rang that idiotic conversation, so exactly did it tally with our experience of those types as they are, or with our imagination of them as they must be, that the play (which was not a play) never for a moment palled on us. The authentic manner of the middle-class—not of those extreme wings which we call the upper-middle and the lower-middle, but rather of that greater, more secret body which may be defined as the midmost-middle—was revealed to us in all its nakedness; and, as the midmost-middle is the one class which breeds no playgoers, needless to say that everyone in the audience was entranced.

In *Lyre and Lancet* Mr Anstey has provided two groups of types: types of the aristocracy, types of the lower classes. These, however, happen to be not at all delightful. They do not tally with our experience of aristocrats and plebeians as they are, or with our imagination of them as they must be. Even as burlesques, they give us no pleasure, having no discernible basis in fact. As figments, moreover, they are stale. Mr Anstey seeks to initiate us into a house named Wyvern Court, above and below stairs. But either he has never been there, or he has been there blindfold. A pompous butler, dropping his aspirates; a housekeeper, perpetually hoping there will not be a 'contretong'; a chef proclaiming in broken English the glories of his art—we know them to be phantoms, dismal phantoms raised from the yellowing pages of Early-Victorian wags. Above stairs the atmosphere is hardly fresher. We are confronted by the haughty dowager so well known to us in Mr George Edwardes's musical comedies, and by the hearty squire who sees no harm in anyone or anything, and by the heavy dragoon who twists his moustache and says

'What?' at the close of every sentence. In somewhat closer relation to actuality is the nondescript young man whose mission in life is to wear an elaborate smoking-suit and say subacid things about the other people staying in the house. But even he belongs to at least a decade ago, and is no longer a profitable theme: Mr Street, once and for all, wrung out of him, as 'Tubby', all the essential fun. However, the lapse of one decade is better than the lapse of five; and Mr Ernest Lawford, as Bertie Pilliner, has proportionately the chance (which he takes) of shining among the other members of the cast. I was forgetting that there is one other figure which dates no further back than the past decade. This is the figure of a poet who has just published some slight but unpleasant verses 'in a little pink book all over silver cutlets' and is accordingly the talk of the town. The part is well played by Mr Cosmo Stuart, who puts into it an amount of brio worthy of a contemporary cause, and by making up as a French poet of this moment, helps us to forget that he is portraying an English type now obsolete. In the whole play these two are the only characters which are not quite frigid and perfunctory. Phantoms they are, but of men who have existed. The rest are phantoms of figments which were dull even when they were new. I urge Mr Anstey back to the portrayal of that midmost-middle-class which really interests him, and about which he can tell us subtle truths.

The kind of puppets with which the little stage of the Royalty Theatre is so sadly overcrowded would be all very well in a rattling farce. In their first form, both *The Man from Blankley's* and *Lyre and Lancet* appeared in the pages of *Punch*. But, whereas Mr Anstey, translating his first tale to the stage, let the plot of it go hang, he has evidently felt that the plot of his second must never be lost sight of. Conscious of the shortcomings of his puppets, he has called in Mr Kinsey Peile to preserve in dramatic form the farce which he himself had compassed in literary form. Mr Peile has done the job quite neatly. But his skill is all in vain. The materials on which he was set to work precluded success. The farce invented by Mr Anstey was not rattling; or, rather, its rattle was too dry, too hollow. What could be drier, hollower than the sound of this? A squire telegraphs for a vet to come and prescribe for one of his horses. On the same day is expected by his wife the poet whom I have already mentioned. The vet has lately bred a prize bull-dog. It is named 'Andromeda'. The title of the poet's volume is also *Andromeda*. The vet arrives at the house before the poet, and is mistaken for him. The poet is subsequently mistaken for the vet. Each is treated accordingly, and cannot understand why.

I do not make the assumption that a case of mistaken identity can yield no fun. *Vice Versa* itself was founded on such a case. But in *Vice Versa* the two mistaken characters were conscious of the mistake, and the greater part of the fun was in the frantic endeavours of the one character to reveal himself, and in the stolid pleasure which the other took in continuing the mystification. Here the fun is chiefly the fun of verbal cross-purposes. The vet is asked when the next edition of *Andromeda* may be expected; the poet is asked if he has a horse of his own, and replies that he has one which soars on wings to the empyrean; and so on, and so on, endlessly. Of course, as in *Vice Versa*, there is the fun that comes of one character being treated with greater deference than he is used to, and the other with less. But in *Vice Versa* there was the strong contrast between what is expected by an elderly parent and what is expected by a brat of a boy at a private school. Here the difference is merely between a third-rate poet and a first-rate vet. The fun is accordingly moderate. And it is quite a relief when the authors, failing in further invention, cause their characters to dance the lancers and have done with it.

Next time, let Mr Anstey rely again on himself, and not on Mr Kinsey Peile and the lancers. Let him lend again to dramaturgy his true talent. 'Rubbish may be shot here' is too often the motto that haunts a clever writer who comes to the threshold of the theatre. To shoot that rubbish is for him not even commercially remunerative. No dramatist who does less than his best can hope to thrive. The rubbish that succeeds is always that of rubbishy writers. Two demons confront the clever writer who gives himself to theatrical work. The one demon is there to prevent his best work from being appreciated, the other to prevent his second-best work from being appreciated. The one demon occasionally relents: did it not relent over *The Man from Blankley's?* The other is always inexorable.

[*22 November 1902*]

## A PLAY IN A SUBURB

Last Monday evening, in the ante-hall of Victoria Station, might have been seen a solitary figure in travelling costume. To you, perhaps, it might not have seemed solitary, for it was in the midst of a myriad of others hustling for departure. But the extremest form of of solitude is, notoriously, that which one experiences in a crowd; and to me this figure, being my own, was fraught with a very real pathos, inasmuch as—but for your better understanding I resume the direct narrative. A porter, miraculously disengaged, perceived the figure, approached and accosted it. 'Paris, sir?' he asked. 'No', I answered, 'Camberwell', and turned on my heel. No doubt the man had meant well, but the contrast between his conjecture and the actual fact intensified too much for tears the actual fact's poignancy. To be asked if one were soaring far on pleasure's rosy and gauzy pinions, when one was only fluttering a little way on the broken wing of duty.... Not in itself unpleasant, the duty of seeing a new play by Mr Fredrick Fenn, whom I knew to be a promising dramatist. *Judged by Appearances*, written by him alone, I remembered as a really ingenious little farce, and *Liz's Baby*, written by him in collaboration with Mr Richard Pryce, had been by far the best play of low life yet seen on the English stage—or rather, the one and only play yet inspired by a sympathetic effort to reproduce for us low life in its crude and interesting reality. Moreover, I knew that at the St James's Theatre (after the run of Mr Justin Huntly M'Carthy's delicate and delightful variations on the theme of Villon) Mr George Alexander meant to produce a new Fenn-and-Pryce play. And thus ... but it is a far cry from the St James's to Camberwell High Street. Against the suburbs, as such, I have no unmitigated prejudice. I can imagine that they are delightful to live in. I can imagine that 'the return of the native' to Camberwell, or to one of Camberwell's equivalents, after long years of absence, or even after the day's work within the metropolis, is an occasion of true sentiment, even of ecstasy. But for the non-resident, for the mere casual visitor, the suburbs dangle no dear attraction. We shun them. Only under protest, in full sulks, do we go to them—patronise them, we should prefer to say. We feel that we are removing ourselves from the centre and focus of things, yet not removing ourselves far enough to feel the joy of change. A great provincial town is pleasant as another (albeit an inferior) centre of things. The depth of the country is delicious as being (at least to our narrow vision) utterly outside that cosmic radius in whose centre our place habitually is. Such a city as that which the porter at Victoria cruelly suggested as my goal is delicious as being a centre superior in almost every respect to our own. But a suburb—what is a suburb to us, but a sordid, unmeaning little effort in the mimicry of ourselves? It may be very silly of us, bu, the fact remains that we have scant patience with the suburbs; and the spleen at our hearts, when we visit them, is like to be vented on whatever we find there—even on a masterpiece of dramatic art. The dramatic critics, last Monday evening, were called from the Metropolis to Camberwell. Like the relatives of Captain Reece, they 'attended there as they were bid: it was their duty and they did'. But Mr Fenn must not take seriously such strictures as they may have made on his play. They were in no humour to do justice to it. At any rate, I was not. And any strictures which I may be going to make must be taken by Mr Fenn with due regard to my admission.

He seems to me to have made one radical and fatal mistake in his scheme. He has given a frivolous development to a serious story, evidently expecting that we shall, nevertheless, be able to take the story seriously all the while, and be illuded and moved by it. Let me suggest by an hypothesis what exactly it is that he has done. I take it that most of my readers have beheld, at one time or another, Miss Vesta Tilley (is not she officially described as 'London's Idol'?) and that her name conjures up for them a definite image— the foot-lit image of a very feminine lady strutting in costume of the latest masculine pattern, and celebrating, in impassioned song, the mystic beauty of the life led by her as 'one of the boys.' Well! suppose that Miss Vesta Tilley were driving through a country lane, conspicuous in the habiliments in which London idolises her, and suppose that (*absit omen*) she were thrown out of the dog-cart and sprained her ankle, and suppose that she was carried to the house of a local baronet, and suppose that she had some good reason for not wishing the inmates of the house to suspect her real sex. From this series of suppositions what situation do you deduce? You say you imagine the local baronet throwing up his hands and exclaiming 'Why, this is none other than London's Idol'? You cannot imagine him, and his relations, and his servants, being completely deceived by Miss Tilley's pretension to be an ordinary young man of fashion? You cannot imagine Miss Tilley staying in the baronet's house for a whole month, all the while being accepted all round as the best of good fellows? You cannot imagine her host inviting her, furthermore, to go and shoot big game with him in Africa? Then Mr Fenn was too sanguine. For he expected of your imaginations no lower a flight than all this. Mrs Kent, his heroine, is unhappily married. She is half-separated from the drunkard who is her husband. He wishes to resume cohabitation. She, to elude him, orders a masculine outfit, cuts her curly hair, and goes into the depths of the country. One day, as she is driving a dog-cart through a country lane, the horse stumbles, and she ... for an account of her subsequent adventures, refer to my hypothesis of Miss Tilley. Here, perhaps, Mr Fenn would interrupt me, protesting that there is nothing inherently impossible in the notion of a woman palming herself off as a man, and that, in point of fact, there are in modern history several well-known instances of a woman palming herself off as a man for many years. Quite so. But these deceivers have been, invariably, women of a peculiar kind—women whose nature was more masculine than feminine, and who chose a masculine life, not by caprice, but because a feminine life dissatisfied them. But Mrs Kent is quite an ordinary woman, and she falls duly in love with the baronet who harbours her. Being an ordinary woman, she is bound to look more than ever womanly in masculine attire, and could not for a moment impose on anyone except on a blind man; and even this blind man, unless he happened to be also deaf, might have his doubts of her. Convinced that the situation is thus impossible and incredible, Mr Fenn might yet accuse me of unfairness in dragging in Miss Tilley. He might urge that he had not conceived his heroine as looking like Miss Tilley, and that if, in point of fact, the lady cast for the part looked like Miss Tilley the fault was not his. But again Mr Fenn would be grounded. The point is that he *ought* to have conceived his heroine as looking like Miss Tilley. She could not possibly (unless she were one of the irrelevant monsters whom I have mentioned) look like anyone else but Miss Tilley. Take any real woman; send her to have her hair cut, and a suit of clothes cut, in the current mode for men, and the inevitable result will be one Idol the more for London. No one, for instance, could be less like Miss Tilley as we know her than is Miss Beryl Faber as she appears in the first and last acts of

*A Married Woman.* Yet in the second and third acts the illusion of identity was complete. And thus the situation was not merely incredible but also ludicrous. If the play had been a farce, neither of these two qualities would have been deprecable. But the play is conceived in all earnest. The characters are meant to be quite real to us. Unless we believe, and are moved, the whole play must fall to the ground. As we are but incredulous chucklers, it falls even so. A pity! for there is much that is good in it. The scenes between Mr and Mrs Kent are admirably written, Mr Fenn shirking neither the good qualities of the unsympathetic man nor the bad qualities of the sympathetic woman. For this kind of conscience one must needs be grateful to any dramatist, even though it be displayed outside the four-mile radius. Many other good points the play had, though they were blunted for us by the duffers who had the making of them. True, Mr Titheradge and Miss Beryl Faber, as Mr and Mrs Kent, played with keen spirit and intelligence; and Miss Edith Craig, in a lesser part, grafted the Terry charm on a brusque and un-Terryish realism, all her own. But the others ... I leave them in unsalted relish of whatever praises they may have won from the critics of the local journals.

[*29 November 1902*]


## A FEUILLETON-PLAY

I have never, to the best of my belief, met one of the many thousands of souls who read daily, with fervid gusto, the feuilletons printed in the halfpenny morning papers. Nor has whatever time I may have wasted been wasted after the fashion of these folk. But I have, now and again, read an instalment of a feuilleton, with the synopsis which is there to comfort those who have been travelling abroad, or who have only learnt to read, since the tale began. These casual studies have made me no scoffer. I think that to write one of these feuilletons must be quite a difficult task, requiring a special gift specially developed. To project a number of absolutely unreal but strongly-defined characters, to involve them in a sad, lurid, happily-ending story, and to throw round them an atmosphere which shall be undeniably 'wholesome', is by no means all that our feuilletonist must do. He must so unfold his story that when it is cut up into small sections of uniform length every section shall have in itself something to hit the reader straight between the eyes and to be clearly remembered by him for the rest of the day, making him long for tomorrow morning. The peculiar conditions under which he works prevent him from indulging in didactic philosophy. Brief interludes of broad comic relief he may give us; but not his to teach us that the Church of Rome is wicked or that Society is hollow. Such profound lessons as these can be inculcated only in the form of a book. And as it is for them alone that the British public really respects an author, the poor feuilletonist lives and dies obscure, inglorious. He gives an immense amount of pleasure, but he gets sadly little in return. His name is on no man's lips. Where he lives or what he looks like, no man knows or cares. Except a slight emolument, his sole guerdon is in the perfection of his work. He is a type, albeit a humble type, of sheer artistry.

Last week I found (where, you shall learn anon) an excellent idea for a feuilleton. The right scheme and the right atmosphere were both suggested to me so forcibly that at a feuilleton I mean to try my hand. I do not suppose I shall be capable of developing it in the truly professional manner; but (law of copyright permitting) I mean to try. Some fragments of it I have already written, and, in order that I may the better gauge their quality before I proceed further, I will here submit them to the test of print.... Young Henry Traquair was the spoilt child of fortune. From his cradle he had not known what it is to want for anything. Wealthy, healthy, handsome, no wonder he was envied by all the men and admired by all the ladies of his numerous acquaintance.... At the time our story opens... the gay city... engaging a luxurious apartment in the Hôtel St Charles in the Champs Elysées, fit for a princess. And indeed was it not a princess he was expecting, the princess of his heart—sweet Margaret Fielding, whom he loved with an ennobling passion.... Cruel parent... run-away match.... The waiter threw open the door. 'A lady for *Monsieur*.' [*To be continued to-morrow.*] 'Harry!' 'Margaret!' He thought she had never looked so beautiful as now.... 'Tomorrow, dearest, is our wedding-day.'... 'Let us step out on to the balcony.'... Two gentlemen were shown in to the apartment. The taller of the two was Captain Richard Haynes, the shorter was the Rev. Walter Maxwell, both old friends of Henry.... They espied the two figures linked arm in arm on the balcony. 'By

Jove, what a beautiful woman!' ... For an instant Henry Traquair stood silent. Then 'Gentlemen', said he, 'allow me to present you to my wife!' [*To be continued to-morrow.*] 'Seen the papers?' asked the Captain. 'Awful bank-smash, that.' 'What bank?' asked Traquair listlessly.... His face was ghastly to behold. 'Every penny I had in the world' he muttered hoarsely.... 'But', Margaret pleaded, 'I love you none the less dearly because you are not wealthy. You can work. With me ever at your side'.... Work? He? He who had never yet turned his hand to anything—he to whom self-indulgence had become a second nature? He pushed her from him almost roughly. 'You will just have time to catch the boat-train back to England' ... At the door she paused. His head was still sunk in his hands. Ah, had he even then looked round, who knows but that ... The door closed ... He rose and touched the electric bell. He bade the waiter bring him his dressing-case—there was something in it that he needed. He seated himself at the writing-table and commenced to write. 'Bring me some sealing-wax', he said, as the waiter re-entered the apartment. 'Here is a stick of black sealing-wax, but perhaps Monsieur would prefer red?' The black will do,' said Traquair without looking up from his task...

I find that these verbatim fragments would overfill my space if I persisted in them. Accordingly, I must give you the rest of the story in the form of a synopsis. Three years elapse after the suicide of Henry Traquair. Margaret Fielding is safely at home. No one knows her to have been the heroine of that painful escapade. Even the Rev. Walter Maxwell (who is now vicar of the parish in which she lives) suspects nothing, for he has become blind. His blindness does not prevent him from loving her. He makes her an offer of marriage, which she accepts. They are very happy in their married life. But Captain Haynes comes to visit his old friend and recognises in his old friend's wife the lady whom his other old friend had introduced as his wife. Mrs Maxwell persists in denying that Captain Haynes has ever met her before. She does not carry conviction. To make matters worse, in steps an eminent oculist. Her husband regains his eyesight. He shrinks from her in horror. She is too proud to explain to him that she is not what he takes her for. But Captain Haynes was the recipient of the letter written by Traquair before his suicide, and this letter, which clears Mrs Maxwell's reputation, he tardily produces. So all ends happily.

## A FEUILLETON-PLAY

Now, I think you will agree that my feuilleton promises well. If it fail, it will fail through my own technical inexperience, not through any flaw in its scheme. But in any case I shall be much surprised if it be treated as literature by the literary critics. I dare not hope, for example, that Mr W. L. Courtney will devote to it a column of discrimination in the *Daily Telegraph*. I dare not hope that he will say of it that, though it is in no sense a great book, 'it is in the best sense of the words a conventional book—good convention being, as we understand the matter, an indispensable element in every good book', or that he will be moved by it to reflect that 'the absence of human foresight is the novelist's opportunity, and the headlong acceptance of every event as it comes is the very essence of romantic fiction', or that he will picture my readers as 'dimly anticipating the complications which Destiny has in store'. Thus my modesty brings me to the point at which I have been aiming—the very different standards which are applied to drama and to literature. The scheme of my feuilleton was suggested by a play produced last week, with very great success, at the Haymarket Theatre. The author of this play is Captain Marshall, and its title (which will be also the catchy title of my feuilleton) is *The Unforeseen*. The style in which my tentative fragments are written does not, of course, echo the style in which Captain Marshall has written his dialogue. The only fault to found with Captain Marshall's dialogue is that it is too literary: his characters are apt to talk more like books than like human beings. But, for the rest, my feuilleton is his play accurately translated into terms of fiction. Suppose, just suppose, that Mr Courtney will be condemned to read my feuilleton, when it is published, and to write a column about it; and then imagine what he will say of it! And yet my instances of what he could not conceivably say of it are accurate transcripts of what he has said of Captain Marshall's original version. (I have merely substituted 'book' for 'play', 'novelist' for 'dramatist', 'fiction' for 'drama'.) I do not for a moment suggest that Mr Courtney is not so sincere a dramatic critic as he is a literary critic. Nor am I so blind as not to see in Captain Marshall a born playwright. But I think it lamentable that one of our half-dozen born playwrights should be content to squander his talent so unworthily. And I think there would be more chance of his reformation in particular, and of our drama's reformation in general, if Mr Courtney and the other literary-dramatic critics would judge him and his fellow-playwrights by a standard somewhat less remote from the standard by which they judge even the humblest writers of books.

[*13 December 1902*]

## 'OTHELLO' RE-INTERPRETED

It needs no courage to say that as a dramatist, in the narrow sense of the word, Shakespeare has had his day. Those crude farces and melodramas, native or exotic, used by him as vessels for his genius, are not good enough for this sophisticated age. What thrill for us in the strange adventures of the Prince of Denmark or the Thane of Cawdor or the Venetian usurer? These were the kind of things that made Shakespeare popular in his own day. They were fashionable then, and accordingly are out of fashion now. What interests us in Shakespeare's plays is not the plays themselves, but the (strictly irrelevant) truth and beauty that he poured into them. We love them for their matchless poetry and their matchless insight into the human soul. *Hamlet* is for us nothing but the study of a contemplative man distracted by the necessity to be up and doing; *Macbeth*, the study of a noble mind degraded by ambition: *The Merchant of Venice*, the study of racial strength against contempt and persecution. Nothing to us now, the actual framework of these studies; everything, the studies themselves, and the language in which they are set forth. Our pleasure in the production of a Shakespearean play is according solely to the illuminative rightness of the conception of the chief character, and to the sonorous beauty with which the verse is declaimed by all. Let us see whether we can be pleased by *Othello* as now enacted at the Lyric Theatre.

Our whole interest in *Othello* is divided between two studies: on the one hand a study of natural villainy; on the other, a study of a grand, primitive soul lashed to overwhelming rage by jealousy. *Othello* is a two-part play, and of the two parts in it the more deeply interesting is not the title-part: its really central figure is Iago, and *Iago* it ought really to have been called. It would, assuredly, have been called so, had Shakespeare conceived it for himself, and not merely 'lifted' it in his usual manner. Not before he had worked some way through his version, did Shakespeare begin to see Iago with his own eyes. I take it that in the Italian story Iago was a commonplace scoundrel, compassing Othello's ruin because he had reason to hate Othello. It is as a commonplace scoundrel that we see Iago at first. He is angry that Othello has preferred to him in military rank Cassio, the less capable soldier; also, he believes that Othello has seduced Emilia, his wife; and these motives prick him to the task of ruining his master's happiness. But gradually, as the play proceeds, and as Shakespeare's own creative genius takes possession of himself, we begin to see that Iago is not really pricked at all by desire for vengeance. He is villainous for villainy's sake—a philosophic villain, planning havoc as a curious intellectual gratification to himself. Against Othello he has no more ill-will than against Cassio or Roderigo or any other pawns. If he has any feeling at all in relation to Othello, it is a feeling of pity—a dry, intellectual pity for one who, like the rest, is his inferior in intellect; and even this pity is eclipsed by sense of humour. Othello is amusing: and the more he suffer, the more amusing must he become. For that reason, and only for that reason, is Iago Othello's enemy. If some yet nobler and more stupendous fool hove in sight, Iago would straightway leave Othello in peace. All the energy of his mind is centred on the contrivance of mischief. For the art of war he has no enthusiasm: he is a capable soldier, because he happens to be a soldier, but he sees no romance in his profession. Neither does conquest in love allure him. He confesses to Roderigo an abstract interest in 'our raging motions, our carnal stings, our unbitted lusts, whereof I take this that you call love to be a sect or scion'. But himself is above such follies. Speaking of Othello's love for Desdemona, he says 'I do love her too', grimly adding that he loves her in so far as she is the instrument prepared for Othello's downfall, and 'not out of absolute lust, though peradventure I stand accountant for as great a sin'—for all he knows, he *may* have a sexual passion for her; but that were neither here nor there. Now and again, he reverts to Emilia's infidelity as his motive in mischief. This is not, as some too subtle writers have suggested, a sign that he is so subtle as to deceive even himself: he sees himself as clearly as he sees everyone else, and the only difference between his vision of himself and his vision of his fellows is that he does not think himself ridiculous. His harping on Emilia is an inconsistency not in himself, but in Shakespeare, who did not wholly untrammel his own finished Iago from the Iago in the first perfunctory sketch. What the poet was too lazy to do, we do for him; and Iago stands out for us as a perfect type of philosophic villainy. A great part, this, needing a great actor. A very difficult part, also, needing a very accomplished actor. To Othello and to most of the other characters Iago must seem simply a bluff, straightforward soldier—'honest Iago', and all that. But to the audience he must seem always the great villain that he is. 'I am not what I am', he confides to Roderigo, and from time to time he reveals himself in soliloquy. But the actor must not rely on these devices: he must be always the true Iago to the audience and the false Iago to the *dramatis personae*. Much skill is needed for this dual suggestion. Much skill might be expected of so clever and experienced an actor as Mr Herbert Waring, who plays Iago in this revival. Much skill is not, however, what Mr Waring shows us. To the audience and to the dramatis personae he is the same creature. The great villain? The bluff, straightforward soldier— Alas, neither. Nothing, alas, that we have not seen in romantic dramas when Mr Waring was playing the hero. A strutting, chin-in-the-air figure, with a fixed smile, and with much squaring of elbows and twirling of wrists—that is the sole impression left by Mr Waring's Iago. Of Iago as a good fellow on the one hand, or as a bad fellow on the other, there is no impression at all. One sees simply a frigid repetition of what was (or, as I think, wasn't) all very well in *Under the Red Robe* and kindred masterpieces. You will hardly believe me when I tell you that at the close of the first act, after speaking the terrible words:

> 'I have't. It is engender'd. Hell and night
> Must bring this monstrous birth to the world's light'

the actor performs his well-known trick of raising his hat by the back of its brim and whirling it round his head till it falls back into position. Throughout, the actor's one aim seems to be the display of a quite irrelevant virtuosity. 'Decorations by Waring'! They should have been countermanded.

The demands made on an actor by the part of Iago are wholly intellectual. The chief need of the part of Othello is a special kind of physique. As I have suggested, there was no reason to expect that Mr Waring would not be a very capable Iago. There was, however, no doubt that Mr Forbes Robertson ought not to appear as the Moor.

His performance has, at least, the advantage of being no dissappointment. It is essential that Othello be a man of solid bulk—a magnificent animal, stately in repose, savagely terrible in passion. When Mr Robertson came on the stage, one felt that here was not Othello, arraigned before the Senators, but Hamlet playing an Oriental part in some play before the dons at the University of Wittenberg. Instead of the calm, majestic Moor, we saw a quick-witted, highly-strung, highly-refined student, who might subsequently be goaded to the verge of hysteria, but hardly through dark depths of passion to the committing of crime. Mr Robertson's conception of Othello is, no doubt, impeccable. But Nature debars him from showing it to us. He cannot suggest the brute grandeur or the brute passion of Othello. In the scene of Desdemona's murder he is at his best, but he is so because here Othello ceases to be Othello, avowing that he will slay his wife not because she has betrayed his trust in her, but as an act of moral precaution—'else she'll betray more men'. Admirable, again, is he when, at last, Othello is subdued by the ruin that he has wrought and by his impending suicide. But in the other scenes—the earlier, needing the extreme of static force, and the later, needing the extreme of dynamic force—Mr Robertson merely fails to perform an impossible task.

Intellectually and emotionally, then, we cannot be pleased by *Othello* as now enacted at the Lyric Theatre. Instead of a giant caught in the toils of a devil, we see a student scored off by a fop. There remains the question of auric pleasure—is the poetry well treated by the company? Needless to say that Mr Robertson so declaims it that every phrase and cadence has its due beauty. Pleasant to add that Miss Gertrude Elliott, as Desdemona, speaks it very prettily, and that Mr Sydney Valentine, as Brabantio, rolls it out impressively. Horrid not to be able to acquit any other one of letting it go hang.

[20 *December 1902*]

## DRAMA FOR EPICURES

The scholars, artists and other such personages in our midst are often chidden for their churlishness in not going habitually and publicly to the theatre. It is pointed out to them that great drama must be ever that which catches in a common enthusiasm all classes of the community And it is assumed that, if all classes went to the theatre, something might turn up and produce a common enthusiasm. Semi-private and unpopular affairs like the Stage Society are declared to be useless in the long run: great drama cannot be produced without an appeal to the ruck of humanity. On the other hand, it is urged, how can the 'giddy vulgar' be lured into a state of fine aesthetic receptivity except by rubbing shoulders with the scholars, artists, and other distinguished personages? Well, no one would be gladder than I to get great drama. But I do not agree with the theorists as to the likeliest way of getting it. The lion might lie down with the lamb, but there would be no satisfactory offspring. It is quite true that great drama has sometimes 'drawn' a whole community. The Athenians, for instance, all went to the play; and so did the Elizabethans. But did the average man of Athens sit out the plays of Aeschylus and Sophocles because their power and beauty compelled him? He sat them out simply because they were a part of the religious devotions expected of him as a good citizen. Even so, the average Elizabethan sat out Shakespeare and lesser masters for sake of the much that they deliberately foisted in to impress him as an admirable substitute for brawling and bear-baiting. Great drama, as such, never has been and never will be loved except by a small minority of playgoers. If a heaven-born and sky-towering school of dramatists arise in our midst, and find some means of being also popular, then, we may be sure, our 'intellectuals' will become playgoers. Meanwhile, we cannot blame these gentlemen for attending only the 'experiments' of such and such an esoteric 'society'. It is from that quarter, and under those conditions, that great drama is least unlikely to crop up. In any case, let us dismiss the fond notion that a nightly complement of spectacles and long hair in the auditoria of theatres which are controlled by Mob and Mammon would bring us one inch the nearer to the threshold of our desire.

For anyone who is yet loth to dismiss this fond notion it may be some comfort to know that I have discovered among the younger and lighter 'intellectuals' quite a cult for that dramatic form which is alleged to make the surest appeal to the greatest number. The other day, introduced into the company of some young poets, painters and dilettanti, I was surprised to find that most of their conversation hinged on 'the drama', and I was humiliated to find that for them this phrase connoted something of which I was wholly ignorant. They bandied, freely and knowingly, the names of theatres, plays, authors and mimes heard by me for the first time. Mystified, quite 'out of it', but caught by their enthusiasm, I begged for enlightenment. I then learned from them that 'the drama' must be sought not in the trite area known as the West End, but in the remote, mysterious, inclement North, East and South Ends, of this city. I said I should seek it forthwith. They smiled at my impetuous ignorance: 'the drama' was utterly suspended just now, owing to the 'panto season': no, stay! one fortress there was, impregnable by 'panto'—the dear old Standard. At the Standard Theatre (Bishopsgate and Shoreditch, E.) was due on Boxing Day a new drama by Frederick Melville. Most of the young 'intellectuals' were leaving town for Christmas, but one of them, a painter, was remaining, and he very kindly offered to convey me to the première of *Between Two Women*.

My anxiety was not so much to see this play as to see the effect of it on my guide. There could be no doubt of his enthusiasm, and of his peers' enthusiasm, for 'the drama' by it exemplified. Here was no mere affectation of enthusiasm: no theory of affectation could be made to square with the constant habit of travelling very long distances, by night, to and from very lugubrious districts. And so, throughout the performance of *Between Two Women* I kept one eye and ear for the stage and the other for my guide's face and comments. The action of the play began on a cliff in 'Poppyland, near Cromer'. After a comic scene between a rustic and a seafaring man, a clergyman entered. My friend joined in the general applause. This, he explained to me, was Albert Ward, perhaps the strongest actor in the Standard's company. The clergyman declared to the audience his intention of saving his friend Harry Millard, son of the Earl of Millard, from the toils of Carmen de Siveraux, that abominable woman. My guide praised the choice of names—'Frederick Melville', he said, 'may always be trusted in the choice of names'.

The fore-shadowing of the plot—just enough, not too much—was also commended. It appeared that Mr Frederick Melville always had been adept in the art of preparation. Presently a shadow crossed my guide's face, and a sigh escaped him. The clergyman had just laid his hand on Harry Millard's shoulder, saying 'Harry, how complex you are! A mixture of the athlete and the artist, the idealist and the man of the world!' I supposed that my guide was wincing at this strange misassociation of ideas. But 'That is the worst of Frederick Melville', was the grievance; 'he is always slipping into subtlety. Walter Melville is incomparably the better man'. It seemed that there were two brothers, Frederick and Walter, sons of Mrs A. Melville, the proprietress and manageress of the Standard, and that Walter, like Frederick, was a famous maker of melodramas. Some people gave the palm to Frederick, others to Walter. My friend admitted that, in breadth of comic relief and in depth of homely sentiment, Frederick was perhaps the better man. But in straightforward virility of conception and execution Frederick fell far below his brother's level. Walter never hesitated, never hedged. His heroes and heroines were heroes and heroines without a blemish; his villains, male and female, were dyed black all over and to the very core. Frederick, on the other hand, was always sneaking away to hold the mirror up to what he took for Nature. 'I have no patience', said my guide, 'with Frederick. I believe he has it in him to do really fine work. But—there! what did I tell you?' And there, to be sure, was Carmen de Siveraux bewailing the long loss of a little blind son whom she had once loved with all the finest passion of maternity. 'So much,' said my guide, 'for Carmen de Siveraux—neither one thing nor the other! Oh for one hour of Walter!' The two male villains acted as a slight emollient. Each was unmitigated from first to last. Walter himself might have been proud to father them. One incident in their career pleased my guide especially. To them, honoured guests at a garden party given by the Earl of Millard, entered the long-lost blind boy, begging bread. The second villain roughly intimated that trespassers would be prosecuted. The first villain, more subtly, drew his hand from his pocket, saying 'I have here two coins—a half-crown and a penny', and threw the penny at the boy's head. 'Well,' he said sharply, 'why don't you pick it up?' 'I cannot, sir' replied the boy, 'I am blind. 'Oh, you're blind, are you?' repoined the villain, proceeding to enunciate the theory that afflicted creatures should be killed at birth, and concluding with a threat that if the blind boy did not go away he would be 'given in charge'. 'Oh, sir', pleaded the boy, 'you could not be so cruel'. 'What', cried the first villain, raising his ebony walking-stick, 'you impudent young rascal, I'll'— but at that moment entered the heroine, taking the blind boy under her protection and saying some plain things about villains in general. My guide, by the way, objected that throughout the play the heroine had rather too sharp a tongue—was not gentle enough in indignation at the iniquities around her. Many other objections did my guide make, of a more highly technical kind. Not all of them did I understand fully. But I understood his general attitude, and the general nature of his pleasure, and of the pleasure taken by the other young intellectuals, in this kind of drama.

On the way back to civilisation, I suggested to him that this attitude and this pleasure were essentially frivolous. 'Why?' he retorted. 'We are lovers of the theatre, lovers of the dramatic form. In the theatres that *you* go to we find no really sincere or beautiful work— only second-rate charades, cleverly enough faked to deceive people who are not very clever. We should delight in good work, if we could find it. As it is, we get from frankly bad work a lesser, an indirect pleasure. Mediocrity is the one negligible thing in art. The extremes are jolly thngs—the things to go for.' I did not try to refute him. I would try now, only I am no sophist.

[*3 January 1903*]

## MR ARTHUR COLLINS AS SYMBOLIST

Not so has Mr Arthur Collins been accounted hitherto. And indeed, if you take down from its place in your library the bound 'book' of any past pantomime in which Mr Collins has collaborated, you will find little that is not quite simple and forthright in the poetry and in the action. The form is modelled carefully according to the precepts of the late Sir Augustus Harris; and there was not, as you know, much literary nonsense about that Augustan age in which Mr Collins was a malleable boy. Yet must there have been deep down in the breast of Master Arthur some seeds of symbolism. One such seed has peeped up, modestly but unmistakably, to blossom, in Mr Collins's latest work; and I do not suppose it can have been the sole implanted one. Who shall prophesy Mr Collins's final place in drama's history? Maeterlinck is gradually enubilating himself from those enchanted mists in which first he strayed, smoothing out the folds of the cloak that wraps his soul about, preparing himself, it would seem, for a brisk walk along the well-lit beaten track of modern drama. But there is not the necessary man. One symbolist goes down, another comes up smiling, or sighing. And the more I think about Mr Collins, the more convinced am I that his ultimate destiny... but such speculations are outside the scope of this criticism. Let me but tell you of the actual little flower of symbolism in *Mother Goose*. You behold 'The Hall of Gold', wherein the suddenly enriched dame is banqueting her friends and relatives. You have never beheld anything like it outside Drury Lane, and inside Drury Lane you have seldom beheld anything not exactly like it. To say that you behold it is perhaps misleading. Without smoked glasses you can but blink at it, furtively, from time to time. So dazzling is it, so blinding in (that which, if I were on the staff of a morning-paper, my proprietor would prefer me to call) its beauty. The world in chaos, hastily overhauled and gilded and prismatised to look like what Early-Victorian persons supposed Heaven to look like—there you have the Drurian idea of beauty, exemplified now as in the past. Needless to say, the British audience blinks at it with eyelids entranced, ponders it with brains entranced by the impossibility of conceiving how much it must have cost. (If, by the way, these scenes were half so expensive as they look, bailiffs would long have been the sole inmates of our National Theatre. But the public does not want Mr Collins to ruin himself in its service. It wants only the illusion that Mr Collins is ruining himself in its service. And that illusion it annually gets. A gross, materialistic, very unkind gratification, doubtless; but Mr Collins, thriving on it, cannot be resentful.) Needless to say, Mother Goose herself, not less than the audience, is entranced by her surroundings. She waves her arms this way and that in an ecstasy of pride and happiness, glorying in the envy of her friends. But suddenly her palace is darkened, and a hush falls. Blanching, she beholds in an uncertain light the Demon King. He sneers at her. He tells her that the palace which has taken her fancy is decorated and upholstered in the worst possible taste. She cowers before him. If (he continues) she wishes to see something really fine and artistic, let her pay a visit to the palace occupied by himself. Here, thought I, was Mr Collins the symbolist. And I was right Only the symbol turned out not as I anticipated. I supposed that Mr Collins was deploring his own estate—deploring that he, with his love of beauty, must provide only that dreadful thing which is mistaken for beauty by his patrons. I supposed that in the palace of the Demon King would be displayed to us a really beautiful scene, such as Mr Collins could always give us were we but capable of appreciating it—displayed to us on the off-chance that we might take kindly to it and so enable Mr Collins to thrive evermore without violence to his ideals. I supposed, in fact, that Mr Collins's symbol was pathetic. It turned out to be a grimly ironic symbol. Mr Collins was apologising only in the original Greek sense of the word. He sought to justify himself. His attitude was one of pride, of conscious rectitude, of defiance to the likes of me. His drift was this: 'You talk of vulgar display? You urge me to give Art a chance? Very well then. I will take you at your word, sirs. I will hoist you with your own petard, sirs, I will show you what Art is. You think you know? You don't. I do. Here it is. How do you like it?' And forthwith we, beholding the palace of the Demon King, were bound to admit that we did not like it at all. For none but Demons did it seem to us fit. It was very much worse than the Hall of Gold, because it was pretentious. It was, in fact, an elaborate display of what is now known to all Europe as *'L'Art Nouveau'*—that thing than which commercial vulgarity never has produced, and surely never will produce, a viler abomination. You have seen isolated specimens of *'L'Art Nouveau'*, seen them and, I hope, sickened at the coarse and garish pretentiousness of them. You may have seen a whole shop-window crowded with various specimens of *'L'Art Nouveau'*, and have, I hope, thought that fate held in store for you no sight so degrading. But you have never seen (unless you have already been to this year's pantomime) a huge stage, with a *'L'Art Nouveau'* background, danced on by a *'L'Art Nouveau'* ballet. Imagine a whole corps de ballet bearing aloft huge samples of those iridescent drain-pipes, and those lilies in debased and discoloured scroll-work, and all those other fearsome objects which *'L'Art Nouveau'* throws on the market. No, no, Mr Collins, your symbolical apology was conceived with a daring that does you credit; but you have not silenced me. And my voice must still raise to you its annual cry in the wilderness—its faint and piteous cry for an experiment in Art. If the experiment fail, if the public really cannot be converted from its love of splosh for splosh's sake, then, certainly, I will take a back seat—I should prefer it as far back from the stage as possible—and never again blame you for persisting in your present policy. But do let the experiment be made. I suppose you are already evolving the scheme of next year's pantomime? Why not call into your council-chamber Mr Gordon Craig, and give him leave to arrange one of the scenes for you? Doubtless, Mr Craig's ideas would involve but a slight expenditure of money, and the British public, guessing this horrid truth, might sulk a little. But all could be set right by an announcement that every farthing of the balance had been spent in glorifying the other scenes. My own belief is that there would be no sulkiness at all. I believe that the public would welcome any change after all these years—even one that might not seem to it a change for the better. And as for the public's children, whose rude breasts are susceptible to simple fantasy, and unstirred as yet by the notion of vast expenditure, I am sure that from them you would win wild and unstinted applause for your originality.

My readers must not suppose that *Mother Goose* is primarily a vehicle for the veiled enunciation of Mr Collins's theories of Art. These, though I have dealt with them at such length, occupy but a small space in the play. It is rather as a vehicle for Mr Dan Leno's genius that the play should be considered. For my part, I prefer Mr Leno in a music hall, which I take to be his native element. Drury Lane is too vast for his peculiar method: he does not, as does Mr Herbert Campbell, 'carry' far enough. Moreover, being, by dint of long practice and inherent genius, supremely able to make his effects without aid from anyone else, he does not blend rightly with the other characters on the stage. He is alone, and yet not alone, an element disturbing and disturbed. Nor is his heart in the buffooneries which he must perform. His is essentially a psychological humour. And such soul-state as is here assigned to him is a misfit. His especial power is in portraying for us comically a humble man (or woman) perplexed but undaunted in the struggle for life. That corrugated brow; that nervous palm outstretched; that tight mouth, whose corners Care pins down vainly, so surely comes Courage and twitches them up into a smile; that voice, half croak, half chirp, and that general air of physical fatigue overcome by spiritual energy, of faint-ness undeterrible from the pursuit—do not these things incarnate for us in Mr Leno the spirit of the small tradesman, the spirit of the charwoman, and of all cognate types? In suggesting worldly success Mr Leno is not himself. So soon as the goose in this pantomime lays the golden eggs, Mr Leno's true self is lost to us.

[*10 January 1903*]


'FIAMMA'

Like the rest of us, Mr J. T. Grein talks and writes much about the futility of the commercial drama. He holds the common view that 'something must be done', and differs from the rest of us only in that he does actually do something. He keeps us in a state of constant wonder what he will do next, and we are always quite sure that, whatever it may be, it will be a bold thing, a thing to interest us and make us sit up. It was with a beating heart, therefore, that I went one afternoon last week, at Mr Grein's bidding, to the Prince of Wales's Theatre. The play, *Fiamma*; the author, one Mario Uchard. I kept all my wits closely about me. I was determined (poor confident fool!) to be surprised by nothing. *Fiamma*! Evidently a powerful very modern affair; morbid perhaps, but justifying itself through its ardent truthfulness. 'Mario Uchard'! The obvious name of a young genius, undiscovered yesterday, but to-day on the lips of all Paris. Almost intolerable, the suspense in which I waited for the curtain to rise. At length it rose. A studio in Paris. A middle-aged man at his easel, talking to a youth. David Lambert, the world-famed painter, and Henri, his son, a poet of high promise. No signs of a mother. But presently a reference to Fiamma, the world-famed soprano, now for the first time giving the Parisians a taste of her quality. And finally the father's confession that the mother of Henri is no less a personage than Fiamma. As the curtain fell I wondered what would be the strange development of this striking theme. Fond father and outraged husband, faithless wife and callous mother, innocent and idealistic child; and, at the same time, pre-eminent painter, incomparable soprano, *the* poet of the future. I scented some triple tragedy of the artistic temperament, and passed out into the foyer. There I met a certain citizen of the world, and asked him

'What sort of a man is Mario Uchard?' ' "Is"? he laughed. 'Why, of course he died years ago.' 'Dead!' I exclaimed. 'Then this play is posthumous! How very sad! Nothing is so sad as to think of a young man dying obscure, dying ignorant of the fame that will so soon be his.' Then I learned that Uchard had been quite conscious of success, having witnessed the first performance of *Fiamma* in the year of grace 1849. And then, gradually, it dawned on me that the first act was very old-fashioned. This apocalypse involved two mysteries: (1) Why had Mr Grein produced the play? (2) Why had I not at the time been conscious of the play's antiquity? I suppose the explanation of the first mystery to be that Mr Grein's energy is so exuberant that the cause of dramatic progress is not a vessel large enough to contain the whole outpouring of it: there is an overflow which trickles down and becomes reactionary. As to the second mystery, I can only assume that plays do not 'date' so quickly and surely as we imagine, and that we deem a play old-fashioned rather because we know it to be old than because virtue has actually gone out of it. The last three acts of *Fiamma* seemed to me, as I watched them, as antediluvian as the first seemed to me in retrospect. My notice of the play here must be written according to that impression. But I cannot lay my hand on my heart and swear that *Fiamma* is not quite abreast of our time, or even ahead of it. Perhaps, therefore, Mr Grein does not need the excuse just made by me for his latest exploit.

Assuming that *Fiamma* really is old-fashioned, let us consider what makes it so. What is the difference between the play as it is and the play as it would be if Uchard were a '*jeune féroce*' lately unearthed by Antoine? The theme, roughly, is a conflict between the maternal and domestic instinct on the one hand, and the artistic instinct and the desire for fame on the other hand. Fiamma, many years before the action of the play begins, left her husband and child, regarding them as an obstacle to the career on which she had set her heart. She made for herself a great name throughout Europe, and, incidentally, was for ten years the mistress of an English nobleman. Coming with him, at length, to Paris, she happened to meet her son in the house of some friends. She fainted at sight of him. Thenceforth her one desire was to take up her motherhood where she had dropped it. Her husband, in view of her previous conduct, did not offer re-union. But she announced her intention of leaving the operatic stage, and, at the same time, sent the English nobleman to the right about. And the husband hinted that after a decent lapse of time he might consider the question of re-union. This is a quite fair and full account of *Fiamma* on the psychological side. It is, however, hardly an account at all of the play. If I tried to describe the play as it is actually set forth, I should stagger through an ingenious labyrinth of intrigue—recognitions, confrontations, overhearings, prospects of bloodshed, and all the rest of it. These, fifty years ago, were the end of every dramatist's desire, and it was to contrive them effectively, not at all to illustrate his theme truly, that the late M. Uchard was striving. He made the father a pre-eminent painter, and the mother an incomparable soprano, and the son *the* poet of the future; but (barring the bare mention of the mother's motive for leaving home) he did not attempt to make them behave as such. For all that they say and feel and do, they might just as well be quite ordinary, inartistic persons. Just as our own inferior modern English plays are filled irrelevantly with Lords and Ladies, because Lords and Ladies are the folk who appeal most surely to the national imagination, so did M. Uchard drag in artists for the benefit of a city which has always been excited by matters of art. David Lambert explains how it is that he became a great painter. The process was strangely simple. He loved the son whom his wife had so cruelly abandoned, and determined to bequeath to this child an illustrious name. I am no expert in the art of painting, but I do not think that 'D.S.M.' could adduce any instance of a great painter who has been made according to this delightful recipe. How it is that the son is becoming a great poet we are not told. Perhaps it is through the passionate love he cherishes for the mother who discarded him in his cradle. But the point is that the conduct and temperament of neither son nor father bear the slightest trace of his peculiar genius. Similarly, we are asked to suppose that a prima donna who has for a long period of years wholly lacked moral sense in general and maternal sense in particular, and has cared only for her art and for her triumphs in her art, needs but a glimpse of her son to make her the most moral and maternal and inartistically selfless creature in the world. In fact, such psycholology as the play contains is all nonsense. It is merely 'padding' for the intrigue. And that is why the play seems antediluvian. Had it been written in our period, it might not be a masterpiece of psychological truth. But there would, at least, be an effort to make the characters live, and to work out through them the theme of the maternal instinct as affected by the instinct for art. The play would be conditioned mainly by that effort. And it is probable that its whole action would be laid in the time of Fiamma's early hesitation between her art and her home. Instead of merely translating the play, Mr Grein should have written it all over again. As it is, the play is better suited to a theatrical museum than to a theatre, except in so far as it is a showy vehicle for the talent of an actress. And for the talent of Miss Lilian Eldée it seemed, alas! rather too showy a vehicle. The talent was in it, indubitably, but one had to take it on trust, as one might have to take on trust a very small princess passing in a very large state-coach.

[*17 January 1903*]


IBSEN'S 'EPILOGUE'

Even as the lusty street-loafer, if haply you ask him to carry across your threshold and up your stairs the light portmanteau with which you have been travelling, clenches his teeth manfully, and tests the strength of his either wrist with the fingers of his other hand, and squares and bows his shoulders as though he were Atlas receiving from a cab-roof the terrestrial globe, and beneath his burden staggers and stumbles, puffs and blows, till you deem no tip large enough to compensate him for the permanent injury to his health, so, often, does the critic, in his wish to be credited with profound insight prefatorily pretend that some quite simple and obvious work of art is fraught with all manner of brain-wracking and heart-breaking obscurities. This favourite trick has its complement in that other by which, in face of some truly difficult work of art, the critic assumes an air of brazen and off-hand knowingness, cloaking his bewilderment under the pretence that all is as clear as noontide. I think that of these two tricks the latter is always the likelier success. The man who is 'terribly at ease in Zion' is a more plausible rogue than he who, at Hyde Park Corner, grasps you by the arm, exclaiming 'Poor waif! Heaven only knows in what dark and devious district you are groping. But, if you will give me time to think, perhaps—I say *perhaps*—I shall be able to enlighten you'.

Take an example. *When We Dead Awaken* was produced the

other day by the Stage Society, and the critics, with one voice, have been assuring us (as they assured us when it was published as a book) that it is a terribly abstruse and nebulous piece of work, overlaid with a symbolism that is unintelligible either by reason of its too arrogant subtlety or because the author in his eld had lost the power of fitting his symbols to his meanings. And evidently they expect high honour for daring to conjecture what Ibsen was driving at. They are doomed to disappointment. For to no one who has read the play, or who has read merely such précis of it as have been made by the critics, does Ibsen's meaning or his method offer the slightest mystery. Palpably 'faint glimpses into the obvious' are the critics' conjectures. Hyde Park Corner itself is not less baffling, does not stare us more familiarly in the face, than *When We Dead Awaken*.

Ibsen has discovered that the great artist is always inhuman, and on this discovery his play is founded. A simple thesis, surely. Who supposed that the great artist could ever be human? All the passion of a great artist's nature goes into his work. Exactly that same energy of emotion which other men concentrate on life is in his case diverted from life into art. Unless he were absorbedly in love with it, his work could not become great. But, though he is thus detached, he cannot dispense with life. Life is a necessary means to his end. He cannot gain inspiration except through experience. He must have his human models, his human documents. Except as models, as documents, they do not interest him. But it may happen that one of them becomes very much interested in him. A human female may happen to fall in love with him. Then one of two complications is in store; and both of them are equally tragic. Perhaps he will be by the woman's love warned to a temporary love for her. His art will seem to him a poor thing in comparison with this strange feeling. Proportionately, his work will decline, losing its strength and magic. After a time, his true nature will re-assert itself. He will cease, slowly but surely, to be human, and will return to his first love, leaving the second love forlorn. Such is the process worked out in Zola's *L'Oeuvre*, and in many other more or less modern novels. The other process is worked out (retrospectively, as is Ibsen's way) in *When We Dead Awaken*. Here the artist does not respond to the passion of the woman who is his inspiring model. So soon as he has finished the great statute, she leaves him, with her heart broken by his indifference to her womanhood. He tells her that, at all events, his acquaintance with her has been for him 'a priceless episode'. So far, the process of the story has well illustrated the inhumanity of great artists in general. If such illustration had been Ibsen's one aim, then the rest of the play would have shown us merely the sculptor finding other models and creating fresh masterpieces and perhaps fresh tragedies. But Ibsen had another and dearer aim. To portray was not enough: he must also preach. And the gist of his sermon was to be that the great artist is not less pathetic a figure than his victims, in that he never knows the joy of life—a joy incomparably greater than the joy of art. In order that he might point this moral the more sharply, Ibsen manufactured a good deal of the evidence. Rubek, the sculptor, ceased to be a type, and became a peculiar example. After the withdrawal of his particular model, he ceased to care for his art, and devoted himself to pot-boilers. 'All the talk about the artist's vocation and the artist's mission, and so forth, began to strike' him 'as being very empty, and hollow, and meaningless at bottom.' What he wanted was 'life'—that 'life in sunshine and in beauty, which is a hundred times better worth while than to wear yourself out in a perpetual struggle with lumps of clay and blocks of stone.' He married a commonplace girl, and bored her and was bored by her. After a few years (and here the action of the play begins) he met again the woman who had been his model. She, through his treatment of her, had lost her reason. But mad or sane, an Ibsen woman may always be trusted to score off an Ibsen man. Irene (for that is her name) makes very short work of Rubek's half-hearted apologies for art and for the artistic temperament. Rubek's wife has already gone up to the mountains (which are, obviously, symbols for freedom and reality of life) in the company of a full-blooded huntsman, Rubek begs Irene will go up with him to the mountains. They go, but are overwhelmed by an avalanche, while the wife and the huntsman escape unharmed. This business of the avalanche is treated by the critics as something quite inenubilable. Yet what could be plainer than Ibsen's meaning?—that there was a time when Rubek and Irene might have lived their lives, but that now it is too late: that a man can never regain the chance he has once thrown away. The meaning may not be profound, and the symbolism may be a trifle crude; but there is no other possible objection to them. From first to last the play is as clear as it can be. If anything, it is too clear: there is too much expression of its meaning. The characters express, in varying terms, the same thoughts and the same feelings over and over again. There is not really enough in them to fill an evening bill. Nor can we wonder, remembering that this is the latest and last play of a very old man.

There is another sense in which *When We Dead Awaken* is essentially an old man's work. I have suggested that it is rather a sermon than a presentment. The great artist in his prime does not, like Rubek, hanker after 'life'. It is only when his power for art has decayed that he, looking back, realises that perhaps he has foregone the true happiness. In this 'epilogue' Ibsen speaks to us, I doubt not, of himself.

Our relations with foreign Powers continue to be of a friendly character.... You think me abrupt, even cryptic? Perhaps, then, you neither attended nor read a report of Mr Wilson Barrett's valedictory performance at the Adelphi Theatre last Saturday, and know not that at the fall of the curtain the audience was by Mr Wilson Barrett assured that 'the colonies—especially South Africa—were knitting themselves by ever closer bonds to the Mother Country'. True, I have not lately been impersonating an English king, and so cannot imagine that my words will carry such weight as is attached to the words of an actual King of England. But no excuse is needed. Why should a man mind his own business? Even at the risk of making a fool of himself, he ought not thus meanly to hoard the powers with which Heaven has graced him. All honour to the greathearted actor who, instead of rushing to wash off his grease-paint, tarries to allay the fears of a nervous nation. I, fired by his example, feel that this weekly criticism of mine would be incomplete if I appended nothing about other, larger issues. I repeat, emphatically, that our relations with foreign Powers continue to be of a friendly character.

[*7 February 1903*]


## A CHAOTIC PLAY

Mr Carton is our nearest equivalent to M. Capus. In lightness and deftness of touch he is unrivalled by any of the other gentlemen who are writing our comedies. And the atmosphere breathed by his characters is just that atmosphere of irresponsibility, of non-morality, breathed by the characters of M. Capus. And yet it seems absurd to mention his and M. Capus's names in the same breath. The most rabid patriot among us would not dare pretend that the work of this Englishman does not shrivel under comparison with that Frenchman's work. What is the secret of their difference? Why is it that after seeing a play by M. Capus we go away glowing with a sense of delicate repletion and exhilaration, while from a play by Mr Carton we seem to go empty away? The reason, surely, is that M. Capus always means something, whereas Mr Carton never means anything. M. Capus always has some idea about life—not perhaps a very profound, or irrefragable, or even original idea, but still an idea. And round it his characters and incidents revolve, illustrating it, and by it brought into artistic unity. His every play is a criticism of life. He is a man of the world, and has something to say about the world, and says it. Mr Carton may be a man of the world, but I gather that the world does not interest him. If he has anything to say about the world, he certainly does not say it. That ladies wear pretty frocks, that gentlemen wear well-cut frock-coats, and that ladies and gentlemen are not always in love with their own husbands and wives, and that they do not always pay their tradesmen's bills punctually—such is the full extent of Mr Carton's message to us. And it is not enough. We knew it before. We want some sort of deduction from the evidence. We want to know what Mr Carton is thinking. We want to know what Mr Carton is driving at. He is thoughtless. He is driving at nothing. And that is why his plays, once seen, are so soon forgotten. It is not necessary that a writer of comedies should have a solid philosophy of life, though, if he have that (with enough artistic sense to keep it in the background, visible but unobtrusive) so much the better. But some sort of attitude towards life he must have. I conjure Mr Carton to strike some sort of attitude.

In *A Clean Slate*, the play now on view at the Criterion Theatre, I find not even that technical neatness which Mr Carton has hitherto displayed. It is a chaotic play. It is a farce conceived as a comedy, and executed partly as a comedy and partly as a farce. Farcical, rather than comic, is the main scheme—a women divorcing her husband because she wants to marry the co-respondent's husband. Mr Carton, however, has drawn two of the 'parties' as comic characters without a touch of farce in them. These are the petitioner and the

# A CHAOTIC PLAY

co-respondent's husband. And the reason, no doubt, why they are purely comic is that one of them was to be, and is, impersonated by Miss Compton. Now, it is quite possible to treat a farcical idea in a purely comic spirit, and to produce thereby a quite passable imitation of a comedy. But it is difficult to play this trick. The farcical idea is always tripping you up, unless you are very careful. It has tripped Mr Carton up. The respondent and the co-respondent are more farcical than comic. And the whole trend of events, after the first act, is wholly farcical. The decree of divorce has been made absolute. Thes petitioner is staying in a cottage, where she is visited by the co-respondent's husband, eager for immediate marriage. She is visited also by the respondent, who has parted from the co-respondent, and is eager for immediate re-marriage. She is visited also by the co-respondent and the co-respondent's mother, who are anxious to know the respondent's address, and then the fun becomes what is technically known as fast and furious—everyone setting everyone else by the ears, in the approved manner. And, as none of the characters is wholly farcical, and some of them are not at all so, the fastness and furiousness of the fun does not exhilarate us. We merely raise our eyebrows, and hope that next time Mr Carton will go to work on some purely comic scheme. No one would wish him to write a thorough farce. We do not wish Miss Compton to be excluded. She is so delightful and peculiar an actress that she is quite worthy to have plays written uxoriously round her. If Mr Carton had to choose between writing plays round a wife and writing them round an intellectual idea, I should urge him to the latter course. But no choice is forced on him. There is no reason why he should not write round both. It only remains for him, having found the one, to find the other.

I chose an unlucky evening on which to see Miss Compton's performance. The first line she speaks is 'Thanks, I'm quite well. I never allow the weather to affect me.' That is a line characteristic of all Miss Compton's impersonations. A genial, comfortable imperturbability is the keynote of them all. But alas, Miss Compton's voice belied her words. It was obvious that she had allowed the weather to affect her, and so strongly to affect her that one could hardly catch a word she was saying, or rather whispering. The extrinsic pity thus evoked from us might have deepened our delight in another kind of performance. But Miss Compton and pathos do not blend well. She ceases to exist when she does not seem immune from discomfort. I hope she has recovered her voice, but, even so, I doubt whether she can be seen at her best. An actress of her kind needs an actor of a similar kind to bring out her full qualities. The only actor whose manner really matches Miss Compton's is Mr Charles Hawtrey. He alone possesses the full secret of that imperturbability. Together in *Lord and Lady Algy* the two were irresistible. But in *A Clean Slate* Miss Compton's coadjutor is Mr Brandon Thomas, whose manner is the very antithesis of hers. He is essentially perturbable, emotional, pathetic. He plays here the part of an old admiral, in whom is a strong vein of sentiment. And this strong vein he works so assiduously, with so much more strength that Mr Carton can have intended, that Miss Compton must inevitably be scouted by the audience as a very monster of heartlessness. And heartlessness is quite out of the character which now, as always, she is illustrating. Can it be that, the other night, she was but feigning voicelessness, in order to redress, for once, the balance of sympathy? If so, I can only say that the stratagem was inartistic.

The chaos of the play is positively cosmic in comparison with the chaos of the cast. One would suppose that Mr Carton, or whoever selected the cast, had sworn to show us a sample of every different style of acting to be found at this moment in Great Britain. As though the duel between Miss Compton and Mr Brandon Thomas were not enough excitement for us, we have champions of all the other various schools fighting it out between themselves. An exciting, even an instructive, spectacle! But one is sorry for the poor trampled-on play. Or rather, one thinks with sorrow of all those other, better plays, which one has seen trampled on with a similar ruthlessness. The great difficulty in casting a play nowadays is not that there are few good mimes, but that the mimes are good in so many divergent and irreconcileable manners. It is seldom that one finds in London, as one finds so easily in Paris, a company of which every member blends with every other member, thus producing that unity of impression which a company ought to produce on us. Almost always there is a sense of discord. Happily, however, there is not often a sense of such complete discord as now at the Criterion.

The Stage Society has done well in producing *A Man of Honour*, a tragi-comedy written by Mr W. S. Maugham. It is the story of a young man who, for reasons of conscience, married a barmaid. The second act, in which husband and wife are bickering, is admirably conceived and written; and the third act is a fine piece of emotional drama. The rest of the play falls to pieces. Mr Maugham becomes too bitter. In the first three acts he draws without prejudice a weak and well-meaning young man. And then suddenly the young man becomes a monster. His wife has thrown herself into the river. Her body lies in the room next to that in which he is sitting. After a little while, he makes no secret of his joy. He pulls up the window-blind and sends a messenger for the lady with whom he is in love, and by reason of whom his wife drowned herself. In real life, no doubt, this young man might be glad, in his inmost heart, from the first. But he would loathe himself for his gladness (though, doubtless, he would love himself for loathing it). He would try to keep it a secret from himself and, more especially, from other people. Thus, since there could be no dramatic revelation, Mr Maugham should have allowed a few months to elapse between his third and fourth acts. Then we could have all the bitterness that he needed, without any sacrifice of truth.

[*28 February 1903*]


## AT THE GARRICK THEATRE

'A great deal may happen in six months', say a lady in Mr Henry Arthur Jones's new play, *Whitewashing Julia*. 'Sir,' said Dr Johnson to someone who had remarked that turkey was a tastier dish than chicken, 'that is a proposition which no reasonable man would impugn.' In precisely that spirit we 'swallow' the proposition laid down by this lady just before the curtain falls on the second act. A great deal may happen in six months. On the other hand, very little may happen. *C'est selon.* From what Mr Jones has already shown us of life in Shanctonbury we infer that in two months (the period covered by the action of the first two scenes) next to nothing may happen. Shanctonbury is a Cathedral town, and we remember what Sam Weller said about Cathedral towns in general. There is (as every student of Anthony Trollope is aware) a calmness—an ἀταραξία— peculiar to such *milieus*. The life there is just that *'auguste vie quotidienne'* which commends itself to the *'animula vagula blandula'* of

M. Maeterlinck—a life from which all the stress of actual events has been practically eliminated. It is quite conceivable that Shanctonbury might go on for eight months 'solid' without an event. Still, we are (in the manner of Mr Mantalini) 'demd hopeful'. According to what Bossuet was fond of calling '*les lois du hasard*', the very fact that nothing has happened so far makes us the more sanguine of the near future. Before the storm the lull; and we look out for squalls 'in a concatenation according'. After all, Mr Jones is not M. Maeterlinck —far from it. His $\tilde{\eta}\theta o\varsigma$ is kinetic, rather than static. He generally 'makes things hum' for the benefit of 'the average sensual man', even though he merely sets them humming a music-hall ditty. Besides, coming as it does at the end of the second act, the proposition rings like a promise. 'Twopence and up goes the donkey'—'Two acts and in comes the dramatic conflict.' Mr Henry Arthur (like his namesake Tom) Jones is 'no disappointer of human hopes'. Assuredly, a great deal is going to happen in the last act.

What happens, however, is so slight as to be hardly enough to swear by. We feel that we have been 'let in'—decoyed into one of those vacua which art, not less than nature, abhors. This particular void does, at least, 'give furiously to think' about Mr Jones's conception of dramatic art. It may be argued that what Aristotle said *pro suis temporibus* is, like what the soldier said, 'not evidence'. But ... but ... what is all this? Where am I? Whither is my pen running running away with me? I find myself glibly quoting authors whom I have never read, using phrases that never occur to me, manipulating a style quite alien from my own, and expressing, above all, opinions from which I utterly dissent. And all this I am doing unconsciously, doing without effort. To what strange influence am I subject? What unfamiliar spirit has possessed me?... Unfamiliar? Nay, as I con over what I have written, I seem to have seen something of the kind before... Can it be that I am—? Impossible! And yet, who shall say that such soul-transference may not be? We have but lifted the fringe of psychic mysteries. We do but know that we know nothing. And my explanation of my strange state seems the likelier when we remember the doctrine that everything has a potential existence. Even the things that never will be done exist in some strange dimension. How much more definitely, the things that will be done hereafter. And how much more definitely still, the things that would have been done, the things that were on the very verge of being done when some sudden accident prevented them. As with deeds, so with words. Imagine yourself suddenly gagged at the moment when otherwise certain words would have been uttered by you forthwith. What would become of those winged words? What more likely than that they would fly away in quest of someone who could utter them for you? What more likely than that the words destined to be written by Mr Walkley about *Whitewashing Julia* have been circling forlornly, since last Monday night, in the smoke-laden air of London, seeking an utterer, and have condescended, at length, on myself?' I have not uttered them all. Since I broke off to wonder what I was at, the inspiration has left me. The rest of Mr Walkley's article is perhaps being written at this moment by some other hand, and will duly appear in some other paper. Meanwhile, I claim to have rescued its exordium. Perhaps I have not rescued it without hurt. Indeed, the style does seem to me not quite so light, the allusiveness not quite so apt and pat, as usual. But the innumerable readers to whom Tuesday's *Times* seemed even as a blank sheet will be grateful enough to make allowances, I am sure.

Let me try now to disentangle my own from Mr Walkley's impressions. I am modestly conscious that the result must be a bathos. Still, my own impressions have (in the eyes of sceptical materialists) a certain advantage over those others. On the first night at the Garrick I was not diverted into the 'royal room' and thence into the Charing Cross Road. I did actually see *Whitewashing Julia*. By the way, what wicked fairy came to the christening of the comedy and insisted on that very monstrous name? Why did not Mr Jones foresee her coming and warn Mr Bourchier to warn Mr Leveaux to have a 'royal room' ready for her? For a heavy farce the name might be well enough. But, as M. Anatole France has somewhere suggested, '*Il y a des oeuvres qui méritent*' . . . How now? Again the spirit of Mr Walkley is moving me. No; 'tis gone. Snapped for me is the thread of what M. Anatole France has somewhere suggested. What I myself was about to suggest is that *Whitewashing Julia* is a very slight comedy and should have been christened accordingly. It is perhaps the slightest comedy that has ever been seen on the English stage. Mr Jones, always daring, has reduced incident to the vanishing point, and has utterly dispensed with what is known as 'sympathy'. There is not among the persons of his play a single one to whom the public's heart could be expected to go out. Let me enumerate them.

A lady of dubious repute; a middle-aged gentleman who has led a *vie tapateuse* (avaunt, importunate spirit! I would rather finish this article in my own way) and whose proposal to marry the lady of dubious repute is less a sign of grace in himself than a formal concession by his creator to the moral susceptibilities of a British audience; his sister, an hypocritical lady who sacrifices virtuous indignation to the chance of saving her nephew from a *mésalliance*; this nephew, a fool; another nephew, a prig; and two female adventurers. The only characters who are not radically unsympathetic are they who have nothing to do with the plot—if so frail a bubble of a story as Mr Jones has blown for us can be called a plot. Frail, and elusive too! For Mr Jones's especial daring is not in the tenuity of his story but in his refusal to let us know exactly what that story is. We know that there has been a scandal about the lady. We hear vague references to a foreign Royal Duke, to a misplaced puff-box and dressing jacket. But the persons of the play, themselves knowing all about the scandal, take for granted our own knowledge of it. Our vulgar curiosity is always being roused, but is never gratified. Nor do we know, even at the last, whether or not the lady was innocent. Now, it is one of the pet traditions of dramatic criticism that an audience must be omniscient from the outset. More than one dramatist has shown the emptiness of this tradition, keeping his audience ignorant (and interested) throughout the greater part of his play. But I think that no dramatist, except Mr Jones, has kept his audience in the dark even at the final fall of the curtain. I see no intrinsic reason why this trick should not be performed. It might in some cases be very effective. There are, according to M. Faguet, certain *états d'âme* in which—(spirit! next time you interrupt me, I shall throw down my pen.) But the trick must be, obviously annoying if we feel a deeply emotional concern for the characters presented to us. And for Mrs Wren, the compromised lady in this play, we do feel a very deeply emotional concern. The fault is not Mr Jones's. If Mrs Wren were lightly played by a comedian we should take her lightly. But Miss Vanbrugh plays the part. And Miss Vanbrugh's sole idea of comedy is to keep her tragic power in restraint. And the result is an intensely, almost mysteriously, moving impersonation. We are dying to know what manner of woman Mrs Wren really is. We thirst for every detail of the scandal of which she was the heroine. Intolerable, our suspense throughout the play; and at last, when the curtain falls relentlessly on our unenlightenment, we go forth into the night, longing for that trans-sepulchral sphere in which all secrets shall be revealed to us.

Hardly less harmful to the play is Mr Arthur Bourchier, as the lady's lover. Lightest of light comedy is needed from him; but he, as usual, *will* toss the pancake as though it were the caber. 'Sir', said Doctor Johnson, 'I conceive that we should differentiate between—' (I throw down my pen.)

[*7 March 1903*]

'THE PROPHECY'

Edgar Allan Poe was so good as to lay bare for us the inner history of 'The Raven'. And the essay in which he performed this task seems to me one of the most valuable essays ever written, casting, as it does, so sharp and searching a light into the secrets not merely of one particular poem, but also of literary creation in general, and teaching us that the masterpieces which we, beholding them and blinking, account for by the blessèd word 'inspiration', are in truth the result of this or that idle chance tactfully taken and improved and perfected by a highly self-conscious, industrious gentleman, through a series of highly artificial processes. Would that all creators were so frank as Poe, and that every masterpiece could thus have for us, as 'The Raven' has, a double fascination, giving at once its synthetised beauty to our senses, and to our brains the analytical knowledge of how it was done. How it was done, how it came about, must be always a mystery to the beholder of a masterpiece. Indeed, one of the safest tests for a work of art is in its revelation of whence and how it came to be what it is. The less it tells us of such secrets, the better must it be; the more, the worse. And herein is the reason for the delight which we do often take in really inferior work. We can tickle the vanity of our brains by a complete demonstration of how such work was done. This vanity may be rather cheap, akin to that of the child who at juvenile parties embarrasses the conjurer and casts a gloom over the other less sagacious children by explaining in a high key just where the rabbit came from and just where the handkerchief went to. Nevertheless, the pleasure is a real one, not to be foregone.

It is this kind of pleasure which one derives from Mr Dick Ganthony's new play at the Avenue Theatre. By the way, why 'Dick'? Do not imagine that the familiarity is mine. It is thus that Mr Ganthony describes himself on the programme. I suppose he has been studying the plays of Mr H. V. Esmond passim, and has learnt from them that this particular pet-name is a recognised symbol for all those qualities which a British audience holds most dear. Dick!—a magic monosyllable, passport to every heart. If you call a man by it, you are bound to admit that he can do no wrong. On the other hand, there is no law compelling you to call him by it. I, for one, am not to be won over by a self-applied term of endearment. To me Mr Ganthony's name is Richard, and with his work I will deal in as impartial a spirit as with the work of any other dramatist. My pleasure in *The Prophecy* and my objection to it are in the sureness with which I discerned the manner of its inception and of its elaboration. I beheld on the stage a forest; and in this forest were twins, remarkably alike; and these almost indistinguishable forest-twins were very angry with each other; and there was a young lady present. The scene was somehow familiar; but I could not fix exactly what it recalled till the twins passed from verbal to physical violence. 'Agreed to have a battle'—the phrase flashed through my mind, illuminatively. The angry dyad was none other than that of Tweedledum and Tweedledee, with Alice and the forest all complete. True, the young lady called herself Winelfin, and the twins (as though they were mere acrobats) called themselves 'The Lundier Twins'. But they could not impose on me. I knew them; and, knowing them, I knew the genesis of *The Prophecy*. Mr Richard Ganthony had been reading *Alice in Wonderland*, and his soul had been stirred by the romantic element of that combat in the forest. Why, he had thought, should so tense a dramatic situation be left in that atmosphere of absurdity which Lewis Carroll had thrown around it? Why should Tweedledum and Tweedledee be shaped for ever like twin-balloons? Ah, let them grow slim and comely, and be dressed in the becoming fashion of the middle-ages or thereabouts. And let the cause of their discord be something more adequate than a rattle. Let theirs be a noble discord caused by—why, Alice, of course. Only, Alice must be disguised as a grown-up lady of the period, and she must be passionately in love with one of them. Which one? Happy thought! Both. Let them have only one soul between them, and then, when she falls in love with one of them because of his beautiful soul, and is introduced to the other, the fun will be fast and furious indeed. Only, of course, it will be romantic fun—romantic, poetic, human and altogether high-class fun. Brother against brother! Twin against twin! Each against each, and yet two in one! And down sat Mr Ganthony to his desk.

'The conception was a rose'; but, had he paused to examine the flower closely, Mr Ganthony would have detected a fatal canker in it. The play, as schemed, could be neither really romantic nor really dramatic. Strictly speaking, all themes are susceptible of every kind of treatment. Death, for example, which is usually a theme for tragedy, might be made ridiculous in a comic or farcical way, as you willed. But, by reason of certain qualities in the theme itself, such comedy or farce would be painful to us. Conversely, there are other themes which, though they be enveloped in an atmosphere of tragedy, and be themselves made really tragic, will yet tempt us irresistibly to smile. Such a theme, surely, is the theme of twinship. Try as we may, we cannot take twins quite seriously. There is something inherently absurd in a man who is not a unique specimen of himself. He is cheapened for us by our knowledge that we need but look elsewhere to find his fairly exact equivalent. Of course, there are cases in which the one twin is, in physique and in temperament, unlike the other. But such cases are rare. And Mr Ganthony has chosen one of the normal cases. Indeed, as I suggested, he has accentuated the point of unity. True, one of the Lundier twins is fair, the other swart; the one gentle, the other saturnine. But it is insisted that they have only one soul between them, and, though the colour of their hair is not interchangeable, their temperaments do, from time to time, dodge in and out of them. The fair twin, at one moment, suddenly shows a vicious temper; at another moment, the swart twin falls into the melting mood. Thus the difference between them is worth about as much as the difference between the terminations of the names of Tweedledum and Tweedledee. They are one and the same person, and illustrate, as clearly as a two-headed 'freak', a ridiculous fact in life carried to a fantastic extreme. As figures in sentimental romance they will not do at all. And that which makes them un-romantic makes them un-dramatic also. The commonest and most obviously effective form of dramatic conflict is the conflict between two men in love with one woman. And if the two men are bound to each other by ties of affection, drama is intensified by the additional conflict within themselves. And if the woman be in love with both of them, she, too, has an inner conflict with which to help the dramatist. Mr Ganthony, in conceiving *The Prophecy*, must have felt that here was a theme which must inevitably yield fine drama. But, in his eagerness, he over-reached himself. By binding the two men together by the strongest of all human sentiment, which is egoism, he cut from under their feet the only ground on which their conflict could be waged excitingly. We care not whether the swart or the fair twin slay the other, for in either case the victor is the same person. It is simply a case of heads he wins, tails 'tother loses—or tails he loses, heads 'tother wins. (A confused statement? I meant it to be so. I meant it to illustrate the state of mind to which Mr Ganthony's play must inevitably reduce anyone who follows it attentively.) Similarly, it matters nothing to us whether Winelfin in Wonderland finally fix her affections on the fair twin or the swart. We are but amazed by the trouble she takes to oscillate so constantly between two beings whose difference is merely chromatic. Miss Constance Collier plays this part with the full force of her variegated talent; and Mr Lyn Harding and Mr Frank Mills played the twins very picturesquely. But, of course, none of the three parts could, by any conceivable means, be made impressive. The play is, in fact, radically wrong. Mr Ganthony shows a good deal of cleverness in the development of his idea. It is the idea itself that is impossible for the kind of drama in which he develops it. Still, I give him due honour for having had an idea at all. Few of our playwrights are so daring. Next time, I hope, Mr Ganthony will have an idea of the right sort.

[*14 March 1903*]


## THREE PLAYS

There was once a clergyman, who was a famous preacher. So throve he on preaching that he was able to build, *ad maiorem gloriam Dei et sui*, a new church, more beautiful and more commodious than the old one. Thither his flock flocked after him. In reverent whispers it declared the east-window to be a dream of beauty. It was duly awed by the noble proportions of the nave. It found the pews more than comfortable—luxurious. It admired the font immensely, and the lectern, and the railings of the chancel, and the pupit. Ah! the pulpit. There was the hub of interest. On this grandly inaugural occasion, what sermon was the dear preacher going to preach? The dear preacher, I must tell you, did not write his own sermons. He employed admirable experts to write them for him. But he was not held the less dear for that. So subtle his tricks of elocution, so illuminative his gesture and facial play, so magnetic, above all, the man's whole personality, that to sit under him was to be entranced utterly. Besides, as I hinted, he had been always on the look-out for good sermons, and always willing to pay handsomely for them. Thus to his flock edification had come tripping ever hand in hand with rapture. And so now, on this bright Sunday morning, as the flock sat in the new tabernacle, it wondered what new and specially great sermon its ears were to be privileged to drink in. 'My brethren', said the dear preacher, 'this is a grand, a solemn occasion. I should like to preach you a sermon worthy of it. Alas! what with one thing and another, I haven't had time to procure that kind of thing. And so I will treat you to a pretty little sermon which I delivered ten years ago or thereabouts, and which you were good enough to admire at the time'. Then, clearing his throat, he proceeded to preach accordingly. And later, the flock, scattering in all directions to enjoy roast beef, was unanimous in protesting that never had the dear preacher preached more beautifully. There was only one churl to whom occurred any sense of disproportion between the occasion and the sermon preached for it.

Hard by was another church, another dear preacher. The church was an old one, but very beautiful, very commodious, associated with the names of many very great preachers. People flocked to it for its own sake, as well as for the sake of its incumbent, who, though young, was already very dear, and very keen to get the best new sermons going. It chanced that the aforesaid churl, soon after the experience which I have related, strayed into this old church. He found there a large congregation, very fashionable and very rapt, and the young incumbent delivering, with extreme animation, a very long, dry sermon which had been written in the eighteenth century. And the churl whispered to those around him 'Is the art of sermon-writing dead among us?' But those around him frowned and said 'Hush!' For they were being very much edified, nor saw aught amiss in their young incumbent having to fall back on the eighteenth-century's hack-work. A tear, nevertheless, stole down the cheek of the churl.

Not long after, wandering through the town, the churl perceived in a side-street another church—a miserably modest little affair, this, made of corrugated iron. He peeped in. The congregation was rather dowdy; and the preacher was unknown to fame, and not nearly so eloquent as those others, those 'dear' others. But, wonder of wonders! he seemed to be preaching a brand-new sermon, and, more wondrous yet! the sermon seemed to be a good one. The churl stayed to hear the very end of it, and went away much edified. 'It seems', he assured himself, 'that the art of sermon-writing is not dead among us. Only', he reflected angrily, 'why don't those fashionable preachers keep a sharper look-out? Have they lost all sense of anything beyond their own personal skill and their pew-rates? Is their religion nothing to them?'

I need hardly say that the foregoing story is a parable, not a fact. As you must have already have demurred, no fashionable preacher would dare to inaugurate his tenure of a fine new church by preaching a little ten-year-old sermon. Nor would one of his rivals preach what had been written to edify an eighteenth-century congregation —written, moreover, by a hack writer of the period. Such things are impossible. No 'flock', however faithful, would for a moment tolerate them. And yet the narration of them forms an exact parable to what has just been actually happening in the sphere that comes within my special ken—the sphere of the drama. For has not Sir Charles Wyndham just inaugurated his really beautiful new theatre with a revival of *Rosemary*? And has not Mr Cyril Maude just produced *The Clandestine Marriage* at the Haymarket? And has not Mr St John Hankin's comedy *The Two Mr Wetherbys* just been furtively shown to us by the Stage Society? Ir Sir Charles Wyndham had moved, not, with a flourish of trumpets, into a really beautiful new theatre, but silently into a devious barn; and if *The Clandestine Marriage* were a classic masterpiece which no one had seen on the stage, and not a dull rigmarole which many people had seen on the stage and tried vainly to forget; and if *The Two Mr Wetherbys* were a feeble effort of dilettantism, and not, as it is, a sound and solid piece of work, then I should not be at all surprised by the theatrical history of the past week. As it is, the strangest thing is that no one else seems at all surprised. Sir Charles's flock did not on the first night tear up the really beautiful brand-new benches. Since the first night, too, His Majesty the King has visited the theatre. And what did he do? Gather his equerries about him, and withdraw in silent displeasure, thus indicating, with a force which could be compassed by no other mortal, a right sense of the insult to that art on which he is by his people regarded as the highest authority? Nothing of the kind. My morning paper informs me that His Majesty, having sent for Sir Charles, 'expressed himself delighted with the theatre and the play'. And remember, irony has never been a plaything of the House of Hanover. As at the New Theatre, so at the Haymarket. Mr Maude's flock cheered him wildly at the fall of the curtain. And in the flock which goes to the performances of the Stage Society I found not one person who seemed surprised that he was not seeing Mr Hankin's play elsewhere. The dull, mild, hopeless docility of these flocks. Long may I be uninfected by it! If you wish to know what I think of the conduct of Sir Charles, and of Mr Maude, and of the managers who have not scented out *The Two Mr Wetherbys*, refer to my parable, in which the churl is meant to be myself.

To *Rosemary* in itself I make no objection. On the contrary, I think it is a delightful little play, written with a really keen sense for the Early Victorian period. Nor, despite its familiarity, does it seem stale. This is doubtless because of the very fact that it portrays a period so remote from its writers. I suppose it has aged not less surely than any other play written a decade ago. But our sense of period is so preoccupied by its matter as to overlook its manner. Even so, looking at a coat which had been cut a decade ago in the Early Victorian mode, we should not notice its shabbiness, as we should if it had been cut according to the mode of its moment. Mr Pinero has been pleading for a repertory theatre wherein we could see again the plays which recently ceased to interest us—the plays of yesterday. Such plays are tolerable only (except to their writers) when they don't show us yesterday: yesterday is both too like to-day and not like enough, for any proper appreciation of them. The only one of Mr Pinero's past plays that we should care to see now is *Trelawney of the Wells*. That would be still delightful. Yet I would not advise Sir Charles Wyndham to secure it for the inauguration of his next new theatre.

*The Clandestine Marriage* is poor stuff whose sole merit is that it might coax to a better knowledge of eighteenth-century manners and eighteenth-century language those dramatists who from time to time write plays about the eighteenth century. However, as it has long been published in a cheap edition, one must reject even this frail excuse for its production at the Haymarket. I found the mimes there making the best of a bad job, and behaving as though the play were the maddest, merriest fun. Certainly, their antics and frolics seemed to be keeping the audience cheerful. But for me, personally, the inherent grisliness of the affair could not be glossed over. A Saxon at an Irish 'wake' could not have been more inexpressibly shocked than I was, from first to last.

*The Two Mr Wetherbys* differs from most English comedies in being not a farcical comedy but a comedic farce. Mr Hankin evidently set out to write a farce, but the play abounds in scenes of pure and delicate comedy. One of these, in which a lady magnanimously offers to forgive the husband from whom she is separated, and who is not at all anxious for re-union, is quite the best-written scene of comedy vouchsafed to us in recent years. Twenty years hence, if Mr Hankin meanwhile continue to write plays of this quality, the managers may begin to suspect that a young man of some promise has arisen in our midst.

[*21 March 1903*]


## 'OLD HEIDELBERG'

A simple little story, this, and quite a harmless one, if it be taken by us in the proper spirit, with due margin for its nationality. A young man, who is Hereditary Prince of a German state, is sent to Heidelberg. He relishes keenly the change from the formal atmosphere in which he has been brought up. Also, he falls in love with the daughter of an innkeeper. He is recalled to the Court, which is in need of a Regent. He goes reluctantly. He succeeds, in course of time, to the throne, and has to form a suitable 'alliance'. He is bored by this necessity. Before the celebration of his nuptials, he pays a flying visit of sentiment to the university where he had such a good time, and says good-bye again to the daughter of the innkeeper. And that is the conclusion of the whole matter.

I have stated the theme briefly, baldly; but, as you will already have seen there is material in it for some pretty sentiment. Kings are human beings, and there is in the business of kingship much to hamper the free play of a human being's instincts. Also, universities are very nice places, in which there is not much to hamper the free play of a young human male being's instincts. Not much, I say; yet, decidedly more than appears in fond retrospect. And that is just the point. One remembers of the past only the pleasant things that happened. One looks back through a roseate haze. And so one often fancies that youth is a much more delightful time than it actually is. It is quite natural that anyone should look back very fondly on his days at an university. For a king who had been to an university, this fondness would be rather intensified. Here, then, in *Old Heidelberg*, are all the makings of a delightful play. But not, as I shall suggest, the makings of a play which could become delightful in the hands of a thoroughbred German playwright.

The prettiness of *Old Heidelberg* is undeniable. Only, it is a ponderous prettiness—a solemn, slow-moving, square-toed, beer-ballasted, blinking-behind-spectacles prettiness—a German prettiness, in fine. There are, doubtless, even outside the confines of the Fatherland, folk to whom this kind of prettiness appeals. I am not one of them. I prefer a light, spontaneous prettiness. I can imagine the theme of *Old Heidelberg* being quite satisfactorily treated—taken for exactly what it is worth—by a Frenchman. But a German must always bring to bear on his lightest task that magnificent thoroughness for which, in his heavier tasks, we so rightly honour him. All the i's must be always dotted, all the t's always crossed. Nay, every t must be transfixed by a shower of darts, every i must cower beneath a plague of dots. Some years ago, I remember, I was staying in a German household. One afternoon I went out for a walk, leaving my hostess with a cousin, Fräulein Charlotte, who had come to spend the day with her. When I returned, some hours later, the cousin had gone, and my hostess I found lying on the sofa in the '*salon*', very pale, holding in her hand a large bottle of smelling-salts. To my sympathetic inquiries she replied, faintly, in these words: '*Sie und ich haben uns gründlich über Liebe und Freundschaft ausgesprochen*' (She and I have been fundamentally discussing love and friendship). If death and disease had been the topic, this poor lady's exhaustion could not have been more complete. Nor, I am sure, would it have been less complete if she had been merely talking chiffons. For Germans are always equally in earnest about all things. At any rate (which comes to much the same thing) they believe themselves to be so. The morbidness of their famous Romantic Movement was all due to their incapacity for believing that anything could ever be transient or intermittent or superficial—that any man or maid crossed in love had any possible course but to give himself or herself up, heart and soul, and for ever, to the desire for death. I do not suggest that the Germans have more capacity for deep-souled sentiment than have people of other nationalities. The distinction drawn by me is that they have no capacity for sentiment which does not touch their soul-depths. The results of this incapacity are often rather ludicrous. *Old Heidelberg* is one of these rather ludicrous results. Terribly and unmistakably Teutonic it is in the technical method of it—in the ruthless persistence with which everything is explained and confirmed, again and again, till nothing shall have escaped even the slowest brain. To suggest an atmosphere is impossible to a German. He must analyse it and synthesise it before our eyes. Or rather, he must build it up, as a piece of solid architecture, till it be an atmosphere which could not be broken with a pickaxe, still less cut with a knife. The atmosphere of a dull court? So we have a dull Staatsminister, and a dull Hofmarschal, and two dull Kammerherrs, and a dull valet, and a dull footman, all playing lengthily into one another's hands, in case we should suppose that any one of them is not always dull. The atmosphere of a lively university? Students—students—students, all backing one another up, and playing, over and over again, the same set of tricks out of the same little bag. Oh believe me, if you took a deaf and blind barbarian to the St James's Theatre he would come away with a perfect knowledge of what Herr Meyer-Förster had been driving at. Yet the essential Teutonism of the play is not so saliently in its technical method as in its general conception. A reigning prince who has spent four months at Heidelberg—youth and freedom on the one hand, manhood and responsibility on the other: 'Ah', sobs the German, after he has '*gründlich*' considered the situation, 'there is no help for it. The Prince cannot become young again. He cannot even pass his sceptre on to someone else. And so there is nothing,

nothing whatever, for him to do but brood eternally over his lost youth and his lost freedom. He may seem to be bearing up bravely, but we know that inside him all is despair-blackness, and that so will it be till the wonder-beautiful Angels shall him to the Ewigkeit upcarry'.

Well! I maintain that for a sane treatment of the theme a lighter touch was needed. Even in Germany, where court-life is stricter, and university-life more lax, than in England, and where every man is born with a genius for making sentimental mountains out of sentimental molehills, the plight of an ex-student prince would not be in real life nearly so tragic as Herr Meyer-Förster makes it in drama. A real Karl Heinrich of Sachsen-Karlsburg would not be permanently deprived by Heidelberg of all his joy in life. The play, in fact, is a fable for German consumption. I should have supposed that in England, the land of common sense, it would be scouted as a quite absurd fable, interesting only in its side-light on the taste of German playgoers. But one never knows. *Old Heidelberg* seems to have been received here, not as a local fable, but as a very serious criticism of life in general. Falsely sentimental himself, Herr Meyer-Förster has been the cause of an awful outbreak of false sentimentality in the London press. Hardly one of my colleagues in criticism but has been weeping over the discovery that life would not be worth living if he were a king and is hardly worth living since he is not at this moment an undergraduate. I implore my colleagues to dry their eyes and pull themselves together. Kingship, as I admitted, has its drawbacks, and youth is pleasant. But the pity for kings, and the regret for lost youth, may be overdone. When our own King revisits, for some ceremonial purpose, either of those universities whereon erst, *in statu pupillari*, he radiated a brief lustre, tears do not, I imagine, start to his eyes for that here, in 'Old Oxford' or 'Old Cambridge', was passed the only period of his life from which he has contrived to extract the slightest pleasure. Kingship has its compensations, and so has maturity. And the idea that neither is a necessarily disagreeable thing because it entails certain added responsibilities is an idea which I should not wish to see widely accepted. It is a morbid and disheartening idea. Even were it true that to go down from an university is to descend into a pit of everlasting regret, we ought to hush the fact up for fear of blighting even the brief span of happiness which the improvident undergraduates are enjoying. But it is quite obvious that many men do contrive to be happy in the prime of life, and even in old age. And they will continue to perform this feat, unless *Old Heidelberg* produce as lugubrious an effect on the public in general as on my colleagues.

The costumes, the backgrounds and the furniture at the St James's are all very German. The acting of everyone there is very English. (I except Mr Beveridge, who, as the Prince's tutor, makes it hard for us to believe that Heidelberg is not Trinity College, Dublin.) Herr Behrend, besides attending the rehearsals, should have personally conducted the cast on a short tour through Germany, to teach by experience what evidently could not be grasped by imagination. Even so, I doubt whether the brisk, sensible, independent manner of Miss Eva Moore could ever have been toned into harmony with the manner of a sentimental German waitress. Mr Alexander, too, is so English that the grim effort to expatriate himself might have added several years to his age and so have prevented him from appearing as the Prince. He really does look and behave as though he were eighteen years old. Next time, we should not be surprised if he appeared as an infant in arms. But we should be so surprised if he looked the part that we should be thinking all the while about him personally and not about the infant in its dramatic significance. And that is the effect wrought on us, in a lesser degree, by this lesser miracle.

[*28 March 1903*]

'THE ALTAR OF FRIENDSHIP'

Dramaturgy, which in the good old days was as simple a literary form as any other, has become now the most complex and difficult form for a writer to tackle. To write a play which shall pass muster according to the modern standard is as difficult as to perform a fancy-feat in jugglery. Well, some people are born jugglers—born with a certain peculiarity of eye and hand whereby they are able, through constant practice and constant observation of the best models, to keep seven golden balls and an umbrella and a pellet of paper revolving in the air without touching one another or falling to the ground. That is an achievement which compels wonder from us all.

## 'THE ALTAR OF FRIENDSHIP'

When the achiever smiles and bows and kisses his finger-tips to us, we applaud frantically. We should like to know him—to know what manner of man this magician is, apart from his magic. Our wish is gratified. We are asked to meet him at dinner. We are bound to confess, subsequently, that we have been terribly disappointed. Apart from his magic, the magician was a very ordinary person. Indeed, he was rather less than averagely intelligent. But was it not rather foolish of us to build our hopes so high? Surely we might have remembered that so highly specialised a gift as the juggler's must, in all probability, be possessed at the expense of other gifts. A man who can do all that with seven golden balls and an umbrella and a pellet of paper is not the man to take an intelligent interest in things at large. His brain has been used only as a signal-box between his eye and his hand. It would be strange if he were not rather a fool. Similarly, it would be strange if the lady or gentleman who, born with an instinct for the technique of the modern theatre, has developed that instinct until she or he has become an habitually successful playwright, were a very clever lady or gentleman. Of course, there are one or two exceptions. But they do not disprove the very obvious rule. Of our good playwrights (by which phrase I mean those who can be trusted to write technically good plays) not more than two (I give the highest estimate) could, in point of brain-power or sense of beauty or knowledge of life or any other good quality, stand comparison with a novelist of (I give again the highest estimate) fourth rank. Not even two swallows make a summer. Not even the two exceptions (even if we are prepared to grant that, if neither of them were thrown into one scale, Mr Meredith and Mr Henry James and Mr Hardy would have to be thrown into the other scale) make a decent national drama. That is a consummation which will only be devoutly wished for until time and fashion shall have changed our mode of dramaturgy, making it, as in the past, simple, and so accessible to the average man of literary genius.

One of our 'good playwrights' is, beyond dispute, Mrs Madeleine Lucette Ryley. Hers is a sure instinct for the modern stage. The form does not baffle her. She can express through it, without apparent effort, just whatever she wants to express. But it is a saddening task to examine the quality and extent of the things implied by this 'whatever'. Examining her latest play, *The Altar of Friendship*, we succumb to the sad conviction that, if the story of it had been written by Mrs Ryley in the form of a novel, no 'commission' could have been handsome enough to induce even the humblest and greediest publisher to publish it. The hero of the story is a young author. He is acquainted with a young American lady, whose father insists that she shall be married to someone. So, to save trouble, he lets it be announced that the young lady is engaged to himself. Mutual affection dawns duly on the pair. But the dawn is soon overcast. For it seems that the hero is of the self-sacrificing kind. His sister is engaged to be married to a young man who is about to become a clergyman, and who has recently seduced a typist. The father of the typist comes out of penal servitude just in time to interrupt the festivities given in honour of the wedding of the hero's sister and the seducer. In steps the hero, taking the blame on himself. Having ostensibly seduced the typist, he alienates, of course, the lady to whom he had been ostensibly engaged to be married. He suffers terribly. His brother-in-law is inclined to let him go on suffering. However, in the end, all is revealed. The hero is going to marry the heroine, and the ticket-of-leave man thinks magnanimously that his daughter is less to be pitied than the brother-in-law's wife, who, 'perhaps—in time', is going to forgive all. I repeat that a novel based on this story would not be put on the market. On the other hand, of course, many plays based on this story (or, at any rate, on a very similar story) have been produced in theatres, and very successfully produced there. This play is, in fact, of the stage stagey. And here is exemplified one of the dangers inherent in the modern form of dramaturgy. So to develop your instinct as to master that form, you must concentrate your soul on it. You become a highly technical creature, remote from life. The stage becomes your world. As I suggested, by reason of the very fact that you possess this so rare instinct for jugglery, you are not likely to have the power of making profound deductions from life. But the task of developing that instinct keeps you out of the way of even knowing what life is like. I do not say that Richard Arbuthnot, the hero of the play at the Criterion, could not exist in life. But I do say that if he did exist in life his friends and relations would not allow him to be at large. Nor can I imagine anyone with any sense for life regarding him with any sentiment except that pity to which all lunatics have a claim. Nevertheless, he is a typical stage-hero. It is curious that self-sacrifice on the stage is almost invariably a stupid and mischievous act. Richard Arbuthnot would not (I suppose) be nearly so fine a fellow, in the opinion of his creatrix, if his self-sacrifice did not involve inevitably a great deal of additional pain to his sister and a great deal of quite unnecessary pain to his fiancée. Even if it were well that the one woman should be deceived, there is nothing to prevent him from privately undeceiving the other. But it would be a slap in the face for stage tradition if a self-sacrificer were endowed with a grain of the most rudimentary common-sense. And so the touch is withheld. Oddly enough, there is one respect in which this self-sacrificer is unlike his kind. But the difference is not in his favour. It is usual for the self-sacrificer to be a consistently melodramatic person. Here he is melodramatic only when he is on his self-sacrificial beat. For the rest, he is engaged in lightly comedic love. So that, when the moment comes for him to be misjudged, he is not contemned and spurned by her who had lavished on him all the wealth of her woman's love, but merely jilted by the girl he was going to marry. The British Public, I am sure, resents this bathos. It feels that if this was all that was to happen, Arbuthnot might as well have not sacrificed himself at all. I wonder that Mrs Ryley, with her very genuine instinct for the stage, fell into this always fatal error of combining two kinds of manner in one play. Her comedy and her melodrama do equal mischief to each other. I would advise her to shun melodrama in the future, and to devote herself wholly to comedy. She has a keen sense of humour—not a verbal or intellectual humour, but that dramatic humour which is, of course, the most effective on the stage. And this gift she ought not to waste. I would also venture to advise her to cast her next play in a bygone period. *Mice and Men* was delightful. The characters in it were copied from the stage, not from life. But one is always much readier to accept such characters as are remote from the age of which we have a direct knowledge.

Miss Ellis Jeffreys, like Mr Lionel Brough, has cultivated a peculiar laugh, which she introduces whenever there is the slightest pretext for it. I should like to see these two admirable comedians in a laughing dualogue. Unsupported, Miss Jeffreys's laugh seems a trifle too salient. Otherwise, her impersonation of the American girl leaves nothing, except an accent, to be desired. Both she and Mr Paul Arthur handle the comedic scenes very neatly and lightly. When it comes to melodrama, Mr Arthur is rather at a loss. Instead of standing still, with a set white face, in a ray of limelight, he potters around, visibly blushing beneath his make-up. This behaviour so intensifies by contrast the lurid intensity of Mr Mackintosh, who plays the ticket-of-leave man, that we feel as though all the convicts in the United Kingdom had just been set at liberty and amalgamated in the single person of Mr Mackintosh. Miss Lilian Braithwaite, as the hero's sister, plays with all her usual sensibility and charm.

[*4 April 1903*]

## 'EVERYMAN' REVISITED

Where is Mr Redford, our censor? Why is he not inspiring with his presence a cordon of policemen round the Coronet Theatre, Notting Hill? Two years ago, when the Elizabethan Stage Society began to give us *Everyman* in the way of privacy, he was powerless. But one of the first principles on which his office rests is that between drama and sacred subjects there must be no contact; and I supposed him to be chafing at the thought that those wily beasts could thus slither through his meshes, and piously hoping that a time might come when he could catch them and spread their skins at the feet of the Lord Chamberlain, on the pavement of Engine Court. That time actually has come. There is no longer the vaguest pretence to privacy in the production of *Everyman*. You need not subscribe to the Society, or beg a ticket from one of its members. You pay your money at the box office, and walk straight in. Straight into the meshes of Mr Redford that Society has walked, and, this time, is inextricably there. Yet the awful snaresman tarries, comes not to bear his haul away. (It were, of course, absurd to suppose that an official licence has positively been granted for a play in which one of the characters is the First Person of the Trinity.) Personally, being one of the parasites of drama as an art, I resent the theory that any union of religion with drama must needs be unnatural and hideous. I deny that the public can be more corrupted by watching such a play as *Everyman* than by looking at the paintings of sacred subjects which the law of the land allows to be exhibited in the National Gallery. Nor do I deem 'the Mysterious Painting of Christus', about which every hoarding in London now whispers to us, a less objectionable phenomenon that was Mr Laurence Housman's *Bethlehem*. On the contrary, those placards offend me, and I grudge the thousands of shillings which doubtless they divert into the till of a certain shop in Bond Street; whilst Mr Housman's play seemed to me a very beautiful little experiment. I will not deny that religious sentiment may be cheapened by a play, even as by a picture. But I object to the theory that, whilst a painter (or writer) may safely be allowed free play with religion, a dramatist who dares to be inspired by a sacred theme must promptly be suppressed as a blasphemer. However, that is the permanent official theory. As a law-abiding citizen, I am anxious to see administered even those laws which ought, in my opinion, to be repealed. An intermittent administration of them does but aggravate their injustice. I repeat, where is Mr Redford?

My annoyance at his latitation is the keener for that, had he duly asserted himself, I should have been spared a certain disimpression which has now been wrought on me by the performance at the Coronet. When first I saw *Everyman*, the ceiling of the theatre was the sky, the walls were the old grey walls of the quadrangle of the Charterhouse. And that setting, in its antique simplicity, right well accorded to the spirit of the play. But here, in this gilded temple on Notting Hill, the spirit of the play is sorely embarrassed. One is beset by a sense of incongruity, of discord. Do not take this as an admission that there is something essentially incongruous between playhouses and religion, and that so the general policy of the censorship is justified. The incongruity is not essential, but accidental. And the accident is in part the fault of the censorship itself. If theatres, like picture-galleries or libraries, were generally allowed to minister in some degree to our taste for sacred art, we should soon be accustomed to them in that connection. But at present the atmosphere in our theatres is one of stale frivolity. The Coronet is no exception, and I sat there offended, desiderating that other atmosphere, which is charged with nothing cheaper than the last word of Colonel Newcome.

The disimpression would have been less severe if the Elizabethan Stage Society had found a stage-manager so untrammelled as to seek, and so imaginative as to find, means of producing simple and austere effects. In the production at the Coronet there was much conventional tawdriness to make us wince. I have seen few things more dreadful than the attempt to suggest Heaven. This consisted of a young lady, with blonde hair, seated on a step. Her face was illuminated by a particularly strong ray of limelight. And on her shoulders she supported something which seemed at first to be a large screen of pink chiffon, but which one gradually guessed to be meant for a pair of wings. A cheap conception, cheaply and clumsily realised; nor, alas! was it the only one of its kind. The producer of the play seemed to have steeped himself in the sacred art of modern Germany, as familiarised to us vaguely by dreadful photographs in the windows of picture-framers. If he had had the full courage of this predilection, I should have deplored but respected him. As it was, he accentuated his folly by a wild eclecticism. By way of a set-off to the angel from Berlin, he gave us later authentic Burne-Jones angels, in the persons of Strength, Beauty, and Five-Wits. As a set-off to the Early Florentine quaintness of Everyman himself we had in Knowledge a perfect costume-model of the Queen 'in *Hamlet*', or of the Queen in any other Shakespearean play. In trying to please everyone, the producer of the play succeeded only in bewildering everyone. It is much better for a man in that position to be consistently wrong than to be right at moments. Unity of effect is the first thing to be aimed at. Our attention is much less distracted from a play by a panorama of one bad style than by a dissolving view of styles good and bad and indifferent. Nor, in this instance, need there have been any difficulty in selecting the properest style. *Everyman* was first acted in England at the end of the fifteenth century, and the costumes of the characters (except Adonai and Death, for whom, of course, fantasy is needed) should have accorded to our knowledge of what was worn by English men and women in that period.

As in the costumes, so in the acting, chaos. Few of the performances were bad in themselves; but none was good in relation to the rest, for all were jangling in various keys. I will not presume to say dogmatically what is the best method of acting in such a play as *Everyman*. I rather incline to the compromise made by the lady who acted the chief part. She was neither wholly of the stage nor wholly of the Church: or, to put it in another way, neither wholly modern nor wholly ancient. There was throughout her speeches the tone of a consistent chant; but she also gave dramatic significance to the words. Her mood and manner varied illuminatively, and yet were never unrestricted by a quaint convention. I suggest (without insisting) that hers was the right manner—hers the example to be enforced on the other mimes. Yet they had all been allowed to go their own ways. Not one of them joined in the compromise: all went to one or the other of two extremes. Knowledge, for instance, acted up to the costume assigned to her, and was Shakespeare's Queen A or B or C just as impersonated (and very capably inpersonated) by Miss X or Y or Z. Goods, for another instance, gave a strikingly realistic portrait of an usurer. For Shylock it had not quite the true poetic ring; but it would have been capital in a modern drawing-room melodrama. Kindred had a pretty little method of her own, taking the audience into her confidence so winningly that we were fain to condone her rudeness in ignoring utterly her comrades on the stage. So much for the 'stage' side of the combat. On the 'Church' side the leaders were Good-Deeds and Death. Both of them chanted their words scrupulously, without a hint of dramatic inflection. But between them, as between the leaders of the opposite party, there was a specific point of difference. Good-deeds was seriously ecclesiastical, Death was comically so. The one chanted plaintively and prettily, the other assumed and sustained a kind of loud snuffle, terrible and ludicrous to hear. I do not say that there was any intentional irreverence in his performance. But I suggest that a reverent man with no sense of humour is more mischievous than an irreverent man, as being more likely to become a cause of irreverence in others. Even were *Everyman* perfectly performed in all other respects, this interpreter of Death would be enough to ruin it. I do not know whether the whole performance has deteriorated since the year before last. Certainly it seems to have done so. But that may be an illusion. Possibly the discrepancies were always there, but not perceptible under the canopy of the magnanimous sky. Possibly, too, *Everyman* is not so fine a work, worthy to be done so well, as we have imagined it to be. We are apt to over-rate a work done in an early period of our history, even as we are apt to over-rate the saying of a small child, whenever any sense at all can be gleaned from it. But children do sometimes say really good things, and *Everyman* seems to me to have just the peculiar quality of one of those sayings—an artless quality of directness and clearness, whereby it might produce on this vulgar and complex age exactly that strange, uncomfortable, salutary effect which a child's wisdom produces on a party of adults. As one of the grown-up and complicated vulgarians, I feel that a good lesson has been lost to me through the distracting faults in this rendering of *Everyman*.

[*11 April 1903*]

## AT THE IMPERIAL THEATRE

There is seldom the least difficulty in determining why such-and-such play has been produced by such-and-such a manager. The reason, almost always, comes pat: the manager thought the play would draw the public, or thought it less unlikely to draw the public than any other play in his bureau. Occasionally, the motive for production seems to be the desire of an actor-manager to play a certain part at all costs. Rarelier still, the motive is that he admires the play, as a work of art, so profoundly that he must at all costs produce it. Now, Miss Ellen Terry has just initiated her management of the Imperial Theatre by producing Ibsen's *Vikings at Helgeland*. But, oddly enough, none of the aforesaid motives can be held to account for her action. The play is not, as I shall suggest, one which she in her most sanguine mood could have hoped the British public would like. Nor, as I shall suggest also, is Hiördis a part in which she could have hoped to make a personal success. Nor is it likely that she has throughout all these years been cherishing for Ibsen a secret admiration so strong as to compel her to produce, as the firstfruits of her independence, a play which is admitted (even by the straitest sect of the Ibsenites) to belong to Ibsen's immaturity. Why, then, has she done this thing? By process of exhaustion, I conclude that she did it for the sake of her son, Mr Gordon Craig, thinking that thereby he would gain for his new ideas a wider acceptance than they had yet had. The motive is altogether to Miss Terry's credit; and I am glad that she has not been disappointed. Hitherto Mr Craig has had to work in a hole-and-corner way, or else in a subordinate way, with the result that he has been taken less seriously than he deserves. Now, by grace of the strongest of human sentiments, he has had his chance, and has come off with flying colours. For the art of Ibsen and the art of Miss Terry our admiration has not been intensified, but the stage-manager-scene-painter-of-costumes-and-all-the-rest-of-it looms up illustriously with laurels on his brow. On the first night Miss Terry led Mr Craig before the footlights (or rather, before the place where the footlights were before Mr Craig swept them away). It would have seemed more correct, really, if Mr Craig, with an air of grateful acknowledgement, had led Miss Terry.

*The Vikings* is excellently well suited to Mr Craig's theory of stage-arrangement. I do not mean that he is incapable of varying his methods according to the kind of work he is illustrating. On the contrary, nothing could be less like the grim mystery of his Viking effects than was the sunny and childish gaiety of the effects wrought by him for *The Triumph of Love*. But it is obvious that his method has limits to its elasticity. It could not be stretched into realism. Outside fantasy it would snap. The lighting of the stage from one place above, instead of from many places below and on either side, is, of course, a change in the direction of realism. But the abolition of ceiling or 'flies', with the effect that the people on the stage seem to be sunk in a gigantic shaft, utterly precludes any notion of realism. Decoratively, Mr Craig wins from this system very valuable effects. But I am speaking, for the moment, from the standpoint of mere drama. For a modern play, in which the aim is to produce the nearest possible illusion of actuality, Mr Craig's system would be manifestly impossible. Further, it would be inappropriate to any poetic plays in which we are meant to accept the characters primarily as human beings. It could not be applied, for instance, to the plays of Shakespeare, except to those which Shakespeare wrote as fantasies. For his fantasies it would be as much more right than the present system as it were less right for his human plays. It would strike at once the proper keynote, reminding the audience that here they are translated from the plane of what actually does exist to the plane of what actually doesn't and couldn't. And for this very reason it is right for *The Vikings*.

I do not assert that there never actually was an actual race of Vikings. I freely admit that it existed, and that the members of it may have behaved exactly as Ibsen makes them behave. Nor do I deny that by a modern Scandinavian audience this play might not be taken as a play of human passion. But I do say that no modern English audience could regard it as anything but a wild fantasy. The difficulty is not that we are too far away from its period: we are too far away from its climate. Barbarism we can understand, if it be the kind of barbarism that flourished on our own shores or on shores adjacent to us. But the barbarism of the North strikes us as something quite beyond the pale of possibility. It strikes us as definitely inhuman. Living in a land which is never extremely cold, and on which the sun does sometimes shine, we can accept warm-blooded monsters as kindred to us. But we reject those boreal monsters whose blood has been frozen inclemently in their veins. The capacity for what we call 'passion' is the touchstone that we apply to humanity. And the kind of 'passion' that we mean depends on the action of the sun's rays. Where the barometer is always at zero, there is no 'passion' at all. That is what we miss in the modern Scandinavian drama generally. Only the intellectuality of the characters forces us to recognise them as human. Take away that intellectuality, and substitute for it the habit of mere physical violence, and the characters become, forthwith, wholly fantastic. Physical violence, without passion, is the keynote of *The Vikings*. Hiördis has no more love for Sigurd the Strong than she has for Gunnar Headman. It is only his action in killing the white bear that she loves. If the white bear had killed him instead, she would have had quite as much direct sentiment for the white bear. Conversely, we do not feel called on to pity Sigurd for that in the first instance Gunnar gets the credit for the deed, and the hand of Hiördis. We feel that it matters not in the least whom he marries. Finally we experience no pang in the knowledge that Hiördis and Sigurd are parted after death, the one going to the Pagan Valhalla, the other to the Christian Heaven. The one will be in her element, the other will be out of his; but their disunion will detract nothing from the pleasure of the one, nor add aught to the discomfort of the other. These two characters (and the rest are like them) cannot but seem to us monstrous, impossible. The whole play cannot but seem to us a monstrous, impossible fantasy. This being so, the best way to produce it is in the extreme manner of fantasy. Hence the appropriateness of Mr Gordon Craig. The strange, supernatural element which he casts over every scene is justified beyond all cavil. We shudder in unfathomable darknesses, in immemorial frosts. The monsters here, as monsters, become positively real to us. We are positively afraid of them. If they were presented to us in the customary realistic manner, we should merely smile at them as at animals walking on their hind-legs. It is foolish to complain, as many critics have complained, that Mr Craig's system of lighting does not always illuminate the features of the mimes' faces. In the case of a play demanding subtle interpretation this complaint would be justified. But *The Vikings* is a play in which nothing would be lost if all the characters wore masks. Indeed, it would be all the better, if the masks were sufficiently grotesque. The muscles of the face count for nothing in it. The muscles of the arms and legs, however, really are rather important. Both Mr Oscar Asche and Mr Hubert Carter, who play Sigurd and Gunnar, are well developed in this respect; and, as they have, also, very strong voices, and a generally terrific manner, I do not think their respective parts could be better enacted. But it is a melancholy thing to see Miss Ellen Terry, that incarnation of our capricious English sunlight, grappling with the part of Hiördis, and trying so hard not to turn it all 'to favour and to prettiness'. Now and again, she does contrive to break away from herself, and becomes a sort of abstract figure; but, even so, she is always a pleasant, English abstraction—a genial Britannia ruling unfrozen waves.

[*25 April 1903*]

## SARDOU'S ANTIDANTEDOTE

Everyone knows Pascal's saying that, if the nose of Cleopatra had been shorter, the whole face of the earth would have been changed. Had this slight subtraction been made from Sir Henry Irving, I suppose the whole history of the modern stage would have been changed likewise. Of one difference I am sure. *Dante* would not have been written.

There never lived a great man whose life would tempt a dramatist less than the life of Dante. Of his private career we know that he, a small boy, set eyes on a small girl, and fell silently in love with her. He did not again set eyes on her till he was grown up. Then he did once see her crossing a bridge. She bowed, passed on. This time he was not silent about his infatuation. He talked about it to his friends. Rumours of it reached the lady, and she, either because she had a sense of humour or because she had not, was much annoyed. Dante never again set eyes on her. In course of time, she died. Two years later, Dante married. His wife bore him seven children. So much for his romantic privacy. Now, a great deal of nonsense is talked about what is and what it not '*du théâtre*'. I am all for widening the scope of dramaturgy. But here, obviously, in the theme of Dante and Beatrice, in this shy, remote, nebulous, one-sided and eventless love-affair, we have that which not Maeterlinck himself could bring into terms of drama. Prologue: meeting of the two children. Act 1.:

Beatrice bows. Act II., Scene I.: Dante rhapsodises to his friends. Act II., Scene II.: Beatrice is much annoyed. Act III.: Death of Beatrice. Act IV.: Marriage of Dante. That would be rather weak. Could it be stiffened by incidents in the public life of Dante? Well, Dante is known to have been able and energetic in the pettifogging local politics of his period. For political reasons he was banished from his native city, and was unsuccessful in his efforts to return. This embittered him. But he lived his life in great comfort under the roofs of various noblemen, writing poems and philosophic treatises and political pamphlets, and being very much admired. That is all we know. Swift's broomstick were hardly a less promising theme for the dramatist. But say! We do know exactly what Dante looked like. There is the death-mask of him, quite authentic. For bronze substitute flesh and blood, and lo! there, quite authentic, is the fine face of Sir Henry Irving. The only difference is that Dante's upper-lip is a trifle shorter. But what is true of noses is not true of upper-lips. And so we find M. Sardou, with whom is M. Moreau, retained to 'weave a drama around the Florentine bard's sombre career'.

'Around', of course, and, also of course, in a very wide circle, at a very respectful or disrespectful distance from so undramatic a reality. Not that M. Sardou has jettisoned all the facts of the case. He has, in an off-hand way, invoked Clio, and taken quite a number of her tips, to be thrown into his hat and drawn out at random by his inspired fingers. But he holds no great opinion of the lady. With a jaunty wink at us, he claims that his and M. Moreau's Dante 'is not the historical Dante: it is the moral Dante'. I will deal anon with the validity of his claim. To his aim I offer no objection. It were a quite legitimate thing to invent, without violence to historical fact, some story, with Dante as its central figure, Dante revealing his soul through it in action, as he has revealed himself to us in his poetry. By all means let 'the moral Dante' thus walk the boards. But I question whether he would hit the taste of the modern British public. Indeed, I would lay long odds that the modern British public would shy at him, have none of him. He was far from being a delightful person, according to the modern British standard. No jolly good fellow, he, but a harsh, narrow saint—harsh and narrow, you understand, in relation to your own ideal. He was the kind of man whom you, loth to admit that the type exists in England, usually

## SARDOU'S ANTIDANTEDOTE

describe as 'dour' and 'gey ill to live wi' '. And that is not the kind of hero to fill the Theatre Royal, Drury Lane. Filled, and filled for many weeks, that temple had to be. Here was no hole-and-corner production, with a small cast and a few cheap scenes. Hither must be compelled to come the whole of the huge public, by whose huge weak stomach 'the moral Dante', as he actually was, could not for a moment be retained. M. Sardou, whatever one may think of him, knows his business, and knew, therefore, that 'the moral Dante', whom he cynically claims to have illustrated, must at all costs be hustled and smothered out of sight, and a pleasant simulacrum be propped up in his stead. Very cleverly has the job been done. The public stomach, aching at the mere prospect of Dantesque fare, has been set triumphantly at rest. As an antidantedote, *Dante* is all that the most exacting box-office could wish for.

Here is no grim ascetic, with one eye on the memory of a barren ideal and the other on hell-fire. 'Here is one who, though he keeps a warm corner of his heart for Beatrice, is devoted to the Lady Pia dei Tolomei, by whom, in his hot youth, he begat illicitly a girl-child, Gemma. Gemma, before the celebration of her nuptials, is by a villain abducted. Ho there! Dante will not rest till he shall have brought back his 'niece', safe and sound, and bestowed on her a duly veiled parental blessing. He is not so young as he was, but his heart is warm as ever, and the man who would lay hands on a damsel except in the way of kindness must still reckon with him. In the Castle of Malatesta he draws blank: that piercing scream was Francesca's, not Gemma's. Baulked, but undaunted, he pushes on to the convent of San Pietro. The scent grows hot. Swords clash. Dante is wounded, but faints not before he has placed Gemma in the strong arms of Bernardino, her betrothed. Again the hapless Gemma disappears. Again Dante undertakes to find her. His investigations lead him into Hell. There, from various sources, he hears much to the disadvantage of Cardinal Colonna. Also, he hears that Gemma and Bernardino are at Avignon, in that Cardinal's power. He sets out, post-haste, for Avignon. He arrives in the nick of time to frighten that Cardinal out of his cruel designs and to bestow the duly veiled parental blessing on his 'niece'.

Granted, that all this is decent melodrama. Granted, that Mr Laurence Irving's task of translation has been done throughout in a live and forceful way, and often with a kind of rough beauty.

Granted, that the scenery and the dresses are of elaborate loveliness, and that the effects in the Inferno are quite wonderfully illusive. Granted, with all my heart, everything, except that Dante need have been dragged in. Am I unreasonable? I do not argue that Sir Henry Irving ought to have engaged some poet to write for him a large play round the real Dante—a Dante worthy of his own powers—and so to have thrown away every penny spent on the production. I admit that M. Sardou, cheap-jack, was the right man to go to for a large play about Dante. Only, things being as they are, would it not have been better to give Dante the go-by? If the temptation of physical resemblance was so overwhelming, why not have engaged some poet to write round Dante a little play in one act? This little play, performed either before or after some garish contrivance by M. Sardou, would have given Sir Henry the chance he coveted, without doing either commercial or artistic mischief. Perhaps it is not accurate to call this *Dante* artistically mischievous. Such a play is so very remote from art. My objection to it is not so much artistic as sentimental. I am distressed by the cheapening of a great and semi-sacred figure. Such a play as *Sherlock Holmes* mildly amuses me. But when the hero's name is changed from 'Holmes' to 'Dante', without any corresponding change in the nature of his heroism, then I am conscious of a pang. Dante's external life was prosaic, as I have said. But his soul was the soul of a great poet and saint—a fiery and illustrious essence, a pure flame apart. And I do not care to see M. Sardou lighting his gas from it.

However, the mischief is done, and will be vastly popular. Great are the immediate rewards of such unrighteousness. I do not grudge them. I have faith in Time—Time the avenger. I know that he, eight centuries or so hence, will evolve some actor with a striking resemblance to such busts and paintings of Sir Henry Irving as shall still be extant. And into the heart of this future actor shall creep a longing to impersonate that great figure of the antique world. And some flashy dramatist shall he suborn to 'weave a play around' his venerable affinity. And some cock-and-bull story shall be duly 'woven around' a cheap distortion. 'My Irving', the dramatist shall boast, 'is not the historical Irving: it is the artistic Irving'; and, even as now we have Dante descending into the Inferno of his own creation, so shall our remote descendants have Irving revisiting the Lyceum and cross-examining for valuable information the ghosts of Louis XI,

Hamlet, Matthias, Jingle, Charles I., Mephistopheles, and Dr Primrose. Maybe, revengeful Time will not even have endowed the impersonator with those truly great qualities which, in Sir Henry, seem almost to cleanse *Dante* of its irreverence.

[*9 May 1903*]


## DRAMA AT OXFORD

The British Empire (according to a recent inspiration of a minor prophet named Joseph) will 'reach to the skies', some day. Some fine day, we, gazing up into the blue arc of heaven, shall discern two bars of faint red light crossing each other in the blue arc's apex, and thence curving down to the four points of the horizon. Anon, wondering at this unfamiliar rainbow, we shall be aware of two narrower bars of faint red light, meeting in that other cross, and curving down obliquely between those other bars. We shall exchange glances. We shall be afraid. We shall dare to look again, shading our eyes with our hands. Even so, we shall be dazzled. For the faint red will now have glowed to most illustrious scarlet, and the edges will have glowed to not less illustrious white. Pressing our hands to our eyes, we shall be distracted between amazement at the strangeness of the phenomenon and a baffling sense that somehow the phenomenon is not strange at all. And then, suddenly, the truth shall flash into our brains. And we shall clap one another on the back, and grip one another by the hand, and toss our hats into the air, towards that glorious apex, knowing that now, at length, all's right with the world.

As the prophecy came to us here only in the curt form of a cablegram from South Africa, we know not whether its maker fixed any exact date for its fulfilment. Obviously, a good deal will have to happen in the meanwhile. Prayer and fasting are not, indeed, means which one would connect with such an end. But of 'efficiency' and 'hustling' there must needs be much. Our young men must on no account dream dreams, if this one is to come true. They must, in accord to the exhortation of that fiery evangelist, the Prince of Wales, 'wake up'. They must be more American than the Americans— more 'strenuous', more snapful, nervier, quicker in the uptake.

They must not go to Oxford. That would be fatal. At any rate, it would be fatal so long as Oxford were unregenerate. Oxford, therefore, is generally regarded as 'on trial' and 'at the cross-roads'. Will she, the Benign Mother, jerk herself up to date, and qualify to become a mother of commercial heroes, or will she go benignly on, in fondness of her remote traditions, cumbering the earth—that very portion of the earth which is to be levelled up to the sky—with her customary brood of erudite and thoughtful ne'er-do-weels? The difference between what she still gives and what is now demanded of her resolves itself, for me, into the trite distinction between the angels and the apes. Is Oxford to teach us the words that angels sang or the words that apes chatter? Personally, I take the same side as was taken by the inventor of that distinction. Let us hustle up sky-high with all possible speed; only let us, I murmur, agree to sacrifice one rung from our projected ladder. Let us spare Oxford. Let us keep it, that dear place, if only as a curiosity, a relic of our dark ages. It need do no harm. There is the University of Birmingham, to which we can send all the finest flower of our youth, to be tended to the finest pitch of commercial culture. For the rest, let London, Durham, Edinburgh, Cambridge and Glasgow put their hot-houses in order, to receive all the flower that is not quite so fine but is yet worthy of attention. To Oxford we need send only the negligible blossoms. To Oxford need be affiliated as scholars only the halt, the maim, and the blind, the congenitally incapable of hustling our empire upwards—'our failures', in fine. Let Oxford become a home for the incurable, since only so can it preserve its own intrinsic and incomparable charm without standing between us and the sky.

You see I do not ask overmuch. I am not unreasonable, not unpractical. Indeed, I think I am more practical, really, than they who take that epithet as their label. Having regard to the appalling physical degeneracy produced already by that modern mode of life which has only just begun, and which, as the years go on, is to continue in an ever-acuter form, I believe—nay! like any other clear-sighted and far-sighted person, I *know*—that the human race, if it be not adverse from total extinction, will have to cry halt, and right-about-turn to the slow old simple ways from which healthy organisms were evolved. How soon this time will come, I cannot, of course, calculate. It may come later than the fulfilment of Mr Chamberlain's prophecy, or it may come so soon as to prevent that charming prophecy from being fulfilled. But come it will. And so, meanwhile, would it not be well for us to reserve one place where the secrets of the old simple ways can be hoarded—one place, as who should say, for future reference; one place to fall back on?

My own feeling is, not that Oxford is too remote from the stress of modern life, but that it is not nearly remote enough. Its curriculum of study is still ornamental, rather than useful; but its aspect, and its life, have lost much of their peculiar magic, by concession to the *Zeitgeist*. Were I a millionaire, I should straightway buy up all the land round Oxford, and cause to be demolished the whole loathsome congeries of red-brick villas encircling and hiding and profaning Oxford's beauty, so that, as of yore, those spires and towers should stand alone, in their little compass, visible from a great distance, with nothing but the damp green meadows, their proper setting, round them. Were I a Member of Parliament, I should not rest till I had forced into the statute-book a bill I have long drafted in my heart—a bill by which the Great Western Railway Company would be compelled to remove all traces of Oxford Station, and to divert their unhallowed rails in a circuit of not less than twenty miles from the Benign Mother. Then, and not till then, &c.

Such are my sentiments about Oxford; and, though they be expressed with a trifle of fantastic exaggeration, they are quite sincerely held by me. If you do not believe that I would really push Oxford further into the past, you will, at any rate, give me credit for sincerity when I declare my wish that she be not protruded into the future. You will not be surprised that I, a dramatic critic much more interested in modern drama than in any other kind, cordially endorse the rule by which the undergraduate mimes of Oxford are restricted to classic drama. I have always thought it a pity, even, that Dr Jowett (that least Oxfordish of Oxford men) succeeded in establishing a theatre in which undergraduates could attend the performance of modern plays. Were I his successor at Balliol, I should atone by using all my influence to crush the slightest symptom of a movement against the classic restriction laid on the O.U.D.S. I hear vague rumours that the members of this society are, indeed, anxious to be let loose on the drama of to-day. I trust that the authorities will not unbend. It is true that, in recent years, there has been a certain monotony in the society's productions. But this is not the fault of the restriction. It is that the society has not been ranging over the very wide field open to it. In 1890 *Strafford* was performed; two years later, *The Frogs*. But since then, so far as I remember, there has been nothing except Shakespearean drama. Both *Strafford* and *The Frogs* were very popular: the one by reason of Mr H. B. Irving's premature ability; the other by reason of the fun of Aristophanes, unblurred by time. (Who could say that of Shakespeare's fun?) In default of a second Mr H. B. Irving, why not give Aristophanes another trial? Or, if the present members are too vague in their Greek, why not try Ben Jonson? A performance of (say) *The Alchemist* would be delightful. At any rate (and this is what the O.U.D.S. really needs) it would be a change. Very limited is their choice among the plays of Shakespeare. Some of these are impossible, as demanding in some one actor greater power and experience than any amateur can possess. Others are impossible because they could never be popular on the stage. This latter objection would not hold if the society were so endowed and so conducted that the box-office could go hang. But the society has to pay its way, and, judging by the very metropolitan elaborateness of this year's production, I suspect that this way is no bagatelle. So, under the present policy, the society's choice is confined to a very few Shakespearean plays, which everyone has seen performed several times by professionals. This evokes not merely a sense of monotony, but evokes also pleasure-spoiling comparisons. And so a local institution, which might have a lively character of its own, degenerates into a vehicle for copies of what we have seen done much better, and too often, elsewhere.

In one respect, certainly, *The Merchant of Venice*, as produced in Oxford, differs from what we are accustomed to in London. We see the play somewhat more in its Elizabethan proportions. Shylock, of course, was the only thing in it that interested Shakespeare—the only thing on which he bestowed a loving care. Yet—and here is exemplified the mischief of his beholdenment to other people for his plots—Shylock is not the central figure in the play. The silly manoeuvres of Portia and her suitors are quite as prominent as Shylock's soul. We, in this century, are bored by those manoeuvres, and are rapt in that soul. The actor-manager, as Shylock, gratifies our preference, forcing Shylock out of the picture. At Oxford, however, there is a tradition of modesty, and also there is the disability of amateurishness, insomuch that the balance between the two parts of the play is redressed. We see the play as it was written for its age.

We see the Jew that Shakespeare drew, not an adumbration of the Jew that he wanted to draw, and would have drawn had he been living at this hour. Mr B. Forsyth (Christ Church) impersonates Shylock proper with much propriety and intelligence. Mr A. P. Boissier (Balliol), as Launcelot Gobbo, is extremely funny. But Bassanio, and the Princes of Morocco and Aragon, and the other romantic personages, fare ill indeed. One very good reason why the O.U.D.S. should give Shakespeare a rest is that all his plays teem with romantic love-affairs. In public, at any rate, undergraduates do not, and will never, shine as romantic lovers. They cannot conceal the shyness, nor reveal the ardour, of youth.

[*23 May 1903*]

'MUCH ADO' AND MR CRAIG'S SETTING

In an article on *The Vikings*, I said that Mr Gordon Craig's way with the proscenium could not harmonise with any play in which our illusion ought not to be an illusion of sheer fantasy. I said that it could not, for instance, be well applied to an ordinary Shakespearean comedy. Of course, in the playhouse there can be no means of absolute realism. It is fantastic, when we come to think of it, that we should see men and women behind a rectangular gilt frame. But we don't come to think of it, if the frame is of the traditional shape. If the frame is suddenly made tall and narrow, we do come to think of it before all things. In time we might grow accustomed to it, taking it as a matter of course. But I have my doubts. The traditional shape has this advantage over the shape as altered by Mr Craig: it corresponds more nearly with out natural and ordinary range of vision. Well! in the design of *Much Ado About Nothing*, at the Imperial Theatre, Mr Craig has skilfully modified his method in such wise that no objection can be made to it on grounds of drama. (Decoratively, it was beyond reproach—making a much prettier or more impressive picture than we ever got through the old method.) He has not restored the old 'border'. His scenery still towers up beyond the limit of the proscenium itself. But the men and women on the stage no longer symbolise the insignificance of the human race that crawls on our globe's surface. They have regained that fallacious magnitude which is so real to us. For the scenery itself is a sort of inner proscenium. True, in the church scene, the characters are dwarfed in Mr Craig's first manner. But it is realistically right that they should be so. We see them in exactly that proportion to which the nave of a real cathedral would, by its narrow upward stretch into the infinite, so emphatically reduce them. For truth and beauty combined, this dim scene is incomparably finer than any other attempt that has been made to suggest a cathedral on the stage. Whatever the Philistines might urge against Mr Craig's art, they could not deny that it is, at least, the handmaid of religion. In the other scenes, the human race has all its customary aspects of importance. Behold it in the tapestried hall of Leonato's house. There is a vast expanse of tapestry, but it is hung on a wall descending to that side of the hall's ceiling which is nearest to the foot-lights. The ceiling itself is comparatively low. The wall above it is, as I have said, a kind of inner proscenium. The characters are not conscious of it, and so are not measured in proportion to it, any more than, if there were the old-fashioned 'border', they would be measured in proportion to the whole outer proscenium. In the garden of Leonato a similar effect is made by similar means. The characters are set under and between a gigantic treillage of vine, the front of which corresponds in form with that tapestried wall, and bears exactly the same relation to the men and women beneath it. Thus Mr Craig, without any sacrifice of principle, has brought his new theories into harmony with that kind of drama against which one had thought they must needs strike a discord. Apart from the proscenium, be it said that he proves his method to be not only the most decorative, but also the most dramatic, method of illustrating a play. By the elimination of details which in a real scene would be unnoticed, but which become salient on the stage, he gives to the persons of the play a salience never given to them before. Even when he dwarfed them, they were midgets clearly defined by reason of the simplicity surrounding them. Now that he gives them their full size, they are more definitely men and women (and therefore more dramatic) than they could be under any other system. As for beauty, it stands to reason that figures moving or posed before simple backgrounds must create a more beautiful effect than is created by figures moving amongst a lot of objects as definitely salient as themselves. Perhaps the most beautiful of Mr Craig's effects in *Much Ado*, and the most characteristic of his especial style, is when Balthazar sings to the accompaniment of three long-robed minstrels who are seen by us silhouetted against the sky, in the arches of a long straight viaduct of clipped yew. To a certain extent Mr Craig is hampered by dealing with a definite period and place, wherein the dresses must be more or less correct in archaeology. His wildly exquisite inventiveness in costume is one of his strongest points, and it is a pity that he must not always insist on it. In Leonato's masque, indeed, he can and does let himself go. An enchanting sight are the masquers, in their uniform gowns of silver lozenges, with diadems of mistletoe on their heads, and waving in their hands great hoops of green leaves. Otherwise, Mr Craig curbs himself. I hope that ere long, as a reward, he will have another sheerly fantastic play whereon to lavish the fantasy of his own spirit. There are many such plays that need him. Above all, no play of Maeterlinck has yet been entrusted to him. That is to say, Maeterlinck has not yet been staged in the right way by the right man—by the one man who could realise for us those children of mystery, all astray in illimitable spaces and dimness.

If Miss Ellen Terry had offered up her son on the altar of some realistic modern dramatist, one would not have cried 'shame', so utterly and so nobly did she immolate herself for his sake in *The Vikings*. If Mr Craig had not been able to make anything of *Much Ado*, he ought still to have undertaken the job, in gratitude, seeing that there never has been, nor ever will be, so perfect a Beatrice as Miss Terry, and that Miss Terry never will be, nor ever has been, more perfect than as Beatrice. Beatrice, in all her sunniness and jollity; a tease, a romp; a woman with something beyond her generous womanhood—some touch of fairydom in her—here is she incarnate and unrivalled. A pity that she has missed a Benedick to match her. Sir Henry Irving, as I remember him, was too sardonic, too spiritual, not human enough. Mr Oscar Asche is quite human enough, but he lacks those light and subtle graces of humour, those brilliant surface-tricks, without which Benedick becomes a boor. The 'merry war' of words between the young lord of Padua and the young lady of Messina is not, in itself, very merry, though it is undoubtedly war-like. 'You're another' (and usually 'another' very ugly thing, according to modern canons) is the sum of their dialogue, with much of that industrious twisting of words than which (to us) nothing is more tiresome. Yet the dialogue can be shorn both of dullness and of offence if it is treated in the right way. Half of it is so shorn by Miss Terry. The other half, in Mr Asche's hands, continues to bristle. Mr Asche's deportment persuades us that Benedick is not a high-spirited young bachelor, but a very serious widower, with a very large family. So we attach a literal importance to all the words that drop from his lips. They drop so very weightily. They should fly so very mercurially. There is a tradition that Dogberry should be fat; and thus has been wrecked what might have been a delightful performance by Mr Norman Forbes. I suppose the tradition sprang from the belief that stoutness entails a slow wit, and slightness a quick wit. Neither entails either, of course. There is, however, a difference in manner between the stupidity of a stout man and the stupidity of a slight man. Not long ago, Mr Norman Forbes, who is clever and slight, gave a memorable rendering of the stupidity of Sir Andrew Aguecheek. But now, padded to the traditional bulk of Dogberry, and being unable, for all his cleverness, to get out of his own skin, he collapses between what he could do and what he would do. He shows us the stupidity of a slight man in the body of a stout man. The effect is unearthly. Don John is played by Mr William Luff, very intelligently, but one misses the personal weight and magnetism without which that 'plain-dealing villain' is bound to seem slightly—more than slightly—ridiculous. Mr Julian L'Estrange, as Don Pedro, has all the grace and distinction which the Shakespearean grandees need and seldom get. Mr Holman Clark handles the part of Leonato with all the ease of his long experience in such parts. It is a pity he does not more often have, as he had in *The Vikings*, something on which he can imaginatively enlarge. Next to Miss Terry's Beatrice, which most impressed me was the Borachio of Mr Hubert Carter. For good, sound, rollicking Shakespeareanism, nothing, except that Beatrice, could have been better. One bad shock was administered to me in the course of the evening. When Balthazar came on to sing 'Sigh no more', I could hardly believe my eyes. Always I had supposed that the sun might fall into the sea and be extinguished, and the mountains be levelled with the earth, and time and space themselves be whelmed into unmeaning, but that never, never would another than Mr Jack Robertson be Balthazar.

[*30 May 1903*]

## A NEW FARCE

That is to say, a farce that has just been produced. Judged apart from its date, *Just Like Callaghan* is old indeed. Except under a microscope, it is indistinguishable from any of those other British or Gallic-British farces whose ghosts are raised, rather wantonly, in the Souvenir Album presented to every member of the audience on the first night at the Criterion Theatre. Farce is a dramatic form, and, as such, is comprehensive of all phases of human life and human character. Whatever men do is material for farce, as for comedy, tragedy, melodrama. And it is a curious thing that farce is restricted, by our writers of it, to the kind of things that are done by one particular kind of man, or rather to the kind of things that might be done by one particular kind of harmless lunatic. Suppose (a hideous hypothesis) someone whose knowledge of life were derived solely from our farces. Such a person would believe the world to be peopled by husbands who spent their time in desperate efforts to prevent their wives from detecting their perfectly innocent relations with other women. From Parisian farces, of course, he would deduce that every husband really was unfaithful. But London, as having a more prudish population, insists that there must be no hint of actual immorality. Tête-à-têtes in public restaurants—thus far and no further may the hero of a farce urge on his wild career. But, as our farces are either adapted (like *Callaghan*) straight from Parisian farces, or are written on the general Parisian model, the hero's soul-state is ever that of a deeply guilty man. He employs all the wisdom of the serpent to conceal the almost impalpable line between himself and the dove. The other day the Stage Society produced a very witty comedy founded by Mr St John Hankin on the usual farcical basis. And there we had an extreme case of the absurdity that comes of a compromise between Parisian license and British prudery. Mr Hankin's hero did not even lunch with a lady in a restaurant. He went to his club, played a game of billiards, drank a glass of spirits and mineral water, and went to a music-hall. That was the sum of his enormities. Despite his prodigious ingenuity he was detected by his wife. It is, of course, necessary to the game that the wife should take the same view of morals as is taken, though not acted on, by the husband. And in Mr Hankin's play the wife definitely stated that she could no longer live under the same roof with such a man. There the absurdity struck one the more violently because, as I have said, the treatment of the theme was comedic. There was no horse-play, but much witty dialogue in its stead, and much clever delineation of character. The persons of the play were quite real to us; and accordingly their unreality in this one vital respect was all the more irritating. In a pure farce, of course, one is not so exigent. Nevertheless, even there we must have some basis of likelihood. The characters must buffet something more solid than air. And English farces fail to amuse us because we have to supply that something out of our own inner consciousness of what must have happened in the Parisian version. That is one reason. Another, a larger reason, is that we are all heartily sick of the figure of the deceptive husband. We have had enough of him. Let him rest. Of course, you may say that we cannot dispense with him, that he is inherently necessary to farce. If you do, you merely convict yourself of being unable to distinguish between true and false traditions. The only reason why the deceptive husband has undisputed possession of farce is that farce-writers are lazy and imitative, like the rest of us, and prone to the line of least resistance. It is easier to write a play on a trite theme than on a new theme. On the other hand, there comes a time when every theme becomes too trite even for the British public. That time has overtaken the deceptive husband. And thus to write about him is not really for our farce-writers the line of least resistance. Let them look about them, casting their eyes over that vast range of human types, every one of whom is, as I suggested, not less amenable than another to treatment in farce.

Of *Le Coup de Fouet* I know nothing, and from the first act of Mr Cosmo Lennox's adaptation I deduced that it was a play in the manner of *The Two Mr Wetherbys*—a comedic treatment of the theme sacred to farce. Certainly, there was plenty of amusing dialogue in the first act; and I, who had been enjoying it, was rather taken aback when an expert assured me that it 'dragged'. For me the 'dragging' process began anon, when the fun became (as the expert would say) fast and furious. One character going down on all fours, and letting another ride on his back; shouts, screams, yells; doors slamming, and bursting open—in this kind I have no sense of humour. Nor do I delight in a series of entanglements complicated to a pitch when all the persons of the play are tearing their hair in

## A NEW FARCE

a frenzy of mystification. In other words, I don't care, personally, for farce as a dramatic form. I can imagine a child enjoying a romp. I can imagine a child contemplating wistfully a romp from which it is excluded. But I cannot imagine an adult enjoying the contemplation of other adults paid to romp on the other side of a row of footlights. Similarly, I can imagine a child concentrating its brain on such problems as a farce presents to us—why does A ram his hat on his head and dash out of the room after telling B that C is really D, and why does E, at sight of F, swoon under the impression B is A? By keeping one's attention fixed grimly on even the most ingenious of farces, one can, I suppose, master its manifold ramifications. But it seems to me strange that any adult should have so much patience. Many adults, however, have; and doubtless derive through it the subtle kind of gratification afforded by the puzzles in the snippet press. Many of them, too, really are tickled and exhilarated by the sight of carefully rehearsed horseplay. But I maintain that this horseplay and these manifold ramifications are not matters with which a critic can concern himself. I can say that the dialogue in the first act of *Callaghan* was full of amusing little conceits, and that it was so constructed as to leave us in lively anticipation of a contest of wits between two of the principal characters. But I must decline to decide whether the subsequent complications were too complex or not complex enough, too quick or not quick enough, or whether they were just perfect of their kind. Nor have I a standard whereby to appraise the various acts of physical violence with which the complications are studded. The public should do its own criticism of farces.

I am at the same disadvantage in criticising the performance. Even as farce is different from comedy, so should it be differently acted. I conceive that the manner and deportment and elocution of the mimes should be consciously grotesque. Mr O. B. Clarence, in this play, utters odd sounds, and puts his body through odd contortions. And Miss Annie Hughes talks, as usual, in that shrill plaintive monotone which is, at any rate, quite distinct from ordinary human speech. But whether these two artists are really funny I have no means of knowing. They act to an accompaniment of the public's laughter; but that, for aught I know, may be due to the quality of the words spoken by them. Let me give them the benefit of the doubt, and assume that they really are funny. Neither Mr Fred Kerr nor Miss Fanny Brough is funny in voice or manner. Each behaves like a normal human being. Each, therefore, must be amiss here. But I very much prefer comedians in the wrong place to farcists in the right one.

[*6 June 1903*]


A TRIPLE BILL

One of the errors made by England is her persistent veneration of solemnity as the outward and visible sign of inward and spiritual seriousness. In point of fact, only that man is solemn who, not taking things seriously, cannot so take himself. Every man desires to be taken seriously by his fellows. Therefore, every non-serious man cramps his face behind a mask of unalterable solemnity. It is only the inwardly and spiritually serious who can afford to laugh—or, rather, thinks he can afford to: he can't afford to, in England. But, of course, he does not reckon the price he must pay. To him, laughter is a spontaneous, necessary function. It is the inevitable reaction from seriousness. A man who sits still in a chair, doing nothing, needs not to repose and recreate his limbs. Even so, a man who neither thinks nor feels deeply on any subject under heaven needs not to laugh. The harder you work your body, the longer and more tranquilly must it lie at rest; and the deeplier you think and feel, the loudlier and longer you will have to laugh. I suppose there is not under heaven a single subject on which Mr Bernard Shaw has not thought deeply and indignantly. And there you have the reason for that spirit of uproarious merriment which seizes him so often, convulsing him as a man is convulsed by a frightful fit of coughing, and convulsing us, also, and preventing the stupid majority of us from taking him at his own right valuation. In his case, usually, the attacks of this spirit are soon over. He doubles up in agony, so do we; but he recovers himself and resumes the thread of his discourse so quickly that we are still gasping when the next fit overtakes him. *The Admirable Bashville* was a strangely prolonged convulsion, relieved only at infrequent moments by pauses of seriousness. It must have been written just after the completion of some almost wholly serious work which the author has not yet allowed us to see. That the Stage Society has dared to act it is a very good sign for the friends of the Stage Society. As with men, so with institutions. Just as it is only the fool that dares not play the fool, so it is only the safe and solid institution that dares dissolve itself in laughter. This year the Stage Society has made a very good record for itself. It has given us a beautiful play by a foreign dramatist, and has discovered for us two new natives who ought to do excellent work for the stage—three such natives, including Mr S. M. Fox, of whose contribution to last week's triple bill I shall speak anon. And so, inevitably, we are treated to *The Admirable Bashville*. Some of the critics, I note, object to this extravaganza on account of its length. That is a typically English attitude. Our constant protest that 'brevity is the soul of wit' arises simply from our mistrust of wit. We may go on being pompous by the hour; but wit is a dangerous thing, and, if we admit it at all, we stipulate that it be got quickly over. It is pathetic that we should try to give an aesthetic air to our purely moral objection. There is, of course, nothing to prevent a man from being witty for hours together—nothing at all but the likelihood that he is not, as Mr Shaw is, an exuberant wit. My only regret is that *The Admirable Bashville* was not written to fill an evening bill. Other critics object to the joke, not on the score of its elaboration, but because it is not elaborate enough. They deplore its lack of form and polish. Well! I am all for polish and form, and I demand them where they can be forthcoming. But Mr Shaw's is a rude genius. He was born without sense of form, without patience for polish. I take him, and delight in him, as he is. Nay, though I hold that his serious work would be the better for a finer art, I recognise that its very carelessness and clumsiness give to this *jeu d'esprit* a peculiar quality and value. Our laughter comes the more easily for the greater ease of its provocation. Something would be lost if we had the sense that the jester had been grimly determined to lose nothing. In a burlesque, the fun cannot be too rough and ready. Perhaps it is not quite accurate to call *The Admirable Bashville* a burlesque. It contains some of the stiffening of a real satire. We are reminded by it that Mr Shaw really does think Shakespeare's form of drama a ridiculous thing, and really is angry with it. But this, after all, is a faint undercurrent. The whole thing resolves itself into a rollicking burlesque of Shakespeare's method and manner. As such, it has only two faults—faults of omission. There is no song. How delightful would be a song written by G.B.S. on the Shakespearean model!

Also, there is no Shakespearean comic relief. Why was not a second policemen introduced into the scene of the prize-fight? *Second Policeman*: 'Canst tell me of this prize-fight? Is't within law?' *First Policeman:* 'Aye! To't. For what does a man prize highest? A fight. But no man fights what he prizes, else is he no man, being not manly, nor yet unmannerly. Argal, if he fight the prize, then is not the prize his, save in misprision, and 'tis no prize-fight within the meaning of the Act.' *Second Policeman:* 'Marry, I like thy wit', etc., etc.

When the play was published, I enjoyed it so much that I was rather nervous of seeing it on the stage. A carefully organised romp is apt to be a fizzle. One often hears of pleasant house-parties overcast by the well-meaning efforts of some of the guests. But professional skill may triumph where good amateur intentions collapse; and *The Admirable Bashville* amused me last Monday more than ever. The right way to act it is to take it quite seriously, reproducing in all their beauty the sonorous elocution and dignified deportment of the traditional Shakespearean mimes. Pre-eminently well by Miss Fanny Brough, that invaluable lady, this trick was performed. But the mimes were good, too.

The first item of the programme was a little play by Mr Ian Robertson—*The Golden Rose, or the Scarlet Woman*. This was a blend of the spirit of the old Morality with the modern methods of symbolism. The idea was beautiful, and the moral was exemplary, and the symbols were very apt and ingenious, and the stage-craft was quite perfect. Beautiful ideas are not uncommon. Many of us have a pretty taste in symbols. Anyone can point any number of exemplary morals, and anyone with a practical experience of the stage can muster as much stage-craft as is needed for a simple theme. Yet I do not fancy that *The Golden Rose, or the Scarlet Woman* will set a wide fashion. Such a play as this needs something more than the qualities I have enumerated. It must be written beautifully. And rare are they who can write beautifully. Mr Ian Robertson is a clever actor, but his sense of literature is very, very rudimentary. He seems to have aimed at simple diction—the most difficult of all—and the result is mere baldness. I need not quote examples: the title itself is enough to acquit him of any sense for words. And it is only through words beautifully chosen and beautifully delivered that he could give the kind of impression that he wanted to give us. Both Miss Lily

Hanbury and H. H. Ainley, who took the two chief parts, would have been able to fulfil their part of the bargain if the author had fulfilled his. I honour Mr Robertson as a writer of a new kind of play. But I implore him, when next he writes another like it, either to have it delivered in dumb-show or to collaborate with one of the very few people who could set it to such words as it needs.

I have already referred to Mr S. M. Fox. It may be rash to judge from one play in one act, but I am inclined to think that we shall hear a great deal of Mr Fox—supposing that Mr Fox writes other plays as clever as *The Waters of Bitterness*, and supposing that managers think the public clever enough to appreciate them. Anyhow, his is a strong and a bold début. He has made the central figure of his play an old maid, and his play is not a farce but a tragedy. Evidently a feminist, he has dared to present an old maid sympathetically. Not that he has idealised her. On the contrary, he insists on her faults. He abates nothing of her outward primness or of her outward egoism. She is not a clever egoist; indeed she is a fool, an obvious fool. None but herself is interested in her. That she has no sense of humour is the sole reason why she does not join in the universal laugh against her. So far, she is the old maid known to us in a hundred farces. But Mr Fox takes us a step further. With a cunning and tender hand he lays open to us the heart of the old maid, moving our own hearts to compassion. At first sight, there seems nothing so very 'bold' in this achievement. Nobody laughs now at old maids in real life. But that is a comparatively recent improvement in the human race. There was a time when cripples were tortured by their full-grown and up-standing fellow-creatures. Gradually it crept into the head of mankind that this was rather a bad habit. So cripples were merely mocked at. Now they are not mocked at, but pitied. Old maids have come into similar favour. But the change is too recent to have been noticed by those slaves of tradition who write for comic papers or write plays. In comic papers and in plays the old maid is still merely a butt, and the boldness of Mr Fox is that he has defied an immemorial tradition. The strength of that tradition was illustrated by the behaviour of the audience. Presumably, the average member of the Stage Society is more intelligent than the average playgoer. And yet it was hardly till the end of Mr Fox's play, when the old maid went out to take her own life, that the audience ceased to titter heartily at her. It required a pistol to make them realise that an old maid on the stage could be anything but ridiculous. I do not think this was Mr Fox's fault. Though, as I say, he made the lady ridiculous in superficial details, it was quite clear to me, soon after the curtain rose, that she was meant to be taken quite seriously. However, perhaps Mr Fox ought to have blazoned this precaution. Is not the first point in stage-craft to assume that every member of your audience is a fool?

[*13 June 1903*]


ADVICE TO THOSE ABOUT TO TRANSLATE PLAYS

I look forward, with a thrill, to the time when Australia, New Zealand, Canada and the other darling colonies shall be steadily exporting to the Mother Country all the drama she needs to supplement her own limited produce. I long for our glorious Empire to be in all things self-sufficient. My patriotic fingers itch to hold a revolver at the head of Germany, France, Norway and the rest of our arrogant rivals. I am all for an instant Inquiry. I move for a return of the successful plays already written by those kith and kin who, in the dark days of the South African War, leapt to arms while we leapt to the conclusion that blood is thicker than water. I declare my motion carried by acclaim. But the outcome of it, tenderly laid upon the table, is a blank sheet of paper. Our kith and kin, so martial, so commercial, so altogether remarkable and delightful, are yet undistinguished in the arts. I picture them, these poor arts, pouting, languishing, smiling, beckoning, running the whole gamut of wistful coquetry, while our kith and kin, with their clear colonial eyes and their firm colonial mouths, stare stolidly back, not seducible. One or two falls are on record, however. A year or two ago, we had an exhibition of Australian paintings. The experiment is not likely to be repeated, just at present. I have heard that a resident in Toronto has written an oratorio. I have also heard that it is not at all a good oratorio. But I never have heard that any colonist has even attempted to write a play. Australia is fired from end to end with an admiration, almost amounting to idolatry, for Mr Wilson Barrett. But when one has said that, one has said everything that there is to be said about the connexion between dramatic art and our colonial dependencies. Distant, far distant still, I fear, is the time I yearn for. We must continue, in the humiliating meantime, to import plays from decadent and unfriendly Europe, duty free.

It is important that we should make the best of this bad job. And this is not what we are doing. It is important that the foreign plays should be well translated. And the translators leave much to be desired. I am not speaking of the translators of poetic plays. What Mr Alfred Sutro has done for Maeterlinck, and Mr Arthur Symons for D'Annunzio, is outside my present scope. I am speaking merely of those who translate plays of realistic modern life. Their cardinal fault is that we are always kept more or less acutely conscious that their work is a translation. They seem to be afraid lest we forget them, to be always calling our attention to their ingenuity and their profound reverence for the original version. For the most part, their ingenuity consists in finding phrases that could not possibly be used by the average Englishman. In a translated play which I saw this season, one of the characters was thanking another for some political service rendered, and was met with the modest disclaimer 'Oh, as to that...' A dozen similar instances occur to me, but this one is sufficient. It is a perfect example of the average translator's method. The meaning of the phrase is quite clear, and the wording of it is quite good English, and doubtless it is a close translation from the original; but if I were to thank you for being a gentle reader, and you replied 'Oh, as to that...' I should set you down as a lunatic. If, on the other hand, you murmured 'That's all right' or 'Not at all,' or if you merely made a gesture of deprecation, your behaviour would seem to me normal. In the play of which I speak 'Oh, as to that...' was not a good equivalent for the original phrase because it produced an unnatural effect which could not have been produced by the original phrase. The prime aim of a translator should be to make his play sound like an original play. To do that is the best form of reverent fidelity that he can pay to the original writer. Fidelity to the exact words or cadence of the original phrases must inevitably preclude fidelity to the whole work. Nay! there are many cases in which a perfectly idiomatic English equivalent sounds unnatural, not being the kind of thing which would naturally be said by the character into whose mouth it is put. Suppose, for the sake of argument, that Norwegian ladies in reply to inquiries after their health, use some slangy phrase equivalent to 'Going strong'. If an English lady told you that she was going strong, you would doubt her ladyhood. If an English lady, impersonating a Norwegian lady on the stage, said that she was going strong, you would doubt the Norwegian lady's ladyhood. You would have no reason to doubt it if she said 'Very well, thanks'. And that, accordingly, would be a better translation of the original phrase. It might be said, paradoxically, that the further a translator goes from his original the nearer he comes to it. Of course, for purposes of minute study, it is interesting to know the exact phrases, or our exact verbal equivalents for the phrases, used by Ibsen or another—the exact means whereby he, writing in his own language for his own compatriots, gained his effects. By all means, let us have minutely faithful translations; but only on our shelves; not in our theatres.

Fatal is a disregard to the difference between the kind of translation that is all very well to read, for a special purpose, and the kind that is necessary across footlights. And I think that from this disregard Ibsen has suffered in England more signally than any other alien. Fate, with her incorrigible instinct for cheap irony, has ordained that the man who has done the most to promote Ibsen's popularity in England should also have done the most to hinder it. With the best will in the world, one cannot deny that there has been in every English production of Ibsen's work a certain sense of oppression—a toiling, up-hill sense, hard to explain. The fault has not been, surely, in Ibsen himself, that stimulator and illuminator. Nor can it have been in Miss Janet Achurch or Miss Elizabeth Robins or any of the other gifted actresses who have impersonated Ibsen's heroines. Whence, then, that subtle atmosphere of gloom which not even they could dissipate? It came, I think, from the quality of the words they spoke. These words had many a good quality, but not that of being speakable. Mr Archer is an admirable writer. He is always lucid. He is never otiose. His grammar is above suspicion. But his style is rather inflexible. Besides, there is a great difference between what looks well in type and what sounds well on a pair of lips; and the width of this difference Mr Archer has yet to realise. Thus Ibsen's characters in English talk like books, or, at any rate, like newspapers of the better sort; and the mimes are accordingly constrained. But, even if Mr Archer were a reed through which Ibsen's words came in exquisitely vocal music, he would still be a damaging translator. For his heart and soul are rooted in a false theory of translation. On a shelf near me are ranged in a row the versions he has made of Ibsen. No library should be without them. But I have to consider them in reference to the theatre. I take down one of them at random. It happens to be the last—*When We Dead Awaken*. It opens at page 14, where Rubek, the sculptor, is describing his contempt for the subjects of the busts which he has been making since his soul lost inspiration. 'At bottom they are all respectable, pompous horse-faces', he insists, 'and self-opinionated donkey-muzzles, and lop-eared, low-browed dog-skulls, and fatted swine-snouts—and sometimes dull, brutal bull-fronts as well'. A strange passage! Of course, one sees what Mr Archer is driving at. One sees only too clearly that he is driving at an exact reproduction of what Ibsen made Rubek say. But one does not hear, through this exotic gibberish, the voice of Rubek. It has been well said that in translating a foreign author we ought to write exactly as he would have written if he had happened to be (without, of course, any according change in his thoughts or temperament) a true-born Briton. Similarly, in translating a dramatic work we ought to think what a true-born Briton would say if he had exactly the same feelings, character and circumstances, and were expressing the same thoughts, as the character whose words we have to translate. If Mr Archer had projected himself into the soul of an embittered British sculptor, he would have been on the highway to a right rendering of the Norwegian words (though it is true that to reach the goal he would have had to write on the model of De Quincey's darkest manner). A few pages further on, I find another shining example of how not to do it. Ulfheim enters. He is a rich gentleman, devoted to sport, and caring not at all for society. He sees the illustrious Rubek, whom he had met some years before. 'Why', he says, 'blast me if here isn't a country tyke that has strayed into regular tip-top society'. I will not labour the point that the construction of this sentence is opposed to all the requirements of oral speech. I merely insist that the words strike an utterly false note. 'Blast' and 'tyke' and 'regular tip-top' are, no doubt, exact equivalents for the original words. But the whole sentence is a nightmare. Possibly it was a nightmare in Norwegian. In that case, Mr Archer should have tried to improve it. By the way, no author is infallible. There is no reason why the maker of a translation for the stage should not try to correct occasional lapses. A dangerous theory? But I am anxious, at all costs, to cure translators of their exaggerated veneration for original authors. Only so can the original authors get a chance.

[ *18 July 1903* ]


A PLAY WITHOUT WORDS

In the ordinary theatres the past season has given us no new thrill, except *The Admirable Crichton*. Mr Henry Arthur Jones has held his own ground already broken by him. Mr Pinero has been in abeyance. A new playwright has appeared, and is very welcome. But a new playwright seldom gives us a new play, and Mr Hubert Henry Davies has not yet had time to become original. In due course, no doubt, he will crown his technical talent and his humour with a recognisable self, and will not, I hope, become less immediately popular. The many French mimes who have come to us have brought with them no drama not familiar to us. For that sort of thing we have had to look, and not in vain, to the Stage Society, that very prosperous shrine off the beaten track. Mr Philip Carr has given Pastoral Plays; but there, through no fault of his own, the new thrill had too much in common with a rheumatic twinge to be altogether delicious. This week, when I supposed that the theatrical season was quite over, and that all hope of new thrills must be deferred to the autumn, I was directed to the West Theatre of the Albert Hall. There a belated thrill was in store for me.

*Prince Pierrot*, produced on Tuesday evening, was a play without words, and these missing words were from the pen of Mr Reginald Turner, who thus modestly diverted to the stage that very light and bright talent which he has devoted to the writing of novels. The silence of Mr Turner was partially filled with music by Mr Dalhousie Young. And the play was enacted by English ladies and gentlemen. From that last fact came for me the new thrill. From the wordless play itself, obviously, no new thrill can be extracted. The wordless dramatist is confined so strictly to a simple, straightforward story, even if he deal not with Pierrot, that traditional figure. He must eschew all unexplored subtleties of the human soul. He must give us nothing that has not been made elsewhere very familiar to us through words. A pretty variation on old schemes is as much as we can ask from him. From Mr Turner we get as much. His scheme for Pierrot has just the right kind of fanciful simplicity. We behold the garden of the cottage of Monsieur and Madame Perrée. Their daughter, Lisette, comes home from market, bringing presents for them. They are pleased but astonished. Why this bounty? They remember that it is their wedding-day. They embrace. Dinner is ready, and they go into the cottage. (It is, by the way, a Swiss cottage, and its tenants wear Swiss costume. Why? No stage manager has the right to expatriate Pierrot—especially into the one country which is barren of romance. Here, indeed, is a new thrill, but not a pleasant one.) A fiddle is heard in the distance, and presently Pierrot, the travel-worn fiddler, is gazing over the hedge. He sighs at sight of so much shade and comfort. He looks up at the apple-tree. Why should he not take an apple? It would be wrong. As he stands hesitating, one of the apples drops to the ground. He snatches it, bites it, relishes it, lies down to finish it, and falls asleep. Out comes Monsieur Perrée. He perceives the theft. Lisette saves Pierrot from his wrath. Pierrot fiddles to them, making them gay, making them sad. Lisette, before the tune is done, has fallen in love with Pierrot. As he plays the last note, she kisses him. He falls on his knees. Monsieur Perrée drives him out of the garden. Lisette and her mother weep. Monsieur Perrée relents, runs after Pierrot, brings him back, gives his blessing. The tableau is interrupted by the arrival of a very gorgeous procession —heralds, courtiers, trumpeters, a major-domo, all in ermine and gold and purple. The foremost carries a board, on which is inscribed in golden letters 'Lost, Stolen, or Strayed: a Prince'. Pierrot cowers into the background. But another, a tiny Pierrot, who has come in the procession, espies him and runs to him and jumps up to be kissed. Pierrot is led forth, reluctant, and on his head is set a crown, and from his shoulders is hung a princely robe. Monsieur and Madame Perrée begin to give themselves airs. They take a new pleasure in kissing Lisette. The major-domo holds up a warning hand: it is forbidden, on pain of death, to kiss the betrothed of the prince. Lisette cries, and lays her head on Pierrot's shoulder. Again the major-domo intervenes: it is unlawful to lay one's head on the shoulder of the prince. So beset are they all with points of punctilio that they almost lose their wits. A thought strikes Pierrot: he will abdicate. The major-domo consults his book of precedents. He finds that the prince *can* abdicate. Pierrot tears off the symbols of his birthright, and invests with them, very ceremoniously, his little brother. The procession forms up. The major-domo congratulates Pierrot, slapping him on the back. And Pierrot takes up his fiddle, and plays for Lisette and for Monsieur and Madame Perrée another tune—one that has not a note of sadness in it.

Now, if this play had been interpreted by professional French mimes, it would have charmed me even more than it did; but it would not have incidentally thrilled me. I have often seen such mimes acting without words, and I know how well they can do it. But I have never seen amateur English mimes acting without words, and I had not imagined how badly they were bound to do it. The performance startled me. I do not pretend that I did not understand what the performers were driving at. The story was quite clear. But its clarity was in despite of, rather than owing to, its plucky exponents. Deprived of words, they seemed to be deprived of everything. Not for one moment did I get the illusion—the desirable illusion—that they were talking; and not for one moment did I lose the exciting but undesirable illusion that they were persons suddenly struck dumb and making frantic, pathetic efforts to make their wishes known. Imagine a group of sphinxes trying to be communicative, and then you can imagine what this performance was like. The fact is, of course, that a gesture play is hopeless in England, because the English are not a gesticulating people. If you ask your way of the man in the street, he will perhaps jerk his thumb to the right, indicating the right, or to the left, indicating the left. And that very rudimentary kind of gesture is the highest flight that the average Englishman can achieve. As with our hands, so with our faces: we express nothing: we let the words speak for themselves. The Latin races, with eternal quicksilver in their veins, give to every phrase a hundred accentuations and qualifications through natural pantomime. There, as I am always protesting, is the reason for the general inferiority of English to French acting. No doubt, it will be well to have a training-school. But we shall go on training till Doomsday without altering the essential truth that actors are born, and are not —with a very few exceptions—born in England. Experience is better than nothing. Through it can be achieved a colourable imitation of the real thing. An English actor who has been on the stage for some years is able to keep his hands and his face moving in some sort of harmony with his words. The amateur, however, fights an uneven battle with his natural disinclination to let these members assert themselves at all. To take the words out of his mouth is too harsh a discipline, I think. I must except from my strictures the interpreter of Lisette, Mrs A. B. Clifton. She, certainly, had something of the authentic quicksilver. But I dare swear her maiden-name was not an English one.

[*25 July 1903*]

## A CONTRAST IN HOSPITALITY

I often wonder what the American, visiting London for the first time, thinks of us as hosts. The Englishman who goes to New York needs not so much letters of introduction as letters of preservation—letters of entreaty that he be not killed with kindness outright. As his ship steams into harbour, the very statue of Liberty seems to be passionately striving to express through her lips of stone the hope that he will have 'a lovely time'. The very officers of the Customs House, cruelly misunderstood men, hasten to show their simple and barabaric reverence of him by appraising at three times its value his every dutiable impediment. Free, at length, of their embarrassing attentions, he is soon to realise that the whole city is agog to please him—to take him by the hand, and whirl him around, and dazzle him, and, having primed him with a surfeit of rich food and wine, to ask him, in a tone of sober wistfulness, whether it meets with his approval. What, I repeat, can the American visitor think of *us*? How much of his approval can *we* meet with? It never occurs to you to ask that question. You, for whom on his own soil he really has put himself out, piling kindness on kindness, and grudging no time or trouble that shall secure that 'lovely time' for you, take on your own soil precious little notice of *him*. You, who were so promptly made free of any club in New York, perhaps go so far as to put his name down as a temporary member of your own club, from whose secretary he will receive, after a decent interval, the glad tidings that he may come in after payment of a modified subscription. Perhaps you ask him to a meal in a restaurant, 'to meet a few friends' whom you don't take the trouble to invite; and thereafter you sigh with the sense of duty nobly done. This difference in international courtesies offers a problem, surely, to ethnologists. For it cannot be that every Englishman who goes to New York is an angel, and every American who comes to London is an ape. I myself have often, on the platforms of Euston and Waterloo, bidden God's speed to Englishmen whom I wished to remain for ever on the other side of the Atlantic; and I have met here, and been entertained by (for their choice here is between hospitality and isolation), many fascinating Americans. Of course, one must remember the difference between our country and theirs—between what is to be seen by them here and by us there. We neglect to hang out a bush, confident in the quality of the wine. If, for instance, an American is about to visit Westminster Abbey, we do not feel that we must accompany him and point out the beauties: he can see them for himself: there is no doubt about them. On the other hand, the beauties of a twenty-nine-story building are not quite so obvious; and the American is not even sure, in his heart of hearts, that they are beauties at all. Thus he feels that he cannot let an Englishman go alone to and up and down New York's equivalent for a cathedral. He takes care that the Englishman be first flushed and expanded at his expense, and so be in a state to receive the hypnotic suggestion that a twenty-nine-story building really is something for the native to be proud of, and for the alien to envy. He knows well that for every sip of the wine he offers us he must daub a fresh coat of green upon the bush. And he is anxious—ever so wistfully anxious—that we should drink deep. If the historic beauties of London did not appeal to the archaeological and aesthetic senses of the American sightseer, we should not be at all vexed. They do not appeal particularly to us. We take them as a matter of course. We know that they are there, and admirable, and that no visitor's ecstasies can improve them. If we were a young nation, we should take a more explicit pride in them. But if we were a young nation, they would not be there at all. There is the tragedy of a young nation: its anxiety to congratulate itself, and to be congratulated all round, on possession of things which it will not possess till it has ceased to care about them. I have no patience with people who have no patience with what they call the 'brag' and the 'bluster' of Americans. To me our cousins' desire to persuade themselves and us that they have a very romantic and heroic national history, and that there is poetry and beauty in their buildings, is a very agreeable and appealing quality. Be sure that we ourselves, before we grew old and beautiful, bragged and blustered quite as freely. Nor can it be said that the Americans are at all grudging in their recognition of our achievements. They are quite as hearty over what we have done as over what they would like to have done. Quite recently was started in London a little paper whose aim was to quicken our pulses weekly by presenting us with tit-bits of British daring. This seemed to me a shaky foundation for success. We take the business of British daring for granted: we don't want it dinned into our ears for even the small consideration of one penny weekly. But the venture is explained by the fact that it was conceived by an American. And its success, if it does succeed, will be due not to English but to American readers— not to an old and surfeited nation, but to a hungry young one. Youth and age: there, of course, you strike the reason for that difference in hospitality between Americans and Englishmen. The mutual visitors are not judged on their own merits, but according to their backgrounds. Out there the most undesirable Englishman is treated with the interest and the reverence due from youth to age. In here the most desirable American is treated with the superiority which age necessarily feels over youth. Neither this superiority nor that reverence is unmixed. Just as an old man's contempt for youth is tinged with envy and fear of its advantages, and just as a young man's reverence is tinged with pity and mockery, so must we resent Americans for that so much more of the future is in their hands than in ours, and so must Americans feel that they can afford to pamper us, the harmless, the futile. Thus, our inhospitality is not quite so shameful in us, nor is their hospitality quite so admirable in them, as one might at first suppose. Both phenomena, at all events, are explained.

If you will now take this theory from the general sphere to which I have applied it, and tranfer it to the special sphere of dramatic art, you will find, not less certainly, the reason why a successful English play is sure to be received with rapture in New York, whereas the greatest American successes are played here to an audience of upturned noses. Mr Clyde Fitch is the most popular dramatist in America. Some of his most popular plays have been performed in London. Yet Mr Fitch has never received our public's accolade, and has always been lectured on his crudeness and his unscrupulousness by those critics who make it their business to suit their tastes to the tastes of the public. His *Climbers*, at the Comedy, has had the customary reception. On the other hand, Mr H. V. Esmond is one of America's darlings. And he has endeared himself not merely through plays which have been successful in England, but also through plays which, produced first in America, have been subsequently slighted in England. *When We Were Twenty-one* was deemed a masterpiece in America, yet the British public gave it the go-by. Similarly, *Billy's Little Love Affair*, another masterpiece in America, and now to be seen at the Criterion, has set all the heads of the critics shaking very gravely. It seems as though even an English play that comes wreathed with American laurels must necessarily be suspect. For I cannot see that *Billy's Little Love Affair* marks any decline from *The Wilderness* and other of Mr Esmond's plays which these same critics thought so very nice. I am sure they would have purred over it if it had been offered first on native soil. Yet it would have been no worthier of their purrs than is *The Climbers* of their hisses. It would have been the same silly little old story that it is, with no charm to excuse its remoteness from life, and with a great deal of ugliness which is the less tolerable because we are evidently expected to think it charming. Mr Esmond's play and Mr Fitch's have this in common: both are comedies in which we see vulgar people. But, whereas Mr Fitch keenly satirises a vulgarity which he has observed, Mr Esmond asks us to coo with delight over a vulgarity which he has invented. Mr Fitch throws in a lot of stage-tricks in case we should grow tired of his very clever and true study of a gambler. Mr Esmond thinks that if only his heroine be called 'Billy', and write love-letters signed 'Wang' to somebody called 'Toodles', we shall watch with breathless interest the process whereby she is falsely suspected of an intrigue really carried on by the female villain. Had the play been written by an American, it would surely have failed in America. Had *The Climbers* been written by an Englishman, it would surely have been acclaimed in England. The difference of hospitality for plays is the same as it is for persons. Much is made of the English play or person, however undesirable. The American person or play, however desirable, is cold-shouldered. For on either side, plays, like persons, are judged not as in themselves they are, but by wide association.

[*26 September 1903*]

## 'LITTLE MARY'

The critics have paid Mr Barrie many handsome compliments on *Little Mary*, and the handsomest of all is in the general demur that, however delightful it may be as an entertainment, *Little Mary* can scarcely be regarded as a play. This is but another way of telling Mr Barrie that he is now perfect master of the medium in which he works; and the message will not be the less gratifying because it is delivered unconsciously. Mr Barrie has learned how to make his dramatic work the exact expression of his own self—his own 'best self', as Mr Matthew Arnold would have said. His inferior self is a slave to sentimentality, cheap and cloying, such as was already too familiar on the stage before he became a playwright. His 'best self' is a reveller in fantastic humour. Such humour is strange upon the stage, and is very rare anywhere else. Therefore, a play that is compact of it must come as a great surprise, and must, seeming so unlike other plays, seem to be hardly a play at all. When Mr Barrie was praised for *The Little Minister* and rebuked for *The Wedding Guest*, there was no hint that these works were not authentic plays. That is because they were simply 'prentice-work. In them Mr Barrie was learning his craft. He was feeling his way along the line of least resistance, doing what other men had done so as to learn exactly how they did it, and exactly how he, in his good time, would be able to transmit by dramatic form, without friction, his own peculiar little genius. *The Admirable Crichton* was the first sign that he had 'found himself'—or, rather, that he had ventured on self-expression. That, too, was hailed as an 'entertainment', a 'charade', a 'caprice', anything but a play. And yet it was, in form and manner, more conventional than *Little Mary*. By so much the less was it Barryish. Here, at length, we have the veritable Barrydom. And the reason, I suggest, is not that Mr Barrie has neglected his art, but that he has mastered it.

Of course, he had always a natural aptitude for play-writing. The dramatist must be born as well as made. Even in his earlier work, however much one may have been jarred by the sentimentality, one had always the comfortable sense that what he meant to express he would express artistically. Student though he was, and, as a student must be, conventional, he was always skilful. His sketches did not need to be touched up by the drawing-master. His 'form' one could always praise. Now that this is perfect, so that he can afford to give rein to his own 'best self', I think his work is on a higher plane than the work of any other living playwright. He has been compared with Mr Bernard Shaw. And the comparison is inevitable, inasmuch as he and Mr Shaw are the only dramatists whose souls are oddities, distinct from the souls of anyone else. Mr Pinero, Mr Grundy, Mr Carton—one meets them by the score in every thoroughfare of London, or of any provincial town. They are, very strictly, 'men in the street'. They mean nothing, amount to nothing, apart from their artistic skill. Mr Henry Arthur Jones is, except Mr Shaw and Mr Barrie, the only one of our dramatists who has definite ideas and a definite temperament. But he is not, in the true sense, an oddity. He differs from the average man in that he thinks and feels forcefully the things which the average man takes muzzily for granted. He is a personal force; we have to reckon with him, to admire him, but as an oddity, no! For that sort of thing, we must go to Mr Barrie and Mr Shaw. But there the parallel between the two men ceases. There are two ways of expressing a peculiar self through an art-form. One way is Mr Barrie's. The other way is to have no innate sense for the art-form which you select and to disdain any effort at mastery of it. That is Mr Shaw's way. If Mr Shaw tried to be artistic, he would assuredly flounder, and go under, and be lost to view. Luckily, he does not try. But, supposing that Mr Barrie's self is as remarkable and delightful, in its way, as Mr Shaw's, one is bound to place Mr Barrie on the higher pedestal. Personally, I delight more in Mr Shaw's self. I prefer the intellectual fantastic to the sentimental fantastic. Mr Barrie could do with a little more logic. He gives out ideas; and his method of giving them out—that is, by illustrating them in action, as opposed to Mr Shaw's strictly explanatory method—is without doubt the right way. Only, he does not always compass the proper illustrations. He wanders often from the point, and far from it. And though his wanderings lead always to delicious adventures, and might even be defended on the ground that if he were not a wanderer he would not be so distinctly himself, yet one cannot help feeling that one is being done out of what ought to be an intellectual treat. The idea is there, right enough, but not the power to drive it home.

The idea in *Little Mary* is not a new one, but it is a very true one,

## 'LITTLE MARY'

and one that is not generally accepted. That the members of the English upper class eat a great deal is a fact which nobody would deny. But Mr Barrie's point is that they eat a great deal too much. And I believe him to be absolutely right. Why so much is eaten, whence came the habit of such generous daily diet, is not easy to determine. It may be partly due to the subtle influence of the upper classes. One must remember that since it has been considered bad form to drink too much, many people have indulged in the compensating excesses of teetotalism. Whether or not this be the reason why the persons in 'society', or within measurable distance of it, eat so much, it is quite certain that the example set by these persons has been followed generally by the class beneath them. Mr Barrie has not drawn his indictment widely enough. The middle class is quite as gluttonous as the upper. In England the only people who do not over-eat are the people who cannot afford to pay for too much food. And be sure that they, if they could, under the present conditions, over-eat, would be as quickly and furiously responsive as now they are to the cry of 'the big loaf and the little loaf'. (Why do not Cobdenites cry also 'the big *pâté de fois gras* and the little *pâté de fois gras*', and so bring the whole of the wealthy class solidly to their side?) Whether, from the standpoint of national welfare, one should deplore the amount of food consumed by our upper and middle classes, is too complex a question to be settled off-hand. There is no doubt that their habit makes them stupid, or, rather, tends to increase their stupidity. But England has always been a stupid nation, and for some centuries it has been a great nation. National stupidity does not preclude national greatness. Indeed, in favourable circumstances, the one thing tends to foster the other. If a dull, unimaginative race can produce, or attract to itself, a few wise and quick-witted leaders, it is likelier to thrive than a clever, imaginative race, however well led. For it follows its leaders, follows them solidly and obediently. England is stupid, but she has two clever neighbours, the Scotch and the Irish; and these have never failed to ply her with leaders in supplement of her own little stock. And I am inclined to think that less food (and consequently quicker wits) for her inhabitants would be as surely the cause as it would be also the effect of national decline. Nevertheless, I can quite sympathise with the irritation which English gluttony and stupidity must arouse in the quick-witted and abstemious Irishman or Scotchman. And I wish that Mr Barrie had expressed his idea sharplier. Even when it might be dangerous to eradicate a fault, it is wholesome that the fault be clearly realised by the delinquent. Mr Barrie seems to me a little lacking in courage. Not only has he left the middle class out of his indictment, but he has put his indictment into the mouth of an Irish character. I think the English public would have respected him all the more if he had spoken his sentiments directly from his own national standpoint. However, this is a trifling fault. What matters more is the fault to which I have already alluded. Mr Barrie does not fit his illustrations closely enough to his idea. It is possible that a girl might become a *malade imaginaire* simply through overeating, and that a young man might, through the same cause, imagine himself to be in love with someone for whom he does not really care. But these are not typical examples of the stupidity induced by too much food. It would be better if the young man had the chance of marrying some ideal person, whom he did not appreciate until his wits were quickened by the lessening of his diet. Of course, this suggestion sounds pedantic. The play you say is a fantasy, and any fantastic thing can happen in it. But I maintain that all fantasy must be rooted in reality, and that Mr Barrie has not duly correlated his delightful extravagances with the serious notion in the back of his head. The part of Lord Carlton, played by Mr John Hare, is another example of irrelevance. He is the most prominent male character in the play, and yet he has practically nothing to do with Mr Barrie's idea. He ought, surely, to be one of the sufferers whom the girl-doctor wishes to cure. As it is, he is simply a walking-and-talking gentleman, who asks her to marry him just before the curtain falls. Mr Barrie is quite popular enough, quite sufficiently recognised as a sentimentalist, to have omitted that perfunctory touch of sentiment. After the roaring absurdities of the preceding scene, it can have imposed on nobody, and must have jarred on many people. The worst of it is that Lord Carlton might easily be made relevant. If he were the prime glutton in the play, and yet fascinated by the girl-doctor, and if in that final scene between them he had to choose between her and happiness on the one hand and dyspeptic plenty on the other, and if, after a desperate heart-struggle, he chose the latter alternative... but I seem to be mistaking collaboration for criticism.

Mr John Hare's quaint and pungent manner was a corrective to his words in that final scene; and throughout the play he was admirable. One watches him with the same pleasure as one has in sipping a glass of very good dry sherry. Miss Nina Boucicault appears first as a child, and is much the best child that I have ever seen on the stage. Subsequently, she is the girl-doctor, and plays with fine imaginative power, making a very realistic thing of a very fantastic thing, and so doubling the fantasy. Mr Gerald du Maurier, as the son of Lord Carlton, gives us a study of a young Englishman which is all the more amusing because it has been made with a touch of French malice and is instinct with French finesse. Mr Eric Lewis, as an eminent physician, is irresistible.

[*3 October 1903*]


A PLAY WITH AN IDEA

Our earliest instincts is to ask for a story; our latest, to tell one unasked. Human life is bounded at either end by a phrase: 'once upon a time' at one end, 'that reminds me' at the other. Above the first instinct we rise gradually, gradually declining to the second. (When I say 'we' I refer not to mankind in general; for most men, as I shall suggest later, never grow up, except in a physical sense. 'We' must be taken merely as a convenient term for the less imperfect minority.) Not that the narrative sense ever dies in us. Only that in the plentitude of our powers we are not satisfied with a story that is nothing more than a story—a narrative for narration's sake. The mind of a child is all agape for facts; for it is empty, and nothing is so quickly-filling, so easily assimilable, as a dish of facts. Facts of fiction are preferred by the child to actual facts, because they satisfy also its strong imaginative sense. Its moral and intellectual senses are still in abeyance. Deduce from any story 'a moral' or an idea, and the child runs away, rudely. There lies the difference between us and it. Our moral and intellectual senses are flourishing, and by their strength our imagination is proportionately weakened. Grimm is not enough for us. Our moral sense cries aloud for Hans Andersen. Dumas leaves us cold. Our mind needs Balzac. It is not enough for us that once upon a time there were three princesses or three musqueteers who suffered or did some queer things. We want those triads to illustrate, to symbolise, to *mean* something, to corroborate or upset some theory that we have formed, to quicken our mind and affect our conduct. Such are the prime needs of our maturity. Comes Time, mowing away with his scythe our intellectual and moral curiosity; nor does he restore to us our old imagination. He crops us bare of all but experience. Things that have happened—especially (old egoists that we are) the things that have happened to ourselves—are the only things that rouse us from our lethargy. 'Anecdotage' is an ugly phrase. 'Second childhood', less harsh, is not less exactly descriptive. For our last state—the state where narrative is absolute despot—was our first state, too.

Infancy, maturity and eld occur to arts less surely than to us. And similar are the signs on the parallels. The infancy of the novel was in the tales that the cave-men muttered to one another over their fires. Its maturity is in the philosophic fiction of Mr Meredith. Its eld will be when the novelists write such stories as were muttered by the cave-men; or perhaps I should say, rather, when novelists write nothing but their own reminiscences. So with drama. Drama's infancy was when Attic peasants danced round an altar in a field, carolling legends of Dionysus. Came Aeschylus, that moralist, and Euripidies, that philosopher, and made the maturity of Attic drama. Shakespeare, similarly, matured English drama from the pools of blood and claps of thunder that were all it had offered to childish eyes and ears. His chief service was not in that he gave beauty to drama, but in that he gave meaning. In course of time, English drama died. Recently it has been born again. It is still in its infancy. A sickly infant, it may never be reared. On the other hand, we may, with care, pull it through. 'We', I say; but 'we' are differing doctors. Some of us insist that drama should consist of unmeaning little anecdotes, and are very angry at a hint of moral or intellectual significance. Others of us maintain that without such significance drama bores us. Some of us, in fact, never grow up, and so resent the growth of an art; and others of us do grow up, and rejoice in an art's growth. The latter class is, as I have said, in a minority: the general rule is against any decent interval between first and second childhood. But what we lack in number we make up for in vital force. And even now there are signs that modern English drama is being coaxed to maturity. Sparse signs, perhaps; yet reassuring.

## A PLAY WITH AN IDEA

This week, for example, at the Kennington Theatre is a new play entitled *A Man and Himself*, written by Mr Murray Carson and Miss Nora Keith, and permeated by the stimulant of a very good idea. No very good idea can be new, except on the modern stage. I suppose that every thoughtful man, in his middle age, must have often craved the dread fascination of standing eye to eye with himself completely incarnate as he was in his adolescence. He must have craved this encounter, not merely in morbid curiosity for the physical contrast, but also, with a fine humility, for the mortification of his soul. Youth, the accuser! Youth, with clear reproachful eyes, looking its outcome up and down, taking its outcome's measure, scanning in the light of its own large and ardent dreams such fulfilment as the dreams have come to! Youth, the avenger, sneering, cursing, shuddering away, vanishing... Man, in the struggle for life, mostly falls, and is content to crawl as best he can; youth foresees mostly an erect triumphal progress, or even a steadily glorious flight on wings. Poor youth, and, in his presence, poor dear man! But must not the man's humiliation be yet subtler and deeper if in the opinion of his fellow-men he has triumphed enviably, and only his own youth knows that he has failed? *A Man and Himself* is a man in such a case as that. A very popular statesman is Mr John Norton. For years he has been a 'great commoner', moving in central limelight. He has made great speeches, in the House and in the country. He is always reported verbatim. For years he has been most impressive, most magnetic. Everybody believes in him. Only, he has never done anything in particular. His one solid achievement has been in making everyone believe him capable of anything whatever. Himself is the one sceptic. And the conflict of his scepticism with the faith of his youth is a conflict ever raging in him and wearing him away. In his library hangs a portrait of himself as he was at the age of twenty; and always this portrait gazes down on him coldly, reproachfully, mockingly: it seems to him a live thing. He (a private member! but we must allow some licence to stage-politics) has, at length, launched a great scheme of constructive statesmanship. Its fate depends solely on such continuous energy of soul and body as he can muster for it. Will he be strong and conquer? Mentally and physically strained, he tries to nerve himself, tries to concentrate all his powers on that effort whose success shall fulfil the dreams of his youth. He will belie that look of mocking inquiry in the eyes of his early self. But he feels his powers slipping from him. Only by ridding himself of that haunting and malign presence can he hope to conquer. Insanely he seizes a knife, rips the canvas from its frame. As it falls, the door of the library opens, and there enters, full-blooded, the very self that he had thought to destroy. The apparition steadies him. From frenzy he passes to curiosity. He invites the apparition to sit with him, drink with him, open its heart to him. After a while, the old hatred and terror resurge. Creeping behind the apparition, he lays his fingers about its throat, and strangles it. Then, realising what he has done, he takes his own life.

Told thus in brief narrative form, the story sounds as though it had a supernatural element. That would be nothing against it as a serious study. Reality can often be best illustrated by supernatural means. I think that if the apparition of John Norton's youth were supernatural the play would be better even than it is. As a matter of fact, this apparition is Mr Norton's daughter, who much resembles his early portrait, and who has assumed, to amuse him, the Court suit in which he sat for it. The adventure is made plausible by preparation, and it provides a sharply tragic ending for a play which must, in any case, have ended tragically. Still, it is a trick, an improbable coincidence; and I should prefer the 'credible-impossible' scene, as more apt to the serious nature of the play. The appointed tragedy for Mr Norton, and the occasion of his suicide, should be the knowledge of his own madness and of the failure of his dear ambitions. Further tragedy is unneeded, and not relevant.

There is, too, a practical reason why the motive of the daughter's likeness to her father's portrait should have been sacrificed. Leading men on the stage seldom resemble their leading ladies. Mr Murray Carson does not at all resemble Miss Esmé Beringer; nor can we believe that he did so even when he was twenty years old. So how about that all-important 'property', the picture over the mantelpiece, for all our eyes to see? What line was the painter to take? Should he have gone for a likeness of Miss Beringer as she is, or for one of Mr Carson as he may conceivably have appeared some years before that evening on which he was to powder his temples, and paint lines on his face, for a correct semblance of Mr Norton? Apparently, he has tried a compromise between the two courses. He has tried to give a little of each sitter. The result was foredoomed to be unlike either, but for the life of me I cannot see why it should be, as it is, a striking likeness of Doctor Nikola, once so familiar on our hoardings. Surely, with a little more skill... I wonder if I am right in suspecting the omnificent Mr Carson himself of this strange canvas. As part-author he has already been praised by me. I applaud him as a manager for his discrimination in producing so good a play. I applaud him as actor, for that he interprets with strong imaginative intensity the fine part that he has helped to invent. Mr Ben Webster is breezy as a naval lieutenant, in love with Miss Norton, but now and again becomes a trifle operatic—too good to be true. Miss Esmé Beringer plays charmingly as Miss Norton, and the only objection is that in her movements she is a trifle too graceful for a girl at 'the awkward age' of sixteen. A contrary objection may be made to Mrs Macsmore Morris's performance of a Duchess, who, purporting to have reached the awkward age of forty, is quite the débutante. Why, by the way, should there be a Duchess? These eternal Duchesses! I suppose no playwright would condescend to a Marchioness. But might we not have, for a change, a Princess of the blood royal?

[*21 November 1903*]

## 'THE PROFESSOR'S LOVE STORY'

I would advise all lovers of drama to go to the St James's Theatre. I cannot conceive a more cheering entertainment. During the early scenes, to be sure, one gasps a little. But presently supervenes a mood of cordial satisfaction, and this mood is gradually intensified, until, at the final fall of the curtain, one steps breezily out into the night, holding one's head ever so much higher than usual.

And rightly, of course, one must leave some margin for the delusive effect of novelty. It is no law of art that work done to-day is better than work done a decade ago. But it is a law of our nature that we are more quickly susceptible to the former kind. Fashions change, and we with them; and a modish bad things seems to us, if we are not very careful, essentially better than a not worse thing whose mode is past. As I write this sentence, an organ in the street below is grinding out 'Mamie in her Canoe', and I see my left hand artlessly beating time to the music. If the tune were 'Oh Marguerite' or some other favourite of ten years since, I suppose no answering gesture would be evoked. My musical colleague would very likely say that the new tune marked no absolute advance from the old. He might even pronounce the old a masterpiece, and the new a wretched imposture. But the mere difference in date is enough for me. For me, unsophisticated, the one tune is alive, the other dead. Passing from an art of which I know nothing in particular, I predicate of the arts in general that sometimes they progress, sometimes they retrogress, sometimes (though their superficial fashions are always varying) they merely mark time. Our tendency is always to imagine them progressive. Once in three times, on an average, the tendency is right. And the cheerfulness of *The Professor's Love Story* is in itself very definite proof that we are right in thinking that the British drama is progressing, or, at least, that it has been progressing in the past decade.

I admit that the difference between this play as it is and this play as it would be if it were new work is partly due to the difference between the mature and the immature author. I sympathise with Mr Barrie on the sudden and sorry resurrection of his old self. It must be very tragic for a man of mature genius (and Mr Barrie is that, though his genius is on a little scale, and his maturity has, luckily for us, not put away childish things) to be brought face to face with his old self's image. He must shrink away, horrified, not less horrified than would be a beautiful girl suddenly confronted by the image of herself in extreme old age. For Mr Barrie what Highland fastness were too remote a refuge from the study of such unripe humour and such ignorance of life as are flaunted now at the St James's? The difference between *The Professor's Love Story* and *Little Mary* is all the more salient for that there are occasional points of likeness. Compare the two doctors in *Little Mary*, those delightful figures, with the two doctors in the earlier play, laboriously and frigidly bandying the phrase '*cherchez la femme*'. The Scotch peasants are well enough; Mr Barrie had studied them at first hand, and managed to express through them some of his inherent humour. But the smart people! Compare them with those who are in *Little Mary*. What dull and pointless figments from the novelettes! The Dowager Lady Gilding, resentfully eyeing a typist in the Professor's service, exclaims in a high voice 'You may present the young person to me!' And that is a fair sample of the satire throughout the play. Yet the intention of the play was to reproduce actual life. Nowadays Mr Barrie treats life in a frankly fantastic manner. But he sees what he twists. The reality is there, right enough, despite the mode of its presentment. *Life shown as it isn't, and yet—life* is the formula for Mr Barrie's recent work. And here we have an exhilarating development from his early work, whose formula is *Nothing that exists, porporting to be life.*

But the special cause for gladness is not so much the advance of Mr Barrie as the advance of drama in general. The point is not that Mr Barrie could not now write such poor stuff as *The Professor's Love Story*, but that no neophyte could do so. At least, if any neophyte did contrive to do so, he could not hope that his play would be accepted by any manager. Of the neophytes at this moment one may presume that few indeed have in them the germs of such talent as Mr Barrie's. But no matter. They are bound to be doing, however badly, a better thing than was done by him. They are using their wits more freely than did he in observation of life. They are tackling a genuine material, where he tackled a false one. Stage-figures, stage-motives, stage-sentiments, stage-language, were what Mr Barrie had to study and reproduce in order to write a successful comedy. The comedy written conscientiously on those lines would be slated now by even the most retrospective critics. We are not nearly so far away from false convention as (I hope) we shall be hereafter. But we are, anyhow, at a little distance from it—enough for perspective—and not stuck in the thick of it, as we were when *The Professor's Love Story* was tolerable. The soliloquies, the asides, the exposition when the curtain rises, help to make this play seem old-fashioned. But to them I make no objection. On the contrary, as I have from time to time suggested, I think it a pity that we are so intolerant of these devices—a pity that they should mar illusion. That they do now mar illusion is no sign of better taste in us. But very definitely such a sign is that we will none of the stage-savant who is so absent-minded that he does not know that he is under the spell of love's young dream; none of the stage-spinster who is very bitter against matrimony, until the finding of a long-lost letter, in which an early suitor for her hand is proved to have been faithful after all, causes her to become very genial; none of the stage-doctors and other puppets, as already described; none of the stage-offer of marriage, with its flatulent rhetoric; none of the stage-suitor's incurable impression that the lady who is accepting him is thinking of 'another'. All these things Time has swept gently away. They are lumber. Comedy (and *The Professor's Love Story* was, and for old sake's sake is, called a comedy) has no use at all for them. They have been made over to farce. Farce has taken them in hand, to the neglect of slammed doors and smashed cucumber frames. In the future decade, I hope, comedy will make over to farce certain other things which now seem appropriate to her. That is always the test of dramatic progress.

*The Professor's Love Story* ought now, of course, to be performed consistently as a farce. But the mimes at the St James's have not been duly coaxed to this effect. Some of them are in the right key. Perhaps the most satisfactory performance is that of Mr A. S. Homewood, who, as Sir George Gilding, frankly dissociates himself from every known or imagined type of humanity. He does not amuse me, but his manner harmonises exactly with the part. The spinster is played by Miss Helen Ferrers, who tries to make the character natural, but atones by her firm resolution not to make it pathetic. Mr Willard throws himself with serious enthusiasm into the part of the Professor. But he is not really suited to it, and would not be so even if a sentimentally comedic rendering were the right one. His strong point is in forceful emotion. He is not a comedian. As the Professor, he makes his points very cleverly, but one sees him making them, and even going to make them, every time. Lightness and elasticity are not his, And even he does not take the part so seriously as to force it within range of his real powers.

[ *12 December 1903* ]

# INDEX

Abingdon, William, 51
*Absent-Minded Beggar, The,* 214–218
Achurch, Janet, 586
*Actor and his Art, The,* 206–209
*Actors of the Century,* 90–92
Addison, Carlotta, 252, 377
*Admirable Bashville, The,* 580–582
*Admirable Crichton, The,* 588, 595
*Admiral Guinea,* 70
*Adventure of Lady Ursula, The,* 61–62, 98
Æschylus, 133, 142, 522, 600
  *Agamemnon,* 323–327
  *Choephoroe,* 324
Ainley, Henry, 448, 583
Ainslie, Douglas, 400
*Alchemist, The,* 572
Alexander, George, 32, 105, 122, 138, 236–237, 250, 252, 278, 282, 285, 351–352, 445, 448, 465, 511, 554
Alexander, Janet, 384
*Ali Baba,* 92–95
*Alladine et Palomides,* 120–121
Allen, Marsh, 202, 282, 388
*All's Well that Ends Well,* 113
*Altar of Friendship, The,* 554–558
*Ambassador, The,* 30–35, 122, 250, 328, 329
*American Beauty, An,* 262
*American Citizen, An,* 159, 186
Anderson, Percy, 54
Anstey, F.
  *Lyre and Lancet,* 507–510
  *The Man from Blankley's,* 370–373, 508–510
*Antigone,* 285
*Antony and Cleopatra,* 255–256
Archer, William, 17, 22, 24, 26, 27, 34, 55, 62–64, 104–109, 120, 123, 188, 210, 246, 254, 309, 377–381, 456, 478, 586–587
Archimedes, 481
Argyll, Duke of, 318
Aristophanes, 572
Aristotle, 81, 459, 540
Arliss, George, 269
  *The Wild Rabbit,* 177–179
  *There and Back,* 470
*Arms and the Man,* 25, 267
Arnold, Matthew, 373, 395–396, 454, 595
*Art Nouveau,* 527
Art Workers' Guild, 162
Arthur, Paul, 36, 65–66, 229, 557
Arthur-Jones, Ethelwyn, 452
Asche, Oscar, 344, 375, 436, 565, 575–576
Ashton Jonson, Mrs
  *The Hedonists,* 487–488
Ashwell, Lena, 150, 197, 244, 287, 297, 298, 300, 444, 489, 492
Atterbury, Bishop, 256
*Au Téléphone,* 442–443
*Auld Lang Syne,* 301
Austen, Jane, 364–366
*Awakening, The,* 350–352
Aynesworth, Allan, 36, 54, 201, 432

Bailey, William, 357
Baird, Dorothea, 110
Balfour, Arthur, 485
Bancroft, George
  *Teresa,* 52–54, 110
  *What will the World Say?,* 110–111
Bancroft, Squire, 209, 471
Bandmann-Palmer, Mrs, 61, 63

# INDEX

Barker, Granville
   *The Weather-Hen*, 171–172
Barnes, J. H., 51, 87
Barrett, Oscar, 92, 94, 95
Barrett, Wilson, 63, 119, 183, 356, 535, 584
   *Man and his Makers*, 195–198
   *The Daughters of Babylon*, 45
   *The Sign of the Cross*, 119, 443
Barrie, J. M.
   *Little Mary*, 595, 599, 604
   *The Admirable Crichton*, 588, 595
   *The Little Minister*, 413, 595
   *The Professor's Love Story*, 603–606
   *The Wedding Guest*, 595
Bateman, Jessie, 322, 373, 473
Bearne, Arthur, 357
*Beauty Stone, The*, 27–30
Beere, Mrs Bernard, 187, 456
Belasco, David
   *Zaza*, 256, 258–259, 264
Bell, George, 90
*Belle of New York, The*, 59, 80, 262, 370
Bellew, Kyrle, 80, 185
*Ben Hur*, 452–454
*Benefit of the Doubt, The*, 227
*Bennets, The*, 364–366
Benson, F. R., 245–248, 255–256, 339–342, 343, 345, 359, 362–363, 365, 448
Benson, Mrs F. R., 255–256, 341
Beringer, Esmé, 45, 138, 252, 376, 602, 603
Bernhardt, Sarah, 41–42, 61, 392, 394, 474–475
Besant, Sir Walter, 94
*Bethlehem*, 558–559
*Between Two Women*, 523–525
Beveridge, J. D., 110, 185, 287, 554

*Beyond Human Power*, 418–421
*Billy's Little Love Affair*, 594
Birrell, Augustine, 206, 263
Bishop, Alfred, 240, 455
*Bishop's Move, The*, 471–473
Bisson, A.
   *On and Off (Le Contrôleur des Wagons-Lits)*, 87–88
   *The Masked Ball*, 227–228
Bjornson, Bjornstjerne, 174
   *Beyond Human Power*, 418–421
*Black Tulip, The*, 203–204
*Blanchette*, 88
Boissier, A. P., 573
*Bonnie Dundee*, 241–245
*Botticelli*, 453
Boucicault, Aubrey
   *A Court Scandal*, 109–110
Boucicault, Dion, 111, 272
   *Rip Van Winkle*, 269–273
Boucicault, Dion G., 36, 150, 202, 259–261
Boucicault, Nina, 118, 353, 495, 599
Bourchier, Arthur, 54, 110, 150, 227, 262, 406, 440, 473, 503, 541, 543
Bowles, Gibson, 263
*Boy Bob*, 195
Boyne, Leonard, 385, 442
Bradfield College, 323–324
Bradfield, Louis, 495
Braithwaite, Lilian, 467, 506, 558
Brandes, Georg, 174–177
Brayton, Lily, 348, 429
Bridges, Robert, 208
Brieux, Eugène
   *Blanchette*, 88
*Brixton Burglary, The*, 85–87
Broadhurst, G. H.
   *The Last Chapter*, 183
   *The Wrong Mr Wright*, 209

608

# INDEX

Brooke, Cynthia, 387
Brookfield, Charles, 124
  *Kenyon's Widow*, 266
Brough, Fanny, 228, 373, 579, 582
Brough, Lionel, 59, 349, 473, 557
Brough, Sydney, 138
Broughton, Phyllis, 425
Brown-Potter, Mrs, 137, 185
Browne, Graham, 172, 489, 490–491
Browning, Robert, 174, 391, 461, 572
Buchanan, Robert, 232
  *Two Little Maids from School*, 82–84
Buckley, F. Rawson, 258
Bulwer Lytton, E., 34, 218, 303
  *Richelieu*, 159–160
Burnand, F. C.
  *The Lady of Ostend*, 167–169
Burnett, Mrs Hodgson, 126
Byron, H. J., 303, 343

*Cabinet Minister, The*, 65
*Caesar and Cleopatra*, 271
*Caesar's Wife*, 443–444
Caine, Hall
  *The Christian*, 199–201, 226
Calderon, Pedro, 145
Calhoun, Eleanor, 195, 322, 344
Calvert, Louis, 425
Calvert, Mrs, 253, 309–310
Cambridge, 323–327
Campbell, Herbert, 528
Campbell, Mrs Patrick, 40, 121, 160, 161, 194, 212, 266, 269, 310, 314, 383, 421
*Canary, The*, 210–212, 254
*Candida*, 26
*Candy, Mr*, 300
*Captain Birchell's Luck*, 204–206

*Captain Brassbound's Conversion*, 335–337
Capus, Alfred, 535–536
Carados, *see* Morton, E. A.
Carlisle, Sybil, 330, 394
Carlyle, Thomas, 109
*Carlyon Sahib*, 160–162
*Carnac Sahib*, 134, 136–137, 271, 422
Carr, J. Comyns, 301
  *The Beauty Stone*, 27–30
Carr, Philip, 337, 588
Carroll, Lewis, 425, 544, 545
Carson, Murray, 20, 51, 63, 98, 128, 159–160, 186–187, 270, 287
  *A Man and Himself*, 601–603
  *Rosemary*, 81, 98, 548–549
  *The Bishop's Move*, 471–473
  *The Jest*, 77–81
  *The Termagant*, 48–51, 81
Carson, Mrs, 187
Carter, Hubert, 565, 576
Carter, Mrs Leslie, 258–259
Carton, R. C., 117, 152, 153, 180, 270, 385, 596
  *A Clean Slate*, 535–538
  *Lady Huntworth's Experiment*, 259–262, 278
  *Liberty Hall*, 147
  *Lord and Lady Algy*, 117, 147, 148, 261, 538
  *Sunlight and Shadow*, 147
  *The Tree of Knowledge*, 147
  *The Undercurrent*, 402, 404–406
  *Wheels within Wheels*, 147–150, 151, 153, 227, 383–384
Cartwright, Charles, 387–388
  *Colonel Cromwell*, 288–289
  *Case of Rebellious Susan, The*, 75, 148, 383–384
*Caste*, 128, 459

## INDEX

Cavalazzi, Madame, 201
Cecil, Lord Hugh, 263
*Celles qu'on Respecte*, 386
*Cenci, The*, 70, 478
Chamberlain, Joseph, 467, 569, 570
Chambers, Haddon, 270, 346, 385
   *The Awakening*, 350–352
   *The Tyranny of Tears*, 128–130, 350
*Chance the Idol*, 488–492
*Charley's Aunt*, 178
Charrington, Mr, 38
Cheatham, Kitty, 388
*Chemineau, Le*, 272
Chester, Elsie, 366
Chesterton, G. K., 456
*Children of the Ghetto*, 218–221
*Christian, The*, 199–201, 226
Chudleigh, Arthur, 36, 85
Churchill, M. L.
   *Blanchette*, 88
Cicero, 116
*Cigarette-Maker's Romance, A*, 353–355, 357–358
Cinquevalli, 89
*Clandestine Marriage, The*, 548, 550
Clarence, O. B., 579
Clarendon, Lord, 478
Clark, Holman, 576
*Clean Slate, A*, 535–538
Clements, Miriam, 417
Clifford, Mrs W. K.
   *The Likeness of the Night*, 415, 417–418
Clifton, Mrs A. B., 591
*Climbers, The*, 593–594
Cockerell, Una, 115
Coffin, Hayden, 112
Coleman, Fanny, 117
Collier, Constance, 386, 436, 546
Collins, Arthur, 57–59, 92–95, 187–189, 293–295, 452, 525–529
Colman, George
   *The Clandestine Marriage*, 548, 550
   *Colonel Cromwell*, 288–289
Compton, Miss, 150, 260–262, 383, 405, 537–538
Connell, F. N., 88
*Contrôleur des Wagons-Lits, Le*, 87–88
*Convert, The*, 36–38
Coolus, Romain
   *Lysiane*, 41–42
Coquelin, aîné, 166, 171, 392–394, 482
Corelli, Marie, 30
*Coriolanus*, 366–367
*Countess Cathleen, The*, 105, 106, 141–144, 145
*Coup de Fouet, Le*, 578
*Court Scandal, A*, 109–110
Courtney, W. L., 517
*Cowboy and the Lady, The*, 154–156, 158, 159
Cox, R. K., 440
Crace, J. F., 326
Craig, Edith, 514
Craig, Gordon, 11, 528, 562–564, 573–576
Craigie, Mrs, 98, 331, 378
   *A Repentance*, 122–123
   *The Ambassador*, 30–35, 122, 250, 328, 329
   *The Bishop's Move*, 471–473
   *The Wisdom of the Wise*, 327–329
Crane, Walter, 164–165
Cranfield, May, 424
Craven, Hawes, 231
Crawford, F. Marion
   *Francesca da Rimini*, 475–477

## INDEX

*Crusaders, The*, 76
*Cuckoo, The*, 123–124
Cunninghame Graham, R. B., 22, 24
*Cupboard Love*, 85, 98
Cutler, Kate, 59
*Cyrano de Bergerac*, 166, 266–267, 482

Dagnall, Ellis, 190
*Daily Chronicle*, 17, 22, 104, 107, 188
*Daily Telegraph*, 43, 181–183, 245, 297, 312, 327, 330, 380, 430, 517
*Dandy Dick*, 237–241
D'Annunzio, Gabriele, 475, 585
Dante, 475, 476, 565–569
*Dante* (Sardou), 565–569
*Daughters of Babylon, The*, 45
Davidson, John
  *Godfrida*, 69–71
Davies, Hubert Henry, 588
Davis, Fay, 32, 138, 237, 252, 283, 284, 285, 351, 444
Dayle, Gilbert
  *What Would a Gentleman Do?*, 492–495
De Bray, Mlle, 477
De Lussan, Zélie, 61
De Max, Edouard, 477
De Quincey, Thomas, 587
De Winton, Alice, 384
*Debt of Honour, A*, 281–285
Decourcelles, Pierre
  *Self and Lady*, 291–292
*Degenerates, The*, 179–183
Denny, W. H., 240–241, 376
*Devil's Disciple, The*, 21, 335
*Dick Whittington*, 92, 94
Diderot, 92
*Dido in the Dumps*, 93

Diogenes, 175, 176
Disraeli, Benjamin, 34, 49
*Divided Way, The*, 85
Dodsworth, Charles, 41
*Doigts de Fée, Les*, 429–432
*Don Juan*, 223, 371
*Don Juan's Last Wager*, 353
*Don Quixote*, 107
D'Orsay, Lawrence, 217
D'Oyly Carte, Rupert, 30
Dreyfus, Captain, 96
Drury Lane, 56–59, 92–96, 134, 187–190, 292–295, 452–454, 525–529
D.S.M., *see* MacColl
Du Maurier, Gerald, 269, 314, 414, 599
Dumas *père*, 54–56, 134, 180
  *Les Demoiselles de St Cyr*, 82–84
  *The Black Tulip*, 203–204
Dunville, T. E., 397–398
Duse, Eleonora, 266, 285

Eastlake, Mary, 183
Echegaray, José
  *Mariana*, 381–383
Edouin, Willie, 59
Edward VII, 454, 483–484, 549
Edwardes, George, 223, 508
*El Capitan*, 169–171, 221
Eldée, Lilian, 532
*Eleanor*, 503–507
*Electra*, 285
*Elixir of Youth, The*, 186
Elizabethan Stage Society, 144–147, 222–223, 256, 332–333, 391, 447, 453, 558, 559
Elliot, Gertrude, 156, 202, 439, 487, 521
Elliot, Maxine, 156, 159, 186, 404
Emery, Polly, 262

# INDEX

Emery, Winifred, 72, 77, 204, 227, 229, 253–255, 394, 413
*End of a Story, The*, 454–456
*English Nell*, 292
*Enigme, L'*, 443–444, 479
Epicurus, 487
Erlanger, A. L., 452
Erskine, James, 36, 202, 377
Esmond, H. V., 33, 98, 270, 283, 405, 440, 489, 491, 544
   *Billy's Little Love Affair*, 594
   *Cupboard Love*, 85, 98
   *Grierson's Way*, 160, 169, 270, 404
   *My Lady Virtue*, 499–503
   *The Divided Way*, 85
   *The Sentimentalist*, 415–417
   *The Wilderness*, 429, 594
   *When We Were Twenty-One*, 402–404, 594
*Everyman*, 398–401, 453, 558–561

Faber, Beryl, 513–514
Faber, Leslie, 506
*Family Herald*, 151, 356
*Fantasticks, The*, 266–269
Farr, Florence, 144
*Faust*, 93, 457–459
*Faust Up to Date*, 93
Fenn, Frederick
   *A Married Woman*, 511–514
   *Judged by Appearances*, 511
   *Liz's Baby*, 511
Fay, Elfie, 498
Fernald, C. B.
   *The Moonlight Blossom*, 193–195
Ferrar, Beatrice, 190, 470
Ferrers, Helen, 606
Feydeau, Georges
   *The Girl from Maxim's*, 478
*Fiamma*, 529–532

Filippi, Rosina, 54, 195, 212, 506
   *The Bennets*, 364–366
*Finding of Nancy, The*, 463–467
Fitch, Clyde
   *The Climbers*, 593–594
   *The Cowboy and the Lady*, 154–156, 158, 159
   *The Masked Ball*, 227–228
Fitzgerald, Aubrey, 202
FitzGerald, Edward, 145, 146
Flaubert, Gustave, 19
Fletcher, Constance
   *The Canary*, 210–212, 254
   *The Fantasticks*, 266–269
Flintwinch, Mr (*Little Dorrit*), 137
Forbes, Norman, 349, 429, 576
Forbes Robertson, *see* Robertson, J. F.
Forsyth, B., 573
Fortescue, May, 132
Foss, George, 172
Fox, Bernard, 506
Fox, S. M., 581
   *The Waters of Bitterness*, 583–584
Fragonard, 481
France, Anatole, 541
*Francesca da Rimini*, 475–477
Fraser, Winifred, 269
Freear, Louie, 195, 232
Frere, S. O. N., 414
Frith, W. P., 248–249
Frith, Walter
   *The Man of Forty*, 248–252
*Frocks and Frills*, 429–432
Frohman, Charles, 290, 292, 428, 429
Fry, C. B., 57
Fulda, Ludwig
   *The Twin Sister*, 425–429
Fuller, Loie, 323

## INDEX

Fulton, Charles, 61, 201, 244, 436
Fuseli, 231

Ganthony, Richard
   *A Message from Mars*, 212–213
   *The Prophecy*, 544–546
Garden, E. W., 269
Gatti, A. & S., 290, 292
*Gay Lord Quex, The*, 128, 130–132, 151, 264, 350
*Ghetto, The*, 184–185
Giddens, George, 87, 186, 229, 240, 386, 459
Gigia, Miss, 54
Gilbert, Francis, 357
Gilbert, W. S., 25, 29, 30, 35, 238, 239, 309, 512
Gilchrist, Connie, 33
Gilliat, J. F. G., 440
Gillmore, Frank, 117
*Gipsy Earl, The*, 47–48
*Girl from Maxim's, The*, 478
*Girl from Up There, The*, 369–370
Gladstone, W. E., 219–220
*Globe, The*, 305
Godfrey, Charles, 228
Goethe, 93, 174, 175, 458, 481
*Golden Rose, The*, 582–583
Goldsmith, Oliver, 253
   *She Stoops to Conquer*, 228–229
Goodheart, Mr, 72
Goodwin, Nat, 156, 158–159, 170, 186, 404
Gordon Lennox, Cosmo, *see* Stuart, Cosmo
Gosse, Edmund, 236, 257
Gottschalk, Ferdinand, 87
Gould, Nutcombe, 63, 161–162
Graham, J. M., 381
Gran, Albert, 375
Granville, Miss, 252

*Great Ruby, The*, 56–59
*Greek Slave, A*, 111–112
Grein, J. T., 352, 353, 529–532
   *Blanchette*, 88
*Grierson's Way*, 160, 169, 270, 404
Grossmith, Weedon, 168
   *The Night of the Party*, 375–376
Groves, Fred, 433
Grundy, Lily, 183
Grundy, Sydney, 71, 82, 98, 159, 270, 285, 311, 464, 489, 596
   *A Debt of Honour*, 281–285
   *A Pair of Spectacles*, 432–433
   *Frocks and Frills*, 429–432
   *The Black Tulip*, 203–204
   *The Degenerates*, 179–183
   *The Marriage of Convenience*, 82
   *The Silver Key*, 82
*Gudgeons*, 81, 98
Gurney, Edmund, 72
*Guy Domville*, 109, 307–308

Haig Brown, Dr, 398
Hall, Owen, 23
Halstan, Margaret, 38, 146–147
Hamilton, Henry, 343
   *The Great Ruby*, 56–59
   *The Three Musketeers*, 54–56, 71–72
*Hamlet*, 62–64, 246, 339, 359–363, 485–487, 518, 560
Hanbury, Lily, 183, 273, 341, 436, 582–583
Hankin, St John, 577
   *The Two Mr Wetherbys*, 548–550, 578
*Happy Thoughts*, 167
Harding, Lyn, 546
Hardwicke, Lord, 12
Hardy, Thomas, 378, 555
Hare, Gilbert, 132

# INDEX

Hare, John, 116–117, 128, 132, 264, 433, 459, 598
Harley, Adrian (*Richard Feverel*), 487
Harmsworth, Alfred, 355
Harris, Sir Augustus, 293, 356, 525
Harris, Frank, 12
   *Mr & Mrs Daventry*, 310–314
Harrison, Frederick, 72, 331, 412–413, 431
Harrison, Mr, 77, 204
Harvey, Martin, 40, 119, 121, 353–355, 399, 438
Hauptmann, Gerhart
   *Lonely Lives*, 364–366
Hawtrey, Charles, 124, 183, 212, 213, 373, 385, 463, 467–470, 538
Hazlitt, William, 81
*Heard at the Telephone*, 442–443
Hearn, James, 40
*Hearts are Trumps*, 187–190
*Heather Field, The*, 104–109, 119, 144, 147, 154, 156–158, 160
*Hedonists, The*, 487–488
Heijermans, Herman
   *The Ghetto*, 184–185
Heinemann, William
   *Summer Moths*, 17–21
Held, Anna, 276
Henderson, Isaac
   *The Mummy and the Humming Bird*, 407–409
Henley, W. E., 90, 393, 462
*Henry V*, 247, 339, 340, 347
*Her Royal Highness*, 51–52
*Herod*, 315–323, 330, 389, 435
Hervieu, Paul
   *L'Enigme*, 443–444, 479
Herz, R. C., 377, 387, 425
Hichens, Robert, 117
Hicks, Seymour, 110, 228, 301, 368

*His Excellency the Governor*, 35–36, 202
*His Last Legs*, 442
Hobbes, John Oliver, *see* Craigie, Mrs
Hodge, Harold, 12
Hoffmann, Heinrich, 338
Homer, 433–436
Homewood, A. S., 606
*Homme aux Poupées, L'*, 482
Hood, Basil, 438–439
   *Her Royal Highness*, 51–52
   *Sweet and Twenty*, 368–369, 438
Hope, Anthony, 98
   *English Nell*, 292
   *Pilkerton's Peerage*, 439–440
   *Rupert of Hentzau*, 233–237
   *The Adventure of Lady Ursula*, 61–62, 98
   *When a Man's in Love*, 65–68
Hopetoun, Lord, 263–265, 478
Hoppe, Charles, 172–173
Hopper, De Wolf, 169–170, 221
Horace, 219
Housman, Laurence
   *Bethlehem*, 558–559
Hughes, Annie, 83, 87, 102, 579
Hurlbert, William, 300

Ibsen, 18, 19, 20, 43, 84, 111, 142, 173–177, 353, 586–587
   *The Pillars of Society*, 374–375
   *The Vikings at Helgeland*, 562–565, 573, 576
   *When We Dead Awaken*, 532–535, 587
*Ideal Husband, An*, 334
Image, Selwyn, 163
*Importance of Being Earnest, The*, 178, 334
*In Days of Old*, 137–140
*Interrupted Honeymoon, An*, 195

614

# INDEX

*Irish Assurance*, 442
Irving, Sir Henry, 63, 134, 136, 271, 345, 366–367, 399, 440, 458–459, 566, 568, 575
Irving, H. B., 32, 33, 138, 237, 252, 352, 429, 452, 572
Irving, Laurence, 38, 54, 135–136, 279–280, 458, 567
*Bonnie Dundee*, 241–245

James, Henry, 105, 233–234, 457–458, 462, 555
*Guy Domville*, 109, 307–308
Jeffreys, Ellis, 186, 386, 432, 557
Jeffries, Maud, 183, 198, 317, 322, 348
Jerome, J. K., 220
*Miss Hobbs*, 224–226
*Jest, The*, 77–81
Jesus Christ, 176
J.F.R., *see* Runciman
Johnson, Dr, 378, 539, 543
Jones, Henry Arthur, 20, 98, 105, 152, 180, 270, 271, 295, 305, 329, 381, 385, 431, 588, 596
*Carnac Sahib*, 134, 136–137, 271, 422
*Chance the Idol*, 488–492
*Mrs Dane's Defence*, 297–300, 330, 492
*The Case of Rebellious Susan*, 75, 148, 383–384
*The Crusaders*, 76
*The Lackey's Carnival*, 297
*The Liars*, 75, 148, 150, 151
*The Manoeuvres of Jane*, 72–77, 297
*The Masqueraders*, 67
*The Princess's Nose*, 448–452
*The Silver King*, 183, 196, 197
*Whitewashing Julia*, 539–543
Jones, Stanley, 206–209

Jonson, Ben
*The Alchemist*, 572
Jowett, Dr, 571
*Judged by Appearances*, 511
*Julius Caesar*, 98–99, 230, 285–288, 295–296
*Just Like Callaghan*, 577–580

*Katawampus*, 423–425
Keats, John, 142
Keith, Nora
*A Man and Himself*, 601–603
Kemble, Henry, 473
Kendal, Madge, 417, 418, 432, 474
Kendal, W. H., 418
Kenworthy-Browne, E., 440
Kenyon, Leslie, 183
*Kenyon's Widow*, 266
Kerr, Fred, 117, 130, 314, 376, 385–387, 579
*King John*, 191–193, 230, 269, 340, 347, 348
Kinghorne, Mark, 204
Kingsley, Mary, 88
Kingston, Gertrude, 77, 352, 376, 452
Kingston, Thomas, 157
Kipling, Rudyard, 156, 203, 209, 214–217, 219, 423, 493
Kitchener, Lord, 89
Klaw, Marc, 452
Knowles, Sheridan, 303

Labiche, Eugène, 20
*Lackey's Carnival, The*, 297
*Lady from Texas, A*, 386–388
*Lady Huntworth's Experiment*, 259–262, 278
*Lady of Ostend, The*, 167–169
*Lady Windermere's Fan*, 34, 76
Lamb, Charles, 219, 349
Landor, W. S., 378

## INDEX

Lane, Grace, 432
Lane, John, 70
Lang, Andrew, 242, 282
Langton, G. P., 384
Langtry, Lily, 183
*Last Chapter, The*, 183
Latham, Frederick, 301
Lauri, Charles, 121
Lawford, Ernest, 509
Lawrence, Gerald, 436
Lawson, Sir Edward, 380
Leader, Mr, 105
Leclercq, Rose, 77
Lee, Sidney, 232–233, 447
Legouvé, Ernest
  *Les Doigts de Fée*, 429–432
Leigh, Mrs Henry, 102
Leno, Dan, 60–61, 274, 528–529
Leonard, Martia, 88, 352–353
L'Estrange, Julian, 576
Levey, Sisters, 72
Lewis, Eric, 150, 202, 262, 432, 599
*Liars, The*, 75, 148, 150, 151
*Liberty Hall*, 147
*Likeness of the Night, The*, 415, 417–418
Lind, Letty, 112
*Little Mary*, 595–599, 604
*Little Minister, The*, 413, 595
*Little Miss Nobody*, 59
*Little Ray of Sunshine, A*, 97
*Liz's Baby*, 511
Loftus, Cecilia, 458–459
Loftus, Kitty, 52, 255
Logue, Cardinal, 141
*Lonely Lives*, 364–366
*Lord and Lady Algy*, 117, 147, 148, 261, 538
*Lost for Russia*, 37
Louise, Princess, 398
Lucas, F. H., 326
Luff, William, 576

Lyndal, Percy, 61
*Lyre and Lancet*, 507–510
*Lysiane*, 41–42
Lysons, the Rev. Dr, 94

*Macbeth*, 62–63, 518
Macbeth, Helen, 470
MacColl, D. S., 162, 165, 335, 410, 531
Macdermott, The Great, 215
Mackail, J. W., 40
Mackintosh, William, 558
*Madame Delphine*, 279–280
*Mademoiselle Mars*, 448
Maesmore Morris, Mrs, 252, 440, 603
Maeterlinck, Maurice, 43, 51, 111, 120–121, 142, 143, 353, 475, 526, 540, 575, 585
  *Alladine et Palomides*, 120–121
  *Monna Vanna*, 477–481
  *Pelleas and Melisande*, 38–41, 43, 84, 99, 120, 446
*Magistrate, The*, 20, 178
Magnier, Pierre, 475, 477
*Main, La*, 482
Malet, Lucas, 416
Mallock, W. H., 34
*Man and Himself, A*, 601–603
*Man and his Makers*, 195–198
*Man from Blankley's, The*, 370–373, 508–510
*Man of Forty, The*, 248–252
*Man of Honour, A*, 538–539
*Man who Stole the Castle, The*, 338
*Manoeuvres of Jane, The*, 72–77, 297
Mantalini, Mr (*Nicholas Nickleby*), 540
*Mariana*, 381–383
*Marmion*, 332

616

# INDEX

Marlowe, Charles
  *Two Little Maids from School,*
    82–84
*Marriage of Convenience, The,* 82
*Married Woman, A,* 511–514
Marshall, Captain R., 327, 331,
    422–423
  *A Royal Family,* 201–202, 329
  *His Excellency the Governor,*
    35–36, 202
  *The Noble Lord,* 309–310
  *The Second in Command,* 329–
    330, 394, 413, 422
  *The Unforeseen,* 517–518
Martyn, Edward
  *The Heather Field,* 104–109,
    119, 144, 147, 154, 156–158,
    160
Martyn, May, 384
*Masked Ball, The,* 227–228
Maskelyne & Cook (conjurers), 26,
    213
*Masqueraders, The,* 67
*Matches,* 102–104
Mather, Anna, 144
Maude, Cyril, 72, 77, 203, 229,
    255, 330, 331, 394, 412–413,
    431, 432, 459, 548, 549
Maude, Mrs, *see* Emery, Winifred
Maugham, W. S.
  *A Man of Honour,* 538–539
Maupassant, Guy de, 18, 19, 24,
    105, 235
Maurice, Edmund, 102, 183, 440
May, Edna, 370
*Mayflower, The,* 127–128
Mayo, Winifred, 366
M'Carthy, Justin Huntly, 511
McCarthy, Lillah, 217
McIntosh, Burr, 156
McIntosh, Madge, 172, 467
McLeay, Franklin, 273, 287

*Meadow Sweet,* 45
Melville, Frederick
  *Between Two Women,* 523–525
Melville, Walter, 524
*Merchant of Venice, The,* 343–345,
    347, 518, 572–573
Meredith, George, 18, 19, 29, 32,
    33, 99, 235, 310, 415, 461, 480,
    487, 555
Merrick, Leonard
  *A Woman in the Case,* 375–377,
    385
  *The Elixir of Youth,* 186
*Merry Wives of Windsor, The,*
    473–474
*Message from Mars, A,* 212–213
Meyer, Guillaume, 126
Meyer-Förster, Wilhelm
  *Old Heidelberg,* 550–554
*Mice and Men,* 437–439, 557
*Midsummer Night's Dream, A,*
    113–116, 230–233, 269
Millard, Evelyn, 61, 201, 225, 332,
    448
Millett, Maude, 118, 130
Mills, Frank, 495, 546
*Milord Sir Smith,* 89–90
Milton, John
  *Samson Agonistes,* 256–258
*Miss Bramshott's Engagement,*
    462–463
*Miss Hobbs,* 224–226
Mitchell, Chalmers, 46
Molière
  *Don Juan,* 223, 371
  *Les Précieuses Ridicules,* 352,
    392–394
Mollison, William, 340
Mommsen, 174, 295
Monckton, Lionel, 326
*Monde où l'on s'ennuie, Le,* 352–
    353

617

## INDEX

Monkhouse, Harry, 23
*Monna Vanna*, 477–481
*Moonlight Blossom, The*, 193–195
Moore, Decima, 425
Moore, Eva, 503, 554
Moore, George, 104–109, 119, 144, 206, 262, 466
Moore, Mary, 78, 80, 130, 384, 440, 455
Moreau, E., 566
Morgan, J. Dudley
 *The End of a Story*, 454–456
Morton, E. A., 43
*Mother Goose*, 526–529
*Mr and Mrs Daventry*, 310–314
*Mrs Dane's Defence*, 297–300, 330, 492
*Mrs Warren's Profession*, 21–24, 25, 70
*Much Ado About Nothing*, 113, 370, 384, 573–576
Mulholland, J. B., 82
*Mummy and the Humming Bird, The*, 407–409
Murray, Gilbert
 *Carlyon Sahib*, 160–162
Music Halls, 273–277, 280–281, 395–398
*My Lady Virtue*, 499, 503
*Mystical Miss, The*, 221

Neilson, Julia, 47–48, 231
Nesville, Juliette, 186
Nethersole, Olga, 51
Newman, J. H., 174, 453
Nicholls, Harry, 102
*Night of the Party, The*, 375–376
Nihilism, 36–38
*Noble Lord, The*, 309–310
*Notorious Mrs Ebbsmith, The*, 19, 20, 28, 65
*Nurse*, 264

O'Connor, T. P., 32–33, 263
O'Connor, Mrs T. P.
 *A Lady from Texas*, 386–388
 *Madame Delphine*, 279–280
O'Donnell, F. H., 141
*Oedipus Rex*, 478
Ogilvie, Stuart, 267
*Old Heidelberg*, 550–554
*On and Off*, 87–88
*Only Way, The*, 118–119, 353
Opp, Julie, 138, 237, 252, 282, 283, 285
Ordonneau, Maurice
 *The Royal Star*, 59
*Othello*, 247, 518–521
O.U.D.S., 114–116, 370, 384, 440, 571–573
*Ours*, 116, 117, 128, 459
Oxford, 113–116, 384, 569–573

Pailleron, Edouard
 *Le Monde où l'on s'ennuie*, 352–353
*Pair of Spectacles, A*, 432–433
*Pall Mall Gazette*, 329
*Pall Mall Magazine*, 377–381
*Paolo and Francesca*, 315–316, 445–447, 506
Parker, Louis N., 20, 75, 98, 267, 270, 272
 *Captain Birchell's Luck*, 204–206
 *Gudgeons*, 81, 98
 *Man and his Makers*, 195–198
 *Rosemary*, 81, 98, 548–549
 *The Jest*, 77–81
 *The Mayflower*, 127–128
 *The Swashbuckler*, 331–332
 *The Termagant*, 48–51, 81
 *The Twin Sister*, 425–429
Parry, Hubert, 326

# INDEX

Parry, Judge
  *Katawampus*, 423–425
Pascal, 565
Passmore, Walter, 30
Pater, Walter, 99, 231, 333, 402, 474
Patterne, Sir Willoughby (*The Egoist*), 29
Paulton, Mr, 51
Pawle, Lennox, 452
Peile, Kinsey
  *An Interrupted Honeymoon*, 195
  *Lyre and Lancet*, 507–510
*Pelleas and Melisande*, 38–41, 43, 84, 99, 120, 446
Penley, W. S., 60, 97
Pennell, Joseph, 162
Percyval, T. W., 183
*Peril*, 377
Pettit, Henry, 336, 343
*Phèdre*, 391–392
*Philanderer, The*, 21
Phillips, Stephen, 278, 324, 377–381, 389, 444–445, 475
  *Herod*, 315–323, 330, 389, 435
  *Paolo and Francesca*, 315–316, 445–447, 506
  *Ulysses*, 433–436, 446
*Pilkerton's Peerage*, 439–440
*Pillars of Society, The*, 374–375
Pinero, A. W., 19, 20, 34, 64–65, 76, 98, 105, 152, 180, 270, 271, 298, 334, 378, 385, 431, 464, 478, 588, 596
  *Dandy Dick*, 237–241
  *Sweet Lavender*, 20, 65, 117–118
  *The Beauty Stone*, 27–30
  *The Benefit of the Doubt*, 227
  *The Cabinet Minister*, 65
  *The Gay Lord Quex*, 128, 130–132, 151, 264, 350

  *The Magistrate*, 20, 178
  *The Notorious Mrs Ebbsmith*, 19, 20, 28, 65
  *The Princess and the Butterfly*, 130, 250
  *The Profligate*, 130
  *The Second Mrs Tanqueray*, 19, 20, 28, 65, 108
  *Trelawney of the Wells*, 549
Plato, 26, 206, 378
Playfair, Nigel, 337
*Plays Pleasant and Unpleasant*, 11
Poe, Edgar Allan, 543
Poel, William, 145–146, 222, 256–258, 333, 398, 401
Pope, Alexander, 256
Portugal Street (Bankruptcy Court) 355
Potter, Paul
  *Trilby*, 54–55
Pounds, Courtice, 349, 424
Poynter, Sir Edward, 463
*Précieuses Ridicules, Les*, 352, 392–394
*President, The*, 463
*Price of Peace, The*, 292–295
*Pride and Prejudice*, 364–366
*Prince Pierrot*, 588–591
*Princess and the Butterfly, The*, 130, 250
*Princess's Nose, The*, 448–452
*Prisoner of Zenda, The*, 54
*Professor's Love Story, The*, 603–606
*Profligate, The*, 130
*Prophecy, The*, 544–546
Pryce, Richard
  *Liz's Baby*, 511
*Punch*, 253, 260, 290

Quartermaine, Charles, 348, 375
*Queen's Double, The*, 373–374

619

## INDEX

Racine
  *Phèdre*, 391–392
*Ragged Robin*, 42–43
Raleigh, Cecil, 356
  *Hearts are Trumps*, 187–190
  *The Great Ruby*, 56–59
  *The Price of Peace*, 292–295
Raleigh, Prof. Walter, 388–391
Randall, Harry, 274
Ranjitsinhji, Prince, 56, 57
Ray, Ruby, 288
*Real Conversations*, 377–381
*Red Lamp, The* (W. O. Tristram), 37
Redford, George Alexander, 108, 123–124, 264–265, 398, 399, 427, 428, 477–481, 558–559
Reece, Captain (W. S. Gilbert), 512
Reeve, Ada, 90, 91
Réjane, 258, 259
Renan, Ernest, 174
*Repentance, A*, 122–123
*Revolted Daughter, The*, 359
*Richard II*, 247–248
*Richard III*, 186–187, 247
Richardson, Francis
  *The Royal Star*, 59
*Richelieu*, 159–160
Richepin, Jean, 74
  *Ragged Robin*, 42–43
Ridley, Sir Matthew, 263
Righton, Edward, 44
*Rip Van Winkle*, 269–273
*Rivals, The*, 252–255
Rivers, Hilda, 33
Roberts, Arthur, 60, 89–90
Robertshaw, Jerrold, 45, 440
Robertson, Ian, 487
  *The Golden Rose*, 582–583
Robertson, Jack, 576
Robertson, Johnston Forbes, 40, 59, 63, 70, 99, 121, 194, 437, 439, 486–487, 521
Robertson, Tom, 20, 84, 110, 111, 116, 117, 118, 147, 327, 330, 380
  *Caste*, 128, 459
  *Ours*, 116, 117, 128, 459
  *School*, 116, 128
Robespierre, 134–136
Robey, George, 274
Robins, Elizabeth, 447–448, 506, 586
Roe, Bassett, 72
*Romanesques, Les*, 266–269
*Romeo and Juliet*, 62, 247
Rorke, Miss, 227
Rose, Edward, 159
  *English Nell*, 292
  *In Days of Old*, 137–140
  *Under the Red Robe*, 54, 332, 413, 520
  *When a Man's in Love*, 65–68
*Rose Ponpon*, 277
Rosebery, Lord, 106, 298
*Rosemary*, 81, 98, 548–549
Ross, Adrian, 29
Rossetti, D. G., 208
Rostand, Edmond, 324
  *Cyrano de Bergerac*, 166, 266–267, 482
  *Les Romanesques*, 266–269
*Royal Family, A*, 201–202, 329
*Royal Star, The*, 59
Royston, Arthur, 138
Runciman, J. F., 12, 139, 335, 410
*Rupert of Hentzau*, 233–237
Ruskin, John, 175, 176
Ryley, Madeline L.
  *An American Citizen*, 159, 186
  *Mice and Men*, 437–439, 557

# INDEX

Ryley, Madeline L. (cont'd)
  *The Altar of Friendship*, 554–558
Salisbury, Lord, 36, 294
*Samson Agonistes*, 256–258
Sardou, Victorien, 53, 110, 430
  *Dante*, 565–569
  *La Tosca*, 443
  *Peril*, 377
  *Robespierre*, 134–136
*School*, 116, 128
*School for Scandal, The*, 229
Scott, Clement, 116, 419–421
Scribe, Eugène, 50
  *Les Doigts de Fée*, 429–432
Seaman, Owen, 471
*Second in Command, The*, 329–330, 394, 413, 422
*Second Mrs Tanqueray, The*, 19, 20, 28, 65
*Secret Track, The*, 37
Sefton, Charles, 156–157
*Self and Lady*, 291–292
*Sentimentalist, The*, 415–417
Serjeantson, Kate, 489
Shakespeare, William, 139, 142, 160, 174, 175, 178, 222, 225, 245–248, 169, 277, 278, 324, 338–339, 342–343, 399, 444–447, 522, 560–561, 563, 572, 581, 600
  *A Midsummer Night's Dream*, 113–116, 230–233, 269
  *All's Well that Ends Well*, 113
  *Antony and Cleopatra*, 255–256
  *Coriolanus*, 366–367
  *Hamlet*, 62–64, 246, 339, 359–363, 485–487, 518, 560
  *Henry V*, 247, 339, 340, 347
  *Julius Caesar*, 98–99, 230, 285–288, 295–296

Shakespeare, William (cont'd)
  *King John*, 191–193, 230, 269, 340, 347, 348
  *Macbeth*, 62–63, 518
  *Much Ado about Nothing*, 113, 370, 384, 573–576
  *Othello*, 247, 518–521
  *Richard II*, 247–248
  *Richard III*, 186–187, 247
  *Romeo and Juliet*, 62, 247
  *The Merchant of Venice*, 343–345, 347, 518, 572–573
  *The Merry Wives of Windsor*, 473–474
  *The Taming of the Shrew*, 339–342, 347
  *The Tempest*, 247, 347
  *Twelfth Night*, 248, 346–350
  *Two Gentlemen of Verona*, 440
Shaw, George Bernard, 11, 12, 13, 17–27, 35, 71, 271, 385, 477, 596
  *Arms and the Man*, 25, 267
  *Caesar and Cleopatra*, 271
  *Candida*, 26
  *Captain Brassbound's Conversion*, 335–337
  *Mrs Warren's Profession*, 21–24, 25, 70
  *Plays Pleasant & Unpleasant*, 11
  *The Admirable Bashville*, 580–582
  *The Devil's Disciple*, 21, 335
  *The Philanderer*, 21
  *Widowers' Houses*, 21, 25
  *You Never Can Tell*, 25, 26, 278, 336
*She Stoops to Conquer*, 228–229
Sheldon, Suzanne, 244
Sheridan, R. B., 277
  *The Rivals*, 252–255
  *The School for Scandal*, 229

621

## INDEX

*Sherlock Holmes*, 568
Shillingford, Osmond
   *A Court Scandal*, 109–110
Shirley, Arthur
   *The Absent-Minded Beggar*, 214–218
Siddons, Mrs, 90, 91
Sidney, Fred W.
   *The Brixton Burglary*, 85–87
*Sign of the Cross, The*, 119, 443
*Silver Key, The*, 82
*Silver King, The*, 183, 196, 197
Sims, G. R.
   *A Woman in the Case*, 375–377, 385
   *Faust Up to Date*, 93
   *The Elixir of Youth*, 186
   *The Gipsy Earl*, 47–48
Smith, Aubrey, 467
Smith, S. (M.P.), 263, 265
Smith, Sydney, 341
Socrates, 74, 176
Somerset, C. W., 322, 417
Sophocles, 285, 522
Standing, Herbert, 387
Stanford, H. B., 458
Steer, Janette, 374
Stepniak, Sergius
   *The Convert*, 36–38
Stevenson, R. L., 233–236, 294–295, 308–309
Stirling, Richard, 156
Storey, Fred, 273
*Strafford*, 572
Street, G. S., 509
   *Miss Bramshott's Engagement*, 462–463
*Struwwelpeter*, 337–338
Stuart, Cosmo, 61, 452, 509
   *Just Like Callaghan*, 577–580
*Such Stuff as Dreams*, 144–147
*Summer Moths*, 17–21

*Sunlight and Shadow*, 147
Sutro, Alfred, 120, 585
*Swashbuckler, The*, 331–332
*Sweet and Twenty*, 368–369, 438
*Sweet Lavender*, 20, 65, 117–118
Swete, E. Lyall, 248, 363–364, 365, 366
Swift, Jonathan, 176
Swinburne, A. C., 480
*Swineherd and the Princess, The*, 425
Symons, Arthur, 585
Syrett, Netta
   *The Finding of Nancy*, 463–467

Taber, Robert, 241, 244, 287, 348
Taine, Hippolyte, 175
Talbot, E. K., 115
Talleyrand, 356
*Taming of the Shrew, The*, 339–342, 347
Tempest, Marie, 112, 292, 459
*Tempest, The*, 247, 347
Tennent, H. M., 384
*Teresa*, 52–54, 110
*Termagant, The*, 48–51, 81
Terriss, Ellaline, 227, 228
Terriss, William, 217
Terry, Edward, 110, 111, 117–118
Terry, Ellen, 135, 367, 458, 474, 562, 565, 575, 576
Terry, Fred, 33, 48
Terry, Marion, 65, 506
Terry-Lewis, Mabel, 117, 387
Thackeray, W. M., 168, 212, 215–216, 253, 372, 403, 461, 559
Thalberg, T. B., 150
Tharp, Norman, 323
*There and Back*, 470
Thomas, Berte
   *The Weather-Hen*, 171–172

622

## INDEX

Thomas, Brandon, 110, 156, 538
  *Charley's Aunt*, 178
  *Women Are so Serious*, 385–387
Thorne, Fred, 44
Thorpe, Courtenay, 172, 353
*Three Musketeers, The*, 54–56, 71–72
Tilley, Vesta, 512–513
*Times, The*, 245, 265, 504, 541
Titherage, G. S., 185, 383, 514
Tiverton, Lord, 440
Tolstoi, Leo, 174, 175, 176, 226
*Tommy Dodd*, 46
*Tosca, La*, 443
Townsend, Stephen, 126
Toynbee, William, 119
Tree, H. Beerbohm, 63, 99, 137, 230–231, 269–273, 278, 286, 321, 323, 350, 385, 436, 473
Tree, Mrs, 231, 287, 418, 442, 443–444, 474
*Tree of Knowledge, The*, 147
*Trelawney of the Wells*, 549
Trevelyan, G. O., 218
*Trilby*, 54–55
*Trip to Midget-Town, A*, 183
*Triumph of Love, The*, 563
Trollope, Anthony, 391, 539
Tsar of Russia, 356
Turgeneff, Ivan, 174
Turner, Reginald
  *Prince Pierrot*, 588–591
Twain, Mark, 170
*Twelfth Night*, 248, 346–350
*Twin Sister, The*, 425–429
*Two Gentlemen of Verona*, 440
*Two Little Maids from School*, 82–84
*Two Mr Wetherbys, The*, 548–550, 578
*Tyranny of Tears, The*, 128–130, 350

Uchard, Mario
  *Fiamma*, 529–532
*Ulysses*, 433–436, 446
*Under False Colours*, 357–359
*Under the Red Robe*, 54, 332, 413, 520
*Undercurrent, The*, 402, 404–406
*Unforeseen, The*, 517–518

Valentine, Sydney, 204, 521
Vanbrugh, Irene, 36, 132, 452
Vanbrugh, Violet, 33, 54, 138, 189, 190, 240, 405, 473, 503, 542
Vaughan, Susie, 353
Vergil, 93, 174
Vernon, W. H., 283
*Vicar's Dilemma, The*, 44–45
*Vice Versa*, 507, 510
Victor, Mary Anne, 229
*Vida es Sueño, La* (Calderon), 144–147
*Vikings at Helgeland, The*, 562–565, 573, 575, 576

Wagner, Richard, 18, 19
Wakefield, Bishop of, 132
Walkley, A. B., 43, 104, 313, 336, 361, 491
  Parodied by Max, 539–543
Wallace, Sir Donald Mackenzie, 460–462
Waller, Lewis, 55, 72, 137, 340, 341, 417, 448
Wallerton, Myles, 357
Ward, Albert, 523
Ward, Mrs Humphry, 461
  *Eleanor*, 503–507
Waring, Herbert, 61, 199, 201, 225, 332, 520
Warner, Charles, 442, 443
Warner, Grace, 50, 187
Warner, H. B., 217, 473

# INDEX

*Waters of Bitterness, The*, 583–584
Watson, Henrietta, 470
Watteau, 222
*Weather-Hen, The*, 171–172
Webster, Annie, 375
Webster, Ben, 67, 201, 603
*Wedding Guest, The*, 595
Weir, George R., 248
Welsh, James, 86–87, 195
Wells, H. G., 213
*What will the World Say?*, 110–111
*What Would a Gentleman Do?*, 492–495
*Wheels within Wheels*, 147–150, 151, 153, 227, 383–384
*When a Man's in Love*, 65–68
*When We Dead Awaken*, 532–535, 587
*When We Were Twenty-One*, 402–404, 594
*Where's the Cat?*, 227
*Whitewashing Julia*, 539–543
Whitty, May, 144, 157
Whyte, Frederic, 90–92
*Widowers' Houses*, 21, 25
Wiehe, Charlotte, 323, 482
*Wild Rabbit, The*, 177–179
Wilde, Oscar, 21, 150, 333–334
  *A Woman of No Importance*, 334
  *An Ideal Husband*, 334
  *Lady Windermere's Fan*, 34, 76
  *The Importance of Being Earnest*, 178, 334
*Wilderness, The*, 429, 594
Wilkinson, Spencer, 460
Willard, E. S., 183, 606

Williams, Arthur, 470
Williams, Harcourt, 366
Wills, Freeman, 438
Wills, W. G., 343, 399
  *Faust*, 93, 457–459
Wilson, Beatrice, 45
Winter, John Strange, 330
*Wisdom of the Wise, The*, 327–329
*Woman in the Case, A*, 375–377, 385
*Woman of No Importance, A*, 334
*Women Are so Serious*, 385–387
Wood, Florence, 186
Wood, Mr, 88
Woodward, H. M. M., 115
*World, The*, 62
*Worldham M.P.*, 448
Wright, Huntley, 112
Wright, Mrs Theodore, 88
*Wrong Mr Wright, The*, 209
Wyndham, Charles, 77–79, 130, 177, 266, 297, 298, 300, 383, 385, 386, 390, 407, 408, 455, 548–549


Yeats, W. B., 105, 175
  *The Countess Cathleen*, 105, 106, 141–144, 145
  *You Never Can Tell*, 25, 26, 278, 336
Young, Dalhousie, 588


Zangwill, Israel
  *Children of the Ghetto*, 218–221
  *The Revolted Daughter*, 359
*Zaza*, 256, 258–259, 264
Zola, Emile, 533